The Decade of the Great War

# The Decade of the Great War

*Japan and the Wider World in the 1910s*

*Edited by*

Tosh Minohara
Tze-ki Hon
Evan Dawley

## BRILL

LEIDEN | BOSTON

Cover illustration: *Shashinkiroku: Nihongaikōshi* (Tokyo: Nihotoshosenta, 2007), p. 111. (background); http://www.loc.gov/pictures/item/93517421/. Library of Congress, Prints and Photographs Division, Washington, D.C. 20540, USA (foreground)

The decade of the Great War : Japan and the wider world in the 1910s / edited by Tosh Minohara, Tze-ki Hon, Evan Dawley.
    pages cm.
  Includes index.
  ISBN 978-90-04-27001-5 (hardback : alk. paper) -- ISBN 978-90-04-27427-3 (e-book)  1. Japan--Foreign relations--1912-1926. 2. Japan--Foreign relations--1868-1912. I. Minohara, Toshihiro, 1971- editor, author. II. Hon, Tze-Ki, 1958- editor, author. III. Dawley, Evan N., editor, author.

  DS885.48.D43 2014
  940.3'2252--dc23

2014010479

This publication has been typeset in the multilingual "Brill" typeface. With over 5,100 characters covering Latin, IPA, Greek, and Cyrillic, this typeface is especially suitable for use in the humanities.
For more information, please see www.brill.com/brill-typeface.

ISBN 978-90-04-30262-4 (paperback, 2015)
ISBN 978-90-04-27001-5 (hardback, 2014)
ISBN 978-90-04-27427-3 (e-book, 2014)

# Contents

SECTION 2

## National and Transnational Networks

# Preface

The genesis of this project, almost a decade ago, can be traced back to the time when I was on sabbatical leave at the Nissan Institute of Japanese Studies, St. Antony's College, University of Oxford. A memo dated July 2006 indicates the initial ideas that I had jotted down, regarding the launch of a collaborative research project that would bring together a group of international scholars who would join me in reassessing what the 1910s meant for Japan. The catalyst of this project, after arriving in Oxford in September 2005, was my realization of the deeply profound impact that the Great War had upon Britain. As a scholar primarily concerned with US-Japan relations, in my mind, the "War" had always been the Second World War, in particular the Pacific theater of that conflict. My time spent in Britain, in addition to my frequent travels to numerous other countries in Europe, had allowed me for the first time to properly grasp a sense of the magnitude of the Great War. Even the smallest town had some sort of commemoration of the First World War. The same was not true about the Second World War, which saw its most brutal fighting on the Eastern Front and on the islands of the Pacific.

Despite its nomenclature, being the first "World War," scholarship of this global conflict has for a large part been placed in a wholly European context. This seemed awkward to me as it seemed that it did not reflect the true nature of the War, since it had also brought forth a tremendous wave of transformation in East Asia. As a matter of fact, it was the Great War that had launched Japan as an economic and military power, and by 1919 she was a proud member of the Big Five powers. So, thus began the process of putting together a viable team of highly competent and ambitious scholars, which ended up becoming twenty-three in all. The chapters that follow are the fruits of their dedication and labor. Many of the contributors are scholars that I had met and come to respect during my two years residing in Britain and the Netherlands. However, the sheer scope of this project simply made it impossible for a single individual to manage. To this end, I was extremely fortunate to be able to enlist the assistance of Professor Hon Tze-ki, whom I had met during my tenure as a visiting professor to the International Institute for Asian Studies at the University of Leiden.

As a specialist on China, Professor Hon was able to fill in the wide gaps that existed in my expertise. Surrounded by the scenic canals and windmills of Leiden, and over a glass of beer, together we drafted a detailed project proposal and began the process of contacting prospective contributors. At the same time we also arrived at the conclusion that the project would benefit through the addition one other project manager, who would also be our third and final co-editor. Finding the perfect individual for such a task was not difficult, for Professor Evan Dawley had always been a highly reliable and capable scholar, from the time I first met him when he was a graduate student at Harvard. Over the years, he has not only become a good friend, but has also contributed to my past projects, the most recent being the publication of *Tumultuous Decade: Empire, Society, and Diplomacy in 1930s Japan,* University of Toronto Press, 2013. Therefore, this volume is very much the outcome of the three editors working closely together as a team, along with the contributors.

# Acknowledgements

First and foremost, I would like to extend my greatest appreciation to my two capable co-editors, Professors Hon and Dawley, for without their wisdom and support, this book would never have seen the light of day. By working on this project over the span of nearly six years, we came to appreciate and learn from our differences in our approaches to the study of history. We were also cognizant of the fact that if we combined our strengths, we could create a multidisciplinary (and international) volume that would illuminate Japan during the decade of the Great War in a new light. So with Professors Hon and Dawley onboard, the very first project meeting was held in the quaint town of Geneseo, located in upstate New York, during September 2008. As we wanted to be certain of publishing this volume in time for the First World War centennial, our deadline was clear from the start: the summer of 2014.

To this end, I was fortunate that I had secured a reputable academic publisher prior to the conference in Geneseo. Brill was the natural choice as I was residing in Leiden at that time (2006–07), and even more good fortune befell me when I met a highly dedicated and experienced editor, Julian Deahl, who enthusiastically embraced the project from the moment I shared my ideas with him over a beer. Since then, I have truly come to appreciate and respect his skills as a senior editor. He not only made sure that the project would be completed on schedule, but he also provided many insightful suggestions that improved the final quality of the volume. I also tip my hat to him for coming out to see me every time my travels brought me to Europe, from Amsterdam and Brussels to Budapest. I am also indebted to his highly competent staff editor at Brill, Marcella Mulder, who was always on the ball. Not only was she always responsive and supportive, but she was also extremely generous in providing her knowledge and expertise in making this volume even better.

Organizing a volume consisting of 23 contributors required numerous conferences which followed after Geneseo at regular intervals: Tokyo and Qingdao in June 2009, Philadelphia in March 2010, Seoul in April 2010, Jeju in June 2010, Arima (Kobe) in November 2010, Honolulu in March 2011, Budapest and Sarajevo in August 2011, Kansas City and Toronto in March 2012, Brussels and Ypres in October 2012, San Diego in March 2013, and finally New York in September 2013, not to mention the many other smaller meetings that took place when one of the editors would pass through each other's cities, such as Kobe and Washington D.C. During many of these meetings we also visited sites related to the First World War; various hosts did their utmost not only to provide a warm welcome but greatly assisted in facilitating our research. However, two individuals at the National World War I Museum in Kansas City deserve special mention: Senior Curator Doran Cart and Museum Archivist Jonathan Casey, as they bent over backwards in response to our request for photos from the museum collections.

Of course, the success of any volume ultimately rests not upon the abilities of editors or even the publisher, but with the essays of the contributors. To this regard, I would like to thank this highly international cadre of scholars for not only being responsive at all times and keeping to the tight schedule, but also for submitting quality manuscripts. It was their level of commitment that made the task of creating this volume a very enjoyable one for the editors.

It also goes without saying that the success of a project of this scope also rests on the vast amounts of generous outside help received over the years. I would therefore like to take this opportunity to express my deepest gratitude to the Shibusawa Eiichi Memorial Foundation who supported this project generously, giving financial and logistical support, and who also graciously hosted our final gala in Paris in September 2014. In particular, I would like to extend my personal thanks to Masahide Shibusawa, the president of the foundation, who possesses a tremendous vision in supporting collaborative academic projects in the humanities. Tomoaki Shimane, Director of the Japan Foundation Cultural Office in Paris, also deserves special mention for facilitating our book launch symposium in *La Ville-Lumière* commemorating the centennial of the Great War.

Many people have read the manuscript in whole or in part, offering helpful comments and suggestions. An anonymous reader read the entire manuscript with great care and in a review which was, on the whole, very positive, provided insightful comments on to how to better sharpen the individual chapters as well as the volume itself. The process of revising the manuscripts to reflect these comments has been a fruitful exercise and has also undoubtedly served to refine the final published volume. To this end, I am extremely grateful. Other individuals contributed to the volume by providing invaluable insight by sharing their knowledge about the 1910s, such as Professors Frederick Dickinson, Noriko Kawaguchi, Akira Iriye, Kenneth Pyle, and Stephen Vlastos, to name just a few. I should not forget to mention my graduate students who assisted in gathering various source materials: Hayato Yukawa and Sho Akahoshi. My administrative assistant, Ayumi Ito – always eager to assist – did a superb job of taking care of all the scanning and photocopying that was needed in order to get the volume ready for publication. Last but by no means least, this work benefitted greatly from the excellent copy-editing done by Sara Elin Roberts. I am grateful to all these individuals.

Finally, a word on the rendering of the text: utilizing international sources requires adopting a few standard conventions, and for purposes of this volume I have chosen to incorporate Romanized transliterations for non-Western names, words, phrases, and titles, rather than use Japanese, Chinese, or Korean characters. We have also adopted the traditional Japanese, Chinese, and Korean practice of putting family or surnames first, except in the case of individuals who regularly use the Western format for their names or are well-known in the West. For Korean names, as it is both acceptable to hyphenate personal names or to capitalize them, I have permitted the contributors to utilize either format. As a general rule, Chinese names (people and places) appear in Pinyin except for when the name is commonly recognized in Wades-Giles. Hence, this volume uses *Taipei* instead of *Taibei*. Finally, in order to conserve space, all Asian-language sources cited have been presented using Romanized versions of the original titles.

I would of course like to end with the standard disclaimer that the opinions expressed within this volume, and any errors that remain, are the sole responsibility of the authors alone, and not those of the organizations or individuals who have supported our work.

*Tosh Minohara*
Kobe University

# List of Tables

# List of Figures

## Cover

## Tosh Minohara

## Masato Kimura

## Ewa Pałasz-Rutkowska

# List of Volume Editors and Contributors

*Tosh Minohara*

Ph.D. (1998), Graduate School of Law, Kobe University, is Professor of US-Japan Relations at that university. He also holds a joint appointment with the Graduate School of International Cooperation Studies. He has published many monographs, compiled volumes, journal articles, and reviews on prewar US-Japan relations and Japanese diplomacy, including [in Japanese] *The Japanese Exclusion Act and US-Japan Relations* (Iwanamishoten, 2002), which was awarded the 2003 Japanese Association for American Studies *Shimizu Hiroshi Prize*. He is also the co-editor of *Tumultuous Decade: Empire, Society, and Diplomacy in 1930s Japan* (Toronto University Press, 2013).

*Tze-ki Hon*

Ph.D. (1992), University of Chicago, is Professor of History at State University of New York at Geneseo. He has published monographs, book chapters, and articles on pre-modern and modern China, including *The Yijing and Chinese Politics: Classical Commentary and Literati Activism in the Northern Song Period, 960–1127* (SUNY, 2005) and *Revolution as Restoration: Guocui Xuebao and the Chinese Nationalist Modernity* (Brill, 2013). He is also the co-editor of *The Politics of Historical Production in Late Qing and Republican China* (Brill, 2007) and *Beyond the May Fourth Paradigm: In Search of Chinese Modernity* (Lexington Books, 2008).

*Evan Dawley*

Ph.D. (2006), Harvard University, is Assistant Professor of History at Goucher College. He has published articles and book reviews on Taiwan's history. He has contributed an essay on social work in Taiwan to *Tumultuous Decade: Empire, Society, and Diplomacy in 1930s Japan* (Toronto University Press, 2013), and a review essay entitled "The Question of Identity in Recent Scholarship on the History of Taiwan," *The China Quarterly* (June 2009). He is currently completing a book manuscript tentatively titled, "Becoming Taiwanese: Ethnic Identity at the Border of China and Japan."

### Yuehtsen Juliette Chung

Ph.D. (1999), University of Chicago, is Associate Professor of Chinese history at National Tsing Hua University, Taiwan. She has published monographs and articles, including *Struggle for National Survival: Eugenics in Sino-Japanese Contexts, 1896–1945* (Routledge, 2002).

### Martin Dusinberre

Ph.D. (2008), University of Oxford, is Lecturer in Modern Japanese history at Newcastle University, United Kingdom. He has published monographs and articles on Japanese history, including, *Hard Times in the Hometown: A History of Community Survival in Modern Japan* (University of Hawai'i Press, 2012).

### Bert Edström

Ph.D. (1988), Stockholm University, is Senior Research Fellow at the Institute for Security and Development Policy. He has published monographs and articles on Japan's foreign and domestic policy, including *Japan's Evolving Foreign Policy Doctrine* (Macmillan, 1999).

### Selçuk Esenbel

Ph.D. (1981), Boğaziçi University, is Professor of Japanese history and Asian studies at that University. She has published many monographs and articles on modern Japanese-Islamic relations, including *Turkey, and the World of Islam* (Brill, 2011).

### Rustin Gates

Ph.D. (2007), Harvard University, is Assistant Professor of history at Bradley University. A specialist in the history of Japan's international relations, his research has appeared in such places as *The Journal of Japanese Studies* and *Diplomacy & Statecraft*.

### Isao Chiba

Ph.D. (2000), Tokyo University, is Professor of Japanese modern history at Gakushuin University, Tokyo. He has published monographs and articles on Japanese modern history, including [in Japanese] *The Formation of Old Diplomacy: Japanese Diplomacy 1900–1919* (Tokyo: Keisō shobō, 2008).

### Masato Kimura

Ph.D. (1989), Keio University, is Director of Research Department, Shibusawa Eiichi Memorial Foundation. He has published monographs and articles on the history of US-Japan relations, including [in Japanese] *Zaikai Networks and US-Japan Diplomatic Relations* (Yamakawa shuppansha, 1997).

### Chaisung Lim

Ph.D. (2002), University of Tokyo, is Associate Professor at Seoul National University. He has published monographs and articles on the economic history of Northeast Asia, including [in Japanese] *A Wartime Economy and Railroad Management* (University of Tokyo Press, 2005).

### John Meehan, S.J.

Ph.D. (2000), University of Toronto, is President of Campion College at the University of Regina, Canada. He has published many monographs and articles on Canada's relations with East Asia, including *The Dominion and the Rising Sun: Canada Encounters Japan, 1929–1941* (University of British Columbia Press, 2004; Japanese edition by Sairyūsha, 2006).

### Hiromi Mizuno

Ph.D. (2001), University of California at Los Angeles, is Associate Professor of history at the University of Minnesota. She has published monographs and articles on science history, including *Science for the Empire: Scientific Nationalism in Modern Japan* (Stanford University Press, 2009).

### Tadashi Nakatani

Ph.D. (2008), Doshisha University, is Assistant Professor of Diplomatic history at that university. He has published articles on US-Japanese and Anglo-Japanese Relations, including [in Japanese] "Wilson and Japan," *Doshisha Hōgaku* 56-2 (2004).

### Yoshiko Okamoto

Ph.D. (2013), International Christian University, Tokyo, is Research Fellow of the Institute of Asian Cultural Studies at that university. She has published many articles on Okakura Kakuzō [Tenshin], including a chapter [in Japanese] in *Okakura Tenshin: Thoughts and Action* (Yoshikawa kōbunkan, 2013).

### Sumiko Otsubo

Ph.D. (1998), Ohio State University, is Associate Professor of history at Metropolitan State University. Her publications include "Engendering Eugenics: Feminists and Marriage Restriction Legislation in the 1920s," in *Gendering Modern Japanese History* (Harvard University Asia Center, 2005).

### Ewa Pałasz-Rutkowska

Ph.D. (1987), University of Warsaw, is Professor of Japanese history at that university. She has published many monographs and articles on Japanese history, including [in Japanese] *History of Polish-Japanese Relations 1904–1945* (Sairyūsha, 2009).

### Caroline Rose

Ph.D. (1995), University of Leeds, is Professor of Sino-Japanese relations at that university. She has published monographs and articles on the history of Japan and Sino-Japanese relations, including *Sino-Japanese Relations: Facing the Past, Looking to the Future?* (RoutledgeCurzon, 2004).

### J. Charles Schencking

Ph.D. (1998), Cambridge University, is Professor of History at the University of Hong Kong. He has published many monographs and articles on modern Japanese history, including *The Great Kantō Earthquake and Chimera of National Reconstruction in Japan* (Columbia, 2013).

### Chika Shinohara

Ph.D. (2008), University of Minnesota, is Associate Professor of Sociology at Momoyama Gakuin University (St. Andrew's University), Osaka. A specialist on legal and social developments of civil society, her research has appeared in such places as *The Asian Journal of Social Science* and *The Asia-Pacific Journal*.

### Naraoka Sōchi

Ph.D. (2004), Kyoto University, is Associate Professor of Japanese History at that university. He has published monographs and articles on Japan, including [in Japanese] *Katō Takaaki and Party Politics* (Yamakawa shuppansha, 2006).

### Shusuke Takahara

Ph.D. (2002), Kobe University, is Associate Professor of the history of American foreign relations at Kyoto Sangyo University. He has published monographs and articles on the history of Japan-US relations, including [in Japanese] *Wilson Diplomacy and Japan* (Sōbunsha, 2006).

### Susan C. Townsend

Ph.D. (1995), University of Sheffield, is Associate Professor of Japanese history at University of Nottingham. She has published monographs and articles on Japanese intellectual history, including *Miki Kiyoshi, 1897–1945* (Brill, 2009).

East Asia on the Eve of the Great War (1914)

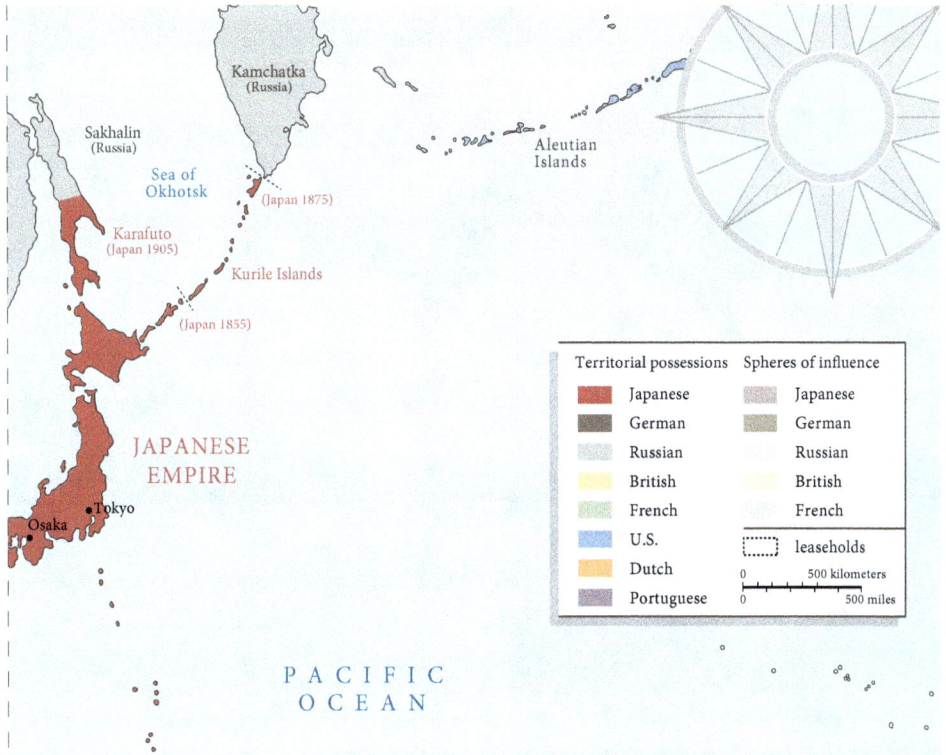
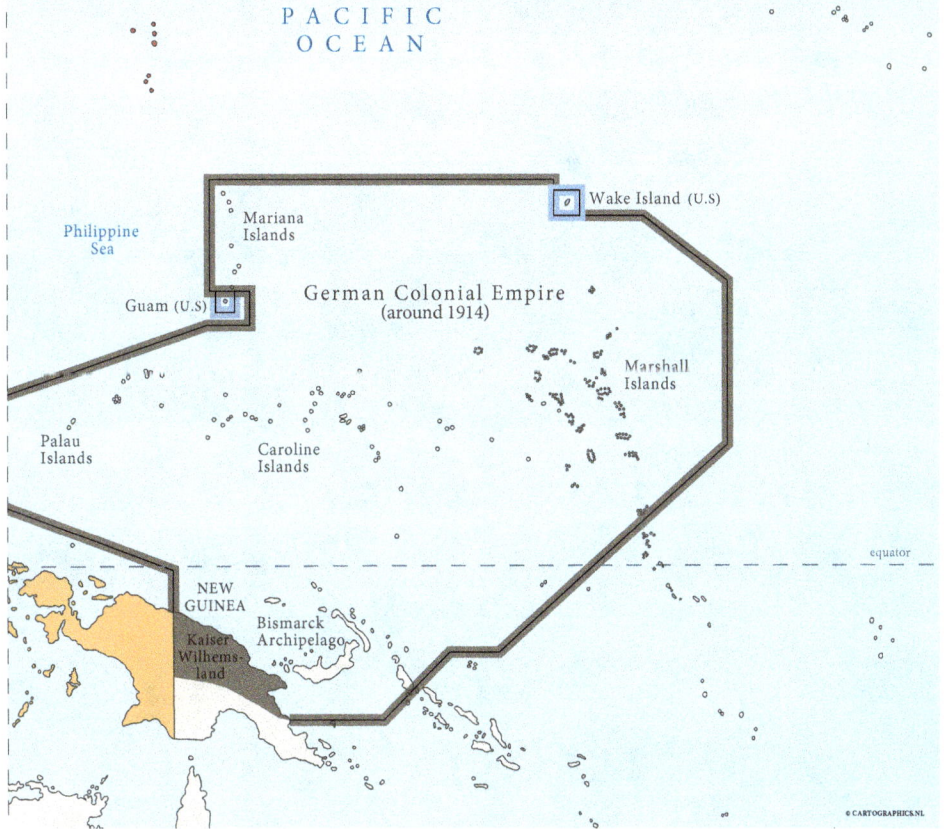

Kamchatka
(Russia)

Sakhalin
(Russia)

Sea of
Okhotsk

(Japan 1875)

Karafuto
(Japan 1905)

Kurile Islands

(Japan 1855)

Aleutian
Islands

JAPANESE
EMPIRE

Osaka •Tokyo

| Territorial possessions | Spheres of influence |
|---|---|
| Japanese | Japanese |
| German | German |
| Russian | Russian |
| British | British |
| French | French |
| U.S. | leaseholds |
| Dutch | 0          500 kilometers |
| Portuguese | 0          500 miles |

PACIFIC
OCEAN

Wake Island (U.S)

Mariana
Islands

Philippine
Sea

German Colonial Empire
(around 1914)

Guam (U.S)

Marshall
Islands

Palau
Islands

Caroline
Islands

equator

NEW
GUINEA

Bismarck
Archipelago

Kaiser
Wilhems-
land

© CARTOGRAPHICS.NL

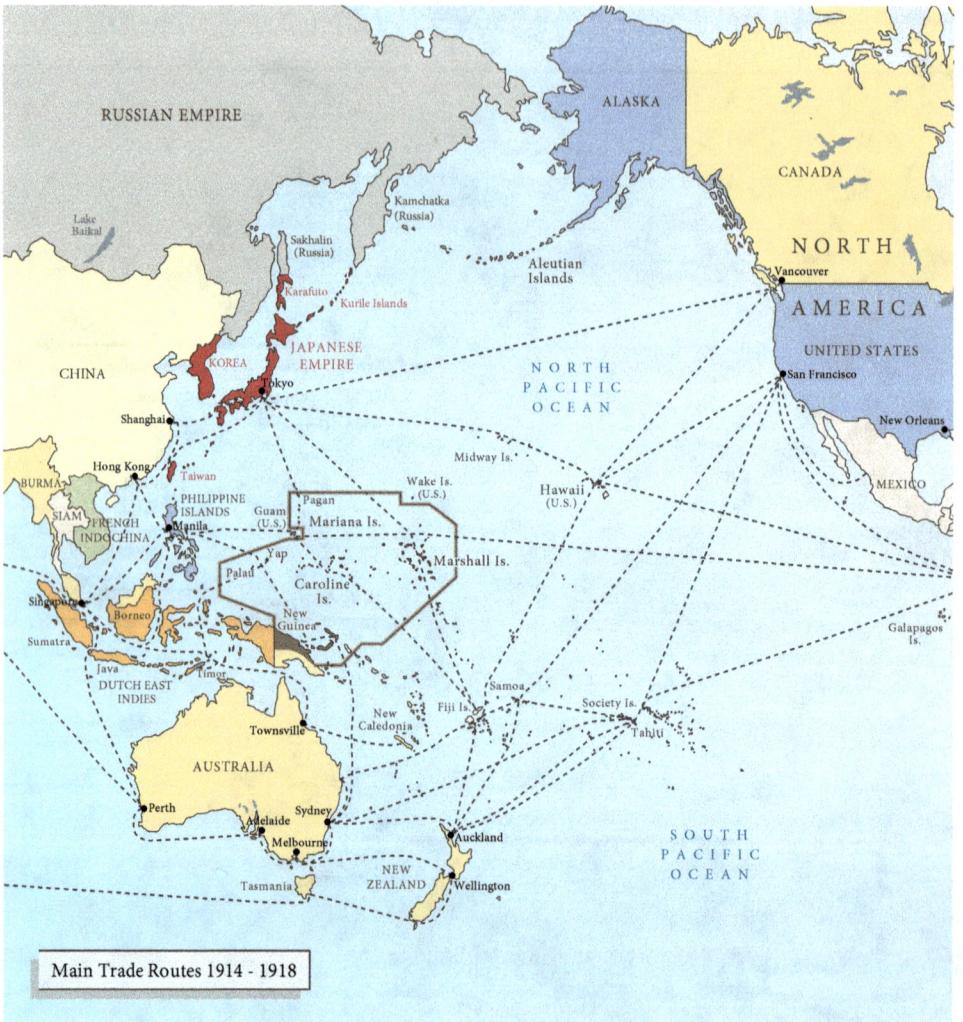

RUSSIAN EMPIRE

Lake Baikal

Kamchatka (Russia)

Sakhalin (Russia)

Karafuto

Kurile Islands

KOREA

JAPANESE EMPIRE

Tokyo

CHINA

Shanghai

Hong Kong

Taiwan

BURMA

SIAM

FRENCH INDOCHINA

PHILIPPINE ISLANDS

Manila

Guam (U.S.)

Pagan

Mariana Is.

Yap

Palau

Caroline Is.

New Guinea

Singapore

Borneo

Sumatra

Java

DUTCH EAST INDIES

Timor

AUSTRALIA

Perth

Adelaide

Melbourne

Sydney

Townsville

Tasmania

NEW ZEALAND

Auckland

Wellington

New Caledonia

Fiji Is.

Samoa

Society Is.

Tahiti

Wake Is. (U.S.)

Marshall Is.

Midway Is.

Hawaii (U.S.)

NORTH PACIFIC OCEAN

Aleutian Islands

ALASKA

CANADA

NORTH

AMERICA

UNITED STATES

Vancouver

San Francisco

New Orleans

MEXICO

Galapagos Is.

SOUTH PACIFIC OCEAN

Main Trade Routes 1914 - 1918

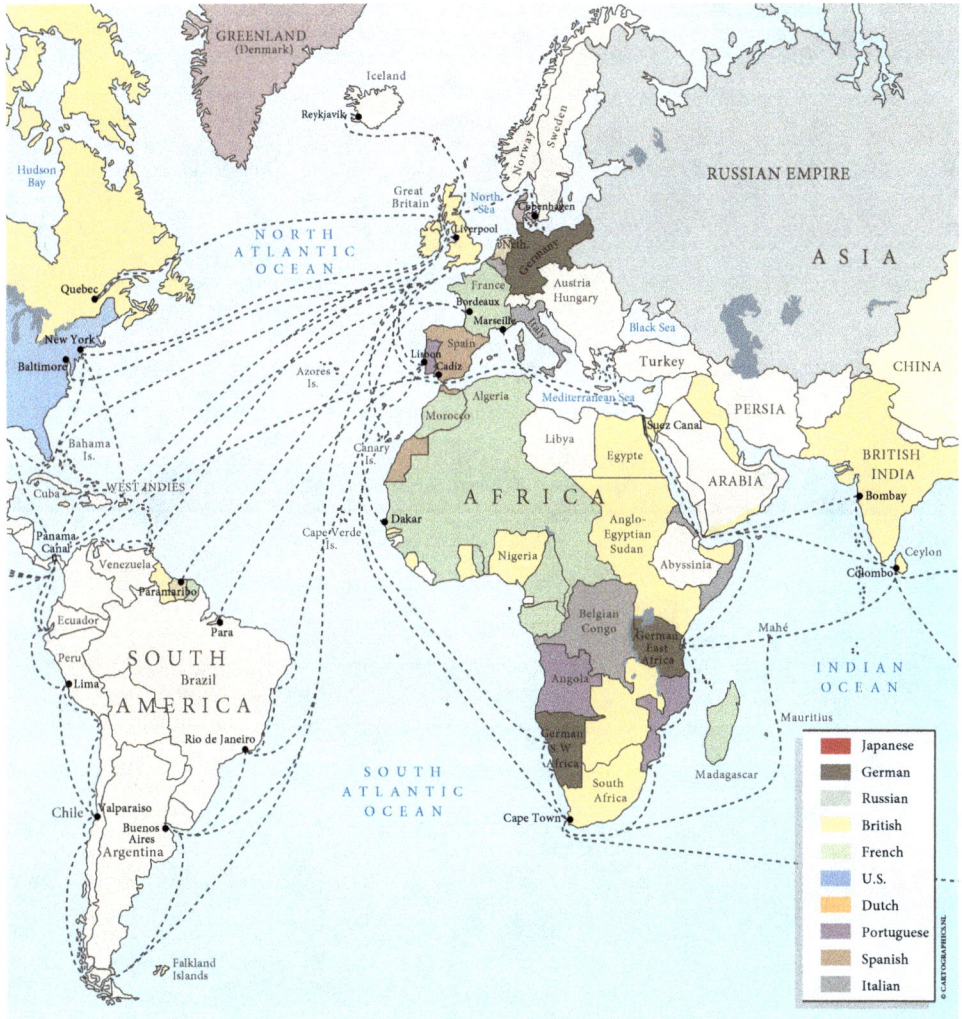

# Japan and the Wider World in the Decade of the Great War

*Introduction*

### The 1910s and the Periodization of World History

How does the decade of the 1910s fit into the broader narratives of world history? It has generally been seen as a bifurcated period, divided between an early half that was the final stretch of the "long nineteenth century," and a latter half when the Great War raged in Europe and transformed the globe. Hobsbawm's classic formulation of that periodization, running from the French Revolution of 1789 through to the outbreak of hostilities in 1914, defined the era.[1] Scholarship on the 1910s has been dominated by two main questions: a search for the origins of the Great War,[2] and an inquiry into the formation and impact of the peace settlement.[3] In this view of the past, Europe is the center and the motivating force of human history, which is seen as an evolutionary process that progressed in stages from medieval through Renaissance and Enlightenment, ultimately bringing modernity into the world. The First World War marked the endpoint, or perhaps the beginning of the end, of that

---

1 Eric Hobsbawm, *The Age of Revolution, 1789–1848* (New York: New American Library, 1964); *The Age of Capital, 1848–1875* (New York: Scribner, 1975); and *The Age of Empire, 1875–1914* (New York: Vintage, 1989).

2 Without attempting to give an exhaustive survey of scholarship on this question, a few examples should suffice: Barbara Tuchman, *The Guns of August* (New York: Macmillan, 1962); James Joll, *The Origins of the First World War*, 2nd Edition (Harlow, UK: Pearson Education Limited, 1992); Niall Ferguson, *The Pity of War: Explaining World War I* (New York: Basic Books, 1999); Richard F. Hamilton and Holger H. Herwig, eds., *The Origins of World War I* (Cambridge: Cambridge University Press, 2003); Sean McMeekin, *The Russian Origins of the First World War* (Cambridge, MA: The Belknap Press of Harvard University Press, 2011); and Ian F.W. Beckett, *The Making of the First World War* (New Haven: Yale University Press, 2012).

3 For example, Thomas A. Bailey, *Woodrow Wilson and the Lost Peace* (Chicago: Quadrangle Books, 1963); Arno J. Mayer, *Politics and Diplomacy of Peacemaking: Containment and Counterrevolution at Versailles, 1918–1919* (New York: Knopf, 1967); Thomas J. Knock, *To End All Wars: Woodrow Wilson and the Quest for a New World Order* (New York: Oxford University Press, 1992); John Milton Cooper, Jr., *Breaking the Heart of the World: Woodrow Wilson and the Fight for the League of Nations* (Cambridge: Cambridge University Press, 2001); Margaret MacMillan, *Paris 1919: Six Months that Changed the World* (New York: Random House, 2002); Norman A. Graebner and Edward M. Bennett, *The Versailles Treaty and Its Legacy: The Failure of the Wilsonian Vision* (Cambridge: Cambridge University Press, 2011).

© KONINKLIJKE BRILL NV, LEIDEN, 2014 | DOI 10.1163/9789004274273_002

historical arc, because it was the moment when the nation-states of Europe and their affiliated empires began to destroy each other and themselves. A few recent works have attempted to globalize the study of the 1910s,[4] but even here, perhaps because of the overwhelming focus on the war and its peace, the Western world and the sense of rupture have remained the primary focus for most scholars.

However, this Eurocentric vision is, quite simply, insufficient for understanding recent world history because it does not account for the fundamental changes that occurred in East Asia – within individual states, in the relations among those states, and in the connections between East Asia and the wider world – over the course of several decades. In contrast to the above narrative, this volume argues that the 1910s should be primarily conceived of as the interplay between two conceptions of time. One is the more traditional narrative, and what we might refer to as the "short 1910s," in which the war and its immediate aftermath had a transformative impact on both domestic and international contexts. The other is the "long 1910s," an era that stretched backwards and forwards beyond the chronological limits of 1910–1919.[5] As a whole, the essays show that the events of those ten years accentuated trends that had been underway since the late nineteenth century, and that the Great War itself was a catalyst for some subsequent transformations, but largely peripheral to other crucial developments. By looking beyond Europe, and beyond diplomatic and military relations, this volume describes the 1910s as a pivotal period with deep connections both to the imperialist heyday of the 1880s–1890s, and to the vibrant global politics, commercial expansion, and social movements of the 1920s.

For East Asia, the most important transition of this broad era was its shift from being a China-centric to a Japan-centric region. This regional restructuring

---

4  Charles Emmerson, *1913: In Search of the World Before the Great War* (New York: Public Affairs, 2103); and, most significantly, Erez Manela, *The Wilsonian Moment: Self-Determination and the International Origins of Anti-Colonial Nationalism* (Oxford: Oxford University Press, 2007). Hamilton and Herwig, *Origins*, cited above, includes a chapter on Japan and the War by Frederick Dickinson. An intriguing effort is underway to expand the study of World War I to a truly global scope through the production of an on-line "International Encyclopedia of the First World War;" see <http://www.1914-1918-online.net/>.

5  This interpretation of the 1910s was first developed at a roundtable at the Association of Asian Studies annual conference in March 2011, in Honolulu, HI. The presenters on that panel were Evan Dawley, David Howland, Youngran Hur, and Guoqi Xu, with commentary by Akira Iriye. The editors would like to thank them for their participation in that roundtable, which was essential to the development of the ideas presented in this volume. Comments by members of the audience at that panel were also extremely helpful.

occurred within the context of a wave of globalization that dated back to the latter half of the nineteenth century. The new and stronger global linkages derived from three main sources: the expansion of world empires outward from the metropolitan cores of modern nation-states; massive human migration, some of it voluntary and some of it forced, across the globe; and the creation and pursuit of the "universal West" as a model for modern development by individuals, groups, and governments across Asia.[6] The imperialist incursions associated with globalization destabilized the existing order in East Asia, opening the door for Japan to emerge as a significant international force. As it rose, Japan displaced China as the intra-regional leader, gained control over new territories and populations, and challenged the Western nation-states to acknowledge the existence of an Asian peer. Japan's ascendance in East Asia had global effects, as smaller states and societies in Europe and Asia sought links to Japan that might enhance their status or security vis-à-vis the major European powers.

The turn of the twentieth century within East Asia saw both the final de-centering of China, and the beginnings of the displacement of European states by Japan and the United States. Since the middle decades of the nineteenth century, Western nation-states had gradually shifted the global economic, military, and cultural center of gravity from the Qing Empire to Europe. Within East Asia, Meiji Japan upset the China-centered order in stages, and in the process began to challenge aspects of European dominance. Japan detached the Liuqiu/Ryukyu Kingdom from the Qing tributary orbit and annexed it as Okinawa Prefecture around 1880. Some fifteen years later, it defeated China in war, removing China's political influence from the Korean Peninsula and acquiring Taiwan as a colony in the process. Ten years after that, it drove Russian influence out of Korea, over which it established a protectorate, and assumed control of some Russian rail lines and other interests in Manchuria. These acts not only reduced China's status and significance, but also shattered the myth of European superiority. Meanwhile, the United States highlighted the transition from old to new powers by defeating Spain in 1898 and acquiring its colonies in the Caribbean and Western Pacific, and by issuing the Open Door Notes in 1899 and 1900 to forestall further imperialist acquisition of Chinese territory. Both Japan and the United States acted with the approval of

---

6   Cemil Aydin argues that reformist intellectuals, officials, and other elites in various parts of Asia helped to create the idea that Western modernity of the nineteenth century was something that could be emulated by all national societies. However, around the dawn of the twentieth century, the pursuit of the universal West slowly gave way to anti-Western pan-Asianism. See Aydin, *The Politics of Anti-Westernism in Asia* (New York: Columbia University Press, 2007).

the global hegemon, Great Britain, but their actions nevertheless heralded a major reshuffling of powers. The evolving orders in Asia and Europe overlapped with the formation of the Anglo-Japanese Alliance in 1902, and with the crucial role of the United States in brokering the peace between Japan and Russia. In short, the world had begun to change before it entered the chronological 1910s, thus what the Eurocentric narrative of the long nineteenth century has framed as the cataclysmic impact of First World War was, in some important structural ways, the continuation of more long-term shifts.

Scholars of East Asian affairs have not ignored the 1910s in general, and the Great War in particular. The earliest work on this period, by historians including James Morley, Albert White, Marius Jansen, and Paul Dull, focused on the most prominent examples of Japan's new assertiveness: the Siberian Intervention and China-Japan relations, especially in the context of the Twenty-One Demands. Dull, in a brief but important essay on Katō Takaaki's (Kōmei) efforts to forge a diplomatic solution to Japan's difficulties with China, argues that the combined influence of Japanese militarists, businessmen, political parties, and religious leaders essentially doomed Katō's attempt to forestall future military expansion.[7] Jansen, in his multi-sided exploration of the unstable alliances between Chinese and Japanese nationalists, stresses the importance of Japanese domestic politics for facilitating Japanese aid to Sun Yat-sen's revolutionary movements.[8] Similarly, all four of the elements that Morley stresses in motivating Japan's participation in the Siberian Intervention – Japan's domestic power structure, Japanese perceptions of global affairs, Japanese knowledge of Western actions and objectives, and Japan's leaders' responses to domestic and international pressures – are essentially part of an explanation of Japanese foreign relations as the extension of domestic politics.[9] Only White, working without the benefit of Japanese sources, sees Japan's actions in Siberia as primarily conditioned by external factors, with war in Europe and revolution in Russia facilitating the Intervention as an extension of Japan's existing policies in China and Manchuria.[10]

However, the interpretations developed during the context of the 1950s are in need of revision, for two main reasons. First, Dull, White, and Morley all

---

7    Paul S. Dull, "Count Kato Komei and the Twenty-one Demands," *Pacific Historical Review* 19:2 (May 1950): 151–161.

8    Marius Jansen, *The Japanese and Sun Yat-sen* (Cambridge, MA: Harvard University Press, 1954).

9    James William Morley, *The Japanese Thrust into Siberia* (New York: Columbia University Press, 1957).

10   John Albert White, *The Siberian Intervention* (Princeton: Princeton University Press, 1950).

approached their topics from the perspective of early Cold War superpower rivalries and US-led efforts to contain the spread of communism. This agenda seems to have led to a more favorable image of Japanese expansionist activities than was warranted. New sources and new perspectives require that we revisit these topics, and in fact scholars such as Frederick Dickinson and Noriko Kawamura have begun to revise the older interpretations and have significantly complicated our understanding of Japanese diplomacy. Kawamura argues that the war both catalyzed a shift in Japanese strategic attention from Europe to the United States, and pushed Japanese leaders toward a particularistic regionalism that contrasted sharply with Wilsonian universalism.[11] Dickinson offers a compelling interpretation of the global effects of the Great War. In his first book, he updated the earlier studies on the domestic drivers of Japanese foreign policy by framing the wartime ascendancy of militarists and expansionists as part of a long standing conflict between leading political factions.[12] He goes further in a more recent work, arguing forcefully that the Great War fundamentally restructured international politics, demarcated the transition from the nineteenth to the twentieth centuries, and thrust Japan into the status of a global power. Much as Commodore Perry's visits had sparked a debate over national construction in the nineteenth century, the war prompted new discussions over national reconstruction in the interwar years. Into the early 1930s, Japanese political actors firmly embraced Wilsonian principles of liberal internationalism, democracy, and peace.[13] About half of the essays in this volume continue this revisionist process and in so doing sometimes challenge both the older and newer interpretations.

The second reason for the need to return to this era in regional and world history is that the vast majority of existing scholarship, from White through Dickinson, has examined Japanese involvement in the world primarily through the lenses of domestic politics and the roles played by important political actors (with Dickinson taking a much broader view of this segment of society than did his predecessors). As important as this diplomatic, leader-oriented history remains, the present volume looks intentionally at relations with the wider world from a variety of perspectives in order to understand the breadth and depth of the shifts that occurred across the long 1910s. Thus individual

11    Noriko Kawamura, *Turbulence in the Pacific: Japanese-U.S. Relations during World War I* (Westport, CT: Praeger, 2000).

12    Frederick R. Dickinson, *War and National Reinvention: Japan in the Great War, 1914–1919* (Cambridge, MA: Harvard University Press, 1999).

13    Frederick R. Dickinson, *World War I and the Triumph of a New Japan, 1919–1930* (Cambridge: Cambridge University Press, 2013).

chapters examine trade, migration, religious activism, disease and hygiene, the spread of ideas, and the interpretation and presentation of history. Our combination of approaches reveals strong continuities that indicate the salience of the longer chronological framework.

In spite of the world historical significance of the 1910s, in both its long and short forms, most of the recent scholarship on East Asia during the late nineteenth and early twentieth centuries has been nation-centric and has overlooked the importance of the decade. In the study of Chinese history, the Xinhai Revolution of 1911 has been seen as the endpoint of a much longer dynastic cycle, and scholars have viewed the 1910s as a period of domestic disarray when the conflicting interests of local warlords tore the country into conflicting satrapies. With the exception of numerous works on the cultural and political transformations of the May Fourth era, and Xu Guoqi's exploration of how China used the First World War to advance its standing in global affairs,[14] the decade has generally been passed over as a chaotic interlude between the death throes of the Qing (1890–1911) and the rise of both Nationalists and Communists during the 1920s. For Japan, the 1910s have been skimmed over in favor of the revolutions of the earlier Meiji Era (1868–1912) and the social and political movements that extended from the Rice Riots of 1918 through to the assassination politics of the early 1930s. Narratives of recent Korean history focus on the years leading up to annexation by Japan in 1910, and then jump ahead to the explosion of anti-colonial resistance in 1919 and the more open conditions under civilian rule of the 1920s. In these histories of nation building, the 1910s are largely disconnected from what came before and after, and thus the decade has not received the careful scrutiny it deserves.

This neglect is unfortunate, to say the least, given that the events of the chronological 1910s built upon existing trends and promoted the ongoing construction of a Japan-centric region. Japan formally acquired a new colony when it annexed Korea; it played significant regional and international roles during the war years; it extended its presence on the Chinese mainland, including the Manchurian railway zone; it gradually transformed the nature of its rule in Taiwan; and it asserted Japanese equality in the international arena. Following the end of China's dynastic order, Japan was one of two locally based states that retained an appreciable measure of autonomy, internal coherence, and international standing (the other was Siam). In light of the gap

---

14    Xu Guoqi, *China and the Great War: China's Pursuit of a New National Identity and Internationlization* (Cambridge: Cambridge University Press, 2005); and *Strangers on the Western Front: Chinese Workers in the Great War* (Cambridge, MA: Harvard University Press, 2011).

between Japan's actual involvement in regional and world affairs, and the amount of scholarly attention to those subjects, the present volume is a much-needed exploration of the emergence of a Japan-centric East Asia. Moreover, it assesses the global realignment of national power, as various states in Europe and Asia enhanced their relationships with Japan in an attempt to counter or limit the influence of Russia (or the new Soviet Union), England, and/or Germany.

However, as the essays in this volume suggest, we must view "the 1910s" through two lenses, both the wide-ranging effects of the Great War, and the longer temporal framework that goes beyond the chronological confines of 1910–1919. For East Asia, the 1910s were the high-water mark of a particular type of international relations, in which Japan saw itself, and was seen by others, as a role model for nation-building projects across the region, even as Japanese foreign policy worked largely in cooperation with that of the dominant Anglo-American powers. It was the period in which Japan achieved the early Meiji objective of acceptance among the ranks of imperial powers and during which it acted within the confines of the order established by the leading Western states, even as it asserted greater political, economic, and cultural influence within East Asia.[15] Moreover, these years encompassed the apogee of Japanese hegemony in the Gramscian sense, when other countries acceded to Japan's leadership. Not all Asian states and societies accepted Japan's regional ascendance, some Western states opposed Japan's rise, and some Japanese leaders chafed against the restrictions imposed by Western global leadership. Nevertheless, in broad terms, positive perceptions of Japan's regional ascendancy combined with Japanese confidence in a collaborative approach to define East Asia's long 1910s. Although it is difficult to fix the precise limits of this era, it extended from the early 1890s through to the late 1920s, with prior roots and later effects. The events of 1910–1919, and particularly the Great War, concentrated and focused the characteristics of the longer period, hence our extension of the nominal decade over a prolonged timeframe.

The chapters in this volume approach the transition from a China-centric to a Japan-centric region through new research and with original analytical perspectives that, as a group, necessitated our reinterpretation of the 1910s. To be sure, many of the papers highlight the significance of the Great War in facilitating this regional transformation and allowing at least some East Asian states to expand their relations with other parts of the globe. In so doing, they make the

---

15　For Japan's multi-faceted, incremental, and ultimately fundamental challenge to that order, see Masato Kimura and Tosh Minohara, eds., *Tumultuous Decade: Empire, Society and Diplomacy in 1930s Japan* (Toronto: University of Toronto Press, 2013).

crucial point that a Western-centric perspective is insufficient to fully understanding that global conflict. However, the authors also tend to show that, in
many regards, the First World War had a circumstantial, rather than a catalytic,
importance for Japan, and East Asia more generally. That is, the War did not
cause a fundamental transformation or dramatic shift in intra- and extra-
regional interactions. Rather, it either promoted the intensification of existing
relationships and tendencies, or it facilitated the pursuit, and in some cases
the at least partial fulfillment, of objectives that had hitherto been unattain-
able. In addition, as some chapters will show, the War was entirely peripheral
to significant aspects of the activities undertaken by East Asians abroad, and to
the connections between those undertakings and the national development of
various states. The volume is divided into two sections on the basis of the subject matter and approach of each essay. The first, which contains chapters that
look at Japan's diplomatic and military relations, offers both a reexamination
of some of the issues addressed in the earlier scholarship on the war years and
a needed sense of the breadth of Japan's new international relations.[16] The second comprises chapters that adopt transnational approaches to the study of
Japan's domestic, intra-imperial, and foreign affairs. Together, the two sections
provide a much-needed reassessment of both Japan's global connections and
the place of East Asia in modern global history. The following overview will
survey the chapters in terms of how they address the interaction between the
two chronological frames of the short and long 1910s.

### East Asia's Short 1910s

As many of the essays in this volume show, the Great War was an important
event for East Asia, challenging the Western-centric view that the conflict was
significant mostly for Europe and the United States. Our intention is not to
argue that the war did not revolve around the nation-states of Europe
and North America. Britain, Germany, France, Austria-Hungary, Russia, the

---

16   A recent volume provides a sense of the expanding state-to-state ties between Japan and
     European nations, from the early Tokugawa period through the Cold War. See Bert
     Edström, ed., *The Japanese and Europe: Images and Perceptions* (Richmond, UK: The Japan
     Library, 2000). Dick Stegewerns's essay "The Break with Europe: Japanese Views of the Old
     World after the First World War," is especially relevant to the present volume. He argues
     that as Japanese shapers of opinions on foreign policy viewed the war, they abandoned
     their earlier vision of Europe as the epitome of advanced civilization and began to focus
     more on Asia as the primary arena for Japanese foreign relations.

United States, and others unquestionably played the largest roles and felt the most immediate effects of the war and the peace. Rather, we seek to emphasize that the war was global in nature, that crucial aspects of it took place outside of the North Atlantic and Eastern European region, and that Asian states and societies experienced profound domestic and international changes as a result of the war.

The narrative of the "short 1910s" is most pronounced in the shifting diplomatic terrain, as Asian countries altered their relationships with each other, and with European nations in the context of wartime alliances and opportunities. In his study of Foreign Minister Uchida Yasuya (Kōsai), who took over that post in 1918, Rustin Gates shows that the War provided the context for two shifts in Japanese foreign policy thinking. The first, which took place early in the war, brought increased expansionism on the Asian mainland and less consideration of the interests of Britain and the United States. The second occurred under Uchida and is described by Gates as the replacement of the "new" by the "old" diplomacy, with its greater reliance on cultivating smooth relations with the Anglo-American powers. John Meehan, in his essay on the Anglo-Japanese Alliance in the context of changing relations between Britain and the Pacific Dominions – Canada, Australia and New Zealand – highlights the first of the shifts that Gates describes. He finds that, as the Dominions gained more control over their foreign relations during the war, Japan began to expand its connections to these increasingly autonomous states. For Meehan, Britain's distraction from the Pacific was essential for Japan's ability to exploit these new diplomatic ties.

Two chapters address this theme of changing diplomatic connections in the context of the peace negotiations by exploring Japan's relations with the United States and Britain. Both Tadashi Nakatani and Shusuke Takahara look at the talks in Paris and find that Japan made some important gains there that marked an evolution in its interactions with the United States, and, to a lesser extent, with Britain. Nakatani argues, as Gates does, that Japan shifted its diplomatic approach during the war years, first to deepen its practice of great power diplomacy in seizing the German possessions in Shandong and the Western Pacific, and then seemingly to embrace Wilson's New Diplomacy, embodied in the League of Nations. However, his key finding is that Japan supported the League at Paris primarily to secure Wilson's agreement to Japanese retention of the formerly German territories. Takahara's multi-perspective study of the origins of the mandate system similarly shows that Japanese aggressiveness and determination during the negotiations ultimately overcame US objections and shaped the agreement in a way that was very much in Japan's favor.

Several of the essays show that Japan both altered existing bilateral relationships considerably and developed new ones during the war years. Isao Chiba's
examination of the role of Gotō Shimpei in shaping Russo-Japanese relations
during the 1910s indicates that the war facilitated the high point of cooperation
between the two countries, with the entente of July 1916. However, following
the Russian withdrawal from the War, Gotō argued forcefully in favor of
Japanese leadership in the Siberian Intervention, in part to reverse the
Bolshevik takeover and in part to give Japan leverage over the United States.
After the October Revolution, Japan deepened its relations with two of Russia's
neighbors, Turkey and Poland, partly to keep closer watch on the new Soviet
Union. Selçuk Esenbel argues that Japan took an active role in the formulation
of the Treaty of Sèvres that dismantled the Ottoman Empire, in order to gain
for itself a place in the shipping routes of the Eastern Mediterranean and Black
Seas, and to contain Soviet Russia. Although remaining openly in line with
British policies in Turkey, Japanese officials in Tokyo and Ankara pursued an
independent "twilight diplomacy" through which they supported Turkish
nationalists, with whom they shared emerging pan-Asianist ideas. Similarly, as
Ewa Pałasz-Rutkowska shows in her essay on the origins of Polish-Japanese
relations, Japanese military and diplomatic officers gained favorable impressions of Poland in battles in Siberia and Warsaw. As a result of these wartime
interactions, Japan openly supported Poland's post-war independence.

Two of the essays show that the latter half of the 1910s provided unprecedented opportunities for Japan's maritime expansion. On the military front,
Charles Schencking clearly demonstrates how the leaders of the Japanese navy
took advantage of the Great War to seize coveted territories in the Pacific and
obtain larger and larger budgets from the national treasury, which they used to
challenge US and British naval supremacy. According to Schencking, these
naval officials viewed Europe's tragedy as "divine aid" for their own plans for
Japanese expansion. Masato Kimura's trilateral study of the influence of the
opening of the Panama Canal on Japan, the US, and the UK also adheres, in
part, to the "short 1910s" narrative, although he diverges from Schencking in
that he de-emphasizes the importance of the war itself. Instead, Kimura argues
that the canal's opening in the summer of 1914 dramatically affected all three
maritime nations. It boosted Japanese trade with, and migration to, South
America, and allowed for closer interactions with the US in the trans-Pacific
trade. Nevertheless, the overall impact of the canal was to reorient global trade
networks away from the UK and towards the US.

The Great War had a strong effect on relations within East Asia, as several of
the chapters attest. Both Yoshiko Okamoto and Sōchi Naraoka examine
changes to China-Japan relations after Japan's seizure of German concessions

in Shandong Province, and especially after Japan issued its Twenty-One Demands in January 1915. Okamoto shows how Japanese Buddhist organizations latched onto the expansion of Japanese imperial influence in order to spread their own networks throughout the region, and especially in China. This imperialist Buddhism stood in contrast to the message of spreading world peace that Japanese Buddhists used to promote themselves in the United States, and it exacerbated tensions with China when Japan pushed for the right to proselytize in Group V of the Twenty-One Demands. Naraoka takes a multilateral diplomatic approach to the Demands, and finds that their issuance not only prompted a downward spiral in relations with China, which used them to promote nationalism at home and gain sympathy abroad, but also caused problems for Japanese interactions with the US and Britain. Significantly, Naraoka finds that the Demands were largely the product of Japanese domestic politics and popular opinion, with expansionists in the Army General Staff pressuring the Foreign Ministry to issue the demands, and segments of the public harshly criticizing Foreign Minister Katō Takaaki for withdrawing Group V in the face of Chinese, US, and British objections.

The narrative of the short 1910s is also seen in several chapters that stress the domestic effects of the First World War. Both Hiromi Mizuno and Chika Shinohara show how the Japanese educational system went through substantive changes during and after the war. Mizuno demonstrates through a careful study of the Taishō era science curriculum that the Great War was a turning point for Japanese education, in that it promoted greater attention to the hands-on study of the sciences from the 1920s onwards. Shinohara examines the role of Tsuda Umeko in promoting girls' education in Japan across the Meiji era and beyond, and finds that the war prompted three key changes that facilitated the expansion of educational opportunities. She argues that the latter half of the 1910s saw changes in gender identity, women's expectations of rights and careers, and an overall acceptance of difference within Japanese society. Sumiko Otsubo shares with Mizuno an emphasis on science as she explores the intersection of Japanese epidemiology, the Siberian Intervention, and the Spanish Influenza pandemic. Through her analysis of the spread and study of the disease, Otsubo finds that the Great War contributed significantly to the expansion of Japan's global networks. Lim Chaisung also looks at the issues of transportation and hygiene, but he focuses on domestic transit networks rather than the overseas routes that brought pandemic influenza to Japan. Lim investigates the war's impact on Japanese railway companies, and finds that the demands and opportunities of the conflict forced railway owners to navigate between the rising demands of long-distance transportation and the need to keep both workers and customers healthy. Finally, Tze-ki Hon looks primarily at Chinese images of the world, and describes a dramatic shift that occurred as a result of Chinese observations of the combat in Europe. Specifically, he argues that the decisions at Versailles regarding Shandong Province revealed to Chinese intellectuals that the global order was defined by military aggression, diplomatic manipulation, and above all, imperialistic domination. Similar to Mizuno's analysis, the war thus marked a turning point in Chinese history, after which Chinese reconsidered their place in the world.

These essays, which constitute roughly two-thirds of the volume, present a strong argument for the salience of the short 1910s. Collectively, they show that the Great War caused or facilitated key shifts in Japanese diplomacy, East Asian international relations, and the domestic environments of Asian societies. More concretely, they show how Japan asserted its dominance over China, and sought to enhance its standing in great power affairs by attempting to determine the course of events in Russia, pursuing new allies in Europe and the Pacific, and both subtly and directly challenging Anglo-American predominance. However, during the war and its aftermath, as a national unit Japan did not seek to upset the established order or forge a global pan-Asianist movement; rather, it restored its own faith in the importance of working with Britain and the United States. Although the significance of the years of war and peace in these chapters is undeniable, it should be emphasized that most of these authors place that short-term significance within a much longer temporal framework. That is, they highlight the greater importance of the interplay between the short and long 1910s.

### East Asia's Long 1910s

Although the Great War and the Treaty of Versailles certainly influenced events in East Asia and affected Japan's relations with European nations and the United States, the contributions to this volume show that the narrative of the long 1910s held equal if not greater salience for East Asian history. Within this temporal view, it appears that many of the events and trends that defined the rupture of the war years were, in fact, linked to longer processes of historic change that extended before and after the chronological decade. Earlier authors, such as Jansen, Morley, White, and Dickinson, all place their wartime subjects within longer foreign and domestic contexts, so our framework is not without precedent. However, in contrast to these older works, several of the present essays describe important developments for East Asian history that were at most tangentially affected by the Great War.

The chapters by Charles Schencking, Shusuke Takahara, Tadashi Nakatani, and Selçuk Esenbel all show that, while Japan tested the limits of Anglo-American preeminence by trying to expand its own influence in international affairs, it consistently stopped short of outright disagreement, let alone open conflict, with Britain and the United States. Schencking argues that the Japanese navy willingly accepted the constraints imposed on its size and budgets through the Washington Treaty System in 1922, because it realized that Japan could not at that time sustain a naval construction program large enough to match US shipbuilding capacity. Similarly, both Takahara and Nakatani demonstrate that Japan had to be very careful in its efforts to secure its territorial gains in China and the Pacific, lest it raise the objections of either Britain or, especially, the United States. In fact, in order to achieve its diplomatic successes in Paris, Japan had to sign onto Wilson's most sought-after goal, the League of Nations. Esenbel also argues that, although Japan's Minister in Istanbul, Uchida Sadatsuchi, recognized the potential significance of Turkish nationalism and took independent action in cultivating relations with the nationalists, he never overstepped the limits of "prudent diplomacy," as she puts it.

This theme – of pushing, but also staying within, the diplomatic and military boundaries defined by the Anglo-American powers – recurs throughout the volume. For example, Tosh Minohara, in his examination of the tensions between Japan and the United States over Japanese immigration, shows that the problem became a diplomatic crisis following California's passage of the 1913 Alien Land Law. Minohara argues that this dispute was the culmination of difficulties that had been mounting as Japanese immigration to Hawai'i and California had increased since the 1890s. The outbreak of war gave both countries a distraction from this point of conflict, and they were able to overcome the further disagreement when Wilson rejected Japan's proposal to insert a racial equality clause into the Treaty of Versailles. In this light, Minohara, Schencking, Takahara, Nakatani, and Esenbel all seem to agree with John Meehan's point that, even as the Dominions sought more autonomous foreign policies, the Anglo-Japanese alliance remained the dominant framework for Japan's foreign relations into the 1920s. This point also reinforces Rustin Gates's main argument that, even though the war years witnessed an important temporary shift in Japan's overseas orientation, Uchida's term as Foreign Minister (1918–1923) showed the overall continuity between Meiji and Taishō era diplomacy.

Several other contributors to the volume share Minohara's emphasis on the long-term roots of Japanese diplomatic relations in the 1910s. In Esenbel's chapter on Japanese-Turkish relations, it is clear that the steps taken between the two countries after the war were only possible because of positive contacts going back to Japanese assistance to the survivors of the *Ertuğrul* incident in 1890, as well as the pre-war efforts of General Utsunomiya Tarō to build connections to Turkish pan-Islamists under the banner of pan-Asianism. Ewa Pałasz-Rutkowska similarly argues that Japanese-Polish relations of the late-1910s were, in fact, built on a deeper foundation of writings on Poland by Japanese travelers that received a widespread readership in Japan, and on long-standing Polish suggestions that Japan and Poland aid each other in their respective conflicts with Tsarist Russia. Bert Edström agrees with both Esenbel and Pałasz-Rutkowska on the centrality of Russia in Japan's evolving strategic concerns from the late-nineteenth century onwards. His study of the origins of relations between Japan and the Scandinavian countries – Denmark, Sweden, and Norway – shows that a mutual concern with Russian expansion was a central motivation for Japan and these "distant friends" to forge relationships that were low-intensity but nonetheless significant. From the perspective of the European states, intra-Scandinavian rivalries and their relative interests in both China and Japan determined the depth of these new connections. On the subject of Russia, Isao Chiba's chapter on the vagaries of Russo-Japanese relations during and immediately after the Great War demonstrates that those developments were in keeping with a longer history of ups and downs that began even before the Russo-Japanese War of 1904–05. Chiba situates the 1916 Entente and the Siberian Intervention firmly within this longer history of bilateral contestation in Northeast Asia.

The long-1910s narrative is even clearer in the context of intra-East Asian relations. Sōchi Naraoka's study of the Twenty-One Demands highlights this volume's contention that the central event for East Asia in this historic era was the transition from a China-centric to a Japan-centric set of regional relations. China's efforts to deflect Japanese pressure by relying on Western assistance clearly displayed Japan's ascendance over the former regional hegemon. Likewise, Yoshiko Okamoto argues that Japanese Buddhists merely took advantage of the conditions of the mid-1910s in order to push their long-standing agenda of proselytization and sect-expansion in China and Korea. In other words, the Great War may have had a circumstantial, rather than catalytic, impact. Yuehtsen Juliette Chung makes a similar argument in her study of Chinese and Japanese quarantine regimes and disease control networks. While Sumiko Otsubo emphasizes the short 1910s periodization in controlling pandemic influenza, Chung argues that the cooperation between China and Japan in containing cholera outbreaks during the 1910s was the result of a process of building quarantine institutions and sharing information on preventing the spread of epidemic disease that began in China's treaty ports decades earlier. In fact, although Otsubo stresses the significance of the Siberian Intervention, she also shows that Japanese advances in knowledge and control depended upon pre-war research conducted in the Manchurian Railway zone.

Japan's colonies also experienced the 1910s as part of longer-term historic changes. In the case of Taiwan, Evan Dawley examines Japanese views of themselves as colonizers through the lens of women settlers and the varying roles they played in promoting Japanese colonial rule. Dawley's study of the Patriotic Ladies' Association (*Aikoku fujinkai*) shows that, as women migrated to Taiwan in greater numbers beginning in around 1905, they brought with them a "softer" brand of Japanese imperialism that focused more on social and cultural reform than it did on military domination and police control. He connects this to the civilizing mission that had been present within Japanese expansionism since at least the 1874 Taiwan Expedition.

The transnational flows of people, goods, and ideas also took place in ways largely unrelated to the history of the Great War. As noted above, Masato Kimura argues that it was the opening of the Panama Canal, rather than the outbreak of the war with which it coincided, that instigated new patterns of trade and migration and allowed the United States and Japan to reorient the global economy away from its nineteenth-century epicenter in the UK. Martin Dusinberre, in his study of the links between Japanese settlers in Korea and Hawai'i and their hometown (*furusato*) in Japan, finds patterns of behavior that were almost completely disconnected from the war. Dusinberre argues that Japan's engagement with the wider world through its growing Meiji-period diaspora was fundamentally connected to, and influenced, the tensions between center and locality that emerged in Japan's domestic nation-building. Although large-scale emigration began in the 1880s, it was only during the 1910s that these overseas Japanese had the financial wherewithal to contribute financially to the construction of hometown and nation. Susan Townsend, in her comparative work on urban planning in Japan and England during the 1910s, finds that England's Garden City Movement had a profound effect on Japanese urban planners. Townsend makes use of travelling theory to show that Japanese planners like Seki Hajime and Shibusawa Eiichi, among others, adapted English ideas on social reform and incorporating green spaces into expanding urban areas to Japanese patterns of urbanization and historic experience with city planning. After the war it seems that Japanese planners turned more towards an urban-suburban divide, but Townsend argues that this shift was the end result of past modifications rather than a complete departure from the British model. Similarly, Chika Shinohara's chapter indicates that the Taishō-era transformation of girls' education derived from long-term experimentation with models acquired overseas. In all of these cases, the events of the 1910s concentrated and refined existing trends.

Finally, a number of chapters show that the concept of the long 1910s arises not only from roots that extended well before the start of the chronological decade, but also from effects that went on into the 1920s and 1930s. Many of the essays discussed above display this transitional nature. For Minohara, the unresolved problem of Japanese immigration was reinforced by the 1924 US Immigration Act, which banned the Japanese and became a rallying cry for those who sought to "leave the West, and enter Asia" in the 1930s. The expansionism of the Japanese navy outlined by Schencking would return in full form after the collapse of the 1930 London Naval Conference, while the return of the "old diplomacy," detailed by Gates, would remain in force for almost two decades. Esenbel and Pałasz-Rutkowska both argue that the small-scale relationships formed in the 1910s became much more significant during the 1930s as Japan became increasingly concerned with the Soviet Union. The changed Chinese worldview that Hon describes, and the Chinese reaction against the Twenty-One Demands detailed by Naraoka, both influenced the rise of Chinese nationalism and China's resistance against Japan before and during the Second Sino-Japanese War (1937–45). Dawley argues that the events of the 1910s influenced the subsequent institutionalization of more lenient colonial policies that facilitated the florescence of public discourse during the 1920s. Mizuno clearly demonstrates how the changes of the 1910s brought a new curriculum to Japanese education, which in turn contributed to the vibrancy of late-Taishō society.

Further examples could be drawn from throughout the volume, but perhaps the most intriguing example of the long-term effects of the 1910s is provided by Caroline Rose in her chapter on Chinese and Japanese textbooks across the twentieth century. Rose finds that, in the wake of the Twenty-One Demands, Chinese textbooks almost immediately adopted a narrative of victimization at Japanese hands, a narrative that persisted even as the 1910s were eclipsed by the 1930s and 1940s as the locus of that victimization, only to return again in textbooks of the 1980s. On the Japanese side, scholars have treated the 1910s as one element in a highly contingent process that produced the conflict of the 1930s, in contrast to a Chinese narrative of inevitability, and have viewed the decade as part of a larger history of global social movements, without connecting events in China to any specific Japanese actions. Although the 1910s seem to have faded into the footnotes of the most recent textbooks of the early 21st century, Rose argues that the decade nevertheless had a tremendous influence on subsequent China-Japan relations.

## Conclusion

The foregoing survey of the chapters in this volume reveals the deep interplay between the contrasting narratives of the short and long 1910s. The former emphasizes that the most significant events of the decade were inextricably linked to the outbreak, conduct, and resolution of the First World War, while the latter stresses that both these short-term developments as well as a range of other historic trends extended long before and after the chronological 1910s, and were often only tangentially affected by the war and peace. In fact, the vast majority of essays touch on both of these narratives, suggesting that they cannot be conceived of independently of one another. This conclusion is in stark contrast to the conventional, Eurocentric narrative of the war, and also of the 1910s in general. As described above, this standard interpretation frames 1914 as the endpoint of a long nineteenth century, during which Europe was the prime motivator in human affairs, and views the war as significant only for Europe and the United States. The present volume argues strongly against that perception of history, and in doing so it joins with the *longue durée* approach of some of the earlier scholarship on East Asia during the war years, although it departs from much of that scholarship in significant ways. On the basis of 23 essays that adopt a wide-range of perspectives on relations within Asia and between Asian, European, and North American states, this volume argues that the 1910s fit into the narrative of world history as a long, transitional period in which Japan replaced China as the core of East Asia. Moreover, it was the era in which Japan and the United States displaced Europe and began to shift the epicenter of global affairs from the Atlantic to the Pacific.

The Editors
*Tosh Minohara, Tze-ki Hon and Evan Dawley*

# SECTION 1

## *Diplomacy and Foreign Relations*

∵

# The Clash of Pride and Prejudice
### *The Immigration Issue and US-Japan Relations in the 1910s*

*Tosh Minohara*

## Introduction

Without a doubt, the 1910s was a turbulent decade. This was not merely due to the outbreak of the first truly global war that engulfed much of Europe for over four years, but also due to political turmoil in other parts of the world, such as the 1911 Xinhai Revolution in China and the 1917 Russian Revolution. On the contrary, however, the relationship between the US and Japan during the same period is perceived to have been relatively amicable, despite a few bumps along the way over differences in Japan's policies toward China, Manchuria, and later Siberia.[1] Such differences, however significant they may have been during times of peace, were completely overshadowed by the Great War. In this bloody conflict, Japan and the US (after April 1917) would fight together as allies against the Central Powers. Under such circumstances, it made perfect sense to set aside minor issues and instead deal with the main task on hand: fighting a war. This was the prevailing spirit that led to the signing of the 1917 Lansing-Ishii Agreement which momentarily set aside the China problem.

In the context of US-Japan relations, the decade of the 1910s began with the 1911 US-Japan Navigation and Trade Treaty that restored tariff autonomy to Japan and shed most of the "unequal" aspects of the former 1894 treaty that it replaced. Therefore this was a decade in which Japan finally attained "equality" vis-à-vis the Western powers, and the primary foreign policy objective since 1856 of this island nation had been achieved. It was also a decade when cultural modernity blossomed, witnessed by Japan's very first Western style theater – with its grand renaissance architecture – opening its doors in 1911.

The catalyst for this dynamic transformation had been Japan's victory against Russia during the war of 1904–05, that catapulted the nation onto the global stage as the first non-White power. Despite Japan having joined the club of first-rate powers, it still only occupied the bottom rung of the ladder and thus Japan was extremely sensitive to being accorded the status of an equal

---

1   For an overview of US-Japan relations during the 1910s, see Minohara Toshihiro et al., "Daiichijisekaitaisen to nichibeikankei no saichōsei, 1909–19," in Iokibe Makoto eds., *Nichibeikankeishi*, (Tokyo: Yūhikaku, 2008).

partner in order to preserve its national dignity. This rang even more true when
it came to the issue of race, as no amount of modernization, industrialization,
or military prowess could alter one's race. However, during the 1910s, US-Japan
relations had finally reached the phase of maturity, bringing to a close the
earlier mentor-mentee phase beginning with the arrival of Commodore
Mathew C. Perry in 1853.

The maturing of diplomatic relations also meant that Japan was now viewed
as a competitor to the US and this naturally led to the surfacing of friction that
did not exist in the past. Specifically, in the case of the US and Japan, this friction manifested itself in racial discrimination that took shape in the form of
maltreatment of Japanese immigrants. This problem manifested itself primarily in California as it was the state which had the largest population of immigrants from Japan.

With this as a backdrop, this chapter will examine the so-called immigration problem in the context of US-Japanese relations during the 1910s which
became a serious point of contention in what was otherwise a relatively stable
bilateral relationship. By doing so, the chapter will attempt dispel the notion of
a "quiet 1910s" in US-Japan relations that was largely overshadowed by the war
in Europe.[2] Although there is no denying that the First World War was the seminal event of the decade – which unmistakably had a profound impact upon
both the United States and Japan – this chapter will reveal that there existed
another important issue that would gradually cast a dark shadow upon the
relationship of the two nations straddling the Pacific.[3]

## 1        The Roots of the Japanese Immigration Problem

The roots of the so-called Japanese immigration issue can be traced back
much earlier than the decade of the 1910s. Legal discrimination against Asians
in general has an even longer history, dating back to the events leading

---

2  Besides the Great War, another reason for the "quiet 1910s" was due to the 1911 Xinhai
Revolution. Had China not been thrown into a state of turmoil, there would have been much
more room for conflict between the US and Japan over China. For example, Japan certainly
would have felt threatened by the Four Powers Banking Consortium that was led by the US
and to which it was not a member.

3  For a full impact of the relationship of the Japanese immigration issue upon US-Japan
relations, see Minohara Toshihiro, *Hainichi iminhō to nichibeikankei*, (Tokyo: Iwanamishoten, 2002); and idem., *Kariforuniashu no hainichiundō to nichibeikankei* (Tokyo: Yuhikaku,
2006).

to Chinese exclusion in 1882.[4] However, at that time the Japanese were spared from exclusion as their numbers were still small and the scarcity of laborers created by the legal exclusion measure of Chinese immigrants had led to a momentary lull in anti-Asian sentiment. Moreover, the main thrust of Japanese immigration during the late 19th century was directed toward the Kingdom of Hawai'i – which embraced the Japanese as a crucial source of labor – rather than the United States.

The attitude toward Japanese immigration would change swiftly from the moment Hawai'i was annexed as a US territory in 1898. From then on, a steady flow of Japanese laborers from Hawai'i to the West Coast began in earnest as immigrants sought higher wages on the mainland. They would converge onto San Francisco, then the major gateway to the US on the West Coast. In addition, there was also a significant increase in emigration directly to the US mainland that originated predominantly from the western region of Japan. This was in contrast with earlier Japanese emigration to Hawai'i which had primarily consisted of Okinawans. As the steer passage to the US was not cheap and contract laborers were prohibited unlike in Hawai'i, most of these new immigrants were from families of relatively well-to-do farmers but in which primogeniture had prevented them inheriting adequate plots of land.

During this time, the American West was growing at a breakneck pace and the influx of Japanese laborers was welcomed by employers while also being tolerated by white laborers. This delicate balance was not to last. The rise of progressivism in California, and particularly in San Francisco, empowered the working class whites who increasingly began to view the Japanese as being a real threat to their economic well-being.[5] Other factors played a role, such as Japan's stunning victory in the Russo-Japanese War, which altered the image of Japan in the eyes of many Americans, as it was now clear that Japan had become a major power in East Asia. Hence, the image of a strong and confident Japan was directly reflected upon Japanese immigrants in the US and as a result their presence became increasingly perceived as a menace. This was exacerbated by the prevailing belief of the time that Asians were of a race that could not be assimilated into American society. Adding to the feeling of

---

4   For details of the passage of the 1882 Chinese Exclusion Act, see Andrew Gyory, *Closing the Gate: Race, Politics, and the Chinese Exclusion Act* (Durham: University of North Carolina Press, 1998); and John Seonnichsen, *The Chinese Exclusion Act of 1882* (Santa Barbara: ABC-Clio, 2011).

5   For the role that progressivism in California had upon Japanese immigration, see Spencer C. Olin, Jr., *California's Prodigal Sons: Hiram Johnson and the Progressives, 1911–1917* (Berkeley and Los Angeles: University of California Press, 1968).

wariness was the strong bond that existed between the Japanese government and its immigrants in the United States.[6] This was a special connection that the Chinese immigrants did not possess, and it changed the very nature of the threat as the Japanese, unlike other Asian immigrants, possessed the backing of a strong home government.

All these factors culminated with the 1906 San Francisco School Board incident in which a measure was passed that prohibited Japanese students from attending the local public schools and instead forced them to relocate to the Oriental School that was the designated school for all Chinese and Korean pupils in the city.[7] This was a serious slight that touched upon the raw nerves of Japanese national sensitivities; both national prestige and pride were at stake as Japan abhorred the idea of being treated on an equal footing with its "second-rate" Asian neighbors.

Strangely, the Japanese government did not for a moment consider the inherent racial paradox that existed in their position. Tokyo was critical of American racism while at the same time it was also propagating racism toward other Asians by insisting upon preferential treatment for itself. This was the irony of Japan's racial sensitivities and national dignity as it was not at all concerned with taking a stand for all Asians, but rather about not tolerating any discrimination towards its own overseas citizens alone.

Thus as long as the Japanese were extended the same terms as their European (or white) brethren, then face was maintained and all was well. As a matter of fact, being treated differently to other Asians was not only favorable, it was the very fact that allowed the Japanese to bask in the glory of national pride; despite similar racial features, this was an crucial way in which one could feel a sense of moral superiority over the Chinese, a nation whom they had soundly defeated in the First Sino-Japanese War of 1894–95.

Fortunately for Japan, at the time of the school board crisis, the president was Theodore Roosevelt. This was an individual who was acutely aware of Japanese racial pride while also realizing the strategic importance of Japan to the US.[8] Dealing with an incident he would later recall as being the most

---

6   Yuji Ichioka, "Japanese Associations and the Japanese Government: A Special Relationship, 1909–1926," *Pacific Historical Review* 46, no. 3 (1977): 436.

7   For a fuller account of the incident, see Thomas Bailey, *Theodore Roosevelt and the Japanese-American Crises: An Account of the International Complications arising from the Race Problem on the Pacific Coast* (Palo Alto: Stanford University Press, 1934).

8   As America's "Achilles's heel," the Philippines, necessitated a strong strategic partnership with Japan, the only reliable partner in East Asia. A. Whitney Griswold, *The Far Eastern Policy of the United States* (New York: Harcourt, 1938), 348.

treacherous of his presidency, he acted resolutely, and skillfully maneuvered to ameliorate both Japanese emotions as well as local sentiments. Roosevelt accomplished this by using his stature as president to appease the local politicians of San Francisco by inviting them to the White House while also coaxing out concrete compromises from Tokyo in exchange for the school board rescinding its decision.

What were the concessions that Roosevelt obtained from Japan? First, the Japanese agreed to allow the US to cease all Japanese immigration to the mainland from Hawai'i. Second, and more importantly, the Japanese government promised that as a solely unilateral measure to be implemented on its own accord, it would limit future emigration of Japanese laborers to the US to less than 500 per year. This was the 1908 Gentlemen's Agreement.[9]

What was crucial to the Japanese, lest their national prestige be injured, was that this restriction should not be forced upon Japan in the manner of a formal treaty. Roosevelt had initially proposed a treaty that mutually excluded the emigration of laborers by both countries but Tokyo rejected this outright on the grounds that this would merely be an unequal treaty in disguise since it was unlikely that an American laborer would want to emigrate to Japan. Tokyo was firm in its position of not allowing any Western power to impose upon it an unequal treaty which still vividly haunted its national memory.

## 2      Cooperation by California: The 1909 Alien Land Bill

One direct ramification of the San Francisco School Board incident was that it prompted many Japanese immigrants to leave the large cities for the rural regions of California. As many had been farmers in Japan, they possessed the experience and skills necessary to excel in farming. Therefore, they actively acquired arable land and soon became quite successful in agriculture to the point where they posed a serious economic threat to competing white farmers. Faced with this reality, it would only be a matter of time before the California legislature began mulling over some sort of legal measure to limit further Japanese expansion into agriculture. Sure enough, during the 1909 legislative session, hardly a year after the Gentlemen's Agreement, a bill was proposed for the first time that would place restrictions on Japanese land ownership.[10]

---

9   For the diplomatic discussions leading to the Gentleman's Agreement, see Gaimushō ed., *Nihon Gaikōmonjo: Taibeiminmondai keikagaiyō* (1972), 171–180.

10  During this time, the California legislature met only every other year, and legislative sessions would convene during odd numbered years.

The bill sponsored by A.M. Drew of Fresno, stipulated that land ownership would be restricted to any alien that failed to naturalize within five years of arriving in the United States.[11] The wording of the bill was ingenious in that it linked land ownership with Federal naturalization laws which were generally understood by the courts at that time to exclude those of Japanese ancestry from acquiring American citizenship. Hence, despite the innocuous name of bill, in truth it was a bill that was aimed squarely at targeting Japanese immigrants. But its intent was much greater in scope than being merely an anti-Japanese land law in disguise. The hidden motive of the legislation was to drastically reduce the overall flow of Japanese immigration by making life more difficult for those already residing or planning to reside in the state. In this way, the proposed alien land law – by making California an unattractive final destination – was actually a thinly veiled immigration restriction bill.[12]

When President Theodore Roosevelt was made aware of this new bill, he was livid. He had recently settled the school board imbroglio that had led to a diplomatic crisis with Japan. This was an ordeal that he would later recall as being the most stressful period of his tenure as president. For Roosevelt, much more was at stake than the issue of local politics as this action by California clearly had implications that would involve foreign relations. Moreover, it was also a matter of personal pride, for he had promised the Japanese government that he would not allow the immigration problem to sour US-Japan relations again while he was in office. In Roosevelt's mind, the land bills being deliberated in the California legislature were not only spurious, but also provided a serious affront to a friendly nation that would surely lead to distrust and animosity towards America. With this in mind, Roosevelt fully committed himself to proactively resolving the matter before the situation spiraled out of control (Figure 1.1).

Across the Pacific, the Japanese government was also keenly following the events transpiring in Sacramento. On January 3, acting Consul General Takahashi Seiichi met with Governor James N. Gillett of California to voice the concerns of his government, and requested his intervention in the matter.[13] In turn, Gillett promised that he would do his utmost to resolve the issue.

---

11    Assembly Bill 78, January 9, 1909.

12    In the landmark decision in the *Passenger Cases*, the Supreme Court had deemed it unconstitutional for states to legislate immigrations laws. This meant that California had no legal means to directly exclude Japanese immigration into its state.

13    Telegram, Takahasahi to Komura, January 3, 1909. In *Nihongaikōmonjo* (1909), vol. 2 (Tokyo: Nihonkokusairengō Kyōkai, 1954), 420. Henceforth cited as *NGM* with corresponding Meiji or Taishō (T) year.

FIGURE 1.1   *Cartoon image: Theodore Roosevelt spanking the dog, California, over the Japanese immigration issue. The caption in Japanese reads, "We Japanese are safe to trust the righteousness of our neighbors."* Reprinted from *Shashinkiroku: Nihonseijishi,* Tokyo: Nihontoshosenta, 2007.

As a Republican and former Congressman, Gillett was sensitive to the interests of Washington and was thus eager to cooperate with the Roosevelt
administration.

On January 14, Japanese ambassador Takahira Kogorō met with Secretary of
State Elihu Root to formally lodge a protest.[14] Root replied to the ambassador
that not only was he carefully following the events in the California, but
because the government was in direct contact with the governor, surely the bill
would not see the light of day. The reason behind Root's confidence in his
assessment was that in Gillett he knew they had a person that could be relied
upon to pull through. True to his word, when Roosevelt sent a telegram requesting Gillett to suspend all deliberations over the bill until he could transmit a
formal correspondence containing the views of the government on the issue,
Gillett promptly acquiesced. As a result, debate of the bill was not resumed
until January 27 by which time Roosevelt's personal letter had arrived.

In accordance with Roosevelt's request, Gillett addressed the legislature and
stressed that the Japanese were not only citizens of a friendly nation, but possessed the same rights as any other alien under California law. He also emphasized the prudence of California not enacting any legislation that could
complicate America's foreign relations. Furthermore, all treaty rights had to be
respected. In Gillett's mind, a bill that essentially targeted one nationality and
discriminated based on that fact only had no solid foundation to become law.
Many fellow Republican legislators, keenly aware that their actions were being
closely monitored by the national administration, concurred with Gillett's
views. When the final vote was taken on February 4, Drew's bill was soundly
defeated 48 to 28.[15] President Roosevelt, on learning of the final vote count,
sighed in relief and jubilantly exclaimed to his Secretary of War and president-
elect William H. Taft that the "Republican machine" had come to his rescue.[16]

In this fashion, the Japanese immigration problem in California during the
tenure of President Roosevelt was amicably resolved due to the swift actions of
a wary president who desperately wanted to avoid another situation similar to
what had transpired in 1906. As such, any action by the legislature that would
interfere with US-Japan relations required firm intervention before it had the
chance to lead to a diplomatic row. It was, however, also self-evident that such
results were only achievable because of an existence of a framework based on

---

14    Telegram, Takahira to Komura, January 14, 1909. In *NGM 42*, 427.

15    Franklin Hichborn, *Story of the Session of the California Legislature of 1909* (San Francisco:
      James J. Barry Company, 1909), 206.

16    Letter, Roosevelt to Taft, February 3, 1909. In Papers of Theodore Roosevelt, Library of
      Congress, Manuscript Division (LCMD).

mutual understanding and cooperation between a Republican national administration and a Republican state administration. In other words, it was far from being a permanent arrangement, and any changes to the political situation at either level would naturally make it considerably more difficult to manage the Japanese immigration problem. Unfortunately, this would be the case during the 1910s.

## 3 Cooperation for a Carrot: The 1911 Alien Land Bill

The 1911 legislative year in California had undergone a remarkable transition. During the 1910 campaign year, state Democrats had launched an aggressive election campaign under the slogan, "Keep California White!" California had long been a state dominated by Republicans but during the elections of 1910, the Democrats came out with a solid showing and went on to grab 44% of the assembly seats.[17] As Republican legislators were more sensitive to the desires of Washington, this political shift would also have a direct impact upon the future course of the anti-Japanese movement in the state. The results of the 1910 elections also left a strong impression upon the state Republican politicians as well, as many had come to realize that the anti-Japanese card was a handy tool in gaining votes within the state with minimal political cost. Hence, 1910 became a watershed for the anti-Japanese movement in California as from this moment forward it would become a much more bipartisan movement within the state.

Another important change that took place in 1910 was the election of a new governor, Hiram W. Johnson, who was a Republican, albeit a progressive. He had reluctantly run for the state's highest office at the behest of the Lincoln-Roosevelt League, an organization that would later play an instrumental role in forming the national Progressive Party (Bull Moose Party) in 1912. Unfortunately, when Johnson took office in 1911, the sitting president was no longer his good friend Roosevelt but Taft, a conservative big-business Republican. This meant that the framework of cooperation between the state and the federal government had also undergone a transformation as well and this would clearly manifest itself in the manner in which the anti-Japanese movement was handled.

---

17   From 1894 to 1938, Republicans continuously held a majority in the state assembly, and it would not be until 1939 that the state would elect Culbert Olson as the first Democratic governor since James Budd who was in office from 1895 to 1899.

With the tide now turned against Japanese immigration, it was no surprise that with the convening of the 1911 legislative session of state assembly, there would be a slew of new anti-Japanese bills put forth for deliberation. Washington also had a watchful eye upon its westernmost state, and President Taft, like his predecessor, was unwilling to allow a local political issue impact the wider bilateral relations between the US and Japan. Fortunately for Taft, Governor Johnson was on very good personal terms with Roosevelt as a fellow progressive. Johnson was not particularly concerned about helping Taft, but when it came to Roosevelt it was a different matter altogether.

Roosevelt had warned Johnson on several occasions that any anti-Japanese legislation was fraught with dangers that could adversely affect American national interests. Johnson therefore took care to assuage the fears of the former president over the latest surge of anti-Japanese legislation in his state by promising that he would do all in his power to prevent any bill from being enacted that could harm US-Japan relations.[18] This promise was conveyed by Roosevelt to Taft, who in turn instructed Secretary of State Philander C. Knox to inform the Japanese Ambassador, Uchida Kōsai. In this way, Washington was conveying a clear message to Tokyo that it was aware of the situation and was closely following the events in the state legislature. Indeed, this indicated how keen the administration was in making sure that another diplomatic crisis would not erupt over the anti-Japanese movement in California.

There was, of course, another vital reason for the additional precaution. In 1911, both the American and Japanese governments were negotiating a new commerce and navigation treaty that would supplant the expiring 1894 treaty. For Taft, signing a new trade treaty with Japan and preserving its most favored nation status was of utmost importance, and he was not about to let events in California derail this crucial diplomatic objective. Fortunately, they had a reluctant ally in Governor Johnson who had chosen to cooperate with the administration out of his friendship toward Roosevelt. As such, the moment Johnson obtained a copy of the pending bill that proposed to limit Japanese land ownership in a manner much similar to that of 1909, he quickly forwarded its content to Secretary Knox and requested instructions on how he should proceed.[19]

Without delay, Knox politely replied that while it was surely within the prerogative of the state to enact such a measure, it would nevertheless be unwise

---

18    Teruko O. Kachi, *The Treaty of 1911 and the Immigration and Alien Land Law Issue between the United States and Japan, 1911–1913* (New York: Arno Press, 1978), 60.

19    Letter, Johnson to Knox, January 6, 1911. In Papers of Hiram W. Johnson, Bancroft Library, University of California at Berkeley (BLCAL).

considering the ongoing discussions over the new trade treaty with Japan. In this way, Knox took the utmost care not to appear as though he was trampling upon the rights of California, while at the same time making it clear that national interests were at stake. Knox endeavored to handle the matter particularly delicately as he was aware of Johnson's difficult personality and bloated ego. As the governor possessed no strong loyalties to the present administration, any misstep could potentially backfire.

If this had been 1909, these measures would have been more than enough to bury the bill. However, the situation in 1911 was made slightly more complicated due to two factors. First, the Democrats had increased their political presence in the state legislature and they were not favorable to the idea of cooperating with a Republican governor. Second, the final bill to reach the floor, the so-called Sanford Bill, had been closely scrutinized in its wording so as to not infringe upon any existing treaty rights. To this effect, an ingenious phrase had been devised: "alien ineligible to citizenship."

By using this legal term the bill no longer needed to single out the Japanese for the target of discrimination and thus it ostensibly had the appearance of being an equitable piece of legislation that applied to all. The truth of the matter, of course, was that only Asians were considered to be "ineligible for citizenship" by most courts in the country at the time, and among this group only the Japanese had significantly large land possessions within the state. Thus the bill in essence was actually targeting Japanese immigrants without having to name them explicitly.

The State Judiciary Committee deliberated upon the Sanford Bill for two months, and on March 15 submitted it to the State Senate for a vote. On March 21, a vote was called and the bill was passed by 29 to 3 upon which it was promptly sent to the State Assembly Judiciary Committee.[20] It was also during this time that Ambassador Uchida met with the Chief of the Far Eastern Section of the Department of State, Ransford S. Miller, and voiced his strong concern should the bill be enacted into law.[21] It is not clear if this is what prompted Washington to apply more pressure on the state, but that is exactly what happened. Feeling the additional heat, Johnson maneuvered to make certain that the bill would not leave the committee. On March 27, with the end of the legislative session, the bill was buried in the committee. The Japanese government, with the full cooperation of Taft and Knox, had prevailed once again.

20    Franklin Hichborn, *Story of the Session of the California Legislature of 1911* (San Francisco: James J. Barry Company, 1911), 342.

21    Telegram, Uchida to Komura, Mach 24, 1911. In *NGM* 44, 427.

Naturally, Taft felt a great sense of relief over how events had transpired and he would soon be further rewarded when the 1911 US-Japan Commerce and Navigation Treaty was put into effect from April 4. Of course, unbeknown to the Japanese, this favorable conclusion had been achieved in the end because Taft had offered a carrot to Johnson. The carrot came in the form of the president's tacit support for San Francisco's bid to host the 1915 Panama-Pacific International Exposition which was also being contested by New Orleans. Taft had gently reminded Johnson that in the event that the alien land law was to be enacted, the image of California would greatly suffer and as a consequence it would surely damage San Francisco's bid.[22] Furthermore, it could be easily surmised that the Japanese would boycott an event that was being hosted by a city that belonged to a state that discriminated against its immigrants.

Interestingly enough, even the Asiatic Exclusion League, which as a pressure group had played an instrumental role in the San Francisco School Board incident five years earlier, now voiced its vehement opposition to the anti-Japanese land law.[23] This clearly shows the nature of the anti-Japanese movement: economic interests consistently took priority over racial discrimination. With Taft's backing, San Francisco was able to emerge as the frontrunner in hosting the world exposition. This was the political backdrop in which the federal government and the state government both reached an agreement not to legislate any anti-Japanese land laws in 1911. It was by all means a delicate arrangement which worked only with the cooperation of both parties and with the presence of a mutually beneficial situation. Unfortunately, as we will see in the next section, the conditions for such a framework of cooperation would cease to exist in the legislative session of 1913.

## 4      Collapse of Cooperation: The 1913 Alien Land Law

Why did the framework of cooperation collapse in 1913? There were three main reasons for this. The first was that a split in the Republican Party had contributed to both Roosevelt's and Taft's defeat in the 1912 presidential elections. Woodrow Wilson emerged victorious, and for the first time in sixteen years a Democrat occupied the White House. Wilson had actively campaigned in California on the platform of respecting state rights as well as the need to exclude the Japanese. The second reason was that in the State of California, Johnson still remained in office as governor. Although a progressive, he was not

---

22    Telegram, Uchida to Komura, March 23, 1911. In *NGM* 44, 456.

23    Telegram, Nagai to Komura, February14, 1911. In *NGM* 44, 444–445.

a Democrat, and he harbored no desire to cooperate with the new administration in Washington.

Moreover, it was not lost on Johnson that Wilson had been his political nem-
esis during the 1912 elections as he had run on the Bull Moose ticket as
Roosevelt's vice presidential candidate. Such strong personal feelings added
another layer that made cooperation between the two parties unlikely. The
third and final reason was that in spite of the 1908 Gentlemen's Agreement, the
Japanese immigrant population in the state had not declined.[24] Of these
Japanese farmers, many had purchased substantial agricultural tracts in
Northern California and were now poised to become fierce competitors to the
white farmers in the state. Posed with this very real economic threat, the anti-
Japanese movement would become much more energized and powerful.

Reflecting the sentiment of white farmers, the opening of the 1913 legislative
session saw a flood of anti-Japanese bills totaling more than thirty.[25] These bills
ranged from those that prevented outright Japanese ownership of private corporations, to bills that proposed segregation of the Japanese similar to the Jim
Crow laws in the South. Many also dealt with Japanese land ownership. With a
Democratic administration taking charge in Washington, state Democratic
legislators felt that the moment was now finally ripe to enact some sort of anti-
Japanese legislation. They had been frustrated for years in this quest through
the repeated intervention by a Republican governor and Republican president,
but now they felt that the moment was for their taking; after all Wilson had
actively campaigned in the state with the premise of supporting such legislation. Adding wind to the sails was the fact that this was a president who
respected states' rights, unlike past Republican presidents who believed that
the interests of the Federal government clearly superseded that of the state.
Wilson would surely stand aside and allow California to legislate freely as
it saw fit.

All these factors contributed to a much different baseline than in 1911. The
governor did not even bother to notify the new administration about the
nature of the impending bills. The defeated Taft knew about the new pending
bills in California by early January, but he also chose to remain silent on the
issue as this was no longer his concern. Thus, Wilson only became aware of
the situation when he assumed office in March, a whole two months after the
bills had been submitted, and only after the Japanese Ambassador, Chinda
Sutemi, had requested to meet with the new president in order to lodge his

---

24    The increase in population was due to natural increases through birth as well as the
      arrival of picture brides from Japan who were exempt from the Gentleman's Agreement.
25    Telegram, Oyama to Katsura, January 22, 1913. In *NGM* T2, 3–7.

deep concern over the situation in California. Wilson promised that he would keep a watchful eye, but he was also mindful to explain to the ambassador that the US Constitution placed limits on how much the federal government could interfere in the individual affairs of states.[26] This was clearly his personal interpretation of the constitution and it marked a clear departure from past Republican presidents.

The Japanese government was fully cognizant of the fact that there was no longer a framework of cooperation between the federal and state governments. Back in February, Chinda had warned Foreign Minister Katō Takaaki that it was no longer realistic to expect Washington to apply pressure upon California.[27] Yet as it was procedurally impossible for the Japanese government to approach and confront the state directly, they had no alternative but to rely upon the good offices of the administration.

Wilson clearly saw the danger of what was at stake over the situation in California. He was not about to sit idly and allow the situation take its natural course, but he was also bound by his campaign pledge of supporting anti-Japanese legislation and not meddling in states' affairs. Because of this, he needed to act very delicately and cautiously in order to avoid a political backlash. He thus deliberately chose not to seek the assistance of Governor Johnson as it was unlikely that he would be given a sympathetic ear.

With the governor absent from his own corner, Wilson's options were limited from the outset, but he was also further hindered by his decision to pursue a course that would limit his exposure. This indirect approach only served to infuriate Johnson all the more as he felt that the president was being a blatant hypocrite. Then what could Wilson do? After mulling over his limited options, he decided to contact his old friend and California's Democratic State Senator, Anthony Caminetti, and enlisted his help in managing the present situation in a manner that would not cause harm to the administration.[28] This required that Caminetti persuade the governor to act on behalf of the president. This was a ridiculous request considering that in the past it had been the Democratic Party of the state that had been the major force behind the anti-Japanese movement in the legislature.

Secretary of State William Jennings Bryan, a seasoned politician, was well aware of the absurdity of this course of action, and he argued against this on the grounds that the governor, a diehard Roosevelt Republican, would never

---

26    Telegram, Chinda to Makino, March 13, 1913. In *NGM* T2, 16.
27    Telegram, Chinda to Katō, February 5, 1913. In *NGM* T2, 9.
28    Roger Daniels, *Politics of Prejudice* (Berkeley and Los Angeles: University of California Press, 1962), 59.

heed such a request.[29] From his past experiences in dealing with Johnson, Bryan suggested that the best possible option was for Wilson to swallow his pride and contact Johnson directly and ask for his help. Bryan felt that a president requiring the help of a governor would surely add to Johnson's inflated ego, and perhaps even lead him into providing the necessary political capital to leverage the situation in favor of the administration. But in the end, Wilson would have none of this, for his own ego would not allow himself to be placed in a compromising situation where he needed to humble himself to Johnson. Such personal pride would ultimately serve to seal the fate of the alien land law bill.

With the president seeking his assistance, Caminetti was placed in a bind.[30] He had a solid track record as being a vehemently anti-Japanese legislator, and during the 1912 state elections, he had come out strongly for the need to pass an anti-Japanese land law. But he also knew that if he cooperated, he would be rewarded for his loyalty with a cushy job at the federal level. Enticed with this offer, Caminetti agreed to act as a go-between and his services would later be awarded amply when Wilson appointed him to the position of Federal Post Commissioner.

Unfortunately for Wilson, his plan quickly unraveled and as Bryan had warned, it instead backfired. Upon receiving a letter from Caminetti, Johnson was livid, for he knew very well that the president was pulling the strings from behind; how else could one explain Caminetti's volte-face on the Japanese immigration issue? As Johnson would confide to his good friend and confidant, Chester H. Rowell, this was the moment that he had decided that it would become his personal mission to ensure the passage of an anti-Japanese land bill in this session.[31] The governor's motivation was purely on a personal level as his sole objective was to place the president in an embarrassing position.

Once Wilson had failed to garner the support of the governor, it was all but assured that some sort of anti-Japanese bill would be passed by the California legislature. Wilson had no carrots to provide either since by this time San Francisco had already been nominated to host the 1915 Panama-Pacific International Exposition. Moreover, Johnson knew via Rowell that the Japanese government had already appropriated a budget to showcase an exhibit at the exposition.[32] It therefore seemed unlikely that the Japanese would pull out at this juncture even if a bill were to pass.

---

29    Roger Daniels, "William Jennings Bryan and the Japanese," *Southern California Quarterly* 48 (1966): 231–232.
30    Letter, Caminetti to Bryan, April 8, 1913. In Papers of William Jennings Bryan, LCMD.
31    Letter, Johnson to Rowell, March 17, 1913. In Papers of Hiram W. Johnson, BLCAL.
32    Telegram, Makino to Chinda, March 19, 1913. In *NGM* T2, 28.

But on the other side of the continent, Wilson remained oblivious to his predicament and on April 7 once again decided to intervene indirectly by enlisting the help of Congressman William Kent, a Democrat from California. Per instructions, Kent promptly transmitted a telegram to Johnson that requested that the land bill under consideration be drafted so that it would not discriminate against the Japanese.[33] The correspondence concluded by stating that although the request reflected the desires of the highest authority of the land, nevertheless, the specific contents were to be kept under strict secrecy.

This only served to add further fuel to the raging fire within Johnson. The enraged governor not only transmitted the confidential letter to Rowell, but in his accompanying note he vowed that he would seek to expose the hypocritical and cowardly president to the public.[34] To Kent, he replied with more restraint, but tersely requested that if the president ever wanted to convey something to him, he should do so in person like the previous administration had. The anti-Japanese issue had now clearly been lost into an abyss of personal animosity; Johnson was going to ram this bill through the legislature out of pure spite.

While Kent did convey the message from Johnson to the president, Wilson still stubbornly refused to get directly in touch with the governor. Instead he relied on Secretary Bryan to propose a solution, but of course this was to no avail. It was during this juncture that the situation took a sudden turn for the worse. On April 17, more than twenty thousand Japanese had amassed in Tokyo to protest about the pending legislation in California, exclaiming that it caused serious injury to national dignity.[35] These jingoes also called out for the Japanese government to send warships to the West Coast as a way to put the Californians back in their place. The American press jumped at this news from Tokyo, and also did not fail to hype it up even further by exaggerating the scope of the anti-American protests.

Those in Washington took this threat seriously, to the point that the military was ordered to devise a plan in the event that hostilities should break out between the two nations. A full-blown diplomatic crisis was now on hand, and Wilson needed to act decisively to diffuse the situation. This meant that he now had no choice but to contact Johnson directly. On April 22, Wilson grudgingly sent a telegram to the governor urging him that the pending bill should be revised so as not to discriminate against the Japanese.[36] He also requested, considering that the bill in its present form infringed upon Japanese treaty

---

33    Letter, Kent to Johnson, April 7, 1913. In Papers of Hiram W. Johnson, BLCAL.
34    Letter, Johnson to Rowell, April 9, 1913. Ibid.
35    *Japan Weekly Chronicle* and the *Japan Times*, April 18, 1913.
36    Telegram, Wilson to Johnson, April 22, 1913. In Papers of Hiram W. Johnson, BLCAL.

rights, that the governor motion to veto it. Wilson also addressed a letter to the California legislature where, for the first time, he came out openly against the anti-Japanese bill; the president had finally reversed his position and Johnson had obtained his political victory.

After a heated debated within his cabinet, Wilson decided to send his Secretary of State to California to meet in person with Johnson as a last ditch effort to avoid passage of the bill.[37] Bryan personally felt that this was a "most thankless task," but nevertheless agreed to do whatever he could for the president.[38] Bryan's reluctance was due to the fact that he had been the leading voice against President Roosevelt's actions when he had sent his Secretary of Labor to California during the San Francisco School Board crisis, arguing that it was an infringement upon states' rights. Hence, Bryan was now shouldered with the burden of having to undertake a task that went against his core beliefs over the relationship between the federal government and the individual states. But as events reveal, his mission was doomed to fail not because of his personal convictions but rather because he had failed to bring any meaningful compromises to the table. One would recall that in 1906, in exchange for cooperation, Roosevelt had promised to restrict future Japanese immigration that culminated into the Gentlemen's Agreement.

As a matter of fact, Johnson had no idea that Bryan was coming to California completely empty-handed, for he was hoping that the administration would make some sort of concession. This was unfortunate, since on April 19, Ambassador Chinda had proposed a Japanese compromise plan to Bryan. Chinda had stated that his government was prepared to halt the issuing of travel documents to picture brides.[39] But this fell on deaf ears – it is quite likely that Bryan did not understand the significance of this gesture – and as a result Bryan had absolutely nothing to offer to the Californians. In fact, he would later reflect that he had merely come to offer "advice" and not to "advise." Of course one can make the argument that if Bryan had really wanted to stop the bill, he could have done a whole lot more. The same can be said about the president. Deep down both were torn between their beliefs in how the American political system should function and managing foreign relations.

---

37   For the details leading to this decision, see Paolo Coletta, "'The Most Thankless Task': Bryan and the California Alien Land Law Legislation," *Pacific Historical Review* 36 (1967): 163–187.

38   David F. Houston, *Eight Years with Wilson's Cabinet, 1913 to 1920*, vol. 1. (Garden City: Doubleday, Page, 1926), 60.

39   Telegram, Makino to Chinda; Telegram, Chinda to Makino, April 20, 1913. In *NGM* T2, 81; 91–93.

It was unfortunate that this dilemma led to half-hearted measures and in the end the only positive result of Wilson's course of action was that he was able to show that he personally held no ill will toward the Japanese.

By the time Bryan had arrived in California on April 28, State Senator Francis J. Heney and State Attorney General Ulysses S. Webb and had collaborated together in rewording the original land bill so that it would no longer infringe upon the 1911 Treaty.[40] The revised legislation became the Heney-Webb Bill, and any direct mention of the Japanese was stricken from the text. In its place new wording was added which based land ownership on the ability to naturalize, much like the Sanford Bill of 1911. In the end, Bryan did gain the support from a few of his fellow Democrats which led to the drafting of the Curtin Resolution that proposed to postpone indefinitely a vote on the Heney-Webb Bill. But in the end this was soundly defeated 26 to 10 along party lines.[41] Johnson would later callously remark that Bryan's visit was utterly meaningless and that he could have attained the same result by simply sending a single telegram rather than coming all the way out to California.[42] Perhaps there was an element of truth to this as the Heney-Webb Bill, upon going through one final round of revision, sailed through both houses of the California State legislature despite Bryan's presence.

It was at this juncture that former president Roosevelt sent a telegram to his good friend Johnson, cautioning him about the perilous path that he was embarking upon.[43] Roosevelt was critical of Wilson, but at the same time he also questioned Johnson's enthusiasm for enacting the bill. Roosevelt reiterated the importance of maintaining solid US-Japan relations and warned that anything that acted against this bilateral relationship would adversely affect American national interests. He therefore warned Johnson that prudence was required when dealing with any anti-Japanese legislation. Although Johnson allowed the bill to be passed despite Roosevelt's concerns, this was the reason he did not concern himself with the numerous legal loopholes that existed in the bill. This fact was not lost upon the local press, who called the actions of the state legislators' mere political bunkum, for it did not completely deny the Japanese from owning land.

Unlike Roosevelt, what Johnson failed to understand was that from the point of view of the Japanese government, the efficacy of the law was immaterial. The very fact that its immigrants were not being treated on an equal basis

40    Telegram, Numano to Makino, April 25, 1913. In *NGM* T2, 126.
41    Telegram, Bryan to Wilson. In Papers of William Jennings Bryan, LCMD.
42    Letter, Johnson to Roosevelt, June 21, 1913. In Papers of Hiram W. Johnson, BLCAL.
43    Telegram, Roosevelt to Johnson, April 28, 1913. In Papers of Hiram W. Johnson, BLCAL.

as other European immigrants was enough to injure national dignity. Although Japan had rapidly modernized through the process of Westernization, race was one factor that it could never overcome no matter how wealthy or powerful the nation might have become. With the traumatic memory of the unequal treaties still fresh in the national psyche, being treated as an equal was a *sine qua non* for Japan to maintain its pride as a modern nation. Tokyo was quite content if the law prevented all aliens from possessing land, but targeting the Japanese and relegating them to the status of second-class citizens was unbearable.

Regardless of the loopholes, Wilson did make one final attempt in requesting Johnson to veto the bill, but the governor casually brushed aside this request, retorting that it was the prerogative of the state to enact any legislation it saw fit so long as it did not interfere with treaty rights.[44] On May 19, Johnson affixed his signature to the bill which would come into effect on August 10 as the 1913 Alien Land Law, effectively limiting Japanese land ownership to a maximum of three years.[45] In Japan this would be referred to as the "First Anti-Japanese Land Law (*Daiichiji hainichi tochihō*)" and it would lead to resentment of Americans by many Japanese. Moreover, this would also be an important turning point in the anti-Japanese movement in California that would eventually culminate into complete Japanese exclusion by the Immigration Act of 1924.

Governor Johnson was mindful of sending a reply to his friend Roosevelt where he outlined the reasons for his actions. In Johnson's mind, the law was necessary in order to expose the hypocritical nature of the Democrats including the president, for they had always actively campaigned for anti-Japanese legislation. Yet when tables were turned, they now conveniently opposed any such measure. Such a dire lack of principles needed to be revealed to the people of the state. Thus the alien land law had been an ideal instrument by which huge political capital had been obtained. Johnson concluded his letter by reassuring Roosevelt that this law would settle, once and for all, the anti-Japanese movement in California.[46] It was his belief that the Japanese immigration problem would never resurface in the state as a political issue.

This assessment would eventually prove to be incorrect. In fact, the anti-Japanese movement was quelled only momentarily, interrupted by the Great War, but it would come roaring back once the world returned to normality in

---

44    Letter, Wilson to Johnson, May 11, 1913. In Papers of Hiram W. Johnson, BLCAL.

45    Telegram, Numano to Makino, May 19, 1913. In *NGM* T2, 216.

46    Letter, Johnson to Roosevelt, June 21, 1913. In Papers of Hiram W. Johnson, BLCAL.

1919. In his capacity as governor, Johnson could not see the far reaching international ramifications of his own actions, for his field of vision was limited to the domain of domestic politics. On the other hand, Roosevelt possessed a much worldlier view and could therefore instantly grasp what was at stake from the perspective of foreign relations. What was unfortunate was that the idealist Wilson was not of the same caliber as Roosevelt, for it was under his tenure that US-Japan relations would feel the stresses of an America that preached liberal democratic values but yet did not act accordingly. Instead what the Japanese saw in America was nation that that had lost its luster and was abandoning its moral leadership as a global power.

## 5    A Diplomatic Crisis: US-Japan Relations after the Passage of Alien Land Law

The 1913 Alien Land Law, in the shape that it was passed, had many loopholes, but this was no consolation for the Japanese government as the issue was over national pride. Therefore, Japan expressed its outrage in a strong note of diplomatic protest – in the tersest language permitted in time of peace – to the secretary of state.[47] As a matter of fact, the wording was so strong that Bryan, fearing a backlash from California when it became public, requested that the ambassador tone down the note. On the following day, Chinda's revised note was received as Japan's formal protest but a delicate diplomatic situation was now on hand.

Although altered, the new note still contained stern language, and on May 13 a concerned President Wilson convened an emergency cabinet meeting to discuss how the administration should respond to Japan's protest. Secretary of Navy Josephus Daniels's diary sheds light on what took place that day. Daniels himself felt that the language used was stronger that necessary, and Secretary of Commerce William C. Redfield felt that it was a clear threat against the US should America not heed Japan's wishes.[48] Nevertheless, in the end it was agreed not to make an issue of the note as it was a reflection of Japan's deep frustration over not being treated on an equal basis.

---

47    Arthur S. Link, *Wilson: The New Freedom* (Princeton: Princeton University Press, 1956), 296; and Ray Stannard Baker, *Woodrow Wilson: Life and Letters, 1913–1914*, vol. 4 (London: William Heinemann, 1932), 80.

48    E. David Cronon, *The Cabinet Diaries of Josephus Daniels, 1911–1921* (Lincoln: University of Nebraska Press, 1962), 52–54.

However, it was the military that objected to such a benign interpretation, and upon learning the nature of the Japanese note, the Aide for Naval Operations Bradley A. Fiske concluded on his own that Japan meant war. He therefore requested that Secretary Daniels gave the order for immediate battle preparations. Fiske was soon joined by Army Chief of Staff Leonard Wood, and together they convened a Joint Board of the Army and Navy conference in which they requested immediate authorization to move warships to the Philippines and also to reinforce American troops stationed on the island.[49]

Wilson's cabinet faced a conundrum on to how to deal with this request. Secretary of War Lindley M. Garrison was of the opinion that it was a prudent defensive measure, and he was seconded by Secretary of the Treasury William G. McAdoo and Attorney General James C. McReynolds. In the opposing group were Secretary of State Bryan, Secretary of the Navy Daniels, Secretary of the Interior Franklin K. Lane, Secretary of Agriculture David F. Houston, and Secretary of Labor William B. Wilson, all of whom believed that such action would further aggravate the Japanese and only serve to escalate tensions.[50]

A heated debate ensued over the proper course of action, but in the end the cooler heads prevailed and Wilson ordered the Joint Board that no troop or ship movements were to be authorized. This should have ended the matter, but the Joint Board, displeased with the outcome, leaked what had transpired to the press in an attempt to rally public opinion in support of American military preparedness. When Wilson learned of this insubordination by his senior commanders, he was outraged. As Commander-in-Chief his decision was final. To make this point clear, Wilson prohibited the Joint Board from convening any further meetings and threatened that he would dissolve the board should it ever again attempt to subvert his authority.[51] This ban on Joint Board meetings would remain in place until America's entry into the First World War.

Wilson also took the precautionary measure of reassuring the Japanese government that the US absolutely did not possess any hostile intentions. Of course Japan had never perceived this incident as a *casus belli* – this very fact was what had led to the strongly worded note in the first place – but Wilson's prompt action did help to dissipate the dark clouds that had gathered above both countries. It was now the task of the diplomats, Bryan and Chinda, to take advantage of this opportunity and enter into discussions that would address the anti-Japanese movement so that it would never again become a

---

49    Ibid., 59.

50    Ibid., 53–54.

51    Josephus Daniels, *The Wilson Era: Years of Peace, 1910–1917* (Chapel Hill, University of North Carolina, 1944), 167.

contentious issue in US-Japan relations. So began the Bryan-Chinda talks that would continue for nearly ten months.

## Conclusion: The Collapse of the Bryan-Chinda Talks

It is important to note that during the Bryan-Chinda talks, on behalf of the American government, Bryan had offered to compensate any losses incurred by Japanese immigrants due to the 1913 Alien Land Law. Chinda refused this in part because he did not want to accept this compromise in lieu of recognizing the validity of the law. But the other reason was that for senior Japanese diplomats of the time, the duress and financial burden endured by the Japanese immigrants was considerably less important than preserving Japan's national dignity. Hence, national pride took precedent over any practical remedy that would offset the material losses incurred by Japanese immigrants.[52]

Had the general interests of the Japanese been that of utmost priority, the Japanese government would surely have pressed for more financial compensation. Yet in the end, this did not occur and instead Japan steadfastly insisted that the Japanese be accorded naturalization rights similar to other European immigrants. The final result of the Bryan-Chinda talks was a draft treaty that proposed to prohibit the passage of any future anti-Japanese legislation in America. It was unlikely that congress would ever agree to such a treaty, but before it even reached that stage it was scuttled by Foreign Minister Katō who was, unlike his predecessor Makino Nobuaki, unwilling to acquiesce to a treaty that was based on acknowledging the de facto premise of the 1913 Alien Land Law.[53] In Katō's view, the offensive and discriminating law had to be first rescinded before the Japanese government would consider any sort of immigration treaty.

In California, however, the feelings toward Japanese immigrants shifted dramatically as the state was in a jubilant mood over successfully hosting the Panama-Pacific Exposition in February 1915. It was not lost upon the local politicians that it was the Japanese pavilion that had saved the day since many of the European exhibits had been canceled due to the Great War. This had the effect of temporarily ameliorating the fears toward the Japanese and as a

---

52    The fact that the Japanese government later agreed to deny travel documents to picture brides also attests to its disregard for the actual wellbeing of Japanese immigrants. With racism prevalent, this had been the only way that Japanese laborers could find a bride and raise a family.

53    Telegram, Chinda to Katō, June 19, 1914. In *NGM* T3, 54.

consequence the anti-Japanese movement also began to subside. Therefore, when a bill was proposed during the 1915 legislature to close the many existing loopholes of the 1913 Alien Land Law, it was never given the opportunity to even reach the floor.

Ultimately, it would be the events across the Atlantic, particularly the sinking of the *Lusitania* on May 7, 1915, that would remove the Japanese immigration problem from the limelight. With war looming over the horizon, the anti-Japanese movement in California rapidly waned and it would not resurface until the conclusion of the First World War in the form of the 1920 Alien Land Law.[54] Moreover, Japan's aggressive imperialistic policies toward China – in the form of the infamous Twenty-One Demands – also momentarily shifted the center of gravity of US-Japan relations from the immigration problem to that of the China problem. Of course even the China problem would be forced backstage in the aftermath of the infamous Zimmerman telegram incident which made America's entry into the "War to end all wars" an imminent reality.

The story of US-Japan relations during the 1910s from the perspective of the immigration problem is a somber one. In a decade when Japan had risen in status to become a pillar of the Big Five powers, she had been rejected by the very nation that had pried open her doors and had guided her through the turbulent waves of modernization. This would have had a profoundly negative impact on the bilateral relations of the two nations, particularly after Japanese exclusion was enacted in 1924, but it would only clearly manifest itself during the 1930s when Japan began to embark on a reverse course in which it sought to "leave the West, and enter Asia (*datsuou nyūa*)" in order to overcome the racial dejection that it had encountered from America, the country it had hitherto most looked up to. Konoe Fumimaro perhaps best described the sentiment of Japan when he proclaimed his rejection of an Anglo-US-centered world as it only sought to preserve their own self-interests.[55] Japan, as the sole great power in East Asia, would seek to create an alternative new order in the form of Pan Asianism. This path, witnessed by Japan's increasingly imperialistic policies toward China, would eventually lock both nations into a collision course.

---

54 For a fuller discussion of the 1920 Alien Land Act, see Tosh Minohara, "The Road to Exclusion: The 1920 California Alien Land Law and US-Japan Relations," *Kobe Law Review* 30 (1996), 39–73.

55 Konoe Fumimaro, "Eibeihon'i no heiwashugi wo haisu," *Nihon oyobi Nihonjin* (December 15, 1918).

One also should not overlook the fact that Emperor Hirohito himself believed that the anti-Japanese movement in California had been an indirect factor that led to the Pacific War.[56] However, during the 1910s, the leaders of Japan still steadfastly maintained a course that was grounded in diplomatic realism and would not allow Japan's foreign policy to stray from cooperation with the US. The First World War was also an opportune distraction that temporarily quelled the anti-Japanese movement. But once the war had concluded, the Japanese immigration problem would once again emerge to the forefront. Japan's persisting sensitivity over this issue became quite apparent when its delegation insisted upon the insertion of a racial equality cause during the discussion over the League of Nations Covenant. Wilson rejected this proposal, but his gravest error was that he failed to offer a separate solution that would settle the Japanese immigration problem once and for all. His inaction, compounded by his inability to comprehend Japanese sensitivities, would sow the seeds of Japan's resentment toward America. The crop from these seeds would eventually be reaped when Japan's internationalist leaders were replaced by a more nationalistic generation of leaders. The 1910s in US-Japan relations, however quiet it may have appeared on the surface, was a precursor to the difficulties that lay ahead.

---

56    Terasaki Hidenari and Mariko Terasaki Miller, eds., *Shōwa Tennō dokuhakuroku* (Tokyo: Bungeishinjū, 1991), 20.

# From Alliance to Conference
## The British Empire, Japan and Pacific Multilateralism, 1911–1921

*John D. Meehan*

### Introduction

For much of the early 1900s, Pacific security loomed large as a concern for Japanese and British decision makers. For Britain's Pacific dominions, namely Canada, Australia and New Zealand, the issue became particularly acute in light of Japan's rising power and Britain's growing focus on Europe. To many, the Anglo-Japanese alliance of 1902 indicated London's reliance on Japanese goodwill to defend its Pacific interests. Japan's newfound status as a great power – as demonstrated by its success in the First Sino-Japanese War (1894–95) and Russo-Japanese War (1904–5) – was a source of pride for some but consternation for others in the dominions. In Western Canada, for instance, railway towns in the newly created province of Saskatchewan were named Mikado, Togo and Kuroki to honor Japan's victory over Russia, the first of a non-Western over a European power.[1] In British Columbia, however, xenophobia culminated in an anti-Asian riot in Vancouver in 1907 that troubled officials in London and Tokyo. Attitudes in the Pacific dominions oscillated between, on the one hand, admiration of Japan's military prowess and, on the other, an underlying wariness of its regional ambitions. Hostility toward Japanese and other Asian immigrants ran high, resulting in demands for exclusionary immigration legislation. In the wake of the Vancouver riot, British and Japanese pressure was such that Ottawa dispatched its labor minister Rodolphe Lemieux to Tokyo to negotiate a gentlemen's agreement that limited Japanese immigration to four hundred laborers and domestics per year. In Australia, such immigration was restricted through short-term stays for students and businessmen as well as dictation tests, a more indirect form of exclusion introduced in 1901.[2]

---

1  John D. Meehan, *The Dominion and the Rising Sun: Canada Encounters Japan, 1929–1941* (Vancouver: University of British Columbia Press, 2004), 2. Published in Japanese as John D. Meehan, *Nikka kankei shi, 1929–1941: Sensou ni mukau nihon kanada no shiza kara*, trans. by Kenki Adachi, Kunihiro Haraguchi and Toshihiro Tanaka (Tokyo: Sairyusha Press, 2006).

2  Meehan, *Dominion and Rising Sun*, 9. As Klaus Pringsheim notes, the number of Japanese immigrants in these two categories never exceeded 253 annually between 1909 and 1921. Klaus H. Pringsheim, *Neighbours Across the Pacific: Canadian-Japanese Relations, 1870–1982* (Oakville, ON: Mosaic Press, 1983), 18. Peter Lowe, *Great Britain and Japan, 1911–15: A Study of British Far Eastern Policy* (London: Macmillan & Co., 1969), 268.

© KONINKLIJKE BRILL NV, LEIDEN, 2014 | DOI 10.1163/9789004274273_004

The First World War marked a major shift in dominion attitudes toward Japan and its role in Pacific affairs. Given the poor state of their Pacific defenses, the dominions were particularly grateful for the protection of Japan's imperial navy. Emboldened by their own substantial wartime sacrifices, the dominions sought a greater role in imperial and international relations, leading to their participation at the Paris peace conference (1919) and its resulting multilateral organization, the League of Nations. Moreover, their rising national consciousness and desire for dominion autonomy resulted in overseas representation and an assertion of "national" interests, albeit within the scope of imperial diplomatic unity. In light of such interests, the dominions soon adopted divergent attitudes on Pacific affairs, particularly in response to Japan's rising status. This chapter analyzes the 1910s as a formative period in this regard as the British Empire moved from bilateral arrangements, notably the Anglo-Japanese alliance, to multilateral forums such as the Washington conference. Shaped by an emerging sense of "national" identity, the dominions sought to influence British policies on Pacific security from the renewal of the alliance in 1911 to the Washington talks of 1921–22. As relatively minor players in Pacific affairs, they came to emphasize the importance of multilateralism and Anglo-American harmony in the region.

### Extending an Alliance

Even prior to the First World War, Britain had begun to consult the dominions on relations with Japan. With the renewal of the Anglo-Japanese alliance in 1905, the dominions appreciated Japanese goodwill in the Pacific.[3] As Britain's foreign secretary Sir Edward Grey later opined, Japan was unlikely to go to war against the United States or the British Empire: "her whole arrangements with Canada show it and I find it in every way."[4] Yet despite the 1908 gentlemen's agreement, the dominions remained sensitive to the possible impact of the Anglo-Japanese pact on the immigration question. For its part, Britain was anxious to avoid exclusionary legislation in the dominions that might antagonize Japan, whose support and protection were beneficial to its interests in Asia. Such concerns emerged in May 1911 at the imperial conference, which London used not only to mark the coronation of King George V but also to

---

3  For more on the first renewal of the alliance, see Ian Nish, *The Anglo-Japanese Alliance: The Diplomacy of Two Island Empires, 1894–1907* (London: Athlone Press, 1968).

4  Grey cited in Ian Nish, *Alliance in Decline: A Study in Anglo-Japanese Relations, 1908–23* (London: Athlone Press, 1972), 7.

consult the dominions on renewing the alliance. As if anticipating the discussion, Philip Kerr, the editor of the well-known imperial review, the *Round Table*, wrote a persuasive article on the Anglo-Japanese alliance in the journal's February issue. Noting the dominions' newfound interest in Pacific and global affairs, Kerr praised the alliance for its obvious military and strategic benefits:

> ...so long as Japan was friendly the Pacific coasts of Canada, Australia, and New Zealand, the sea frontiers of India, and the East coast of Africa were safe from attack, for there was no other power which could reach them with modern ships of war...[5]

The British Empire needed a common policy toward Japan, Kerr argued, one that prevented dominion immigration laws from jeopardizing a crucial alliance. His stance echoed that of the colonial secretary, Lewis Harcourt, who overcame London's initial reluctance to discuss the alliance with the dominions. Even Tokyo had feared the matter might come up at the imperial conference and that dominion concerns over immigration might hinder renewal of the alliance. Given such sensitivities, both in Japan and in the dominions, London decided to hold discussions in private, away from public scrutiny, within the Committee of Imperial Defence (CID) on 26 May. In the secret session, British officials stressed the strategic importance of the alliance, whose expected termination in 1915 would require costly naval forces in the Pacific. With much skill and tact, Grey urged that the alliance be extended for ten years but that it did not impede dominion control of immigration. His stance met with unanimous support from dominion representatives. Yet beneath this consensus, subtle but important divisions were already emerging among the dominions toward Japan due to their particular interests. The Australian prime minister, Andrew Fisher, and his defense secretary George Pearce voiced concerns over Japanese migrants to New Caledonia, territory jointly administered with France. As Pearce explained, Australians were fearful of such immigration and even felt it was "degrading" for their dominion to have an alliance with an Asian nation. Indeed Fisher had caused a stir prior to the conference by publicly declaring Australia's menace was not Germany but rather "in the Pacific." To his dismay, Sir Wilfrid Laurier, the prime minister of Canada, warmly praised Japan for abiding by the Lemieux agreement and hoped friendship with Japan would lead to an alliance lasting fifty or more years. On defense, Fisher and Sir Joseph Ward, the prime minister of New Zealand, advocated a strong naval policy in the Pacific, adding that Laurier's position was not comparable to

---

5   Lowe, *Great Britain and Japan*, 270.

theirs since Canada, in time of need, could always turn to the United States for protection.[6]

Strictly speaking, London's consulting of the dominions had been unnecessary. After all, it had the final say on such matters and, in any case, it had informed Tokyo the previous March of its plan to extend the alliance for ten years. Indeed, some scholars have alleged Britain resorted to "deceitful and sometimes untruthful misrepresentation" to compel the dominions to adhere to its position.[7] Still, dominion consensus marked a significant confirmation of London's decision, even if it belied tensions among them regarding Japan. With satisfaction, Grey soon informed Katō Takaaki, Japan's ambassador to London, that the conference had given "cordial and unanimous" approval to renew the alliance. In return, Japanese officials offered to assuage the dominions on immigration, claiming renewal would foster a desire to regulate the situation more effectively. The revised agreement, signed at London on 13 July 1911 by Grey and Katō, outlined the threefold purpose of the treaty: to maintain peace in East Asia and India, to guarantee the integrity of China and an economic "open door" there, and to defend the interests of both signatories in the region. The inclusion of Article IV, which made the alliance non-binding upon third parties, seemed to allay the concerns of Canada and other dominions of an exclusive bilateral pact that might alienate the United States.[8]

Upon their return home, however, dominion leaders faced stiff opposition. To their chagrin, many of them had misread popular sentiment, especially on the volatile issue of Japanese immigration. In December 1911, Laurier lost a federal election to his Conservative opponent, Robert Borden, mainly over his attempt to forge a reciprocal trade agreement with the United States, but

---

6  Other representatives, such as General Louis Botha of South Africa and Sir Edward Morris of Newfoundland, reflected views of dominions less vitally affected by Pacific concerns. Nish, *Alliance in Decline*, 60–62; Lowe, *Great Britain and Japan*, 272–276; Robert Joseph Gowen, "British Legerdemain at the 1911 Imperial Conference: The Dominions, Defense Planning, and the Renewal of the Anglo-Japanese Alliance," *Journal of Modern History* 52: 3 (Sept. 1980): 389, fn 20.

7  Don Dignan, "Australia and British Relations with Japan, 1914–1921," *Australian Outlook* 21 (1967): 136; Robert Joseph Gowen, "British Legerdemain," 385–386. Gowen claims that British officials intentionally withheld sensitive foreign policy information from the dominions. Gowen, "British Legerdemain," 389.

8  Nish, *Alliance in Decline*, 60–63; L. Harcourt to Earl Grey, 22 July 1911, Library and Archives Canada [hereafter cited as LAC], RG25, vol. 1115, file 883. When imperial leaders met in London in 1921, they affirmed it was "generally understood" that Article IV would not oblige Britain to go to war with the United States. Memorandum entitled "Meeting of Prime Ministers of Empire in London," June 1921, LAC, RG25, vol. 1284, file 42, pt. 2.

Borden was supported by exclusionists in British Columbia.[9] Over the next two years, provincial legislatures in Western Canada passed discriminatory laws banning "oriental" employment of white females and Japanese involvement in the fishing and lumber sectors. Facing protests from Japan, Borden arranged for Canada's adherence in 1913 to the Anglo-Japanese commercial treaty (1911) – something Laurier had been reluctant to do – provided it did not affect domestic immigration laws. In response, Japan's consul general in Ottawa, Nakamura Takashi, assured him Japan would observe the quotas agreed upon in 1908.[10] Even Canadian military planners noted the potential danger of Japanese immigrants, whose military experience, enduring ties with Tokyo and "aggression patriotism" made them "a menace to the Country and to the Empire." In Australia and New Zealand, public sentiment reflected a general wariness of reliance upon Japan for protection. In New Zealand, a new government under William Massey followed Australia's efforts to develop its own fleet, indicating a general frustration with Britain's growing preoccupation with the German threat over Pacific concerns.[11]

### The Alliance in Practice

The outbreak of the First World War in 1914 provided the first real test of the renewed alliance. To its proponents, wartime realities – especially Britain's strategic weakness in the Pacific – only vindicated London's policy toward Japan. When war erupted that August, the poor state of defenses and lack of

---

9    C.P. Stacey, *Canada and the Age of Conflict: A History of Canadian External Policies, vol. I: 1867–1921* (Toronto: Macmillan of Canada, 1977), 146–149. For more on anti-Asian sentiment in British Columbia, see David Sulz, "Transitional Relations: Japanese Immigration and the *Suian Maru* Affair, 1900–11" in Greg Donaghy and Patricia Roy, eds., *Contradictory Impulses: Canada and Japan in the Twentieth Century* (Vancouver: University of British Columbia Press, 2008), 46–61.

10   Nakamura to Borden, 1 March 1913, Canada, Dept. of External Affairs, *Documents on Canadian External Relations* [hereafter cited as *DCER*], vol. I (Ottawa: Queen's Printer, 1967), 747–748. Until it lapsed in 1923, Canadian leaders maintained that the 1911 Anglo-Japanese commercial treaty mainly regulated trade, was "independent and separate from the Alliance," and was subject to the 1908 gentlemen's agreement on immigration. Memorandum entitled "Meeting of the Prime Ministers of the Empire in London, June 1921" in Library and Archives Canada [hereinafter cited as LAC], RG25, vol. 1284, file 42, pt. 2.

11   Peter Lowe, *Great Britain and Japan*, 278–287; Pringsheim, *Neighbours Across the Pacific*, 20; Gregory Johnson and Galen Roger Perras, "A Menace to the Country and the Empire: Perceptions of the Japanese Military Threat to Canada before 1931" in Donaghy and Roy, *Contradictory Impulses*, 65–66.

50                                                                                    MEEHAN

military preparedness in the Pacific dominions were alarming indeed. Australia and New Zealand had heeded Britain's request to contribute to their own defense but their navies were still in their infancy. Amidst heated debate, Canada had begun its own navy in 1910 but French Canadians remained cool to the idea and imperialists favored direct contributions to Britain's Royal Navy. The contentious Naval Service Act (1910) called for a new naval college and eleven warships but Canada began with only two training ships, which Conservative critics lambasted as a "tin-pot navy."[12] Of the navy's 800 officers and men in 1911, most had been on loan from Britain and the force declined to 350 within two years.[13] Canada's Pacific coast was woefully under-defended with only one light cruiser, HMCS *Rainbow*, two British patrol craft and two small submarines recently purchased from the United States.[14] Useful mainly in monitoring sealing activity and, ironically, illegal Asian immigration, the *Rainbow* was outdated, undermanned and poorly armed. Moreover, until the Panama Canal opened in August 1914, the main west coast base at Esquimalt was a 15,000-mile voyage from Britain. Pacific defense thus relied on the transport of troops by the Canadian Pacific Railway and Japanese goodwill through the alliance. American aid was precluded by Washington's initial neutrality in the conflict.[15]

Such minimal defenses were unlikely to deter Germany's faster and better-equipped Pacific squadron under Admiral Graf von Spee. When the British Empire declared war on Germany on 4 August, the *Rainbow* was already at sea seeking British patrol vessels reportedly threatened by a German cruiser. Few expected the Canadian ship to return since it had left Esquimalt without the proper ammunition, which had yet to arrive at Vancouver. Defense staff prepared for the worst, nobly advising the *Rainbow*'s captain to "Remember Nelson and the British Navy. All Canada is watching."[16] Spared from attack, its

---

12    Canadian military historian Desmond Morton has attributed the phrase to Canada's noted satirist, Stephen Leacock. Desmond Morton, *A Military History of Canada*, 4th ed. (Toronto: McClelland & Stewart, 1999), 125–126.

13    Marc Milner, *Canada's Navy: The First Century*, 2nd ed. (Toronto: University of Toronto Press, 1999), 28.

14    The *Rainbow* had been constructed in England in 1891 and purchased by Canada in 1910. The two submarines, originally built for the Chilean navy, had been bought shortly before the outbreak of the war by Richard McBride, the premier of British Columbia. Pringsheim, *Neighbours Across the Pacific*, 20–21.

15    Milner, *Canada's Navy*, 35; Morton, *Military History of Canada*, 130.

16    William Johnston, William G.P. Rawling, Richard H. Gimblett and John MacFarlane, *The Seabound Coast: The Official History of the Royal Canadian Navy, 1867–1939, vol. I* (Toronto: Dundurn Press, 2010), 231–237. Citation is from Milner, *Canada's Navy*, 43.

crew was reassured by Japan's decision to send a battleship and an armored cruiser to defend Pacific shipping lanes. On 25 August, only two days after Japan declared war on Germany, the *Izumo* arrived at Esquimalt, soon joined by a British cruiser, HMS *Newcastle*. While insufficient to defend Canada's entire Pacific coastline, their presence did much to calm fears in British Columbia and deter von Spee's squadron from heading north. Over the next months, a combined British, Australian and Japanese force successfully defended Australia and New Zealand, pushing the German force eastward toward Mexico and South America. After winning a naval battle in November off the coast of Coronel, Chile, von Spee's squadron was defeated by a larger British force near the Falkland Islands in early December. To the dominions, Japan's wartime assistance had clearly demonstrated the value of the Anglo-Japanese alliance in maintaining peace in the Pacific.[17]

For the rest of the war, Japan remained a staunch ally. In Canada, naval planners received helpful advice from Japanese consular officials at Ottawa and enjoyed good relations with Japanese military personnel visiting Esquimalt. The former prime minister, Laurier, noted the irony of those who had cursed his support of the Anglo-Japanese alliance but were "grateful to have the Japanese good-will." Indeed, many who had been wary of Japanese immigration now appreciated the benefits of Japanese protection. British Columbia's premier, Richard McBride, was proven wrong in his warning to Borden that Japan might side with Germany and threaten the west coast should the war go badly for Britain. In early 1915, he thanked Japan for its "immense service" to his province, though his thanks did not extend to some 200 Japanese-Canadians who volunteered to fight for Canada overseas despite their lack of enfranchisement. Able to vote federally while serving in Europe, they were denied the vote upon their return to British Columbia after the war. His praise notwithstanding, McBride harbored lingering fears about Japan's long-term ambitions. "Just as soon as the war ends," he confided to a colleague in 1914, "we shall find Japan in complete control of the Pacific." To a large extent, military and diplomatic realities held parochial forces in check since Canada and Japan remained linked by the Anglo-Japanese alliance, the gentlemen's agreement of 1908 and the trade treaty of 1911. Even in British Columbia, the press thanked the "fortunate stroke of diplomacy from Downing Street" that had made Japan "our ally."[18] Such

---

17    The Battle of Coronel witnessed the first Canadian casualties of the war with the death of four midshipmen. Johnston et al., *Seabound Coast*, 249–258; Pringsheim, *Neighbours Across the Pacific*, 20–21.

18    Patricia E. Roy, *The Oriental Question: Consolidating a White Man's Province, 1914–41* (Vancouver: University of British Columbia Press, 2003), 14–15, 245n4; Pringsheim,

sentiments echoed those of Wilson Crewdson whose popular book, *Japan Our Ally* (1915), extolled the Anglo-Japanese alliance for such wartime protection:

> We are now, after several months of this terrible war, in a position to estimate the great value of the Alliance so happily entered into between England and Japan....The responsibility for the defence of the coasts of these countries has to a large extent been assumed by the navy of Japan, so that their soldiers might be free to fight in Europe. It is in its absolute quietness that the strength of the Japanese Alliance has been proved.[19]

What raised cheers in some quarters aroused suspicion elsewhere. To many, it appeared that Japan's alliance with Britain had enabled it to pursue opportunistic policies in China. In South China, Japanese commercial interests pushed for a more aggressive stance at the expense of British firms. In the north, upon Tokyo's declaration of war, Japanese forces immediately blockaded Qingdao, the German port in Shandong. A combined Anglo-Japanese force took the city that November with British forces serving under Japanese "allied" command. Friction arose between these troops as British soldiers were at times mistaken for Germans and fired upon or mistreated. In early 1915, Japan issued its so-called Twenty-One Demands to China, ostensibly concerning its presence at Qingdao but also strengthening its interests in Manchuria, Fujian and the Yangzi valley. To London, the move indicated Japan's desire to assert its interests in China more vigorously. British attempts to involve China in the war led to sharp rebukes in the Japanese press, the conservative *Yamato* calling for an end to the alliance and racial equality for Japanese living in "Australia, Canada, Africa, India and other self-governing English possessions." As the war progressed, Japan's navy continued to protect the dominions but Tokyo pointed out how politically awkward this was due to ongoing discrimination there against Japanese immigrants. In early 1917, Japan and Britain reached a secret agreement on naval assistance in return for British acceptance of Japanese rights in Shandong and the former German South Sea Islands. By this stage, Australia and New Zealand had also accepted Japan's claims in these territories. After the United States entered the war in April 1917, London feared that Tokyo would exact similar terms from

---

*Neighbours Across the Pacific*, 21–22; Morton, *Military History of Canada*, 126. McBride cited in Johnson and Perras, "Menace to the Country," 67.

19    Wilson Crewdson, *Japan Our Ally* (London: Macmillan & Co., 1915), 31–32.

Washington during a mission there by former foreign minister Ishii Kikujiro later that year.[20]

The Allied intervention in Siberia further tested the limits of Anglo-Japanese collaboration in wartime. In response to the Bolshevik revolution and Russia's withdrawal from the war, Japan joined Britain, the United States and other Western powers in resisting communist advances in Siberia. Yet differences among the Allies soon became apparent. Early in the expedition, Tokyo dispatched a cruiser to Vladivostok, considering Siberia within its sphere of influence. Since Japan accounted for most of the Allied forces there, General Otani Kikuzo was placed in charge of the Siberian operation. The United States, though it had invited Japan to participate, did not place its troops under Otani and opposed attempts by his forces to move beyond Vladivostok. Britain desired a strong presence but, lacking sufficient troops, relied on Canada – the only dominion involved in the Siberian expedition – to direct the British contingents. After sending more than 500 soldiers to Murmansk and Arkhangelsk in northern Russia in 1918, Canada dispatched some 4200 troops to Vladivostok that fall, relying largely on conscripts rather than volunteers. Their presence, which coincided with a Canadian trade mission to the region, became problematic. Firstly, the chain of command was blurred with their Canadian head reporting to General Otani, Ottawa and the War Office in London. Moreover, most of them reached Vladivostok after war in Europe had ended, leading to a dispute between London and Ottawa over the future aim of the mission. To remain in Siberia, as Winston Churchill strongly advocated, amounted to intervention in Russia's internal affairs, a course that Canada's prime minister, Borden, was anxious to avoid. With Canadian opinion opposed to continued intervention, Borden flatly refused Churchill's appeals for military assistance and ordered the withdrawal of Canadian troops by the following spring. Canada's wartime sacrifices had given it a newfound status in relations with Britain. For the first time, a Canadian had commanded a joint Commonwealth force overseas and a Canadian government had declined British requests for military support.[21]

---

20    *Yamato* cited in Nish, *Alliance in Decline,* 167–168. When questioned after the war by congress, US secretary of state Robert Lansing claimed that Ishii had informed him in 1917 that Japan had intended to restore Shandong to China and that it was not until early 1919 that he had learned the agreement contained any reference to Japan's claim there. R.C. Lindsay to Foreign Office, 12 August 1919 in LAC, RG 25, vol. 1246, file 881.

21    Paul E. Dunscomb, *Japan's Siberian Intervention, 1918–1922: "A Great Disobedience Against the People"* (Lanham, MD: Lexington Books, 2011), 67; Jean-David Avenel, *Interventions Alliees pendant la Guerre Civile Russe (1918–1920)* (Paris: Economica, 2001), 116; Stacey,

### An Imperiled Alliance

By 1918, dominion influence on British policies toward Japan had become apparent. During the war, the dominions had earned seats at the imperial war cabinet due to their major commitment of troops, money and war material. This body, formed by the British prime minister David Lloyd George in early 1917, had brought together the leaders of Britain, Canada, Australia, New Zealand, India and other dominions to coordinate the empire's conduct of the war. Under British leadership, its members had agreed that an imperial conference after the war would do much to promote a clearer voice for the dominions in world affairs. No longer seeing themselves as simply junior partners, the dominions participated at the Paris peace talks and the new League of Nations, some later seeking diplomatic representation abroad. Within such forums, they expressed an emerging national identity as well as a growing reticence toward foreign entanglements. In this light, the Anglo-Japanese alliance faced an uncertain future. On the one hand, it seemed to run counter to the new spirit of internationalism that endorsed multilateralism over bilateral and often secret alliances that were blamed for provoking the war. On the other, the dominions themselves were unlikely to continue with support for such arrangements if they did not judge them to be in their own interests. The notable absence of the United States – both from the League of Nations and from a multilateral system of Pacific security – further cast a shadow on the future of the Anglo-Japanese alliance.[22]

For the dominions, much had changed since 1911. At the imperial conference of that year, Britain had consulted them on renewing the alliance for ten years, though it had already made up its mind on the question. On that occasion, as we have seen, its foreign secretary, Sir Edward Grey, had skillfully enabled renewal by emphasizing the pact's strategic value, disassociating it from dominion legislation on Japanese immigration. Yet it was precisely this link that had frustrated Japanese officials during the war, as they had sought to

---

*Canada and Age of Conflict*, vol. I, 276–284; Benjamin Isitt, *From Victoria to Vladivostok: Canada's Siberian Expedition, 1917–19* (Vancouver: University of British Columbia Press, 2010), 111–115; John Swettenham, *Allied Intervention in Russia, 1918–1919* (Toronto: Ryerson Press, 1967), 172–178. While Australia and New Zealand were not formally involved in the Siberian operation, some 150 of their soldiers participated in the northern Russian expedition. For more on their involvement, see Michael Challinger, *Anzacs in Arkhangel: The Untold Story of Australia and the Invasion of Russia, 1918–19* (Melbourne and London: Hardie Grant Books, 2010) and Bruce Muirden, *The Diggers who Signed on for More: Australia's Part in the Russian Wars of Intervention, 1918–1919* (Kent Town, S. Australia: Wakefield Press, 1990).

22    Stacey, *Canada and the Age of Conflict*, vol. I, 206–214, 240–269.

justify to their nation why they were defending British dominions that discriminated against Japanese immigrants. Moreover, the imperial conference of 1911 had shown a growing divergence among the Pacific dominions over Japan's rise to power. In contrast to Canada's desire to renew the alliance – even for fifty years – Australia and New Zealand had been wary of Japanese aims, and British attempts to distance itself from Pacific security. Finally, Anglo-Japanese cooperation in wartime had met with mixed results. While Japan had fulfilled its obligation to protect the Pacific dominions, it had used the war for its own advancement in East Asia, sparring with Allies over joint operations in Shandong and Siberia. Japan's desire to maintain its special interests in China and the South Sea Islands, according to Australia's prime minister William (Billy) Hughes, clearly indicated its ongoing threat to the British Empire. To his dominion counterparts, it became apparent that a more comprehensive approach to Pacific security would be required.[23]

Such concerns assumed greater urgency as the alliance neared its expected termination in 1921. By this stage, Britain had distanced itself from Japan due to commercial and naval rivalries as well as the strong desire of both nations to improve ties with the United States. In 1919, London sent Lord Grey to Washington for this purpose as its new ambassador, though he lamented the US senate's refusal to ratify the Versailles treaty and League covenant the following year. Meanwhile, Britain dispatched its First Sea Lord, Admiral Sir John Jellicoe, to the dominions to survey the state of imperial naval defense. After visiting India, Australia, New Zealand and Canada in 1919–20, Jellicoe came to see Japan as the leading threat in Asia, necessitating a new British fleet to be based at Singapore. His findings echoed those of Canadian military officials who concluded that Japan had become "the most probable enemy of the future" in the Pacific. Their fears were bolstered by a defense memorandum of early 1921 that envisaged a possible war between Japan and the United States in which Canadian neutrality would be difficult to maintain. In Washington, the Anglo-Japanese alliance was regarded with suspicion, officials there blaming it for Japan's injustices against China during the war. The situation was enough to convince Loring Christie, chief legal advisor at Canada's Department of External Affairs, that the United States would be unlikely to accept renewal of the alliance in any form. Since an imperial conference of dominion premiers was expected in the near future, Tokyo and Washington looked to see what Britain and the Pacific dominions would decide.[24]

---

23    Nish, *Alliance in Decline*, 258–259.

24    Alfred Milner to Duke of Devonshire, 28 Jan. 1921, LAC, RG25, vol. 1284, file 42, pt. 1; Nish, *Alliance in Decline*, 277–279, 285; Johnson and Perras, "Menace to the Country," 67–70.

In preparing for the conference, British and dominion leaders weighed the pros and cons of renewal. For some, an appealing alternative was a possible tripartite alliance of Japan, Britain and the United States or perhaps a wider pact that included France. Yet there was little evidence of support for this from the American public or the new Republican administration of Warren Harding, which saw the alliance as an obstacle to naval disarmament. For Britain, renewal was problematic on several counts. It seemed incompatible with Jellicoe's assessment of Japan as the greatest threat in Asia and his calls for a strengthened Pacific fleet and base at Singapore. Moreover, the dominions were believed to be hostile to renewal due to concerns over Japanese immigration. Finally, it was unclear if the alliance would lapse automatically in July 1921 since the parties were obliged to give one year's notice before termination. According to legal experts at the foreign office, such notice had been given in 1920 in a joint statement by Britain and Japan to the League of Nations that the agreement, if renewed, would not be inconsistent with the League covenant. With the imperial conference to be held in London in June, Britain proposed to the dominions in early 1921 that the question of renewal be placed near the top of the agenda and that the alliance be renewed for an additional year to facilitate discussion.[25]

In soliciting the dominions, London recognized their new role in imperial and Pacific affairs. Unlike in 1911, they could no longer be expected simply to confirm decisions already made. In fact, Britain was intentionally open on renewal, claiming that no decision could be reached until dominion leaders had convened. As it canvassed their views, London realized how much dominion interests had changed over the decade, leading to a reversal of positions. Australia, though still wary of Japanese immigration, strongly endorsed renewal due to Britain's weakness in Asia, Prime Minister Hughes publicly praising Japan as "the greatest Power in the East." New Zealand and other dominions also voiced support, mindful of Japanese protection during the war. Canada, on the other hand, firmly opposed renewal as a "barrier to an English speaking concord" between the British Empire and the United States. In contrast to Laurier's earlier enthusiasm for the alliance, Prime Minister Arthur Meighen, whose Conservative government had been elected in 1920, warned against any arrangement that might exclude the United States. Instead, as urged by his advisor Loring Christie, he proposed that a conference of Pacific powers be held, offering to send Sir Robert Borden to Washington to gauge American support for the idea. While the alliance had been useful in the past,

---

25 Winston Churchill to Devonshire, 26 Feb. 1921, LAC, RG25, vol. 1284, file 42, pt. 1; Nish, *Alliance in Decline*, 319–321, 324–325.

Meighen concluded, conditions had changed so that "old motives no longer hold, while the objections have greatly increased." Due to its own major interests in Asia, it was necessary to bring the United States into a wider forum of Pacific security, one consistent with the new internationalism.[26] His arguments, sent to Britain by Canada's governor general, the Duke of Devonshire, were clear and compelling:

> We feel that every possible effort should be made to find some alternative policy to that of renewal....Specifically we think we should terminate the Alliance and endeavour at once to bring about a Conference of Pacific Powers – that is Japan, China, the United States, and the British Empire represented by Great Britain, Canada, Australia and New Zealand – for the purpose of adjusting Pacific and Far Eastern questions. Such a straightforward course would enable us to end the Alliance with good grace and would reconcile our position in respect of China and the United States. It would be a practical application of the principles of the League of Nations. Should it eventually result in a working Pacific Concert the gain to the stability of British-American relations is obvious.[27]

Ottawa's statement had an impact in London. In fact, it arrived just as British officials were debating the future of the Anglo-Japanese alliance. Less than a month earlier, a foreign office committee had recommended the pact be replaced by "a Tripartite Entente" between Britain, Japan and the United States, seeing relations with the latter as "the prime factor" in global stability. The foreign secretary Lord Curzon, though he had commissioned the committee, failed to support its findings, claiming renewal was endorsed by Britain's ambassador to Washington, Sir Auckland Geddes. With the foreign office and Committee of Imperial Defence still studying the question, London advised Meighen to defer any overtures to Washington so as not "to prejudice complete liberty of action" at the imperial conference. In light of Canada's position, Britain soon reduced the proposed temporary extension of the alliance from one year to three months. The move surprised Japanese officials who had not seen the joint statement at the League as a formal notice of termination. Moreover, London reserved judgment on a Pacific conference, an idea that Christie had discussed with Lloyd George during his visit to Europe in late 1920.

---

26    Nish, *Alliance in Decline*, 325–326; Christie memorandum entitled "The Anglo-Japanese Alliance," 1 Feb. 1921, LAC, RG25, vol. 1270, file 680; Devonshire to Churchill, 15 Feb. 1921, LAC, RG25, vol. 1284, file 42, pt. 1.

27    Devonshire to Churchill, 15 Feb. 1921, LAC, RG25, vol. 1284, file 42, pt. 1.

A brilliant lawyer and senior bureaucrat with extensive ties to the American elite, Christie was convinced of Canada's crucial role in the empire as a mediator between Britain and the United States. In deciding the alliance's fate, he argued, the initiative should come from the Pacific dominions due to their "dominant voice" on the question, Canadians having "greater chances of success in dealing with Americans."[28]

London's "wait-and-see" attitude frustrated officials in Ottawa. Indeed, its ambivalence nearly drove Christie to disregard Britain's note by sending Borden to Washington anyway. Dissuading him, Meighen impressed upon London "the very special Canadian position" on the matter and reiterated Canada's opposition to renewal. Facing questions in parliament, his requests to London for information on the conference elicited only vague advice that public comments on the alliance "be worded so as not to give rise to misgivings in the United States or in Japan." In response, Meighen argued that failure to consider options other than renewal would "in itself prejudice the liberty of action" at the imperial conference. The Pacific was a vital region for Britain and the United States and delay in fostering cooperation between them in this area "can only do harm." As Canada was "intimately involved" with such cooperation, he believed resolution of the question would be "the first definitely significant step in post-war British American relations." During a parliamentary debate on the alliance on 27 April, Meighen assured critics that no treaty would bind Canada unless approved by parliament, no less one that might compel Canada to fight the United States.[29] Such factors reinforced Meighen's view of Canadians' special role within the empire in cultivating good relations with Washington:

> In spite of occasional differences their whole experience has been favourable to principle of co-operation and they would recoil from anything to the contrary. They have had special opportunities through intercourse and association to understand and deal with the Americans and they will feel that the advantages of this consideration should not be overlooked. They will be unlikely to be convinced by the conclusions of committees which must necessarily be lacking in the intimate experience

---

28    Churchill to Devonshire, 26 Feb. and 26 April 1921; both in LAC, RG25, vol. 1284, file 42, pt. 1; Stacey, *Canada and Age of Conflict*, vol. I, 335–337.

29    Christie memorandum entitled "The Anglo-Japanese Alliance," 3 March 1921; Churchill to Devonshire, 9 March 1921; Devonshire to Churchill, 1 April 1921; all in LAC, RG25, vol. 1284, file 42, pts. 1–2; Canada, *House of Commons Debates*, vol. LVI, no. 49 (27 April 1921), 2759–2760.

and association essential to a judgment upon the political conditions of this hemisphere.[30]

Diplomatic factors only added to Britain's reluctance to define its position. Not renewing the alliance might antagonize Japan, though London could lay blame for this outcome on the dominions, whose suspicions toward Japanese aims were known in Tokyo. On the other hand, renewing the pact would confirm to critics in America and China that London and Tokyo sought to play by the old rules, endorsing "all the wrongs" inflicted by Japan upon China during the war. Regardless of the decision, British diplomats realized that the Pacific dominions would look increasingly to the United States and not to Britain for protection. Moreover, the alliance seemed to have outlived its original aim of countering Russian influence in Asia. When the British cabinet met on 30 May in a special session to consider the matter, divisions resurfaced among the key players. As foreign secretary, Curzon still ignored the advice of his own committee and supported renewal, albeit in modified form and for a shorter period, though he recognized strong counter-arguments. The colonial secretary, Winston Churchill, favored the "Canadian proposal" of a conference of Pacific powers while naval officials stressed the strategic value of the alliance. Ever the consummate politician, Lloyd George sided with Curzon but believed Britain could support Japan in encouraging a Pacific conference. In the end, cabinet reached a strange, perhaps even paradoxical, compromise. It was agreed the United States should be asked to convene a Pacific conference but only after Japan was reassured of Britain's desire to renew the alliance, albeit for a shorter duration and in conformity with League principles. In light of American sensitivities, talks with the United States and China should be held prior to renewal. How the dominions would react to this position remained to be seen.[31]

Examining British and dominion attitudes prior to the imperial conference of June 1921 provides helpful context for an episode that later aroused much debate among historians. To some, such as John Bartlet Brebner, the conference was a dramatic precedent, "the first notable occasion of a Dominion

---

30   Devonshire to Churchill, 1 April 1921, LAC, RG25, vol. 1284, file 42, pt. 1.
31   Charles Eliot to Curzon, 22 March 1921; memorandum entitled "China and the Anglo-Japanese Alliance" by Bertram Lenox-Simpson to Meighen, 4 May 1921; Christie memorandum, "The Anglo-Japanese Alliance, Notes on Mr. Lloyd George's Telegram of February 26, 1921," dated 3 March 1921; assessment of US Attitudes by British consul-general at New York, forwarded by British foreign office to imperial cabinet, 16 June 1921; all in LAC, RG25, vol. 1284, file 42, pts. 1–2. Nish, *Alliance in Decline*, 328–332.

formulating the policy of the British Empire." Writing only fourteen years after the event, Brebner credited Canada with having checked a general desire at the conference to renew the alliance, thereby marking a turning-point in British policies toward the Pacific. In highlighting Canada's role, Brebner attributed its stance to a "Canadianism" that asserted national aims and a "North Americanism" that reflected continental concerns within what he termed the "North Atlantic triangle." Other historians have disputed Brebner's view, criticizing its nationalist tone. As Ian Nish has observed, every leader who returned from the conference, including Lloyd George himself, claimed to have influenced the outcome. Despite Brebner's portrayal, disputes between Canada and Australia did not undermine the meeting's cordial spirit and extensive common ground. All delegates, including Australia, viewed Anglo-American harmony as the chief concern, seeking a compromise between outright renewal and termination, as J. Chal Vinson has argued. With no one wishing to continue to alliance in its existing form, according to Nish, differences were in priorities and not in substance. More recently, historians have questioned the reasons for renewal, Philips Payson O'Brien claiming its proponents did not envisage a real treaty of mutual defense and Antony Best attributing this to myths about Anglo-Japanese friendship and "old diplomacy."[32]

Amidst the scholarly debate, few historians have argued that the dominions had little influence at the imperial conference. When Lloyd George opened the meeting on 20 June, he carefully outlined Britain's dilemma of keeping Japan's friendship while, at the same time, not alienating the United States and China on Pacific security. After a similarly cautious speech by Meighen, Hughes stated Australia's strong desire for renewal but in a form that was amenable to the United States. New Zealand's premier, W.F. Massey, echoed this conciliatory tone. British ambiguity became apparent when the conference reconvened on 28 June. Curzon was unwilling to abandon the alliance, hoping for a tripartite pact or a renewal of perhaps four years, but Churchill retorted with fresh reports from Washington confirming opposition to renewal in any form. Appealing to the admiralty and Committee of Imperial Defence, Curzon cited the military's view of renewal as being in Britain's best strategic interests.

---

32    J. Bartlet Brebner, "Canada, the Anglo-Japanese Alliance and the Washington Conference,"
       *Political Science Quarterly* 50, no. 1 (1935): 45–58; Nish, *Alliance in Decline*, 333–353;
       J. Chal Vinson, "The Imperial Conference of 1921 and the Anglo-Japanese Alliance," *Pacific
       Historical Review* 31, no. 3 (1962): 257–266; Philips Payson O'Brien, ed., *The Anglo-Japanese
       Alliance, 1902–22* (London: RoutledgeCurzon, 2004), 280–282; Antony Best, "The 'Ghost'
       of the Anglo-Japanese Alliance: An Examination into Historical Myth-Making,"
       *The Historical Journal* 49, no. 3 (Sept. 2006): 811–831.

On the following day, Meighen directly attacked the alliance by emphasizing Anglo-American harmony as "the pivot of our world policy" and making the case for a "broad, inclusive arrangement" due to American interests. He outlined Canada's vulnerability in the event of an Anglo-American conflict and even threatened to pull out of talks if renewal were pursued. His remarks prompted an emotional outburst by Hughes who claimed Meighen had presented not the British case but that of his powerful neighbor "under whose wing the Dominion of Canada can nestle in safety." Australia would back renewal unless the United States could give concretȩ assurances of its protection, a stance supported by New Zealand and India but not explicitly by South Africa.[33]

Meighen's intervention led Britain to change its tack, though not its basic position. When the British cabinet convened on 30 June to revise its stance, Curzon acknowledged that Meighen had opposed renewal "even more strongly than had been anticipated." While not dismissing renewal, it was agreed to give priority to talks with Japan and the United States on reaching an arrangement on Pacific security that was acceptable to all parties. By a stroke of political genius, Lloyd George had Lord Birkenhead, the Lord Chancellor, overturn the foreign office's earlier legal view of the 1920 joint declaration, thus endorsing the Japanese position that neither party had yet given the twelve-month notice of termination. This shrewd move affected the outcome of the conference. The delegates, no longer pressured by the imminent expiry of the alliance, turned to considering the merits of a Pacific conference. On 1 July, they unanimously authorized Curzon to approach the Pacific powers to solicit their interest in such a conference. Should this gathering be unable to amend the alliance to the satisfaction of all parties, the pact could then be renewed along League principles, though few saw this as a likely outcome. The compromise allayed fears regarding Pacific security, expressed by Australia and New Zealand, and concerns of alienating the United States, shared by all but stated most directly by Canada. On 11 July, President Harding publicly announced that he had invited Britain, Japan, France and Italy to Washington for a disarmament conference and a separate meeting on Pacific security. Six months later, the Anglo-Japanese alliance was formally replaced by multilateral treaties on naval strength and China's territorial integrity. Much like the dominions at the imperial conference, the United States saw the gathering as being within its national

---

33  Curzon memorandum entitled "Anglo-Japanese Agreement," 28 June 1921; Curzon to Geddes, 28 June and 30 July 1921; all in LAC, RG25, vol. 1284, file 42, pt. 1; Meighen's speech to delegates, 29 June 1921 in Lovell C. Clark, ed., *DCER*, vol. III (Ottawa: Queen's Printer, 1970), 174–188; Stacey, *Canada and the Age of Conflict*, vol. I, 338–348.

interest, avoiding an unpopular naval arms race while at the same time taking centre stage in deliberations on Pacific security.[34]

### Embracing Multilateralism

From 1911 to 1921, the British Empire moved perceptibly from bilateralism to multilateralism in Pacific affairs. In this process, as this chapter has maintained, the Pacific dominions played a key role, though they were by no means the only or most significant factor. Britain's own declining relative strength in the Pacific, combined with rising American and Japanese influence there, pointed to more significant shifts in power. While the Anglo-Japanese alliance, in retrospect, was unlikely to have survived well into the 1920s, the dominions acted as important agents within British imperial policy. Initially, they were solicited for their views, though Britain technically did not need to consult them on such matters. In 1911, they accepted renewal of the alliance insofar as it did not impinge on domestic immigration legislation. As the 1910s progressed, however, the dominions increasingly realized their emerging national interests and growing status in world affairs. The experience of the First World War was crucial in this regard. On the one hand, their reliance upon Japanese protection demonstrated their strategic weakness and need for a comprehensive security arrangement in the Pacific. On the other, their wartime sacrifice enhanced their voice in imperial and Pacific affairs, causing London to take their views more seriously at the 1921 imperial conference than in 1911.

In becoming global citizens, the British dominions became early advocates of Pacific multilateralism. By 1921, the principal dominions had revised their positions on bilateralism. Anxious of their own vulnerability, Australia and New Zealand, earlier critics of the Anglo-Japanese pact, favored renewal in a form acceptable to the United States. Barring commitments from the latter, they saw Britain as the best guarantor of their security. In Canada, there was little enthusiasm for the alliance, Laurier's earlier hope of a long-term pact being little more than a naive wish. By strongly opposing renewal at the imperial conference, Meighen asserted Canadian, not American, interests in response to political realities at home. The matter had major implications for Canada as a small Pacific power. Public opinion and national interests favored inclusion of the United States, Anglo-American harmony and a wider security arrangement. Cooperation between the English-speaking peoples, as Christie

---

34    Notes from twelfth and thirteenth meetings of prime ministers, 1 July 1921, *DCER*, vol. III, 188–194; Nish, *Alliance in Decline*, 335–339.

observed, was far more than "a trite phrase" due to Canada's dependence on such ties. Moreover, national interests were predicated upon friendly relations with Asia's great powers. As he advised Meighen in early 1921, it was imperative to seek common ground with both Japan, "a great and ambitious nation" that had been faithful to its treaty obligations, and China, whose stability and prosperity were vital for peace in the region. Looking to the future, Christie felt it was "impossible to believe of this vast community that, given a fair chance, the traditions of their ancient civilization will not reassert themselves, or that they can be left out of the reckoning."[35] His words were prophetic indeed. In advancing their national interests, Canada and the other dominions had come to espouse a nascent form of Pacific multilateralism. In light of the subsequent failure of the Washington system and the horrors of the Pacific war, this is a precedent worth considering and consolidating.

---

35    Christie memorandum entitled "Meeting of Prime Ministers of Empire in London," June 1921, LAC, RG25, vol. 1284, file 42, pt. 2.

# Out with the New and in with the Old

## Uchida Yasuya and the Great War as a Turning Point in Japanese Foreign Affairs

Rustin B. Gates

### Introduction

The question of whether the Great War and its aftermath was a turning point in Japanese history is not a new one. Indeed, this question has been the focus of numerous studies by historians of Japanese diplomacy beginning in the 1960s and continuing to the current day.[1] One scholar, for example, argues that following the war the Hara Takashi cabinet (1918–21) reoriented Japanese diplomacy toward cooperation with the United States, which became more important to Japan than Britain.[2] Others agree with this thesis on change, but locate the shift in the new East Asian order created by the Washington Conference treaties of 1921–22.[3] In contrast, a more recent study contends that the Hara cabinet continued the sphere of influence diplomacy it had inherited from earlier, non-party cabinets.[4] Still a third view argues that Japanese foreign policy in the early 1920s was a combination of Old and New diplomacy, a blending of partial adherence to a new emerging order with concrete efforts to retain old imperial interests.[5]

This essay considers the above question of whether the Great War was a turning point in Japanese foreign affairs by examining the policies of post-WWI

---

1 Frederick Dickinson, for example, considers the war a "watershed" event for Japanese national identity. Frederick Dickinson, *War and National Reinvention* (Cambridge, MA: Harvard UP, 1999), 4. Also, see Dick Stegewerns, "The End of World War One as a Turning Point in Modern Japanese History," in *Turning Points in Japanese History*, ed. B. Edstrom (London: Japan Library, 2002), 138–162.

2 Mitani Taichirō, "'Tenkanki' (1918–21) no gaikō shidō," in *Kindai Nihon no seiji shidō* eds., Shinohara Hajime and Mitani Taichirō (Tokyo: Tokyo UP, 1965), 295–297.

3 Akira Iriye, *After Imperialism: The Search for a New Order in the Far East, 1921–1931* (Cambridge, MA: Harvard UP, 1965), 19–20; Hosoya Chihiro, *Ryō taisenkan no Nihon gaikō, 1914–1945* (Tokyo: Iwanami Shoten, 1988), 75.

4 Hattori Ryūji, *Higashi Ajia kokusai kankyō no hendō to Nihon gaikō, 1918–1931* (Tokyo: Yūhikaku, 2001), 3–9.

5 Sadao Asada, "Between the Old Diplomacy and the New, 1918–1922: The Washington System and the Origins of Japanese-American Rapprochement," *Diplomatic History* 30, no. 2 (April 2006): 211; and Thomas W. Burkman, *Japan and the League of Nations: Empire and World Order, 1914–1938* (Honolulu: University of Hawai'i Press, 2008), 212.

Foreign Minister Uchida Yasuya (1865–1936) in relation to his work as minister earlier in the decade. Uchida had a long career in the Japanese Ministry of Foreign Affairs, serving as minister three times (1911–12; 1918–23; and 1932–33). While Uchida was active during the Great War as Ambassador to Russia, he only came to help guide Japanese policy in the war's immediate aftermath. As foreign minister in the Hara Takashi cabinet, Uchida continued to base his policies on the imperatives of cooperation with the Western powers, non-intervention in China, and the maintenance of Japanese interests in Manchuria. To avoid Japanese isolation and continue his policy of cooperation with the powers, Uchida replaced his previous reliance on bilateral alliances and agreements with multilateral ones in the postwar era. He was less open to modifying his Manchuria policy, however. In the immediate postwar period and throughout the decade, Japan succeeded in preserving its sphere of interest in Manchuria by excluding it from international agreements and resisting Chinese attempts to recover its territory. With only slight modification, Uchida was able to continue policies in the 1920s that he had enacted as foreign minister in the early 1910s.

In doing so, Uchida effectively ended Japan's expansion on the mainland that his immediate predecessors had pursued during the war. Following its declaration of war against Germany, Japan displaced the Germans from their colonial possession of Jiaozhou in Shandong province, China, taking the colony for itself in the process. Later, in 1918, Japan occupied northern Manchuria and dispatched troops to Siberia as part of a joint allied expedition. In addition to military action, Japan utilized diplomatic measures as well to expand its position and influence on the mainland. The infamous Twenty-One Demands (1915) and the Nishihara Loans (1917–18) are the two prime examples of Japanese aggrandizement through non-lethal means during the war. By presiding over the return of Shandong to China and the withdrawal of Japanese troops in Siberia as well as by re-instituting his non-intervention policy for China, Uchida replaced the "new" diplomacy of the Terauchi Masatake and Okuma Shigenobu cabinets, with the "old" diplomacy he had practiced in the late Meiji era. Uchida's case, then, does not point to the Great War as turning point in Japanese foreign affairs but rather it offers a striking example of foreign policy continuity in prewar Japan.

### Uchida's First Term as Foreign Minister, 1911–12

While making his way across the Pacific, Uchida, the former ambassador to the US and the newly appointed foreign minister in the second Saionji Kinmochi

cabinet, received word of the outbreak of revolution in China. He was largely
unprepared to deal with this major crisis as his first order of business as foreign
minister. The fact that he was in transit during the first few days of the upheaval
made Uchida feel even more out of his depth. As such, Uchida turned to the
key tenets of his foreign policy, Manchuria and the Anglo-Japanese Alliance,
for guidance. Since instability in China threatened Japan's Manchurian interests, his first impulse was to shore up Japan's position in the region. Unsure of
how to react to the chaos in China proper, Uchida tied Japanese policy for
China to that of its ally, Britain. Both had extensive interests in China and
desired continual calm so as not to interrupt those interests.

After returning to Tokyo, Uchida joined the cabinet to devise a general policy on the revolution in a meeting on 24 October 1911, ten days after the initial
outbreak. The main focus of the policy was Manchuria. The Japanese leadership believed it had a "Manchuria problem" (*Manshū mondai*), a phrase that
represented Japanese efforts to secure and maintain their interests in the
region in the face of anti-imperial policies from the US and failures on the part
of the Qing government to strictly adhere to the spirit of the Peking Treaty of
1905; the treaty provided Chinese recognition of Japanese interests in
Manchuria acquired in the Russo-Japanese War. Uchida had assisted in concluding that treaty in 1905 and thus came to regard solving this "problem" as
crucial to his foreign policy as minister. Because the Chinese revolution presented both complications and opportunities for Japanese efforts to secure its
interests, Uchida and the cabinet essentially took a wait-and-see approach in
the cabinet policy: "we must await the most favorable time for the fundamental solution of the Manchuria problem."[6]

Uchida enacted this policy through various ways. When Minister to China
Ijūin Hikokichi called for the dispatch of Japanese troops, Uchida replied in
the negative, stating that such a movement must be first discussed with the
British.[7] The Qing government made Yuan Shikai premier of the imperial
cabinet in November with the task of putting down the revolutionaries. By this
time, however, the revolutionaries had been so successful that a change in government was a foregone conclusion. The question that arose, of course, was
what type of new government would be established. Both of the possibilities
had Yuan at the top: either a constitutional monarchy, which retained the Qing

6  *Nihon Gaikō nenpyō narabi ni shuyō bunsho*, hereafter NGSB, Vol. 1 (Tokyo: Foreign Ministry,
   1965), 356; for English translation, see Ikei Masaru, "Japan's Response to the Chinese
   Revolution of 1911," *Journal of Japanese Studies* 25, no. 2 (Feb. 1966): 214–215.
7  Uchida Yasuya Denki Hensan Iinkai, ed., *Uchida Yasuya* (Tokyo: Kajima Kenkyūjo Shuppandai,
   1968), 158; Ikei, "Japan's Response," 216.

court but made Yuan the premier and established a representative congress, or a republic with Yuan as president.

Floating on the choppy seas of the revolution, Uchida reached for the life raft of the Anglo-Japanese Alliance to buoy Japanese policy. Uchida sent a note to Britain, and later to the other powers, asking their views on the government situation in China. He concluded by stating that Japan supported the establishment of a constitutional monarchy, which would provide a more conservative and familiar form of government in China than would a republic.[8] Keeping the Qing court in place would temper any radical changes in China's foreign policy that might result if a popular government in the form of a republic took control. In essence, Uchida believed that a constitutional monarchy would protect Japanese interests in China and, most importantly, Manchuria to a much greater extent than a republic.

Uchida's bold initiative to first contact the powers met with total failure. The British buoy proved elusive. Throwing their weight behind the republic proposal, the British convinced Yuan to become president. Uchida was incredulous that his ally had acted without prior consultation and expressed doubts to the British that Yuan as president could solve the China situation. He further suggested that a conference of the powers should be held to discuss the matter.[9]

However, the momentum behind the republic continued to rise to the point where Yuan himself abandoned any talk of a constitutional monarchy. Japan, too, resigned itself to the republic in a cabinet decision on 22 December 1911 in which members unanimously agreed to cease demands for a constitutional monarchy.[10] On 25 December, Uchida met with the British ambassador to express his new position on China. First, while Britain and Japan should work with whatever form of government the Chinese national assembly decided to establish, they must not allow any arbitrary actions by Russia, France, the US or Germany in China. Second, it was not a problem if China established a republic, but if it did so, Britain and Japan would prefer that Manchuria, Mongolia, and Tibet were not included.[11]

---

8    Uchida to Yamaza, 28 November 1911, NGSB, Vol. 1, 357–359. For a similar note to the US, see *Foreign Relations of the United States: 1911* (Washington D.C.: Government Printing Office, 1918), 56–57. Hereafter FRUS.

9    Ikei Masaru, "Nihon no tai-En gaikō (shingai kakumeiki)," *Hōgaku kenkyū* 35, no. 5 (May 1962): 56.

10   Hara Takashi, *Hara Takashi Nikki*, Vol. 4 (Tokyo: Kangensha, 1950), 420–421; Ikei, "Japan's Response," 223.

11   *Uchida Yasuya*, 171.

Uchida ultimately failed to keep Manchuria outside of the new Chinese republic, but he was more successful in securing recognition of Japan's interests in that region. His success originated in a British suggestion that foreign troops secure the Beijing–Mukden railway. Uchida quickly replied in a memorandum to the British foreign office in which Japan claimed the right to guard the section of the railway within Manchuria. In a return note, the British Foreign Secretary Edward Grey offered recognition of the Japanese right to station guards, but explained that they were not necessary at that time.[12] Securing British consent for unilateral Japanese protection of the railway line in Manchuria was, nonetheless, a significant achievement for Uchida in that it amounted to a British acknowledgement of Japanese dominance in China's northeast.[13]

An additional goal of Uchida's Manchuria policy was not to upset Japan's important relationship with Britain. This approach can be seen in Uchida's policy choice for solving the Manchuria problem: he supported the only option that would not damage Anglo–Japanese relations nor those with any other Western power. At the time, there were three plans being circulated in Tokyo. Elder Statesman Yamagata Aritomo hoped to dispatch two Japanese army divisions to maintain order and protect Japanese lives and property within Japan's colonial leasehold in Manchuria. Another plan came from the Japanese General Staff that called for allowing military officers to support Manchurian independence movements. Finally, the foreign ministry suggested reaching a diplomatic agreement with Russia to divide Inner Mongolia into spheres of interest.[14]

Yamagata's troop dispatch plan had raised concerns among the powers. The US and Germany, for example, intimated to Japan that all the powers should maintain a policy of refraining from independent action in Chinese internal affairs. As a result, Saionji and Uchida quashed the plan as detrimental to Japan's international relations. Warnings from the powers also influenced Uchida's opposition to plans for Japanese support of revolutionary movements in Manchuria and Mongolia. The British added to the earlier suggestions from the Germans and Americans by cautioning Uchida against breaking off Manchuria from China through these movements. In March 1912,

---

12      Peter Lowe, *Great Britain and Japan 1911–1915* (London: Macmillan, 1969), 66; Yui Masaomi, "Shingai kakumei to Nihon no taiō," *Rekishigaku kenkyū* 344 (Jan. 1969): 4; Ikei, "Japan's Response," 217. For the cables between Uchida and Yamaza, see Tsunoda Jun, *Manshū mondai to kokubō hoshin* (Tokyo: Hara Shobō, 1967), 755.

13      Ikei, "Japan's Response," 217.

14      Yui, 7.

Uchida and Saionji then pushed through the cabinet an official policy that stated Japanese agents must stop any participation in independence movements.[15]

Rather than dispatching troops or supporting independence movements, Uchida and Saionji enacted the third policy option: a diplomatic agreement with Russia over the division of Inner Mongolia. This option was less radical and supplemented previous Russo–Japanese agreements, two things that made it less likely to elicit protests from the powers. Japan and Russia had already split Manchuria into spheres of influence with Russia in the north and Japan in the south in 1907, and had agreed to work together to defend the status quo in Manchuria against outside intervention in 1910. Now, in early 1912, Uchida pushed a Russo–Japanese agreement through the cabinet that extended their spheres of interest into Inner Mongolia. An official ministry statement commented that "The new entente may be described as second only to the Anglo-Japanese Alliance in its bearing on the Far East Situation."[16] Uchida envisioned his agreement with the Russians would complement the alliance as the backbone of his foreign policy.

While Japan and Russia divvied up Inner Mongolia, a new problem in the form of the China Reorganization Loan Consortium, organized by the powers in response to China's request for funds after Yuan established a republic, threatened to impinge upon Japan's predominant position in Manchuria. Representatives from Britain, the US, Germany, and France originally formed the consortium in 1910 to provide a loan to bolster China's currency reserves. Uchida had been wary of the consortium from its inception. As ambassador to Washington in 1910, Uchida fretted that the loans might be used by China to challenge Japanese interests. American Secretary of State Philander Knox assured him that the consortium would not let that happen. Two years later, Uchida's fears were rekindled; however, he found a friend in Russia, which shared Japan's concerns. The two powers succeeded in joining the consortium and demanded that the loans "not be expended in such a manner as to prejudice their respective rights and interests in Mongolia and Manchuria."[17] The US agreed to the stipulation but only recognized those rights guaranteed

---

15 Knox to German ambassador, 3 February 1912, FRUS 1912, 63–64; Ikei, "Nihon no tai-En gaikō," 80; and Robert Valiant, "Japanese Involvement in Mongol Independence Movements, 1912–1919," *The Mongolian Society Bulletin* 11, no. 2 (Fall 1972): 4–15.

16 Statement quoted in A.M. Pooley, *Japan's Foreign Policies* (London: George Allen and Unwin Ltd., 1920), 77.

17 J.O.P. Bland, *Recent Events and Present Politics in China* (London: William Heinemann, 1912), 401.

by treaties or conventions with China.[18] An agreement was later reached that satisfied the demands of the Russians and Japanese: Manchuria and Mongolia were effectively off-limits for China's use of the loan.

Uchida's approach to the Chinese revolution evolved during his time as minister, but the overarching principles of his foreign policy did not. To be sure, Uchida was taken aback by the unilateral British support for the establishment of a republic. However, the pragmatic Uchida quickly adjusted to the new reality and continued to pursue his two main policy goals, the protection of Japanese interests in Manchuria and Anglo-Japanese coopera-tion. The type of government in China was a minor point in comparison to these two goals.

While Uchida did suffer a certain amount of hostility over this approach at the time, Japanese foreign policy did not experience any real setbacks during the Chinese Revolution. Japan maintained the status quo in Manchuria and remained close to the British via the alliance, both preeminent goals of Uchida diplomacy. It was Uchida's failure to push Japanese interests in China proper that ultimately brought scorn from Diet members and the press. Yet, the long-term effectiveness of Uchida diplomacy proved more resilient than its critics in 1911–12 were willing to credit. Uchida would continue the same basic foreign policy later in the decade as foreign minister from 1918 to 1923.

### Uchida's Second Term as Foreign Minister, 1918–23

Japan's relations with the world were in a dismal state when Uchida became foreign minister in the Hara Takashi cabinet in September 1918. The Japanese occupation of Shandong province in China and Foreign Minister Katō Takaaki's "Twenty-One Demands" in 1915 had enraged the Chinese populace. The Western powers, while grateful for Japanese assistance in the Great War, viewed Japanese troops in China and Siberia with a wary eye. The establishment of Lenin's government in the October Revolution nullified the various Russo-Japanese agreements concerning Manchuria and Inner Mongolia concluded over the past decade. In addition, since Japan had not recognized the new Russian government, relations with Moscow were nonexistent. Thus, the Hara cabinet had a laundry list of diplomatic goals: reestablish Japan's friendly and cooperative relations with the powers, mitigate anti-Japanese sentiment in China, and reaffirm Japanese special interests in Manchuria.

---

18    Knox to German ambassador, 12 May 1912, FRUS 1912, 79.

On 8 January 1918, ten months before the World War I armistice agreement was signed by Germany and the Allies, American president Woodrow Wilson delivered a speech to a joint session of the US Congress in which he outlined a plan for an enduring peace. Later to be known as Wilson's fourteen points, the provisions that he laid out were designed to create a new international order based on such ideals as self-determination, armament reductions, open diplomacy, the lowering of trade barriers, and collective security through the creation of an association of nations. Taken collectively, Wilson's ideals represented a "new" diplomacy that was to replace the "old" that had been determined by imperialist calculations of interest, secret treaties and alliances, and colonial oppression, policies which had led the world to the brink of destruction in the Great War. The power of Wilson's vision was so strong that the fourteen points became the basis for the negotiations for Germany's surrender at the Paris Peace Conference.

In November 1918, Uchida drafted a personal memorandum on the fourteen points as a sort of rough plan for Japanese delegates at the conference.[19] As a member of a generation raised on the principles of the old diplomacy, Uchida unsurprisingly offered a lukewarm reaction to the points. For example, while he agreed with the principle of abolishing secret diplomacy, he continued to believe that "there are cases in which it is suitable to keep secret the progress of negotiations." He was similarly cautious with regard to the removal of economic barriers, stating that "it is difficult to say yes or no unless there is discussion of the details of concrete provisions." Armament reduction enjoyed even less enthusiasm from Uchida, who thought that it was "inadvisable to be restrained" by arms limitations. Regarding the League of Nations, Uchida once again offered approval but remained skeptical:

> The League of Nations is one of the most important problems and the Japanese government supports its ultimate objective. However, because there still exists racial prejudice between nations today, it is a concern that the methods used to achieve the League objective might cause disadvantages to the Empire.

Despite his tepid reaction to the new diplomacy, Uchida did not cling to the old to the point of isolation. Uchida was, if anything, a pragmatist. For nearly all of Wilson's fourteen points, Uchida concluded his opinions by stating that

---

19    Text of Uchida's memorandum can be found in *Uchida Yasuya*, 233–235; and Kobayashi Tatsuo, ed., *Suiusō Nikki* (Tokyo: Hara Shobō, 1965), 285–286.

Japan must not go against the tide at the peace conference in arguing its point. Regarding the abolition of secret diplomacy, Uchida felt that Japan should "go along with the prevailing opinion" at the conference. Similarly, Japanese delegates to Paris should follow "the general trend" of the negotiations on armament limitations. Because of the possible "disadvantages" the League of Nations might create for Japan, Uchida thought that Japanese delegates should postpone discussion of the League as long as possible but, if the League were to be established, "Japan cannot remain isolated outside" of it.

Just as he approached the chaotic situation of the Chinese Revolution in 1911–12, Uchida cautiously set out to reposition Japanese diplomacy before the peace conference. While he believed it would be in Japan's best interests to retain some reservations regarding the principles of Wilson's new diplomacy, such as the League, open diplomacy, and arms reductions, he would not do so to the point of jeopardizing Japan's relations with the powers. With the end of World War I, Uchida had to go along with the trends of the times to pursue his past policy of cooperation. This policy would be tested in Paris over the question of Japanese control of Shandong.

Perhaps the most important issue for the Japanese delegates at Paris was that of Japanese control of Shandong province in China, which Japan had seized from Germany and then occupied during the war. Looking to expand its economic penetration of China, Japan was eager to assume control of Germany's dominant political and economic position in the province. One way Japan sought to assure itself of continued control of Shandong was through foreign minister Katō Takaaki's Twenty-One Demands of China in 1915. In the resulting treaty with Japan, signed on 25 May 1915, China consented to recognize any agreement that Japan might make with Germany concerning its rights and interests in Shandong. This had the effect of a complete transfer of the German concession to Japan. Thus, Japan's main order of business at Paris became assuring that the peace treaty included the formal stipulation that Germany transfer its Shandong concessions to Japan.

Less interested in military expansion than the previous cabinet, Hara and his ministers decided in November 1918 that Japan would return Germany's leased territory in Shandong to China once the Kaiser had unconditionally ceded it to Japan in the peace treaty.[20] They based their decision on the Shandong issue (*Santō mondai*), which referred to the leased territory of

---

20      Cabinet decision in *Nihon Gaikō Monjo* (hereafter NGM): T7, Vol. 3 (Tokyo: Foreign Ministry, 1968), 635. English translation in Russell Fifield, "Japanese Policy toward the Shantung Question at the Paris Peace Conference," *The Journal of Modern History* 23, no. 3. (Sept. 1951): 265–266.

Jiaozhou (Kiaochow) and the Shandong Railway, on the Treaty of 1915 with China. In the treaty, Japan had pledged to return Jiaozhou to China and control the railway jointly once Germany had ceded them to Japan. This move would prevent Germany from directly restoring its rights to China.[21] Japan then hoped to resolve the outstanding Shandong matters through direct negotiations with China following the signing of the peace treaty and without the assistance of the Europeans or Americans.

Having already received pledges from Britain and France to support Japanese claims in Shandong, Uchida was surely pleased when he learned of Chinese foreign minister Lu Zhengxiang's intention to visit Japan on his way to Paris to make "preliminary arrangements" regarding the conference.[22] Uchida decided to "express informally our intentions [to return Jiaozhou] so that China may understand our just attitude. Thus the way will be paved to coordinate the policy of China and Japan in the coming peace conference without any misunderstanding between the two countries."[23] When Lu arrived in Tokyo, Uchida explained Japan's intentions and added that Japan would be true to its word and return Jiaozhou as long as the Chinese did not behave excessively. According to Uchida, Lu was in complete agreement.[24] It appeared as if Japan would enjoy smooth sailing in Paris.

The waters turned choppy, however, when Chinese conference delegate Wellington Koo demanded direct restoration to China of all German rights and territory in Shandong. The overturning of Lu's apparent consent to Japan's plan caused outrage in Tokyo. Feeling betrayed, Uchida cabled the delegation in Paris on 21 April 1919 with instructions to refuse to sign the Covenant of the League of Nations if the conference failed to meet Japan's demands for Shandong.[25] Japan's threat to refuse to sign the Covenant, however, pushed US President Wilson, the main proponent – in addition to the Chinese – of direct restoration, into making a compromise with the Japanese delegates in which Japan would return Jiaozhou in full sovereignty to China, retaining only the economic privileges Germany held and the right to establish a settlement in the city of Qingdao. The Hara cabinet consented to this arrangement and Japan became one of the founding members of the League of Nations.

21 Noriko Kawamura, "Wilsonian Idealism and Japanese Claims at the Paris Peace Conference," *The Pacific Historical Review* 66, no. 4 (Nov. 1997): 521.

22 Kawamura, 514.

23 Translation from Fifield, 266. Original in *Suiuso Nikki*, 316.

24 *Suiuso Nikki*, 348–349; Ikei, "Japan's Response," 220.

25 Fifield, 267; and *NGM* T8, Vol. 3 (Tokyo: Foreign Ministry, 1968), 242.

The establishment of the League of Nations at the Paris peace conference presented a problem for the cornerstone of Japanese diplomacy, the Anglo–Japanese Alliance. One of the purposes of the collective security apparatus of the League was to make such defensive alliances unnecessary. With the changed international environment, both in East Asia with the Russian Revolution and in Europe with the end of German power, the alliance came to be regarded by some as a relic of an age that had passed.

For his part, Uchida had been a strong proponent of the alliance and also of greater policy coordination with Britain. He delighted in the news of the conclusion of the alliance in 1902 while he was minister to China, and attempted to link Japanese diplomacy with the British during the Chinese Revolution in 1911–12. His enthusiasm for Japan's strong relations with Britain continued into his second term as foreign minister. The other Hara cabinet members, while supportive of the alliance, did not hold Uchida's enthusiasm. Hara, in particular, felt that Japan must prioritize relations with the United States considering its new position of power in the post-WWI world. He hoped to supplement the alliance with a tripartite agreement between Japan, the US, and Britain for East Asia.[26]

The alliance became a policy issue soon after the conclusion of the peace conference both because of the League and the fact that it would expire in July 1921. In a meeting with British ambassador Charles Eliot in June 1920, Uchida commented that he personally supported renewing the alliance but that he would have to query the cabinet for the government's position. In a second meeting with Eliot a few days later, Uchida happily reported that the Japanese government was in favor of the alliance's renewal. Eliot was a bit taken aback by this because his original purpose in meeting with Uchida was merely to state that Britain felt the alliance needed some modification to conform to League principles; he was not proposing to renew it.[27] Upon hearing this explanation, the fog of alliance euphoria that had apparently surrounded Uchida, and caused his earlier misunderstanding of the British ambassador's intentions, lifted. He was ready to forget the whole matter, for it was in Japan's interest to maintain the status quo.[28]

The issue remained, however, of amending the alliance to satisfy the League of Nations. The two countries opted first to send a joint note to the League in

26   Ian Nish, *Alliance in Decline* (London: Athlone Press, 1972), 289–290.

27   For a recounting of the two meetings see, Eliot to Curzon, 7 June 1920, *FO 410/68*; and *Documents on British Foreign Policy, Series 1, 1919–1939*, Vol. 14 (London: HMPO, 1966), 28–29 (Hereafter DBFP). For the Japanese side, see *NGM* T9, Vol. 3:2 (Tokyo: Foreign Ministry, 1974), 1093–1095.

28   Nish, 300.

early June 1920 informing it that the alliance would only be continued "in a form which is not inconsistent" with the League Covenant.[29] There was not much movement on the alliance until nearly a year later in May 1921, when British foreign minister George Curzon requested that the alliance be extended three months past its July expiration. Uchida and the foreign ministry were jolted by the realization that Britain was working under the assumption that the June 1920 note to the League served as notice of termination of the alliance. Hurrying to set matters straight, Uchida explained to Eliot in Tokyo that the Japanese government was of the opinion that the alliance would be ended only if one side explicitly requested it. According to Uchida, the League note of last year did not constitute such a request and thus he denied the British request to extend the alliance by three months. Uchida pressed his case even further when he refused to accept Britain's view that the note did in fact constitute notification of termination.[30]

Canadian and American objections forced Uchida to reconsider altering the alliance. Eliot had already floated the idea of including the US in the alliance in June 1921. Uchida replied that he would have no objection to consulting the US so that the new terms of the alliance were not displeasing, but he failed to fully endorse the idea.[31] From this exchange Eliot got the impression that Uchida, out of fear of Japanese isolation, would agree to almost any modification of the alliance so long as it remained in effect. Later, in August, Uchida was gratified to learn from Eliot that Britain did not wish to end the alliance without "good reason" or without "replacing it by something as good, or, if possible, better." According to Eliot, Uchida would not refuse to include the US in the alliance but "would greatly prefer some instrument which should recognize that special ties connect them with Great Britain."[32]

By this time, however, talks of convening a Pacific Conference that would include the US had come to supplant most discussions of renewing the alliance. Japan agreed that such a conference should be held in Washington and should include all of the powers with interests in the Pacific. The Four Power Treaty that resulted from the Washington Conference in 1921 served to replace the Anglo-Japanese Alliance. In the treaty, Britain, Japan, the US and France agreed to consult with the other signatories if a disagreement arose between them regarding their possessions in the Pacific. This collective security arrangement was starkly different in nature from the bilateral, defensive alliance

---

29    *NGM* T9, Vol. 3:2, 1100–1101.
30    DBFP, Vol. 14, 298; and Nish, 326–327.
31    DBFP, Vol. 14, 43.
32    Eliot to Curzon, 15 August 1921, FO 410/71.

between Japan and Britain that it replaced. Still, Uchida, while in part responsible as foreign minister for the Four Power Treaty, pined for the old alliance,
preferring to view the new agreement as a sort of new and improved version.
In talking with the press, Uchida commented that, "The Quadruple Agreement
just concluded may be looked upon as an extension of the Anglo-Japanese
Alliance."[33]

Uchida confronted other issues at the Washington Conference beyond collective security, such as armament reduction and the Open Door. When first
informed of the American proposal for a conference that would bring together
the world's powers, Uchida was awash with feelings of fear and suspicion.
Japanese officials, Uchida included, thought that the US would use the conference to take Japan to task for its policies in Siberia and Shandong, both of
which were still being occupied by Japanese troops. To eliminate this possibility, Uchida informed Eliot that Japan would not be willing to discuss the questions of Shandong and Siberia at the conference.[34]

In addition to Siberia and Shandong, Uchida and the Hara cabinet also
hoped to remove Japan's special interests in Manchuria from consideration at
the conference. Uchida's goal was to maintain the status quo in Manchuria,
which, the Japanese government believed, included American recognition of
those interests. It was not until Japanese ambassador to Washington Shidehara
Kijūrō received the assurance from Secretary of State Charles Evan Hughes
that the US would not corner Japan on the issues of Shandong, Siberia, and
Manchuria in Washington that Uchida offered Japanese approval of the conference agenda. Should Hughes renege, however, Japan reserved the right to
bring up potentially embarrassing subjects for the US, such as racial equality
and immigration.[35]

At the conference, fears held by Uchida and the rest of the Japanese govern-
ment that Japanese policies might be put on trial never materialized. Japan
was able to settle all three issues, Shandong, Manchuria, and the Siberia
Intervention outside of the conference and without pressure from the powers.
Hughes remained true to his word by refusing to allow the Chinese delegation
to bring up the question of Shandong in the open session of the conference.
Instead, Hughes offered his good offices for outside direct talks between the
Japanese and Chinese delegates. Although several thorny issues came up in the

---

33    Eliot to Curzon, 23 January 1922, FO 410/72.
34    Eliot to Curzon, 15 August 1921, FO 410/71.
35    Eliot to Curzon, 15 October 1921, FO 410/71; and Asada Sadao, "Japan's 'Special Interests'
      and the Washington Conference, 1921–22," *The American Historical Review* 67, no. 1 (Oct.
      1961): 64.

talks, the two sides reached an agreement in January 1922 in which Japan would restore the Jiaozhou leasehold in return for China's pledge to make the territory an Open Door port. In addition, the Japanese backed down from an earlier demand that the Shandong railway be operated jointly by both countries and instead sold it outright to China.

Japanese motives at the Washington conference regarding Manchuria were not to return their rights to China, as they did with Shandong, but to continue their policy of obtaining international recognition of those rights. Although recognition of Japan's "special rights" in Manchuria had been secured from the US – in the form of the Lansing-Ishii Agreement of 1917 – the Japanese government feared that the new international environment would spur Washington to more aggressively challenge Japan's position. The assurance from Hughes that he would not press Japan on Manchuria gave Uchida and the Hara cabinet reason for hope, but the danger still remained. Japan's luck continued, however, in the form of the sympathetic Elihu Root, an American delegate to the conference. Root drew up a resolution that became the basis for the conference's Nine Power Treaty, in which nine states, Japan, the US, and Britain among them, agreed to respect Chinese independence and territorial integrity as well as the Open Door. Aware of Japan's past insistence on protecting its special rights in Manchuria, Root inserted a clause into his resolution through which the signatories pledged not to "countenance any action inimical to the security" of another power. Since Japan had previously claimed its rights in Manchuria were vital to its national security, Root essentially precluded Manchuria from the scope of the Nine Power Treaty. Uchida thus came to feel that Japan had achieved its goal of protecting its special position in Manchuria at the Washington Conference. In fact, Japan's success at the conference was so significant that Uchida feared Chinese warlord and ruler of Manchuria, Zhang Zoulin, might join forces with his Chinese enemies in the south to confront Japanese dominance in Manchuria.[36]

With their interests in Manchuria recognized, the only other issue Japan feared the United States might shine the spotlight upon at the conference was the continued Japanese military expedition to Siberia. The US had withdrawn all of its troops by April 1920. With the American withdrawal, then, the chance for US–Japan cooperation – the main reason for undertaking the intervention, at least among the moderate civilian elements in the government – had vanished. Many of those officials, including Uchida, now looked for an opportunity to withdraw all of Japan's forces. The massacre of hundreds of Japanese

---

36    *NGM*: T12, Vol. 2 (Tokyo: Foreign Ministry, 1979), 265–266. English translation in Gavan McCormack, *Chang Tso-lin in Northeast China, 1911–1928* (Stanford, CA: Stanford UP), 63.

civilians in the Russian town of Nikolaevsk in May, however, rekindled some of the fire for the intervention in the government. In retaliation, the Japanese extended the intervention by occupying the northern half of Sakhalin Island, the southern portion of which was already a Japanese possession won in the Russo-Japanese War.

A year later the Japanese troops were still in the Russian Far East. According to one outside observer, the issue had become a tug-of-war between the cabinet – especially Hara, Uchida and finance minister Takahashi Korekiyo – and the army and its political allies. Uchida mentioned to British ambassador Eliot that "something must be done quickly about withdrawal."[37] Something, unfortunately, was not done and the intervention continued into the Washington Conference. There, Shidehara announced to the general approval of the powers that Japan promised to withdraw its troops as soon as possible.[38] However, Takahashi's installment as prime minister, following Hara's assassination, set back this timetable because, unlike his predecessor, he was not as adept in political maneuverings and he had no hopes of swaying the army. Fortunately, Takahashi's cabinet was short-lived and Admiral Kato Tomosaburō's administration was able to bring the troops home. By that time, the intervention had become so costly financially, without anything to show for the expense, that it was completely without popular support. Uchida noted the irony in his diary on the occasion of the withdrawal: "Strange that I was the one who completed the withdrawal of forces from Siberia considering I was against the intervention from the beginning."[39] The intervention had cost Japan any hope of good favor with the new Leninist government in Russia and had alarmed the powers of the possibility of Japanese expansion on the continent. Since both were counter to Uchida's long-standing policies of cooperation and non-intervention, feelings of elation must have accompanied those of astonishment when he wrote in his diary that day.

As noted above, Uchida and the Hara cabinet reversed the previous Terauchi cabinet's policy of intervening in Chinese territory. One example of this was the restoration of Jiaozhou to China in 1922. During negotiations with the Chinese, Uchida actually softened his position by abandoning Japan's demand for the right to establish an exclusive settlement in Qingdao and by selling the Shandong Railway to the Chinese instead of keeping it in Japanese hands.

37    Eliot to Curzon, 28 June 1921, FO 410/71; and Eliot to Curzon, 30 July 1922, FO 410/73.

38    *NGM: Washinton kaigi*, Vol. 2 (Tokyo: Foreign Ministry, 1978), 343–355.

39    Unpublished manuscript of Uchida's biography held at the Diplomatic Records Office of the Ministry of Foreign Affairs, Tokyo. Aoki Arata, *Uchida Yasuya Denki Sōkō*, Vol. 7, part 5, DRO [Diplomatic Records Office, Ministry of Foreign Affairs, Tokyo].

Later, in front of the Diet, Uchida explained that these "minor" concessions improved Sino-Japanese relations and eliminated any Western "misapprehensions" about Japanese designs on China.[40]

The Hara administration also repealed Terauchi's meddling in Chinese domestic politics by using the Nishihara Loans to fund Duan Qirui's Anhui clique. In return for concessions and rights in Northern China, the Terauchi cabinet provided loans to Duan to fund his fight against rival factions for control of the Chinese government in Beijing. Uchida announced to the Diet in January 1919 that Japan would refrain from offering financial assistance to China since it might "foment political complications in that country."[41]

The Hara cabinet, however, did agree to provide assistance through an international financial consortium that also included the United States, Britain, and France. This was the second iteration of the loan consortium that Japan had joined in 1912 while Uchida was foreign minister. The British and American governments hoped to undermine claims of spheres of interest in China by opening the entire country to international development through the loans. Uchida was open to the consortium proposal because ending spheres of influence in China proper, he reasoned, would benefit Japanese economic development on the mainland.[42] Just as he had in 1912, however, Uchida linked Japanese participation in the consortium to the group's agreement to exclude Manchuria and Inner Mongolia from the loan's scope.

Japan's first introduction of a proposal for exclusion, in the form of an informal note to Thomas Lamont, the American representative to the consortium, met with little enthusiasm from Washington and London. The Hara cabinet decided to try again in August 1919 with a formal note to Washington that stated Japan's desire that the consortium would not "prejudice...the special rights and interests possessed by Japan in South Manchuria and Eastern Inner Mongolia."[43] At the same time, Uchida instructed Japanese ambassador to

40    "Dai-46 kai Teikoku Gikai, Kizoku-in iinkai giji sokkiroku," 3rd session, 24 January 1923, 49–52, Tokyo, National Diet Library. Also reported in Eliot to Curzon, 1 February 1923, FO 410/74.

41    "Speech Delivered by Viscount Uchida, Minister for Foreign Affairs, Before the Imperial Diet in January 1919," Diplomatic Records Office, Japanese Ministry of Foreign Affairs, Japan Center for Asian Historical Records (JACAR) reference code B03041472100 (<http://www.jacar.go.jp>).

42    Sadao Asada, "Japan and the United States, 1915–1925" (PhD diss., Yale University, 1963), 87.

43    FRUS, 1919, Vol. 1 (Washington, D.C.: Government Printing Office, 1934), 480; Asada, "Japan and the United States, 1915–1925," 92.

London Chinda Sutemi to press Japan's case at Whitehall.[44] This second attempt experienced the same fate as the first; the US did not consent to the formal note and British foreign secretary Curzon would not accept Chinda's explanation.

The impasse between Japan and the US and Britain lasted into the spring of 1920 when Washington offered an implicit assurance that the consortium would not work against Japanese interests in Manchuria. This assurance plus an explicit guarantee from the US and Britain that the South Manchuria Railway zone would not be subject to the consortium convinced Uchida and the Hara cabinet to join the group.[45] Uchida explained the cabinet's decision to participate to the Diet in July 1920, by commenting that the three other consortium powers "not only contemplated no activities inimical to the vital interests of Japan but they were ready to give a general assurance which would be sufficient to safeguard" Japan's Manchurian interests.[46]

In a further effort to protect Japanese interests, the Hara cabinet had made it policy to offer aid to Chinese warlord Zhang Zuolin in Manchuria. Although ostensibly part of the Republic of China, Zhang and his Fengtian clique ruled Manchuria independently. Zhang's strong rule in Manchuria, which kept it relatively free of the political chaos south of the Great Wall, impressed Hara so much that he tried to make Zhang "an instrument of Japanese policy."[47] Hara offered aid and alliances with Zhang in return for the expansion of Japanese interests in Manchuria.

Following Hara's assassination in November 1921, the new cabinet of Takahashi Koreikyo – a Seiyūkai party member and finance minister in Hara's cabinet – continued the policy of aiding Zhang. However, this policy applied only if he and his Fengtian Army remained inside of Manchuria. In April 1922, Zhang marched his army south in an attempt to supplant rival warlord Wu Peifu and his Zhili army as ruler of North China. Zhang's Japanese advisors had already petitioned Tokyo for military aid months before Zhang moved his troops. Uchida replied with a strongly worded rebuke of the request. In the cable, Uchida explained that Japan would be violating the arms embargo for China that it had agreed to, along with the other powers. This was on top of the fact that the Japanese government had an avowed policy of neutral non-intervention in China. When Zhang's defeat looked imminent in May 1922, Uchida sent another cable reiterating his position of Japanese neutral

44    DBFP, Vol. 6, 700–701.
45    Asada, "Japan and the United States, 1915–1925," 106.
46    "Speech by Uchida Before the Imperial Diet in July 1920."
47    Young, 134.

non-intervention. The reason for this was not only to affirm international trust in Japan, but also for Japan's peaceful economic development in China proper.[48] However, following Zhang's defeat in North China, Uchida and Japan would continue to offer aid, but not financial or military due to international agreements, so long as Zhang remained within Manchuria.[49]

During his tenure as foreign minister in the 1920s, Uchida gave up very little in Manchuria. In nearly all matters related to Manchuria, Uchida played a strong hand to assure that Japanese interests would be protected – first in the loan consortium and then at the Washington Conference. While these assurances were perhaps not as explicit as he would have preferred, Uchida believed them to be sufficient and the benefits to Japan's international standing, resulting from its inclusion in the agreements, were great. Uchida's real concessions came most of all in his China policy, where he was much more flexible. He softened his demands on the Chinese for the restoration of Shandong and he led Japan into multilateral agreements, in the form of the loan consortium and Washington Conference, which guaranteed Chinese sovereignty and territorial integrity. Furthermore, he followed these agreements to the letter by refusing to offer Zhang aid in his war in North China. Just as he had while foreign minister in 1911–12, Uchida pursued a softer policy in China while remaining firm in his protection of Japanese interests in Manchuria.

### Conclusion

It must be noted that Japanese foreign policy did undergo a shift at the conclusion of the Great War. Moving along with the trends of the times, Japan reluctantly abandoned its favored bilateral alliances, most notably the Anglo-Japanese Alliance, in favor of the collective security provided by the League of Nations and the multi-lateral agreements of the Washington Conference.[50] This essay, however, has argued that this shift, while not unimportant, was rooted in an earlier policy of cooperation with the powers that had been a guiding principle of Japanese diplomacy since the early Meiji era. Moreover, in the wake of World War I, Japanese leaders such as Uchida returned to policies for China and Manchuria that they had followed earlier in the decade. Tokyo pledged to not intervene in Chinese internal affairs, but also strongly resisted

---

48   *NGM* T11, Vol. 2 (Tokyo: Foreign Ministry, 1976), 212–213 and 342–343; Hattori, 114.

49   NGSB, Vol. 2 (Tokyo: Foreign Ministry, 1966), 31–32; Hattori, 114.

50   For more on this shift from bilateralism to "Pacific multilateralism," especially with regard to Britain and its dominions, see John Meehan's chapter in this volume.

any outside attempts to limit Japanese rights or interests in Manchuria. Taken as a whole, the revival of these established policies then points not to a new era in Japanese diplomacy in the 1920s but to an older one in which the Meiji-era leaders crafted enduring measures to guide the ship of state in international waters.

The continuities in Uchida's experience between his time as foreign minister in 1911–12 to his second term in 1918–23 suggest, then, that the new era in Japanese diplomacy did not come after World War I, but during it. That is, Japanese foreign policy from 1914 to 1918, characterized by foreign minister Kato Takaaki's Twenty-One Demands and the Terauchi cabinet's Siberian Intervention, appears to have been a marked departure from that which preceded and followed it. In terms of Japan's policy for the continent, Katō and Terauchi both used military intervention to acquire potential territorial concessions. This went against Uchida's refusal to intervene in the Chinese civil war in 1912. And, of course, Uchida reversed these policies as foreign minister following the war. Thus, while it could still be argued that the Great War represented a sea change in Japanese foreign affairs, this shift was short lived and quickly corrected by statesmen who returned Japan to its original course.

# The Imperial Japanese Navy and the First World War

*Unprecedented Opportunities and Harsh Realities*

*J. Charles Schencking*

There are many things going on in many places that I do not at all like: it is an inevitable consequence of being engaged in a huge war – everyone outside it will try to take advantage of the situation.[1]

Foreign Secretary EDWARD GREY

Even if we are given more money for warship construction, we will likely be unable to use it this year [owing to a lack of construction materials and available shipyard capacity].[2]

Navy Minister KATŌ TOMOSABURŌ

## The Great War and the Imperial Japanese Navy

In August 1914, the world's attention focused on Europe. Amidst the atmosphere of escalating aggression, Japanese navy officials cast their gazes to the east and saw an extraordinary chance for betterment. Bound to Britain by an alliance and years of camaraderie, navy bureaucrats believed that a once in a lifetime opportunity had materialized to expand Japan's empire into the Pacific. Navy leaders not only saw the occupation of Germany's colonial territory of the Marianas, Caroline, and Marshall Islands as a chance to secure long-sought Pacific island territory, but they also envisaged acquisition as the means to obtain greater rewards. Seemingly all that stood in their way to territorial expansion, acclaim for military exploits, and larger budgets were a collection of cautious Japanese diplomats and a few weakly defended atolls and islands of Germany's remote Pacific empire. For the Japanese navy, an unprecedented opportunity emerged soon after the guns of August thundered to life halfway across the world.

---

1    Foreign Secretary Edward Grey to British Ambassador to Japan, Conyngham Green, 18 August 1914, London, Public Records Office (P.R.O.), Foreign Office Papers [F.O.] 371/2017.

2    Katō to the Lower House Parliamentary Budget Committee during the Fortieth Session of Parliament (22 December 1917 to 26 March 1918). Cited in Saitō Seiji, "Kaigun ni okeru Dai ichiji taisen kenkyū to sono hado," *Rekishigaku kenkyū* 530 (July 1984): 22.

© KONINKLIJKE BRILL NV, LEIDEN, 2014 | DOI 10.1163/9789004274273_006

The rewards of Japan's participation in the First World War proved extraordinary, greater than anything even the most starry-eyed opportunist envisioned.
In less than two weeks the navy expanded Japan's empire by roughly 4000 km
measured west to east, and 2000 km measured north to south. Leaders thereafter parlayed successful military deployments into larger appropriations. During
the war, navy budgets expanded faster than at any previous time in Japan's history and by 1921 they comprised 32% of the nation's budget: no other institution
received more money than the navy. For a service that had long stood in the
shadow of its chief rival, the Japanese army, the war and the overall economic
growth it generated injected prodigious lifeblood into the navy. To admirals
who had devoted their professional lives to naval expansion, Japan's involvement in the great European tragedy was, beyond doubt, "divine aid."[3]

Why then did numerous navy leaders embrace naval limitations and accept
acute budgetary reductions with the advent of the Washington Treaty System
in 1922? The answer lies in large part with the navy's experiences during and
after the war. The navy's Pacific island acquisitions aroused suspicions, and its
subsequent military expansion fostered an unbridled naval arms race with
America. However grateful Japanese admirals might have been on receiving
larger appropriations, the naval armaments race exposed significant weaknesses in Japan's ability to develop and maintain a maritime defense against a
growing US Navy. The First World War demonstrated the limits of Japan's
industrial capabilities as well as its dependence on overseas resources. Though
Japanese shipyards could produce state-of-the-art warships equal to those
built in America, it could not produce enough of them to keep pace. The war
thus provided the Japanese navy with unparalleled opportunities but likewise
forced its leaders to face the harsh realities of Japan's inherently weaker industrial and economic position vis-à-vis America. Rational, objective-minded
navy officers thus concluded that the cause of naval expansion – the bureaucratic raison d'être of the navy from its inception – would have to be subordinated to naval limitations for the defense of Japan.

## 1914: A Tumultuous Political Year for the Imperial Japanese Navy

Navy Minister Saitō Makoto approached 1914 with a feeling of jubilation. In
February of 1913, for the first time in Japan's twenty-four-year parliamentary
history, an active duty admiral – Yamamoto Gonnohyōe – became prime

---

3   Quote by Inoue Kaoru, cited in Frederick Dickinson, *War and National Reinvention: Japan
    and the Great War, 1914–1919* (Cambridge, MA: Harvard University Press, 1999), 35.

minister. His appointment followed the infamous Taishō Political Crisis in which the pro-army Chōshū political faction led by then Prime Minister Katsura Tarō clashed bitterly with the majority party in parliament, the Seiyūkai.[4] Both opponents fought over issues of army appropriations and Katsura's wanton use of Imperial Rescripts to force opposition MPs to support the government's army expansion plan. In this epic struggle the Seiyūkai and the Japanese navy saw an opening to forge a working relationship cum political alliance to challenge their common political adversaries. They also perceived of the alliance as an opportunity for each to gain power and influence where each wanted it the most: the navy within the Seiyūkai-dominated lower house of parliament where budgets were endorsed or rejected, and the Seiyūkai within the upper echelons of the cabinet and bureaucracy where policies were initiated.

While elite level political opportunism brought the navy and Seiyūkai together, a shared pro-industrial expansion policy gave the relationship endurance. Between 1906 and 1913 Japanese shipbuilding underwent a transformation spurred in large part by naval expansion. During these years, Japanese shipyards produced 78 percent of the navy's warships. Only 2 percent of this total, however, was produced in private shipyards: navy arsenals produced the lion's share of warships.[5] After 1910, private shipyards owned by industrial conglomerates that supported the Seiyūkai – the Mitsubishi shipyard at Nagasaki and the Kawasaki shipyard at Kobe – secured an ever-increasing share of navy construction contracts. By the eve of the First World War private shipbuilders supplied 37 percent of the navy's warships while navy arsenals provided 32 percent: the remainders arrived from overseas shipyards.

For Seiyūkai party leaders who looked to expand party support through a positive industrial policy, championing naval spending at private firms was an ideal vehicle by which to stimulate economic growth and political support.[6] It dovetailed well with other Seiyūkai-backed expansion programs including harbor development, rail expansion, and the expansion of other industrial enterprises. Naval orders encouraged the diffusion of technological know-how from navy arsenals to private shipyards and from overseas shipyards to private

4 The Taishō Political Crisis is discussed in J. Charles Schencking, *Making Waves: Politics, Propaganda, and the Emergence of the Imperial Japanese Navy, 1868–1922* (Stanford: Stanford University Press, 2005), 154–164; Roger Hackett, "Yamagata and the Taishō Political Crisis," in Sidney D. Brown, ed., *Studies on Asia* (Lincoln: University of Nebraska Press, 1962), 21–37.

5 Zōsen kyōkai, *Nihon kinsei zōsen shi* (Tokyo: Hara shobō, 1973), 44–59; Schencking, *Making Waves*, 182–187.

6 Hara Kei'ichirō, ed., *Hara Takashi nikki*, 6 vols. (Tokyo: Fukumura shuppan, 1965–1967). Entry for 7 February 1914, 3: 387–388. Hereafter cited as *Hara Takashi nikki*.

Japanese shipbuilders.[7] Expanding capacity and production in private shipyards as a result of increased naval spending was a win-win situation both for
the navy and for the Seiyūkai.

Not surprisingly, as soon as Yamamoto became prime minister with
Seiyūkai support he introduced fresh naval expansion requests, even though
the very issue of army expansion had triggered the previous political mael-
strom. Though the Seiyūkai had criticized army expansion plans on grounds
of financial largesse and resisted their implementation with open political
warfare, they expressed no similar criticisms against increased naval appropriations that were far larger in scale. Pragmatic politics trumped principle.
With party support, Yamamoto and Saitō believed that 1914 would be the year
in which sizeable multi-year naval expansion programs would be initiated.
Not surprisingly Saitō introduced a whopping ¥352 million naval expansion
budget plan to cabinet colleagues in October 1913. Specifically, this seven-
year plan budgeted funds for the construction of seven *Dreadnought*-
class battleships, two first-class cruisers, five second-class cruisers, twenty-
six destroyers, and ten submarines. When completed in 1921, Saitō suggested
that Japan would possess an eight-six fleet, a fleet with eight battleships
and six first-class cruisers that could safeguard Japan against any likely
opponent.[8]

The day Saitō introduced his proposal, 23 January 1914, navy plans unraveled. Newspapers in Tokyo reported the outcome of a German trial against Carl
Richter, a former Siemens employee in Japan. The court convicted Richter of
stealing documents from Siemens headquarters in Tokyo and for attempting
to extort money from company officials.[9] The documents he removed from
the Siemens headquarters documented the widespread practice of giving
commission bribes to Japanese navy officials who were responsible for granting construction contracts for naval shore facilities and warships. Publication
of Richter's verdict, and discussions concerning the stolen documents that
linked commission bribery to navy officers, not only called into question the
scruples of navy officials, but it also cast doubt over the efficacy of granting
fresh appropriations to a service that engaged in illegal activities. The Siemens
Scandal enabled political forces opposed to the navy-Seiyūkai entente to attack
the government with virtual political immunity.

---

7    Kawasaki jūkōgyō, ed., *Kawasaki jūkōgyō kabushiki kaisha shi* (Kobe: Kawasaki jūkōgyō,
     1959), 70.

8    Saitō shishaku kinenkai, ed. *Saitō Makoto den*, 4 vols. (Tokyo: Saitō shishaku kinenkai, 1941),
     2: 244–247.

9    For details on the Siemens Scandal, see Schencking, *Making Waves*, 187–199.

During the first months of 1914 opposition forces became energized by the revelation of naval corruption. Emboldened by numerous public protests, elites threatened by the navy's political emergence over the previous year demanded that it withdraw new construction plans until after a thorough review of naval procurement procedures was concluded. Though the Seiyūkai remained the navy's unwavering ally and passed the naval expansion budget despite nothing other than a promise by the navy to review its practices and "cleanse itself," Japan's upper house of parliament rejected the budget that earmarked new naval expansion funds. It was not customary for members of the House of Peers to engage in such blatant political intervention and to reject a bill endorsed by the lower house, but their actions were not entirely unexpected: the upper house remained a bastion of pro-army Chōshū faction support that had the most to lose from the navy-Seiyūkai entente. Faced with such an unprecedented decision of the upper house rejecting a bill that had passed the lower house, Yamamoto resigned as prime minister and left the issue of naval expansion to future cabinets. The next cabinet led by Prime Minister Ōkuma Shigenobu refused to consider any large-scale naval expansion plan until a thorough investigation of the navy occurred.

The following five months saw budgetary and political solitude for navy elites. Though banished to political exile, naval leaders lobbied the government to implement what they described as urgently required expansion of naval forces. Their calls, however persistent, fell on deaf ears within Ōkuma's cabinet. As one newspaper reported on 1 August 1914, naval expenditures remained the "Gordian knot" for Prime Minister Ōkuma to cut.[10] Little did the *Japan Times* editors who published this statement know that dramatic events soon to unfold in Europe would provide a golden opportunity for the government to increase expenditures for military expansion, and to do so with popular support. Both in 1894 and 1904, war provided Japan's leaders with the means and motives to increase military expenditures with almost unanimous public backing. The First World War was no exception. Rather, it became Japan's most lucrative war in history and one that the navy would use to secure long-held objectives.

### War and the Politics of Participation

Soon after the European war began, Japan's Anglophile Foreign Minister, Katō Takaaki, sought to involve his country in the conflict. Not wishing to raise

---

10    *Japan Times*, 1 August 1914.

suspicions with British officials by sounding too eager to assist, Katō relayed to British Foreign Secretary Sir Edward Grey that Japan would define its attitude toward the European war only after it had an intimation of what Great Britain thought Japan should do.[11] "If called upon to do so," Katō added, his country would assist Great Britain "with all her strength," while "leaving it entirely to His Majesty's Government to formulate the reasons for, and nature of, the assistance required."[12] Katō, in an attempt to reinforce the sincerity if not the finality of his position, also stated that he had likewise conveyed this position to the German Ambassador in Tokyo.[13]

On 6 August, the British government sought Japanese assistance, but its request was tempered by the realities of Britain's precarious position and divergent interests in Asia. On the one hand, the admiralty office strongly desired Japanese naval assistance.[14] On the other hand, British diplomats in China and Hong Kong believed that Japanese participation would diminish Britain's "future political influence in China" and tarnish its "prestige in Asia generally." Moreover, many diplomats believed that opportunistic Japanese action "would involve deplorable complications now and hereafter."[15] Grey's communiqué of 6 August therefore defined the limited assistance he sought. Specifically, Grey asked only for naval assistance to "hunt out and destroy German armed merchant cruisers in East Asian waters."[16] The next morning, Grey informed Japan's ambassador in London, Inoue Katsunosuke, "His Majesty's government would gladly avail themselves of proffered assistance of the Japanese Government in the direction of protecting British trading vessels."[17]

---

11    Greene to Grey, 3 August 1914, contained in G.P. Gooch and Harold Temperley, eds., *British Documents on the Origins of the War, 1898–1914*, 11 volumes (London: His Majesty's Stationery Office, 1926): 11: No. 571. Hereafter cited as *BD*.

12    Greene to Grey, 3 August 1914, *BD*, 11: No. 571.

13    Luigi Albertini, *The Origins of the War of 1914*, translated by Isabella M. Massey, 3 volumes (London: Oxford University Press, 1957), 3: 694.

14    For a more detailed study of Britain's naval position on the eve of war, see Ian H. Nish, "Admiral Jerram and the German Pacific Fleet, 1913–1915," *Mariner's Mirror* 56 (May 1970): 411–420.

15    For Jordan's belief that fighting would not be necessary in China, see Japanese Foreign Ministry, ed., *Nihon gaikō bunsho*, 3: No 114, *Taishō sannen* [1914]. Hereafter cited as *NGB T.3/III*. For Jordan's concern about a loss of prestige and influence in Asia, see Jordan to Grey, 9 August 1914, London, (P.R.O.), F.O. 371/2016. For May's remarks, see May to Harcourt, 10 August 1914, London, Colonial Office, 1910–1915, box no. 3. See also Peter Lowe, *Great Britain and Japan, 1911–1915* (London: Macmillan, 1969), 183.

16    Grey to Greene, 6 August 1914, *BD*, X: Appendix 2, 823.

17    *NGB*, T.3\III, No. 104.

Though Britain's request was more restrictive than he had hoped for, Katō obtained cabinet approval to enter the war. Within thirty-six hours of receiving the British request, the cabinet, the emperor, and the most influential elder statesmen in Japan had been informed of, and endorsed, albeit begrudgingly in some cases, Katō's policy.[18] From that point on, the language of Katō's communiqués with British officials changed markedly. On 9 August, Katō informed Grey that Japan could not "restrict her action only to the destruction of hostile armed merchant cruisers."[19] Furthermore, Katō concluded that such formal involvement in the conflict would necessitate an independent declaration of war against Germany.[20] The tone of this and nearly all subsequent messages resonated with Katō's newfound confidence. That sureness emanated not only from the fact that he had obtained the domestic political support needed for participation, but also because he believed Great Britain's military position in East Asia was such that Grey's government had no choice but to acquiesce to Japan's military and diplomatic freedom of action. Katō's actions in early August 1914 were masterstrokes of diplomatic opportunism.

By entering the war at the request of Britain, Foreign Minister Katō and Prime Minister Ōkuma saw a unique chance to further Japan's interests in China. Prior to 1914, Katō desired to extend Japanese territorial leasehold in China, informing the Foreign Secretary Grey in 1912 that he would wait for the "right psychological moment" to renegotiate these issues with Chinese leaders.[21] Katō believed that seizing Germany's territorial possessions in Shandong during the opening stages of the war might provide the leverage needed to extend Japan's economic and territorial interests in China.[22]

An examination of Japan's diplomatic communiqués drafted in the first weeks of the war, as well as the statements issued by the government, further reveal Katō and Ōkuma's overriding interest in China. After Katō received Great Britain's military request on 6 August, the foreign minister communicated to Ambassador Greene "that an attack upon Tsingtau [sic] would be the quickest way of settling business."[23] Moreover, Japan's 15 August ultimatum to Germany further illustrated that the government's ambitions lay clearly on the

---

18   See Itō Masanori, ed., *Katō Takaaki den*, 2 vols., (Tokyo: Katō haku denki hensan iinkai, 1929), 2:45–50.
19   *NGB*, T.3/III, No. 108., and Itō, ed., *Katō Takaaki den*, 2:86.
20   *NGB*, T.3/III, No. 108.
21   Itō, ed., *Katō Takaaki den*, 2:133. Katō had previously been Foreign Minister in 1900–01, 1905–06, and February 1913. He was also ambassador in London from 1909 to January 1913.
22   See Japanese Foreign Ministry, PVM 12–5, Series 12, 2599–2607.
23   Greene to Grey, 7 August 1914, *BD*, X: Appendix 2, 823.

continent. Article Two, the only article that mentioned any German territory, specifically advised the German government

> To deliver on a date not later than September 15th, 1914, to the Imperial Japanese Authorities, without compensation, the entire leased territory of Kia-chou [sic] with a view to the eventual restoration of the same to China.[24]

Three days later, when meeting with a group of Japanese businessmen, Ōkuma declared the official reason behind Japan's ultimatum:

> Japan's object is to eliminate from the continent of China the root of German influence, which forms a constant menace to peace in the Far East....Japan's wartime operations will not, therefore, extend beyond the limits necessary for the attainment of that object[ive].[25]

Continental aspirations motivated Katō and Ōkuma and neither expressed any similar desire to expand the war into the Pacific. To both individuals, the German-held islands of present-day Micronesia were of little immediate or potential value. Not everyone, however, shared this view.

A long-held desire of navy personnel since the late 1870s, the acquisition of a South Seas empire had never been more than a hollow dream.[26] The aspirations of many southern advance (nanshin) advocates foundered simply because Japan's navy lacked any realistic opportunity to carve out and secure a Pacific empire. No uncharted islands of any significance existed in the 1880s waiting for intrepid explorers or navy personnel to claim for Japan. The occupation of charted islands would have resulted in military conflict with a previously established colonial power such as Spain, Germany, Britain, or America and such a scenario was out of the question for Japan. The First World War changed all of this overnight.

---

24    NGB, T.3/III, No. 154.

25    NGB, T.3/III, No. 206, pt. 1.

26    For a discussion on the navy's dreams of a South Seas empire, see: J. Charles Schencking, "The Imperial Japanese Navy and the Constructed Consciousness of a South Seas Destiny," *Modern Asian Studies* 33:4 (November 1999): 769–796; Schencking, *Making Waves*, 38–44; Mark R. Peattie, *Nan'yō: The Rise and Fall of the Japanese in Micronesia, 1885–1945* (Honolulu: University of Hawai'i Press, 1987), 5–20; Henry P. Frei, *Japan's Southern Advance and Australia* (Honolulu: University of Hawai'i Press, 1991), 31–47; Shimizu Hajime, "*Nanshinron*: Its Turning Point in World War I," *Developing Economies* 25:4 (December 1987): 386–402; Yano Tōru, *Nanshin no keifu* (Tokyo: Chūō shinso, 1993), 9–47.

The chance to seize territory through naval operations in the Pacific arose when Japan agreed to locate and destroy Admiral Maximilian von Spee's East Asiatic Squadron that had fled its homeport at Qingdao upon the outbreak of war. Believing that von Spee had taken his vessels into Germany's Pacific territory, Japan formed two task forces to pursue von Spee.[27] Task force number one, led by Admiral Yamaya Tanin, put to sea on 14 September, but did so with restrictive orders. Following Foreign Minister Katō's suggestions, Yashiro Rokurō and Vice Navy Minister Suzuki Kantarō emphasized discretion in all Pacific operations, informing Yamaya:

> The Foreign Minister feels that occupation of any German territory in the Pacific would lead to an extremely unfavorable diplomatic situation. Therefore, even if by chance you stop and must land military personnel, do not acquire the islands and hoist the Japanese flag. If Marines (*rikusentai*) become necessary, you must recall them expeditiously.[28]

Yashiro and Suzuki's timidity was not well received by all officers of the Japanese navy, many of whom voiced their concerns directly to the navy minister.

By the end of September numerous factors motivated Yashiro to question then challenge the wishes of his close friend, Katō, and to advocate a more aggressive military policy. First, a cacophony of voices within the navy ridiculed the restrictive guidelines relayed by Yashiro. Captain Katō Kanji, commander of the battleship *Ibuki*, was one of the first individuals to suggest a reevaluation of orders. Almost as soon as restrictive orders were released, Katō communicated his disbelief that the navy would not use the wartime opportunity to acquire territory in the *Nan'yō*.[29] This was followed by a more tersely worded telegram dispatched to naval headquarters on 29 September that advocated the immediate occupation of Germany's South Sea Islands.

---

27    Peattie, *Nan'yō*, 41–43; Kaigun rekishi hozonkai, eds., *Nihon kaigun shi*, 10 vols. (Tokyo: Hatsubai dai'ichi hōkishuppan kabushiki kaisha, 1996), 2: 313–315; Gabe Masaakira, "Nihon Mikuroneshia senryō to nanshin," *Keio daigaku hōgaku kenkyū* 55:7 (July 1982): 83.

28    Yashiro's recommendations to Yamaya are quoted in Gō Takashi, *Nan'yō bōeki go-jūnenshi* (Tokyo: Nan'yō bōeki kabushiki kaisha, 1942), 219; Gabe Masaakira, "Nihon Mikuroneshia," 82. The 12 September orders that called for the destruction of the German fleet and ground facilities in the Pacific, but not for the occupation of territory, can be found in Kaigun rekishi hozonkai, eds., *Nihon kaigun shi*, 2: 313; Hatano Masaru, "Tai-Doku kaisen to Nihon Gaikō," *Keiō daigaku hōgaku kenkyū* 61:8 (August 1988): 67.

29    Kaigun rekishi hozonkai, eds., *Nihon kaigun shi*, 2: 314.

Others within the navy shared Katō's opinions. Shortly before dispatch of the Second South Seas Task Force, Admiral Akiyama Saneyuki met with its commander, Matsumura.[30] Matsumura predicted correctly that Akiyama would question the restrictive orders issued by the navy high command. Everyone in the navy high command knew that Akiyama had been a long time proponent of southern advance. What Matsumura did not expect, however, was for Akiyama to suggest that the newly appointed commander did not necessarily have to pay close attention to the government's stated wishes. Akiyama claimed that it would be impossible to locate German vessels in the vast Pacific without occupying potential German bases. Moreover, Akiyama questioned the financial costs of extended deployment without occupation of Germany's island territories. Lamenting the fact that the first task force had accomplished little and wasted much, Akiyama told Matsumura that "if you do a job that expends large sums of money, at least get some profits" [in return].[31] Akiyama intimated that occupation of phosphate-rich Angaur Island – to name only one – could serve many purposes for Japan and the navy.[32] Stirred by Akiyama's passions, Matsumura proceeded to the Navy General Staff headquarters where vice chief of staff, Admiral Inoue Yoshika, condemned Yashiro's restrictive orders. He pointedly asked Matsumura, "Do you think that you will be able to accomplish what the navy minister suggests in time of war?" He concluded: "as long as the islands are enemy territory what should you be afraid of? I do not think it is the rule of war to withdraw."[33]

As Matsumura departed Japan, the commander of the First South Seas Task Force, Yamaya, implemented his own policy. On 30 September, Yamaya violated his restrictive orders, dispatched a landing force to Jaliut Atoll, and thereby seized what was Germany's commercial headquarters in the central Pacific.[34] Yamaya's actions triggered considerable discussions within the navy

---

30    Akiyama was also one of the brightest naval strategists in the Japanese navy at that time. For more information, see David C. Evans and Mark R. Peattie, *Kaigun: Strategy, Tactics, and Technology in the Imperial Japanese Navy*, (Annapolis: Naval Institute Press, 1997), 69–74.

31    Gō, *Nan'yō bōeki*, 219–220.

32    Hirama Yōichi, "*Akiyama Saneyuki: Nan'yō guntō senryō no suishinsha,*" *Taiheiyō shakai zasshi*, 50:14 (April 1991): 190–191.

33    Gō, *Nan'yō bōeki*, 221–222, and Hatano, "*Tai-Doku kaisen,*" 82.

34    A detailed account of Admiral Yamaya's orders and movements, as well as those of the Second South Seas task force under Admiral Matsumura Tatsuo is given in Kaigun gunreibu, eds., *Taishō san-yonnen kaigun senshi* 5:5 (Tokyo: Kaigun gunreibu, n.d.), 625–650.

between 30 September and 3 October 1914.[35] The debate focused on whether the navy should follow the restrictive course recommended by the foreign minister, the cabinet, and the navy minister and risk that the German-held Pacific territories might fall into the hands of Australian forces, or whether the navy should occupy these islands on their own accord. One day before the navy was set to introduce its initial wartime budget request to the cabinet, Yashiro reversed his initial timid recommendations and endorsed the occupation of all German held islands north of the equator.[36] The navy would soon use its successful exploits to legitimate greater naval appropriations when parliament convened in December 1914.

### War and the Politics of Naval Expansion

Well before Navy Minister Yashiro introduced his expansion requests before the cabinet and parliament, however, the navy used the beginning of hostilities in Europe to secure emergency appropriations. On 4 September, Japan's parliament opened a special session to approve a supplementary war budget. Rather than request funds solely to cover deployments and military operations as had been expected, Admiral Yashiro introduced a bold initiative for fleet expansion.[37] Though his request was small and covered only the construction of ten destroyers, it caught the government by surprise. Before sympathetic Seiyūkai MPs, Yashiro claimed that forty-two of Japan's fifty destroyers were over nine years old and thus could not be considered state-of-the-art for potential military operations against German forces. This fact, he suggested, endangered Japan's naval forces and could potentially restrict operations that Japan might find itself called to undertake in support of its ally, Great Britain. Parliamentarians agreed, and on 9 September they endorsed a request for the immediate construction of ten destroyers. This was just the beginning of the navy's wartime requests.

---

35  See Hirama Yōichi, "*Kaigunshiteki ni mita nanshin no ichi dammen: Nihon kaigun o Mikuronesia senryō ni fumikiraseta haikei,*" *Seiji keizai shigaku,* 250 (February 1987): 95.

36  For a detailed discussion of Yashiro's requests to the cabinet and the related military affairs council, see Kaigunshō, kaigun daijin kanbō, eds., *Kaigun gunbi enkaku* (Tokyo: Gannadō shoten, 1970), 185–193. See also Hatano, "*Tai-Doku kaisen,*" 67; Gabe, "*Nihon Mikuroneshia,*" 82; *NGB,* T.3/III, No. 627; Dickinson, *War and National,* 76. For details concerning the occupation of German held islands, see Kaigun gunreibu, eds., *Kaigun senshi,* 5:5, 640–797.

37  Kaigunshō, *Kaigun gunbi enkaku,* 183–185.

When Japan's regularly scheduled session of parliament convened in early December 1914, military expansion budgets took center stage. The Seiyūkai remained the strongest party in the parliament, and endorsed plans for sizeable budgetary increases for the navy to cover both wartime operating costs associated with warship deployments and funds to enlarge the navy. MPs, however, again refused to support requests made by the Japanese army for expansion despite being at war with Germany.[38] The prime minister thus faced a politically motivated budgetary dilemma similar to what had undermined the Yamamoto cabinet ten months earlier. Rather than resign, the prime minister dissolved parliament and called new elections for 25 March.

Prime Minister Ōkuma did everything in his power, both legal and extralegal, to assure that the next parliament would be more amenable to his government's military expansion program. In one of the most corrupt elections since 1892, Ōkuma and his government eviscerated the Seiyūkai at the polls.[39] The Seiyūkai lost seventy-two seats and pro-government parties increased by eighty-three. Though composition of the new parliament made passage of the army's expansion request more likely, the loss of a Seiyūkai majority worried the navy. The navy minister therefore dispatched Vice Navy Minister Suzuki Kantarō to build alliances within parliament.[40] Suzuki's hard work helped guarantee passage of a ¥94 million naval expansion that the Seiyūkai had endorsed previously in December 1914. The plan supported the continuing construction costs of three battleships first ordered in 1911, and appropriated funds for eight new destroyers and two submarines.[41]

When Katō Tomosaburō replaced Yashiro as navy minister in August 1915, he focused on one goal: securing greater appropriations. Born in Hiroshima in 1861, Katō rose through the ranks of the navy quickly. Katō's most important sea assignment involved service under Admiral Tōgō Heihachirō during the Russo-Japanese War. His skills shone brightest, however, as vice navy minister to Saitō Makoto (1906–1909) and commander of the Kure Naval Base (1909–1914). In short, Katō was an extraordinary naval administrator and politician. Though cadaverously thin to the point of looking frail, Katō possessed a will of iron that he used to further the navy's institutional interests. Just months after becoming navy minister, Katō introduced a ¥364 million, eight-year

---

38    Hara Kei'ichirō, ed., *Hara Takashi nikki*, 22 to 25 December 1914, 4: 81–83.

39    Peter Duus, *Party Rivalry and Political Change in Taishō Japan* (Cambridge, MA: Harvard University Press, 1968), 90–91.

40    Suzuki Hajime, ed., *Suzuki Kantarō jiden* (Tokyo: Ōgikukai shuppanbu: 1949), 196–197.

41    Kaigun daijin kanbō, eds., *Kaigun gunbi enkaku*, 194–198, and Zōsen kyōkai, eds., *Nihon kindai zōsenshi: Taishō jidai* (Tokyo: Hara shobō, 1973), 15–16.

expansion program.[42] Specifically, Katō asked for ¥43 million in additional funding for outlays in 1916 and a firm budgetary and political commitment to dispense ¥321 million between 1917 and 1923 to fund continued expansion.[43] On 24 February 1916, parliament endorsed the navy's expansion request.[44]

Katō's 1916 budgetary success was not an isolated event. Parliamentarians endorsed virtually all of Katō's future requests with little debate – there were many and all were expensive. Katō secured multi-year expansion plans in July 1917 that totaled ¥262 million; ¥225 million in 1918; and over ¥700 million in 1919 to fund expansion between 1920 and 1927 which would culminate with the attainment of an 8–8 Fleet.[45] In short, between 1916 and 1921, the navy found itself awash with yen. The navy had secured so much funding that Prime Minister Hara Takashi and Navy Minister Katō agreed that even if Parliament appropriated additional funds for naval expansion, little more could be accomplished in the near future as all shipyards were producing at 100 per cent capacity.[46]

Numerous factors related to the war helped transform the politics of naval appropriations in Japan. First, with a Pacific empire to defend, the navy could more effectively legitimate expansion requests; a luxury that this service never before possessed. Second, the continued growth of the navy translated into an expansion of expensive industrial contracts and jobs growth in shipbuilding and related industries. A military-industrial complex surrounding the construction of warships and support vessels materialized after 1915 as domestic shipyards constructed all Japanese navy vessels and commercial transports. This made appropriating funds for naval expansion far more appealing to parliamentarians who were supported by business interests and those that represented constituents in urban industrial areas as well as naval bases.

The war, moreover, transformed Japan's economy and infused the nation with capital on a level never before experienced. Japan's economy expanded markedly between 1915 and 1919 with money gained from selling and shipping commodities and manufactured goods to markets dominated previously by the European imperial powers. Kyoto University economist Kojima Shōtarō,

---

42   Kaigun daijin kanbō, eds., *Kaigun gunbi enkaku*, 198–209.
43   Zōsen kyōkai, eds., *Nihon kindai zōsenshi*, 16–18.
44   Kaigun daijin kanbō, eds., *Kaigun gunbi enkaku*, 206–207.
45   Ibid., 227–239; Katō Gensui denki hensan iinkai, eds., *Gensui Katō Tomosaburō den* (Tokyo: Miyata Mitsuo, 1928), 79–91; Zōsen kyōkai, eds., *Nihon kindai zōsenshi*, 19–24; 15 January 1918, *Hara Takashi nikki*, 4: 353.
46   15 January 1918, *Hara Takashi nikki*, 4: 353.

wrote in 1922 that the value of exports more than tripled between 1913 and 1918 while the value of imports doubled.[47] Many statistics support Kojima's assertion. Few areas of the economy showed as much expansion as shipping. Japanese shipping companies came to dominate seaborne transportation in the waters of Asia and the Pacific, reaping enormous profits and investing sizeable fiscal outlays into further expansion. Japanese owned ocean-going steamers totaled 831 vessels in 1913 with 1,320,000 tons displacement. By the end of September 1920, Japanese shipping companies had 1320 vessels at their disposal with a total displacement of 2,580,000 tons. The number of shipping companies increased from twenty-three in 1913 with paid up capital of ¥62 million and annual net earnings of ¥16 million, to sixty-five companies in 1918 with paid up capital of ¥270 million and net earnings of ¥218 million.[48] By 1917, Japan had gained control of more than fifty-five per cent of the total carrying trade in the Pacific; America possessed just two per cent.[49] Not surprisingly, an expansion in the number of Japanese shipyards mirrored the dramatic increase in Japan's seaborne trade capacity: shipyards increased from six to fifty-seven between 1913 and 1918.

Japan's increase in wealth was not related to shipping alone. Rather, industrial production and the sale of manufactured goods resulted in a virtual financial bonanza. In 1912, 15,119 factories employed 864,000 workers, but by 1918, roughly 1.4 million people worked in 23,391 factories.[50] Along with shipyards, factories that produced machinery, chemicals, steel, and textiles expanded rapidly during the war. The sale of war materials to the Entente powers, namely ammunition and small arms to Russia, likewise helped transform Japan from a debtor nation to an international creditor for the first time in its history. Japan's balance of trade between 1915 and 1918 totaled just over ¥1.48 billion in surplus, while foreign specie holdings by the Bank of Japan topped ¥1.3 billion. Japan's national budget reflected this economic emergence, rising from ¥583 million in 1915 to ¥1.5 billion in 1921. According to Kojima, Japan's national wealth quadrupled between 1910 and 1920. As Table 4.1 illustrates, the growth in naval budgets exceeded even this figure and increased by 469 per cent between 1915 and 1921.

---

47    Kojima Shōtarō, "The Influence of the Great War upon Japanese National Economy," *Weltwirtschaftliches Archive* 17. Bd. (1921/22): 527–528.

48    Kojima, "The Influence," 530.

49    Abraham Berglund, "The War and Trans-Pacific Shipping," *American Economic Review*, VII (1917): 553–558; Jeffrey Safford, "Experiment in Containment: The United States Steel Embargo and Japan, 1917–1918," *Pacific Historical Review*, 39:4 (November 1970): 440.

50    Kojima, "The Influence," 530–532.

TABLE 4.1    *Japanese army, navy, and national expenditures and military personnel 1910–1922 (expenditures listed in yen).*

| Year | Army expenditures | Navy expenditures | National expenditures | Army personnel | Navy personnel |
|------|------|------|------|------|------|
| 1910 | ¥101,323,000 | ¥83,840,000 | ¥569,154,000 | 225,000 | 54,731 |
| 1911 | 105,000,000 | 100,463,000 | 585,375,000 | 225,000 | 56,887 |
| 1912 | 104,125,000 | 95,486,000 | 593,596,000 | 227,861 | 59,777 |
| 1913 | 95,440,000 | 96,446,000 | 573,634,000 | 227,260 | 55,940 |
| 1914 | 87,700,000 | 83,700,000 | 648,420,000 | 231,411 | 60,914 |
| 1915 | 84,699,978 | 84,974,783 | ¥583,270,000 | 242,230 | 62,881 |
| 1916 | 94,813,114 | 116,625,000 | 590,795,000 | 248,175 | 67,962 |
| 1917 | 123,436,576 | 162,435,084 | 735,024,000 | 251,600 | 69,428 |
| 1918 | 152,081,959 | 215,903,389 | 1,017,036,000 | 255,887 | 73,328 |
| 1919 | 221,268,029 | 316,419,080 | 1,172,328,000 | 260,753 | 77,626 |
| 1920 | 246,557,000 | 403,202,000 | 1,359,978,000 | 275,028 | 83,668 |
| 1921 | 246,979,000 | 483,590,000 | 1,489,856,000 | 284,819 | 88,161 |
| 1922 | 230,909,000 | 373,892,000 | 1,429,690,000 | 292,612 | 78,837 |

Sources: National expenditures and army and navy personnel are found in Statistics Bureau, *Historical Statistics of Japan*, 5 vols. (Tokyo: Japan Statistical Association, 1987): 5:525, 528. Army and navy expenditure figures are taken from Naikaku tōkeikyoku (Cabinet statistics bureau), *Nihon teikoku tōkei nenkan* (Statistical yearbook of the Japanese empire), 59 vols. (Tokyo: Tokyo ripurinto shuppansha, 1962–1967): 43:507 (1924).

One further development – perhaps the most important – likewise played into the navy's hands and created a groundswell of elite-level support for naval expansion: American naval development. Beginning in early 1916, US President Woodrow Wilson embarked on an elite political and public relations campaign to secure the most dramatic expansion of the US navy in its modern history to date. Speaking before an audience in St. Louis, Missouri, on 2 February 1916, Wilson proclaimed that the US Navy must become "incomparably the greatest navy in the world."[51] Beyond Wilson's rhetoric were plans drawn up by Joseph Daniels, Secretary of the Navy, for America to become a naval leviathan. The 1916 Navy Act appropriated funds for fifty-six warships including eight dread-noughts (four battleships and four battle cruisers), four light cruisers, twenty

---

51    Arthur Link, ed., *The Papers of Woodrow Wilson* (Princeton: Princeton University Press, 1966–1994), 36:120; Roger Dingman, *Power in the Pacific: The Origins of Naval Arms Limitations, 1914–1922* (Chicago: University of Chicago Press, 1976), 34–47.

destroyers, thirty submarines, and four auxiliary craft.[52] However large this
building program was, it paled in comparison to the one requested the following year. The Naval Appropriations Act of 1917, signed by President Wilson in
March 1917, earmarked an additional $517 million (equivalent to ¥1.05 billion)
for naval construction that included an additional battle cruiser, three additional battleships, three additional light cruisers, fifteen more destroyers,
thirty-eight additional submarines, and two further auxiliary craft.[53] Beyond
this, the 1917 act also created a $115 million "Naval Emergency Fund" for future
expansion contingencies. The emergency fund was called upon in less than a
year to construct seventy additional destroyers. The building plan was slowed
only by the fact that little available space existed in US shipyards to finish these
destroyers in the time desired by Secretary Daniels.[54] In just over two years,
America laid the foundation to become the world's preeminent naval power.
Importantly, it possessed the industrial, economic, and resource basis with
which to make these plans a reality.

Initially, Japanese navy leaders relished the prospects of using American
naval increases to further legitimate naval expansion. Speaking before an
assemblage of local governors, elected politicians, and bureaucrats in June
1917, the chief of a naval research bureau that examined the European War,
Captain Yamamoto Eisuke – nephew of navy kingpin, Admiral Yamamoto
Gonnohyōe – argued that Japan faced no alternative but to match US naval
expansion.[55] Many MPs endorsed this assertion and criticized the government
for not appropriating enough money for comparable naval expansion. In late
1917 and into 1918, parliamentarian Inukai Tsuyoshi urged the government not
only to spend more on naval defense, but also to further enlarge Japan's military-industrial complex.[56] Newspapers such as the *Jiji shinpō* and the *Nichi
nichi shimbun* reiterated these themes and published numerous articles on
American naval development between 1916 and 1918.[57] These papers often followed such stories with editorials urging Japan's leaders to increase the size of
the navy. By 1917, it was clear to numerous observers that, although Japan and

52  Harold Sprout and Margaret Sprout, *The Rise of American Naval Power, 1776–1918* (Princeton
     University Press, 1942), 317–346; William J. Williams, "Josephus Daniels and the US Navy's
     Shipbuilding Program During World War I," *The Journal of Military History*, 60:1 (January
     1996): 9–11.
53  Williams, "Josephus Daniels," 12–13. The $517 million Naval Appropriations Act was larger
     than Japan's total national budget for 1917 by roughly thirty per cent.
54  Ibid., 16–17.
55  Saitō, "*Kaigun ni okeru,*" 20.
56  Ibid., 22.
57  Ibid., 19–21.

America were on the same side of a larger conflict, both were likewise engaged in a naval arms race across the Pacific.

### The Chimerical Nature of Naval Defense

Amidst this expanding naval armaments race, Katō Tomosaburō reached a somber realization by 1919. Namely, he concluded that Japan could never match, let alone win, a naval race with America, even if Japanese shipyards continued to produce warships at full capacity.[58] Though the production and appropriations disparities that developed between both countries during the later stages of the conflict proved striking in their own right, Katō knew that other basic factors pointed to Japan's inherently weaker position vis-à-vis America. Katō surmised that Japan did not possess enough raw materials to produce adequate numbers of warships for home island defense against an ever-expanding US navy. America's steel embargo of 1917 pointed to this fact clearly.

During the First World War, high-grade steel became the Japanese navy's Achilles' heel. At its most vulnerable point in 1917, more than ninety percent of Japan's total shipbuilding steel came from America. When steel imports slowed or stopped outright, shipbuilders and the navy suffered. Imports of American steel stopped in 1917 because of a politically motivated embargo.[59] The US Exports Administration Board and later the War Trade Board used the steel embargo to pressurize Japan into releasing more shipping capacity to assist with Atlantic wartime shipping and, as a byproduct, to reduce Japan's growing commercial mastery of the Pacific.[60] While the Mitsui Corporation pressed Japan's government to initiate direct negotiations with President Wilson to lift the steel embargo, envoys from the Kawasaki Corporation approached US steel makers on their own and pleaded for the dispatch of steel to Japan.[61] Neither action influenced American policy makers or steel producers and the embargo was lifted only after the US ambassador to Japan secured an agreement by which America would charter 150,000 tons of Japanese shipping for a six-month period in the Atlantic, and Japan agreed to sell forty-five steel cargo

58    Katō gunsui denki kankōkai, eds., *Katō Tomosaburō den*, 81–83, and Kaigun daijin kanbō, eds., *Kaigun gunbi enkaku*, 238–239; 15 January 1918, *Hara Takashi nikki*, 4: 353.

59    Safford, "Experiment in Containment," 434–452.

60    Safford, "Experiment in Containment," 446–449.

61    Kawasaki jūkōgyō, *Kawasaki jūkōgyō kabushiki kaisha shi* (Kobe: Kwasaki jūkōgyo, 1959), 80–82.

carriers to the United States.[62] As a result, 250,000 tons of steel were released for export in March 1918, nine months after Japanese firms had purchased it on the open market.

Newspapers in Japan expressed outrage over America's belligerent economic action. As historian Jeffrey Safford documented, an *Osaka asahi* editorial of 16 August 1917 declared that "the embargo...is a life and death problem to the Japanese." "It is like giving a cold bath," the editors continued, "to the prosperity-intoxicated people of Japan."[63] The embargo did more than just anger journalists and industrial elites. It worried military and political leaders. Many came to understand that unbridled naval expansion was not a means, in and of itself, to guarantee national security. This was perhaps the most obvious but also the most troublesome "lesson" of the First World War for naval officers who had expended considerable effort to secure fleet expansion. MP Inukai Tsuyoshi understood this point well when he declared in Parliament that "National defense," no longer revolved around military "defense provided by the army and the navy," exclusively, but rather also involved a "coordinated approach whereby commerce and production" was incorporated into this equation.[64] In this regard, he concluded that Japan simply could not match the industrial strength of America nor defend against the military power that America could deploy if both countries continued to build their armaments at current levels.

Foreigners who took an interest in Japan reached similar conclusions. Adventurer-cum-popular writer Frederic Coleman F.R.G.S., who had visited the Western Front and Asia during the war, wrote in his 1918 tome, *Japan Moves North: The Inside Story of the Struggle for Siberia*, that while "jingoes" in Japan continually emphasized her industrial and military greatness, the "advanced Japanese is under little hallucination as to the capability of most Japanese industrial concerns to hold their own on equal terms with the big manufacturers of America, England, or Germany."[65] He concluded that if a future war erupted between Japan and America, American forces would find it difficult to mount an invasion of Japan's home islands, but given the change in the face of warfare, they would not need to do so to destroy Japan. "Should Japan be overwhelmed at sea," he wrote, "and her islands surrounded by a hostile cordon of

62    Safford, "Experiment in Containment," 448–449.
63    *Osaka asahi*, 16 August, 1917. Quoted in Safford, "Experiment in Containment," 442.
64    Speech by Inukai on 25 January 1917. Quoted in Saitō, "*Kaigun ni okeru*," 22.
65    Frederic Coleman, *Japan Moves North: The Inside Story of the Struggle for Siberia* (London: Cassell and Company, Ltd., 1918), 3–8.

battleships and cruisers, her ultimate defeat would be certain."[66] This was precisely what worried Navy Minister Katō.

The navy's "Temporary Naval Affairs Research Committee" established in October 1915 and led by Admirals Yamaya Tanin and Takeshita Isamu reached similar conclusions to those articulated by Inukai and Coleman.[67] Victory in war, or so this committee's findings suggested, was as much about economic and industrial output and civilian mobilization as it was about force levels at a front or on the sea. As a nation dependent upon overseas resources, Japan's economy and industrial complex, they argued, was extremely vulnerable to a war of attrition. Their findings were supported by naval officers who travelled to Europe during the war such as Akiyama Saneyuki, who concluded that industrial strength and a large independent resource base were as fundamental to victory as modern warships in great numbers.[68] In this regard, they concluded that Japan was anything but an economic and industrial superpower that could match American production.

The war, however profitable for Japan and the navy, thus exposed a significant weakness in Japan's industrial capacity and its reliance or near outright dependence upon imports of natural resources and steel. As early as February 1919, Katō admitted as much to Diet representatives who questioned him about, or more precisely criticized him over, the navy's inability to keep pace with American naval increases.[69] Katō informed colleagues that owing to Japan's lack of resources, limited shipbuilding capacity, and the vast richness of America in both regards, Japan simply could neither defend against nor match American naval increases in a competitive way. Moreover, Katō suggested that if Japan continued a naval arms race and America followed suit, naval expansion by the United States could "create such a disparity" in power that the Pacific could be "reduced to an American lake."[70]

Hyperbole aside, Japan's wartime experience convinced Katō that only one viable option existed to safeguard the security of Japan and its new Pacific empire: a combination of international naval limitations and strict agreements

66    Ibid., 8.

67    Saitō, "*Kaigun ni okeru,*" 17–19.

68    Dingman, *Power in the Pacific*, 125.

69    Spoken before the Lower House Budget Subcommittee. Quoted in Saitō, "*Kaigun ni okeru,*" 22; Yamanashi Katsunoshin sensei kinen shuppan iinkai, ed., *Yamanashi Katsunoshin sensei ihōroku* (Tokyo: Yamanashi katsunoshin senei kinen shuppan iinkai, 1968), 66–67.

70    Asada Sadao, "Japanese Admirals and the Politics of Naval Limitation: Katō Tomosaburō vs. Katō Kanji," in Gerald Jordon, ed., *Naval Warfare in the Twentieth Century: 1900–1945*, (London: Croom Helm, 1977), 146.

proscribing US fortification of advance Pacific island bases on Guam or in the
Philippines. If Katō had begun to realize the drawbacks of stiff naval competition with America and the possible benefits of naval limitation, a report issued
by the Navy Ministry's League of Nations Affairs Research Committee in July
1921 might well have solidified his opinions.[71] This committee's findings suggested that limitations coupled with proscriptions on US fortifications could
actually improve Japan's naval position against the United States. On the other
hand, an unlimited naval race would, by 1925, reduce Japan's overall ratio of
capital ships with America to a level far below the seventy percent that many
in the navy believed was critical for Japan's defense.

The notion that Japan needed a fleet size that equated to at least seventy
percent of the total size of its primary hypothetical enemy's fleet had become
dogma with Japanese navy circles in the years immediately following the
Russo-Japanese War. It was a calculation based on a number of untested
hypotheses, but it became orthodox thinking nevertheless.[72] After research
conducted at the Naval Staff College by naval officers Satō Tetsutarō and
Akiyama Saneyuki, both concluded that an attacking fleet would require a fifty
percent superiority (i.e. 1.5 to 1) in firepower to overcome a fleet defending its
home waters; this equated to a 0.67 percent ratio for the defending fleet to successfully repel an aggressor. Satō and Akiyama rounded this figure up to seventy percent and concluded this was the base minimum that Japan's navy
must possess to safely defend itself from attack by America's navy. The absence
of any serious evidence to support such claims was rarely if ever challenged
and the seventy percent ratio became a convenient figure used to legitimate
ever-increasing budget requests by this service.

The question of how Japan could best reach and maintain a seventy
percent level vis-à-vis the emerging naval behemoth, America, proved far
more contentious to resolve. Katō Tomosaburō concluded that pragmatism,
defined by naval limitations, was the surest and most stable way to guarantee
Japan's long-term military, economic, and political security. Not everyone in
the Japanese navy shared Katō's opinions concerning naval limitation.[73]
Foremost among Katō's critics was Katō Kanji (no relation), who in 1921 was a
vice admiral within the navy general staff. Katō Kanji agreed with Katō
Tomosaburō that the First World War demonstrated America's industrial
primacy, particularly when compared to Japan. In Katō Kanji's mind, however,

---

71    Dingman, *Power in the Pacific*, 187–189.
72    Evans and Peattie, 141–144.
73    The most comprehensive discussion of the internal debates over the limitations issue is
      found in Asada, "Japanese Admirals," 141–166.

it made it necessary for Japan to maintain a powerful peacetime fleet that could serve as an unambiguous deterrent. To develop an effective deterrent, he suggested that Japan must continually enlarge its fleet to the maximum level that its economy and industrial base could support.[74] Katō Kanji further articulated that it would be impossible for Japan to enlarge its fleet as quickly as America could expand its navy during a future conflict and that this simple fact required Japan to build and maintain well over a seventy percent naval ratio in peacetime. In Katō Kanji's opinion, accepting any limitations, even at the figure of seventy percent of the American fleet, endangered Japan's future security.

Politics went a long way to determine the resolution of the limitation issue that split the two Katōs. After receiving an invitation by the US government to discuss naval limitations in Washington, Prime Minister Hara appointed Katō Tomosaburō as Japan's chief delegate, the only chief delegate amongst the powers assembled who was an active-duty naval officer. In Hara's mind, Katō, the navy's most successful administrator and champion of fleet expansion, was the only individual who could successfully negotiate naval limitations acceptable to the Japanese navy. Throughout the duration of the Washington Conference, Katō faced strong criticisms and challenges from Katō Kanji who was appointed by the navy general staff to serve as the chief naval specialist to the Japanese delegation. Though Katō Kanji initially argued that any limitations agreement that did not result in parity with the Americans would be a political insult and a military disaster for Japan, he eventually accepted the fact that parity would not be politically or militarily acceptable to the American or British delegates. He thus channeled his energies into convincing Katō Tomosaburō that Japan must accept nothing less than a seventy percent ratio of capital ships with the American and British navies.

Others shared Katō Kanji and Satō's fixation on the seventy percent ratio. The Naval Affairs Research Committee for the League of Nations concurred with Satō's earlier findings and recommended against accepting any ratio that was less than seventy per cent of the American force level. They concluded that, "there can be no room whatsoever for compromise on this issue."[75] The committee also warned that Japan's position in the Western Pacific could be threatened severely by continued US naval expansion and fortifications of advance naval facilities. While Katō Tomosaburō refused to commit to any firm ratio, the committee's recommendation vis-à-vis US fortification resonated

74    Asada Sadao, "The Revolt Against the Washington Treaty: The Imperial Japanese Navy and Naval Limitation, 1921–1927," *Naval War College Review*, (Summer 1993): 86.

75    Asada, "Japanese Admirals," 149.

with Katō's own beliefs and the navy minister decided to hold out for US acceptance of a non-fortification clause in any agreement.

Though angered by Katō Tomosaburō's willingness to accept a sixty percent ratio if a non-fortification clause governing US bases in the Western Pacific accompanied it, Katō Kanji had little room to maneuver in Washington. The resolute Katō Tomosaburō had been given considerable flexibility by Hara to reach any agreement that he deemed reasonable, and he followed pragmatism in Washington as he had done previously in budgetary negotiations in Tokyo. Katō Tomosaburō simply refused to accept the junior Katō's recommendations and followed the course that he saw as a military necessity. Reflecting later that he had been guided by intuition and had acted within the mindset that avoidance of hostilities with the US through diplomatic means was the surest if not the only means to provide for Japan's security, Katō Tomosaburō signed the treaty that aborted the 8–8 Fleet, a fleet that Katō had labored to secure through years of astute and pragmatic political maneuvering.[76]

## Conclusion

At the end of the First World War few institutions reflected Japan's newfound power, confidence, status, and wealth better than the Imperial Japanese Navy. Since its inception in the early 1870s navy leaders had sought greater political power and influence to secure ever-increasing budgetary outlays with which to fund fleet expansion. Establishing a Pacific empire had likewise been a dream of navy officials since the mid Meiji period onward. Political realities and military limitations, however, repeatedly tempered such ambitions.

The First World War changed everything for the navy. While this service had grown considerably stronger from the 1870s to 1914 and emerged as the preeminent military power in the western Pacific, the large financial outlays necessary for it to become a global power remained elusive. In the opening weeks of the war, navy leaders comprehended the unprecedented opportunity that had presented itself. They seized German Pacific territories despite the stated wishes of their longtime ally, Great Britain, and quickly thereafter lobbied for greater wartime appropriations to defend this new empire. When the British government requested further naval assistance in 1917 – asking Japan to send warships to the Mediterranean Sea – the Japanese government and navy agreed, but only on the condition that their claims to island territories

---

76      Asada, "The Revolt," 87.

occupied in 1914 would be supported by Britain after the war.[77] Left with few alternatives, Britain accepted Japan's conditions.

The diplomatic and military confidence that Japan exhibited in 1917 emanated from the fact that both the nation and the navy had grown rich and powerful beyond what even the most starry-eyed opportunists believed possible when war erupted in 1914. Japan became an important economic, military, and political ally in the Entente war effort, and used their newfound position to secure maximum domestic benefit. The war led to an extraordinary influx of wealth into Japan, and in the climate of ever-increasing revenue, politicians readily appropriated funds for military deployments and expansion on a level never before witnessed in Japan. In short, the war was a transformative event for the nation's military, industry, and economy.

The transformations were not all beneficial, however. Ironically, no institution likewise illustrated Japan's modern industrial and military vulnerabilities made apparent by the First World War better than the navy. To construct, deploy, and maintain a world-class battle fleet Japan needed high-grade steel and ever increasing amounts of oil. Japan lacked both. It thus found itself dependent on the importation of these vital commodities in larger quantities than ever before. The precariousness of Japan's resource situation was compounded by the fact that the nation that supplied the lion's share of high grade steel and oil – as well as a plethora of other vital commodities – to Japan, America, was the country that found itself most threatened by the navy's meteoric rise between 1914 and 1918. Spurred in part by Japan's naval growth, and partly as a result of the overall conflict in Europe, America undertook a naval building program far larger than anything Japan could ever hope to match in a similar time frame.

The First World War also amplified trends in the nature of warfare itself that had first become apparent to Japan during the Russo-Japanese War of 1904–05. It became clear to all objective observers of the First World War that modern conflict was no longer an exclusive contest between armies and navies but rather a battle of economies, mobilization, and industrial production. This proved problematic for Japan. Navy leaders such as Katō Tomosaburō realized that a long war of attrition against America would likely end in ruin. Moreover, he and other rational minded leaders understood that unlimited naval expansion was by no means a guarantor of national security. Though he had spent the better part of his distinguished political and administrative career advocating expansion if not unbridled growth of the navy, Japan's wartime experience

---

77    Ian Nish, *Alliance in Decline: A Study in Anglo-Japanese Relations 1908–1923* (London: The Athlone Press, 1972), 202–211.

convinced him that naval expansion would never provide the security that Japan's leaders desired if it resulted in an arms race with America. Katō understood that this was a competition that Japan could never win, given the industrial and economic disparities that existed between both nations. This was perhaps the most important lesson that future navy leaders in the late 1930s could have drawn from this conflict but chose not to. When faced with an even greater naval race after the US Congress passed the Two Ocean Navy Act of 1940 – a program devised to increase the US navy by seventy per cent – Japanese navy leaders chose a different course of action than the one advanced by Katō following the First World War. Predictably, given America's industrial capacity and Japan's continued dependence on overseas resources, the course navy leaders followed after 1940 ended in disaster for this service and the empire it endeavored to protect.

# Securing the Maritime Trade

*Triangular Frictions between the Merchant Marines of the US, UK and Japan*

*Masato Kimura*

### Introduction

From the viewpoint of the history of global sea powers, the 1910s was one of the most fascinating decades because three countries, the UK, US and Japan, competed to strengthen their maritime powers, while at the same time cooperating with each other to promote global trade and commerce, in particular in Pacific Asia. This chapter will clarify the triangular maritime relationships in the 1910s focusing on the merchant marines. I will address in particular the impact of the opening of the Panama Canal on the three countries under review.[1]

Revolutionary advances in transport have had a tremendous impact on world traffic routes and international relations, as well as the conduct of wars. The opening of the Panama Canal in 1914 was a long-cherished dream of the United States because it made the US a true oceanic power by virtue of the links between the Atlantic and the Pacific Oceans. It also initiated new changes and opportunities for expanding commerce, trade and merchant marine activity of both Britain, the strongest sea power since the 17th century, and Japan as a developing sea power subsequent to the Russo-Japanese War in 1904–1905. The Panama Canal, which markedly raised the military and economic priority attached to the Pacific Ocean, both complicated and gave a new dimension to the evolving triangular relationships between the US, UK and Japan. Therefore, one cannot analyze the three-way interaction of these countries in the 1910s without touching upon the effects the opening of the Canal had on them. While this chapter seeks to clarify the impacts of the opening of the Canal on these triangular relationships mainly from the viewpoint of merchant marines, it also has seeks a wider objective: the ways in which World War I influenced the structural change in global society in the 1910s.

---

1 This chapter represents a major revision of my article in Japanese, "The Opening of the Panama Canal and US-Japan Relations," (*Zaikai Network and Japan-United States Diplomatic History*, Tokyo: Yamakawa Shuppansha, 1997), 38–59. In particular, the revision includes detailed presentation of the triangular relationships between the UK, US and Japan.

© KONINKLIJKE BRILL NV, LEIDEN, 2014 | DOI 10.1163/9789004274273_007

There are several possible reasons as to why the proposed research, in focus and methodology, has been largely absent before now from the literature. Firstly, the Panama Canal is located in Central America, far away from Britain and Japan, and these two countries were not directly involved with its construction. Secondly, the opening of the Panama Canal coincided with the outbreak of the First World War. On 28 July 1914, just before the opening of the Panama Canal, the First World War started on the Balkan Peninsula. This conflict, the scale of which would far exceed initial expectations, brought about changes to the political, military and economic structure of the world. This makes it genuinely difficult to bring out and keep separate the impact of the opening of the Panama Canal.

### General Circumstances of Merchant Marines in the Pacific-Asia Region before the Opening of the Panama Canal

1      *Britain*

The so-called British World was created from the 18th century based on global networks associated with overseas migration, markets, consumer cultures, multiple new information channels, and investment, as well as the discriminatory subjugation of indigenous peoples.[2] One can say that Britain governed the seven seas confident that the sun would always rise on its territory and secure in its belief that the navy and merchant navy could maintain its worldwide empire. Not insignificantly, Britain's Navy had been the strongest in the world since 17th century, reinforced by a highly organized and effective merchant navy. Between 1890 and 1914, Britain's merchant navy carried up to 60 percent of the world's trade, and built two-thirds of its ships. The strength of Britain's merchant navy were twofold: maritime steam technology; and coal resources.[3] Steam technology gave Britain powerful economic and naval advantages. Steam ships carried 5,414,000 tons, approximately twice the combined total of 2,293,000 tons for all other leading maritime nations.[4] Coal resources greatly contributed to Britain's power, underpinning the network of Britain's trade. Thanks to the dominant role of the merchant navy, Britain's exports such as textiles, steel and machinery such as railroad equipment, along

---

2  As for the British world, see Gary B. Magee and Andrew S. Thompson, *Empire and Globalization: Networks of People, Goods and Capital in the British World, c. 1850–1914* (Cambridge: Cambridge University Press, 2010).
3  See Nigel Dalziel, *Historical Atlas of the British Empire* (London: Penguin Books, 2006), 86.
4  Ibid.

with immigration, rapidly increased in the early 20th century. Before World War I, Britain's economy was at its peak.

## 2  Japan

Major Japanese political and business leaders such as Okubo Toshimichi, Okuma Shigenobu, Iwasaki Yataro and Shibusawa Eiichi well understood the fundamental impact of a modern merchant marine on modernization and industrialization of Japan, and each played a role in developing the country's merchant marines from the late 19th century. In particular, after the Sino-Japanese War in 1894–1895, Japanese shipping companies such as Nippon Yusen Kaisha (NYK) and Osaka Shosen Kaisha (OSK) rapidly developed trading links with China, India, Europe and the United States. The Meiji government strongly supported their efforts by subsidizing huge amounts of money based on two laws: (1) the Navigation Subsidy Law of 1896; and (2) the Shipbuilding Subsidy Law of 1896. After the Russo-Japanese war, the Japanese merchant marine surpassed America's and severely competed with the British in the Pacific despite the fact that Japan suffered under the burden of a huge debt and trade deficit.

## 3  United States

The US maritime transport industry was in a deep slump at the beginning of the 20th century. Until the second half of the 19th century, the United States had been a great seafaring nation, focusing mainly on sailing ships, reaping huge profits from trade with China. However, at the time of the Civil War the absence of a well-developed rail transport capacity in the US led to heavy reliance on maritime transport, which triggered the development of coastal trade; most vessels formerly engaged in international trade were diverted to such activities. This meant that although the US was third behind Great Britain and Germany in terms of total tonnage volumes, the US was well behind when it came to the international shipping route proportion held by its merchant marine, and the loading ratio of American goods carried by American ships fell to less than 10 percent.[5]

Not surprisingly, the question of rebuilding the maritime industry was debated within the United States not just by the maritime transport industry but by the Federal Government as well. However, such debates did not lead to an actual increase in the number of international vessels. The reasons for this includes the fact that: (1) development of domestic markets was given priority,

---

5  As for the condition of the American merchant marine, see Lloyd W. Maxwell, *Discriminating Duties and the American Merchant Marine* (New York: Wilson, 1926).

with most financiers and capitalists focused on domestic investments, and railways in particular; and (2) there were conflicting opinions within the United States regarding policies for assisting maritime transport.

### The Significance of the Opening of the Panama Canal on Triangular Relationships between Britain, US and Japan

#### 1    *Background*

The Panama Isthmus connects the North and South American continents with a width of only a few dozen kilometers. Opening a canal through this isthmus, an American dream for many years, would allow that country to extend its influence in North America, and further solidify its position as one of the world's leading industrial nations in the latter half of the 19th century. At the same time, the opening of the Panama Canal was expected to have a large impact on Britain and Japan as well; in Britain, the country had entered a period of decline following its involvement in and the consequences of WWI; conversely, in Japan, its fortunes were rising as it occupied a central place in discussions about international politics after the Russo-Japanese War. As John C. Perry pointed out in his book, *Facing West: Americans and the Opening of the Pacific,* "With the formal opening of Panama in 1914, the great age of Suez – and of Britain in world affairs – was over, although most people at the time did not recognize it."[6] As a general observation, the opening of the Panama Canal significantly increased the military and economic value of the Pacific Ocean. As a result, the relations between nations on either side of the Pacific – Japan and the United States in particular – came to have a much greater competitive impact on Britain and the international community. Accordingly, any discussion of the relations between Japan, the United States and the United Kingdom in the second decade of the 20th century requires analysis of the impact of the opening of the Panama Canal on various issues common to Britain, Japan and the United States.

However, little research has been conducted on Japan–US–UK relations in the second decade of the 20th century relative to the Panama Canal's effects in the context of the rapidly changing maritime world. Broadly speaking, Japan-US relations become ever more complex following the Russo-Japanese War and one example of this emerging complexity is the new connection forged by private sector economic diplomacy between the business communities of the two

---

6    See John C. Perry, *Facing West: Americans and the Opening of the Pacific* (Westport: Praeger, 1994), p. 179.

nations.[7] Such analysis confirms that leaders of various sectors in both Japan and the United States believed that the opening of the Panama Canal would have a huge impact on the relations between Japan, the US and China.

A typical expression of this sentiment can be found in the words of Theodore Roosevelt. Looking back at his time as President, he noted, "The feats of the Republic that have made the greatest impressions abroad are the sending of the White Fleet around the world and the construction of the Panama Canal."[8] The people within the United States who held the same impression as Roosevelt were the residents of the Pacific Coast. At the same time, these developments elicited an even greater response in Japan than the Americans had probably expected. Studying these kinds of impressions and responses to the opening of the Panama Canal in the various sectors of society in both Japan and the United States can provide new insights into US-Japan relations in the second decade of the 20th century. And while it is true that Britain did not pay as much attention to the impacts of the opening of the canal, there is considerable documentation of its concern about the costs associated with passage through the Panama Canal.

The sections to follow will consider how the Panama Canal, which was expected to be completed in 1914, would affect Japan-US relations, based on documents from both countries. For example, I would like to point out that the establishment of the Californian Alien Land Law was a turning point that resulted in most Japanese leaders tending to adopt a more hard-line attitude towards the United States.[9] It was very closely related to the opening of the Panama Canal in 1914. I will also clarify the kind of impact the opening of the Panama Canal actually had on various aspects of Japan-US relations. I will conclude with my own view as to the importance of the Panama Canal in Japan–US –UK relations.

2      *The Significance of the Panama Canal for the United States*
What was the significance of the opening of the Panama Canal for the United States? Firstly, from a domestic American perspective, the opening of the Panama Canal would allow the United States to become truly 'a country with

---

7   See Masato Kimura, *Nichibei minkan keizai gaiko 1905–1911* (Tokyo: Keio Tsushin [University of Keio Press], 1991).

8   Theodore Roosevelt, *The New Nationalism* (New York, 1910), 110.

9   As for the conflict on Japanese immigration, see Rodman W. Paul, *The Abrogation of the Gentlemen's Agreement*, (Cambridge: The Society [Harvard Universtiy], 1936); Tosh Minohara, *Kariforunia no hainichiundo to nichibei kankei* (Tokyo: Iwanami shoten, 2002); and *Hainichi iminho to nichibei kankei*, (Tokyo: Yuhikaku, 2006).

two oceans', linking the Atlantic to the east and the Pacific to the west. In other words, the economic development of the West Coast could be advanced and defense could be strengthened. The development of the American West proceeded rapidly in the second half of the 19th century, as symbolized by Frederick Turner's phrase "the disappearance of the frontier," but in the early part of the second decade of the 20th century, the Pacific Coast of the United States was still an undeveloped region, and the East and West Coasts were linked only by the transcontinental railroad. Accordingly, the residents of the Pacific Coast were attempting to gain the attention of the Federal Government and East Coast entrepreneurs in order to further develop the region.[10]

In terms of security, the Pacific Coast was geographically cut off from the East Coast by the Rocky Mountains and – before the completion of the Panama Canal – could not be easily defended from a sea-based attack.[11] In terms of economic potential, the residents of the Pacific Coast attempted to draw the attention of the Federal Government to the development of abundant natural resources, such as petroleum and timber. For the Federal Government, opening the Panama Canal was the most effective means of promoting the security and economic development of the Pacific Coast region, in order to engage with what was happening there, as is plainly indicated by the Federal Government's response to the question of Japanese immigrants. As Alfred Thayer Mahan points out, it was believed that,

> It is clear that by opening the Panama Canal it will become possible to colonize the Pacific Coast even more rapidly, and that that is a good thing. Instead of the expensive and tedious journey across the continent by rail, ships loaded with migrants will be able to take the relatively calm sea route directly to the ports of the Pacific Coast, making an immeasurable contribution to overcoming the problems of population distribution and labor shortages.[12]

10    As for US policy toward the Panama Canal, see John Barrett, *Panama Canal, What it is, What it means (1913)* (Washington D.C.: Pan American Union, 1914); Paul B. Ryan, *The Panama Canal Controversy, U.S. Diplomacy and Defence Interests* (Stanford: Hoover Institution Press, 1977); and Walter Lafeber, *The Panama Canal, the Crisis in Historical Perspective* (New York: Oxford University Press, 1978).

11    This is pointed out in the several books on "Treatise on the Future War between Japan and the United States," such as Homer Lea, *The Valor of Ignorance* (New York: Harper & Brothers, 1909).

12    Alfred Mahan, *The Panama Canal and Sea Power in the Pacific,* (Century Magazine, June 1911).

The second aspect of the significance of the opening of the Panama Canal for the United States is its impact on US policies towards Central and South America. Economically, the opening of the Panama Canal halved the shipping distance to the Pacific Coast of South America, placing South America fully within the economic orbit of the United States. However, at the same time this development opened up South America to other advanced nations such as Britain, Germany and Japan, so that militarily Central America became critically important to the United States.

Let us start by considering the economic aspect. In terms of trade, the opening of the Panama Canal: (1) made transportation more convenient between the Pacific seaboard of the United States and the Atlantic Coast of South America; and (2) shortened transportation between the Pacific Coast of South America and the Atlantic Coast of the United States, the core part of the American heartland (see Figure 5.1). It was believed that this would result in favorable conditions for developing and importing goods from South America – coffee, tobacco and sugar from Brazil and underground resources such as saltpeter (potassium nitrate) from the Pacific Coast of South America. From a military perspective, the Central American region became extremely important in terms of defending the mainland of the United States.

In 1901, the US Government negotiated with Great Britain the annulment of the Clayton-Bulwer Treaty of 1850, which had stipulated the neutrality of any canal through the isthmus, replacing this treaty with the Hay-Pauncefote Treaty. This treaty, signed by the United States and the United Kingdom on 18 November 1901, presaged the creation of the Panama Canal and forced Great Britain to recognize the United States' right to construct, control and defend a canal. The US then purchased the rights to the canal from the French company that had failed to excavate a canal through the Panama Isthmus, and in 1903 concluded a treaty with the Columbian government regarding the management of the canal zone. However, the Columbian parliament did not ratify the treaty.

When the people of Panama rose up to express their dissatisfaction with the failure to ratify the treaty, the United States sent a battleship to force Columbia to recognize the independence of Panama. The United States then concluded a treaty with Panama whereby the United States gained perpetual jurisdiction over the canal zone in exchange for a one-time payment of $10 million and an annuity of $250,000. The canal then took ten years to build, completed in 1914. This sequence of diplomatic strategies on the part of the United States clearly illustrates Roosevelt's "big stick diplomacy."

Incidentally, it can also be observed that the opening of the Panama Canal added a degree of subtlety to the Monroe Doctrine that formed the basis of

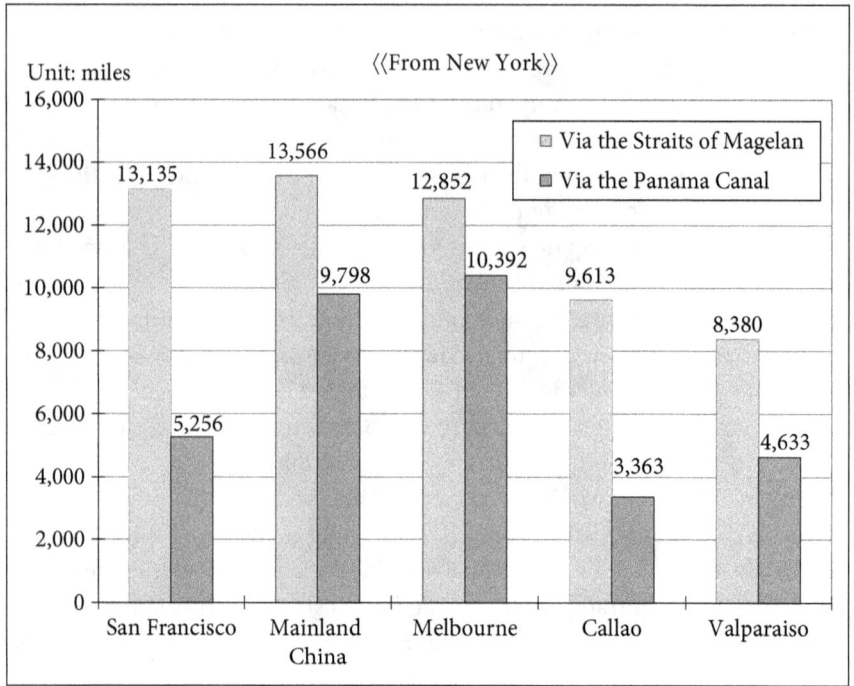

**《From New York》**

Unit: miles

Via the Straits of Magelan
Via the Panama Canal

| | San Francisco | Mainland China | Melbourne | Callao | Valparaiso |
|---|---|---|---|---|---|
| Via the Straits of Magelan | 13,135 | 13,566 | 12,852 | 9,613 | 8,380 |
| Via the Panama Canal | 5,256 | 9,798 | 10,392 | 3,363 | 4,633 |

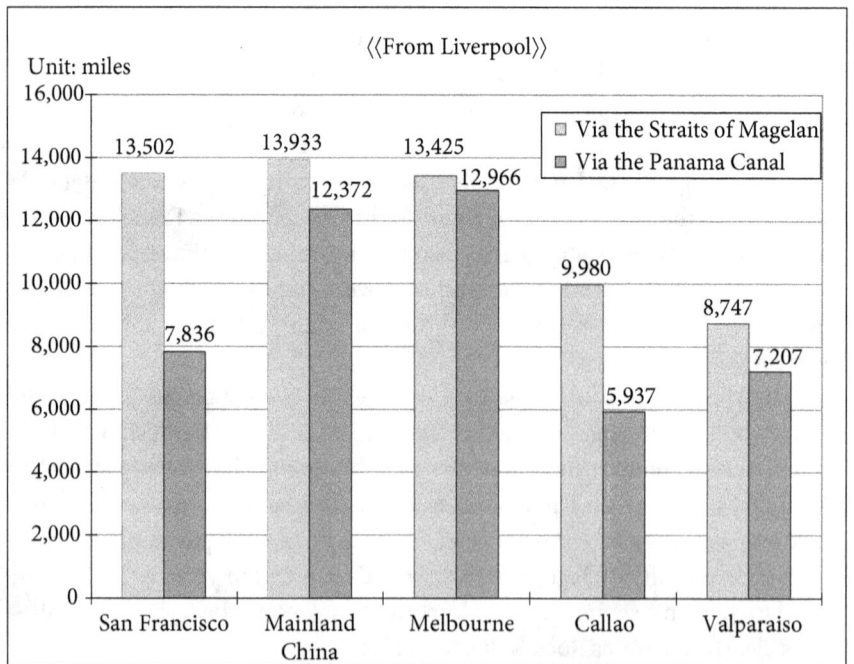

**《From Liverpool》**

Unit: miles

Via the Straits of Magelan
Via the Panama Canal

| | San Francisco | Mainland China | Melbourne | Callao | Valparaiso |
|---|---|---|---|---|---|
| Via the Straits of Magelan | 13,502 | 13,933 | 13,425 | 9,980 | 8,747 |
| Via the Panama Canal | 7,836 | 12,372 | 12,966 | 5,937 | 7,207 |

FIGURE 5.1    *The shortening of shipping distances resulting from the opening of the Panama Canal.*
SOURCE: CREATED BASED ON THE TABLE ON P85 OF PANAMA CANAL, WHAT IT IS, WHAT IT
MEANS, BY J. BARRET (PAN AMERICAN UNION, 1913).

US foreign policy at the time. That is, the primary issues for the United States became explicit: (1) facilitation of US naval supremacy in the Caribbean; and (2) identification of Panama as a base of defense for other countries in the Western hemisphere. We can see the United States' awareness of the increasing importance of the Central American region from statements by President Taft. One illustration is,

> The Monroe Doctrine has a vitally important significance in the area surrounding the Panama Canal and in the Caribbean region.[13]

Even by the time of the Wilson administration, such thinking persisted regarding Central American policy. At the time of the Mexican Revolution, the United States refused to recognize the Mexican administration on the grounds that it was a military dictatorship and actively interfered with domestic Mexican politics, eventually taking advantage of the murder of an American citizen as an opportunity to dispatch the United States Army. This incident can be explained as part of Wilson's "ideological diplomacy," but we should not overlook the background to this incident, namely the increased strategic importance of the Central American region resulting from the opening of the Panama Canal.

The opening of the Panama Canal also facilitated the US expansion into the Pacific. As can be seen from Figure 5.1, the shipping route from New York to the Chinese mainland was shortened by 3768 miles, or about nine days' traveling time. At the same time, the US Navy's ability to engage in Hawai'i Guam and the Philippines was correspondingly deepened. Economically, the shortening of shipping routes also resulted in cheaper freight rates, which became an inducement for expanding exports to Asian markets. Each of these points will be discussed further, below.

It terms of specific economic impact expected, the US was particularly hopeful that the opening of the Panama Canal would lead to economic expansion into the Chinese market. At the beginning of the 20th century, US trade with China was not growing smoothly. By the second decade of the 20th century, US trade with China was sluggish. An itemization of US exports at the time would include such products as petroleum, cotton goods, railway materials, and machinery. With the exception of cotton, all of these products were extremely heavy and required a huge amount of space. Apart from petroleum, all of these products were uncompetitive if they had to rely on the transcontinental railroad and its expensive freight rates; as a result, they were

---

13   See Annual Message 3 December 1912 (James D. Richardson, *A Compilation of the messages and papers of the Presidents, vol. XVI* (Washington D.C., 1914).

shipped to the Chinese market from the Atlantic coast, via the Suez Canal. This meant that shipping rates were relatively expensive compared to the rates for European countries, let alone Japan. However, as can be seen from Table 5.1, the opening of the Panama Canal would allow the journey to be shortened by about 3800 miles, resulting in substantial cost reductions in terms of savings on shipping rates and interest payments. Accordingly, it was expected that the opening of the Panama Canal would produce favorable conditions for dramatic growth in trade with China.

TABLE 5.1    *Comparison of the distances for shipping routes through the Panama and Suez canals (Unit: miles).*

| End points | Intermediate ports | Panama route | Suez route | Difference | Comment |
| --- | --- | --- | --- | --- | --- |
| New York – Yokohama | San Francisco | 9798 | 13,647 | 3849 | The Panama route is shorter |
| New York – Kobe | San Francisco, Yokohama | 10,152 | 13,293 | 3141 | The Panama route is shorter |
| New York – Nagasaki | San Francisco, Yokohama, Kobe | 10,537 | 12,908 | 2371 | The Panama route is shorter |
| New York – Shanghai | San Francisco, Yokohama, Kobe, Nagasaki | 10,997 | 12,248 | 1251 | The Panama route is shorter |
| New York – Hong Kong | San Francisco, Yokohama, Kobe, Nagasaki, Shanghai | 11,317 | 11,628 | 311 | The Panama route is shorter |
| New York – Singapore | San Francisco, Yokohama, Kobe, Nagasaki, Shanghai, Hong Kong | 13,271 | 10,174 | 3097 | The Panama route is shorter |
| New Orleans – Yokohama | San Francisco | 9219 | 14,924 | 5705 | The Panama route is shorter |
| New Orleans – Shanghai | San Francisco, Kobe, Nagasaki, Yokohama | 10,418 | 13,851 | 3433 | The Panama route is shorter |
| New Orleans – Hong Kong | San Francisco, Kobe, Nagasaki, Yokohama, Shanghai | 11,238 | 13,031 | 1793 | The Panama route is shorter |

*Source:* Created based on p91 of *Panama Unga no Kaitsuu ga Nihon ni Oyobosu Keizai-jou no Eikyou* ("The Economic Impact on Japan of the Opening of the Panama Canal") by the Ministry of Agriculture and Commerce (Sanshusha, 1914).

As well as benefiting commerce, the reduction in shipping distances to the Asia Pacific region from the Atlantic Coast of the United States was expected to increase the military influence of the United States. That is, the opening of the Panama Canal – which would become "a key base on the route connecting America to China, along with Hawai'i and the Philippines"[14] – facilitated US actions in Asia, dramatically increasing US influence in the Asia Pacific region while also strengthening the defense of American territories in the Pacific, such as Hawai'i, Guam and the Philippines.

The opening of the Panama Canal was also regarded as an excellent opportunity to rebuild the American merchant marine. Once the prospect of the completion of the Panama Canal began to appear likely, policies for rebuilding the American maritime industry began to take on a degree of concreteness. If the Panama Canal could be completed, not only would there be an increased flow of domestic goods linking the Atlantic and Pacific, but there would also be an increasing need for many international ships to connect with Europe and Asia. The industries that stood to benefit most were the maritime transport industry and the shipbuilding industry in the United States. The opening of the Panama Canal would increase the demand for merchant vessels, which under different circumstances would otherwise not have been operating at full capacity. Accordingly there was a high level of enthusiasm for rebuilding the maritime industry throughout the country.[15]

## 3      *The Significance of the Panama Canal for Japan*

The Japanese Government took considerable interest in the development of the Panama Canal from the beginning of the 20th century, and both the Ministry of Foreign Affairs and the Ministry of Agriculture and Commerce initiated their own investigations when it began to appear likely that the canal would be completed in the near future, after President Roosevelt launched full-scale construction efforts.[16] The following two points emerged as a result.

Japanese trade at the beginning of the 20th century was expanding steadily, but the United States was the primary export destination. Based on the results of a 1913 survey, the Ministry of Agriculture and Commerce found that 96 percent of trade with the Americas was with the United States, and that

---

14      Alfred Mahan, *The Problem of Asia and Its Effects upon International Policies* (Boston: Little Brown, 1900).

15      As for the plan for rebuilding American merchant marine, see Samuel H. Walker, *The Panama Canal and Restoration of American Merchant Marine* (Washington: 1912).

16      See Minegishi Shigetaro, *Report on the visit to the Panama Canal, 1903,* Japanese Foreign Ministry's Archives.

more than 98 percent of Japan's export destinations in the Americas were in the United States. Accordingly, it was considered that, "Of all the countries in North and South America, the country that will generate the most important economic relations with the Japanese Empire as a result of the opening of the Panama Canal will be none other than the United States of America."[17] This was also the view of the business community.[18]

The opening of the Panama Canal would bring about huge changes in the routes that Japan used for trading with the United States. That is, the shipping routes linking Japan to the Atlantic Coast of the United States, which was a massive consuming region and Japan's largest export market, would be shortened enormously, as indicated in Table 5.1. For example, the route between Yokohama and New York would be cut by 3849 miles, or about one quarter. Prior to the opening of the Panama Canal, there were two shipping routes for transporting goods between Japan and the United States: (1) "sea-rail dual post," whereby goods were sent across the Pacific on steamships and then transferred to the transcontinental railroad; and (2) the "Suez line," whereby goods were shipped across the Indian Ocean and then on to the Atlantic via the Suez Canal. However, as can be inferred from Table 5.1, shipping goods via the Panama Canal would save about ten days in comparison to the Suez route. For this reason the consensus in Japan was that trade between Japan and the United States would expand rapidly.

Incidentally, a key issue here was the question of freight rates. If freight rates were too high despite the opening of the Panama Canal then Japanese goods would not be competitive. This point can be illustrated in a comparison with the existing trade routes at the time, starting with exports to the United States. The main export items at the time included such things as raw silk, tea, and chinaware. The freight rates for these items are shown in Table 5.2. Consider the case of a merchant sending raw silk from Japan to New York, for example. If the merchant were to send the goods to the West Coast of the United States via ship and then use the transcontinental railroad for the rest of the route, he would have been charged a total of six dollars in freight charges; however, by sending the goods via the Panama Canal there is no need to pay four dollars for the freight rates for the transcontinental railroad. Therefore the route via the Panama Canal would result in much cheaper freight charges.

Turning next to imports from the United States to Japan, the items imported included cotton, petroleum, machinery, and wheat. Most of these items were

---

17    Ibid.
18    See Yokohama Customs Office, *Report of the Visit to the Panama Canal* (Yokohama: Yokohama Customs, 1904).

TABLE 5.2    *Freight rates for major export products to the United States (Units: USD).*

| Freight rate | Raw silk | | Tea | | Chinaware | | Floral mats | |
|---|---|---|---|---|---|---|---|---|
| | Japan | China | Japan | China | Japan | China | Japan | China |
| Steamship | 2.00 | 2.00 | 0.63 | 0.50 | 0.63 | 0.50 | 0.30 | 0.40 |
| North American railroad | 4.00 | 4.00 | 1.00 | 1.00 | 0.95 | 0.95 | 1.00 | 1.00 |
| Total rate | 6.00 | 6.00 | 1.63 | 1.50 | 1.58 | 1.45 | 1.30 | 1.40 |

*Note:* Conference freight rates apply to the rates for the Pacific shipping route, and the rates for the North American railroad are the rates per 100 pounds where the goods take up less than one carload (being the minimum cargo volume in order for carload discount rates to apply). *Source:* The Ministry of Agriculture and Commerce, op. cit. Created based on p167.

produced in the Atlantic seaboard region, or in the southern part of the United States near the Gulf of Mexico, with only wheat and timber originating from the Pacific Coast. Cotton, for example, which accounted for as much as 35 percent of the value of all imports from the United States, used to be sent by rail to the Pacific Coast before being sent to Japan by steamship from San Francisco or Los Angeles. However, the opening of the Panama Canal would make it possible to send cotton down the Mississippi River to New Orleans or one of the other ports on the Gulf Coast, from where it could be shipped directly to Japan.

Pursuing this line of reasoning, it becomes apparent that the opening of the Panama Canal had the potential to change US-Japan trade routes massively. Thus the next critical point becomes the question of how the rates for freight sent via the Panama Canal were set. Freight sent via the Panama Canal was influenced by two main factors: (1) the number of shipping companies competing along the Panama shipping route; and (2) the fees for transit along the Panama Canal itself. Numerous shipping companies were expected to use the Panama shipping route, including Japan, Great Britain and Germany, but ultimately the number of shipping companies plying this route would depend on the transit fees. Thus the issue of the fees for transit on the Panama Canal became the focus of attention for each of the countries involved.

As recorded in the memoirs of Shidehara Kijuro,[19] the ambassador to the United States at the time, the United States attempted to impose a transit tax on all foreign vessels. Great Britain protested strongly against this move, invoking the Hay-Pauncefote Treaty, which forbid discriminatory treatment between

---

19    Shidehara Kijyuro, *Fifty Years of Life as Diplomat* (Tokyo: Chuokoronsha, 1987), 48–52.

British and US vessels. At one point a transit tax bill passed the US Senate but this bill was scrapped soon after the outbreak of the First World War. Thus this legislation did not produce any great impediment to transit of the Panama Canal once it had been opened. If the issue of transit fees could be resolved reasonably in this way, then the opening of the Panama Canal was expected to be advantageous to Japan in all respects, such as lower risk and a reduction in the number of days spent at sea.

The second point to emerge from the studies by the Ministry for Foreign Affairs and the Ministry for Agriculture and Commerce was that the opening of the Panama Canal would enable Japan to pursue full-scale trade expansion into South America. Japan's relationship with South America was centered on migration and trade, but the volume of trade was not large. In 1905 the Osaka Shosen shipping company had established a regular route to Valparaiso in Chile, but the opening of the Panama Canal was expected to facilitate expansion to the Atlantic Coast of South America as well. A report by Minegishi Eitaro commissioned by the Ministry for Agriculture and Commerce points out that once the Panama Canal opened, Japan should adopt a policy of expanding trade with the United States, and then went on to point out that Japan should "work towards the economic development of Japan by establishing commercial colonies in Central and South America."[20] A March 1914 report by the Department of Commerce within the Ministry of Agriculture and Commerce illustrates the situation within Central and South America as follows:

> South America takes the form of an enormous triangle, connected to North America by the Panama Isthmus,...so we should be aware that it is crucial for Japan to make preparations to dispatch troops to South America in the event that there is a chance to seize the opportunity.[21]

Japan was aware that the situation in the South American region was one where "the influence of Europeans, and particularly those from Northern Europe, is extremely substantial, and consequentially the core group of enterprises in each industry is almost entirely dominated by such people."[22] At the same time, the general social organization in South America was different to

---

20   See Minegishi Shigetarō, *A Report on the visit to the Panama Canal in 1903* (Tokyo: The Diplomatic Record Office of the Ministry of Foreign Affairs [MOFA]).
21   See Ministry of Agriculture and Commerce in Japan, *The Economic Effects of the Opening of the Panama Canal on Japan* (Tokyo, Sanshusha, 1914), 241.
22   Ibid., 244.

that in North America, so that "It is exceptionally rare for migrants to South America to be naturalized."[23] Accordingly, "Despite the fact that a shortage of labor has already been reported in the major nations of South America, migrants from Asia are not welcome because of racial differences."[24] The conclusion drawn was that "As for commercial discrimination on the basis of nationality, let alone race, it is likely that relations between the Americas and East Asia shall eventually lead to a complete change [i.e., improvement] in the social standing [of Japanese migrants] as passage [between East and West] becomes increasingly more commonplace following the opening of the Panama Canal in the future."[25]

Specifically, then, what Japan hoped to gain from its relationships with Central and South America were trade and immigration opportunities. With regard to the actual situation of trade with South America at the time, the total value of trade with South America was extremely small and as noted earlier, trade flow focused on the US. This sum was no more than 3 percent of the total value of Japanese trade at the time. Apart from Argentina, these countries nonetheless all had ports on the Pacific Coast of South America, and were linked to Japan by regular shipping routes.

The opening of the Panama Canal was expected to make transportation to the countries on the Atlantic Coast of South America, such as Brazil, far more convenient. The journey from Japan to Rio de Janeiro, for example, was shortened by about 4800 miles, or about 30 percent of the distance in comparison to shipping via the Suez Canal. Shortening the distance between Japan and Brazil would also have a huge impact on immigration. Japanese immigration to South America has a long history; in 1913 there were about 7400 Japanese migrants living in Brazil. Once the Panama Canal was completed, it would become possible to have regular passenger vessels carrying migrants back and forth between Japan and Brazil, leading to rapid potential increases in the number of Japanese people immigrating to Brazil.[26] From this perspective, it was believed that the opening of the Panama Canal would "provide Japanese immigrants in South America with great benefit, but it will also promote better use of South America's abundant natural resources and lead to closer ties, both economically and in terms of two-way trade, and in the future there is a good

---

23    Ibid.
24    Ibid., 246.
25    Ibid.
26    As for the impacts of the opening of the Panama Canal on Japan-Brazil relationships, see Matsuo Otojirō, *The Opening of the Panama Canal and the Wealth in South America and Mexico* (Tokyo: Hokubunkan, 1914).

chance that it will result in the discovery of good markets for Japanese products."[27]


## Japan-US-UK Relations: Expectations and Effects

I will now turn to the question of how the opening of the Panama Canal was expected to affect Japan-US-UK relations, and specifically how these expectations were projected on to Japan-US-UK relations up until the canal was actually completed in August 1914. I will also clarify the results of those expectations after the opening of the Panama Canal through the 1910s.

As discussed above, we have already seen that on the Japanese side both the government and business circles expected the economic relationship with the US to become increasingly close-knit. In terms of exports, as the distance to the Atlantic coast of the United States became shorter, there was an expectation that Japanese exports would make greater inroads into the US market. At the same time, the freight rates for US imports such as cotton and petroleum would become cheaper. Not only was this advantageous to Japanese importers, it would also make it easier for US exporters to enter the Japanese market. On the other hand, the Panama Canal was expected to bring little benefit to European countries such as Britain in terms of their trade with Asia.[28] This made the supremacy of US products in the Japanese market clear. Cotton, for example, which accounted for 35 percent of all Japanese imports at the time, was dominated by imports from India prior to the opening of the Panama Canal, but it was expected that "American cotton will take an extremely advantageous position relative to cotton from India and Egypt."[29]

The US had been running a trade deficit with Japan, and so US business circles generally regarded the opening of the Panama Canal as desirable in order to rectify trade imbalances, as they would be able to export large volumes of cotton and petroleum to the Japanese market. The US maritime transport industry was alone in being concerned about more intense competition along Pacific routes from ships traveling via Panama unless the United States were to engage in a full-scale rebuilding of the maritime industry after the opening of the Panama Canal.[30]

---

27    Ibid., 185.

28    The Ministry of Agriculture and Commerce ed., *Panama unga kaitsu ga nihon ni oyobosu keizaiteki eikyo* (Tokyo: Sanshusha, 1914), 66–67.

29    Ibid., 93.

30    See Mihara Shigekichi, Panama keiyu koro ni tsuite no shiken (Tokyo: a pamphlet, 1921).

What most concerned Japan was an intensification of economic competition with the United States in the Chinese market. Opinion in Japan was greatly divided regarding US expansion into China following the opening of the Panama Canal. One theory was that US economic expansion represented a threat, the gist of which was to exaggerate the influence of the US in Asian markets: "Unless Japan can establish commercial rights regarding China, Korea, Siberia and so on, within the next ten years (that is, prior to the completion of the [Panama] canal), we are likely to eventually find ourselves trapped in the unfortunate circumstances of defeat at the hands of young and powerful America."[31]

This kind of argument appeared in the mass media in the years following 1903, when the United States started work on constructing the Panama Canal. However, by the second decade of the 20th century, when it became clear that the so-called "dollar diplomacy" of the Taft administration would not necessarily lead to greater trade between China and the US, the tone of the argument was tuned down somewhat. To the contrary, detailed investigations by the Ministry of Agriculture and Commerce and the business community found that the risk of US expansion would be more than outweighed by the benefits to Japanese manufacturers of being able to purchase cotton at lower prices from the United States – the world's largest cotton producer – following the opening of the Panama Canal, so that Japanese manufacturers would be quite capable of competing with the United States in the Chinese market.

Nonetheless, the Japanese business community remained cautious, considering that there was a possibility that networking between the Chinese and US business communities would lead to moves to exclude Japanese products from the Chinese market. In 1908 and 1909, private sector economic diplomacy developed briskly, focusing mainly on networking between the Japanese and US business communities. Both Japan and the US took advantage of the 1910 Nanking Exposition to send business delegations to network with the Chinese business community. The year 1911 saw the advent of the Xinhai Revolution; three-way networking between Japanese, Chinese and US business communities was interrupted for some time thereafter, but the United States continued to pursue economic exchanges actively with China as anti-Japanese sentiment within China grew. Japan was concerned about these kinds of moves by the US business community as a concrete expression of so-called "dollar diplomacy," but not overly concerned. The Japanese maritime transport industry was also concerned that US shipping companies would take up routes to

---

31    Minegishi, op. cit., 33.

China as the US rebuilt its maritime transport industry following the completion of the Panama Canal.[32]

Despite harboring these kinds of misgivings, the prevailing view within Japan regarding the economic impact resulting from the opening of the Panama Canal was that there would be more advantages than disadvantages. The economic aspects of the opening of the Panama Canal could be predicted, but more troubling for Japan-US relations were the military aspects and the ramifications for the immigration problem.

In terms of the military aspects, the boost to the American Navy resulting from the opening of the Panama Canal is regarded as having had a large impact on the Japanese Navy's strategies towards the United States. In the 1907 report *Teikoku Kokubo Hoshin* ("Policies for the Defense of the Realm"), the United States appears as a hypothetical enemy, ranked second only to Russia. The naval arms race between Japan and the United States also continued to intensify, and it is clear that the opening of the Panama Canal is the implicit premise behind this buildup.[33]

The Americans, for their part, were convinced that Japan wanted a war before the Panama Canal opened, and it was believed that the immigration problem might well be Japan's last good excuse to launch a war against the United States. In Japan, on the other hand, a war with the United States was not considered to be a realistic option. However, there were those who proposed that the United States' objective in opening the Panama Canal was "precisely because they predict that conflict with Japan was inevitable in the near future, and so [want to open the Panama Canal] in order to secure supremacy in the Pacific in order to prevent military conflict before it developed or, in the unlikely event of the outbreak of war, in order to hope for victory in any such conflict,"[34] as stated in an investigative report by the Japanese Army. At the very least, there were some people, such as Tanaka Gi'ichi of the Imperial Japanese Army General Staff, who were aware that the United States might well seize the initiative in international diplomacy in the Far East after the First World War.

---

32  We can find many similar expectations and opinions in Japanese businesses as expressed by several Chambers of Commerce in major Japanese cities. See the Ministry of Agriculture and Commerce, op. cit.; and Yokohama Chamber of Commerce, ed., *Panama unga no kaitsu ni tsuite* (Yokohama: 1921).

33  So far there are no concrete archives on the point either in the Diplomatic Record Office of MOFA or the archives of the National Institute for Defense Studies. These ideas can be found in Mizuno Hironori, *Tsugi no Issen* [*The next war*] (Tokyo: Kaneobuneido, 1914).

34  Itami Matsuo (Colonel), *Panama unga koji shisatsu hokoku* (Ministry of Army, 1911), 60.

For Britain on the other hand, and as illustrated in Figure 5.1, the Panama Canal did not change her trade route to Asia from being equal in significance to that of the Suez Canal in the middle of the 19th century. Furthermore, Britain had little capacity to further incorporate East Asian trade because of World War I.

In terms of the impact of the opening of the Panama Canal on the migration problem that was the source of so much antagonism between the United States and Japan, we can observe the following. In the United States it was generally believed that the fear of Japan on the Pacific Coast lay at the root of the effort to expel Japanese migrants, but that such concerns would subside once the Panama Canal opened, and that the movement to expel migrants would gradually calm down. However, in Japan the opposite view was widespread – that the opening of the Panama Canal would negatively affect the migration problem.

Such reasoning is the background to Japan's many efforts to calm the anti-Japanese sentiment on the Pacific Coast of the United States. For example, for the Panama-Pacific International Exposition in 1915, Japan restrained those with a hard-line position against the United States, instead sending leaders from the business community such as Shibusawa Ei'ichi to encouraging attendance. European countries such as Britain and Germany were unable to attend the exposition because the First World War had started in 1914, and the organizers had great hopes for Japanese participation. The leaders of the Japanese business community participated actively, believing that their presence would have a positive influence on the migration problem and the enlargement of Trans-Pacific trade and commerce. The Japanese migrant community on the Pacific Coast of the United States was also united in hoping for a turnaround in anti-Japanese sentiment.[35] Thus we can see that Japan and the United States adopted totally opposite views as to the likely impact of the opening of the Panama Canal on the question of its impact on Japanese immigrants.

The opening of the Panama Canal dramatically increased US military power, but at the same time it also increased the importance to the United States of the Central America region, such as Mexico and the Caribbean, and the Panama Canal zone in particular. In Japan, the interpretation was that the United States had started to "work toward aggressive expansion by transforming the passive Monroe Doctrine of the past to adopt an assertive foreign policy," and Japanese military officials viewed the United States' objective in opening the Panama Canal was "calculated based on the principles of warfare" rather than being for peaceful purposes. Particular attention was paid to the

---

35    Kitaoka Shin'ichi, Wakakihi no Kiyosawa Kiyoshi-San Francisco Hojishi "Shinsekai" yori (*Shisō*, March 1988), 67.

fact that the United States had intervened to ensure Panamanian independence and make the canal zone into a permanent territory and then stationed
a powerful field army to defend it, which was taken as a clear indication of the
United States' hard-line stance of being prepared to exercise military force to
ensure the security of the Central American region. On the Japanese side,
these kinds of responses by the United States were understood and there was
no criticism of the argument that the Panama Canal Zone was "a possession
[of the United States] both nominally and as a matter of fact, and there is
surely almost no doubt that the United States will extend its remaining energies to the other nations of Central America."[36] This issue may well have overlapped with the China Question, which would later become a significant
matter of concern between Japan and the United States.

As the US Navy strengthened in the Caribbean Sea and South America,
thanks to the ability to transit the Panama Canal, Britain's sea power declined,
hand in hand with the effects of World War I. Britain worried about the future
of her effectiveness in Central and South America, but was obliged to accept
the reality.

In the discussion above I have analyzed, from various angles, the impact
that the opening of the Panama Canal was expected to have on Japan-US-UK
relations in the first half of the second decade of the 20th century in terms of:
(1) the enormity of the economic benefits that the opening of the Panama
Canal would bring to the US and Japan; (2) the more limited economic benefits
accruing to Britain; and (3) the anticipated opening resulting in ever-increasing military tensions, in particular between Japan and the US.

While statistical data only partially portray the impact of the opening of the
Panama Canal, as summarized by Figure 5.1 and Table 5.1, there are three areas
in which it seems clear that Japan-US-UK relations were transformed.

Firstly, in the United States the argument that Japan represented a threat to
the Pacific Coast began to fade, whereas within Japan there was much talk of
the threat posed by the United States. Following the opening of the Panama
Canal the immigration problem continued unresolved, but in the United States
at least the fear of war as a background factor abated. The argument that
Japanese Navy represented a threat, which had previously been observed even
in the otherwise realistic business community, furthermore, disappeared. At
the same time, the economy of the Pacific Coast of the United States grew at a
dramatic rate, and the value of business dealings with Japan also increased.
The irony, however, is that as viewed from Japan the immigration problem
and the opening of the Panama Canal were linked, so that the argument was

---

36    Itami Matsuo, op. cit., 61.

developed at every opportunity that "by opening the Panama Canal, the United States had arrogantly decided to expel immigrants."[37]

Secondly, there were now direct shipping routes via the Panama Canal to the Atlantic Coast of the United States, and so the relative importance of the Pacific Coast to Japan-US trade and diplomatic relations declined. The importance of the Pacific Coast for commercial routes and as a point of contact f or trade between US and Japan did not decline in absolute terms, but the Eastern Coast of the United States, which was the core economic zone of the United States, 'moved closer' to Japan, both psychologically and in terms of actual distance; as a result, Japanese interest directed towards the Eastern United States became dominant. For the people on the Pacific Coast of the US, relations with Japan become more normalized, although the immigration problem was not fully resolved. However, the political role of the Pacific Coast in Japan-US relations can be described as having declined. As a diplomatic channel, communication between Tokyo-Washington deepened.[38]

The third area is the impact on Japan-US-UK relations concerning Japan's policies in China. The fact that the Panama Canal was built by the United States and that the canal zone continued to be occupied by the United States even after Panamanian independence, together with the exercise of US military force evidenced by the US response to the Mexican Revolution, had a large influence on the ideas that informed Japan's policies in China. After the opening of the Panama Canal, Japan pursued increasingly aggressive policies in China as the First World War unfolded. The clearest example of such policies is the "Twenty-One Demands." The events surrounding this incident led to a crisis between Japan and the United States.

Britain, on the other hand, was less concerned about the growth of the American merchant marine as a result of the opening of the Panama Canal. Instead, as an ally Britain had to recognize Japan's aggressive activities toward China concurrent with the outbreak of WWI, while at the same time viewed with trepidation the rapid growth of the Japanese merchant marine and its likely adverse impact on British business interests in East and South East Asia. Britain had neither the opportunity nor power to interfere with Japan's aggressive military and commercial activities in China due to the prolonged war with Germany, Austria-Hungary and Ottoman Empires.

Japan and the United States sought to compromise through the subsequent Lansing-Ishii Agreement, but in Japan it is important to note the degree to

---

37    Aruga Nagao, Panama unga no gunjiteki chii (*Gaiko Jihō*, March 1916), 157.

38    From the military viewpoint, the importance of the West Coast in case of a US war against Japan decreased. See Itami Matsuo, op. cit., 62.

which comments and actions were cognizant of US policies in Panama. The key point to be emphasized in the discussions between Japanese Special Envoy Ishii Kikujiro and the US Secretary of State is the implication for Japanese foreign policy, looking forward, of the phrase "...the countries of Central and South America should be grateful for the fact that the United States takes a special interest in them," suggesting an awareness in Japan that the fact that the United States had engaged in building the Panama Canal contributed enormously to the development of the South and Central American regions.

Such thinking appears frequently in the Japanese mass media in the second decade of the 20th century. That is, contrary to the idea that "....the United States has already annexed Hawai'i and appropriated Guam and Samoa, and – insofar as the United States is able to open the Panama Canal – will launch out into the Pacific to attempt to implement imperialism,"[39] there is the opinion that, "Although it may appear that the United States is attempting to suppress Japan in the Pacific, to do so would be reckless and foolish, and this is probably not what the prudent US officials are trying to do." The reason given for this position is that, before the United States can develop excessive political and economic influence in Asia, "[the United States] has many things that it must do in Central and South America."[40]

In this way the idea formed in Japan that the United States should understand that there are complexities within Japan's policies in China, and that Manchuria is a region of particularly vital importance for Japan. This can be described as one of the factors that made Japan-US cooperation concerning China all the more difficult foreshadowing a number of future problems for the triangular relationships between UK, US and Japan.

### Conclusion: A New 'Path' for Japan–US –UK relations

Okuma Shigenobu, one of Japan's great early modern leaders, has pointed out that the opening of the Panama Canal was extremely desirable for a trading nation such as Japan because it "shortened shipping routes by linking the Pacific and the Atlantic, so that all the ships circumnavigating the globe will gather in Japan."[41] However, the opening of the Panama Canal was actually far more important for the United States than it was for Japan. The greatest transformation brought about by the opening of the Panama Canal was to redraw

---

39    Ibid.
40    Kanbe Masao, Nichibei kankeiron (*Taiyo*, Vo. 21, No. 2, February 1915), 82.
41    Ōkuma Shigenobu, An address at Yokohama Chamber of Commerce, January 1915.

the trade maps of the world so as to be centered on the United States. Together with the First World War, which coincidentally started in the same year, the opening of the Panama Canal turned the United States into the world's greatest superpower. Thus the fact that the Panama Canal was built by America is highly symbolic. US diplomacy towards Panama is a perfect example of the so-called dualistic nature of US foreign policy, being both idealistic and realistic. 'Idealistic' because it deepened friendship and trade ties for both North and South America. 'Realistic' because the United States stood to gain many billions dollars' worth of Pan-Pacific trade with Central and South America. To this end the United States was prepared to exercise military force to obtain a permanent lease of part of Panama, and to interfere with the Mexican Revolution.

The changes to the United States resulting from the opening of the Panama Canal also produced changes in Japan-US relations. Japan-US relations grew ever closer, focused mainly on economic relations and, in terms of diplomacy, relations between Tokyo and Washington became closer and more broad-based. The opening of the Panama Canal also had a substantial effect on the arguments for Japanese expansion in China in general and Manchuria in par-ticular. That is, the argument that Manchuria was a lifeline for Japan just as the Panama Canal was a lifeline for the United States appears to have become established throughout Japanese society. With the outbreak of the First World War immediately after the opening of the Panama Canal and Japan's participa-tion in that war, the attention of Japanese foreign policy was to become riveted on China, such that interest in the Panama Canal itself can be said to have faded rapidly as it became a *fait accompli.*

The Panama Canal that is described as the greatest project of the beginning of the 20th century became a new 'path' linking the Pacific and the Atlantic, leading to the development of new kinds of international relations. Naturally enough, the Panama Canal also created a new path for the relations between Japan and the United States as they faced off across the Pacific. The change in the relationships between those two countries both pushed and pulled the UK into a new Pacific-centric orbit, as well. The opening of the Panama Canal can be fairly described as highly significant because the fundamental structure of British Atlantic-oriented governance of the world was destroyed and the Trans-Pacific relationships between Japan and the United States became more important in the world. When considering international political economy, we are liable to take the development of transportation as a given, tending only to be transfixed by wars and other incidents, but due attention should be paid to the construction of railways or the establishment of shipping routes or canals that transform global transport routes. They, too, are significant factors that shake international relationships from their foundations.

# From Cooperation to Conflict
*Japanese-Russian Relations from the Formation of the Russo-Japanese Entente to the Siberian Intervention*

*Isao Chiba*

## Gotō Shimpei and the Relationship between Japan and Russia

At the beginning of the 20th century, the Russo-Japanese War broke out between Japan and Russia because of a failure to reconcile the interests of the Korean Peninsula and northeastern China (Manchuria). After the war, Japan and Russia remained wary of each other, and Japan considered Russia its greatest potential enemy. On the other hand, China's demands that Japan and Russia concede parts of Manchuria caused the two countries to cooperate in some matters of foreign policy because of their shared opposition to Chinese nationalism. Therefore, the first, second, and third Russo-Japanese Ententes ended with the joint participation of the two countries in the First World War. And concluding the fourth Russo-Japanese Entente in July 1916, Japan allied with Russia; however, the following year the Russian Revolution began and Japan waged an intervention war with the other alliance countries, which resulted in renewed conflict between Japan and Russia. Thus, the relationship between Japan and Russia at the beginning of the 20th century would alternate between enmity and cooperation. With this in mind, we will focus on the relationship between Japan and Russia in the 1910s, viewed through the lens of Gotō Shimpei, who first became involved in foreign policy as a colonial government official, not as a diplomat. The colonial governments at this time tended to intervene in the foreign policies of the ministry of foreign affairs, because the colonial governments had international relations with neighboring countries (e.g., China). After he served as the first president of the Manchurian Railway, which was established after the Russo-Japanese War, he became a member of the temporary Foreign Affairs Investigation Committee during the First World War. Then, even though he was not a diplomat, he served as Foreign Minister and was responsible for the Siberian Intervention. Meanwhile, he focused on economic cooperation between Japan and Russia as vice-president from 1911–20, and later as president from 1920–29, of the Russo-Japanese Friendship Association. Why did he insist upon the Siberian Intervention? To understand this, we will analyze the complexity of the relationship between Japan and Russia in the 1910s by following Gotō's career, beginning with the events leading up to the Russo-Japanese War and concluding with the end of the First World War.

### From the Russo-Japanese War to Russo-Japanese Entente

Gotō Shimpei (1857–1929) was from the Tōhoku District, which was seen as an enemy of the court clans during the Meiji Restoration. He started his career as a government official overseeing public health, which was considered to be in the technical department, while men from Satsuma or Chōsyu Districts held the power because of their districts' role during the Meiji Restoration. During the Sino-Japanese War (1894–95), Gotō enjoyed the favor of Kodama Gentarō from Chōsyu. When Kodama was appointed Governor-General of Taiwan in 1898, Gotō assumed the position of head of the Government Section of the Governor-General (later Civil Governor).

Gotō decided to create a Japanese sphere of influence in the opposite side of Taiwan, Fujian. Then the Boxer Rebellion spreading to Fujian led to the Amoy Incident in 1900. When the Honganji missionary temple in Amoy was destroyed by arson (planned by the Governor-General of Taiwan), Gotō recommended dispatching land troops to the Taiwan Army Chief of Staff of the Governor-General, and he made plans to occupy batteries with the Amoy consul and captains of the navy ships. "All of the related members were outraged" when the government in Tokyo reversed orders to dispatch troops due to the interference of great-power countries, including England. Gotō appealed to Kodama to cancel Tokyo's reversal but was unsuccessful, and he lamented the deterioration of the situation. Thus he was enthusiastic for a Japanese "advance to the south" through the other side of Taiwan to southern China, and he also thought that Japan should abandon its status in Korea, even if Japan must appease Russia, who had ambitions on Korea, for future security when Japan headed southward.[1]

After that, however, Gotō's concern over international affairs turned his attention from southern China to Korea and Manchuria. For example, when Russia failed to honor a second deadline to withdraw from Manchuria in April 1903, relations were strained. Russia instead presented withdrawal conditions from Manchuria to China. During May and June Gotō wanted Japan to have complete access to land and sea transportation, as well as

---

1  Diary entries for 1 July, 27 August, and 31 August 1900, in *Documents on Gotō Shimpei* (YŪSHŌDO CO., LTD, 1980), Microfilm, 31-1-17. Publication Association of Diary of Konoe Atsumaro ed., "Supplement," in *Diary of Konoe Atsumaro* (Kajima Printing, 1969), 64.

banking facilities in China and Korea, in order to secure Japan's trade and commerce.[2]

Russo-Japanese negotiations started on August 12 in 1903 after Kurino Shinichirō, minister to Russia, presented a draft of the Russo-Japanese Entente. Gotō and Kodama, the Governor-General of Taiwan, maintained a firmer attitude toward Russia than that of the Katsura Tarō Cabinet at the time. For instance, Gotō wrote in his diary, "Russia finally gave an answer to the suggestions which were provided on August 12 by Japan. The response was extremely rude and egoistic of Russia. Russia regarded Manchuria as outside of the extent of the Russo-Japanese Entente. The Japanese government negotiated with Russia by yielding slightly." He blamed the Katsura Cabinet for the tone of Russia's response.[3]

Gotō lamented in his diary on 11 December 1903 that "the reply from Russia is coming. Russia does not actually make any concessions. We agree with the Governor-General of Taiwan, Kodama, that a declaration of war is unavoidable. The Japanese government is still undecided and is not prepared for war." Kodama, who had served as the Governor-General of Taiwan, and Vice Chief of the General Staff since October, and who made strong assertions concerning the campaigns against Russia, was not qualified to attend the meeting of elder statesmen (the joint meeting of elder statesmen and major cabinet ministers is the decision-making body superior to cabinet meetings, and is attended by the Emperor). In this meeting, the government decided that the negotiators should continue to ask Russia to reconsider. Gotō felt deeply resentful, saying that the Japanese government agreed to ask Russia to reconsider and this agreement "chagrined us and other companions."[4]

At the 12 January 1904 meeting of elder statesmen and major cabinet ministers with the Emperor, there were heated discussions between the elder statesmen and the Cabinet; in the end, the Cabinet forced its way by affirming that negotiations would continue with Russia, and Russia should be pressed to reconsider. Gotō lamented that what was determined was to again ask Russia for reconsideration. A reply from Russia was delayed, and Japan finally severed diplomatic relations with Russia on 6 February. After that, Japanese naval forces attacked the Port Arthur fleet on 8 and 9 February 1904, resulting in the outbreak of the Russo-Japanese War.[5]

---

2  Tsurumi Yūsuke, *Authentic Biography: Gotō Shimpei*, vol. 3 (Fujiwara-shoten, 2005), 736–745.

3  *Gotō's diary*, 3 September 1903. For Japan's foreign policy, see Chiba Isao, *The Formation of Old Diplomacy: Japanese Diplomacy 1900–1919* (Keisō Shobō, 2008).

4  *Gotō's diary*, 11 and 21 December 1903. Chiba, *The Formation of Old Diplomacy*, 119–130.

5  *Gotō's diary*, 5 January 1904, 6 and 8 February 1904. Chiba, *The Formation of Old Diplomacy*, 133–141.

Gotō, like many, was nervous about the course of the war. What was distinctive about Gotō was his recognition that the Russo-Japanese War was really an economic and financial battle between Russia and Japan. Gotō advised Prime Minister Katsura to dispatch a well-qualified person to the United States to contact newspapers or to connect with influential people in economic circles in order to bring down the Russian bond prices in the markets of Paris and so on. Gotō recommended arranging interference by friendly countries as a method to shorten the war, rather than actually waging war. Specifically, Gotō reminded the authorities to take diplomatic steps that would create positive feelings between the German Emperor and Japan, under the condition that Japan would help him realize his requests of Turkey and Persia.[6]

Gotō was concerned that Russia would change the dismissive attitude toward Japan due to a series of defeats, and he feared that they might discover a means of striking Japan's weak points. War was expected to be prolonged because both Russia and her rulers wrongly believed that the final victory would be Russia's. Even when Japan and Russia made peace, he thought that Japan should not see it as an eternal peace, but rather as a temporary cease-fire. Gotō presented these concerns to Prime Minister Katsura again on 27 December 1904. Gotō pointed out the necessity of making fiscal arrangements for the Russo-Japanese War to continue for three to five years. To this end, he requested that the Cabinet nationalize railways and carry out a monopoly on sugar as well as issuing large amounts of foreign bonds by collateralizing the income from railways and selling sugar as the best measure for this.[7]

A peace conference was held on 10 August 1905 between Japan and Russia at Portsmouth in the United States. The most challenging issues to be discussed were cession of territories and compensation of war expenditures. Gotō recognized that as long as Japan pursued these policies It could cause bad feelings with the great powers.[8] Although Gotō had taken a firm stand when the Russo-Japanese War started, he advocated for the "theory of early peace" when Japan and Russia made peace, and the treaty signed during the peace conference was acceptable to Gotō.

As an outcome of the Russo-Japanese War, Japan acquired interests in south Manchuria from Russia, including the South Manchurian Railway Co., Ltd., a semi-official special company established in 1906 to manage the southern

---

6  *Gotō's diary*, 19 and 20 June 1904. *Authentic Biography*, vol. 3, 748–761.

7  *Authentic Biography*, vol. 3, 762–765, 771–784.

8  *Authentic Biography*, vol. 3, 784–798.

branch line of the Chinese Eastern Railway (Changchun to Port Arthur) as well as other incidental businesses. It was like a Japanese version of the "East India Company." Kodama persuaded Gotō to serve as its first president.

Immediately before his appointment, Gotō sent management plans for Manchuria and Korea to the elder statesman Yamagata Aritomo. In the plans, Gotō urged the government to set up sufficient land bases in Manchuria and Korea using immigrants and implanting the latest technology in order to prevent the coming war between Japan and Russia – and then to obtain final victory even if the Russo-Japanese War broke out again and Japan temporarily lost. According to Gotō's management plan of Manchuria and Korea, massive amounts of investment would be necessary, but it was Japan's great responsibility as victor.[9]

Gotō next sought cooperation with Russia which, just a few years previously, had been at war with Japan over Manchuria. For example, in a report that Gotō made after visiting Beijing in May and June 1907, he insisted on isolating China from the great powers as a means for Japan to win without fighting, while at the same time suggesting the possibility of "a second Sino-Japanese War" with Qing, where recovery of rights and anti-foreignism was widespread. He also recommended isolating Germany from Europe – and China from Asia – by bringing the United States, France, and Russia over to Japan's side in addition to the Anglo-Japanese Alliance.[10] According to Gotō's perspective, the Russo-Japanese Entente and Franco-Japanese Entente should be welcomed.

After the conclusion of the Franco-Japanese Entente (10 June 1907) and the first Russo-Japanese Entente (30 July 1907), Gotō indicated that he considered Germany's instigation of Russia a key factor in the Russo-Japanese War. He also expressed concern that Germany and China would be close to each other while Japan, England, Russia, and France were making an association, and the United States was also showing a favor to that association. Hence, the priority of Japanese foreign diplomacy was to encourage China to cooperate with Japan, England, Russia, and France.[11]

On the other hand, a variety of disputes had occurred between Japan and China around the time of the conclusion of the Russo-Japanese and the

---

9    Letter dated 9 June 1906, from Gotō Shimpei to Yamagata Aritomo, in Shōyū Club Editing Committee ed., *Documents related to Yamagata Aritomo*, vol. 2 (Yamakawa Shuppansha Ltd., 2006), 117–118. *Authentic Biography*, vol. 3, 811–824.

10   Tsurumi Yūsuke, *Authentic Biography: Gotō Shimpei*, vol. 4 (Fujiwara shoten, 2005), 433–448.

11   *Authentic Biography*, vol. 4, 448–468.

Franco-Japanese Ententes. The substantiation of the Convention of Peking (concluded in 1905) made China accept the devolution of interests in Manchuria from Russia to Japan. Still, for Katsura Tarō, Foreign Minister Hayashi Tadasu's diplomacy on behalf of the first Saionji Kinmochi Cabinet moved too slowly.[12]

The famous episode *Itsukushima Yowa* (Gotō Shimpei and Itō Hirobumi talked over Japanese policy on Eastern Asia for three days in Itsukushima) gives us a sense of Gotō's thinking at this time. It describes talks held between Gotō and Itō Hirobumi, an elder statesman who served as Resident-General of Korea in September 1907. Gotō recommended that Itō travel around China and talk to influential people about "Asianism." He also suggested the second measure, "Theory for Confrontation between New and Old Worlds," to Itō in case he had difficulty in understanding Chinese politicians or in talking about "Asianism." This meant controlling the potential threat of the United States in advance by cooperating with countries in Europe (especially England, Russia, France, and Germany), as the future trend in the world would lead to confrontation between the Old and New Worlds.

In the "Theory for Confrontation between New and Old Worlds," the target that Japan had to keep an eye on changed from Germany to the United States, which was different from the opinion just a few months earlier. Kitaoka Shinichi stressed that Gotō did not believe that the United States was hostile toward Japan, and could interact with Japan constructively through an economic relationship. "Theory for Confrontation between New and Old Worlds" is not a theory of a balance of power in the wake of conflict in international relations, but rather a view of international relations as an opportunity for integration.[13]

On the basis of this theory, Gotō visited Russia from April to May 1908 to foster Russo-Japanese partnership, despite the fact that the political atmosphere was leaning toward another Russo-Japanese War. His official purpose for visiting was to inspect factories in Russia and to order rails for the Manchurian Railway, but this visit was seen as a first step in Russo-Japanese partnership. Gotō had talks with Prime Minister Petr A. Stolypin, and Finance

---

12    Letter from Katsura Tarō to Gotō Shimpei dated 31 August 1907, in Chiba Isao ed., *The Letters of Katsura Tarō* (University of Tokyo Press, 2011), 195–196. After the sudden death of Kodama Gentarō in 1906, Katsura, the fellow and senior of Kodama, became the political mentor of Gotō. Thus Katsura's ideas would have been shared by Gotō.

13    *Authentic Biography*, vol. 4, 487–514. Kitaoka Shinichi, "Gotō Shimpei as a diplomacy leader," Modern Japan Research Society ed., *Annual Report Study on Modern Japan 2: Modern Japan and East Asia* (Yamakawa Shuppansha Ltd., 1980), 75, 93. Later this article was expanded and published as *Gotō Shimpei: Diplomacy and Vision* (Chūōkōron-sha, 1988). As the volume does not contain notes, I will refer to the article.

Minister Vladimir N. Kokovtsov at Saint Petersburg. Joint connections were
made between the Manchurian Railway, the Chinese Eastern Railway, and the
Trans-Siberian Railway as a sign of their cooperative relationship.[14]

On the other hand, Sino-Japanese relations were ambiguous for Gotō.
He stood on the side of "Theory for Confrontation between New and Old
Worlds" and pursued a Sino-Japanese partnership based on the platform of
"the same language and same race for China." When Gotō visited Beijing in
1907 he spoke with Yuan Shikai about the "chopstick alliance," but he
strongly objected when China attempted to infringe on Japan's interests in
South Manchuria. He disagreed with abandoning the rights specified by
the Japanese treaty, such as the expansion of the new Railway from
Hsinmintun to Fakumen, saying that "A concession of one inch leads to the
concession of one foot," or "disasters brought on by infringement of the
treaty [by China] would not stop." Under these circumstances, resorting a
second Sino-Japanese War with inflexible China may be favorable to
Japan.[15]

### Russo-Japanese Economic Cooperation and Russo-Japanese Alliance

When the second Katsura Tarō Cabinet was established in July 1908, Gotō
joined the Cabinet as Minister of Communication and Transportation. In this
capacity he further strengthened Japan's relationship with Russia.

In 1908 Gregory Wilenkin, Russia's financial commissioner to Japan, made a
plan in which the Chinese Eastern Railway and the Manchurian Railway would
be merged, and an international syndicate would manage the merged company. Wilenkin consulted on the idea with Jacob H. Schiff, a chairman of Kuhn,
Loeb & Co. in New York, who saw it as a means to bring US capital into Japan's
management of Manchuria. In addition, after Wilenkin proposed the idea to
Minister of Finance Kokovtsov in Russia, it was changed to enable the Chinese
Government to buy shares of the Chinese Eastern Railway and the Manchurian

14    *Authentic Biography*, vol. 4, 580–599. Vasily Molodyakov, *Gotō Shimpei and History of Russo-Japanese Relations: New Opinion Based on New Russian Documents*, (Fujiwara-shoten, 2009), 28–40. Translated by Hiroshi Kimura.
15    Tsurumi Yūsuke, *Authentic Biography: Gotō Shimpei*, vol. 5 (Fujiwara shoten, 2005), 58–74. *Authentic Biography*, vol. 4, 653. Tsunoda Jun, *Manchuria Problems and National Defense Policy: Changes in National Defense Environment in the Late Meiji Era*, (Hara Shobō, 1967), 406.

Railway using funds provided for by the international syndicate, whose owner was Kuhn, Loeb & Co.[16]

The following year, on 19 February 1909, Gotō met with Wilenkin, who had returned to Tokyo on 17 February. Wilenkin recommended that the Chinese Eastern and Manchurian Railways be sold simultaneously, but Gotō was not willing to accept this suggestion.[17]

Later, Itō visited Russia, as Gotō had recommended, in order to meet with Kokovtsov for Russo-Japanese partnership; however, Itō was assassinated on 26 October while he was in Harbin, so Gotō's efforts failed. In spite of the incident, Gotō had several meetings in November and December with the Russian ambassador to Japan, Nikolai A. Malevskii-Malevich. Gotō thought it wise for Japan and Russia to be tied up against China over the issues of the railway and trade. This was characteristic of Gotō's approach, to focus on economic issues instead of political issues with Russia.[18]

Japan's decision to approach Russia was fostered by US Secretary of State Philander C. Knox's suggestion to neutralize the Manchurian Railways. Malevskii-Malevich visited Gotō on 23 December to talk about diplomatic correspondence from Russian Foreign Minister Aleksandr P. Izvol'skii. Gotō wrote a memo concerning these talks. Finally, on 21 January 1910, Japan and Russia jointly rejected the suggestion made by the US.[19]

Later, Schiff protected the plan to neutralize the Manchurian Railway in a formal letter exchanged with Takahashi Korekiyo, vice president of the Bank of Japan and head of Yokohama Specie Bank, Ltd. In the letter, Schiff reminded Takahashi of the fact that the United States had provided moral and financial aid to Japan during the Russo-Japanese War, and stressed the necessity of establishing neutral areas in Manchuria to prevent trouble between Japan and Russia. Even though a year and a half previously Schiff had reported Wilenkin's plan to sell the Chinese Eastern and Manchurian Railways to the Japanese government, Schiff criticized Gotō for using the report to attack American bankers in the newspapers.[20]

---

16    *Authentic Biography: Gotō Shimpei,* vol. 5, 494–548.

17    *Gotō's diary,* 17 and 19 February 1909. *Authentic Biography: Gotō Shimpei,* vol. 5, 494–499.

18    Kitaoka, "Gotō Shimpei as a diplomacy leader," 79. In Komatsu Midori, *The Secret Story of Diplomacy in the Meiji Era,* (Chikura Publishing Co., Ltd., 1936), 408–419. *Authentic Biography: Gotō Shimpei,* vol. 5, 499–510.

19    *Gotō's diary,* 23 December 1909 and 21 January 1910. The closer relationship between Japan and Russia was triggered by the neutralization of Manchurian Railways suggested by the US, evolved into conclusion of the 2nd Russo-Japanese Entente (4 July 1910).

20    Letter from Jacob H. Schiff to Takahashi Korekiyo, 24 February 1910 (translated into Japanese), in Documents related to Inoue Kaoru, 665–667, National Diet Library

In October 1911 when the Chinese Revolution broke out, Gotō was no longer in office; however, he appealed to Katsura for a partnership with Germany. Gotō realized that the incident in China could be a good opportunity to approach Germany, as England was becoming more decrepit by the day. Gotō had the "Theory for Confrontation between New and Old Worlds" in mind, in which Japan was resistant to the New World (the United States), while attempting to maintain the territorial integrity of China by collaborating with the Old World (England, Russia, France and Germany). He put more attention on partnership with Germany because the benefits of the Anglo-Japanese Alliance were fading.[21]

In July 1912 when the Chinese Revolution died down, Katsura visited Europe and Gotō accompanied him. Gotō said that the purpose of Katsura's visit to Europe was to "study world policy," specifically "to obtain acceptance from each government in England, France and Russia, as well as the German Emperor, for policies relating to China."[22] However, Katsura's delegation had to return to Japan in the middle of their visit due to the sudden death of the Meiji Emperor.

Gotō joined the third Katsura Cabinet, which was established immediately afterwards, as Minister of Communication and Transportation. Katō Takaaki, Ambassador to Great Britain, was slated for the Foreign Minister, but Gotō strongly objected his induction because Katō was a member of "the Mitsubishi family and had passive prejudiced opinions," and Gotō feared that Katō's "senile British remarks" would serve to continue the unchanged passive policies with Manchuria.[23]

But in the manuscript of a political speech[24] drafted for Prime Minister Katsura, Gotō said that we needed to respect the Anglo-Japanese Alliance, Russo-Japanese Entente, and the Franco-Japanese Entente and endeavor to exercise their spirit. Aside from Gotō's arguments, the Katsura Cabinet continued to honor the Anglo-Japanese Alliance in its diplomatic policies.

The Katsura Cabinet soon collapsed due to the Taishō Political Crisis. After the collapse, Gotō joined the Katsura New Party (Rikken Dōshikai) begun by Katsura, but left after Katsura's death. Katō then became the president of the

Constitutional Materials Room. Tsunoda, *Manchuria Problems and National Defense Policy,* 471–473.

21  Letter from Gotō Shimpei to Katsura Tarō, 12 November 1911, in Chiba Isao ed., *Selected Papers of Katsura Tarō* (University of Tokyo Press, 2010), 173–175.

22  Tokutomi Sohō, *Biography of Duke Katsura Tarō,* vol.2 (Hara Shobo, 1967), 564. *Authentic Biography: Gotō Shimpei, vol. 5,* 586.

23  Letter from Gotō Shimpei to Katsura Tarō, 14 December 1913, *Selected Papers,* 182–183.

24  Letter from Gotō Shimpei to Katsura Tarō, 30 December 1912, *Selected Papers,* 185–187.

Rikken Doshikai. The second Ōkuma Shigenobu Cabinet was established in April 1914 while the Rikken Dōshikai was the ruling party, and Katō was appointed Foreign Minister.

Immediately after, the First World War broke out and Russia and France offered to join the Anglo-Japanese Alliance. Elder statesmen Yamagata Aritomo and Inoue Kaoru agreed with the Russo-Japanese Alliance, but Foreign Minister Katō, who was concerned about the decreasing effects of the Anglo-Japanese Alliance, was not willing to conclude the Russo-Japanese Alliance. On 22 June Gotō visited Ambassador Nikolai A. Malevskii-Malevich to explain the intricacies of Japan's internal affairs. It is said that Gotō told the Ambassador the following: Yamagata and Inoue would like to conclude the Russo-Japanese Alliance as soon as possible, but Foreign Minister Katō, who implemented a shortsighted foreign policy, refused. The successors of Itō, two elder statesmen, became frustrated with the Ministry of Foreign Affairs and determined to change the foreign policy of the Cabinet by all available means. If the Ōkuma Cabinet continued to oppose the foreign policy that the elder statesmen suggested, Yamagata would resolve it himself.[25]

Foreign Minister Katō forcibly participated in the First World War under the guise of the Anglo-Japanese Alliance, and submitted the Twenty-One Demands to the Chinese Government while he waited for the moment that the European great powers' influence retreated from Asia. Gotō and the elder statesmen corresponded with each other, as they were strongly offended by Katō's foreign policy.

The second Ōkuma Cabinet then reshuffled the Cabinet and Ishii Kikujiro, Japanese Ambassador to France, replaced Katō Takaaki as Foreign Minister. When Gotō visited Ambassador Malevskii-Malevich in September 1915, Gotō told him that the Japanese Government would start negotiations to conclude the Russo-Japanese Alliance when the new Foreign Minister Ishii returned to Japan.[26] On the other hand, during the First World War, Russia was willing to conclude the Russo-Japanese Alliance; Grand Duke Georgie Mikhailovich's visit to Japan in January of 1916 triggered new negotiations on the Russo-Japanese Alliance.

Gotō's opinions on the Russo-Japanese Alliance are described in *On Japan's Expansionism*, published in February 1916. In the book, Gotō insisted that the Anglo-Japanese Alliance no longer conformed with the national interests of Japan. He focused on the one-sided characteristics of the Alliance, and criticized

---

25  Baryshev Eduard, *The Epoch of Russo-Japanese Alliance, 1914 to 1917: The Truth about an "Exceptional Friendship"* (Hana Shoin, 2007), 137.

26  Ibid., 153.

the pro-English attitude in which Japan followed other countries without question, accepting a servile position. Gotō maintained that Japan must follow the great powers unquestioningly, and was always at threat of isolation from them, because Japan did not interact well with other countries; specifically, the emotional and political connection with China and Russia was insufficient.[27]

For Gotō, the Russo-Japanese Alliance itself was not the goal but rather a means to get to the real purpose, an autonomous foreign policy for Japan. According to his article "Theory of Friendship between Japan and Russia," in the October 1915 issue of *Chūōkōron*, he was enthusiastic about promoting "a friendly relationship between Japan and Russia" in trade relations by declaring regions from Lake Baikal to the coast of River Amur as commerce areas; however, he was very cautious about starting further relations.[28]

In March 1916 when the Japanese Government and Russian Government were engaged in negotiations on the Alliance, Gotō visited Ambassador Malevskii-Malevich and presented a note informing him of the establishment of a Russo-Japanese bank in Japan, by people involved in Japan's commerce and finance. The capital for this Russo-Japanese bank was ¥30 million and the major activity proposed was to make loans to munitions factories and support trade between Japan and Russia.[29]

In July 1916, the 4th Russo-Japanese Entente was concluded, which Gotō welcomed because Japan's autonomous foreign policy was established. In other words, the Russo-Japanese Alliance was not an alternative to the Anglo-Japanese Alliance, but was welcomed because Japanese independence was promoted by modifying the one-sided structure of the Anglo-Japanese Alliance.[30]

On the other hand, Gotō pointed out that the Ōkuma Cabinet entered the Agreement three years late because of its hesitation about their foreign policy to Russia. Gotō, whose major focus was on East Asia, still focused on cooperation between Japan and Russia, which was centered on the Chinese Eastern Railway, the main artery of traffic in the world.[31]

---

27  Gotō Shimpei, *On Japan's Expansionism* (Popular university meeting, 1916), 177–179, 199, 228–230. Baryshev, *The Epoch of Russo-Japanese Alliance*, 217–218.

28  Gotō Shimpei, "Theory of friendship between Japan and Russia," *Chūōkōron*, October 1st 1915, 72–73. Baryshev, *The Epoch of Russo-Japanese Alliance*, 218–219.

29  Baryshev, *The Epoch of Russo-Japanese Alliance*, 219.

30  Gotō Shimpei, "The Russo-Japanese Entente is the expansion of the Anglo-Japanese Alliance," *Tokyo Nichinichi Shimbun*, 8 July 1916. Baryshev, *The Epoch of Russo-Japanese Alliance*, 252–253.

31  "I am a slug in the political world: Baron Gotō wearing a yukata talks big" *Tokyo Nichinichi Shimbun* 10 July 1916. Yoshimura Michio, *Japan and Russia* (Hara Shōbō, 1968), 309. Baryshev, *The Epoch of Russo-Japanese Alliance*, 253.

Gotō strongly criticized the Ōkuma Cabinet's decision to overthrow the Yuan Shikai Government in China in 1915–16,[32] which inspired him to approach Governor-General of Korea Terauchi Masatake, who took a similar stance. When the Terauchi Cabinet was established in October 1916, Gotō became Home Minister.

Prime Minister Terauchi and Home Minister Gotō attempted to use the Russo-Japanese Friendship Association as a measure enter the Russian market to compete with the expansion of US capital. Terauchi served as chairman of the Association and Gotō was vice chairman. The Russo-Japanese Friendship Association issued a newsletter, *Bulletin of Russo-Japanese Friendship Association,* and encouraged Japanese industries to enter into the Russia market, rather than promoting friendly relations between Japan and Russia. The Japanese Government decided to establish the Russo-Japanese in response to the affirmation made by the Russo-Japanese Friendship Association, and the basic agreement was made as a result of preliminary talks with the Russian side. The head office of the Russo-Japanese bank was located in Saint Petersburg, the capital of Russia, and several branches of the bank were located in Tokyo.[33]

### Gotō and the Siberian Intervention

The following year, in June 1917, Temporary Foreign Affairs Investigation Committee was established. Gotō was appointed as a member of the Committee and participated in meetings.

In 1917, Home Minister Gotō wrote statements concerning the Cabinet's domestic and foreign policies, including the Siberian Intervention during the November Revolution in Russia, and presented those statements to Prime Minister Terauchi. Gotō said that Japan should not dispatch troops without reason, even if it was driven by the current of the times; or, if Japan had to dispatch troops, the Japanese Government should not make any mistakes anticipating the withdrawal of the troops. Gotō suggested two policies to be implemented: one was to buy cereal grains in order to control prices, with half of the grain to be consumed domestically and the other half to be given to the poor in Russia along the Trans-Siberian Railroad; the other was to dispatch large-scale Red Cross groups to give free medical treatment to the wounded

---

32    Letter from Gotō Shimpei to Terauchi Masatake, 4 April and 1 May 1916, in Documents related to Terauchi Masatake, 27–43, 27–44, National Diet Library Constitutional Materials Room.

33    Baryshev, *The Epoch of Russo-Japanese Alliance,* 314–315.

and injured along the Trans-Siberian Railroad. According to these plans, if any hindrance occurred in the implementation of this rescue project, Japan would occupy Siberia with force, which meant that a large neutralized area, or buffer zone, could be established in Russia. Gotō advocated imitating the same paradoxical humanitarian policies used by the United States to contain the "hypocritical monster U.S.A. under the cloak of humanitarianism," who held "moral aggressive policies" on other countries. That is, Gotō found justification for the exercise of military force in the activities of nonmilitary and humanitarian efforts in the region, including food and medical support.[34]

The Bolshevik regime, which was established as a result of the Russian November Revolution, negotiated a cease-fire with Germany and seceded from the Allies in December 1919. England and France continued to ask Japan and the United States to dispatch troops to re-build the Eastern battle line. The United States was always cautious about troops dispatched by the Japanese Government, thinking that it would lead to a full-scale dispatch.

Meanwhile, on 5 February 1918, Foreign Minister Motono Ichirō – without permission from Prime Minister Terauchi – unofficially questioned the United States on the Siberian Intervention. This aggravated the relationship between Motono and Terauchi. Gotō, who agreed with Terauchi, said that the idea of immediately dispatching troops, in accordance with the requests from the great powers (including England and France), was, as Motono said, different from the opinions held by the Prime Minister. From the viewpoints of Terauchi and Gotō, even if Japan did dispatch troops, the decision had to be autonomous. "The opinion of Motono on dispatching troops is a joint operation with England and France, not self defense" said Gotō. Motono's opinion on dispatching troops was in keeping with that of England and France, so Gotō saw it as a deviation from the goal of defending Japan.[35]

In the Temporary Foreign Affairs Investigation Committee held on 9 and 17 March, Motono's opinions were rejected and a decision was adopted that Japan would not comply with the request – even from England and France – for dispatching troops, if self-defense was not necessary. Gotō reported to the elder statesman Yamagata, who was concerned about opposition from the

---

34    "Papers of Count Itō Miyoji; the opinion of the Home Minister, Gotō" ("Documents collected by constitutional history editing committee" 589, stored in the National Diet Library Constitutional Materials Room). Izao Tomio, *Study on Primary Siberian Intervention: Appearance and Development of New Salvation Army* (Kyūshū University Press, 2003), 18–22.

35    Tsurumi Yūsuke, *Authentic Biography,* vol. 6 (Fujiwara Shoten, 2005) 453–454. *Gotō's diary,* "Documents related to Gotō Shimpei," 31-2-16.

United States and was very careful about dispatching Japanese troops, that "fortunately there was no point in today's decision which disagreed with your opinions and the discussions were very practical and carefully thought out. The decision made in this discussion should be welcomed."[36]

Motono resigned from the role of Foreign Minister in April. Three people, Chinda Sutemi, Uchida Yasuya (Kōsai), and Itō Miyoji, were nominated as successors to Motono. Itō rejected the nominations and recommended Gotō, who was appointed the first Foreign Minister from a non-diplomat agency in the 20th century, which was a bolt out of the blue for the Foreign Ministry.

However Gotō, who had been considered "heretic" by the Foreign Ministry, began to be influenced by the ideas of the Foreign Ministry almost as soon as he joined. In the Foreign Ministry, even after Motono resigned, Matsuoka Yōsuke and Kimura Eiichi strongly agreed to the Siberian Intervention. In June, Gotō changed his principle to not seeking approval from the United States before making decisions. Gotō had Kimura make a statement on the Siberian Intervention; however, the details of the statement were similar to those written by Motono. The statement was as follows: it would be a plan for the distant future that the basis of Japanese diplomacy was still the Anglo-Japanese Alliance even after the First World War, and insufficient areas in the Anglo-Japanese Alliance were covered with the American-Japanese Entente. The Siberian Intervention would be necessary to strengthen the "basis of the Japan-England-US alliance. If England, France and Italy persuaded the US and joint suggestions were made by those four countries, it would be hard to reject implementing the Siberian Intervention."[37]

Gotō added wording about a "counter plan against activities of the US in Siberia," which was not in the statement put out previously by Motono. This phrase meant that there was no doubt that the United States would carry out considerable economic activities over the Far East Russian Territory using large amounts of capital, even though the US insisted that the US had no ambition over Siberia. Hence, it was necessary for Japan now to take a powerful

---

36   Hara Keiichirō ed., *Diary of Hara Takashi*, vol. 4, 9 March and 17 March 1918 (Fukumura Shuppan, 1965). Letter from Gotō Shimpei to Yamagata Aritomo, 17 March 1918, *Documents related to Yamagata Aritomo*, vol. 2, 122–123.

37   "The Documents on Japanese Foreign Policy" 1918, vol. 1 (Ministry of Foreign Affairs of Japan, in 1968), 848–859. "*Authentic Biography, vol. 6*, 483–512. Hosoya Chihiro, *Historic Study on Siberian Intervention* (Iwanami shoten, 2005), 159–160. Hara Teruyuki, *Siberian Intervention: Revolution and Interference, 1917–1922* (Chikumashobō, 1989), 292. Izao Tomio, *Study on Primary Siberian Intervention*, 26.

stand in Siberia, regardless of whether Japan would make a partnership with or oppose the US in the future.

To oppose the US dispatching technicians to rescue Russians, Gotō enthusiastically started talking about rescuing Russia. During a June 28 meeting, Gotō told Russo-Asian Bank President Aleksei I. Putilov that food and clothes would be sent to Russia as a project by the Russo-Japanese Friendship Association and the Red Cross.[38]

Although the US did not appear to agree with Japan dispatching troops, Gotō tried to overcome the Temporary Foreign Affairs Investigation Committee to support the Siberian Intervention. When Gotō talked on July 2 with Itō Miyoji, who participated in the Committee as a representative of the Privy Council, he stated that he believed that now was the best time for Japan to establish another autonomous policy without being bound by diplomacy which emphasized the US on the issue of dispatching troops, and to move forward within Japanese statements until then. He also stated that rescuing Russians should be added to the goals for the dispatching of troops, along with the goal of Japan's self-defense.[39]

Foreign Minister Gotō ordered that the State Affairs Bureau of the Foreign Ministry should present a report on Japan's Russia policy as it related to Czechoslovakia. The report insisted that Japan should dispatch troops based on a sense of caution against the US's moving into Russia, and presented a plan for dispatching troops to rescue the Czecho-Slavik Army. As enemy activity could not be confirmed, dispatching troops for self-defense was not an adequate reason. The principle of dispatching troops only for self-defense, on which Gotō depended when he criticized Motono, was no longer an absolute requirement.[40]

Under this situation, the July 8 suggestion made by the US to rescue the Czecho-Slavik Army by dispatching troops jointly, meant the removal of the greatest hindrance for "opposition from the US" on Japan's dispatching troops. After this, in Japan, there were discussions on which should be adopted: "limited dispatch of troops," where the number of soldiers was 7000 as requested by US with the area of dispatch to be Vladivostok and the surrounding area, or a "full-scale dispatch of troops," where the area to be dispatched was expanded

38    Izao Tomio, *Study on Primary Siberian Intervention,* 31.

39    Ibid. *Authentic Biography,* vol. 6, 517–528.

40    "The Documents on Japanese Foreign Policy" 1918, vol. 1, 894–898. Izao Tomio, *Study on Primary Siberian Intervention,* 27.

to eastern Siberia and all regions of northern Manchuria to the east of Lake Baikal, with the number of soldiers to be increased.[41]

When Itō Miyoji and Foreign Minister Gotō met on 10 July, they agreed with each other because both of them intended to carry out the suggestion of the US immediately – as well as "full-scale dispatch of troops" to Vladivostok and Siberia. They defined the decision as sending one division, with the understanding that when reinforcement would become necessary, they would double that. The reply given to the US was based on the following opinions of Foreign Minister Gotō, and adopted in an extraordinary cabinet meeting on July 12: (1) dispatching the same number of troops as the US was not acceptable, and the Japanese military force should be in the superior position and have command; and (2) the areas where troops were dispatched should not be limited to Vladivostok.[42]

In the Temporary Foreign Affairs Investigation Committee held on 16 to 18 July in the emperor's court, Hara Takashi and Makino Nobuaki, who supported the idea of a limited dispatch of troops, opposed Terauchi, Gotō, and Itō, who were in favor of a full-scale dispatch of troops. In an effort to prevent sounding too blatant in the reply to the US, Hara's assertions were added to the reply modified by Itō. It was then signed by all of the committee members. From the draft made by Foreign Minister Gotō, Itō eliminated the following statements, to avoid provoking the US: concerning troop strength, "when dispatching troops to Vladivostok, the Japanese Government would like to believe that the US Government does not intend to make it a condition that the Japanese Army have the same number of soldiers as the American Army," and concerning the geographical range of the troops, "the Japanese Government has determined to immediately dispatch troops to areas other than Vladivostok as needed."[43]

On July 25, the reply to Japan from the US was given by the acting Secretary of State, to Ambassador to the US Ishii Kikujirō. The reply said that the number of Japanese soldiers dispatched first should be within from 10,000 to 12,000, and that Japan must consult with the US to increase that number.[44] Also, the US wanted to "limit the dispatch of troops" to Vladivostok. The number of Japanese

41    Hosoya, *Historic Study on Siberian Intervention,* 165–166.

42    Kobayashi Tatsuo ed., *Suiusō Diary: Record of Temporary Foreign Affairs Investigation Committee* (Hara Shobō, 1966), 126–128. *Authentic Biography,* vol. 6, 534. *Hara Diary,* 13 July 1918. Hosoya, *Historic Study on Siberian Intervention,* 166–169.

43    *Suiusō Diary,* 135–161,189–90. *Hara Diaryō* 16, 17, and 18 July 1918. *Documents on Japanese Foreign Policy, 1918,* vol. 1, 919–921. Hosoya, *Historic Study on Siberian Intervention,* 173–187.

44    *Documents on Japanese Foreign Policy, 1918,* vol. 1, 930–934.

soldiers the US requested, 12,000 (equivalent to a mixed brigade), was about one-fourth of the upper limit (two divisions) of troops promised by Terauchi during the Temporary Foreign Affairs Investigation Committee meeting.

Gotō was very disappointed when he heard from American Ambassador Rolland S. Morris through his son-in-law Tsurumi Yūsuke that American President T. Woodrow Wilson disagreed with the proposed increase in the number of soldiers. The next day, Gotō reconsidered, and told Tsurumi that he did not care if the American President disagreed with the increase, and he would "make the things be carried out in the way which he intended to." Gotō summarized opinions of the Japanese Government again, and he finally decided to go through with the Siberian Intervention under the US conditions described in the reply from the US.[45]

Inside of the Terauchi Cabinet, there were complaints that the Temporary Foreign Affairs Investigation Committee, having political power even though it was just an advisory body, had decided to dispatch troops jointly with US. Then, conflict erupted when the American Government made a special request to Japan concerning the reply by Gotō. In the cabinet meeting on 31 July, Foreign Minister Gotō advocated for US and Japan to dispatch the troops jointly; other cabinet members criticized Gotō. Ultimately the draft declaration on dispatching troops, which contained one sentence implying possibility of Japan's voluntary dispatching of troops, was presented to the Temporary Foreign Affairs Investigation Committee on 1 August.

Itō Miyoji's creative and acrobatic compromises solved the problem. On 1 August, the Temporary Foreign Affairs Investigation Committee consented to the US reply on condition that Japanese troops were expected to be dispatched to areas other than Vladivostok to rescue the Czecho-Slavik Army, and to be increased if state of affairs changed. This enabled the committee to allow the US reply to stand. For any Siberian Intervention other than Vladivostok, Hara considered that a prior discussion with the US was necessary, whereas Prime Minister Terauchi thought that after-the-fact notice was enough. This was a very equivocal decision.[46]

---

45    *Authentic Biography,* vol. 6, 544–551.
46    *Diary of Den Kenjirō,* 18, 19, and 31 July 1918 and 1 August 1918 (National Diet Library Constitutional Materials Room). Izao Tomio, *Study on Primary Siberian Intervention,* 29, 45–46. On August 7th, Gotō left in the middle of the Cabinet meeting and announced his resignation, because he had mistakenly got the idea that sarcastic remarks were made to him, due to misunderstanding criticism of the US by cabinet ministers including the Prime Minister, Terauchi (*Den Diary,* 7 August 1918). *Documents on Japanese Foreign Policy, 1918,* vol.1 935–936. *Suiusō Diary,* 169–180. *Hara Diary,* 1 August 1918 and 16

Once Japan began to dispatch troops, the military started self-rotation operations, resulting in an increase in the number of soldiers. As a result, the
expansion troops outside of Vladivostok, and the increase in the number of
soldiers without prior discussion with the Temporary Foreign Affairs
Investigating Committee or the US, the number of Japanese Army soldiers dispatched to Siberia or northern Manchuria increased to about 73,400, until the
successor to the Terauchi Cabinet, the Hara Cabinet took action to decrease
the number. Foreign diplomacy was subject to military needs.[47]

Foreign Minister Gotō's speech that was made during the first meeting of
the Temporary Siberia Economic Aid Committee on 21 August suggested that
the Siberian Intervention was a foreign war prosecuted for a new justice. Gotō
stated that these troops comprised of armies from various countries, mainly
Japan and the US, were a "new Salvation Army," "in accordance with the new
principle of people of the world being all brothers," and that their goals were
completely different from that of a punitive expedition and invasion. The
Allied force mainly comprised of Japan and US Armies would rescue the
Czecho-Slavik Army, which was a member of the allied force, and supported
the cause of self-determination. The Siberian Intervention was justified as providing aid to Russians exhausted from revolutions.[48]

To obtain local Siberian support for Japan, a materials supply project was
conducted, while the Japanese Army in the field and the Temporary Siberia
Economic Aid Committee in Japan cooperated with each other. A large amount
of money was injected for economic aid to Siberia because of negative propaganda against Japan resulting from its invasion of Russia. As Foreign Minister,
Gotō was deeply involved in these activities.[49]

## Conclusion

Why did Gotō, who was "Pro-Russian," force the Siberian Intervention? Kitaoka
Shinichi said that there were few politicians who had the correct view of
the epochal characteristics of the Russian Revolution, and the potency of the

_____

     September 1918. Hosoya, *Historic Study on Siberian Intervention,* 191–197. Hara, *Siberian
     Intervention,* 364–365.

47    Hosoya, *Historic Study on Siberian Intervention,* 207–208. Hara, *Siberian Intervention,*
     378–381.

48    *Authentic Biography,* vol. 6, 584–590. Izao Tomio, *Study on Primary Siberian Intervention,*
     34–35.

49    Izao Tomio, *Study on Primary Siberian Intervention,* 143–146.

revolutionary regime. He said that Gotō saw the revolutionary regime as a temporary regime that had no real foundation. He also assumed that Gotō was horrified at the possibilities, considering the external policies of the Russian Revolution, and that China and Russia were connected with each other because of their anti-imperialism and anti-Japanese feelings and would threaten the Japanese interests in Manchuria, including the Manchurian Railway.

The real reason why Gotō, who promoted economic association with Russia after the Russo-Japanese War, carried out the Siberian Intervention, has not yet been conclusively identified. As we can understand from the process described in this paper and the assumptions made by Kitaoka, Gotō's policies relating to Russia were not limited simply to Japan's relationship to Russia, but there is little doubt that the policies were a "function" of those related to China, and related to England and the US (as represented in the autonomous foreign diplomacy theory).

Gotō carried out the Siberian Intervention because he misread the revolutionary administrative power in the Russian Revolution as transient. When he discovered that dispatching troops failed, and that the revolutionary administrative power was strong, he began to seek partnership with Russia again. In 1923, Gotō, then mayor of Tokyo city, invited the Bolshevik diplomat Adolf Ioffe and seized the opportunity for the resumption of diplomatic ties with Russia. The turbulent relationship between Japan and Russia, of opposition and cooperation in the 1910s can be clearly seen from a study of Gotō's life.

# The Wilson Administration and the Mandate Question in the Pacific

*Struggle among the Powers over the Disposition of Former German Colonies*

Shusuke Takahara

### The US Mandate Plan and the Allies' Resistance

During the Paris Peace Conference of 1919, there was controversy among the victorious Powers over whether the former German islands in the South Pacific north of the equator should be transferred to Japan. It was one of the most important points of dispute regarding the territories in East Asia and the Pacific. Much scholarship exists on the disposition of these islands in the Pacific, and it focuses on either connections to Japan's advance to the south (*Nanshin-ron*) or on the validity of the mandate system itself.[1] However, most previous studies have been Europe-centric and only shed light on the decision-making process involving the European Powers. Few studies have elucidated how US policymakers observed and dealt with this question,[2] and most scholarship haphazardly assesses the

---

1   Some important contributions have appeared in recent Japanese scholarship. Sakai described Japan's position in Asia and the Pacific on the basis of findings in the Australian archives, while Tomatsu focused upon the entire period of Japan's role as a mandatory from the Japanese perspective. Gabe Masaaki, "Nihon no Micuroneshia senryō to 'Nanshin' (1), (2)," *Hōgaku kenkyū* 55–57 (July 1982): 70–89; 55–58 (August 1982): 67–87; Imaizumi Yumiko, "Nanyō guntō inin tōchi seisaku no keisei," in *Iwanami kōza kindai Nihon to shokuminchi 4: Tōgo to shihai no ronri* (Tokyo: Iwanami Shoten, 1992), pp. 51–81; Sakai Kazuomi, *Kindai Nihon gaikō to Ajia Taiheiyō chitsujo* (Kyoto: Shōwadō, 2009), chapter 4; Tōmatsu Haruo, *Nihon Teikoku to inin tōchi* (Nagoya: Nagoya Daigaku Shuppankai, 2011), chapter 2.

2   Fifield and Pomeroy brilliantly clarified US policy in the Pacific but paid little attention to Japanese policy makers. Only this author's work covers both the US and Japanese perspectives. Russell Fifield, "Disposal of the Carolines, Marshalls, and Marianas at the Paris Peace Conference," *American Historical Review* 51–53 (April 1946): 472–479; Earl S. Pomeroy, "American Policy Respecting the Marshalls, Carolines, and Marianas, 1898–1941," *Pacific Historical Review* 17–21 (February 1948): 43–53; Takahara Shusuke, *Wiruson gaikō to Nihon: risō to genjitsu no aida, 1913–1921* [Wilson Diplomacy and Japan: Ideal and Reality, 1913–1921] (Tokyo: Sōbunsha, 2006), chapter 4.

© KONINKLIJKE BRILL NV, LEIDEN, 2014 | DOI 10.1163/9789004274273_009

intentions of Japanese policymakers. This study takes a multiperspective, multinational approach that both addresses Japan's assertive diplomacy and shows that Japanese obstinacy, together with a similar stance from the British Dominions, helped force the Woodrow Wilson administration to resolve the mandate question.

## US Views of the Japanese Military Occupation in the Pacific

In August 1914, Japan declared war against Germany and occupied Germany's Pacific islands north of the equator. The Japanese Foreign Ministry feared that the occupation would aggravate Japan-US relations, while the Imperial Japanese Navy actively implemented the occupation to promote trade with the islands and expand Japan's defensive perimeter against the United States. From 1915 to 1917, Japan asserted its territorial rights in communications with Britain, France, and Russia, and secured the authority to claim territorial sovereignty over the German Pacific islands at the upcoming Peace Conference. The diplomatic blunder over the Triple Intervention of 1895 had imprinted an indelible impression on Japanese policymakers; hence, in this case Japan ensured that it established its position as a participant in "secret diplomacy" and "imperial diplomacy."[3]

Initially, the United States did not criticize the Japanese occupation of the islands, but, upon realizing the strategic importance of the Pacific islands, US policymakers gradually took precautions against Japan's territorial expansion in the region. They generally agreed that they would not overlook the Japanese occupation of the islands after the Great War. However, their proposed measures for the disposition of the islands varied widely.

President Wilson was reluctant to agree to the United States assuming ownership of these German territories, but he stridently opposed their annexation by Japan, in part because he realized that Japanese occupation could pose a danger to US interests in the Philippines. Moreover, while Wilson believed that the United States could enlighten the Filipinos through the implementation of policies imbued with supposedly universal virtues, such as freedom and

---

3  Gaimusho tsūshō kyoku hen, *Dokuryō nanyō shoto jijyō* (June, 1915), 2–10; Imaizumi Yumiko, "Nihon no gunsei ki nanyō guntō tōchi (1914–1922)," *Kokusai kankeigaku kenkyū* 17 (Supl.) (1990): 1–20; Hirama Yōichi, *Daiichiji Sekai Taisen to Nihon Kaigun* (Tokyo: Keiō Gijyuku Daigaku Shuppankai, 1998), chapter 2; J. Charles Schencking, "Bureaucratic Politics, Military Budgets and Japan's Southern Advance: The Imperial Navy's Seizure of German Micronesia in the First World War," *War in History* 5–3 (July 1998): 308–326.

democracy, he doubted that Japan could accomplish the same if it claimed the former German islands.

US strategic outposts such as Guam and the Philippines would be endangered if Japan occupied the German Pacific islands. Wilson "had shown that he was by no means prepared to accept the Japanese Treaty, and was doubtful whether Japan could be admitted there even in the capacity of a mandatory power."[4] Besides, he was deeply concerned with the situation because the islands, which could serve as a Japanese naval base, were located between Hawai'i and the Philippines, and were much closer to Hawai'i than the Pacific coast.[5] The president sought to avoid such an old-fashioned disposal as "annexation" by the victorious Powers, as he groped for the best possible solution to remove a threat to US national security right from the start.

The US Naval Planning Board had, from early on, warned of the Japanese military administration of the Pacific islands. During the war, Japan had prohibited foreign vessels (including those belonging to Britain, Japan's ally) from calling at the islands without prior permission. This situation alarmed the staff members of the US Naval Intelligence Division (NID) and Army War Plans Division (WPD) that were engaged in the strategic planning of the US military effort. In order to check Japanese activity, the NID proposed an inspection tour of the islands by US naval officers stationed in Guam.[6] The WPD argued that it would be extremely difficult for the United States to seize the islands if Japan completely fortified them, and suggested that the United States occupy at least the Marianas.[7] Anti-Japanese alarmists in the navy argued that the United States must block Japan's occupation and fortification of the Pacific islands in order to secure a US naval base in the Pacific. To this end, they proposed placing the islands under US or international control.

Nevertheless, the US naval delegation at the Paris Peace Conference regarded the anti-Japanese alarmists' argument as merely the basic principles of naval strategy, and concluded that the claims derived from the parochial interests of

---

4 "Draft Minutes of Meeting of the Imperial War Cabinet 47," 30 December 1918, in Arthur S. Link, ed., *The Papers of Woodrow Wilson* (hereafter cited as *PWW*), Vol. *53* (Princeton, NJ: Princeton University Press, 1985), 562–563.

5 Entry in the diary of David Hunter Miller, dated 30 January 1919, in David Hunter Miller, *My Diary at the Conference of Paris, Vol. 1* (New York, 1924), 100.

6 "Memorandum for the Chief of Naval Operations," by Rear Admiral Roger Welles, 25 July 1918, RG 45, Naval Records Collection of the Office of Naval Records and Library, C-45-12, National Archives (hereafter cited as NA).

7 Planning Commander to Chief of Naval Operations, "The Terms and Conditions that Should be Insisted Upon by the United States in Armistice and Peace Conference Following the Present War, Problem Fall 1918," RG 80, Navy Department, General Board Papers, Box 438, NA.

the Navy. The Chief of Naval Operations, William S. Benson, a US naval representative at the Paris Peace Conference, maintained that nonfortification of the islands would not create a problem even if Japan conquered them. In addition, William Sims, an Anglophile Commander of the US naval forces operating in Europe, dismissed the threat of Japanese expansion on the grounds that Japan could only initiate a surprise attack, not a full-scale war, in the Pacific.[8] Therefore, high-ranking US naval officers reached a compromise to include the nonfortification and indirect administration of the islands through a mandate system under the League of Nations, which went on to become the primary argument of the US Navy. At the Paris Peace Conference, the anti-Japanese posture assumed by middle-ranking US naval officers was considered a trivial matter and thus was excluded.

Some US naval officers considered the Japanese acquisition of the Pacific islands to be a military threat, while the State Department officials reviewed the case from both diplomatic and military viewpoints. The Third Assistant Secretary of State, Breckinridge Long, was extremely concerned about the commercial disadvantage faced by the United States.[9] Since Germany had no naval power and would take years to recover from its defeat in the Great War, according to Long, the islands should be temporarily returned to Germany and later transferred to the United States. Long regarded Guam not as a naval base but as the key location for trans-Pacific cable and telegraphic communication. The cable station in Guam, established in 1917, had often experienced problems with its civilian telegraphic link to the Philippines, which forced the US naval cable station to act as its substitute. Therefore, the United States sought additional cable-connecting points in the Pacific in addition to those in Guam, which led to its claim for free access to Yap.[10] Long looked upon the problem of a defective network along the cable stations with seriousness and proposed its significant improvement as a top priority.

While Long maintained US rule over the Pacific islands, Stanley K. Hornbeck and Edward T. Williams, who were Far Eastern specialists in the State Department, argued that the islands should be administered under a more

---

8    William Sims to Bradley Fiske, 8 October, 1920, William Sims Papers, Box 69, Manuscript
     Division, Library of Congress (hereafter cited as MDLC).

9    "Memorandum on International Telegraphic Communication" by Breckinridge Long
     (enclosed in a letter from Long to Lansing dated 25 November 1918), *FRUS, 1919: Paris Peace
     Conference* (hereafter cited as *PPC*), *Vol. 1* (Washington, D.C.: Government Printing Office,
     1942), 535–538.

10   "Memorandum on Wire and Radio Communications" by Walter S. Rogers of the
     Committee on Public Information, February 12 1919, Woodrow Wilson Papers, Series 5B,
     Reel 393, MDLC.

universal system and institution. They particularly highlighted the resonance between the Pacific islands and Shandong problem. Hornbeck believed that the islands should be administered under a system of Anglo-American support. However, since he was aware of the difficulty in achieving that arrangement, he offered an alternative plan. Neither independence nor the restoration of control to Germany would benefit the natives, so the only realistic solution was that "the islands should be put under the jurisdiction of the League of Nations."[11] He advocated that the islands should be controlled by more than one mandatory power, guaranteeing an open door, and nonfortification of the islands. In this respect, Hornbeck's recommendation was comprehensive and expressed grave concerns to Long and the navy advisors. Further, Long was anxious about America's commercial disadvantage. The naval advisors, vigilant against Japan's military threat, frowned upon the concept of international administration.

Williams doubted the recommendations offered by Long and Hornbeck. He opposed Long's argument for US control following the brief restoration of German ownership. He contended that "if the islands held by Japan must be returned to Germany, why not also those taken by Great Britain?...Consistency requires that the two groups of islands should be treated upon the same principle." Williams believed that Australia would not accept the return of German New Guinea to Germany. He also suggested that "it should be done without any intention upon our [American] part to purchase the islands subsequently from Germany if the islands should be returned to Germany...Such action would at once subject us to the charge of bad faith."[12] Williams almost agreed with Hornbeck's plan owing to his deep-seated distrust of Japan; however, he did not admit to Japan's position as mandatory of the Pacific islands north of the equator. Japan's mandate over of the islands would necessarily pose an enormous strategic threat to Hawai'i and the Philippines. He claimed that Japan's mandate should be denied on moral, not legal, grounds.[13] Williams thought it would be advisable to place all the islands "under the protection of the proposed League of Nations to be governed by some organ to be created by the League."[14]

11    Stanley Hornbeck and Edward Williams, "Far East – Problems and Recommendations," undated, Hornbeck Papers, Box 329, Stanford University.

12    "Memorandum" by Edward Williams, (enclosed in a letter from Williams to Lansing, dated 13 January 1919), undated, Lansing Papers, Box 3, Princeton University.

13    Williams to Commissioners, 14 March 1919, 185.1151/6, RG 59, Department of State, NA.

14    "Memorandum" by Edward Williams, undated, Hornbeck Papers, Box 330, Stanford University.

Secretary of State Robert Lansing objected to the disposition of the Pacific islands through the mandate system under the League of Nations and submitted a memorandum to President Wilson outlining the problem of the mandate plan in February 1919.[15] Lansing doubted whether the League could indeed exercise the powers of a sovereign state as the mandate system implied. The system needed further definition regarding the relationship between the League and a sovereign state. He also believed it would be advisable to separate the Peace Treaty with the Central Powers from the deliberations over the League Covenant. The mandate system needed to be carefully discussed together with the League Covenant.[16] As a specialist in international law, Lansing doubted that the League could assume the sovereign powers of a nation-state. He preferred to transfer the territories by treaty rather than through the mandate system.

As shown above, the policymakers of the Wilson administration had differing views regarding the disposition of the Pacific islands north of the equator. Middle-class naval officers feared that a mandate would allow de facto occupation of the islands by Japan from a strategic perspective. Not every policymaker, however, shared these concerns. Everyone seemed vigilant against Japan's control of the islands, but their understanding of the situation and their proposed measures for resolving this problem varied. As the deliberation of the mandate question progressed, the US plans, together with the conditions, converged toward the mandate system.

## The Making of the Mandate Plan

### Origins of the Mandate Plan

The argument over the mandates emerged in Britain just before the outbreak of the Great War. Mainly expressed by the Liberal and Labour Parties in Britain, they emphasized the international responsibility to safeguard the less-developed peoples. John Hobson and Philip Kerr, who presided over the well-known British political magazine, *The Round Table*, played a central role in this discussion. Kerr, who became the private secretary of British Prime Minister David Lloyd George in June 1914, proposed the formulation of a system that enabled the development of the backward peoples under the tutelage of

---

15    "Some Problems of the Mandatory System," 2 February 1919, Lansing Papers, Private Memoranda, Box 64, MDLC.

16    Lansing to Wilson, 31 January 1919, *PWW, Vol. 54* (Princeton, NJ: Princeton University Press, 1986), 400–402.

advanced nations. The Labour Party adopted this argument in 1917 and became the most influential advocate of the mandate system the following year. This plan had a profound effect on the origins of the Smuts plan.

President Wilson also strongly supported the mandate principle well before the Peace Conference. He approved of the Cobb-Lippmann memorandum, which specifically defined the contents of the Fourteen Points in October 1918.[17] Article 5 of the memorandum prescribed the following:

> A colonial power acts not as owner of its colonies, but as trustee for the natives and for the interests of the society of nations....The terms on which colonial administration is conducted are a matter of international concern...and the peace conference may, therefore, write a code of colonial conduct binding upon all colonial powers.[18]

For Wilson, the mandate system had many attractive features. It was ideal for defeated Germany because it meant that the former German colonies were to be handed over not to the enemy but to the League. When the time came, Germany – as a member of the League – could recover its voice in administering them. Liberal reformers around the world also welcomed this system as a symbol of self-determination requested by the subordinated peoples. The great powers expected that the disposition of former German colonies through the League would not make them imperialistic but would, rather, create a favorable impression on world opinion.

In this way, US and British policymakers, bearing in mind its idealistic character, admitted the needs of the mandate system and agreed to the plan in principle. As they lacked territorial ambition over the European continent, the United States and Britain could set a high moral standard for France and Italy, who regarded the territorial issue as crucial. Anglo-American cooperation in the colonial disposition, however, was not so strong. They had no common understanding of the practical application of the mandate system.

### The Smuts Plan and Wilson

If the mandate plan seemed perfect in general theory, problems quickly arose when it came to working out the particulars. In the Council of Ten of 24 January 1919, Australian Prime Minister William Hughes requested New Guinea;

---

17    House to Wilson, 29 October 1918, *PWW, Vol. 51*, (Princeton, NJ: Princeton University Press, 1985), 495–504.

18    Lawrence Gelfand, *The Inquiry: American Preparations for Peace, 1917–1919* (New Haven, CT: Yale University Press, 1963), 229.

New Zealand Prime Minister William Massey called for Samoa; and South African Prime Minister Louis Botha asked for the former German colonies in Southwest Africa.[19] On the other hand, President Wilson asserted "nonannexation" and "self-determination." At this point, their antagonism reached a climax. Lloyd George was worried about the situation and sought help to ensure that the Dominions would not wreck the conference. On the part of the Unites States, George Beer of the American Commission to Negotiate Peace at Paris, following the President's instructions, worked toward Anglo-American negotiation.[20]

The above paragraphs give a brief background to the creation of the mandate plan, also known as the Smuts plan. The Smuts plan was a scheme drafted by South African Foreign Minister General Jan Smuts, for the disposal of colonies. While it affirmed the mandate principles, it divided the mandated areas into three parts (Class A, Class B, and Class C) and determined the administrative policy and mandatory state for each in proportion to their political and economic conditions and location.[21] There were exceptions in some regions, but the basic objects were "nonannexation" and "self-determination." While persuading the Dominions to concede, Lloyd George suggested a compromise to the Smuts plan and tried to break the stalemate.

The birth of the Smuts plan dates back to before the peace conference. In December 1918, Smuts wrote a pamphlet entitled "The League of Nations: A Practical Suggestion," which contained the outlines of the mandate system. In fact, about one-third of this pamphlet dealt with the mandate plan under the League. Its contents were rather innovative and epochal, considering that imperialism was quite common for the majority of the people at the time.[22]

---

19   The Council of Ten implies the conference of the Big Five held in the French foreign ministry (Quai d'Orsay). The Council, which was initiated on 20 January 1919, comprised the heads of government and foreign ministers of the five major Powers – Britain, France, the United States, Italy, and Japan – and discussed major issues. It ended with the opening of the Council of the Big Four, which was established by a proposal by Wilson and Clemenceau in March 1919. Thomas A. Bailey, *Woodrow Wilson and the Lost Peace* (New York: Macmillan Co., 1944), p.137; The Council of Ten, 24 January 1919, *FRUS, 1919: PPC, Vol. 3*, 718–728; Entry in the diary of George L. Beer, dated 29 January 1919, in James T. Shotwell Papers, Rare Book and Manuscript Library, Columbia University.

20   Entry in the diary of George L. Beer, dated 29 January 1919, James T. Shotwell Papers, Rare Book and Manuscript Library, Columbia University.

21   "Draft Resolutions in Reference to Mandates," 30 January 1919, in *FRUS, 1919: PPC, Vol. 3*, 795–796.

22   Elizabeth Van Maanen-Helmer, *The Mandates System in Relation to Africa & the Pacific Islands* (London: P.S. King, 1929), chapter 2; George Curry, "Woodrow Wilson, Jan Smuts, and the Versailles Settlement," *American Historical Review* 66–74 (July 1961): 968–986.

Wilson focused on the Smuts proposal and decided to incorporate it into the League Covenant, which was still being drafted, although he made some substantive changes, such as the omission of Russia and Austria-Hungary, and the addition of a clause for former German colonies.[23]

However, it should be pointed out that the Smuts plan was adopted beyond the drafter's intention. The original plan intended to apply the mandate system only to Hungary, Turkey, and the countries separated from Russia. It considered the former German colonies, such as those in Africa and the Pacific, as not applicable to the plan. Nevertheless, Wilson oversimplified the Smuts plan and gave it a universal and fundamental application without exception.

However, there was a difference in what the Powers and Wilson expected from the Smuts plan. The Powers recognized the value of the plan as annexation with diversity depending upon the area and the extent of cultural development. Wilson recognized the value of the plan as nonannexation, which set the applicable scope of the mandate system under the League of Nations. As seen above, the Smuts plan originally included variations in the types of mandates. However, both Wilson and the Powers regarded it as having a singular character, the former seeing the essence as nonannexation, the latter as annexation. This gap triggered a conflict between the United States and the British Dominions.

### Various Responses to the Mandate Plan

*Wilson's Mandate Plan: "Nonannexation" and "Self-determination"*
During the pre-conference discussion with Britain in December 1918, President Wilson explained the contents of Point 5 of his Fourteen Points. He maintained that former German colonies should not be ceded fully to one specific country. Wilson urged that all colonies formerly belonging to Germany should come under the trusteeship of the League of Nations and be administered by mandatories. He believed that former German colonies were the common property of the League and that they should be governed by small nations under specific international supervision. Wilson's original plan supposed neutral nations like Holland and those in Scandinavia to be the mandatories.[24]

---

23  According to the diary of Edith Benham Helms (Wilson's private secretary), Wilson carried the Smuts pamphlet on his visit to Italy and began reading it on 1 January 1919. Entry in the diary of Edith Benham Helms dated 2 January 1919, *PWW, Vol. 53*, 588–589; Entry in the diary of Dr. Grayson dated 6 January 1919, *PWW, Vol. 53*, 621–622; Entry in the diary of Edward M. House dated 8 January 1919, House Diary, House Papers, Yale University.

24  Charles Seymour, *Letters from the Paris Peace Conference* (New Haven: Yale University Press, 1965), p.25; Bailey, op. cit., 168.

At the same time, the mandate plan closely matched the US tradition of trusteeship and provisional conservation. Both its historic origins in the rejection of British rule and its experience in Cuba and the Philippines left the United States wary of rule by external powers. However, these experiences also induced the country to retain a missionary sense. Thus, at the time, most people in the United States felt that progressivism and imperialism complemented each other. Wilson, who relied heavily on idealistic and humanitarian measures to spread democracy and commerce, sympathized with such beliefs. In its earliest days, the weak and vulnerable government that existed under the Articles of Confederation had maintained the unity of the first thirteen states in part because it had been the trustee for a much larger expanse of land. For the same reason, Wilson believed that the mandate plan would guarantee the success of the League of Nations. Moreover, Wilson's political thought was shaped by various factors: his Presbyterian background, William E. Gladstone's British liberalism, and his sympathy for Edmund Burke's conservatism. Besides, "as a Virginian and a Southern Democrat, he believed in the right of secession in his bones."[25] Therefore, Wilson was largely sympathetic to the rights and liberties of small nations.

With this mindset, Wilson defined the mandate system as follows: "It was not intended to exploit any people" nor was it intended "to exercise arbitrary sovereignty over any people"; if anything, it meant that "the world was acting as trustee through a mandatory" and the League "would be in charge of the whole administration until the day when the true wishes of the inhabitants could be ascertained." Wilson extolled the development of the colonies under British support, rather than the large costs Britain expended on its colonies. Stating that General Smuts "had rightly compared the British Empire to a League of Nations," he criticized the argument for annexation.[26]

Wilson did not seek to apply the principle of self-determination to the former colonies without restriction. He granted the rights of self-determination to developed areas like Czechoslovakia, but not to non-European areas, because he believed that the people living there were not civilized. Wilson regarded the creation of a new nation as a progressive process of historical development. He believed that a strong political leadership and sense of

---

25    Alfred Cobban, *National Self-Determination* (London: Oxford University Press, 1944), 62–66.

26    The Council of Ten, "Minutes of Meeting," 27 January 1919, *FRUS, 1919: PPC, Vol. 3*, 740–741, 747–748.

unified history, rather than a common race and language, were essential for the development of a nation.[27]

However, his principle of self-determination had inherent defects: it had no specific standard, and it contained no guidelines about how the borders of a state should be fixed. It seems that applying the principle of self-determination with ambiguous criteria would only exacerbate the variety of conflicting ethnic problems.[28] Wilson's original mandate plan was to make the "newborn" League of Nations play an essential role as the governing actor, but the victorious Powers viewed this situation as unacceptable and unrealistic. The representatives of the Powers endeavored to ensure the disposition of territories by annexation, lest the principle of self-determination should be applied to the former German colonies.

### British Response: Joint Writing of "Nonannexation" and "Annexation"

The British understood the necessity of the mandate system from early on. However, owing to concerns within the Dominions, the system's contents had yet to be defined. Hence, well before the Paris Peace Conference, the British conveyed to the Unites States the possibility that the Dominions' strong opposition might limit their support for the mandate system. For example, at a meeting with Colonel Edward House, Lloyd George expressed his sympathy for the principle of the mandate system and hoped that the United States would become a mandatory of a former German colony in East Africa. Meanwhile, he claimed that Southwest Africa should be transferred to South Africa and the Pacific islands south of the equator should be handed over to Australia. Otherwise, Lloyd George maintained that the British would confront a "revolution" by the Dominions.[29]

The British Empire at the end of the Great War faced many difficulties. The Dominions' contribution to the war effort was significant, sending about 800,000 men to the war. The disposition of German colonies may have been a peripheral issue to London, but it was a central issue with regard to the

---

27    Kusama Hidesaburo, *Wiruson no kokusai shakai seisaku kōsō* (Nagoya: Nagoya Daigaku Shuppankai, 1990), pp. 84–85; Lloyd Ambrosius, *Wilsonianism: Woodrow Wilson and His Legacy in American Foreign Relations* (New York: Palgrave Macmillan, 2002), 128–131.

28    Harry Notter, *The Origins of the Foreign Policy of Woodrow Wilson* (Baltimore: Johns Hopkins Press, 1937), 651–654; Derek Heater, *National Self-Determination* (London: Macmillan, 1994), 207–209; Betty Miller Unterberger, "Self-Determination," in Alexander DeConde, et al. eds., *Encyclopedia of American Foreign Policy, Vol. 3, Second Edition* (New York: Scribner, 2002), 461–467.

29    Letter from House to Wilson, 30 October 1918, *FRUS, 1919: PPC, Vol. 1*, 407.

Dominions. While the Dominions were not yet fully independent from their home country at the time, they began to act against Britain.

Above all, before the Peace Conference, Australia and New Zealand took for granted that they would receive the Pacific islands south of the equator in return for their contributions. Under these circumstances, in the meetings of the Imperial War Cabinet from November to December 1918, the British held discussions with the Dominions about the disposition of the former German colonies. British and Canadian representatives clearly stated that they would not seek any territory and argued that, in light of a recent surge of global anti-imperialism, if the Dominions laid additional claims for annexation, it would present an unfavorable impression to the world. In order to win US favor regarding the colonial problem, the British and Canadians were ready to accept the mandate plan proposed by the United States. In the meantime, members of Australia, New Zealand, and South Africa strongly requested that they be given the former German colonies. Hughes protested that if the British government abided by its promise to Japan concerning the Pacific islands north of the equator, then it must also keep its promise to the Dominions and allow them to annex the areas in which they had fought during the war. Hughes viewed the Pacific islands as a package and his argument seemed to sway the British government. The Imperial War Cabinet finally agreed to apply the non-annexationist principles of the mandate system to former German colonies except those in Southwest Africa and the Pacific islands.

Opinions in the British Empire were also divided with regard to the reinforcement of US naval power in the Pacific. Britain and Canada, although distrusting the US naval-building program, gave priority to cooperation with the United States, considering the importance of the country in the League of Nations in the postwar world order. Meanwhile, Australia and New Zealand felt threatened by Japan, and supported the Anglo-Japanese Alliance rather than a partnership with the United States as the best measure for peace and stability in the Pacific. Both countries supported this alliance until it was abrogated after the Washington Conference in 1921–22.

In this way, as long as the Empire was not jeopardized, Britain was able to adopt a flexible global policy. It could grant some discretionary powers to the Dominions to satisfy their territorial interests and it could support the League of Nations and seek a cooperative policy with the United States.

### The Japanese Response: A Passive Stance

The emergence of the mandate plan was unexpected and surprising for Japan because it had not only captured the Pacific islands north of the equator, but was, in reality, already controlling them. Moreover, Japan had signed a secret agreement with Britain, France, and Italy after its annexation of the territories that confirmed its possession. Therefore, the Japanese took it for granted that the Pacific islands, as well as Shandong, would be formally ceded to them.[30] In his report after the revelation of the mandate plan, Marquis Saionji Kinmochi, head of the Japanese delegation, confessed that Japan "faced unexpected difficulties" in solving this problem, and the members of the Japanese delegation in Paris were astonished by the unexpected obstacles they now faced in the annexation of the islands.[31]

The Smuts plan attracted the attention of almost all members of the Council of Ten, so they were inclined to accept the plan. With no particular reason for objection, it was difficult for Japan alone to oppose the plan. The Japanese government sought a compromise and accepted the plan after February 1919, because the Japanese delegation began to realize that Wilson's argument was losing support in the Council of Ten.[32] When the disposition of the Smuts plan was officially recognized, on 3 February 1919, the Japanese government forwarded its basic policy to the delegation in Paris, and directed them toward accepting Japan's policy in the Council of Ten. The main points were (1) if Japan requests the transfer of islands, it will have no intention to fortify them and will not deny the principles of equal opportunity; (2) Japan will never accept the occupation or control of the islands by other Powers; and (3) Japan hopes to receive the cooperation of other Powers in this case and has no objection to controlling the islands if the Powers approve of the mandate plan.[33]

In fact, the Japanese delegation in Paris did not disclose its policy for the disposition of the Pacific islands. This reserved tendency can be easily found in

30    Gaimushō rinji chōsabu, *Doku ryō shokuminchi mondai* (17 October 1918), 1–16;. Katō Yōko, "Daiichiji Sekai Taisen chū no 'sengo' kōsō: Kōwa Junbi Iinkai to Shidehara Kijūrō," in Jie Liu and Kawashima Shin, eds., *Between Conflict and Co-Existence Historical Understanding* (Tokyo: University of Tokyo Press, 2013), 127–150.

31    In his report on the deliberation of the mandate plan at Paris, Vice Minister for Foreign Affairs Shidehara Kijyurō mentioned that "needless to say, as for the Pacific islands, the principle of self-determination would not be applied." In Kobayashi Tatsuo, ed., *Suiusō nikki* (Tokyo: Hara Shobō, 1966), 390; Saionji kōwa zenken iin jōsō bun, 27 August 1919, in Gaimushō, *Nihon Gaikō Bunsho* (hereafter cited as *NGB*), *1919, Vol. 3, pt. 1* (Tokyo: Gaimushō, 1970), 781; Gaimushō kōwa junbi iinkai, "Santō shō oyobi dokuryō nanyō shotō sengo shobun ni kansuru torikime" (November 1918), Papers of Makino Nobuaki, Document #346, National Diet Library of Japan.

32    "Memorandum" by Kimura Eiichi, 22 June 1919, in Gaimushō, *NGB, 1919, Vol. 3, pt. 1* (Tokyo: Gaimushō, 1970), 790–791; Ambassador Matsui Keishirō to Foreign Minister Uchida Yasuya, 1 February 1919, in ibid., 381.

33    Uchida to Matsui, 3 February 1919, in ibid., 381–382.

documents on Japanese Foreign Policy at that time. For example, when Baron Makino Nobuaki was asked for his opinion about the Smuts plan, he replied that Japan could only accept it provisionally, since he had not received permission from Tokyo.[34] The victorious Powers agreed with the overall concept of the mandate system, which was incorporated in Article 19 of the League Covenant by the League of Nations Commission. Even after this, however, Matsui Keishirō suggested that Japan should not agree to the mandate system voluntarily and should postpone the decision until the last moment.[35] Indeed, owing to the considerable geographical distance between Paris and Tokyo, the Japanese delegation needed to wait for directives from Tokyo. At the same time, there was also a strategic reason for the Japanese reticence in replying: prolonging acceptance of the mandate plan could improve Japan's chances of gaining de facto annexation.[36] In any case, the negotiation style of the Japanese delegation in Paris was strikingly different from those of the other Powers. Baron Makino pointed out the Japanese delegation's tendency to delay. He cautioned that should the Japanese delegates, on grounds that they must wait for directives from Tokyo, fail to make their attitude clear, they would arouse the suspicion of the other Powers.[37] Prince Konoye Fumimaro, who accompanied the Japanese delegation, recalled that the Japanese focus was narrow, their interest was limited to the Far East, and that they tended to feel indifferent toward problems that were outside of their immediate area.[38] Generally speaking, Japan's delegates focused on the Shandong problem and the Pacific islands north of the equator, but were indifferent about and disinterested in other former German colonies. They "remained constantly silent and observant," but at the same time, "they kept their eyes fixed on the goal."[39]

Japan finally approved of the overall concept of the mandate plan, but with some reservations, since there was no possibility of the other Powers occupying the Pacific islands. However, after its tentative agreement to the Smuts plan, Japan requested a revision of the plan in three places when applying it to

---

34    Matsui to Uchida, 1 February 1919, in ibid., 380.

35    Matsui to Uchida, 24 February 1919, in ibid., 384.

36    Hosoya Chihiro, *Nihon gaikō no zahyō* (Tokyo: Chūō Kōronsha, 1979), 9; Michael Blaker, *Japanese International Negotiating Style* (New York: Columbia University Press, 1977), 113–114.

37    Gaimushō, *NGB: Pari kōwa kaigi keika gaiyō* (Tokyo: Gaimushō, 1970), p. 68; Kumamoto Fumio, *Taisenkanki no tai Chūgoku bunka gaikō* (Tokyo: Yoshikawa Kōbunkan, 2013), 1–4, 36–44.

38    Konoye Fumimaro, *Sengo ōbei kenbunroku* (Tokyo: Chūō Kōronsha, 1981), 48.

39    Emile Dillon, *The Inside Story of the Peace Conference* (New York: Harper & Brothers Publishers, 1920), 78.

the islands. The first point was whether a provision of "equal opportunity" should be included in the definition of Class C mandates. The Smuts plan obliged the Class B mandates to secure the equal opportunity of commerce, but did not extend that obligation to those in Class C. Japan requested that this provision apply to Class C, since it desired to evade commercial discrimination from Australia in the Pacific. However, since Australia and New Zealand were aware of Japan's expansion plans, Japan's request was denied.

The second point was a demand to modify the text of the mandate plan. The original text of the plan, dated 30 January 1919, stated that the territories were to be administered under the laws of the mandatory state "as integral portions" thereof. However, the final text of 8 February 1919 stated that they were to be administered under the laws of the mandatory state "as if integral portions" thereof. This change in the text clearly indicated that the mandatory approved the obvious differences between national territory and the mandated area, but such a distinction could jeopardize the character of annexation. Baron Makino requested a revision of the final plan, and it was accepted.[40]

The third point was the control of the communication cable on the small island of Yap in the Caroline Islands. Yap, located about 380 km southeast of Guam, played the important role of a cable station connecting Guam, Manado, and Shanghai.[41] President Wilson insisted that Yap "be internationalized because if it belonged to the Japanese, they could cut communications between different parts of the Pacific whenever they liked."[42] However, Japan refused Wilson's request as it was impossible to give special treatment only to Yap. Since even the British representatives did not support Wilson's claim, his demand was eventually dismissed. In May 1919, it was finally confirmed that Yap would be placed under the administration of Japan as a Class C mandate.[43]

---

40    Makino Nobuaki, *Kaikoroku, Vol. 2* (Tokyo: Chūō Kōronsha, 1977), 211; Ambassador Matsui to Uchida, 24 February 1919, *NGB: 1919, Vol. 3, pt. 1,* 384–385; Gaimushō, *NGB: Nihon gaiko tsuikairoku (1900–1935)* (Tokyo: Gaimushō, 1982), 459.

41    Walter Rogers of the Committee on Public Information had already sent President Wilson a memorandum at the end of January 1919 on the importance of Yap and the communication cables. "Memorandum" by Walter Rogers, 30 January 1919, *PPW, Vol. 54,* pp. 381–382.

42    "34th Meeting of the Council of Four," 15 April 1919; "38th Meeting of the Council of Four," 18 April 1919; "41st Meeting of the Council of Four," 21 April 1919, in Paul Mantoix, *The Deliberations of the Council of Four (March 24-June 28, 1919), Vol. 1* (Princeton: Princeton University Press, 1992), 250, 275, 312.

43    The question of Yap was discussed during the Washington Conference of 1921–22. It was finally resolved while the Japanese mandate for Yap was reconfirmed and the United States obtained free access to the cable communications there. Samuel F. Bemis, "The Yap

In deliberations on the mandate question concerning the Pacific islands, Japan followed the annexationist claims of the southern Dominions and assumed a wait-and-see attitude. Japan carefully avoided direct conflicts with the Wilsonian principles of "nonannexation" and "self-determination" while it observed the negotiations among the Powers. By asking for the annexation, Japan entrusted the British Dominions with the role of fighting against Wilson. However, Wilson vehemently opposed the annexation, so the British compromised on the Smuts proposal. Japan had already shrewdly understood that the victorious Powers would approve of the mandate plan. Therefore, after accepting the Smuts plan, Japan requested a minor revision of the aspects of the proposal that directly affected its own interest. Japanese diplomacy was, in the narrow sense of promoting its own national interest, technically a triumph. Japan as a member of the victorious Powers called the Big Five, however, lacked a future vision that the other interested parties had, and lost sight of its responsible role to construct the postwar international order.

## Wilson's Compromise and the Establishment of the Mandate System

### Battle over the Smuts Plan

The Smuts plan helped moderate the conflict between the United States and British Dominions. However, both parties were not fully receptive to the plan. President Wilson stated that while he took the Smuts plan to be a compromise that would prevail until the League of Nations had begun operations, if more priority was given to the disposition of the colonies, it would be difficult for the mandate system to function properly. He maintained that the mandate plan should be discussed after the birth of the League. On the other hand, Australia and New Zealand regarded the Smuts plan to be incomplete for the securing of greater discretionary power in the Pacific islands. In other words, both parties expressed discontent over a lack of practicality in the mandate plan.[44]

---

Island Controversy," *Pacific Review* 2-2 (September 1921): 308–328; Sumitra Rattan, "The Yap Controversy and Its Significance," *Journal of Pacific History* 7-1 (Spring 1972): 124–136; Timothy Maga, "Prelude to War?: The United States, Japan, and the Yap Crisis, 1918–1922," *Diplomatic History* 9-3 (Summer 1985): 215–231.

44    The Council of Ten, "Minutes of Meeting," 30 January 1919, *FRUS, 1919: PPC Vol. 3*, 789–790; William R. Louis, *Great Britain and Germany's Lost Colonies, 1914–1919* (Oxford: Clarendon Press 1967), 130.

THE WILSON ADMINISTRATION AND THE MANDATE QUESTION

The conflict over the Smuts plan continued, but a hopeful solution seemed likely. In place of Lloyd George, who failed to persuade the southern Dominions, the Canadian Prime Minister Sir Robert Borden and South African Prime Minister General Louis Botha served as mediators. Between the deliberations of the Council of Ten in the morning and afternoon of 30 January, Borden urged Hughes of Australia and Massey of New Zealand to alter their firm attitudes, and explained Lloyd George's difficult position to Wilson, while he also praised Wilson's lofty ideals. By introducing his personal experience after the Boer War, Botha suggested that the Council should concede trivial things and guide various peoples to lofty ideals. He finally announced that South Africa would renounce its demand for the annexation of South West Africa and accept the mandate plan.[45] With Canadian and South African persuasion, Australia and New Zealand eventually decided to approve the mandate plan.

### Some Restraints for Wilson

Although the mandate plan forced the annexationists to retreat, there was not a complete congruence between the American proposal and the final mandate system. In reality, the Wilson administration was constrained when it came to the disposition of the former German colonies. At least three factors limited Wilson's actions regarding the Pacific islands. First, the Pacific islands north of the equator were actually under Japanese military administration. Therefore, it was impossible for the United States to ask Japan to relinquish the islands. Wilson was confident that persuasion without military pressure would not result in Japan's withdrawal from the Pacific islands, but the United States had no real intention to use military power in this matter after the war.[46] Second, the US government could not both deny the Japanese mandate for the islands north of the equator, and also concede the mandate of the islands south of the equator to Australia and New Zealand. Since the mandate system had to be uniformly applied to the colonies, Wilson was unable to object to this resolution.[47] Third, should the discussion of the Pacific islands rouse disputes among the Powers, Britain, France, and Japan would not only oppose the mandate plan but would also withdraw their support from the League of Nations.

---

45   The Council of Ten, "Minutes of Meeting," 30 January 1919, *FRUS, 1919: PPC Vol. 3,* 800–802.

46   "Black Book 2: Outline of Tentative Report and Recommendations" prepared by the Intelligence Section in Accordance with Instructions, for the President and the Plenipotentiaries, 13 February 1919, Wilson Papers, Series 5B, Reel 393, MDLC.

47   Seth Tillman, *Anglo-American Relations at the Paris Peace Conference of 1919* (Princeton: Princeton University Press, 1961), 100.

Wilson's top priority was to establish the League, and he believed that the cooperation of the Powers was indispensable to its creation, therefore he strongly felt that the United States must not jeopardize that cooperation.[48]

Under the circumstances, it was wise for the United States to avoid a direct confrontation with Japan and accept its request. Therefore, as a conciliatory resolution, President Wilson favored a Japanese mandate of the Pacific islands north of the equator rather than Japan's annexation of the islands.

After the compromise between the United States and British Dominions, their earlier conflict was soon resolved and the Council of Ten approved the Smuts plan on 30 January 1919.[49] Wilson accepted the plan on the condition that it must be revised should it lose its consistency with the League Covenant. These slight modifications to the mandate plan ultimately saved the League Covenant and the peace conference itself. After the deliberation of the League of Nations Commission, the mandate plan was recorded in Article 22 of the League Covenant and on 7 May 1919, and the Supreme War Council allocated mandates for the German colonies. Under the Smuts plan, Japan assumed the Pacific islands north of the equator as a Class C mandate.[50] Even though from the US perspective this was only the second-best resolution – the best would have been formal nonannexation – President Wilson had sought not only to eliminate a security threat to the United States in the Pacific, but also to maintain consistency between the mandate system and the concept of the League of Nations.

### Conclusion

President Wilson regarded "nonannexation" and "self-determination" as authoritative principles under which the United States endeavored to apply the mandate system to the former German islands in the Pacific as a practical function of the League of Nations. However, Wilson's proposal was rejected owing to vehement objections from the annexationists of southern British Dominions that had a stake in those territories. A compromise proposal based on "the Smuts plan" broke the stalemate. This proposal, while it claimed the administration of mandates under the League, simultaneously approved the

---

48   Entry in the diary of William Wiseman, dated 27 January 1919, William Wiseman Papers, Series I, Box 7, Yale University.

49   The Council of Ten, "Minutes of Meeting," 30 January 1919, *FRUS, 1919: PPC Vol. 3*, 803.

50   Records of the Supreme War Council, 7 May 1919, 180.03401/149. RG 256, General Records of the American Commission to Negotiate Peace, 1918–1931, Reel 113, NA.

annexation of the islands by the victorious Powers. In effect, the mandate system meant a disposition through annexation by the mandatory countries. Thus the national interests of the victorious Powers provided a major setback to the new Wilsonian vision of mandates under the League itself.

Peculiarly, it was the southern British Dominions, such as Australia and New Zealand, rather than Japan that sharply confronted the United States. Moreover, other British Dominions that were not interested parties, such as South Africa and Canada, helped break the deadlock. How can we understand the relation between Japan's silence and Wilson's final compromise regarding the former German islands in the Pacific?

Once Britain conformed to the United States' vision of the mandate system, Japan abandoned its pursuit of the direct annexation of the islands. When it appeared that the contents of the proposal came close to a disposition through annexation, however, Japan took an interest in becoming the administrator of the islands. Japan's first priority was to block the involvement of the League of Nations and any third power in the administration of the former German islands in the north Pacific. In order to keep the islands under Japan's control, Japan kept in step with Britain's stance and got Australia and New Zealand to speak on behalf of Japan's intentions. In this case, Japan made full use of traditional diplomatic methods (old diplomacy), such as signing a secret treaty and agreement, and thereby achieved its aim.

President Wilson undertook to enhance the influence of the League of Nations as the base for a postwar international system, by applying the mandate system as a comprehensive solution to the colonial question. However, he also intended to block the expansion of Japan's presence in the western Pacific, which posed a threat to the immediate national interest of the United States. Wilson's mandate proposal was a hybrid policy of universal idealism (anticolonialism) and US national interest (national security). However, the establishment of the League of Nations, which was Wilson's first priority, was still uncertain and his plan lacked a practicable strategy for implementation. Moreover, Japan's claim over the islands tied with the interests of the Allied Powers in the disposition of other former German colonies. Therefore, the final draft of the mandate system took on the character of annexation.

# What Peace Meant to Japan
## The Changeover at Paris in 1919

*Tadashi Nakatani*

## 1   A Clash of Diplomacies?

At the 1919 Paris Peace Conference, the United States and Japan entered an intense diplomatic dispute over the disposition of ex-German possessions and interests in China and its colonial islands in the Pacific. Many previous works evaluate this dispute as one of the typical representations of, in a manner of speaking, a "Clash of Diplomacies" between the new and old systems in the wake of the first "total war" in human history – World War One.[1]

Indeed, it is difficult to reduce this meeting at Paris to a mere conflict between two great powers who, despite contradictory national interests, were able to come to a compromise through give-and-take. Japan and the United States, and especially their political leaders, had come to hold widely differing opinions of international politics and envisaged peace from different viewpoints when the Great War ended. Most Japanese political leaders recognized the outbreak of the war as "one chance in a thousand" to obtain new territories in the western Pacific and, in particular, enhance its interests and "spheres of influence" in China. Spheres of influence were the geographical areas in China in which a particular great power virtually monopolized important economic interests and privileges. For example, the Yangtze Valley, with Shanghai at the mouth of the river, was a sphere of influence for the United Kingdom; Canton

---

\*   This chapter is based on my presentation at the session 539, April 2, the Joint Conference of the Association for Asian Studies & International Convention of Asia Scholars, March 31–April 3, 2011, Honolulu, Hawai'i, USA. I would especially like to thank the discussant, Stephen Vlastos, and the chair, Tosh Minoara, and the other presenters and the audience in our session, all of whom provided impressive comments and questions on my research. In preparing the presentation, Masato Kimura made valuable suggestions, and my British, American and Japanese friends, Jennefer Hodges, William Carr and Wataru Yamaguchi, were very helpful.

1   For previous and related major works in English, see Selected Bibliography for Chapter 8 and note 23, 26. For the Japanese research, refer to endnotes of Tadashi Nakatani, "Wilson to Nippon: Pari Kōwa-kaigi to Santō-mondai," *Dōshisha Hōgaku*, 56(2) (July 2004) and the bibliography of Shūsuke Takahara, *Wilson-Gaikō to Nippon: Risō to Genjitsu no Aida 1913–1921* (Tokyo: Sōbunsha, 2006).

for France; Shandong for Germany; South Manchuria for Japan; and North Manchuria for the Russian Empire. The United States never had a sphere of influence nor approved of them formally, continuing to give a tacit nod to them until the advent of Wilson's New Diplomacy.[2]

In contrast, Woodrow Wilson, who had assumed the American presidency in 1913, repeatedly denounced the traditional features of international politics based on military alliances, secret agreements, colonial rules, unequal treatment of "backward" countries, and the "balance of power" as the war dragged on, giving such diplomatic ways the generic name of the "old diplomacy," because he considered it the main cause of the war. "To end all wars," the President believed in changing the entire sphere of international politics through innovation, although he hardly intended to progress radical changes.[3] This is Wilson's interpretation of "New Diplomacy," and he left very little room for allowing the Japanese to enjoy the fruits of their wartime old diplomacy when the peace conference opened.

As a natural consequence, during the course of the peace negotiations, Japan persistently claimed ownership of ex-German possessions and interests in China and the Pacific, of which it had already seized control by force early in the war. The United States openly opposed this, trying hard to ensure that the disputed assets came under international control of the victorious great powers, led by the United States, for the sake of China and its own principles of New Diplomacy.

The outcome appears, however, to have largely satisfied Japan's claims. The Treaty of Versailles clearly stated that all ex-German possessions and privileges in Shandong, which included the leased territory and the main railroad, should be transferred legally to Japan with no reservations, and that all ex-German islands north of the equator in the Pacific were to be put under a trusteeship rule of Japan, which would enable the Japanese to govern the islands as if they were their own territories.

---

2 See note 14.

3 On Wilson's New Diplomacy, see Arno J. Mayer, *Politics and Diplomacy of Peacemaking: Containment and Counterrevolution at Versailles, 1918–1919* (New York: A.A. Knopf, 1967); N. Gordon Levine, Jr., *Woodrow Wilson and World Politics: America's Response to War and Revolution*. Reprint ed. (New York: Oxford University Press, 1970 [first published in 1968 by Oxford University Press]); Arthur S. Link, *Woodrow Wilson: Revolution, War, and Peace* (Arlington Heights, IL: AHM Pub. Co., 1979); Jules Cambon, "Old and New Diplomacy: A Debate Revisited." *Review of International Studies*, 14 (July 1988), 195–211; Tomas J. Knock, *To End All Wars: Woodrow Wilson and the Quest for a New Order* (Princeton: Princeton University Press, 1992); Erez Manela, *The Wilsonian Moment: Self-determination and the International Origins of Anticolonial Nationalism* (Oxford: Oxford University Press, 2007).

What brought Wilson, who had been eager to apply the principles of his New Diplomacy to East Asia as well as Europe, to such concessions? The arrangement for Shandong looked particularly one-sided. Many previous works have provided a simple answer to this question: Wilson managed to protect the most cherished proposal in his New Diplomacy, the League of Nations. The Japanese delegation often hinted at their withdrawal from the peace negotiations, stating that they would not be able to commit to the peace treaty if their claims on Shandong were not accepted, and Wilson genuinely feared that Japan's retreat would mean that the League was unworkable.

Nevertheless, in hindsight, Wilson's decision on this matter may have been an error of judgment in terms of the success of his League program per se. It meant that he lost his good reputation in China and much of his ground in the US delegation and State Department, which contributed to his downfall in American domestic politics. The Chinese had expected Wilson to repel any Japanese imperialistic ambitions and, on witnessing his "betrayal" on Shandong, they refused to sign the peace treaty. Most members of the American delegation, and almost all experts on East Asia in the State Department, had no doubt that the Japanese threat was a bluff and that they would have no choice but to submit if the United States stood firm.[4]

Against this backdrop, consider the above question in a different way. What brought Wilson to the decision to go against all opposition from the Chinese and his advisers and experts who were, based on Wilson's own New Diplomacy, opposed to yielding to Japan's imperialistic demands? Did he back the wrong horse and sacrifice American ideals quite unnecessarily, or did Wilson carry out his responsibility as the President to make a tough decision and preserve the future of the League at the temporary expense of some of his principles? Of course, Wilson himself would have supported the latter explanation. In fact, he believed that the result of the Shandong controversy at Paris was not one-sided but "fifty-fifty"[5] and, as this chapter later explains, including Japan in the League as one of the original member states would be essential for the entire postwar program he envisioned. However, he could not convince his advisers and experts, let alone the Chinese delegation, that the deal with Japan was

---

4   See, for example, Burton F. Beers, *Vain Endeavor: Robert Lansing's Attempts to End the American-Japanese Rivalry* (Durham, N. C.: Duke University Press, 1962); Noel H. Pugach, *Paul S. Reinsch: Open Door Diplomat in Action* (Mill Wood, NY: KTO Press, 1979); Stephen G. Graft, "John Bassett Moore, Robert Lansing, and the Shandong Question," *The Pacific Historical Review*, 66 (May 1997), 231–249.

5   From the Diary of Grayson, 30 April 1919, Arthur S. Link, ed., *The Papers of Woodrow Wilson*, vol. 58 (Princeton, NJ: Princeton University Press, 1988), 244–245 (cited hereafter as *PWW*).

necessary. Why were they and the President at odds with each other despite sharing the basic ideas of what a postwar world order should be?

If we only consider the question within the framework of the "Clash of Diplomacies," then it is difficult to decipher Wilson's behavior and the meaning and consequences of the US-Japanese diplomatic dispute over China at Paris. As the peace negotiations progressed, Wilson began to view Japan in a different light from the Chinese delegation, his advisers and experts, and this is what most previous works have failed to grasp. In the closing days of the conference, he came to believe that Japanese diplomacy was changing gradually in a favorable way, and in some ways coming close to his own ideals.

Therefore, the main topic of this chapter is the stance of Japan at Paris in 1919, taking a new look at Japanese diplomacy in the aftermath of the Great War. Through this re-examination, the study provides three major findings concerning US-Japanese relations and the Shandong controversy at the Paris Peace Conference.

First, it shows that Japan's diplomatic shift had actually happened and begun before the war ended, which was similar in nature to what Wilson supposed at Paris. The paper explains the background and forces that brought about this important policy shift within the Japanese government, especially in the Foreign Ministry. Second, it describes how the Japanese delegation's oft-expressed assertion that they supported the basic principles of the New Diplomacy encouraged Wilson to deal with them at the conference. He felt strongly that including Japan in the League was essential for a new, stable, just order in East Asia and, by extension, for world peace, and that the inclusion must not simply be the product of a reluctant diplomatic compromise. Finally, in light of these new views, the study argues that what the peace of the Great War meant to Japan, US-Japanese relations, and international politics in East Asia was not simply a "Clash of Diplomacies." Instead, it was the beginning of the final process of tearing down the old framework of great-power diplomacy, which had dominated East Asia from the late 19th century, under the influence of Wilson's New Diplomacy model.

## 2     A Wilsonian World for Japan

### What World Would Be Best?

Hagihara Nobutoshi, the late, renowned Japanese historian, stated that, "Japan did not really experience World War I," so "[the] Japanese were unable to cope with the ideas and forces released by the war." One of the ideas and forces he referred to here was Wilson's New Diplomacy (in his phraseology,

"American idealistic internationalism").[6] Considering the First World War only cost the Japanese some three hundred lives, and that they never experienced a total war or "Great War" in the true sense until they attacked Pearl Harbor in 1941, this view is justifiable. Similarly, other major previous studies emphasize the adverse reaction of the Japanese to Wilson's Fourteen Points, the President's famous address manifesting his principles for peace in January 1918. It is argued that the Japanese never grasped the true meaning of Wilson's new thinking, even after the war ended, continuing to stand for the old diplomacy and their self-serving agendas throughout the peace conference. Therefore, in taking this position, the peace meant only the end of the "one chance in a thousand" to Japan.

Indeed, as the basis of the first general instructions to the delegation, the government worked out "three principles for the peace," which asked Japan's plenipotentiaries: 1) to call on the unconditional cession of all ex-German privileges and interests in China and its islands in the Western Pacific to Japan; 2) not to interfere unnecessarily in any negotiation in which the Japanese Empire had no direct interest; and 3) when responding to problems in which all Allied and Associated Powers had a common interest, to cooperate with the majority of the powers. In addition, in responding specifically to Wilson's Fourteen Points, the government ordered the delegation to delay the establishment of the League program as far as possible, although it reluctantly allowed them to give Japan's basic approval to each of the Fourteen Points. Finally, they were supposed to lay a course in concert with the United Kingdom, Japan's ally, or follow the majority of the powers. Generally, the Japanese government seemed to lack a clear plan and enthusiasm for the general peace process, and its concern about the peace appeared limited and introspective.

However, appearances can be deceptive, and previous works oversimplify the policy debates within the Japanese government that produced these principles and positions. Although a number of Japan's political leaders and diplomats, and the military establishment, were wary of Wilson's New Diplomacy, especially the League program, it could be misleading to think that they were considering the peace problems within the dichotomy of the old and New Diplomacy. Facing the end of "one chance in a thousand," they seriously contemplated the possibilities for the world order that would emerge in the wake of the first total war, having three main images in mind.

---

6  The other "ideas and forces" are "Chinese nationalism" and "Soviet communism." Nobutoshi Hagihara, "What Japan Means to the Twentieth Century," in Hagihara et al. (eds.), *Experiencing the Twentieth Century* (Tokyo: The University of Tokyo Press, 1985), 20.

1.  The restoration of an old international order, in which great powers would dominate world politics and compete with each other for the extension of powers and interests in "backward" areas but, at the same time, giving serious consideration to other powers' existing interests, privileges, and spheres of influence, as they did before the Great War.[7]

2.  The emergence of a Wilsonian world, which would not only end the acquisition of new colonies or territories by force or threat, but also rule out any mutual recognition of exclusive interests and privileges as a means of regulating their relationships; it would call on them to remove any economic barriers as far as possible, official or unofficial, at home and abroad, to promote international free trade.

3.  A stable international order would fail to emerge as the European great powers, from experience of the war, were naturally expected to attach importance to state control of economic activities and strive to enclose their own market wherever possible, which would strictly limit the possibility of Japan's economic development at home and expansion abroad.

What most Japanese leaders hoped for was the first scenario, as some previous works have assumed. They realized that the favorable international environment, which had allowed Japan to expand its interests and influences at the expense of China and the European powers after the outbreak of the war, had gone. The "one chance in a thousand" had already ended before the armistice, or at least that was what most of the Japanese leaders felt. Japan's vigorous expansionist policy, led by the notorious Twenty-One Demands imposed on China in 1915, could only last until late 1916. The country made further efforts to expand or solidify its interests and sphere of influence in China during the final throes of the war, but this did not bring the results the policymakers had expected. This was largely due to strong objections from the United States, China's unstable situation owing to a civil war and corruption in its central government, and Japan's lack of sufficient financial resources. In addition, the elder statesmen had serious fears that such an exclusive and selfish policy was likely to ruin Japan's name, which was already blackened by the Twenty-One Demands and subsequent policies, and anger its allies in the United Kingdom and the Russian Empire.

Consequently, the political leaders came to the basic consensus that Japan would require some form of cooperation with other great powers in the

---

7   See Akira Iriye, *After Imperialism: The Search for a New Order in the Far East 1921–1931* (Chicago, IL: Imprint Publications Inc., 1990 [first published in 1965 by Harvard University Press]), 4–13, in particular 4–5.

postwar era. Although it had achieved eye-catching economic growth, boosted by a huge increase in exports thanks to the Great War, they realized that Japan did not possess the economic, financial, and political power to maintain its own economic activities if depending only on its own markets.

Without doubt, the Japanese believed that the final scenario would be the worst for their interests, being eager to prevent protectionism from spreading and dividing the world economy into blocs. Its domestic market, colonies (Korea and Taiwan), and sphere of influence in China (mainly the southern area of Manchuria) paled on every count compared to other great powers, especially the United Kingdom.

However, the Japanese could not be certain that the first scenario would prevail after the end of the war, and this uncertainty should be taken into account when evaluating Japan's reaction to Wilson's New Diplomacy, despite many previous works largely failing to do so. As a matter of course, the Japanese did not welcome the New Diplomacy with open arms, primarily because of its obvious incompatibility with the first, preferred scenario. In fact, the Wilson administration once or twice unofficially proposed to Japan the abolition of the spheres of influence in China during the time of war. A realization of a Wilsonian world in some form, however, would not be a disaster for Japan given the circumstances, because it could provide the most dependable barrier against the worst scenario: the proliferation of protectionism.[8] Because of the uncertainty about what it would mean for the country, Japan failed to reach a solid consensus on the possibility and meaning of a Wilsonian world, which gave rise to extensive discussions within the government around the time of the peace conference.

### Japan's Peace Policy Debates

Japan's policy-making process of those days is complicated to trace. This difficulty stems partly from a change in administration around a month before the armistice, from the cabinet headed by Masatake Terauchi, a general of the army, to the cabinet led by Takashi Hara, the head of the main party, Seiyūkai,

---

8  Kōwa no Kiso-jōken no Tōyō ni okeru Teikoku no Chii ni Oyobosu Eikyō ni tsuite, sealed by Komura, undated [supposedly October 1918], Shina Seiken Zassan, vol. 3, The Foreign Ministry's Record: 1.1.2–77, Diplomatic Archives of the Ministry of Foreign Affairs of Japan (cited hereafter as FMR). This document is also available as B03030277800 from the website of Japan Center for Asian Historical Records, National Archives of Japan < http://www.jacar .go.jp/english/> (cited hereafter as JACAR); A Memorandum on the League program in the Foreign Ministry, sealed by Kijūrō Shidehara, the Permanent Under Secretary of the Foreign Ministry, and others, undated [supposedly at the early stages of the peace conference], ibid., vol. 3, FMR: 1.1.2–77 and JACAR: B03030278700.

and the first Japanese Prime Minister who had a seat in the House of Representatives (the lower house).

To begin with, it was not the cabinet but another body that held responsibility for the discussions to prepare for the peace conference. The organization was "the Provisional Committee of Investigation on Foreign Affairs" (mentioned hereafter as the diplomatic committee). Founded by the Terauchi cabinet in 1917, it comprised some key cabinet members, including the army and navy ministers, some privy councilors and the leaders of the major parties (however, Takaaki Katō, the leader of Kenseikai, the party second to Seiyūkai, refused to participate because the committee could be a breach of the constitution). The body was formed through a combination of the initiative of Terauchi and some of his political colleagues' designs in the hope that it would play a role as a so-called all-nation cabinet, limited to foreign affairs, with the chair assumed by the Prime Minister. However, the committee became independent of the cabinet over time, going so far as to criticize the latter and the Foreign Ministry on many occasions, even before Terauchi left office (legally, it was not under the cabinet's control but bore a direct responsibility for the Emperor). In particular, Miyoji Itō, a privy councilor and one of those who drafted the Meiji constitution of 1889, distinguished himself as the typical outspoken critic of the cabinet's foreign policy, and he would be the primary objector to the New Diplomacy in the peace debates within the government.

Therefore, the Foreign Ministry, an organization supposed to have the prime responsibility for planning and conducting foreign policies, found its power and influence undermined in the policy-making process. This was largely due to the influence of the diplomatic committee and the fact that, during the last days of his cabinet, Terauchi relied heavily on personal and unusual diplomatic approaches in his China policy using secret military agencies in China, a few officials of the Finance Department, and his private agents. (The Foreign Ministry's loss of power was not peculiar for Japan but common for the belligerents as the conduct of a total war inevitably raised the ability and influence in foreign affairs of existing other or newly established administrative bodies, though the country's war effort was nowhere near what the mobilizations by the Europeans and Americans needed.)

The new Prime Minister, Hara, was a political leader who started his career in official circles as a diplomat and clerk in the Foreign Ministry. He attached great importance to cooperating with the United States, and was willing to cast aside the former cabinet's diplomatic goals and approaches that had resulted in an overly ambitious economic expansion policy in China and the deterioration in relations with the United States and China (although part of the policy was implemented as the Nishihara Loan of 1918). Hara also wanted to give foreign policy power back to the cabinet and the Foreign Ministry, despite him being a member of the diplomatic committee since before assuming the premiership. However, it was only after the peace conference opened that the Prime Minister and the Foreign Ministry started to take the initiative on foreign affairs.

Finally, and importantly, this abnormality and uncertainty in the policy-making process within the Japanese government during a period of transition means that it is difficult to establish precisely the value of its policy debates; there was not only a dispute over which diplomatic goals to pursue, but also a power struggle to gain control of foreign policy in the postwar era. Behind the division of opinion among the policymakers and governmental organizations were differences not only in their sense of values on diplomacy but also in their political and organizational interests in domestic politics.

The Japanese debates before the peace conference climaxed at a meeting of the diplomatic committee held on 8 December, which saw a heated exchange about the New Diplomacy.[9] It had two main actors: one was the previously mentioned Itō, the other was Nobuaki Makino, Itō's colleague in the Emperor's Privy Council but a close friend of the Prime Minister. He also had substantial experience in the diplomatic service, at one time holding the portfolio of Foreign Minister, and was scheduled to leave for Paris as the de facto chief of the plenipotentiaries.[10]

Previous works (especially the Japanese research) have frequently preferred to depict the debate as an important episode that demonstrated how old-fashioned realism prevailed against a noble, but pure-minded, idealism, and that this resulted in the intense diplomatic dispute between Japan and the United States in Paris. Naturally, Itō's arguments represented the former and Makino stood for the latter. However, this dichotomy is less precise when reviewed from three different viewpoints.

First, Makino stressed not only the New Diplomacy's high moral value but also the economic and political positives for Japan when he insisted on a more positive approach to Wilson's New Diplomacy, especially the League program. He also expressed his firm belief that the establishment of the

---

9    Tatsuo Kobayashi (ed.), *Suiusō nikki: Itōke monjo rinji gaikō chōsa iinkai kaigihikki tō* (Tokyo: Hara Shobō, 1966), 333–346 (cited hereafter as *Suiusō Diary*).

10   The actual chief of the plenipotentiaries was Kinmochi Saionji, a blue-blooded statesman who used to name his cabinets twice before the Great War and the former leader of Seiyūkai, and well known as the last Genrō (the elder statesmen the Emperor himself appointed to consult with on his affairs of state from the founders of Modern Japan). He did not arrive in Paris until early March.

League of Nations would help Japan overcome the obstacles of differences in races, religions, and nations to attain the just treatment that the Western powers enjoyed in the international community. In other words, he did not specifically claim the necessity of sacrificing some part of Japan's individual interest to devote itself to a universal idealism or adapting to the one-sided demands of a stronger country, but instead asked the Japanese to shift their focus and realize that its self-interests could be compatible with, and extended in, a Wilsonian world.

Second, when offering counterarguments against Makino, Itō's greatest concern was to maintain the existing international frameworks as far as possible and to cooperate with victorious great powers, especially the United Kingdom, rather than to leave room for Japan's future expansionist policy (although he perhaps had some regrets about the latter). He could scarcely understand why Makino believed so firmly in the effectiveness of Wilson's New Diplomacy and doubted whether the League could be anything more than an organization primarily serving the Western powers, especially the Anglo-Saxons. With this uncertainty regarding the League, he believed that Japan's positive approval of it might lead to the country being deprived of traditional methods and without any alternative means to survive within great power politics, in particular the Anglo-Japanese alliance, the only official alliance it maintained at that time (Japan had already lost its de facto alliance with Russia due to the collapse of the Russian Empire and the final success of the Bolshevik revolution in 1917). In short, the main issue of the two privy councilors' debate was how to cooperate rather than compete with other powers in a postwar world for the sake of Japan's national interests. The most important point here is that they both recognized that Japan's expansionist policy toward China during the war largely deviated from a traditional, important rule of great-power politics in East Asia: a mutual recognition of privileges and interests in China, and in particular spheres of influence.

Third, Makino's arguments for the New Diplomacy were not an example of his grandstanding, but largely fitted with the contentions of the Foreign Ministry officials in charge of Japanese policy toward China on a practical level. The representative example of the officials was Kin'ichi Komura, the 36-year-old chief of the first section (China section) in the state affairs bureau (*Seimukyoku*) of the Ministry (he was the eldest son of Jutarō Komura, the well-known Foreign Minister around the period of the Russo-Japanese War). Komura insisted from the midpoint of the war that there was an urgent need to establish a new set of policies that would enable the country to cooperate mainly with the United States. Before seeing the Fourteen Points, let alone the armistice, he accurately forecasted that Wilson's idealism would have a major bearing on the peace negotiations that were eventually to come.[11] This was in contrast with the policymakers and senior officials in the Foreign Ministry who, regretting a series of self-seeking expansion policies which had injured relations with not only China but also other great powers in the initial stages of the war, were largely concerned with returning Japan's foreign policy to a traditional framework that prioritized a mutual respect for each sphere of influence in China. In Makino and Komura's opinion, however, returning to such a traditional method would prevent Japan from cooperating with Wilson's United States. In addition to this concurrence of opinions, the two men were desperate to recover the position of the Foreign Ministry by making clear Japan's approval of Wilson's New Diplomacy. While Makino stressed the need for the Ministry to control all diplomatic activities, Komura also invoked Wilson's denouncing of militarism to justify the same point.[12] Both stances were an implicit attack not only on the measures the former cabinet, led by a general of the army, often used in its China policy, but also on the value of the diplomatic committee.

For these reasons, it is fair to assume that there was some communication between the two men, and that the policy visions of Komura and the China section stood behind Makino's arguments, although there is no direct evidence to prove that Komura or his junior staff were involved with Makino's statement, and it was the Foreign Ministry itself that drafted the first instruction to the delegation, which Makino criticized as being too inadequate to cope with the peace negotiations. This clearly coincided with the political interests of the Prime Minister, who intended to reduce the diplomatic committee to a nominal status and eliminate the former cabinet's influence. Meanwhile, Itō also needed to refute Makino's claims to protect not only what he considered to be the national interest, but also his own power and position in foreign affairs.

Itō's realism arguably prevailed prior to the peace conference but, as explained above, its triumph was not as definitive as previous works assumed when considering the Japanese government's floating power structure at that time and the complex character of the peace debates within it. Although his strong statements to the diplomatic committee have often been aligned with the Japanese government's preferences in foreign affairs (arguably thanks to the huge amount of records of the committee which were left by Itō),[13] his influence was neither strong nor stable, and he did not enjoy the

---

11    Kin'ichi Komura, *Shina ni okeru Seiryokuhan'i no Teppai ni tsuite*, September 1917, *Shina Seiken Zassan*, vol. 3, FMR: 1.1.2–77 and JACAR: B03030276900.

12    See note 8.

13    The record was published as part of *Suiusō Diary*. See note 9.

overwhelming support of other policymakers. However, his view was old-fashioned, which meant that they could understand his logic. Other than voicing the typical anxieties of the Japanese leaders, it had no concrete vision to cope with the new stream of thought that was pervading world politics. Moreover, the arguments Makino or Komura presented were not so radical that others would not understand them. In the framework of the old diplomacy, Japan was able to enjoy a relatively stable international order in and around East Asia after the Russo-Japanese War of 1904–1905, but its chances to expand economically, let alone territorially, were naturally limited because European great powers, especially the United Kingdom, had already captured promising areas as their colonies or, in particular in China, spheres of influence. To give way to the possessor in each sphere of influence, even regarding economic activities, was one of the old diplomacy rules for cooperation. As previously mentioned, the United States was unique in not *fully* supporting, if not positively denying, this unwritten rule, but widely accepted and sometimes reflected in international agreements, in great-power politics in East Asia from the beginning – the only great power which had no clear-cut sphere of influence in China, even though as a favored nation it enjoyed prerogative rights and privileges as other powers did.[14] In this regard, Japan and the United States potentially shared the same interests in opening the doors of European areas in the region, despite the continuing presence of major differences which they needed to overcome. For these reasons, Japan's original reluctant response to Wilson's New Diplomacy was not inflexible and, in fact, the peace negotiations would see a change in Japanese diplomacy as it proceeded to the US-Japanese talks.

## 3      The Changeover at Paris

From the beginning of the peace conference, Wilson was unwilling to accept any Japanese claims on Shandong. For example, in a private meeting on March 24 with Gu Weijun (better known by his Western name of Wellington Koo), the Chinese Minister to the United States and one of the plenipotentiaries of China, the President commented that "he was quite clear in his mind on principles involved in the question" and "he did not think it necessary" that "the

---

14    On the question of the Imperialism in American diplomacy in East Asia, see James C. Thomson Jr., Peter W. Stanley, and John Curtis Perry, *Sentimental Imperialists: The American Experience in East Asia* (New York: Harper Torchbooks, 1981) and Iriye, op. cit., 10–11.

council [the Council of Four] would call for another hearing from both sides."[15] Thus far, Wilson had held several private meetings with the Minister in Washington and Paris, but there had been little chance for the Japanese to talk with the President on the question in a concrete form, except for one or two meetings in the Council of Ten. Although he never gave the Chinese a clear promise, Wilson obviously sympathized with their assertion that all German possessions and privileges in Shandong should be returned instantly, without any condition, and not through any third party, to China. He set great store on applying the principles of his New Diplomacy to East Asia because the next big world crisis could occur there, rather than in Europe, due to the region being unfamiliar with what a total war meant.[16] His experts in the delegation and State Department naturally assumed a similar position.

Japan's basic position toward the peace negotiations, however, had begun to change by the time the Council of Four – the supreme body of the peace conference composed of Wilson; David Lloyd George, the British Prime Minister; Georges Clemenceau, the Premier of France; and Vittorio E. Orlando, the Premier of Italy (briefly out of the council due to the Fiume problem) – deliberated the Shandong question from mid-April. On February 4, to meet Makino's request, the Japanese government sent a new instruction that called on its plenipotentiaries "upon not only important issues, including the China problems, that are directly related to the interests of the Empire, but also everything else, strive to deliver your opinions [at the negotiations] whenever your excellences believe they would be fair and in the interest of justice, and then improve the standing of Japan," without waiting for instructions from home.[17] This was intended not only to save time in communicating between Tokyo and Paris but also allow Makino and the other plenipotentiaries to attempt to talk Wilson into accepting the Japanese claims by using Makino's arguments supporting the New Diplomacy. At the meeting of the diplomatic committee that discussed the Foreign Ministry's draft of the instruction, and on other

15    Memorandum by Vi Kyuin Wellington Koo, 24 March 1919, *PWW*, vol. 57, 637.

16    Memorandum by Vi Kyuin Wellington Koo, 26 November 1918, *PWW*, vol. 57, 634–635; Arthur S. Link, trans. and ed. with the assistance of Manfred F. Beomeke, *The Deliberations of the Council of Four: Note of the Official Interpreter Paul Mantoux*, vol. I (Princeton: Princeton University Press, 1992), 250–251 (cited hereafter as *The Council of Four*).

17    Yasuya Uchida, the Foreign Minister, to Keishirō Matsui, the ambassador to France, 4 February 1919, *Nippon Gaikō Bunsho: Taishō 8 [A.D. 1919]*, volume 3, no.1 (Tokyo: The Foreign Ministry, 1967), 125 (cited hereafter as *NGB*); Uchida to Makino, 6 February 1919, Makino Nobuaki Monjo[Papers], 291–292, Kensei-shiryōshitsu, the Tokyo main library of the National Diet Library, Tokyo, Japan.

occasions, Itō repeatedly scourged Makino's performance in Paris up to that point, but he was unable to stand in the way of the instruction's adoption.[18]

The Japanese Foreign Ministry was also in the process of revisiting and reviewing its general policy for peace problems around that time, and Komura and his junior staff at the China section took the initiative. Through the senior officials, they had asked the Foreign Minister, Yasuya Uchida, to allow the Japanese delegation to first put forward what they called "the four leading polices on China" at the peace conference. They insisted in fact that Japan take the initiative in suggesting that all related powers including the United States and Japan commonly and simultaneously execute those China policies that were the abolition of foreign powers' extraterritorial rights; the removal of the spheres of influence; the withdrawal of foreign troops arising from the Boxer Rebellion in 1900; and the abandonment of the indemnity arising from the rebellion.[19] The Minister and senior officials did not adopt their policy recommendation as it was, but Uchida finally telegraphed the delegation, without referring it to the diplomatic committee, explaining that they could express a favorable attitude toward the same kind of policies on a personal basis if other powers proposed them, until an official decision on the questions was reached within the Japanese government.[20] It might have been easy for Makino to reconstruct the original intention from the actual instruction that Komura had envisaged and, arguably, Komura and his junior staff could have expected him to do so. As a result, he was to come through.

Japan's original reluctance to approve the policy of the League program had brought poor results in the early peace negotiations, which was a catalyst for these changes. For their coming to ask the government to rethink its peace policies, it was the deciding factor that the Japanese delegation knew that they had made Wilson greatly disappointed, during the talks on the mandatory rules on ex-German and other defeated nations' colonies, with their passivity and repeated delay in revealing Japan's attitude.

In addition, China's unquestionably hostile attitude towards Japan was much more robust than the Japanese leaders and senior officials of the Foreign Ministry had anticipated, which served to undermine their confidence in the

---

18    *Suiusō Diary*, 393–397 and 399.

19    Komura to Masanao Hanihara, the head of the state affairs bureau in the Foreign Ministry, 30 December [1918], Shina Seiken Zassan, vol. 3, FMR: 1.2.2–77 and JACAR: B03030278700. Makino's statement on December 8 also included those contents in it, except the removal of the spheres of influence, arguably based on Komura's opinion.

20    Uchida to Matsui, 28 March 1919, *NGB: Taishō 8*, vol. 3, no. 1, 204–205. Thanks to Toshihiro Nishida, the author was able to find out about this document.

early instructions to the delegation (the Chinese Foreign Minister had earlier promised to cooperate with Japan at the peace conference when stopping over in Japan on his way to Paris).

The Japanese government, however, would not make any concession on Shandong, and the Prime Minister shared this stance.[21] In the course of talks on the question, the delegation had strict instructions that an unconditional legal transfer of all ex-German possessions and privileges in Shandong to Japan was "the ultimate decision of the Imperial Government and there could never be any room to alter it," so that, if any part of the Japanese claims was not accepted, the delegation had to "refrain from affixing its seal to the League of Nations Covenant and seek the government's directions on it." The government was adamant that there was no other choice, even if the plenipotentiaries had already made some commitment breaching this governmental policy in the negotiations.[22]

It was in this situation that Makino and his colleagues in the delegation strived to secure Japan's demands on Shandong but at the same time avoid breaking ties and, wherever possible, improve relations with the United States. To carry out this apparently impossible mission, Makino adopted two approaches during negotiations with the Council of Four or in private meetings with Wilson, while at the same time hinting at Japan's possible withdrawal from the conference.

One was to make factual concessions on the conditions of the final return from Japan to China of ex-German interests. Since occupying the Peninsula by force, it had been Japan's consistent official position that it intended to ultimately hand back all ex-German possessions and privileges to China, apart from some remaining economic rights, but only after all were devolved from Germany to Japan at the peace negotiations. The economic rights included the joint management authority with China of the main railroad in Shandong and the right to set up Japan's exclusive settlement in the central port city of the province, Tsingtao, located within the leased territory, under the same conditions as existing foreign settlements in China. The former had been officially arranged in the form of an exchange of notes between the two governments in 1918, and Wilson did not know of their existence until the middle of the peace conference.[23]

---

21    *Suiusō Diary*: 467; Keiichirō Hara, ed., *Hara Kei [Takashi] Nikki [Diary]*, 2nd ed. vol. 5 (Tokyo: Fukumura Shuppan, 1981), 21 April 1919, 86.

22    Uchida to Matsui, 4 April 1919, *NGB, Taishō 8*, vol. 3, no. 1, 242; *Suiusō Diary*, 467–468.

23    Bruce A. Elleman, *Wilson and China: A Revised History of the Shandong Question* (Armonk, NY; London, England: M.E. Sharpe, 2002), 60. Japan's Foreign Ministry did not fail, however, to notify the State Department the exchange of the notes with rapidity and

While emphasizing the importance of the sacredness of treaties to secure a stable international order, Makino used his own judgment to specify the actual conditions in a form advantageous for China. He expressed, for example, the intention to set up an international settlement instead of the exclusive one, in which anyone, including the Chinese, would have the same rights as the Japanese, regardless of their nationality, and committed to have all Japanese forces retreat from Shandong as soon as possible if the peace treaty came into force. On the joint management of the railroad, he made a promise, again without consulting home, not to use Japanese but only Chinese nationals as transport police officials and that the Chinese government would have the authority to appoint the Japanese railway police adviser, who was to be employed by the joint railway company. He eventually delivered a statement that pledged publicly to adhere to all of those agreements with the Council of Four on the request of Wilson.[24]

The other approach Makino used was to make clear Japan's basic approval of the New Diplomacy and stressed his opinion to Wilson that it was the overall structure of great power politics in East Asia, rather than Japan's individual policies, that had caused China's predicament. At a private meeting between Wilson and the Japanese plenipotentiaries on April 22, the first meeting between the two parties to talk specifically about the Shandong problem, Makino at first refused a collective management plan on the ex-German interests by the five victorious great powers, which Wilson proposed as a compromise scheme (the Chinese were not about to accept it either, until they had seen Japanese claims accepted by the Council of Four). He then accused the Chinese of being inaccurate and breaching trust when claiming that any Sino-Japanese treaties and arrangements concluded during the war were no longer good because Japan had imposed them on China by force and threat. In the course of the talks, however, Makino explained carefully to Wilson the changeover of Japanese diplomacy that had just started. Within the Japanese government, he insisted, the influence of the hard-liners had waned gradually since the final stages of the war, and the current cabinet was composed of "those who should be called the true supporters of the Sino-Japanese rapprochement." He also referred to the "fact" that the previously mentioned four

---

giving an accurate summary of it. The Japanese Embassy to the Department of State, Handed to the Secretary by the Ambassador, 30 October 1918, U.S. Department of State (ed.), *Papers Relating to the Foreign Relations of the United States, 1918* (Washington, D.C.: U.S. Government Printing Office, 1930), 205.

24    Hankey's Notes of a Meeting of the Council of Four, 30 April 1919, *PWW*, vol. 58, 257. The Japanese version is in *NGB, Taishō 8*, vol. 3, no. 2, 289.

leading policies on China were garnering support from the policymakers and influential persons in the political arena of Japan. According to Makino, Wilson paid particular attention to his explanation of the fundamental cause of China's problems and commented at the end of the meeting that "we should have chances to exchange opinions on this question again one of these days, and...today's meeting with you was very profitable and I was able to learn a lot of the facts and the backgrounds from it."[25]

Makino's approach to negotiation did not utterly convince Wilson that compromising with the Japanese would be right and not equate to a breach of trust for the Chinese and his own principles. He lost sleep over the decision and continued to work hard to secure better conditions for China, as far as he could, to the last.[26]

Makino succeeded, however, in altering Wilson's basic acknowledgment of the Shandong problem in two ways. First, he argued well that Japan could provide China and other countries with better treatment than Germany had in Shandong by specifying the conditions on how and to what extent Japan would return ex-German possessions and interests to China after the peace conference. This became one of the reasons, or perhaps "excuses," for the President to accept the Japanese claims.

Second, and more meaningfully, he provided the President with another view of international politics in East Asia, and it sat well with Wilson's fundamental concern for China and wider world politics. At a meeting of the Council of Four following the private US-Japanese talks on the same day, Makino's remarks about the China problem again attracted the interest of Wilson. He had implicitly blamed the present difficult situation in China on "the advanced countries in the West" and said "we even have an instruction from the government, according to circumstances, not to hesitate to have a discussion with the related powers on the subjects of the abolition of the extraterritorial rights and spheres of influence; the withdrawing of foreign troops; and the exemption of indemnity for the Boxer Rebellion."[27] This was clearly exaggerated by Makino, but it was enough to prompt Wilson to advance a suggestion to Lloyd George and Clemenceau on 25 April, at another meeting of the council without Japan and China, that "the Japanese declared themselves ready to give up the special

---

25    Matsui to Uchida, 22 April 1919, *NGB: Taishō 8*, vol. 3, no. 2: 244–247. As far as the author
        knows, there is no specific record of the meeting in the US documents.

26    Wilson's efforts for China at the peace conference are dealt with well in Elleman, ibid.

27    Matsui to Uchida, 22 April 1919, *NGB: Taishō 8*, vol. 3, no. 2, 249–250; Hankey's Notes of a
        Meeting of the Council of Four, 22 April 1919, *PWW*, vol. 57, 607–608; *The Council of Four*,
        vol. I, 325–326.

rights of foreigners in China if we ourselves did the same. If they accept the transfer, pure and simple, of the German rights to Japan and really want to discuss with us the change of the terms we imposed on China, we can find a solution to the problem." Wilson had virtually declared himself ready to make a concession on the Shandong problem, but in exchange for the commitment by not only Japan but also the United Kingdom and France – European powers with a great deal of interests and a sphere of influence in and around the country – that they would work hard together in the near future "to liberate China from the chains which weigh on her"; needless to say, this meant within the framework of the League of Nations.[28]

The British Prime Minister and Wilson's experts were offended by Wilson's judgment, but on clearly different grounds. Lloyd George, who had recommended that the President make some concessions to Japan, a British ally, reacted sharply against the suggestion, stating, "we couldn't agree to give up our special rights in the Yangtze Valley if Japan retained a privileged position in Shantung. What we can propose is a perfect equality of treatment." This reaction, however, might have served to endorse the accuracy of Wilson's awareness of the issue. He replied to the Prime Minister, "the question is whether or not this equality, which would open the Yangtze Valley to the Japanese, would be advantageous to China."[29]

The criticism from his experts, advisers, and other plenipotentiaries in the American delegation must have struck Wilson as serious, because it focused on the grounds of his own New Diplomacy. However, Wilson did not accept their opinions and stuck to his guns, and he signed the Treaty of Versailles on 28 June. Another factor, of course, influenced his judgment on Shandong: the secret treaties that Japan concluded with the United Kingdom and France during the war to secure its claims on German interests. Wilson expressed to his attending physician his strong fear that Japan's withdrawal from the peace conference would finally lead to the collapse of the League program.[30] At the same time, he also had to prepare for "the treaty fight" to come in the American political arena.[31] In this difficult situation, however, Wilson was never about to

---

28    *The Council of Four*, vol. I, 379. See also Hankey's Notes of a Meeting of the Council of Four, 25 April 1919, *PWW*, vol. 58, 131.

29    Ibid, 131.

30    From the Diary of Dr. Grayson, 25 April 1919, *PWW*, vol. 58, 112–113.

31    Lloyd E. Ambrosius, *Woodrow Wilson and the American Diplomatic Tradition: The Treaty Fight in Perspective* (Cambridge, UK: Cambridge University Press, 1987); Widenor C. William "The United States and the Versailles Peace Settlement" in John M. Carroll and George C. Herring. eds., *Modern American Diplomacy*, revised and enlarged ed. (Wilmington, DE: Scholarly Resources Inc., 1996), 35–51; John Milton Cooper, Jr., *Breaking*

revert to the original position he had held on the Chinese problems before the direct talks with the Japanese at the peace conference. On the day the Shandong question was finally settled in the Council of Four, he summed it up as cited below, after saying that it was not ideal but "the best that could be gotten out of a dirty past."

> The only hope was, somehow, to keep the world together, get the League of Nations with Japan in it and then try *to secure justice for the Chinese not only as regards Japan but as regarding England, Russia, France, and America, all of whom had concessions in China.* If Japan went home[,] there was a danger of a Japanese-Russian-German-alliance[*sic*] – and a return of the old "balance of power" system in the world... [Italicized by the author][32]

Clearly coming to see the problem from the point of view emphasized by Makino in the talks, he decided to settle the problem as the impetus for reshaping the entire structure of great-power politics in East Asia. Wilson judged that program would require the cooperation of all related powers, and putting into question only Japan's behavior would fall pitifully short in meeting his purpose "to liberate China from the chains."

## 4     Conclusion

What did peace mean to Japan and international politics in East Asia? Did it bring about something that, to some small extent, measured up to Wilson's New Diplomacy? According to Ray Stannard Baker, the Press Secretary in the American mission, the delegation's judgment was clearly negative. Baker remarked that "[our] whole delegation, except Col. House [Wilson's 'right arm' but his opinion seems to have had little influence on the settlement, in sharp contrast with what most of the American mission, including Baker, were firmly convinced of.],...is for the Chinese case, and declare [sic] Wilson has made a terrible mistake." He himself could hardly understand the settlement Wilson reached with the Japanese, despite probably having the most sympathy among the Americans for the President, whom he knew had faced a tough choice.[33]

the Heart of the World: Woodrow Wilson and the Fight for the League of Nations (Cambridge, UK: Cambridge University Press, 2001).

32     From the Diary of Baker, 30 April 1919, PWW, Vol. 58, 270.

33     From the Diary of Baker, 29 April 1919 and 1 May 1919, PWW, vol. 58, 229 and 327.

(Ironically, Wilson's "secret diplomacy" in the Council of Four made it much harder for his experts and advisers to grasp his fundamental reasoning behind the settlement).

It was not only the Chinese refusal to sign the peace treaty and the people's uprising in China that Wilson's "terrible mistake" brought about in East Asia, however. He arguably succeeded in giving rise to two important changes in international politics in the region, which in comprehending, refocuses our attention on Japanese diplomacy.

First, because of the US-Japanese talks on Shandong at the peace conference, Japanese diplomacy clearly switched from Itō's realism to the new framework to come into line with American New Diplomacy that Makino and Komura had insisted on from the outset. This did not mean that Japan decided to abandon its own sphere of influence or privileges in China as the pioneer of all great powers. What they resolved was to accept Wilson's basic insistence to cast away the old rule of great-power politics in East Asia, which had called on mutual respect for each sphere of influence in China, and, instead, to protect and extend Japanese diplomatic and economic interests by acting on the principles of the New Diplomacy that stood for vigorous economic interaction open to all, even though they knew many problems remained to be solved both at home and abroad.

That is, the Japanese decided to abandon a traditional way of cooperating with other powers, which showed that the Japanese leaders and officials in the Foreign Ministry came to think more, through the peace negotiations, about how to cooperate with the United States, the advocate of the new principles, than the United Kingdom, the old champion of world politics, Japan's only ally at that time, and the country that had been the most important diplomatic partner in and around China over the nearly two decades. In addition, the refusal of the Japanese racial equality proposal, another important issue for the two countries at the peace conference, did not stand in the way of Japan's rapprochement with the United States. Although Wilson was the chair of the special committee that finally settled on it, the Japanese plenipotentiaries realized this was not a peculiar flaw inherent in his New Diplomacy and that the strongest objection to the proposal came from within the British Empire, that is, Australia.[34]

This Japanese diplomatic changeover meant not only a character change of an important player in great-power politics in East Asia, but also the beginning

---

34     Memorandum by the delegation for the report on the mission to the peace negotiations, 22 July 1919, *NGB, Taishō 8*, Vol. 3, no. 1, 789–790; Nobuaki Makino, *Kaikoroku*, vol. 2 (Tokyo: Chūōkōronsha, 1978), 203–211.

of the old international order's replacement in the region by a new one, and this is the second consequence of Wilson's "terrible mistake" at the peace conference. It took a few more years to see some concrete results as international treaties, which were negotiated at the Washington Naval Conference in 1921–22. What should be noted here is that it was an factor for the success of the conference that Japan had never made any attempt to come into line with the United Kingdom in the old manner to handle American demands concerning China and other issues since the peace was concluded at Paris in 1919, even when its old ally hoped it would do so.

Consequently, the old order in the region was incapable of reproducing itself given the changeover of Japanese diplomacy following the collapse of the Russian Empire and the defeat of Germany. Taking into account the influence and power of France too, there were no great powers willing *and* capable to cooperate with the United Kingdom in the manner of the old diplomacy in China, whatever policy the United Kingdom might have hoped to adopt in such a situation.

After the Paris Peace Conference, East Asia continued to witness conflict between states, nations, and ethnic groups, as other regions did, and the liberation of China from "the chains" was not smooth. However, the peace clearly changed the way in which the Japanese policymakers, and especially the officials in the Foreign Ministry, thought about "international cooperation." This, if not in the exact way Wilson had hoped at Paris, virtually ended the great-power politics in which international cooperation had been largely equated with a mutual recognition of each sphere of influence at the expense of China in the previous few decades.

# A New Look at Japan's Twenty-One Demands
*Reconsidering Katō Takaaki's Motives in 1915*

*Sōchi Naraoka*

## The Twenty-One Demands: A Turning Point in Japanese Diplomatic History

The issue of the Twenty-One Demands, which Japan proposed to China in 1915, is known to be a turning point in Japanese diplomatic history. By concluding a treaty with China based on these demands, Japan succeeded in gaining a secure place in Manchuria. On the other hand, China resisted Japan fiercely in these negotiations, which was a catalyst for increasing Chinese nationalism. From 1915 onwards, May 9, the day when the Chinese government accepted the Demands, was named as "a National Day of Humiliation." The Twenty-One Demands in retrospect are regarded as the herald of Japanese expansion on the Continent which accelerated in the 1930s.

The Twenty-One Demands resulted in Japan's deterioration in its relations not only with China but also with Europe and America. The United States was opposed to Japan's rejection of the "Open Door" in China. Secretary of State William Bryan expressed serious concern over Japan's infringement of Chinese sovereignty. Great Britain, Japan's ally, also began to develop a deep-rooted distrust towards the government in Tokyo. This had a great impact in that it became one of the main causes of the demise of the Anglo-Japanese alliance.

Why were the Demands so problematic? The first reason was that the Japanese requests were too vast. The Twenty-One Demands were divided into five groups. Most of the articles in Groups I to IV could be and were approved by the Great Powers, considering the imperialism and sprit of the times. However, Group V brought much criticism because it attempted to violate Chinese sovereignty and clashed with existing British privileges. In short, the Japanese demands were against the practice of imperial politics.

The second reason was that the Japanese government tried to conceal the most controversial part, Group V, from the interested Great Powers including Britain. When the negotiations started, the Japanese government requested the Chinese government to keep Group V secret and did not notify the Great Powers of its existence. However, the Chinese government leaked this information in order to resist the Japanese and it led to the distrust towards the Japanese government in China, Europe, America and even within Japan itself. In the end, the Japanese government succeeded in concluding a treaty with

China through the threat of military force. Nevertheless, it can be said that the Chinese government also achieved a measure of success in that it forced Japan to withdraw Group V.

Why did the Japanese government include such problematic requests? Why specifically did Katō Takaaki, the then Japanese Foreign Minister of the Okuma administration, insert Group V? There have been many studies about the Twenty-One Demands, but clear answers to these questions have not yet been given. This paper attempts to answer these questions, based mainly on the primary sources in Japan and Britain. We will examine three points of view which have been neglected. The first is the process in which Group V was made, concealed and revealed. The second is the reaction of the Chinese government, and the third is the role of the media in Japan, China and Britain.

Before proceeding to the main issues, it is of use to briefly review previous studies.[1] The most reliable works on this topic are the books written by Peter Lowe and Ian Nish. These revealed the process of negotiations and evaluated the leadership of Foreign Minister Katō mainly using British sources. In Japan, the books written by Horikawa Takeo and Usui Katsumi are reliable.

---

1  The studies which will be mentioned are as follows. Peter Lowe, *Great Britain and Japan, 1911–1915: A Study of British Far Eastern Policy* (London: Macmillan, 1969); Ian Nish, *Alliance in decline: a study in Anglo-Japanese relations, 1908–23* (London: Athlone Press, 1972); Ian Nish, *Japanese Foreign Policy, 1869–1942: Kasumigaseki to Miyakezaka* (London and Boston: Routledge and Kegan Paul, 1977); Horikawa Takeo, *Kyokuto Kokusaiseijisi Josetsu* (Tokyo: Yuhikaku, 1958); Usui Katsumi, *Nippon to Chugoku* (Tokyo: Hara Shobo, 1972); Arthur S. Link, *Wilson: The Struggle for Neutrality, 1914–1915* (Princeton: Princeton University Press, 1960); Noel H. Pugach, *Paul S. Reinsch: Open Door Diplomat in Action* (New York: KTO Press, 1979); James Reed, *The Missionary Mind and American East Asia Policy 1911–1915* (Cambridge, Mass.: the Council on East Asian Studies at Harvard University, 1983); Noriko Kawamura, *Turbulence in the Pacific: Japan-U.S. relations during World War I* (Westport, Washington: Praeger Publishers, 2000); Takahara Shusuke, *Wilson Gaiko to Nippon: Riso to Genjitsu no Aida 1913–1921* (Tokyo: Sobunsha, 2006); Yu Xintun, *Xinghai Geming Jie Zhong-Ri Waijiaoshi* (Tianjing, Tianjing Renmin Chubanshe, 2000) [the Japanese version is *Shingai Kakumeiki no Chunichi Gaikoshi Kenkyu* (Tokyo: Tohoshoten, 2002)]; Chan Lau Kit-Ching, *Anglo-Chinese Diplomacy in the careers of Sir John Jordan and Yuan Shih-k'ai 1906–1920* (Hong Kong: Hong Kong University Press, 1978); Kawashima Shin, *Chugoku Kindaigaiko no Keisei* (Nagoya: Nagoyadaigaku shuppankai, 2004); Kawashima Shin, *Kindaikokka eno Mosaku 1894–1925* (Tokyo: Iwanami shoten, 2010); Kitaoka Shin-ichi, "Nijuikkajo Saiko: Nichibei Gaiko no Sogosayo," *Nenpo Kindainihon Kenkyu*, vol. 7 (1985); Shimada Yoichi, "Taika Nijuikkajo Yokyu," *Seijikeizai Shigaku*, vol. 259, 260 (1987); Frederick R. Dickinson, *War and National Reinvention: Japan in the Great War, 1914–1919* (Cambridge, Mass.: Harvard University Asia Center, 1999). For Katō as political leader, see Naraoka Sochi, *Kato Takaaki to Seito Seiji: Nidai Seitosei eno Michi* (Tokyo: Yamakawa shuppansha, 2006).

They analyzed the Demands focusing mainly on Japanese sources. For American responses, Arthur S. Link, Noel H. Pugach, James Reed, Noriko Kawamura and Takahara Shusuke examined the making of the "non-recognition" policy. For Chinese reactions, Yu Xin-tun examined the situation based mainly on Japanese sources, and Chan Lau, Kit-Ching based their study mainly on British sources, but unfortunately few Chinese primary sources were used. Kawashima Shin's recent studies imply that the Twenty-One Demands should be studied more in terms of Chinese diplomacy.

As previously indicated, the issue of Group V is the most important topic. Regarding this, Kitaoka Shin-ichi and Shimada Yoichi published important articles, and Frederick Dickinson also examined Group V in his book. This paper will refer to these in detail later.

### What Is Group V?

On 18 January 1915, Hioki Eki, the Japanese Minister in Beijing, met Yuan Shi-Kai and proposed the Twenty-One Demands to him. Yuan did not express his opinion but was very angry. On the following day he asked his military adviser why the Japanese government were dealing with China as if it were a slave.[2]

The Twenty-One Demands were divided into five groups. Group I concerned Shantung province, which Japan had acquired from Germany after the breakout of the Great War. It requested that China allow Japan to succeed to the German rights and concessions in Shantung. Group II concerned Manchuria and requested that China agree to the extension of the lease over Port Arthur, Dairen, and the South Manchurian Railway for a further ninety-nine years. Group III requested that China allow Japan to invest in the Hanyeping Company, one of the largest mine companies, so that it would become a joint Sino-Japanese firm. Group IV was a declaration that China would not grant any further ports as concessions to any foreign power.

The fifth group was the most notorious and controversial. It included the following articles. China was to engage some influential Japanese people as political, financial and military advisers (article 1); Sino-Japanese control of the police was to be implemented where necessary (article 3); and China was to grant Japan the right to construct railways in the Yangtze (article 5). The Japanese government said they were not "demands" but "wishes," and pushed the Chinese government not to leak them to other foreign countries.

---

2  Hioki to Katō, Jan 20 1915, in Gaimusho ed., *Nihon Gaiko Monjo* (hereafter NGM, Tokyo: Gaimusho, 1966), 1915, Vol. 3–1.

The Japanese government drafted the Demands after the Japanese army had beaten Germany in Shantung province and begun occupation in November 1914. Japan had to negotiate with China in order to decide who should govern the area because the latter had sovereignty there. However, Foreign Minister Katō did not confine his negotiations with China to Shantung province. He also wanted to take the opportunity to negotiate and solve various problems which had arisen since the Russo-Japanese War, so he included them in the Demands as Groups II to IV. Katō believed the most important issue was the problem of the extension of the lease in Manchuria to which Japan had succeeded after the Russo-Japanese War. The original Russian lease had been for twenty-five years, and therefore Japan had to return them to China after 1923. For this reason Katō, as the Ambassador to Britain, had already discussed this issue with Sir Edward Grey, the British Foreign Secretary, in London in January 1913 and obtained his agreement to an extension.[3]

Groups I to IV were generally based on existing Japanese interests, but they also requested that Japan's interests be extended. As he thought it would not be easy to persuade the Chinese government, Katō intended to make concessions on Group I. In short, Katō planned to persuade China to accept the other requests in exchange for a promise to return Shantung province in the near future. Katō thought this was virtually his only bargaining chip and his best trump card, so he repeatedly outlined this plan to Hioki.[4] Among the Army and journalists, there were a lot of hardliners who did not want to return the Shantung province,[5] but Katō did not agree with them. It can be said that his attitude towards Groups I to IV was consistent.

On the other hand, his attitude toward Group V was rather ambiguous. Surprisingly he did not outline how to implement it in the negotiations. Most of the articles of Group V, unlike those of Groups I to IV, were not based on existing Japanese interests and were likely to conflict with the sovereignty of China and the existing interests of Britain and other countries. Kitaoka Shin-ichi has proposed the hypothesis that Katō dared to insert those articles because he intended to use Group V as a bargaining chip.[6] I agree in part with him. I believe that Katō had a vague plan to threaten Yuan Shi-kai with Group

3  Ito Masanori ed., *Kato Takaaki*, vol. 2 (Tokyo: Katotakaakihaku dennkihensaniinkai, 1929), 132–147.

4  Katō to Hioki, Jan 11, Feb 16, 1915, *NGM*, 1915, Vol. 3–1.

5  For example, Machida Keiu, a military attaché in Beijing, and Japanese political pressure groups such as Toa-doshikai and Taishi-Rengokai made such proposals to the Foreign Office (*NGM*, 1914, Vol. 2).

6  Kitaoka Shin-ichi, op. cit.

V with the intention of dropping some parts in order to persuade him to accept the more important Groups I to IV. In fact, at the Cabinet Meeting on 16 February, he decided to give up the inclusion of most of Group V in the treaty and hoped to conclude a kind of agreement with, or statement from, the Chinese Government as a compromise.[7]

However, as Shimada Yoichi has made clear, Katō was not consistent in his handling of Group V. He continued to try to press for some demands to be implemented in the following negotiations. As discussed in detail later in this paper, I think Katō did not have a clear map with Group V but only had a loose plan to be flexible in negotiations according to Yuan's attitudes.


### How Was Group V Made? (1) Katō vs. the Army

Why was Katō's attitude so ambiguous? The key to the question is in the way Group V came about. The origins of Group V were that its contents came as requests from the general staff of the Army and various domestic pressure groups to the Foreign Ministry. The late Dr. Peter Lowe said in his work *Great Britain and Japan* that it appears most likely that the fifth group was a concession to the pressure being exerted on Katō. I am basically of the same opinion. Unfortunately there are very few materials which confirm this conclusion, but this study will attempt to reconstruct the circumstances at the time by referring to primary sources in Japan.

Requests from many factions in Japan were made after the start of the war. In particular, the Army insisted on taking active steps to acquire more interests on the Continent while the European powers were busily occupied with war.[8] Soon after the start of the war, Akashi Motojirō, the Vice Chief of the General Staff, insisted that China should entrust the reform of its administration and military to Japan, and that if it gave concessions to, or asked for loans from, foreign countries, China should consult Japan beforehand. Tanaka Giichi, of

---

7   Katō to Hioki, Feb 16 1915, *NGM*, 1915, Vol. 3.

8   For the plans of policy towards China in the Army just after the breakout of the First World War, see Kobayashi Michihiko, Sekaitaisen to Tairikuseisaku no Henyo: 1914–1916, *Rekishigaku Kenkyu*, vol. 656 (1994). For the views of the hardliners in the Army, see the following documents. Akashi Motojiro to Oka Ichinosuke (the War Minister) Aug 16 1914, Oka Papers, The National Diet Library of Japan (hereafter NDL), Tokyo, Japan, Tanaka Giichi to Oka Ichinosuke, Aug 1914 (estimated), Oka Papers, the summary of the draft of Sino-Japanese Agreement written on Aug 7 1915 by Fukuda Masataro, the memorandum written on Aug 24 1915 by Oshima Ken-ichi, *NGM*, 1914 Vol. 2, Terauchi Masatake to Akashi, Aug 22 1914, Akashi Papers, NDL.

the General Staff, Oshima Ken-ichi, the Permanent Under-secretary of the War
Office, and Fukushima Masataro, the head of the second section of the General
Staff Office, also took a hard line and sent their opinions to the Foreign Ministry.
Meanwhile General Terauchi Masatake, the Governor-General of Korea,
insisted that Japan should establish "the Asian Monroe Doctrine." It seems that
Katō and the Foreign Ministry faced serious difficulties in coordinating the
draft, considering that there were such hardliners in the Army.

In contrast with the latter, Katō was not at ease in presenting such wide-
ranging demands to China. He was critical of Japanese expansion to the
Continent after the Russo-Japanese War. After the Xinghai Revolution in 1911,
China had lapsed into a state of civil war and some Japanese political and
military leaders had been tempted to intervene in the interior in order to
maintain Japanese special interests in China. However Katō did not think that
Japanese interests should be upheld by military actions or interventions.
From April to June 1913, Katō visited China and met Yuan Shikai and Sun
Yatsen. In an interview after he had returned to Japan, he emphasized that
Japan should not intervene in the conflict in China. When Japanese men were
killed in China and hardliners insisted on taking military action in the autumn
of 1913, Katō supported the non-intervention policy of Makino Nobuaki, the
Foreign Minister in the Yamamoto administration.

For Katō, whose policy towards China was originally moderate, the coordination of these far-reaching requests was thus very difficult. On November 11,
1914, he finished the task and presented the draft of the instructions to the
Minister in Beijing at a special cabinet meeting. This first draft of the demands
to the Chinese government consisted of seventeen demands and there was no
distinction between "requests" and "wishes."[9]

### How Was Group V Made? (2) Katō and Yamagata

The draft was agreed by all the Ministers in the cabinet but Katō had to ask for
the consent of the Army, Navy and other branches of the government. Katō
expressed his true feelings to the Chief of the Tokyo Metropolitan Police
Department in his letter of November 14 as follows.[10] This letter is the only
private letter in which he referred to the origins of the Twenty-One Demands.

---

9      Obata Yukichi Denkikankokai ed., *Obata Yukichi* (Tokyo: Obata Yukichi Denkikankokai,
       1957), 95–96.
10     Katō to Kawakami Chikaharu, Nov 13 1914(estimated) in Kohara (or Ohara) Ryuma, *Seinan
       Hishi: Kawakami Chikaharu Ouden* (Kagoshima: Kagoshimaken Kajikicho Shidankai,
       1942), 274.

I imagine there will be various demands on diplomatic matters from now. It is needless to say I can't include all of them, so I feel very nervous.

On November 18, Katō visited the genro, Yamagata Aritomo. The latter had already retired from the front line of politics but maintained potentially strong influence on politicians and the military as an elder statesman, Field Marshal and Duke. Fortunately there is a record of this meeting written by the secretary of Yamagata. According to this, Katō explained the content of the demands without handing over the draft to him. On hearing them, Yamagata told Katō as follows:[11]

As for the policy towards China, my opinion is fundamentally different from yours...The articles which you explained now cover too wide a range of topics. I heard there are articles such as requesting China to consult Japan on important diplomatic matters and to entrust Japan on financial matters, but I believe the Chinese government cannot approve them because they treat it as a subject state. Can the Government request such things at all?

Katō replied to him as follows:

These were made by collecting opinions in many quarters such as the Army and the Navy. The Government has the intention of requesting only what is important.

Katō forced Yamagata to tell him whether he agreed to the policy of the government or not. Yamagata answered as follows:

As I have said, my opinion is fundamentally different from yours. But I could say I agree to most parts.

This appears to be contradictory, but Yamagata was consistent in that he thought the articles which were included in Group V were unnecessary. What he thought important was to extend the lease in South Manchuria, and he explained this not only to Katō but also to Oka Ichinosuke, the War Minister and to Hara Takashi, the leader of the opposition party.[12]

---

11    The note of Yamagata's talking, No. 5, Futagami Papers, NDL. This note has recently been published as Shoyu Club ed. *Taishoshoki Yamagata Aritomo Danwahikki Zoku* (Tokyo: Fuyoshobo Shuppan, 2011).
12    Ibid., Hara Keiichiro ed., *Hara Kei Nikki, Vol. 4* (Tokyo: Fukumura Shuppan, 1965), the descriptions in Nov 29 1914, July 8 1915.

Historians have expressed different interpretations of Yamagata's views on Group V,[13] but we can discover his real opinion from this record which has not previously been cited. It indicates that Yamagata was not at ease with the articles which would later be arranged as Group V, although officially he was not strongly opposed to the draft. We can conclude that if Katō had asked Yamagata to persuade the General Staff, Group V might have been moderated to some degree. However, Katō did not do so as he believed their role to be unconstitutional and undemocratic. Equally, the elder statesman was also not eager to support Katō, who had been hostile to him. Yamagata did not take any action to calm these demands from generals of the Army, although he later implied he might have done so if Katō had asked him to.[14]

Katō and the Foreign Ministry revised the draft between November and January. Primary sources, which remain in fragments, imply that they made efforts to tame the hardliners.[15] For example, some articles in the first draft were deleted in December. However, in contrast, some harsh conditions were also added in December. For example, the notorious articles on the Sino-Japanese joint control of the police were now inserted.

In particular the most difficult obstacles were the many hardliners in the General Staff. For example, in the first draft in November, the requests from Akashi Motojiro were toned down regarding the adoption of Japanese advisers and loans from foreign countries. But the General Staff is believed not to have accepted this and to have pushed the Foreign Ministry to revise this scheme. As a result, the final version of Group V which was proposed to China in January included Akashi's requests as articles 1 and 7. The final version is believed to have been a result of the rivalry between the Foreign Ministry and the Army. Coordination was difficult partly because of the situation of the party in the Government, Rikken Doshikai (Constitutionalists' Party). The party was disorganized and lacked maturity because it had been founded only two years before. There were many expansionists in the party who tended to be sympathetic towards the increase of Japanese influence on the Continent. The leader of the party, Katō, could not control them fully. Had Katō ignored their opinions, he might have been driven to resign as leader of the party. Katō, who had political ambition to become Prime Minister, had to meet requests from the party.

---

13    Kitaoka, Dickinson insist that Yamagata was not opposed to Group V, while Shimada
      points out Yamagata was opposed to it.
14    Hara Keiichiro, op. cit., the descriptions in July 8 1915.
15    Ito Masanori, op. cit., 198–214, Obata Yukichi Denkikankokai, op. cit., chap.5, NGM, 1914,
      Vol. 2, 865–953, Vol. 3, 541–597. See also the documents in footnote 8.

Pressure from many factions in Japan, especially the Army, were therefore a huge influence on the presentation of the Twenty-One Demands. Group V was made for the reason that Katō and the Foreign Ministry could not reject these requests. It is likely that Katō felt it would be difficult to get China to approve Group V and that it might provoke an angry response from Europe and America. That is the reason that Katō distinguished Groups I to IV from Group V and called the latter "wishes." However, he did not expect that Chinese resistance would be so strong and skilful and he did not imagine that Europe and America would be so angry. It could be said that his reading of the situation and his approach was too optimistic.

### Why Was Group V Concealed?

Why did Katō conceal Group V from the Great Powers including Japan's ally, Britain, when he started the negotiations with China? Katō told Yuan Shikai not to leak "the wishes" to other countries, even though it was quite possible and even probable that Yuan would leak them. Did Katō not consider this possibility?

"To control barbarians by using barbarians" was the traditional way in Chinese diplomacy and the Chinese government often tried to make foreign countries compete with each other.

For example, at the conference at Shimonoseki after the Sino-Japanese War in 1895, Li Hongzhang, the representative of the Qing Dynasty, tried to leak the draft of the peace treaty, although it was interrupted by Japan.[16] A similar example is also seen in 1900. In this year Russia concluded the Russo-Chinese Secret Agreement in order to justify its occupation of Manchuria; however it was soon leaked by the Chinese government to George Morrison, the Beijing correspondent of *The Times*, which led to the agreement being reported around the world. Katō, the then Foreign Minister, protested strongly, pressing Russia into promising to retreat from Manchuria.[17] Therefore the Japanese politicians and diplomats including Katō must have understood that the Chinese may well try to follow this practice in the negotiations in order to take advantage of the competition between the Powers.

---

16    Ito Masanori, op. cit., vol. 1, 246–249, Nakatsuka Akira, *Nissin Senso no Kenkyu* (Tokyo: Aokishoten, 1968), 286–287.

17    Ito Masanori, op. cit., vol. 1, 402–447, Eiko Woodhouse, *Nichiro Senso wo Enshutsusita Otoko Morrison*, vol. 1 (Tokyo: Toyokeizaisinposha, 1988), 4–47.

However, the Japanese had lately developed a feeling of contempt towards China after Japan had defeated Russia in the Russo-Japanese War. Japan became too confident after its victory and its approach in diplomatic matters often became arrogant. We can see a good example of this in the case of the conclusion of the Sino-Japanese Agreement in 1905.

Following the treaty of Portsmouth in September 1905, in which Japan gained possession of the Russian concessions in Manchuria, Japan also had to conclude a treaty with the Chinese Government, as China still had ultimate sovereignty over Manchuria. The negotiations were undertaken in Beijing. The representative of Japan, Komura Jutaro, requested that the talks should be held secretly, and Prince Yikuang and Yuan Shikai, the representatives of China, accepted this. The negotiations continued for about one month and as Japan had intended, the process was kept from the outside world. The representatives of China were unusually weak and did not appear to offer any resistance.

The treaty and an attached agreement were concluded in December 1905. It should be noted that the agreement was made in addition to the treaty and kept strictly secret. It listed the details of the concessions to Japan in Manchuria regarding railways, telegraphic lines, mines and so on. Japan ensured that detailed minutes were also kept in order to guarantee the Japanese position in Manchuria. Britain and the other Powers were unaware of the secret agreement and minutes.[18] The fact that the negotiations were held in secret and were completed quickly was of great benefit to Japan, with the result that the Powers did not intervene following the example of the Triple Intervention after the Sino-Japanese War.

It is possible that this success was the model for the Twenty-One Demands. The way in which Katō negotiated was not new but rather followed the precedent set in 1905. As Japan had succeeded fully then, Katō did not worry too much about the possibility of the Chinese leaking information. He seems to have thought that it would not be problematic if he informed the British government of the treaty after he had finished the negotiations. Of course, he was too optimistic. The terms included in Group V were more severe than the Sino-Japanese Treaty in 1905. Moreover, Chinese nationalism had become much stronger after the Xinghai Revolution, and journalism was developing quickly in China and an informed public was emerging. This became clear soon after Japan proposed the Twenty-One Demands.

---

18    Gaimusho ed., *Komura Gaikoshi* (Tokyo: Harashobo, 1966), chap. 8 Sect. 9.

### How Did China Resist?

The Japanese government proposed the Twenty-One Demands to Yuan Shikai on 18 January 1915. He called his staff the next day. According to the memoir of the Vice-Minister,[19] Cao Rulin, Yuan thought "Japan was trying to conquer China," and said "Because Group V means Japan is treating China as Korea, we must not negotiate with Japan." Yuan ordered to Cao Rulin that Group V "must not be discussed." Skillfully, Yuan took four measures to defend China. Over the following months he prolonged the negotiations, encouraged Chinese journalists to inspire anti-Japanese sentiments in China, leaked information to foreign newspapers, and invited intervention from Europe and America.

The first of the actions that Yuan took was to prolong the negotiations. He dismissed his Foreign Minister on the pretext of illness, and appointed Lu Zhengxiang as his successor. Lu, the ex-Foreign Minister, had also served as a Chinese representative in Europe for a long time and had much experience in diplomatic matters. He did not respond to the Japanese offers to start the negotiations, delaying the first meeting until February 2. The Japanese minister in Beijing, Hioki, was irritated at this because the delay put Japan in a greatly disadvantageous position.[20]

Secondly, Yuan approached the media in China in order to inspire anti-Japanese sentiments. Chinese newspapers began to report the Japanese demands on January 27. The first of these to do so was the *Yaxiya Ri Bao* (Asian Daily News), according to the information that Foreign Ministry in Japan collected. The paper insisted that the demands from the Japanese government would lead to the violation of the sovereignty of China, and so could not be discussed under any circumstances. Other Chinese newspapers such as the *Min Shi Bao* (People's Report), and English newspapers in China such as the *Peking Daily News* and *Peking Gazette* also started to criticize Japan before the first conference was held.[21] It is most probable that the Chinese government leaked information to the newspapers. An example of this can be seen with *Shen Bao* (Shanghai News), the most influential newspaper in China at the time. On January 28 it reported correctly that the Japanese demands consisted of twenty-one articles.

Yuan gave an interview to one of the most famous Chinese journalists, Liang Qichao. After the interview Liang wrote articles for some Chinese newspapers.

---

19    Cao Ruin, *Issho no Kaioku* (Tokyo: Kashimakenkyujo Shuppankai, 1967), 71–73.
20    Hioki to Katō, Jan 29, Feb 3, 1915, *NGM*, 1915, Vol. 3–1.
21    Ariyoshi Akira (the Consul-General in Shanghai) to Katō, Jan 29 1915, Hioki to Katō Feb 1 1915 in *NGM*, 1915, Vol. 3–1.

He criticized the Japanese demands and warned the Japanese not to mistake China for "a second Korea."[22] On February 2 Chinese newspapers reported that nineteen warlords, such as Duan Qirui, Feng Guozhang, had sent telegrams to Yuan in order to declare themselves opposed to the Japanese demands. According to Kanda Masao, the Japanese correspondent in Beijing of the *Tokyo Asahi Shimbun*, one of the leading newspapers in Japan,[23] the truth is said to have been that Yuan himself ordered them to do so. Along with other newspapers, *Tokyo Asahi Shimbun* criticized these actions for "doing harm to the friendship between the two countries." It led to the rapid rise of anti-Chinese sentiment in Japan in February.[24]

### The Response of Journalism

The third action Yuan Shikai took was to leak information to foreign newspapers. Yuan had no intention whatsoever of keeping the secrecy which Japan had requested of him. In his memoir, the Japanese journalist, Kanda Masao, later recalled:[25]

> It was too naïve of the Japanese government to think it possible to make the Chinese government keep secrecy by saying it is a diplomatic rule. It was impossible to do so because leaking was beneficial to the Chinese government. Leaking was the traditional way of the Chinese.

How were the Japanese demands leaked? Yuan is believed to have leaked them not only to Chinese but also foreign journalists almost immediately after he had received them.

The situation was complicated regarding Japanese newspapers. Straight after presenting the demands, Foreign Minister Katō gathered the editors of all the major newspapers in Japan, and secretly told them the outline of the negotiations. Katō requested them to refrain from reporting the negotiations, to which they agreed.[26] Therefore, most of the newspapers in Japan did not go so

---

22   *Osaka Asahi Shimbun*, Feb 4–5 1915, Kanda Masao, "Taisho 4 nen Nisshi Kosho Shiryo" in Keiogijuku Mochizuki Kikin Shinakenkkyukai ed., *Shina Kenkyu* (Tokyo: Iwanamishoten, 1930): 206–207. For Liang's criticism of the Twenty-One Demands, see Chen Lixin, *Liang Richao and journalism* (Tokyo: Fuyoshobo shuppan, 2009), 245–248.
23   Hioki to Katō, Feb 5 1915, NGM, 1915, Vol. 3–1, Apr 27 1915, *Tokyo Asahi Shimbun*.
24   For example, see Feb 5 1915 *Osaka Asahi Shimbun, Tokyo Nichinichi Shimbun*.
25   Kanda Masao, op. cit., 205.
26   Katō to Hioki, Jan 22 1915, NGM, 1915, Vol. 3–1.

far as to report the detail of the negotiations. However some of them did fall into the temptation to report in full, possibly stimulated by leaking from the Chinese.

For example, on January 23, *the Tokyo and Osaka Asahi Shimbun* reported the scoop in a special edition. This special edition was based on information which Kanda had acquired in Beijing. It classified the Japanese demands into three categories; the problems of Manchuria, Shungtong and China as a whole. Kanda seems to have received the outline of the demands from Chinese sources, as he later recalled that Japanese journalists understood the contents of the demands very easily through Chinese leaks. The Foreign Ministry in Japan regarded the special edition of *the Asahi Shimbun* as extremely problematic. As a result, it was cancelled with the notice that the report about the negotiations was different from the facts.[27]

Chinese leaking caused a greater sensation in newspapers in Europe and America. On January 27, *The New York Times* reported correctly that the Japanese minister in Beijing had presented "requests made up of twenty-one demands." Around that time correspondents of other newspapers in China, such as Frederic Moor of the American *Associated Press*, began to report that Japan wished to expand its interests in the Yangzi valley and Fujian.[28] In contrast, there was also much conflicting information. Some newspapers reported that the Japanese demands were not contrary to China's territorial integrity, the "open door" and equality of opportunity.[29] The Japanese government could not and did not reply to them effectively. For example, the minister in Beijing, Hioki, gave very few interviews, and so he was nicknamed "I don't know."[30] It can be guessed that the name of the "Twenty-One Demands" prevailed as the content was revealed by newspapers.

*The Times*, the most influential newspaper in Britain, reported Japan's presentation of the demands to China on January 18, but then refrained from reporting further until the situation had developed. This may have been due to the fact that it had traditionally had good relations with the Japanese government and had emphasized the importance of the Anglo-Japanese Alliance.

27    Yamamoto Tadashi, "Taishoki Nippon no Kaigai Tokuhain Hodo," *Nihon Daigaku Daigakuin Sogo Shakaijoho Kenkyujo Kiyo*, vol. 4 (2003). For the reports of the Twenty-One Demands in the Asahi Shimbun, see Goto Takao, *Singai Kakumei kara Manshu Jihen e* (Tokyo: Misuzushobo, 1987), 87–99.

28    Debuchi Katsuji, "Nijuikkajo Mondai" in Hirose Yoshihiro ed. *Kindaigaiko Kaikoroku*, vol. 4 (Tokyo: Yumanishobo, 2000), 202–203, Kanda Masao, op. cit., 210–212.

29    Jan 29, Feb 3–4 1915, *Osaka Asahi Shimbun*, Jan 29, Feb 7 1915, *Tokyo Nichinichi Shimbun*.

30    Kanda Masao, op. cit., 210.

George Morrison, who had been a correspondent of *The Times* in China until 1912, was now a political adviser to Yuan Shikai.[31] He was deeply concerned about the Japanese expansion to China. On January 28, he asked Cai Tinggan, an officer in the Presidential Office, to give him the full text of the Japanese demands and proposed that it should be published. He did not know the exact contents of the demands, and so he wrote in his diary "I am as ignorant as ordinary people."[32] On February 4, Cai visited Morrison and revealed the contents of the demands from Japan "very secretly." He did not give the full text, but at the meeting did tell Morrison that the demands consisted of twenty-one articles. In Morrison's diary, the words "21 demands" were underlined with an explanation of the contents. We can assume it shocked him very much.

The following day, Yuan summoned Morrison. Yuan talked frankly with him about the situation in which the demands had been presented, how the negotiations had been progressing, and confirmed that the demands were made up of twenty-one articles. Morrison wrote as follows in a memorandum after the meeting.[33]

> The president suggests to me that the keenness of the Japanese to keep the demands secret may be prompted by the desire to be in a position to deny the extreme nature of the demands should negotiations fail, as they will fail.

Morrison had a great influence on not only *The Times* but also the British government from that time on. Over the coming months, Morrison's support for China strengthened.

### The Response of the British Government

The fourth and the most effective action Yuan Shikai took was to invite interventions from the Great Powers. He understood that he had to rely on them in order to resist Japan. The country which seemed the best to approach was

---

31    For Morrison, see Eiko Woodhouse, *The Chinese Hsinhai Revolution: G.E. Morrison and Anglo-Japanese relations, 1897–1920* (London: RoutledgeCurzon, 2004).

32    Memorandum by George Morrison, Jan 28 1915, Morrison Papers, Mitchell Library, State Library of New South Wales, Sydney, Australia.

33    Feb 4–5 1915, Morrison's Diary, Memorandum by George Morrison, Feb 5 1915, Morrison Papers.

America, because Britain was Japan's ally and France and Russia were busy at war. According to the memoir of Paul Reinsch, the American minister in Beijing, Yuan revealed to him the outline of the Japanese demands as early as January 22. Keenly pro-Chinese, he committed himself to supporting China from that point.[34]

On January 22, the Japanese Ambassador in London, Inoue Katsunosuke, presented the British Foreign Secretary, Sir Edward Grey, with the translated text of the Japanese demands, although crucially without Group V. As is already well known, the existence of Group V was concealed by Katō not only to Britain but also to Japanese diplomats in Europe and America. Grey replied to Inoue that he recognized that he had implied the approval of the extension of the Japanese lease in South Manchuria when Katō had spoken to him about this issue before leaving London in 1913. But he stated that there was a great deal in the text with which he was not familiar, and so he could not say anything about it until he had it considered by the Foreign Office.[35] In addition, he expressed his anxiety about the deterioration of relations between China and Japan. According to the document of the British Foreign Office, Grey told Inoue as follows.

> My chief anxiety was that Japan should not get into bad relations with China: because we, as Japan's Ally, would have to settle what line we were to take with regard to any negotiations between Japan and China; if we gave Japan diplomatic support, it would be very inconvenient to us to be dragged into bad relations with China at this moment.

What is interesting is that the important point of the meeting was misinterpreted by Inoue. According to the document of the Japanese Foreign Ministry, Inoue reported to Katō that Grey's reply at the meeting as follows:[36]

> On the whole it is not too bad. I believe we have no objection as far as British interests are concerned.

Inoue seems to have been optimistic and had not correctly understood Grey's cautious attitude.

---

34    Noel H. Pugach, op. cit., Paul Samuel Reinsch, *An American Diplomat in China* (Garden City, New York and Toronto: Doubleday, Page & co., 1922), 129–149.

35    Grey to Greene, Jan 22 1915, Foreign Office Papers (hereafter FO) 371/2322, The National Archives, London, UK.

36    Inoue to Katō, Jan 22 1915, *NGM* 1915 Vol. 3–1.

On January 25, Katō also presented the translated text without Group V to the British ambassador in Tokyo, Sir Conyngham Greene. Greene reported to Grey that Katō had said that the Japanese demands "were not as far-reaching as some parties in Japan desired."[37]

On 29 in Beijing, Hioki explained to Jordan the outline of the demands, although the text was not handed over. Jordan reported to Grey "So far as I can judge from knowledge thus obtained, demands do not seriously affect British material interests in China, and may be regarded as inevitable outcome of recent events."[38]

In short, the British government adopted a cautious approach, but did not immediately express opposition, instead stating the need for further consideration to Groups I to IV before taking a clear position. Russia also did not appear to be opposed to the demands in Groups I to IV. Greene reported that the Russian ambassador in Tokyo, Malevskii-Malevich, had told him that "the Japanese demands are reasonable."[39] It could be argued that if it had not been for Group V, the Japanese demands would have been skilful diplomacy in a time of imperialism, and that the Chinese government and the Great Powers would have been forced to accept them. As mentioned earlier, Group V was the root cause of the outrage felt by China and the Great Powers, which led the negotiations to deadlock.[40]

Kitaoka Shin-ichi speaks of the Twenty-One Demands as "using every technique of classic diplomacy in the times of imperialism." Frederick Dickinson says "Katō saw himself as playing the game of imperial politics by rules that were widely accepted in the capitals of Europe and even in Washington." I believe these are contrary to the facts. As we saw and will see later, Katō was neither confident nor consistent in the negotiations, and Group V was not approved by the Great Powers even in terms of the rules of imperialism.

The first British diplomat who received information about Group V was Jordan in Beijing. He sent a telegram to Grey on 29 January, in which he reported the information that he had acquired from the Russian minister in

---

37    Greene to Grey, Jan 25 1915, FO371/2322.

38    Jordan to Grey, Jan 29 1915, FO371/2322.

39    Greene to Grey, Feb 8 1915, FO371/2322.

40    Kitaoka Shin-ichi speaks of the Twenty-One Demands as "using every diplomatic technique of classic diplomacy in the time of imperialism," and Frederick Dickinson says "Katō saw himself, in other words, as playing the game of imperial politics by rules that were widely accepted in the capitals of Europe and even in Washington." But, as we saw and see later, Katō was not confident and consistent in the negotiations, and Group V was not approved by Great Powers even in terms of the standard of imperialism.

China who had told him that among the Japanese demands, there were wide-ranging articles.

Similar information was also given to the British ambassador in St. Petersburg, Sir George Buchanan. On February 3, he was told by the Russian Foreign Minister, Sergey Sazonov, that Japan had presented demands that were too far-reaching. Sazonov told Buchanan that the Russian minister in China had acquired this information from "a secret source," and invited him to comment. On receiving the telegrams from Jordan and Buchanan, Grey pointed out that compared with the text given to him by Inoue on January 22, "the version of Japanese demands supplied to the Russian Government is very much exaggerated."[41]

However, Grey received much clearer information a few days later. On February 6, the British ambassador in Washington, Sir Cecil Spring-Rice, reported to Grey that the American Secretary of State, William Bryan, had shown him a telegram from Reinsch in Beijing.[42] It indicated that the Japanese demands included "Sino-Japanese joint control of police in China," and "the adoption of Japanese advisers in the Chinese Government."

On the same day, Jordan in Beijing reported to Grey that he had been told by Morrison that the Japanese demands consisted of "twenty-one articles."[43] Morrison had been asked to do this by Yuan Shikai. Morrison told Jordan the concrete contents of Group V and informed him that the Japanese Minister "was insisting that the demands must be accepted as a whole in principle before they could be any discussion of the detail." As Jordan reported to Grey, Morrison had also told him that "the President realized that resistance was hopeless, but the country would be ruined by the acceptance of the Japanese terms, and a military occupation, which he expects if they are refused, would apparently be preferable in his opinion."

On the same day, February 6, Katō summoned Greene and told him that wrong information about the Japanese demands was prevailing abroad. On receiving a telegram from Greene, Grey continued to watch the situation without getting involved. On February 8, he told Spring-Rice in Washington that "according to our information, reports from Chinese sources of Japanese demands are much exaggerated, but Secretary of State had better get the information direct from Japan."[44]

---

41    Buchanan to Grey, Feb 3 1915, FO371/2322, Grey to Greene, Feb 4 1915, FO371/2322.
42    Spring-Rice to Grey, Feb 4 1915, FO371/2322.
43    Jordan to Grey, Feb 6 1915, FO371/2322.
44    Greene to Grey, Feb 7–8 1915, FO371/2322, the minutes of the meeting of Katō and Greene, Feb 6 1915, *NGM*, 1915, Vol. 3–1, Grey to Spring-Rice, Feb 8 1915, FO371/2322.

Prior to these events, Grey had basically trusted Katō. Japan was a British ally, and he had acted primarily based on the information from Japan. But Katō had lied completely, concealing Group V, which was soon to become all too clear.

### The Deadlock in Negotiations

The negotiations started between Japan and China on February 2. On 5 February, a second conference was held, but it did not make progress as opinions were sharply divided on the schedule and the procedure for the talks between the two countries.

The Chinese government took the offensive after the second conference. On February 9, Jordan was visited by a young Wellington Koo, who acted as a diplomat under the Yuan administration after graduating from Columbia University in the US. According to Koo's "informal" communications, the Japanese demands consisted of twenty-one articles and were divided into five groups. He told Jordan the exact contents of all the demands including Group V, and explained that this information was as presented in the documents handed over by the Japanese government. Jordan did not fully believe this, but conveyed the details of the conversation to Grey.[45]

The Japanese government gradually noticed that the existence of group V seemed to have been leaked. On February 2, the Japanese ambassador in St. Petersburg reported to Katō that "various rumors" had been passed from China to Russia. On February 5, Inoue in London informed Katō that the British Foreign Office had received inaccurate news that Japan had presented far-reaching demands. On 8, Hioki in Beijing pointed out in a telegram to Katō that Jordan had already become aware of the existence of Group V, although only vaguely. Hioki also reported that British correspondents in Beijing of *The Times* and *the Daily Telegraph* were trying to object to the Japanese demands.[46] The news that even *The Times* was becoming critical must have been shocking to Katō.

It was only at this point that Katō decided to notify the existence of Group V to the Great Powers. On February 9, Katō confessed the existence of Group V to

---

45    Jordan to Alston, Feb 10 1915, FO371/2322. For Wellington Koo during the First World War, Stephen G. Craft, *V.K. Wellington Koo and the Emergence of Modern China* (Lexington, Kentucky: The University Press of Kentucky, 2004), 30–60.

46    Motono Ichiro to Katō, Feb 2 1915, Inoue to Katō, Feb 6 1915, Hioki to Katō, Feb 8 1915, NGM, 1915, Vol. 3–1.

David Fraser, the Beijing correspondent of *The Times* who was visiting Tokyo briefly. Fraser immediately reported this to Greene. Greene was so greatly shocked that he visited Katō the following day. He protested to Katō, complaining that he was "in a considerably difficult position" as there appeared to be some articles of which he had not been notified. Nevertheless, Katō, also in a difficult position, arrogantly explained that "there were no demands outside those in the memorandum but there were certain wishes which he had laid before the Chinese Government with a view to settlement of outstanding questions," "I did not talk to you about them because it had no relation with the interests of your country." Greene, greatly disappointed, reported to Grey as follows:[47]

> I can see no difference personally between the 'demands' and the so-called 'wishes' except that Baron Katō did not intend to communicate the latter to you at all.

Greene felt he had been deceived by Katō, as he had trusted the Foreign Minister. Katō also explained Group V to the Russian ambassador, Malevski, but his explanation gave the impression of "being very ambiguous."[48]

On February 13, another correspondent of *The Times* in Beijing, William Henry Donald, reported the "rumor" of the Japanese demands including Group V, but at the same time the head office in London published an editorial which doubted the existence of Group V and supported the exiting Japanese demands.[49] It can be guessed that this was because the content of Group V was still unclear and the foreign editor of *The Times*, Henry Wickham Steed, thought the Anglo-Japanese Alliance was important. The editorial of *The Times* was widely criticized in China. Sir John Jordan and George Morrison in Beijing were also critical of this editorial.[50] On the contrary, Japanese newspapers welcomed this report and publicized the legitimacy of the Japanese demands without referring to Group V.[51]

Yuan then took a bold step, handing over the full translated text of the demands to Morrison. Morrison reported this immediately to Jordan, who

---

47    The minutes of the meeting between Katō and Greene, Feb 10 1915, NGM, 1915, Vol. 3–1, Greene to Grey, Feb 10 1915, FO371/2322.
48    Yoshimura Michio, *Zoho Nippon to Rosia* (Tokyo: Nihonkeizaihyoronsha, 1991), 188.
49    *The Times*, Feb 13 1915, Inoue to Katō, Feb 13 1915, NGM, 1915, Vol. 3–1.
50    Jordan to Grey, Feb 16 1915, FO371/2322, a letter from Morrison to Tsai Ting-Kan, Feb 16 1915, Morrison Papers.
51    *Osaka Asahi Shimbun, Tokyo Nichinichi Shimbun.*

likewise immediately told Grey.[52] Grey, much disappointed with Katō, decided to request Japan to act in accordance with the aims of the Anglo-Japanese alliance on February 20. At this point Katō's plans, which had been based on the assumption that the negotiations would be done secretly and quickly, collapsed.

What follows is an outline of the negotiations after this time. The British government warned Japan to be more careful in respecting existing British interests and the sovereignty of China. In Britain, Japan's actions were criticized in parliament and even criticism of the Anglo-Japanese alliance appeared in the newspapers. The United States was more critical of Japan, as is well known. In March the American government published the Bryan Statement which expressed strong opposition to some articles in Group V. The Chinese government, which felt encouraged by these, continued to resist Japan.

Katō should not have clung to Group V after his original plan collapsed, but he continued to push some parts, partly because he mistakenly felt that the opposition from Britain and America was not so strong, and partly because he misunderstood in assuming that China would accept them. However, the resistance of the Chinese government was stronger than Katō had expected, and so the Japanese government was eventually forced to withdraw Group V. Those who insisted strongly on the withdrawal were the elder statesmen who favored a more cautious approach, such as Yamagata Aritomo and Inoue Kaoru. On May 7, the Japanese government issued an ultimatum which demanded China to accept the draft of the Treaty based on Groups I to IV or face military action. The negotiations ended when the Chinese government accepted the final draft on May 9.

## Conclusion

This paper has reevaluated the process of the diplomatic negotiations on Japan's Twenty-One Demands. The Japanese Foreign Minister, Katō Takaaki's handling was inept. He included demands which were too far-reaching in Group V. He was not consistent in his handling of the demands and tried to conceal them from the Great Powers.

Debuchi Katsuji engaged in the negotiations as a secretary in the Japanese legation in Beijing. He later recalled as follows,[53] which can be believed to be an accurate evaluation.

52    Morrison's Diary, Feb 15 1915, a letter from Morrison to Tsai Ting-Kan, Feb 15 1915, Jordan to Grey, Feb 16 1915, FO371/2322.
53    Debuchi Katsuji, op. cit., 216–217.

In short, the reason why the negotiations failed was that Japan displayed as many as twenty-one demands like wares in a supermarket, and did not distinguish the most important from those that were less so. In addition, Japan was impolitic in the way it notified foreign countries. Even when considered in the most favorable light, it must be said that the Foreign Office lacked due care in its preparation and in the negotiations.

We have examined three points of view which have been neglected. First, this study focused on Japan's domestic political process in which Group V was inserted into the demands. The origins of Group V are located in the huge pressure exerted by many factions in Japan. After the outbreak of the Great War, various groups approached and pressured the government. In the government itself, the Army, and in particular the General Staff, were aggressive. Katō and the Foreign Ministry were simply not able to control them.

Those who might have had the power to control the requests were the elder statesmen such as Yamagata Aritomo and Inoue Kaoru. However, Katō did not communicate with them as he believed their role to be unconstitutional and undemocratic. Equally, the elder statesmen were not eager to support Katō who had been hostile to them. Although they eventually took actions in May 1915 to delete Group V, I believe that it might have been moderated to some extent had Katō managed to cooperate with the elder statesmen.

It is well known that Katō was severely criticized in the parliament and by newspapers over the demands. Many of this criticism came from groups and individuals who held more extreme views than Katō. Those who had rational and moderate opinions, such as Hara Takashi, and Ishibashi Tanzan, were in the minority. Even a figure such as Yoshino Sakuzo, a famous scholar of politics and a well-known champion of Taisho Democracy, regarded the deletion of Group V as "regrettable." It should be remembered that these pressures were the background to the presentation of the Twenty-One Demands.

The second point of focus was the proactive reaction of the Yuan Shikai administration. Foreign Minister Katō aimed to negotiate secretly and quickly as with negotiations for the Sino-Japanese Treaty in 1905. However, China, where nationalism was developing after the Xinghai Revolution, was no longer passive towards Japanese expansion.

Instead Yuan prolonged negotiations and inspired anti-Japanese sentiments inside and outside China. Lu Zhengxiang, Cai Tinggan and Wellington Koo who were familiar with Europe, and America, supported Yuan in the government. Yuan failed to achieve a Great Power intervention, but succeeded in arousing international criticism towards Japan such as the Bryan Statement. This contributed to the withdrawal of Group V, the most problematic set of demands. It can be concluded that the resistance by the Yuan Shikai government was skilful and effective to a certain extent.

Thirdly, this paper analyzed the role of journalism. The negotiations on the Twenty-One Demands were battles not only of diplomacy but also of publicity. The Japanese government succeeded in controlling the domestic press to some degree but it was not good at communicating with newspapers abroad. In contrast, the Chinese government succeeded in inspiring nationalism by leaking Group V at home. In addition, it also leaked information about the demands to George Morrison and Western journalists sympathetic to China, which in turn inspired anti-Japanese sentiments abroad. The Japanese government could not effectively resist these anti-Japanese campaigns. The criticism of Japan by foreign newspapers was widely reported in Japan from February onwards and became one of the factors which forced the Japanese government to delete Group V.

Finally, to place the Twenty-one Demands in complete perspective, it is important to recall the developments that followed. The Twenty-one Demands greatly disappointed Britain and damaged Anglo-Japanese relations. Sir Edward Grey had expected better things of Katō and did not conceal his opinion that the Alliance had been shaken. The Demands did not immediately break the Alliance as Britain was busily occupied with the Great War, but the continuance of the Alliance in a post-war world started to come into question. It is generally accepted that the Twenty-One Demands accelerated the annulment of the Alliance.

Katō resigned as Foreign Minister three months after the conclusion of the Treaty with China, and the Okuma administration collapsed the following year. Katō remained as the leader of the opposition party for about ten years after that. He attacked the governments in order to justify his own actions when the problems concerning Shantung were discussed in the Paris Peace Conference and the Washington Conference. However, by 1923 he had changed his stance and his foreign policy followed a moderate line. He became Prime Minister in 1924, appointed Kijuro Shidehara as Foreign Minister, and guided a new moderate form of foreign relations known as "Shidehara Diplomacy."

# Japan as a Distant Friend

## Scandinavian Countries Adjusting to Japan's Emergence as a Great Power

*Bert Edström*

### Origins of Japan-Scandinavia Relations

Despite a flurry of interest among the Scandinavian countries in Japan after the latter began to open its doors to the outside world during the middle of the 19th century, relations between Japan and Scandinavia developed very slowly. Three main factors drove the intensification of relations during the early 20th century: one, a shared concern with their mutual neighbor, Russia; two, rivalries among the Scandinavian states; and three, fluctuating evaluations of the relative importance of China and Japan for Scandinavian interests. In all cases, Japan's rapid transformation into a great power conditioned the nature of the relationships that emerged at this time. These themes emerged in the earliest phases of Japanese-Scandinavian interactions.

Relations between Japan and the Scandinavian countries have long been marked by the vast distance separating them, both geographically as well as in economic and psychological terms. Limited contacts and exchanges were not only the result of this distance, however; more important was Japan's seclusion policy during the Tokugawa era. This policy derailed in the wake of Japan's opening up as a result of US gunboat diplomacy. In 1853 Commodore Matthew Perry aboard his "black ships" delivered an ultimatum from the US president that forced the Tokugawa regime to establish diplomatic relations with the United States. The result of this exercise of raw power was a vindication of the use of gunboat diplomacy as an efficient means for securing foreign policy goals vis-à-vis Japan. It whetted the appetite of the Danish government, moreover, which proposed to Sweden in 1859 that the two countries send men-of-war to Japan. Sweden at this time had entered the throes of industrialization and was also increasingly affected by mass emigration to the United States. As a result, the Swedish government was not ready for such a venture, nor in a

* Research for this paper was partly conducted during the author's stay as a visiting scholar at Keio University, Tokyo, in summer 2010. A generous travel grant from the Birgit and Gad Rausing Foundation is gratefully acknowledged.

position to afford it, and the plan did not materialize.[1] Significant instead was that the most famous Swedish ship to come to Japan was not a man-of-war, but the scientist Adolf Erik Nordenskiöld's *Vega* after having successfully traversed the Northeast Passage in 1878–1879.

Japan and Denmark established diplomatic relations in 1867, and Japan and Sweden-Norway followed suit the next year. The bright prospects for trade with Japan lured Swedish trade and shipping circles, but the diplomatic treaties signed did not result in the expected expansion of exports to Japan. Not even the visit to Denmark and Sweden of the Iwakura Embassy in 1873 on its round the world tour did much to increase trade. And yet, growing curiosity about this exotic country in the Far East was visible after Japan's opening up, when a number of Scandinavians began to travel to Japan. Some of them even settled in cities like Yokohama, Kobe and Osaka. At the time of the *Vega*'s visit to Kobe, Captain Louis Palander noted in his diary that three Swedes resided in the city.[2]

Around the turn of the 20th century, in the wake of a number of military and political developments, the small Scandinavian countries came under pressure from the great powers and found themselves increasingly drawn into the great power diplomacy. Most exposed was Finland, which had been under the yoke of Russian domination since 1809; Sweden-Norway, meanwhile, shared a long border with Russia, and Denmark with Germany. In the aftermath of Japan's victory over China in the war of 1894–1895, the world's attention came to rest on Japan, the Scandinavian countries being no exception. Japan's name was "on everybody's lips," as the Swedish journal *Ny illustrerad tidning* wrote in its introduction to a series of articles on Japan published in 1895.[3] In the Scandinavian press, a majority of reports on Japan reproduced articles from the international press but in some cases were authored by Scandinavians who had travelled to Japan, or had lived there for shorter or longer periods. One of them was Ida Trotzig. She arrived in Japan in 1888, and filed war reports to Swedish newspapers during the Sino-Japanese and the

---

1  Olof G. Lidin, "Japanese-Danish Official Contacts," in *Danes in Japan 1868 to 1940: Aspects of Early Danish-Japanese Contacts*, ed. Mette Laderrière (Copenhagen: Akademisk Forlag, 1984), 16f.

2  "Dagboksanteckningar från Vegas ishavsexpedition 1878–1880, scrivner av Louis Palander," Sjöhistoriska museets arkiv [Stockholm], 1955:008/2. One of the three Kobe residents was Herman Trotzig, who arrived in Japan in 1859 and became municipal superintendent in the Kobe Foreign Settlement in 1872.

3  Åke Holmberg, *Världen bortom västerlandet: Svensk syn på fjärran länder och folk från 1700-talet till första världskriget* (Göteborg: Kungl. Vetenskaps- och Vitterhets-Samhället, 1988), 345.

Russo-Japanese wars. Indeed, advances in communication saw the Russo-Japanese War become the most reported war in history until then.[4] It was also a war that influenced Scandinavian policies.

Domestic pressures such as economic development necessitated a reorganization of the foreign policies of the Scandinavian countries. The key to industrial success was seen to reside in finding new markets for their growing industrial production. In Sweden-Norway, pressure for change stemmed not only from economic factors, but also from nationalism and the movement for independence that was becoming stronger in Norway. Popular protests in Norway agitated against the union with Sweden that had been in place since 1814, with the verbal exchanges between the Norwegians and their Swedish overlords becoming increasingly bitter in the 1890s. The question of consular representation both contributed to the death knell of the Swedish-Norwegian union, and affected relations with Japan. Gradually, this issue took center stage in the political showdown between Stockholm and Oslo. Whereas Sweden and Norway up until this point had had joint consulates, in light of Norway's increasing commercial interests, a Norwegian committee proposed the establishment of separate Norwegian consulates, and the *Storting* (the Norwegian parliament) decided in accordance with the committee's proposal in 1892. In response, the Swedish court wanted to go to war with Norway in order to defend the king's powers, but lacked support in the *Riksdag* (the Swedish parliament).[5] Swedish nationalists and hawkish social circles fulminated at the government's feeblemindedness and military impotence.

The Swedish conservative political scientist Rudolf Kjellén was one of the most prolific critics of the "submissive" governmental policies toward the Norwegians. He contrasted Swedish decrepitude with Norwegian youthfulness and Japanese vitality.[6] At the beginning of the new century, when Sweden experienced increasing problems in controlling Norway and a split looked more and more likely with war imminent, Kjellén called upon the Swedish government to stand firm and not give in to the Norwegian demands for independence. It was to no avail, however: the *Storting* declared the union dissolved in June 1905, resulting in Norway's unilateral secession. After some

---

4  Ben-Ami Shillony and Rotem Kowner, "The Memory and Significance of the Russo-Japanese War from a Centennial Perspective," in *Rethinking the Russo-Japanese War, 1904–05, vol. 1: Centennial Perspectives*, ed. Rotem Kowner (Kent: Global Oriental, 2007), 1.

5  Narve Bjørgo, Øystein Rian and Alf Kaartvedt, *Norsk utenrikspolitikks historie, vol. 1: Selvstendighet og union: fra middelalderen til 1905* (Oslo: Universitetsforlaget, 1995), 349f.

6  Bert Edström, "Rudolf Kjellén och Japan," *Orientaliska studier* 89 (1996): 18.

less than enthusiastic saber rattling,[7] Sweden accepted the dissolution on 26 October 1905.

The termination of the Swedish-Norwegian union occurred the same year as the Russo-Japanese War ended. Japan's victory had repercussions world-wide; reports of the war dominated the newspapers to the degree that a Japanese "boom" could be noted in both Sweden and Norway. One of those particularly excited by Japan's entrance on the world stage was Rudolf Kjellén. Japan's triumph against China in 1895 prompted him to proclaim that Japan had initiated a new chapter in world history. He argued that Japan's subse-quent military success had important ramifications for Sweden, since it elimi-nated the threat from Russia, which had been traditionally central to the formulation of Swedish defense policy.[8] However, according to Kjellén, the implications were far greater than this. When it was beyond doubt that Russia had been defeated by Japan, he noted that one should consider "that what stopped Russia's fight was the power of a non-European and, up to now, despised tribe. ...A jolt pervades all parts of the world suppressed by white men...the colored races shall not be condemned forever to serve the whites like the animals serve men."[9] In 1907, he wrote about the fight "between races and religions" and argued that a new historical epoch had started based on the greatness of the Japanese nation and Japan's deeds on the battlefield: "Japan's victory in 1905 seems to be the beginning of what may be the most important dialogue in history."[10]

Sweden's political and military leadership followed developments in East Asia carefully.[11] At the end of the 19th century they had concluded that Russia and Japan would, in all likelihood, eventually clash, which was bound to affect Sweden. After all, Russia was Sweden's historical archenemy and, in spite of the fact that Sweden's last war with Russia had taken place in 1808–1809, it contin-ued to be seen as posing the main threat. With a long border in the north that Sweden shared with Finland – a grand duchy in the Russian empire – the threat from the east was the key parameter in Swedish defense planning.

7    Försvarsstabens krigshistoriska avdelning, *Militärt kring 1905: en skildring av militära för-beredelser och åtgärder i samband med unionskrisen* (Stockholm: Hörsta förlag, 1958).
8    Rudolf Kjellén, "Don Quixote eller Catilina?" *Svenska Dagbladet*, 11 January 1897; "Sverige, Ryssland och Japan, I–II," *Svenska Dagbladet*, 31 January, 2 February 1897.
9    Rudolf Kjellén, "Världshändelsen för dagen," *Göteborgs Aftonblad*, 3 January 1905.
10   Rudolf Kjellén, "Världshistoriska repliker" (1907), reprinted in Rudolf Kjellén, *Politiska essayer: första samlingen* (Stockholm: Hugo Gebers förlag, 1914), 127.
11   Gunnar Åselius, *The "Russian Menace" to Sweden: The Belief System of a Small Power Security Élite in the Age of Imperialism* (Stockholm: Almqvist & Wiksell International, 1994).

Swedes held strong anti-Russian sentiments and looked with sympathy on Japan in its struggle with the Russian bear.

When the Russo-Japanese War broke out in 1904, Colonel Akashi Motojirō transferred from the Japanese legation in St. Petersburg to serve as military attaché at a new legation that was hurriedly set up in Stockholm. He took up the post under the direct control of the Japanese General Staff in order to coordinate intelligence activities in Europe.[12] Akashi befriended some officers in the Swedish General Staff, who agreed to help him obtain Russian military intelligence.[13] One of them was Captain Nils David Edlund, the officer in charge of reconnaissance regarding Russia. His friendship was a windfall for Japan, since the Swedish government later sent him to the war front in Russia.[14] Edlund promised to arrange for military spies to serve Japan in Russia.[15] Edlund and others in the General Staff may have seen this assistance as appropriate; Swedish military authorities were in no doubt that Russian espionage activities on Swedish soil had increased.[16] Japanese intelligence activities targeting Russia became an inspiration for the efforts of the Swedish military to build up an intelligence organization.[17]

Akashi's intelligence operations focused on Russia. One of the countries under the czarist yoke was Finland. In the 1890s, the policy of Russification intensified and met increasing resistance from workers, peasants, and radical intellectuals. One of the opponents to Russian oppression was Konni Zilliacus, a Swedish-speaking lawyer who earned his living as a journalist and writer. He had lived in Japan for two and a half years and realized that it could be a strong and important ally in the Finnish fight for independence. When Akashi arrived in Stockholm, he met Zilliacus, who had moved there in order to escape the Russian secret police, and who published the newspaper *Fria Ord* or "Free Words," which he smuggled to Finland to encourage the anti-Russian struggle. He also took part in, and organized, secret meetings of European revolutionaries and radicals and published books and pamphlets that discussed the end of czarism and the

12    Kurobane Shigeru, *NichiRō sensō to Akashi kōsaku* (Tokyo: Nansōsha, 1976 [1983]), 73ff.
13    Akashi Motojirō, *Rakka ryūsui: Colonel Akashi's Report on His Secret Cooperation with the Russian Revolutionary Parties during the Russo-Japanese War.* Selected chapters translated by Inaba Chiharu, ed. Olavi K. Fält and Antti Kujala (Helsinki: Finnish Historical Society, 1988), 35.
14    Gunnar Åselius, "Militärattachéerna i S:t Petersburg: En undersökning av det svenska underrättelseväsendets professionalisering 1885–1917," *Militärhistorisk Tidskrift* (1990), 22.
15    Akashi, *Rakka ryūsui*, 171.
16    Åselius, *The "Russian Menace" to Sweden*, 266–268.
17    Jan Ottosson and Lars Magnusson, *Hemliga makter: Svensk militär underrättesetjänst från unionskrisen till det kalla kriget* (Stockholm: Tidens förlag, 1991), 20.

liberation of oppressed peoples. Akashi realized that Russia could be seriously weakened by Japanese support to Zilliacus and his collaborators. In an attempt to undermine Russia by promoting anti-czarist parties and organizations, Akashi received the go-ahead from the Japanese General Staff to initiate Japan's first large-scale intervention in European domestic politics.[18] The General Staff, through Akashi, made available huge sums to Zilliacus and other European anti-czarist parties and organizations.[19] A part of the money was used to fund arms procurements for opponents of Russia. Most spectacular was a large shipment of arms, intended for revolutionaries in Moscow, shipped on the *John Grafton,* which sailed from London to Kemi but ran aground and had to be blown up.[20] Japanese assistance to the Finnish independence movement did not last long, however. The Japanese army essentially used the Finns and other European anti-czarists as mercenaries and, in reality, did not care about the fate of the opposition forces. Shortly before it concluded peace with Russia, with the war already won, it cut off the flow of aid.[21]

### Post-1905 Relations

Japan's victory in the war against Russia influenced its relations with the Scandinavian countries. With its primary focus on the great powers, Japan did not pay much attention to small countries like those of Scandinavia. Even Denmark experienced Japan's lack of interest, despite the fact that diplomatic relations between the two dated back to 1867 (the unequal treaty signed had been renegotiated in 1895). Denmark bore some responsibility for this state of affairs because of its stance. It fought a war with its powerful neighbor Germany as recently as 1864, and endured competing pressures from both Germany and another large power, Great Britain. The German emperor revealed in February 1905 "a burning desire" for a German-Danish alliance in order to avoid a British attack on the Kiel Channel or harbors in the Baltic Sea, but nothing came of it, since any Danish government agreeing to such an alliance would have been

---

18    Inaba Chiharu, "The Politics of Subversion: Japanese Aid to Opposition Groups in Russia during the Russo-Japanese War," in Akashi, *Rakka ryūsui*, 83.

19    Kurobane has estimated that Akashi spent one million yen, see Kurobane, *NichiRō sensō to Akashi kōsaku*, 86. This is equal to US $75 million according to Inaba Chiharu and Rotem Kowner, "The Secret Factor: Japanese Network of Intelligence-gathering on Russia during the War," in *Rethinking the Russo-Japanese War, 1904–05*, Kowner, ed., 92.

20    Akashi, *Rakka ryūsui*, 46–52; Konni Zilliacus, *Från ofärdstid och oroliga år* (Stockholm: Lindqvist, 1960), 133ff, 142ff.

21    Inaba, "The Politics of Subversion," 82ff.

ousted.[22] While Denmark continued its policy of neutrality when the Russo-Japanese War broke out, it argued for the right of neutrals to provide pilots for the ships of belligerent countries. In practice, this favored Russia, a fact that provoked Japan's displeasure.[23] In fact, a distancing between Denmark and Japan could already be observed in the 1870s when, in the build-up to a war between Japan and China, Denmark had chosen to support the latter.[24]

In 1906, the Danish foreign ministry established a commission to look into the organization of its foreign policy. The modest measures proposed reflected the foreign ministry's small size: in 1905, the total number of officials was only 36.[25] In considering its interests in East Asia, the Danish government decided to open a legation in Beijing in 1912, with its *chargé d'affaires* also assuming responsibility for Tokyo. This arrangement reflected that it was China and not Japan that counted in the eyes of the Danish government, despite Japan's victory over Russia. Furthermore, Denmark had previously been represented in Beijing by Russia, an arrangement that did not change despite Japan's victory in the war against Russia.[26]

The Swedish and Norwegian governments saw things differently than the Danish. The dissolution of the union made it urgent for them to find positions of their own between the great-power alliances. To Kjellén and many other Swedes, Japan's victory over Russia – heralding the former's emergence as a new great power – meant that the Russian threat had abated; the Norwegians, in contrast, viewed Russia's defeat in the east as increasing its threat to northern Norway in the west. Above all, however, a more acute threat to Norway was seen to come from Sweden.[27]

---

22    Troels Fink, *Spillet om dansk neutralitet 1905–09: L.C.F. Lütken og dansk udenrigs- og forsvarspolitik: Fremstilling, Lütkens selvbiografier, breve og aktstykker* (Aarhus: Universitetsforlaget i Aarhus, 1959), 23f.

23    Carsten Holbraad, *Danish Neutrality: A Study in the Foreign Policy of a Small State* (Oxford: Clarendon Press, 1991), 49.

24    Claus Bjørn and Carsten Due-Nielsen, *Dansk udenrigspolitiks historie 3: Fra helstat till nationalstat, 1814–1914* (København: Gyldendal Leksikon Danmarks nationalleksikon, 2003), 378.

25    Stefan Håkansson, *Konsulerna och exporten 1905–1921: Ett "Government Failure"?* (Lund: Lund University Press, 1989), 218.

26    Mads Kirkebæk, "Trade in Command: Denmark's China Policy 1912–49," in *China and Denmark: Relations since 1674*, ed. Kjeld Erik Brødsgaard and Mads Kirkebæk (Copenhagen: Nordic Institute of Asian Studies, 2000), 92.

27    Roald Berg, "Norsk utenrikspolitikks historie, 1905–1920" (PhD diss., Høgskolesenteret i Rogaland, 1994), 58; Harald Hals, "Regjeringen Michelsen og Sverige 1905–1907," *Scandia* 71 (2005): 221ff.

The Norwegian government was eager to obtain diplomatic recognition and moved quickly, albeit with a certain proviso. The official view was that "the foreign services should concentrate on looking after Norway's interests, to the virtual exclusion of all other activities normally associated with foreign policy."[28] Norway became one of the world's largest shipping nations in the 1870s and it was among Japan's largest trading partners. With shipping, fishing, and whaling all key industrial sectors, Japan promised to become commercially important for independent Norway.[29]

It turned out that developments played into the hands of the Norwegians. When the Swedish-Norwegian union ended, four out of twelve envoys and 17 of 27 employed consuls in the joint consular organization were Norwegians.[30] Thus, Norway already had a cadre of well-trained diplomats at its disposal. These diplomats enabled the Norwegian government to take quick action to gain recognition as an independent country, which Japan swiftly granted on 31 October 1905. On 4 November 1905, the Norwegian government appointed the former Swedish-Norwegian legation counselor in Tokyo, Peder Bernt Anker, its *chargé d'affaires* for Tokyo and consul-general for Japan. The enthusiasm felt by Anker at the new opportunities was not reciprocated on the home front, however. The foreign ministry wanted to keep costs low and preferred a *chargé d'affaires* to a minister, reflecting that Japan was seen as commercially important to Norway but largely irrelevant in terms of political interaction. To his annoyance, Anker initially had to accept that Norway's representation office was not situated in the capital Tokyo but in Yokohama, until the office was moved to Tokyo after a year.[31]

For Sweden, foreign policy had not changed much since the mid-19th century, despite the rapid expansion of foreign trade that resulted in an increasing workload for its foreign service. An overhaul was long overdue and became urgent after Norway's separation. In 1905 the Diplomatic and Consular

28    Erik-Wilhelm Norman, "Norway: The Royal Norwegian Ministry of Foreign Affairs," in *The Times Survey of Foreign Ministries of the World*, ed. Zara S. Steiner (London: Times Books, 1982), 395.

29    In 1907, Norway was the fourth-largest shipping nation to Japan with 348 ships arriving, compared to 24 Danish and four Swedish ships, respectively. See Eldrid Ingebjørg Mageli, *Towards Friendship: The Relationship between Norway and Japan, 1905–2005* (Oslo: Oslo Academic Press, 2006), 80. Norwegian ships were also very active in coastal trade both in Japan and China, and Hjalmar Cassel saw Norwegian enterprise and energy as a model for other small countries like Sweden. See Hjalmar Cassel, *Det nya Östasien* (Stockholm: Alberts Bonniers Förlag, 1905), 335, 344.

30    Berg, "Norsk utenrikspolitikks historie, 1905–1920," 51.

31    Mageli, *Towards Friendship*, 23, 46f, 26ff.

Committee was appointed to work out proposals for a reorganization of the Swedish foreign service. The committee focused on the promotion of trade and commercial interests. With foreign markets accounting for an increasing share of production at the expense of the domestic market, expansion on the world market was seen as necessary. The committee argued that a legation in East Asia should be situated in Japan "because of the role that [Japan] plays in world politics nowadays, and because of the commercial relations, which have already been established and further can be expected to be developed with it."[32] While Sweden had posted a consul-general to Kobe since 1901 (Dutch diplomats represented Swedish interests in Tokyo), Sweden's new trade ambitions meant that this representation was seen as inadequate and in need of being upgraded concomitant with Japan's rise in power. Based on the recommendation of the committee, therefore, Japan became one of thirteen countries where Sweden was represented by a minister.[33] When it opened a legation in Tokyo in 1906, Sweden reciprocated a step that Japan had already taken. Since 1880, Japan had side-accredited its minister to Russia to Sweden as well, but following the outbreak of the war with Russia in 1904, the Japanese government stationed a minister in Stockholm. This minister was also responsible for Oslo, Copenhagen (from 1917), and Helsinki (from 1921). Until 1917, Japanese diplomats in the Netherlands covered Denmark, except for a period during the First World War, when Japan's legation in Stockholm took over.[34]

The Diplomatic and Consular Committee recognized the need to make the foreign ministry better equipped to serve Sweden's economic interests. Recruitment of diplomats was to rest on the principle of "the strict selection of able people at all levels." In its bill to the *Riksdag,* the government proposed that personnel should be familiar with Swedish conditions and the needs of Swedish industry and have practical skills, gained through previous experience in the export business.[35] Although in 1900, 70 percent of foreign ministry employees came from aristocratic families, the new edict heralded a great change in the makeup of the ministry.[36] It was no accident, therefore, that the government appointed G.O. Wallenberg as envoy to the important new market

32    *1905 års diplomat- och konsulatskommittés betänkande* (Stockholm 1906), 101.

33    Torsten Gihl, "Utrikesförvaltningen från 1809 till närvarande tid," in Sven Tunberg et al., *Den svenska utrikesförvaltningens historia* (Uppsala 1935), 459.

34    Yoshitake Nobuhiko, "Nihon-Hokuō seiji kankei no shiteki tenkai: Nihon kara mita Hokuō," *Chiiki seisaku kenkyū* 3:1 (July 2000): 23.

35    *1905 års diplomat- och konsulatskommittés betänkande*, 6; *Kungl. Maj:t Nådiga Proposition 1906:143* (Stockholm 1906), 12ff.

36    Åselius, *The "Russian Menace" to Sweden*, 15f. In 1917, the proportion of the nobility occupying positions in the foreign service had decreased to 47 percent, see ibid., 16.

of Japan. Wallenberg was not a career diplomat but a well-known ship owner belonging to an illustrious financial dynasty and a noted member of the *Riksdag*. He epitomized the new type of diplomat that the committee wanted to recruit.[37]

In his instructions to Wallenberg, Foreign Minister Arvid Trolle emphasized that the development of trade relations with Japan "must be seen as the main purpose of the newly-established representation."[38] In a lengthy memorandum submitted to the foreign ministry in 1908, Wallenberg outlined a plan for the development and organization of Swedish trade in East Asia. It comprised increased diplomatic representation, creating new posts for consuls, and the establishment of trading companies and retail trade activities. Moreover, it emphasized the need for collaboration between Swedish diplomats and traders in East Asia. Most important, however, it stressed that adaptability, in addition to knowledge and experience of the market, was essential to success.[39] Wallenberg repeatedly preached the line that different markets needed different approaches, and he criticized the use of methods that suited Sweden but did not take into account the conditions prevailing in that of the trading partner.[40]

Wallenberg worked incessantly to ensure that Sweden made inroads into the Japanese market, but he had no intention of limiting his work to trade only. While his main task was to expand trade, he was aware that Japan was also becoming an important power in East Asia. In a letter to Trolle's successor Arvid Taube, Wallenberg wrote in 1910 that the Swedish interests in the new emerging markets were "the same as for all other nations – to sell our products. But, in addition, something else is dear to a small country, to become famous and noticed; to be equal to those bigger than herself." These ideas became

37    Bert Edström, "Storsvensken i Yttersta Östern: G. O. Wallenberg som svenskt sändebud i Japan, 1906–1918," University of Stockholm, Center for Pacific Asia Studies, *Working Paper* 52 (August 1999): 6–10.

38    Utrikesdepartementet, "Framställning af ministern i Tokio om tillstånd att vistas i Sverige 4 månader innevarande år m.m." (memorandum), 12 April 1907, Riksarkivet, UD:s arkiv 1902 års dossiersystem [National Archives, Foreign Ministry Archives, 1902 file system; hereafter: FM], vol. 435.

39    "Om Sveriges representation i Östern," no date, FM, vol. 493a; G.O. Wallenberg, "Sverige i Ostasien," in Erik Nyström, *Det nya Kina, senare delen* (Stockholm: P.A. Norstedt & Söners förlag, 1914), 198; Wallenberg to foreign minister, 14 December 1910, File: Brev rapporter m.m. Japansk politik 1910–1911, G.O. Wallenbergs personal archives kept by his grandchild Gustaf Söderlund, Uppsala [hereafter: WA].

40    Wallenberg to foreign minister, 18 November 1914, File: Japan: Brev och skrivelser, tidn. klipp 1914, WA.

lodestars for him as Sweden's envoy to Japan and China. Soon after his arrival in Japan, he began to find his feet and reported to the foreign ministry that one had to go from merely making sounds to actually doing things.[41] In 1908 he found that prospects for successful business and profits could hardly be better; in 1909 he described trade exchange between Sweden and Japan as singularly beneficial to Sweden; and in 1912 he reported that future prospects for doing business in China were excellent.[42]

Whereas Wallenberg continually argued that trade expansion rested on the support of the Swedish public and their understanding of the importance of the markets and their development potential,[43] he found that his advice to Swedish authorities and businessmen largely fell on deaf ears: many of them viewed Japan as too distant to really matter. He found ample reason to believe that the lack of interest at home for the rapidly growing markets in East Asia resided in the marked difference between his assessments of the situation and opportunities and the priorities prevailing in the foreign ministry in Stockholm. Indeed, what Wallenberg saw, as envoy in Japan, to be important matters were sometimes treated as mere trifles in Sweden.[44]

In his illuminating description of the situation in East Asia prevailing in 1905, the journalist Hjalmar Cassel pointed out that there was an advantage for a small country like Sweden to trade with countries in East Asia.[45] Wallenberg was also struck by the opportunities and saw the advantages to Sweden and Swedish companies of approaching Japan's financial and commercial circles. Not only would it increase exports to Japan, but it would also provide good opportunities for making inroads into the markets of Korea, Manchuria, and China, where the Japanese were better organized than other countries. Wallenberg reported to his brother Knut that

---

41    Wallenberg to foreign minister, 18 November 1914, File: Japan: Brev och skrivelser, tidn. klipp 1914; Wallenberg to Foreign Minister Taube, 8 June 1910, File: 1912: Bomull, fr. Bäckman, Svedbergs; Wallenberg to foreign minister, no date, File: Diverse 1907, WA.

42    Wallenberg to foreign minister, 18 November 1914, File: Japan: Brev och skrivelser, tidn. klipp 1914; Wallenberg to Foreign Minister Taube, 8 June 1910, File: 1912: Bomull, fr. Bäckman, Svedbergs; Wallenberg to foreign minister, no date, File: Diverse 1907; "Anteckningar om ett samtal med Herr Mac. Lindskog, Chef för Wijks East-Asiatish-Agency i Shanghai," 5 October 1908, File: Wijks Göteborg affären Ostasien 1908; Wallenberg to foreign minister, 27 March 1909, File: Japan Politik 1909; Wallenberg to foreign minister, 31 May 1912, File: Handelsfrågor och handelsintressen i Östern 1912, WA.

43    Wallenberg, "Sverige i Ostasien," 183.

44    Wallenberg to Dan Broström, 9 April 1910, in G.O. Wallenberg, Kopiebok 10/11 1909--31/12 1910, 185; Wallenberg to Carl Hultgren, 6 September 1910, ibid., 307, WA.

45    Cassel, Det nya Östasien, 332.

the Japanese, but above all the Chinese, have a knee-jerk reaction against doing business with the great powers and their subjects protected by cannons and bayonets. I have been told repeatedly that they would prefer to do business with the lesser states of Europe, since they, especially in dealings with the Germans, have had nasty experiences of the solidarity prevailing between diplomats and businessmen and which have given the former reasons to interfere, or at least opportunities to exert political pressure.[46]

For Wallenberg, it was important not only to improve mutual understanding but also to derive benefits for Sweden from East Asia's growing markets. He also argued that involvement with Japan augured well for opening up new exciting prospects for Swedish expansion into other East Asian markets. With one quarter of the world's population, China had enormous needs that Japanese industry could meet. The logic was that if Sweden could become a supplier to Japan, then it would automatically result in an upsurge in Swedish exports as a result of the rapid growth of Japan's exports. He pointed out to Foreign Minister Trolle that one argument that had been effective in his discussions with Chinese leaders over how China could benefit from Swedish experience, was that Sweden was "one of the small [countries] that has not caused damage to China and has not had anything to do with great power politics." Later, he argued that the same approach could also benefit Sweden in regard to the Russian market, which was considerable and increasing.[47]

## Japan as a Model and Threat

Already at the time of his appointment, Wallenberg had formed his impression of the Japanese as being "a civilized people striving forwards and who, no doubt, can give our people and our country several beneficial impulses by its youth, its force and its initiative. For certain, we have a great deal to learn from the capable Japanese people, both from a commercial and a cultural viewpoint."[48] Expressing wonder at Japanese deeds in battle was not unusual in Wallenberg's dispatches back home, and, after some time in Japan, he reported to Foreign Minister Trolle that such admiration was justified: "One cannot but be surprised," he wrote in 1907, "at the *results* which have been gained, and this

46   Wallenberg to K.A. Wallenberg, 2 May 1908, File: Japan: Finansfrågan 1908, WA.
47   Wallenberg to foreign minister, 5 May 1907, FM, vol. 493a; Wallenberg, "Sverige i Ostasien," 176.
48   "Sverige och Japan: Ett samtal med den nye ministern," *Svenska Dagbladet*, 3 October 1906.

naturally awakens a striving to profit by what seems to have contributed to this, for the good of one's own country."[49] Wallenberg told the British ambassador to Japan, Sir Claude MacDonald, that he had learned "to esteem their patriotism, their thrift, their anxiousness for adopting all the good of w[e]stern civilization, and the unparalleled development of their country." In letters and dispatches he disclosed his "great sympathies for the energy and capabilities of the Japanese," as he wrote to his brother Knut, who had been appointed Swedish foreign minister.[50]

Arriving in Japan at the end of 1906, Wallenberg wrote later that he found himself in "a terrible situation," since he represented "a country that was totally unknown."[51] This was something that had to be changed if Swedish trade ambitions were to be fulfilled. When one of Japan's leading statesmen, Count Makino Nobuaki, complained to Wallenberg that Europeans ridiculed the Japanese as being interested in nothing but war and strife. Wallenberg struck upon the idea to propose that the world-famous Swedish explorer Sven Hedin be invited to visit Japan to deliver some lectures in order so that his fame could "spill over" to the Japanese and demonstrate them – through their interest in Hedin's exploits – to be a civilized people. Makino found it a good idea.[52] Hedin's subsequent visit pleased Wallenberg, since Hedin received an overwhelming reception.[53]

Before Wallenberg became a diplomat, he had been active as a politician, and as Sweden's envoy to Tokyo he continued to harbor ambitions of making an imprint on the political front at home. He saw how visits like that of Hedin could be used to bridge contradictions in Swedish society and turn developments in Sweden onto paths that he saw as positive. In a letter in December 1908 to King Gustav V, Wallenberg reported that he was trying to persuade Rudolf Kjellén to visit Japan

> in order to, based on conditions [in Japan] that are developing more favorably than at home in Sweden...publish a book that, under the guise of interest in the development of a modern civilized state, provides Swedish readers with an opportunity to make comparisons

49  Wallenberg to foreign minister, 26 January 1907, FM, vol. 35.
50  Wallenberg to Sir Claude MacDonald, 21 October 1912, File: Japan: Konsulatsfrågan 1913–19, WA; Wallenberg to foreign minister, 24 February 1907, FM, vol. 35; Wallenberg to Foreign Minister K.A. Wallenberg, 23 November 1915, FM, vol. 36.
51  Wallenberg to Marcus Wallenberg, 6 November 1930, File: Svensk utrikeshandel 1931–32, WA.
52  G.O. Wallenberg, "Då jag kom till Japan," ms (1935), 2.
53  Edström, "Storsvensken i Yttersta Östern," 33.

unconsciously and draw conclusions concerning our most pressing questions that in many cases have suffered from the predilections of our
nation for self-righteousness and self-assuredness based on the great
deeds of our forefathers, and limited knowledge of the wide-ranging
developments occurring in the rest of the world.[54]

In a letter to Kjellén, Hedin wrote after his visit to Japan that what was needed
was "someone who shakes up our crofters and opens their eyes to perspectives
beyond our own rocky islets."[55] It was obvious to him that Kjellén was such a
man. After the astounding victory of the "yellow" people in the East over the
great "white" great power of the West in 1905, he had emerged as a spokesman
for Swedes of a nationalist and conservative creed, hailing Japan as a model.
Already after Japan's victory over China, he had expressed his longing for
Swedes to become a people "full of vitality like the Japanese, developing their
national uniqueness and self-confidence in isolation from foreign influence."[56]
In an outline of a program for conservatism he had portrayed Japan as a
model.[57] This was a tune to Wallenberg's liking and he invited Kjellén to undertake an extended trip to Japan.

Rudolf Kjellén was not only a leading conservative and nationalistic ideo-
logue and a celebrity of his time, but also the father of geopolitics. He had
depicted Japan as a success story in the first edition of *Stormakterna* [The great
powers] in which he analyzed world politics and in which Japan was included
among the great powers, albeit belonging to the second tier.[58] When he travelled to Japan in 1909, he was able to scrutinize at first hand the new great
power that he had described four years previously. The weeks that he spent in
Japan confirmed in his eyes what he had long argued: that the Japanese

---

54    Wallenberg to Gustaf V, 10 December 1908, FM, vol. 435.

55    Quoted in Ruth Kjellén-Björkquist, *Rudolf Kjellén: En människa i tiden kring sekelskiftet*,
      vol. 2 (Stockholm: Verbum, 1970), 80.

56    Rudolf Kjellén, "Skandinavism på bakvägar," *Göteborgs Aftonblad*, 28 July 1897.

57    Rudolf Kjellén, *Nationell samling: Politiska och etiska fragment* (Stockholm: Hugo Gebers
      Förlag, 1906), 31.

58    Rudolf Kjellén, *Stormakterna*, vol. 2 (Stockholm: Hugo Gebers förlag, 1905), 208–253. In an
      interesting parallel, Japan's status as an ascending great power was also stressed by Harald
      Hjärne in his posthumously published *Japan: Historisk öfversikt* (Upsala: Arvid Svenson,
      1923). Hjärne was Sweden's leading historian and, similar to Kjellén, took up Japan stud-
      ies. See Ragnar Björk, "Japan Enters Great Power Politics: Swedish scholars analyzing a sea
      change in the world-system at the turn of the century 1900," in *Contacts and Encounters:
      Essays in Honour of Seung-bog Cho*, ed. Bert Edström and Staffan Rosén, *Orientaliska stud-
      ier* 121 (2007): 139–154.

were "men of the dawning sun" who had a burning national sentiment that manifested itself in an awe-inspiring ambition that he had hitherto admired from afar.[59]

But Kjellén also found reason to raise a warning flag. In *Stormakterna,* the work that made him an internationally renowned scholar, he also analyzed the contemporaneous debate concerning the so-called yellow peril, the concept made popular by Kaiser Wilhelm II. It was a timely topic for Kjellén, strongly influenced as he was by the debate in Germany, and he sided with the fêted author Viktor Rydberg, who argued that the white race had an almost hopelessly bleak future.[60] Kjellén's visit to Japan thus confirmed in his eyes Western fears. In the first edition of *Stormakterna,* he cautioned that a combination of China and Japan would be formidable: "Japan's soul in the Chinese body would mean a world empire that would put in the shade even Russia and the United States."[61] In *Den stora Orienten* [The great Orient], the travelogue he published after his return from Japan, Sweden's by now famous "planetary professor" wrote that the yellow peril was "nothing less than the approaching struggle for world hegemony between the white and the yellow peoples, between the main camps of mankind, Western Europe-America and East Asia."[62] He returned to the theme in the second edition of *Stormakterna,* and wrote of the ominous prospects for the Western world. He described how the outbreak of the Russo-Japanese War heralded "a struggle between the yellow and white races, between Asia and Europe, between Buddha and Christ; and for the first time success seems in earnest to desert the representatives of the white race."[63]

## The Scandinavian Countries, Japan, and the First World War

At the time of Rudolf Kjellén's visit to Japan in 1909, relations between the Scandinavian countries and Japan had expanded after their initial diplomatic encounters in the 1860s, but the long-awaited "take-off" that proponents had hoped for had not yet materialized. In the run-up to the First World War,

59    Mayre Lehtilä-Olsson, *K G Ossiannilsson och arbetarrörelsen: En studie i en ideologisk kon-frontation* (Göteborg 1982), 43.
60    Rudolf Kjellén, *Stormakterna,* vol. 2, 2nd rev. and expanded ed. (Stockholm: Hugo Gebers förlag, 1913), 228. Rydberg aired his view in his introduction to the translation into Swedish of Benjamin Kidd's *Social Evolution* (1895).
61    Kjellén, *Stormakterna,* vol. 4 (1913): 227.
62    Rudolf Kjellén, *Den stora Orienten: Resestudier i Östervåg* (Göteborg: Åhlén & Åkerlunds förlag, 1911), 257.
63    Kjellén, *Stormakterna,* vol. 1 (1913): 7.

as well as during the war, the key interests of Sweden, Norway, and Denmark were to keep out of future wars and further their own economic interests. They tried to avoid entanglement by adhering to a policy of neutrality. Aloofness also characterized Japan to a certain extent, although during the war it used the opportunity to consolidate and expand its interests on the Asian continent.[64]

Denmark's interest in East Asia was directed less at Japan than at China. When Denmark established a diplomatic representation in East Asia in 1912, it was not to Tokyo but Beijing that a minister was dispatched. Its choice of Beijing was based on the large Danish telegraph interests in China. Wallenberg saw Sweden's position as the leading Scandinavian country in the region threatened, and proposed collaboration between Sweden and Denmark. His main objective was to stop a partnership between Denmark and Norway from developing that would threaten Swedish economic interests. Eventually, Sweden and Denmark decided, in March 1914, to initiate collaborative efforts, after companies from both countries had tried to obtain telephone concessions in China.[65]

After his appointment, Norway's *chargé d'affaires*, Peder Bernt Anker, found himself facing an uphill struggle in Japan. The auspicious start to relations in 1905, which had seen rapid mutual recognition, soon faded. In 1918 when Anker left, there was still only one Norwegian company in Japan, Aall & Co in Yokohama, and Norway's consuls in the country were of German or British origin. Even though Norway and Japan had similar interests in sectors like shipping and whaling, Oslo displayed a distinct lack of interest in launching a trade offensive with Tokyo. Suspicion that the Japanese would try and emulate their products (something the Japanese were renowned for) made Norwegian companies reluctant even to send products to Japan. Accordingly, Anker found that his efforts to promote Norwegian interests resulted in very little in concrete terms. Ironically, shipping, the backbone of Norwegian industry, even showed a decrease in the number of ships calling at Japanese ports soon after relations with Japan had been established. In 1915, the number of ships making port calls had decreased to only 10.[66]

Anker despaired. He could only note the lack of interest in Japan among Norway's political and commercial circles. During his years as consul-general

---

64    Frederick R. Dickinson, *War and National Reinvention: Japan in the Great War, 1914–1919* (Cambridge, MA: Harvard University Press, 1999), 2.

65    Jan Larsson, *Diplomati och industriellt genombrott: Svenska exportsträvanden på Kina 1906–1916* (Uppsala 1977), 105f.

66    Mageli, *Towards Friendship*, 28, 54, 88.

he wrote lengthy reports complaining about his salary and living conditions, and his dissatisfaction with his country's diplomatic and consular activities. The inescapable truth was that for politicians and businessmen alike, whether in Oslo or Copenhagen, it was China that really counted. In 1919, the Norwegian government closed its office of *chargé d'affaires* and consulate general in Tokyo, and opened a combined post of minister and consul-general in Beijing; it appointed a Norwegian businessman honorary consul in Tokyo. This decision reflected Oslo's view that Japan was secondary to China, irrespective of the fact that Norway's exports to Japan were far larger than to China during the First World War; in any case, Norwegian exports to Japan had decreased sharply during the war years.[67] Norwegian disinterest was reciprocated: Japan did not send any diplomats to Oslo but tasked its Stockholm envoy with representing interests in Oslo.

To Norwegian diplomats in Tokyo, their contrasting fortunes with Sweden were a source of annoyance. In a dispatch to Oslo the *chargé d'affaires* noted with envy how "the indefatigable Wallenberg [was] always on the lookout for more firms, more work to be done for Sweden."[68] Wallenberg's activities were so bustling and his dispatches so long and frequent that he was advised by his brother Marcus not to do more than other Swedish diplomats.[69]

Sweden faced the danger of becoming entangled in war, notwithstanding its official declaration of neutrality, as evidenced by an incident involving Wallenberg that seriously jeopardized Sweden's policy of neutrality. He was side accredited to China, and on a visit there in 1917, he had made a number of German-friendly statements, declaring also that England would be defeated by the submarine war and that Germany would capture Petrograd. The Chinese reported his statements to the British who found them outrageous and accused him of having used the diplomatic pouch to carry German messages. The Japanese minister to Sweden, Uchida Sadatsuchi, told Foreign

---

67   Ibid., 28ff.

68   The Norwegian Office for Information about the Industries to the Norwegian foreign ministry, 29 January 1911, quoted in Mageli, *Towards Friendship*, 55. About the same time, Wallenberg is described in a dispatch to the British foreign minister as having shown "great activity in promoting the commercial interests of his country," and upon his return after leave in 1913, he was "as active as ever." Sir C. Greene to Sir Edward Grey, 10 January 1914, in *British Documents on Foreign Affairs. Reports and papers from the Foreign Office confidential print. Part I, From the mid-nineteenth century to the First World War. Series E, Asia, 1860–1914, vol. 10: North-East Asia after the Russo-Japanese War, 1905–1914*, ed. Ian Nish (Frederick, MD: University Publications of America, 1989), 360.

69   Marcus Wallenberg to G.O. Wallenberg, 28 October 1912, quoted in Larsson, *Diplomati och industriellt genombrott*, 104.

Minister Johannes Hellner that Wallenberg had been severely criticized by the British and US envoys. His situation was such that Uchida advised that Wallenberg be given a leave, at least until the war was over. The cable ordering him to return to Stockholm "for consultations" reached the legation in Tokyo two days later, and he started packing immediately. The subsequent investigation showed that the accusations regarding the diplomatic pouch were unfounded; despite this, Hellner recounted in his memoirs that Wallenberg had occasionally failed to observe the discretion that was absolutely necessary for a diplomat, and had been instructed to be more cautious in the future.[70]

Among the Scandinavian countries, perhaps Finland had benefited most from the First World War. Czarist Russia's collapse and the coming to power of the Bolsheviks resulted in Finland's declaration of independence in 1917; the Peace Conference finally recognized Finnish independence in the spring of 1919. And while it had been a long time since Japan had extended help to Finland in its fight for independence in 1903–1905, the latter had learnt an important lesson from Japan: a small country, if united, could defeat a great power.[71]

### Conclusion

Any indications of deepening Scandinavian-Japanese relations linked to Japan's opening to the world eventually faded away after the initial establishment of diplomatic relations in the 1860s. However, after the turn of the 20th century, the break-up of the union between Norway and Sweden spurred an activism in their respective foreign policies that saw a greater engagement with Japan, albeit to a much more limited extent in the case of Norway. Only Sweden, through its indefatigable envoy Wallenberg, seized the chance to bolster its relations with Japan. For its part, Japan as a new great power had no particular reason to pay much attention to the small countries on the periphery of Europe unless they, however small and weak, augmented the strength of the European great powers that Japan had to take into account. With war approaching, the need for Scandinavians to keep out of war heightened their

70 *Minnen och dagböcker: Joh. Hellner med inledning och kommentar*, ed. Wilhelm Odelberg (Stockholm: P.A. Norstedt & Söners förlag, 1960), 444ff; Telegram from Foreign Ministry to Wallenberg, 6 April 1918, File: Handlingar rörande Envyén Wallenbergs återkallande till Sverige, hemresan, m.m., WA.

71 Hirama Yōichi, *NichiRō sensō ga kaeta sekaishi* (Tokyo: Fuyō shobō shuppan, 2005), 104.

urge for aloofness. With Japan and Scandinavia geographically remote from each other, the concerns and priorities of their political leaders understandably lay elsewhere. The onset of the First World War, rather than bringing them together, marked a growing gulf between them.

Relations were asymmetric with the great-power focus of both determining their views. Japan had an urge to become a member of the club of great powers. Consequently, its focus was on countries that were already members of this elite club. On the other hand, the small Scandinavian powers pursued a myopic policy, keenly aware of the effect that the great-power play could have on them, and based their foreign policies on the concept of neutrality in order to avoid entanglements. They succeeded in the sense that they avoided being dragged into the war.

That Scandinavian-Japanese relations were asymmetric is evidenced by the fact that Sweden was the only Scandinavian country where Tokyo felt a need to place an envoy. Based on her studies of the Norwegian relationship with Japan, Eldrid Mageli finds that it "is most aptly characterised as a non-relationship" during the period from 1905 to the 1930s.[72] In a similar way, Denmark more or less disregarded Japan. Mads Kirkebæk has described Denmark's policy toward countries in East Asia during this period as a "non-policy"; Denmark's economic interests were squarely focused on one country in the region: China.[73]

Sweden therefore stands out among the Scandinavian countries in their relations with Japan. Furthermore, Swedish "awareness" of Japan differed from that of European great powers like France, Germany, and England, for the very reason that Sweden was not a great power. While the relations between Japan and the European great powers were conducted through the prism of great power politics, Sweden's policy towards Japan was that of a trader. Economic and commercial interests also swayed Norwegian and Danish interests but, unlike Sweden, China – not Japan – was the priority partner. For Finland, meanwhile, Japan had been important during the Russo-Japanese War, when Akashi collaborated with Zilliacus and other influential figures striving for independence, but cooperation proved short-lived. Assistance to Finland was a tool for Japan to weaken Russia, and once the latter had been defeated, Japan ended its support to the Finns. In short, mutual concern over Russian power did not prove strong enough to pull Japan and the Scandinavian countries together in a meaningful way, at least not prior to the 1917 Russian Revolution.

---

72    Mageli, *Towards Friendship*, 47.

73    Mads Kirkebæk, "Fortiter in re, suaviter in modo: En undersøgelse af udvalgte dele af Danmarks Kinapolitik 1912–1945" (PhD diss., University of Copenhagen, 1998).

Nor did the Scandinavian rivalries provoke much lasting competition for the Japan market, which Sweden dominated as Norway and Denmark turned to China. Although Japan's emergence as a great power brought it greater awareness among the Scandinavians, only Sweden and Japan forged substantial bonds during the decade of the 1910s.

# The Making of a European Friend
*Japan's Recognition of Independent Poland*

*Ewa Pałasz-Rutkowska*

## Polish-Japanese Relations up to 1919

Because of geographic distance and the unfavorable course of history, Poland and Japan did not maintain official contacts before 1919.[1] After the Third Partition in 1795, Poland was divided by three occupying powers – Russia, Prussia and Austria – and did not exist as a sovereign state until after World War I. From the mid-17th century, Japan existed in isolation from the world for over 200 years. It became interested in the Western world, including Poland, only after the opening up of its frontiers in the second half of the 19th century, when it was eager to absorb patterns of modernization from abroad. But rapid westernization required caution. Attempts were made to avoid mistakes committed by other nations and to protect the sovereignty of a still weak country. Toward that end, in 1885 Tōkai Sanshi published the novel *Kajin no kigu* (Unexpected Meetings with Beautiful Ladies), in which appeared the first Japanese references to the tragedy of the Polish nation, and references to the partitions and the independence movement. The author, emphasizing his solidarity with the long-suffering Polish nation, attempted to warn Japan, which was just initiating its contacts with the world, about the great powers and their policies of colonization. In the same spirit, in 1893 the poet Ochiai Naobumi wrote the poem *Pōrando kaiko* (Reminiscence of Poland), part of a longer epic poem *Kiba ryokō* (Journey on Horseback). He was inspired by the memoirs and reports of Major Fukushima Yasumasa (1852–1919) on his lonely horseback journey from Berlin to Vladivostok (1892–1893). Fukushima sought information about modern European armies, particularly that of Japan's then most dangerous neighbor – Russia (Figure 11.1). Fukushima, who was the first representative of the Japanese government to establish contacts with Poles, believed that they could give him valuable information based upon their long years of conflict with the Russian occupiers. The information he gathered was put to good use over a dozen years later, during the Russo-Japanese War (1904–1905).

---

1  More on this topic: Ewa Pałasz-Rutkowska, Andrzej T. Romer, *Nihon Pōrando kankeishi*, transl. Shiba Riko (Tokyo: Sairyūsha, 2009), 7–64.

FIGURE 11.1    *Major Fukushima Yasumasa during his lonely horseback journey from Berlin to Vladivostok (1892–1893) (collection of Ewa Pałasz-Rutkowska).*

At that time there was also a significant increase in Polish interest in Japan; the victories of Japanese armed forces impressed Polish political activists. Some of them believed that the war would weaken Russia and change Russia's attitude toward Poland. Józef Piłsudski (1867–1935) of the Polish Socialist Party and others thought that the war could be used as a means to regain independence. They hoped that Japanese financial assistance could support the organization of an armed insurrection in the Russian-ruled Kingdom of Poland, forcing Russia to send reinforcements to Europe and weaken the czarist army in the Far East. They also proposed sabotaging the Trans-Siberian Railway, which was the main means of transporting Russian soldiers and military supplies to the front in Manchuria, by contacting Poles who worked on the railroad, particularly in Siberia. In addition, they promised to spread revolutionary literature among the Polish soldiers in the Russian forces, urging them to desert. The emissary to Europe of Japan's Army General Staff, Col. Akashi Motojirō (1864–1919), strongly supported such activities, but Roman Dmowski (1864–1939) and

FIGURE 11.2
*Józef Piłsudski* (Tygodnik
Ilustrowany, *no. 32/1919*).

the National League opposed them on the grounds that an insurrection in
the Kingdom would only result in yet another tragedy for Poland, and gain
no advantage for Japan. The Russians would quickly deal with the insurgents and then have more forces to transfer to the Far East. Both politicians,
Dmowski and Piłsudski, traveled to Tokyo for consultations. Although they
did not establish broad cooperation at that time, the warm feelings then
engendered in Poles toward Japan survived the years of war and dominated the
foreign policy of a newly independent Poland after World War I (Figures 11.2
and 11.3).

## Japan's Recognition of Independent Poland

The victory of the Entente powers in the Great War and the October
Revolution in Russia led to significant changes in the political map of
Europe. The empires of Germany, Russia and Austria-Hungary ceased to exist.
Czechoslovakia, the Republic of Hungary, the People's Republic of Western

FIGURE 11.3
*Roman Dmowski* (Tygodnik Ilustrowany,
*no. 47/1919*).

Ukraine, and Yugoslavia, the country of Slovenes, Croatians and Serbs, were
created. Lithuania, Latvia, Estonia, Finland and also Poland returned to the
map of Europe. The first demands for reconstructing an independent Poland,
which had been occupied for 123 years, were presented to the Allies by Roman
Dmowski in March of 1917. In August he led the Polish National Committee
(Komitet Narodowy Polski; KNP), which by the end of that year was recognized as the official Polish representative by France, Great Britain, Italy and
the United States, the most important countries then deciding the fate of
the world.[2] The Committee took charge of Polish armed units being created
in France, then in other parts of the world, including eastern Russia and
Siberia.

On 19 September 1918, the representatives of the KNP in Paris asked
Ambassador Matsui Keishirō (1868–1946) if the Japanese government would
also recognize the Committee as the official representative of Polish interests,
and the Polish units in Siberia as fighting under the leadership of this

---

2  Ishii's cable no. 69 to Uchida (31 Jan. 1919), in: 1.4.3.17, Gaimushō gaikō shiryōkan (hereafter,
   GGS), Tokyo.

Committee and in cooperation with Allied units.[3] The Poles knew that Japan recognized the Czechoslovak National Council as the official Czech representative in the international arena on 16 September. On 15 October, the Japanese Minister of Foreign Affairs, Uchida Kōsai (1865–1936), responded negatively, believing that it was too early because "the Polish national movement does not have direct contacts with the Empire of Japan and therefore presents a totally different image in the awareness of the Japanese nation than the Czech movement."[4] The main reason for such a response was the unfavorable assessment of Polish involvement in the so-called Siberian expedition – the intervention against the Bolshevik revolution. The Japanese government considered that the aims of the Japanese military coincided with those of the Czechoslovak Corps, and thus felt it advantageous to provide assistance to the Czech and Slovak units in eastern Siberia. However, it was concerned about the activities of the Poles in that region. According to the Japanese, creating Polish units that enlisted Poles working on the Trans-Siberian Railway could lead to disruptions in transportation that was also necessary for Japanese forces.[5]

### Siberian Intervention: Polish Troops and Japan

How did these Allied and Polish forces find themselves in Siberia? In August of 1918, the United States, Great Britain, France, and Japan decided to join the fight in that area against the Bolsheviks, who were rapidly gaining control of Russia. Forces landed in the Far East in Murmansk and Vladivostok. The immediate pretext for this intervention was assistance for units of the Czechoslovak Corps, formed in 1915 from deserters and prisoners from Austro-Hungarian armies captured by the Russians and under the jurisdiction of the Czechoslovak National Council. After Russia signed the Treaty of Brest with the Central Powers (3 March 1918), and on the basis of an agreement with the Entente, the Corps was to be transported to Vladivostok and then to France, where it was to enter action on the side of the Allies. But when the Bolsheviks began to disarm the soldiers, they rose up against the Russians and moved eastward along the Trans-Siberian Railroad to Vladivostok, in support of the counter-revolutionary operations of the forces of Admiral Alexander Kolchak (1874–1920), cutting off Moscow's connection with the Far East.

---

3   Matsui's cables no. 431 (20 Sept. 1918) and no. 432 (21 Sept. 1918) to Gotō, ibid.
4   Uchida's cable no. 40 to Matsui, ibid.
5   Gotō to Matsui, draft (undated), ibid.

In the second half of July 1918, the command of the Czechoslovak Corps entered into an agreement with the Polish War Committee for Russia, created in Omsk, to establish a Polish division. The Committee, a branch of the Polish government in Siberia, took on the task of recruiting volunteers, among which were Poles residing in Russia, prisoners from the German and Austrian armies, political exiles and their descendants. The operation was directed by Colonel Walerian Czuma (1890–1962), who soon became the Commander of Polish Armed Forces in Eastern Russia and Siberia. The 5th Division of Polish Riflemen, also known as the Siberian Division, was formed in January 1919, headed by Colonel Kazimierz Rumsza (1886–1970). The Siberian Division was formally part of the Polish army being formed in France, which at the direction of the Polish National Committee, was headed by General Józef Haller (1873–1960). The Entente powers recognized the Division as an independent and allied unit, and placed it under the jurisdiction of the chief of the French military mission, General Pierre Janin (1862–1946), together with all of the forces in Siberia.

One of the major tasks of the Siberian Division was the protection of the western section of the Trans-Siberian Railroad, on the stretch from Novonikolaiev (Novosibirsk Obl.) to Klukviennaia station. But the Bolshevik offensive in the autumn of 1919 and the defeat of Kolchak's army forced the counterrevolutionary forces in Siberia to retreat. English, French and Czechoslovak units were withdrawn to the east, and subsequently out of Siberia, with rear-guard action assigned to the 5th Division, which fought fierce battles with units of the Red Army. However, the Corps delayed its evacuation and blocked the rail line, which placed the Polish units in an impossible situation, forcing them to engage in constant heavy fighting. Colonel Czuma requested from General Janin that the Siberian Division be replaced with Czech forces, but Janin did not issue such orders and the Poles retreated to Klukviennaia station, where the Bolsheviks cut off their rear. Neither the Czechoslovak Corps nor the recently independent Polish home government chose to, or could, lend support, and on 10 January 1920 Colonel Czuma decided to capitulate. Most Polish soldiers became prisoners – officers went to prisoner-of-war camps, soldiers to work in mines. Many of them died there because of very harsh conditions and cruel treatment, and those that survived returned to Poland in 1921. But not everyone surrendered, and some of the officers and men, led by Colonel Rumsza, made their way to Harbin in Manchuria.

From March 1920, the repatriation of those who fled to Manchuria was overseen by a special Polish mission headed by Józef Targowski (1883–1956), High Commissioner of the Republic of Poland and Minister Plenipotentiary for

THE MAKING OF A EUROPEAN FRIEND

Siberia and the Far East.[6] The Polish soldiers were placed under the command of General Antoni Baranowski (1854–1922), head of the military mission accompanying Targowski.[7] Although the decision to dispatch the mission and authorize Targowski to establish relations with the Kolchak regime and its foreign allies was made on 27 August 1919, the mission arrived in the Far East too late. The Kolchak government had fallen, and in January 1920 the Czechoslovak Corps turned Kolchak over to the Bolsheviks, who eventually shot him. The fall of Kolchak greatly complicated Targowski's mission to repatriate the Polish forces, which he noted in his memoirs:

> In the face of the disaster of the 5th Division the only course of action is to create an outpost, or perhaps a series of Polish outposts, which could take care of the remaining forces and refugees, and could conduct repatriation...Obviously, that brings up the most important matter, that is, how to go about obtaining official authorization for acting. I decided to first attempt to get recognition of the Polish state by China.[8]

### Peace Conference in Paris: Japan and Poland

On 18 January 1919, while the Siberian intervention was still going on, the peace conference began in Paris, where the most important decisions about the post-war world were made. Representatives of 27 allied and associated countries took part, but only Great Britain, France, the United States, Italy, and Japan (recognized after the war as a world power) were considered to have so-called "universal interests." Delegates of these countries, as opposed to those from the remaining participants with "limited interests," sat on all of the commissions, and above all in the Supreme Council. The official Japanese delegation, led by the statesman Saionji Kinmochi (1849–1940), included: politician and diplomat Makino Nobuaki (1861–1949), Ambassador to Great Britain Chinda Sutemi (1856–1929), Ambassador to France Matsui Keishirō, and Ambassador to Italy Ijūin Hikokichi (1864–1924). Poland was represented by Roman Dmowski and Prime Minister Ignacy Paderewski (1860–1941).

The general directives for the Japanese delegation, as established by the government in Tokyo, were relayed by Minister Uchida to Makino on

---

6   Józef Targowski, *Pamiętniki 1883–1921* (typewritten manuscript; hereafter, JT), 162–165.
7   Ibid., 169.
8   Ibid., 221–222.

9 December 1918.[9] More detailed instructions were sent later to Chinda.[10] The initial directives included, "Three Main Principles for Making Peace (Kōwa no sandai hōshin)" and clearly specified what conditions should be set by the Japanese delegation in matters which were (1) of interest solely to Japan, (2) of no interest to Japan, and (3) of interest to Japan and the allied and associated powers. Point (1) included, among other things, stating that Japan was to demand the cession – without any compensation – of territories it had taken from the Germans at the beginning of the war, meaning Qingdao, Shandong, and also Pacific islands lying north of the equator. The instructions stressed that, in all matters, the Japanese delegates should proceed as far as possible in agreement with the major powers, respecting their demands regarding taking possession of other territories. In point (2), the government instructed the delegation to avoid taking part in discussions about the terms of peace. Point (3) suggested proceeding in harmony with the stand of the powers and the overall situation at the conference. The Japanese were thus mostly interested in Far Eastern matters, above all the China question, so they practically took no part in discussions of European, including Polish, matters. Nevertheless, the delegates applied these principles to the case of Poland when they made Japan the last of the five major powers to recognize the independent Polish state.

On 16 November 1918, Józef Piłsudski, acting as the head of state and commander of Polish armed forces, prepared a telegram "notifying the President of the United States and the governments of England, France, Italy, Japan, Germany, and all of the warring states, of the establishment of the Polish state."[11] A day later, the head of the Ministry of Foreign Affairs (MOFA) of Poland, then in the process of being created, sent this telegram along with a cover letter to the foreign ministries of the mentioned countries, with a proposal to exchange official diplomatic representatives. In late January 1919 the United States became the first to officially recognize the independent Polish state and the cabinet of Ignacy Paderewski. Next, between 24 and 27 February, France, Great Britain and Italy all extended recognition. Finally on 6 March, the Japanese government made the decision to recognize the Polish government.[12] Matsui relayed this information to Roman Dmowski, head of the KNP,

---

9    *Nihon gaikō bunsho*, 1918/vol. 3 (Tokyo: Nihon kokusai rengō kyōkai, 1969), 649–650.
10   Ibid., 665–678.
11   *Dokumenty z dziejów polskiej polityki zagranicznej 1918–1939*, vol. 1 (Warsaw: PAX, 1989), 27.
12   "Taishō hachinen sangatsu muika no kakugi kettei" 1.4.3.17, GGS.

on 22 March, and that is why Polish documents record that date as the day on which Japan *de jure* recognized independent Poland.[13]

### Establishment of Diplomatic Relations

#### *Japanese Legation in Warsaw*

To formalize their relationship, Poland and Japan began to exchange diplomats. In March 1919, the Japanese Ministry of Foreign Affairs prepared a "Proposal Concerning Sending of Representatives of the Empire to Various Countries, Including Finland, Southern Russia, Poland, «Czechoslovakia»," meaning to the countries newly created or re-established in Central and Eastern Europe after the war.[14] At that point, MOFA saw consulates general in Helsinki, Kiev, and Odessa as essential, because they could provide current information about Russia's periphery, while it included Poland and Czechoslovakia because, as a world power, Japan should have representatives in Central Europe. However, these proposals were not implemented, because Minister Uchida felt that Japan did not have the appropriate persons to staff those posts. The matter was reconsidered in August of 1919 on the intervention of Ambassador Matsui who, being familiar with the politics of the great powers, asserted that Japan should send representatives to all the countries in Europe as quickly as possible. In a cable to Minister Uchida, he wrote:

> The situation in Europe indicates that international conflicts will occur over the next decade. In connection with that, it is imperative that we send our representatives to the appropriate regions of Europe. We must properly understand their situation and react to it quickly. Besides, we must realize that Japan is one of the most important members of the League of Nations and because of that must react seriously and with dignity to international events.[15]

In response to this cable, in September MOFA prepared a more detailed document, "Reasons for the Necessity of Establishing Legations and Consulates

13   Matsui's cable no. 94 to Dmowski (22 March 1919), 1.4.3.17, GGS; Cf. documents in the file "Komitet Narodowy Polski – Paryż," 31–35, Archiwum Akt Nowych (hereafter, AAN), Warsaw.
14   "Finrando, Nanro, Pōrando, «Chekosurovakku» nado no shokoku ni teikoku daihyōsha saken ni kansuru an," 1.4.3.5, GGS. Brackets in original.
15   Matsui's cable no. 1755 to Uchida (30 July 1919), 6.1.2.72, GGS.

after the End of the War."[16] It mentioned the countries of Eastern, Central and Southern Europe, agreeing that legations should be established in Poland, Czechoslovakia, Yugoslavia, Romania, Turkey and Greece, and consulates general in Hungary, Bulgaria and Finland. Two main reasons were given for this decision. First, the Ministry assumed that the newly established countries would themselves turn to Japan proposing an exchange of representatives, so Japan should be prepared. Second, as a world power, Japan should have representatives in all of the countries in which other powers had representation, in order to know the situation in Europe accurately and thus be able to take appropriate positions on matters concerning this region. The document also mentioned Poland's significant role in any possible changes in the European political situation. In this connection, it stated that a legation in Poland, thanks to the possibility of providing current information about political trends and about the intentions of the powers in that part of the world, could be a point of departure for creating a Japanese policy toward Europe. However, due to a lack of appropriately trained cadres, and also due to financial limitations, Japan delayed sending its first official representative to Poland, which caused concern on the Polish side. Debuchi Katsuji (1878–1947), Counselor and *chargé d'affaires* of the Japanese embassy in Berlin, informed Uchida about a meeting he had with the Polish representative to Germany.[17] He reported that the Polish delegate, Ignacy Szebeko (1860–1937), spoke of Poland's dissatisfaction with Japan's delay in opening a legation, and mentioned that one Japanese officer was staying in Warsaw.

That officer was Captain Yamawaki Masataka (1886–1974), who, on assignment from the Army General Staff and with the agreement of the Polish government, came to Warsaw in June 1919.[18] In the 1920s and 30s he would play a very important role in shaping Japanese policy toward Poland, both as military *attaché* in Poland (1921–1922; 1934–1935) and as a pro-Polish representative of the highest military authorities in Tokyo. His main task was to observe Russia from the West, and he also relayed much valuable information and opinions about Poland, which the Army passed on to MOFA. Knowing of the preparations for opening a Japanese legation in Warsaw, Yamawaki sent the following cable to the General Staff:

> From information in the press I find out that Japan will soon name her representative in Poland. In that connection, I would like to submit my suggestions regarding the makeup of the mission:

---

16    "Taisen no kekka kōshikan ryōjikan nado shinsetsu no hitsuyō riyū," ibid.

17    Debuchi's cable no. 78 to Uchida (10 May 1920), 6.1.8.4-23, GGS.

18    Doc. no. 49 (14 May 1919), "Komitet Narodowy Polski – Paryż," AAN.

1.    Poles use the Polish language. Many of them know German or Russian, but for a diplomat it is not sufficient to know only one of these, he should understand them both.

2.    Many representatives of the Polish government and intellectuals speak French and do not like to use either Russian or German. For this reason knowledge of French by a diplomat posted here is essential. Very few Poles know English.

3.    It is better not to send Russian specialists, because Poles in general do not like Russia and are quite sensitive on that point. Therefore the posting of such persons could raise suspicions and cause unnecessary difficulties in other matters. I believe that it would be better to send as the representative a diplomat who has no connection with Russia, and to place one such specialist in the auxiliary staff of the mission.[19]

Nevertheless, for almost the entire following year MOFA did not make a decision about establishing a legation in Warsaw. The main reason was the continuing lack of an appropriate candidate to head the mission, but it could be supposed that Japan delayed also because of concerns about the outcome of the Polish-Soviet war, waged since February 1919.

Japan did not abandon its interest in opening a legation in Warsaw, as seen in a January 1921 cable from the ambassador in Paris, Ishii Kikujirō (1866–1945), to Minister Uchida.[20] He wrote about a report by Ueda [Sentarō], a Russian specialist who in early 1921 paid official visits to Poland, the Baltic States and Finland. Ishii noted that those countries were excellent locations for observing and gathering information about the Soviet Union, which could fundamentally influence the creation of an appropriate Japanese foreign policy toward the region. This opinion probably hastened the decision to open a diplomatic mission in Warsaw, which finally occurred on 6 May 1921.[21] Japan's first official representative in Poland was Kawakami Toshitsune (1861–1935) who, despite the suggestions of Yamawaki, was a Russian specialist. But Polish affairs were not foreign to him because, as interpreter for Dmowski and Piłsudski during their talks with authorities in Tokyo in 1904, he became familiar with the issues of concern to Poles. Although 26 months had passed since Japan recognized the Polish state, Poland was, in fact, the first of the Central and Eastern European countries in which a

---

19    Yamawaki's cable no. 81 to Fukuda Masatarō (15 Sept. 1920), 1.1.4.1-14, GGS.
20    Ishii's cable no. 59 to Uchida (17 Jan. 1921), 6.1.5.8-15, GGS.
21    *Nihon gaikōshi jiten* (Tokyo: Yamakawa Shuppansha, 1992), 82.

Japanese legation was established.[22] Japan had finally realized the fact that Poland was an ideal strategic location, situated between Soviet Russia and Western Europe.

### Polish Legation in Tokyo

The government of the reborn Polish state was more eager than that of Japan to quickly establish diplomatic relations between the two countries and to post an official representative to Tokyo. But even here many difficulties were encountered. First of all, Poland was only now, after over a century of partitions, creating the independent diplomatic service of a sovereign country. Appropriate candidates were sought to fill the newly created positions. The diplomatic cadres came from varied political, social and educational backgrounds. The majority were former officials from the Austrian partition, activists of the Polish National Committee allied with Dmowski, or supporters of Piłsudski. After the dissolution of KNP in April 1919, close collaborators of Piłsudski decided that the number of Dmowski supporters posted to diplomatic posts abroad should be limited. Therefore there was much maneuvering among various factions, among persons of various political convictions and different connections. The issue of naming a Polish representative to Japan was a case in point.

The first candidate for the post in Tokyo was a doctor of philosophy, Adam Żółtowski (1881–1958).[23] French Ambassador to Japan, Constant Bapst (1858–1934), passed along word of his candidacy to Tokyo, as did Ambassador Matsui in a cable to Minister Uchida.[24] He wrote:

> The Captain [Yamawaki] spoke with the Polish Vice-Minister of Foreign Affairs Skrzyński [Władysław] from whom he learned that for the Polish government and for its future foreign policy, London, Washington and Tokyo are very important. That is why he wants to send 'Zorutuisuki'.[25]

---

22  The only earlier legation was in Turkey on 18 Apr. 1921, subsequently in Czechoslovakia, 17 Oct., Romania 12 Mar. 1922, Greece 31 Oct. The role of the Japanese representative in Hungary was filled from 30 Dec. 1920 by the Japanese representative in Austria, in Finland from 14 Mar. 1921 by the representative in Sweden, in Yugoslavia from 4 Feb. 1924 by the representative in Romania. In Bulgaria a legation was opened on 4 Dec. 1939. Ibid., 64–94.

23  Janina Żółtowska, *Inne czasy, inni ludzie* (typewritten manuscript). Documents at the Diplomatic Archives of the MOFA of Japan (GGS). His name appears there as "Zolotowski" or "Zorutuisuki."

24  See: Bapst's cable to Hanihara (16 Mar. 1919); cable no. 287 (12 Nov. 1919), no. 312 (26 Nov. 1919), no. 333 (12 Dec. 1919), no. 343 (24 Dec. 1919), 6.1.8.4-30, GGS.

25  Matsui's cable no. 312 to Uchida (28 Nov. 1919), 6.1.8.4-30, GGS.

However, with the passage of time, the political position of Piłsudski and his supporters strengthened, and that was no doubt the major reason that Żółtowski's nomination was withdrawn. In January 1920, Ambassador Chinda wrote from London about the possibility of naming a new Polish envoy to Tokyo, and on 31 March, Ambassador Matsui mentioned as the first candidate the acting chief of the Polish mission *ad interim*, Józef Targowski (Figure 11.4).[26]

FIGURE 11.4    *Józef Targowski, High Commissioner of the Republic of Poland and minister plenipotentiary for Siberia and the Far East and first chargé d'affaires ad interim in Japan (collection of Ewa Pałasz-Rutkowska).*

---

26    Chinda's cable no. 1 to Uchida (5 Jan. 1920); Matsui's cable no. 568 to Uchida (31 Mar. 1920), ibid.

From Targowski's memoirs it appears that, before his departure for Siberia, he knew nothing of the possibility of his taking over the mission in Japan. In mid-1919 he even suggested that, simultaneously with his mission, an envoy should be sent to Tokyo, because that diplomatic post could provide good support for his activities in Siberia. Head of state Piłsudski officially nominated Targowski to the post of *chargé d'affaires ad interim* in Japan on 7 April 1920.[27] This nomination served as the basis for creating a legation of the Republic of Poland in Tokyo. Targowski wrote this about the nomination:

> In Shanghai I was surprised by a cable naming me representative of Poland to China and Japan, while retaining my current authority as High Commissioner for Siberia. That is a vast territory of activity.[28]

The Japanese government accepted the candidate on 17 May,[29] but that information did not reach Targowski until 28 July, when he was still in Shanghai:

> Yesterday evening Jezierski [Władysław, director-in-chief of the Russian-Asiatic Bank in China] returned from his trip. In Beijing he met Obata [Yūkichi, Japanese envoy to China], who asked how long have I been in Tokyo...When he saw Jezierski's evident surprise, he said that *agrément* came immediately after the inquiry from the embassy in Paris. And Warsaw, despite my cables, said nothing of this to me. Of course I decided to leave on the first ship to Yokohama.[30]

Józef Targowski arrived in Tokyo on 10 August, and on the 13th he presented letters of credence, signed by the Minister of Foreign Affairs of the Republic of Poland, Stanisław Patek (1866–1945), to Minister Uchida.[31]

### Difficult Beginnings: The Polish-Soviet War and Japan

Immediately after assuming his post in Tokyo as the first representative of Poland in Japan, Targowski had to articulate a position on the Polish-Soviet

27  *Archiwum Akt Nowych w Warszawie. Przewodnik po zasobie archiwalnym* (Warsaw: PWN, 1973), 94.
28  JT, 259.
29  Uchida's cable to Bapst (23 Jul. 1920), 6.1.8.4-30, GGS.
30  JT, 310. Published also in *Japonica* no. 1 (1993): 124–125 (hereafter, JTJ).
31  JT, 312–313 (JTJ no. 1 (1993): 126–127); Uchida's cable to Hara (16 Aug. 1920), 6.1.8.4-30, GGS.

War and Poland's policy toward the East – this despite a dearth of information from his country. The armed conflict between Poland and Soviet Russia lasted from February 1919 until October 1920, and was ended by the signing of the Treaty of Riga in March of 1921. Yet the first major action of this war is considered to be Marshal Piłsudski's excursion against Kiev, which began on 25 April 1920. After the Polish victories on the Ukrainian front and the occupation of Kiev, the Red Army launched a counter-offensive under the command of Marshals Mikhail Tukhachevsky (1893–1937) and Siemion Budionny (1883–1973), forcing the Polish forces to retreat on the entire length of the front. Soon the Red Army entered ethnically Polish territory. The turning point of the war occurred between 13 and 26 August, when the Red Army met stiffer resistance and a battle was joined that determined the fate of Poland and her eastern border. Polish forces broke through the front and advanced eastward, pushing the Soviets past Minsk.

Limited information about the war reached Targowski while he was still in China and even after he arrived in Japan. On 21 June he wrote from China:

> Just now they brought from Shanghai a cable from Warsaw...with the sad news of giving up Kiev. ...It is difficult to officiate in my conditions, when without any directives and assistance from my country I must handle all circumstances and not make mistakes.[32]

However, before news of the Polish victory and Soviet retreat reached Tokyo, Targowski found himself defending Polish actions to his counterparts in Japan. On 14 and 19 August he wrote:

> The news, particularly that coming through Berlin, has been nothing but the worst for the past two days. According to the news service of the 'Kokusai' agency, which twice a day sends packets of dispatches to all of the legations, Russian forces have entered the Lublin region. Vice Minister Hanihara [Masanao], and also Bapst, in a delicate but nevertheless unpleasant manner, reproach me. Why did we start a war that we are losing? ...We work practically around the clock, because there are constant telephones, primarily from editorial offices of newspapers, asking for news. And here we get nothing from the home country, we are left only with the agency dispatches. ...Visits to Prime Minister Hara [Takashi] and the English ambassador occurred at the time of the worst news. And

---

32    JT, 289.

again these slightly critical but very unpleasant questions. And how am I to explain to these people here?[33]

*Japan Advertiser*, the largest English-language daily in the Far East, published articles containing fragments of conversations with Targowski regarding the reasons for Poland's embarking on the war with Soviet Russia. The most important, in his view, was the desire to preempt an attack, already in preparation, by the Red Army on Ukraine and Lithuania, territories neighboring Poland.

> 'The charges that Poland desires one foot more of territory for herself are false' – said Minister Targowski – 'and many of them are just a bit of propaganda. The truth about the «imperialistic charge» against Poland lies in the simple fact that Poland knew her neighbours were about to attack and Poland, with the knowledge, attacked first.' ...'Poland is now in her sixth year of war' – said Mr. Targowski – 'Few people of the world stop to realize that our nation has been fighting longer than any of the countries of Europe. And for what is Poland fighting? Herself alone? I think not. My country does not feel that she is begging the world at all when she asks for help in this present crisis. We feel that our war is one in which the world is vitally interested and that unless we are given help now the Bolshevist advance will continue into other European countries.'[34]

In a subsequent interview printed in *Japan Advertiser*, Targowski needed to express a position on the information that reached the *Nichinichi Shimbun* on 16 August from a correspondent in Berlin, about an alleged occupation of Warsaw by the Soviets.

> 'Until I have official notification of the capital's fall I can issue no formal statement.' ...*The Japan Advertiser*'s special correspondence dated August 16...describes the battle as still outside of Warsaw «ranging on a semicircular 15 miles front 5 miles from Warsaw». 'The 5 miles mentioned in *The Japan Advertiser*'s report' – said Targowski – 'mean a great deal more to the Polish reader than they do to the average foreigner in Tokyo. The attacking forces must cross a wide and deep river before they are on the

---

33    JT, 313–314; JTJ, no. 1 (1993): 127.
34    "Charge of Imperialistic Hopes in Poland Denied by Minister," *Japan Advertiser*, 15 Aug. 1920, 7. Brackets in original.

outside of the defenses of Warsaw and undoubtedly they are some defenses, even though they are temporary. I am inclined to think that the reported fall may be an exaggeration.'

Commenting on the submissive quality of the Polish people... Targowski said that the Polish people had not adopted Bolshevism, as reports reaching Tokyo would indicate. ...The Polish people are not Bolshevistic in their tendencies, and he has no fear of their accepting the teachings of the barbarians from Russia.[35]

That same day, in fact, *Japan Advertiser* reported on the successes of the Polish forces, adding that, "the news of Warsaw's fall is evidently of Soviet origin."[36] This news caused a total change of attitude toward Poland among representatives of the Japanese government and of foreign countries accredited in Tokyo. On August 19 Targowski wrote:

When noon was striking, in rolled Prime Minister Hara in top hat and formal wear, Minister Count Uchida and the chief of protocol of the Foreign Ministry; all...expressed very warm congratulations to the Polish government for the splendid victory of our forces. Since yesterday we breathed a little easier after the latest news, but this visit gave us enormous joy as one more, unquestionable, confirmation of victory. I achieved a great personal success, being considered, after my denial in *Japan Advertiser*, one of the better-informed diplomats in Tokyo. What irony of fate and comedy of reality.[37]

Japan, for its part, had adopted the opinion of the Western powers, mainly England and France, about the Polish-Soviet conflict, as evidenced by articles in the Japanese press. Allied leaders observed the developing situation in Poland with great unease, fearing the breakdown of the Versailles order in the event of Poland's defeat. Such a situation could lead to Soviet-German cooperation, which in turn would hamper the enforcement of war reparations from Germany. The Allies' critical views of Polish military operations derived from their distrust of Marshal Piłsudski. He had been, after all, a socialist and revolutionary conspirator, and the creator of the Polish Legions, which in the first phases of the war fought alongside Austria against the Entente. He was

35 "Pole Envoy Doubts Occupation Report," ibid., 19 Aug. 1920, 1.
36 "Pole Counter Attack Drives Soviet Forces away from Warsaw," ibid., 1.
37 JT, 315; JTJ, no. 1 (1993): 128. See also, "Premier Hara Expresses Friendship for Poland," *Japan Advertiser*, 20 Aug. 1920, 5.

suspected of being a Germanophile, and the Allies assumed that, as a socialist, he would come to an agreement with the Soviets. That is why the Allied powers faulted Piłsudski for the Polish failures on the front and sent a special mission to Poland for the purpose of convincing the Marshal to utilize allied officers in the Polish army. The Polish government finally agreed on 27 July to the naming of General Maxime Weygand (1867–1965) as official advisor to the Polish Chief of Staff, General Tadeusz Rozwadowski (1866–1928). Following the Polish victory at Warsaw, the French press and, due to false information and propaganda, many American, British and Japanese newspapers gave Weygand the credit for the triumph, claiming that he was responsible for the strategic plan for the battle, the reorganization of the Polish army and even commanding it during the battle.[38]

Today it is known that the main author of the victory in the Battle of Warsaw was Piłsudski,[39] and at the time one key eyewitness of the "Miracle on the Vistula," Captain Yamawaki, shared that opinion. In an interview many years later, he said:

> I asked Piłsudski for permission to remain at headquarters. The defense of Warsaw began. ...The victory was the result solely and completely of the Polish plan. It was Piłsudski's plan...Piłsudski had not only great experience and knowledge in military matters, but also a good sense and understanding of foreign policy and internal affairs of the country.[40]

In summary, the attitude of Japanese authorities toward the Polish-Soviet conflict was mostly the same as that of the Western powers, which was a result of Japan's earlier alliances and political sympathies and of principles established even before the Paris peace conference. Accordingly, in matters that did not involve the country directly, Japan – a young and inexperienced world power – acted in concert with the other powers, relying on their politics and experience. However, when the Polish forces were victorious over the Soviets, the Japanese government hurried to send its congratulations, realizing that Poland would play a significant role on the European political scene. But this, of course, was not indicative of a change in the general attitude.

---

38  See: *Japan Advertiser*, 25, 26 Aug. 1920, 1.

39  *Rok 1920. Wojna polsko-radziecka we wspomnieniach i innych dokumentach* (Warsaw: PIW, 1990), 304–308; Mieczysław Pruszyński, *Wojna 1920: Dramat Piłsudskiego* (Warsaw: "BGW," 1995).

40  E. Pałasz-Rutkowska, A.T. Romer, 85–86.

## Stabilization of Bilateral Relations

### The Issue of Upper Silesia

An excellent example of such policy was the issue of Upper Silesia. The Versailles Treaty established that Upper Silesia's belonging to Poland or Germany was to be decided by a plebiscite. The dissatisfaction of the Polish inhabitants and increasing persecution by Germans led to the outbreak of two insurrections (August 1919 and August 1920). Fear that a division of Silesia after the plebiscite of March 1921 would be unfavorable to Poland, arising from a difference of opinion between Great Britain and France, led to a third Silesian insurrection. France, wanting to weaken Germany as much as possible, sought to grant Poland larger and more industrialized regions of Upper Silesia, while Great Britain, being generally pro-German, displayed an anti-Polish attitude.

The Polish government, in light of its respect for the Versailles Treaty, could not extend direct assistance to the insurgents, but attempted to gain understanding in Paris, London and Tokyo for the patriotic strivings of Silesians. Targowski received an instruction in this regard in mid-June 1920, but he could not act officially, because he was still in Shanghai waiting for *agrément* from Japan.[41] The issue was taken up by his deputy in Tokyo (February-September 1921), *chargé d'affaires* Otton Sas-Hubicki (1888-?). Several times, at the end of May and beginning of June, he visited the Ministry of Foreign Affairs, meeting with Minister Uchida or his deputy Hanihara Masanao (1876–1934) to explain the position of Poland on the insurrection and the significance to Poland of Upper Silesia.[42] Minister Uchida stated that in his directives to the Japanese Ambassador in Paris he stressed the necessity of proceeding according to the Versailles Treaty and according to "commonly appropriate direction." He also added that, "Japan is not especially interested in this issue and must maintain neutrality."

Hubicki, in his report to the Minister of Foreign Affairs in Warsaw, accurately evaluated the reasons for Japan's position:

> [T]he position of the Japanese government on this issue was to some extent established by the British policy on this matter. ...A strong anti-Polish-French stance in the matter of Upper Silesia was plainly evident in the statement by Lloyd George. It should be clear that Japan, because of its desire for an alliance with Britain, must take British policies into

41    JT, 283–284.
42    Sas-Hubicki's cable no. T/99/2/pol (6 Jun. 1921), file "Ministerstwo Spraw Zagranicznych," no. 5953, 5–10, AAN.

consideration...Although on my part I have done everything to convince the shapers of Japanese foreign policy, as did Minister Targowski...in connection with the argument that our common enemy – Bolshevism – means that a strong Poland is in Japan's interest, and Poland cannot be strong without Silesia. But on the other hand, it must be realized that Japan does not have any specific interest in finding a solution to the Silesian question that is favorable to Poland. I must conclude this report with the opinion that more cannot be expected from Count Uchida other than maintaining neutrality and a generalized stance of applying the Versailles Treaty to the matter of Silesia.[43]

It is worth noting that Japan, although generally conducting its politics in accordance with the diplomacy of its greatest ally, Great Britain, maintained its neutral attitude on the issue of Upper Silesia, rather than adopting the anti-Polish stance of London. It might be added that Japan took a similar stance in the matter of Poland's eastern borders.[44] On 12 October the Inter-Allied Commission reached a decision about the partition of Upper Silesia that was favorable to Poland. The Conference of Ambassadors accepted it on 20 October.[45] Japan's strict neutrality might have helped to turn the Commission in Poland's favor.

### Trade Treaty

Seeking potential future benefits, Japan was more active in pursuing the establishment of trade relations with Poland. This decision was connected with a document prepared within MOFA by the Commission for Studying and Revision of Treaties (*Jōyaku kaisei chōsa iinkai*), titled *Proposed Principles for Entering Into Treaties With Newly-Established Countries* (21 November 1921).[46] It addressed, among other issues, how countries resurrected or newly-created after World War I were gaining stability and thus were interested in developing international trade. These countries had already reached agreements with some European trading partners, and negotiations were continuing with others. The report recommended that Japan should do the same, but it pointed out that, before Japan initiated trade with these countries, it must

---

43    Ibid., 10.

44    *Prawo międzynarodowe i historia dyplomatyczna. Wybór dokumentów*, comp. L. Gelberg (Warsaw: PWN , 1958), vol. 2, 204–208.

45    Stanisław Sierpowski, *Źródła do historii powszechnej okresu międzywojennego*, vol. 1 (Poznań: Wydawnictwa Naukowe UAM, 1991), 229–236.

46    "Shinkōkoku ni taisuru jōyaku teiketsu hōshin'an," 2.5.1.107, GGS.

first review other treaties which were in effect before the war and which took on different meanings after the abrupt changes on the international scene after the war.

It seems that the Japanese government completed this review and then began the process of negotiations over a trade treaty.[47] In August 1922, Japan presented a draft of a document that had been the subject of discussion from mid-October 1921. The final Trade and Navigation Treaty (*Tsūshō kōkai jōyaku*)[48] was signed in Warsaw on 7 December, and the exchange of ratification documents occurred also in Warsaw on 8 January 1925. The treaty went into effect ten days later.

The purpose of the treaty was to strengthen the existing bonds of friendship and to develop trade relations. Theoretically, the treaty created conditions for broad trade exchanges and economic cooperation, but in practice the commercial contacts between Poland and Japan, similar to their political contacts, were sporadic. The intermittent nature of relations was primarily the result of the large distance separating the two countries, and the lack of significant interest from Japan.

### Repatriation of Polish Children from Siberia

Japanese authorities displayed a different, much more active, attitude in the matter of repatriating Polish children from Siberia and Manchuria. This determination arose from the conviction that Japan, as a new power on the international scene, should also participate in humanitarian actions. This matter began even before the establishment of the Polish diplomatic mission in Tokyo, with an initiative of the Polish Relief Committee, which was created in 1919 in Vladivostok on the initiative of Anna Bielkiewicz (1877–1936). Initially, aid to the children was to be provided by the American Red Cross, but due to the departure of American troops from Siberia after the failed military intervention, the Red Cross care center was also closed. The Relief Committee then began to seek assistance in Japan. In June 1920, Bielkiewicz went to the Ministry of Foreign Affairs in Tokyo, which directed the Japanese Red Cross to investigate the matter. On 5 July, after gaining the support of the Army Minister Tanaka Giichi (1864–1929) and the Navy Minister Katō Tomosaburō (1861–1923), a representative of the Red Cross notified Minister Uchida that assistance from Japan "is necessary, because

---

47    See: Kawakami's cable no. 80 to Uchida (26 Jun. 1922), 2.5.1.113, GGS.
48    *Jōyaku isan*, vol. 1 (Tokyo: Gaimushō jōyakukyoku, 1925), 1059–1072; cf., Juljan Makowski, *Umowy międzynarodowe Polski 1919–1934* (Warsaw: Drukarnia W. Łazarskiego, 1935), 102.

FIGURE 11.5     *Polish children from Siberia (collection of Matsumoto Teruo; used by permission).*

of the enormous significance of this matter both in the diplomatic and humanitarian aspects (Figure 11.5)."[49]

The first group of young repatriates sailed from Vladivostok to Tsuruga on 20 July 1920, and by July of 1921, 375 orphans were transported to Tokyo. A year later, in 1922 another 390 Polish children landed in Osaka. After spending some time in Japan, the Japanese Red Cross transported the Siberian children by ship from Japan to the United States and Britain, from where they left for Poland, to Gdańsk. The last such transport left Kobe on 6 September 1922. While they remained in Japan, the Japanese Red Cross managed their care, and the Imperial Household also became involved, under the leadership of Empress Teimei (1884–1951). The Japanese primarily offered the Poles medical care, but also organized rest and recreation. Anna Bielkiewicz published a series of articles about Poland in the Japanese press. From September 1921 till May 1922 the *Echo Dalekiego Wschodu* (*Kyokutō no sakebi, Echo of the Far East*) appeared bi-weekly. This publication (in Polish, Japanese and English) was sold in Tokyo, Kyoto, Osaka, Kobe and Yokohama. It informed the Japanese about Poland, its history, the current situation of Poles in Siberia, and about the orphans and the progress of repatriation (Figure 11.6).

---

49     Matsumoto Teruo, "Pōrando no Siberia kojitachi," *Polonica*, 5 (1994): 71.

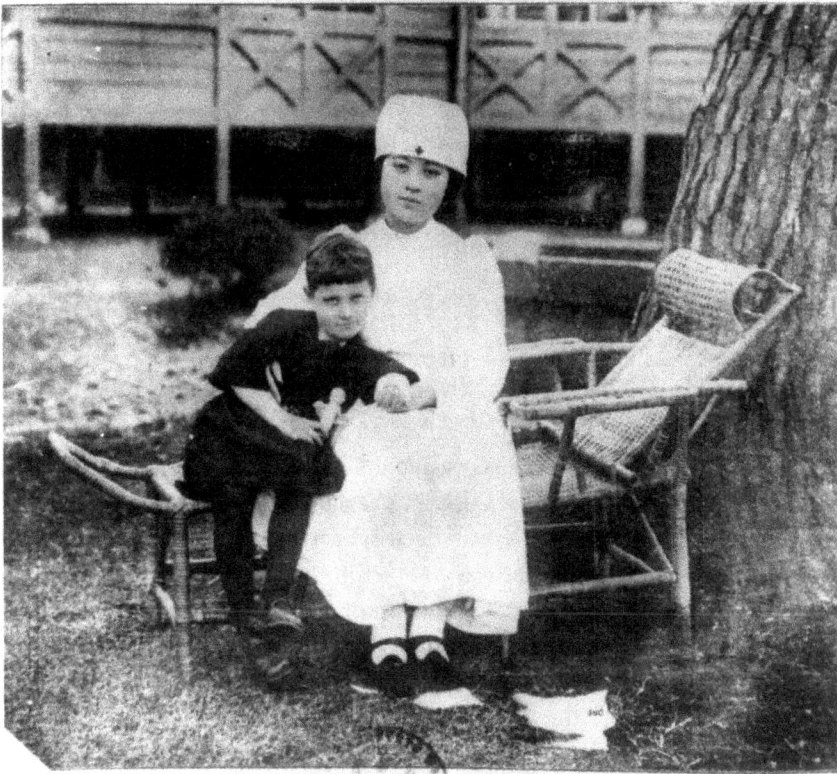

極東の叫び

本邦印刷 大正十一年四月二十八日 〔第三種郵便物認可〕大正十年十月一日 大正十一年五月一日發行

（第拾號）號念記社字十赤本日

定價十五錢

日本赤十字社病院看護婦と波蘭孤兒

Siostra Miłosierdzia Jap. Czerw. Krzyża z sierotą polską z Syberii.

A nurse of Japanese Red Cross with a Polish orphan from Siberia.

FIGURE 11.6 *Kyokutō no sakebi, Echo of the Far East, May 1922 (collection of Matsumoto Teruo; used by permission).*

## Conclusion

Official relations between Poland and Japan began with Poland's regaining of independence and Japan's recognition of it as a sovereign country in March 1919. Although the beginnings of bilateral contacts were dependent on the international situation and big-power politics, in which the government in Tokyo was involved, they were not as difficult as could be expected on the basis of geopolitical distance. This no doubt resulted from the conflict-free history of earlier unofficial contacts, and the sympathy that both nations felt for each other. But closer cooperation, independent of the efforts of the Polish side, could arise only on the condition that Japan increased its attention to Central Europe.

In the 1920s, Poland lay beyond the scope of the direct interests of Japan's foreign policy, which is demonstrated by the very small collection of documents dealing with that subject in the Diplomatic Archives of the MOFA in Tokyo. Japan's policy toward Poland was in keeping with the principles established at the peace conference in Paris – it did not meddle in affairs that were not of direct interest. Whenever Japan's representatives had to speak in the international arena, mainly in the League of Nations, they expressed a favorable neutrality toward Poland. But they avoided taking positions counter to that of other powers, especially Great Britain, with which Japan had the longest relationship, having been bound by a bilateral treaty since 1902.

This attitude toward Poland, arising from a lack of earlier official relations, influenced, as we saw, a delay in establishing a diplomatic mission in Warsaw. There were no Poland specialists in Japan, so the first minister to Warsaw, Kawakami, as well as his successors, were specialists on Russia. The Ministry of Foreign Affairs realized that it was necessary to educate professionals who knew various cultures, but that was not possible within Japan. There were no institutions that could undertake that task in a professional manner. It was agreed that students would be sent to appropriate countries to learn the language and gain general knowledge of society.[50] But when exactly the Polish language was added to the list of languages recommended by MOFA cannot be determined definitely, because the documents relating to this matter are incomplete. It may only be surmised that the appropriate directives were issued in the early 1920s, and on that basis two students came to Poland for three years, Suzuki Toranosuke and Oda Toranosuke.[51] After the three years, in accordance with the practice of the Foreign Ministry, they remained with the

---

50    See various documents in 6.1.2.12, GGS.

51    Uchida's cable no. 264 to Kawakami (10 June 1922); Ida to Uchida (5 May 1923), 6.1.7.6-4-1, GGS.

mission to deepen their knowledge of the language. But beyond these two, no one else was sent to Poland in the 1920s, yet more proof that Poland was not in the center of attention of Japan's foreign policy.

Nevertheless, there was a reason why the General Staff became interested in Poland: its proximity to the Soviet Union. Poland was the best vantage point for observing this neighbor that was so dangerous to Japan. Staff officers were very well aware that, in the realm of cryptology, the Japanese army was behind other powers, including Poland, which through the years of struggle with the Russian occupier became specialized in this field. So they were eager for cooperation. Talks in this regard were begun with Section II (Intelligence) of the General Staff in Warsaw by the first Japanese military attaché, the aforementioned Yamawaki Masataka, and continued in 1922–1925 by his successor Okabe Naosaburō (1887–1946).[52] Section II was chiefly represented by Colonel Wacław Jędrzejewicz (1893–1993), who in 1925 would become the first official military attaché of Poland in Tokyo. The immediate reason for the Japanese General Staff's decision to seek cooperation in cryptography were Japan's experiences during the first round of talks about establishing relations with Soviet Russia (earlier contacts had been severed in 1917 during the October Revolution), held in Dairen from the autumn of 1921 to April 1922. It turned out the Japanese intelligence officers posted there by the Staff were unable to decode cables intercepted from Moscow. They were then sent to Okabe in Warsaw, who was assisted by specialists of the Polish General Staff. The fact that the Poles decoded the messages within a week convinced the representatives of the Japanese General Staff of the high level of Polish cryptology. As a result, in early 1923, on the official invitation of the Japanese General Staff, Captain Jan Kowalewski (1892–1965), came to Tokyo.[53] He was an outstanding cryptologist of Soviet ciphers, whose capabilities were used to good advantage during the 1920 war. He lectured personnel of Section II of the General Staff on Soviet ciphers, general principles of decoding, and structures of diplomatic ciphers. In order to deepen this cooperation, staff officers were posted to Poland, and others came for working visits. It should be emphasized that most of these officers were interested in Poland only in the context of intelligence about the Soviet Union.

---

52     Ariga Tsutao, *Nihon rikukaigun no jōhō kikō to sono katsudō* (Tokyo: Kindai Bunsha, 1994), 140–141.

53     For details see: Ōkubo Shunjirō, *Tairo angō kaidoku ni kansuru sōshi narabi ni senkun nado ni kansuru shiryō* in, *Manshū. Shūsenji nissosen* (Tokyo: Bōei kenkyūjo senshi kenkyū sentā shiryō etsuranshitsu). Cf., Gen. Sikorski's cable no. 32105/II inf.II.A.5 to Kowalewski (13 Dec. 1922), file: "Oddział II Sztabu Głównego," no. 616/57, AAN.

Following on the positive diplomatic and personal contacts of the preceding years, military cooperation begun in the 1920s would blossom in the following decade, when Poland became a key strategic location for garnering intelligence from the east (Soviet Union) and west (Germany) in the new European international climate. That climate would create significantly greater interest in Poland on the part of the Japanese Ministry of Foreign Affairs.

# Friends in Opposite Camps or Enemies from Afar
## Japanese and Ottoman Turkish Relations in the Great War

*Selçuk Esenbel*

## The Origins of Japan's Involvement in the Near East

The effects of the Great War on Japan's role in the Near East have not been studied in depth, with existing studies limited to a few accounts of Japanese diplomats who served in Turkey.[1] There are ample references to the Japanese delegation members in the records of the Paris Peace Conference, and in the documents relating to the Treaty of Sèvres of 10 August 1920, that dismantled the Ottoman Empire in favor of British and French mandates and Allied occupation of most of Anatolia and the imperial capital, Istanbul. Japanese also appear in the accounts of the negotiations for the Lausanne Treaty of 24 June 1923, through which the Allies discarded the Sèvres agreement and reached a new settlement with the Turkish nationalist government in Ankara.[2] All of these documents contain rich data on Japanese involvement, but there has not yet been a full monograph study on the topic. Perhaps the subject has not attracted as much attention as has Japan's participation on the East Asian front, because its formal posture was of noninvolvement in the Near Eastern Question, choosing to remain an observer in the partitioning of Turkey as the defeated ally of Germany.

Given the dearth of scholarship, this preliminary study will survey the field and argue that Japan's activities on the Near Eastern front of the Great War, and especially during the Turkish war of independence (1920–1923), derived from Meiji Japan's interests in securing a place for itself in the Ottoman world in order to gain access to the commerce of the Mediterranean and Black Seas region. More significantly, the primary Japanese motivation throughout these years was to use Istanbul as a location for keeping watch on Russia. The imperial capital, situated along the Bosphorus and Dardanelles Straits, was the perfect location from which to achieve this goal.

---

1  Matsutani Hironao, *Nihon-Toruko kōshō-shi kaisetsu to shiryō* (Tokyo: Okazaki kenkyūjō, 1999). Klaus Kreiser, "Vom Untergang der *Ertoghrul* bis zur Mission Abdurrashid Efendis-Die türkisch-japanischen Beziehungen zwischen 1890 und 1915" in Joseph Kreiner, ed., *Japan und die Mittelmächte* (Bonn: Bouvier Verlag Herbert Grundmann Studium Universale, 1986), pp. 235–247.

2  *Gaikōmonjō*, 1921 Volume III Part I Section 2. "Dōmei oyobi rengōkoku to To-koku to no Se-buru jōyaku gunjiyō jōkō nado jisshi narabi Gi-To ryōkokukan suru ken." This paper is based on the documents on pp. 28–46.

258 ESENBEL

After the 1868 Meiji Restoration, Japanese leaders increasingly saw the Ottoman Empire's position between the Balkans and the Middle East as a key site for monitoring Imperial Russia. Field Marshal and Prime Minister Yamagata Aritomo (1838–1922), who more than any other figure shaped modern Japan's geo-political strategy, in 1890 defined Japan's imperial sphere of interest to include North Asian territories up to the Amur River, including the Korean peninsula. Yamagata and his Foreign Minister, Aoki Shūzō, feared Romanov Russia as the major threat to Japan's security zone. In their memoranda to the Diet and cabinet members, both expressed particular concern over the construction of the Trans-Siberian Railway, beginning in 1891, because it intensified Russia's threat to the Korean monarchy and Japanese security. Some Meiji leaders thought that "Japan had to struggle for survival by following the path of the Great Powers"[3] that had plunged into the Near East and the Balkans to replace what they saw as the corrupt and declining Ottoman Empire. Accordingly, Japan viewed the Ottoman realm partly in terms of the troubling "Eastern Question" that addressed the future of territories now rife with nationalist conflict. A 1911 classified report by Japan's Ministry of Foreign Affairs on conditions in Turkey discussed the ethnic problems, nationalism, and decline in terms that reflected the imperialist thinking of the British Foreign Office, and addressed the prospects of Japanese interests in the event of a Great Power-takeover of formerly Ottoman territories.[4]

In addition, Japanese leaders wanted to use the Ottoman territories to keep watch on the global rivalry between Great Britain and Russia and, more important to Japan's core interests, to monitor Russian actions in the Balkans. Japanese strategists argued that the Russian empire could not simultaneously engage in operations in both the Balkans in the West, and in North Asia and Korea in the East. The eminent pre-war Japanese scholar of Ottoman and Turkish history, Naitō Chishū (1886–1984), explained that the Balkans were important for two reasons: nationalist conflict there troubled the weakened Ottoman empire, and Russia had a long-standing interest in accessing the region's warm water ports, through conflict if necessary. As Naitō knew from the time he had spent working at Japan's embassy in Ankara during the 1920s,

---

3  Akira Iriye, "Japan's Drive for Great Power Status," in *The Cambridge History of Japan Volume 5 The Nineteenth Century*, Marius B. Jansen, ed. (Cambridge: Cambridge University Press, 1989 online 2008), 763.

4  Ian Nish, *Japanese Foreign Policy, 1869–1942: Kasumigaseki to Miyakezaka* (London: Routledge, 2002), 45; Iriye, "Japan's Drive," 739, 764; Roger F. Hackett. *Yamagata Aritomo in the Rise of Modern Japan, 1868–1922* (Cambridge: Harvard University Press, 1971), 139–139; Ministry of Foreign Affairs, *Toruko jijō* (Tokyo: Gaimushō seimukyoku dainika, 1911), 100–104, 246–248.

the prevailing assumption among Japanese diplomats and military officers was that, if the Russian authorities pushed an expansionist policy in the Balkans, they would leave the Far East alone. However, if Russia were to pull back from the Near East it would likely be a prelude to an expansionary policy in East Asia, which could threaten Japan.[5] By the early 20th century, the Meiji leadership approached the Near East from the Great Power perspective of the disposition of former Ottoman territories, as well as out of its concerns with the potential threat that Imperial Russia posed to Japan's expanding global interests. For these and other reasons, Japan sought to enhance and transform its relationship with the waning Ottoman Empire during the first decades of the 20th century.

### Extraterritoriality and Pan-Asianism

Meiji leaders also pursued relations with the Istanbul authorities to enhance the international recognition of Japan's new status as a "Western power" after the promulgation of the Meiji Constitution in 1889. After 1868, the Meiji government frantically pushed for treaty revision in order to attain equal status with the Western Powers, a goal it achieved with the 1894 Anglo-Japanese treaty of navigation that abolished extraterritoriality in Japan and signaled British recognition of Japan as a partner against Russia. Foreign Minister Aoki is alleged to have encouraged the young merchant Yamada Torajirō (1866–1957), manager of the Nakamura Shoten's offices in the international commercial Pera district of Istanbul, to pursue contacts among the Turkish officials. The Nakamura Shoten subsequently served as the center of unofficial Japanese-Turkish relations and Yamada became the primary conduit for informal "twilight diplomacy" between the two countries, even as he expanded a profitable trade between Japan, the Ottoman Empire, and the neighboring regions from Russia to the Balkans to the Middle East. Yamada worked as an intermediary who frequently passed messages back and forth between Tokyo and Istanbul, and arranged visits by numerous distinguished figures from Japan.[6]

---

5    Naitō Chishū, *Nitto kōshō shi* (Tokyo: Izumi shōin, 1931), 1–2; Shingo Minamizuka, "A Non-European Analysis of the Balkan Situation," in Maria Couroucli and Dionigi Albera, eds., *The Balkan Ethnic and Cultural Crossroads: Educational and Cultural Aspects* (Strasbourg: Council of Europe Press, 1997), 79–80; Riko Shiba, "Images of the Balkans in the Japanese Media of the Meiji Period," *Annual for Social History* 3 (2011), 7–16.

6    Selçuk Esenbel, project manager, *The Crescent and the Sun Three Japanese in Istanbul: Yamada Torajirō, Itō Chūta, Ōtani Kōzui* (Istanbul: Istanbul Research Institute, 2010); Selçuk Esenbel

Nevertheless, the two countries failed to reach an agreement on a treaty of commerce and diplomatic relations, largely because of a dispute over the question of extraterritoriality. In its drive for equality with the imperialist nations, and encouraged by its partnership with Britain, Japan sought the same rights and privileges that the Great Powers held under the terms of the capitulatory treaties they had signed with the Ottoman government, beginning with the British in 1838.[7] However, the Ottoman government was reluctant to sign a similar agreement with a new state, and Japan could not muster the military strength to force the issue.

The Ottoman authorities politely refused the Japanese demands, which surfaced with increasing frequency during the terms of foreign ministers Aoki Shūzō and Mutsu Munemitsu (1844–1897). The Turkish leaders were concerned by the Japanese requests because the nineteenth-century European practice of the "unequal treaties" had primarily facilitated the political and economic expansionism of the major Western powers at the expense of other parties under the cover of diplomatic and trade relations. The Ottoman government felt that extending such privileges to Japan would seriously compromise its hard-earned recognition as a member of the European Concert in the 1856 Treaty of Paris, following the Crimean War victory against Russia. This small triumph had been achieved because the Ottoman Empire had joined Great Britain as an ally against Russia. According to the Treaty, the Ottoman government gained the right to *gradually abolish* extraterritoriality and other privileges of the existing capitulatory treaties, and, perhaps more importantly, the Ottomans also received recognition of their right to sign treaties of reciprocity and equality with new countries, which fit the case of Japan.[8] Due to this prolonged dispute over extraterritoriality, when the Ottomans and the Japanese entered the Great War in 1914 in opposite camps, they had not yet established formal relations.

However, one event occurred that would have a long-term impact on Turkish-Japanese relations. During the autocratic reign of Sultan Abdulhamid (1876–1908), Prince Komatsu, the uncle of the Meiji Emperor, paid a visit to the Ottoman court in 1886, which the Sultan reciprocated three years later by

---

and Inaba Chiharu, *The Rising Sun and the Turkish Crescent: New Perspectives on the History of Japanese-Turkish Relations* (Istanbul: Bogazici University Press, 2003), 7–41; Selçuk Esenbel, *Japan, Turkey, and the World of Islam: The Writings of Selçuk Esenbel* (Folkestone: Brill Global Oriental, 2011), 108–129, 130–147.

7   Resat Kasaba, "Treaties and Friendships: British Imperialism, The Ottoman Empire, and China in the Nineteenth Century," *Journal of World History*, IV:2 (Fall 1993), 215–241.

8   Selçuk Esenbel, "A Fin de Siecle Japanese Romantic in Istanbul: Yamada Torajirō and the Nakamura Shoten, Japon Magazasi of Pera," in *The Crescent and the Sun*, 13–68.

sending the naval frigate *Ertuğrul* on a goodwill mission. After an arduous journey, the vessel's commander, Osman Pasha, and his crew completed their mission in the summer of 1890. While en route back to Turkey, the voyage ended in tragedy when it encountered a typhoon and foundered on the rocks off the southeast coast of Japan, near Kushimoto in Wakayama prefecture. Most of the 633 crew members and the commanding officer died in the incident, but the Japanese government returned the 69 survivors to Turkey on its own naval frigates in 1891, an act that was well-remembered on both sides and promoted more regular contacts in subsequent years.[9]

By the outbreak of the Great War in 1914, the Japanese authorities already had a well-established network of informants in Ottoman Istanbul and other sites in the region, under the oversight of the Japanese legation in Vienna, to monitor regional developments with an emphasis on the activities of the Great Powers, particularly Imperial Russia. In particular, Minister Makino Nobuaki in Vienna, who was in charge of intelligence activities regarding Russian activities in the Balkans, conducted operations through contacts in Sophia, Odessa, and Istanbul, where he engaged Yamada Torajirō. Japanese Naval intelligence also stationed an officer in disguise in Port Said to monitor the comings and goings of vessels through the Suez Canal. Colonel Fukushima Yasumasa (1852–1919) of the Intelligence Bureau of the General Staff of the Japanese Army visited Istanbul a number of times in 1896 to gather information that would help to establish the Japanese military's trans-Asian intelligence network. He is thought to have incorporated Istanbul into that network when it was activated on the eve of the Russo-Japanese War.[10] During the Russo-Japanese War (1904–1905) there was a marked surge in Japanese intelligence activities in the region as the Japanese authorities made effective use of Yamada and his partner, Nakamura Kenjirō, in Istanbul to follow the movements of the Russian Black Sea Volunteer Fleet.[11]

Both the Ministry of Foreign Affairs and the Japanese Army General Staff designated Istanbul as an important site for gathering information on Russia and a key to Japan's emerging global strategy. General Utsunomiya Tarō,

9    Esenbel, *Japan, Turkey,* 108–129, 130–147.
10   Inaba Chiharu, "The Question of the Bosporus and Dardanelles during the Russo-Japanese War," in Esenbel and Inaba, eds., *The Rising Sun,* 122–145; Esenbel, "A Fin de Siecle," in *The Crescent and the Sun,* 41. 261; for Colonel Fukushima Yasumasa's postcards to Yamada, see the Yamada Family Archives.
11   Esenbel, "A Fin de Siecle," in *The Crescent and the Sun,* 45–46; for telegram and postal invoices from Yamada to Makino and other Japanese in the Vienna Legation, and Yamada's hand-written list, see the Yamada Family Archives.

who was the head of the Second Bureau for Intelligence in the Imperial Army General Staff, began to dispatch military attachés in 1907 who always came from the Russia Bureau of the General Staff. Since the two governments had no formal relations, the presence of these Japanese military officials must have been due to an informal arrangement that embodied the practice of "twilight diplomacy."[12] For the Japanese side, at least, informal diplomacy was the accepted mode of Japanese-Turkish relations. According to Utsunomiya's notes for 21 January 1909, the Japanese Army paid the unofficial military attachés in Istanbul (Japanese officials followed European practice in using the old name of Constantinople) the same amount that other governments paid their formal representatives. He also acknowledged that the Army funded the local intelligence network as a matter of course.[13] Utsunomiya, who would later be known for his embrace of Asianism, advocated for the military advantages of forging close ties with Turkey, based on the principle of "befriending a distant state while attacking a neighbor." He urged the Ministry of Foreign Affairs to be the first to abolish extraterritoriality in Turkey, in return for favorable opportunities for Japanese immigration and possible attractive concessions. He even argued in favor of a military alliance. Utsunomiya's vision was not immediately applicable to the situation at hand, but it showed that the Japanese understanding of the Ottoman world was shifting from the Westernist treaty-oriented stance of the Ministry of Foreign Affairs to the geo-political strategic perspective of the Japanese Army.[14]

To solidify relations with Turkey, Utsunomiya and others forged connections with pan-Islamist activists like Abdürreşid Ibrahim (1853–1944), the religious leader and political revolutionary of Romanov Russia's Muslim intelligentsia.

12 Merthan A. Dündar and Nobuo Misawa, "A Case Study of Human Relations at Nakamura Store in Istanbul: Torajirō Yamada's Letters to Sōhō Tokutomi," *The Bulletin of Faculty of Sociology*, Tokyo University 46:2 (March 2009): 181–220.

13 Utsunomiya Tarō, *Nihon rikugun to Ajia seisaku rikugun taishō: Utsunomiya Tarō nikki* (Tokyo: Iwanami shoten, 2007), 3 volumes, Vol. 1, 213, 258.

14 Hatano Masaru, "Eruto-rurugo jiken wo meguru Nitto kankei," in Ikei Masaru and Sakamoto Tsutomu, *Kindai Nihon to Toruko sekai* (Tokyo: Keisōshobō, 1999), 62. In the quote above, General Utsunomiya is referring to one of the 36 Stratagems included in the Book of Qi from the Qi dynasty (479–502), believed to be part of the military teaching of Sunzi (Sun Tzu, 544–496 BC), from the Spring and Autumn Period of ancient China. Recent scholarship suggests that the above work that was attributed to Sunzi was probably a collection of older oral and written teachings. Utsunomiya's reference indicates that Sunzi's teachings have remained popular in East Asia. Here, Utsunomiya is arguing the popular Japanese Army Staff view that the friendship of Ottoman Turkey, a country far away from Japan, could be used to attack Japan's near enemy, Russia.

A long-lasting friend of Japanese pan-Asianists, Ibrahim visited Japan in 1908–1909 and began spreading the message that Japan supported Muslim emancipation in Asia. While in Japan, Ibrahim and other political émigré Muslims communicated with Japanese Army officers, including members of the pan-Asianist Kokuryūkai, popularly known as the Black Dragons, who were actively participating in revolution and rebellion in China and Korea. This "Islam circle" of Japanese officers and foreign Muslims formed the *Ajia gikai* (Asian Reawakening) society that functioned as Japan's global public relations organization in the Islamic world.[15] Moreover, as Utsunomiya's diary revealed, the Japanese government used this transnational pan-Asianist and pan-Islamist network to enhance its intelligence operations and overseas activities. Utsunomiya's bureau financially supported the revolutionary activities of Sun Yat-sen in China, and funded Ibrahim's activities in Japan and his return voyage to Istanbul between 1909–1910. During his year-long journey, Ibrahim visited Muslim communities in China, South East Asia, and India. Most significantly he introduced Yamaoka Kotarō, a young Kokuryūkai member and Russian language agent whom Ibrahim had converted to Islam and named *Omar*, to Arab notables in Mecca and Medina. Utsunomiya also supported other Muslim political activists who sought political exile in Japan. The Japanese military's turn toward the Turks and Muslims as new targets for pro-Japanese networking was the spark for future Japanese outreach among Muslims in Asia as part of a geo-political strategy that surfaced in the 1930s in the context of Asianist internationalism.[16]

### Japan's Participation in the Great War

As war approached in Europe, Enver Pasha and the other recently ascendant "Young Turks" had to choose sides. Although the Ottoman Empire had joined Great Britain to fight Russia in the Crimean War, the two governments had become estranged since the latter had occupied Egypt in 1881. More recently, Russia, Britain, and France had proposed to settle the "Eastern Question" by dismembering the Ottoman Empire. When the Great War erupted in August 1914, the Young Turk leaders quickly joined on the side of the Central Powers. On 28 October Enver Pasha, then Minister of War, ordered the German battle

---

15    Selçuk Esenbel, "Japan's Global Claim to Asia and the World of Islam: Transnational Nationalism and World Power, 1900–1945," *The American Historical Review,* 109:4 (October 2004): 1140–1170. Recent version in *Japan, Turkey, and the World of Islam* (2011), 1–27.

16    Utsunomiya Tarō, *Nihon rikugun,* 243, 258, 273.

ships *Goeben* and *Breslau* to sail up the Dardanelles Straits to Istanbul, where he incorporated them into the Ottoman Navy; renamed *Yavuz* and *Midilli*, they proceeded to destroy the Russian Black Sea ports.[17] While the Ottoman military forces, with close to 3 million members, fought in major campaigns of the Near East theater, Turkey perhaps played a more important role by using pan-Islamist propaganda to incite Muslims in the British colonial territories in India, Malaya, Singapore, and outlying regions of Afghanistan.

Japan entered the conflict on the opposite side. On 14 August 1914 it issued an ultimatum to Germany to remove its vessels from Japanese waters and cede territories in China to Japan, which preceded Japan's declaration of war on 23 August. Soon thereafter, British Foreign Minister Edward Grey indicated to the Japanese Ambassador in London that Britain would like Japan to send navy cruisers to challenge the *Goeben* and *Breslau*. The Japanese side initially refused this request on the grounds that it was not capable of such an overseas operation. Yet, the new cabinet of Prime Minister Ōkuma Shigenobu and Foreign Minister Katō Komei decided that it would be opportune for Japan to enter the war "step by step" on the side of Britain in order to gain advantages in the post-war era.[18] However, although Russia, Britain, and France all declared war against Ottoman Turkey between 2 and 5 November, Japan never followed suit. Although Japan and Turkey were in opposite camps, they were merely "informal enemies" as neither declared war against each other and they engaged in no direct confrontation, much as they had previously practiced twilight diplomacy in place of formal relations.[19]

A Turkish journalist and writer from Istanbul, Samizade Süreyya bey, highlighted the absence of Japanese animosity towards Turkey. He visited Japan in 1914 and was there when it entered the war. He reported in an article for the popular Turkish paper *Sabah* that Japan's entrance to the Great War on the side of Britain was due to the influence of the pro-British Foreign Minister Baron Katō on the government, and the unwarranted popularity of the "pompous" Prime Minister Ōkuma Shigenobu. Although he was very critical of what he saw as the expansionist tendencies of the Japanese government, Süreyya found many in Japan who shared his views. He appears to have become acquainted

---

17      Norman Stone, *World War One: A Short History* (London: Allen Lane, 2007); Mustafa Aksakal, *The Ottoman Road to War in 1914: The Ottoman Empire and the First World War* (Cambridge: Cambridge University Press, 2008); Stanford J. Shaw, *The Ottoman Empire in World War I, Volume 2: Triumph and Tragedy, November 1914-July 1916* (Ankara: Turkish Historical Society, 2008).

18      Hirama, *Dai ichiji sekai taisen to Nihon* (Tokyo: Keio gijuku daigaku shuppankai, 1998), 212.

19      Ibid., 211–222.

with a wide circle of anti-war Japanese who were also very critical of the Anglo-Japanese Alliance, perhaps even the same Asianists and members of the Kokuryūkai who had surrounded Ibrahim and other Muslim visitors. His book on Japan, published in 1917 in Istanbul, provided a brief introduction to the history and culture of Japanese society, which was much admired among Turkish people.[20] The book contained a group photograph that depicted the increasingly close ties between Japan and Turkey. It showed four men seated in Japanese formal style wearing male kimono, or *hakama*: Hasan Fehmi bey, the director of education, in Edirne; Yovan effendi, an Armenian merchant; the author Süreyya bey; and the enigmatic figure of Ōkubo Kōji, who was Japan's first Turkologist. Ōkubo later became a specialist in Turkish studies, took charge of Tartar refugee émigrés from Central Asia, and promoted Japan in the Turkish world. During the Second World War, he headed the Kaikyōken-kenkyūjō (Institute of Islamic Area), which became an important Islamic studies center affiliated with Japan's Ministry of Foreign Affairs.

After January 1917, the Japanese side became more directly involved at the war front by providing naval support to the British forces against German submarines in the Mediterranean and the Indian Ocean. The new cabinet formed by Prime Minister General Terauchi adopted a pro-active foreign policy, and advocated sending a fleet to support the Allied naval operations in order to raise the status of the empire and gain access to advanced military technology.[21] When Indian Muslims rebelled against a British order to fight against the Ottoman sultan, a world leader of Muslims, Japan dispatched the *Akashi* cruiser and four destroyers to Singapore to assist the British forces in the Indian Ocean.[22] The Japanese Special Second Squadron fleet of 17 vessels was stationed in Malta under British command, from where it constantly transported Allied troops between Alexandria, Marseille, Taranto, Malta and Salonika, or rescued men from damaged ships. While the Japanese government firmly refused to send troops to the European front, after British insistence, the Army started a profitable trade in ample supplies of arms and ammunition to the British forces.[23]

From the 3 November 1918 Mondros armistice that ended hostilities in Ottoman territories, through the meetings and conferences that produced the Sèvres Treaty, Japanese forces and diplomats participated in the postwar

---

20    Samizade Süreyya (Erdogan), *Day Nippon Büyük Japonya* (Istanbul: Matbaa-I Osmaniye, 1917), 137–144.
21    Hirama, 214.
22    Ibid., 187–189.
23    Ibid., 216–218.

settlement. A small Japanese fleet sailed into Istanbul to join the Allied fleet, under British command, that occupied the imperial capital.[24] The Japanese delegates to the diplomatic talks included Prince Saionji Kinmochi (1849–1940), the Japanese Ambassadors to London and Paris, Viscount Chinda Sutemi (1857–1929) and Matsui Keishirō (1868–1946), and Foreign Minister Makino Nobuaki (1861–1949), who knew the Ottoman Empire well from his previous service in Vienna. On 10 August 1920 Ambassador Matsui signed the Sèvres Treaty that dismembered the Ottoman Empire, left the Sultan's government in Istanbul under Allied occupation, reinstated the capitulatory treaties, and placed the Anatolian heartland under the control of France, Italy, and Greece. The Treaty also betrayed the British promise for Arab independence with the declaration of Syria as a French mandate, and Iraq and Palestine as British mandates, under the authority of the League of Nations.[25] During the preparatory meetings of the Allies at London between 12 February-10 March 1920, Viscount Chinda had set the tone for Japan's non-involvement in European designs for the Near East. On 14 February, in a meeting on the dismemberment of the Ottoman Empire, Chinda commented that Japan, unlike the other Allies, had no direct relation to these matters and would not express an opinion.[26] Generally, the Japanese representatives followed the British agenda of protecting the minority Christian population of Istanbul, establishing a League of Nations representative in the capital, and confirming the Greek administration of the port of Izmir. The Japanese delegates also requested that Japan have its own post office in Istanbul, much as the Allies had.[27]

The Japanese representatives took a strong stand on two key issues in the Sèvres negotiations. The first was Japanese opposition to the Italian proposal to start trade with Bolshevik Russia. The Japanese government had taken a strong anti-Communist position when it embarked upon the Siberian Intervention of 1918, together with Britain, the United States, and Czechoslovakian forces. On 19 February 1920, the Japanese side expressed serious concern that opening trade relations would encourage the survival of the Bolshevik regime.[28] The second issue of particular concern for Japan was the future regulation of navigation and transport through the Dardanelles and the Bosphorus,

---

24    Matsutani, *Nihon-Toruko*, 1–2.

25    Osman Olcay, *Sèvres Andlasmasina Doğru*, (translation from *Documents on British Foreign Policy*, Vol. VII and Vol. VIII) (Ankara: S.B.F. Basin ve yayin Yüksek Okulu Basimevi, 1981), 44.

26    Ibid., 7.

27    Ibid., 275, 390.

28    Nish, 145–147; Olcay, 70.

between the Aegean and the Black Seas. Japan wanted to secure free access to the Black Sea for the sake of Japanese commercial interests in the Mediterranean. On 4 March 1920, Viscount Chinda broke out of his usual silence and proposed that Japan join the Straits Commission that was established to administer the Straits. France and Italy opposed the Japanese entry on the grounds that Japan did not have a frontier in the region, and Britain's delegate, Lord Curzon, argued that Japan, like the United States, never declared war against Turkey and did not fight on land though was much appreciated for her naval support.[29] Japan joined the Straits Commission in the end, however.

Once the treaty had been signed, the Turkish nationalists launched a war of independence in defiance of its terms. The former Ottoman General Mustafa Kemal Pasha, the future President of the Republic who later received the surname Atatürk, led the Turkish forces under authorization from the newly elected Grand Assembly. On 28 January 1920, before moving from Istanbul to Anatolia in April, the Grand Assembly had unanimously issued a National Pact (*Misak-I-Milli*) that outlined non-negotiable terms for peace. These terms included the abolition of the capitulations, the end to Allied occupation, and the reestablishment of Turkish sovereignty over what largely comprises the territory of Turkey today. The defiant National Pact incited the British authorities to dismantle what remained of the Ottoman government, prompting the Grand Assembly to launch military opposition to the Allied occupation.[30] The Ankara-based Turkish regime sought an ally in Bolshevik Russia, which had been at odds with Great Britain and France since its withdrawal from the Great War following the October Revolution of 1917. The two regimes shared an opposition to the European imperialist powers, and on 16 March 1921, the Ankara government signed its first diplomatic treaty with the Soviet Union. In addition to Indian Muslims who sent gold to help the resistance, the Russians started supplying ample amounts of arms and gold to the Turkish nationalist resistance that helped rejuvenate the war-weary Turkish nationalist forces.[31] The Turkish struggle for independence forced a reconsideration of the terms of the Sèvres Treaty.

### The Friendly "Enemy": A Pro-Ankara Japanese Diplomat

On the eve of the meetings that were convened in Paris and London to reformulate the Sèvres Treaty, Foreign Minister Uchida advised Ambassador Ishii

29    Olcay, 203.

30    Nur Bilge Criss, *Istanbul Under Allied Occupation, 1918–1923* (Leiden: Brill, 1999), 1-XI, 16–19.

31    Erik Zurcher, *Turkey: A Modern History* (London: I.B. Tauris, 2005), 151–158.

Kikujirō (1866–1945) in Paris to use discretion on matters that directly concerned Japan: free passage through the Straits, and the revision of the capitulatory treaty privileges. He cautioned Ishii to preserve Japan's status quo position, and argued that revision of the peace treaty remained primarily a European affair that did not bear direct relevance to Japanese national interest. Uchida instructed, "Our policy is that there should be no modification of the Treaty... but also avoid influence in internal matters concerning Greece."[32] However, as the tide of war turned, so, too, did the views of the Great Powers. In March 1921, both France and Italy signed agreements with Turkey to withdraw from the territories they occupied in exchange for some economic privileges.[33] The Italian Foreign Minister Count Sforza went so far as to offer diplomatic support to Ankara out of annoyance with British support for the Greek occupation of Smyrna.[34] The Ottoman government of Sultan Vahdettin, though still technically the legitimate authority to represent Turkey, was powerless.

The Japanese government decided to be more pro-active in the Near Eastern Question when it was clear the Sèvres Treaty would have to be revised now that Ankara's domestic prestige rivaled that of the Ottoman government in Istanbul. The British government, which greatly feared the spread of Bolshevism, was alarmed at Russian support to the Ankara forces. By 1921, Lord Curzon envisioned an anti-Communist strategy that would abolish the Ottoman government and turn Istanbul into an international city; in this radical new vision, the Sultan would remain as the religious head of Islam who would live in the Asia Minor part of the city. From now on the Straits Commission, now including Japan, would have a new charge to control the city and the environs.[35]

Curzon's proposal seemed to offer the opportunity that Japan needed to play a larger role. Having acquired the invitation of Britain in December 1920, Foreign Minister Uchida Yasuya (Kōsai) dispatched the diplomat Uchida Sadatsuchi (1865–1942) to serve as one of the High Commissioners on the Straits Commission. Uchida Sadatsuchi had graduated from Tokyo University and in 1889 joined the Ministry. He became Consul in Seoul in 1893, and in 1902 became Consul General in New York. Uchida worked with Ambassador Komura

---

32    No. 35. *"Se-buru jōyaku kaitei baishū mondai tairo ippan seisaku ni kan suru waga taido ni tsuki kunren no ken,"* 21 January 1921 Telegram 50. Ministry of Foreign Affairs Records on Exchange Between FM and Ambassador Uchida Sadatsuchi in Istanbul, Gaimushō hensan, *Nihon gaikōmonjō* (Tokyo: Gaimushō hakkō, 1975), Volume III Part I, 1921, 28.

33    Zurcher, 154.

34    Yılmaz Altuğ, "Turkish-Italian Diplomatic Relations (1918–1938)," *İstanbul Üniversitesi Siyasal Bilgiler Fakültesi Dergisi*, Number 3-4-5 (1993): 197–208.

35    Criss, 8.

in drawing up the Treaty of Portsmouth. He later served in Argentina, Brazil, and Turkey, where he became Ambassador in 1923. Uchida stayed in Istanbul for close to two years, during which time he formed an unusually close relationship with the Turkish nationalists. His activities invite attention because he went against the grain of Japan's policy of staying out of the conflict. He worked hard to ensure that Japan's participation in the occupation was on a par with that of the Western powers. At the same time, he did not simply follow the British line, but rather took an independent path by forging relations with the Turkish "radicals." In an indication of these close ties, his house in Yokohama still serves as the meeting venue for the Turkish-Japanese Friendship Society of Tokyo.[36]

Uchida arrived in Paris on 14 February 1921 to join the Supreme Allied Council that met to discuss the imminent Treaty revision, before moving to London for meetings with representatives from both Turkish governments, and from Greece. Uchida met with the Ottoman Prime Minister Tevfik Pasha, a supporter of the Ankara resistance, before holding lengthy discussions with Bekir Sami bey, who was the Foreign Minister of the Ankara government. In a report to Tokyo, Uchida noted the generational contrasts between the two Turks: he described Tevfik Pasha as about 70 years old with a gentle and sincere personality, and Bekir Sami bey as a vigorous man of 40 with muscular appearance and energetic speech.[37] It was clear from the tone of Uchida's discussions with both parties that Uchida had decided to take a friendly approach toward the Ankara nationalists. His subsequent frequent meetings in Istanbul with Turkish nationalists representing Ankara reflected the global sympathy that the Turkish nationalists were already receiving as freedom fighters against Western imperialism.[38]

Although the Japanese and Turks were on opposite sides, both Turkish representatives received Uchida with warm words on Japanese-Turkish friendship. This discourse had evolved in the late Ottoman period following the events of the Ertuğrul Frigate disaster in 1890 that inaugurated close relations between the two empires. When Uchida explained that he had been assigned to be the representative of the imperial Japanese government in Istanbul and wished to join the preparation of the future peace treaty, Tevfik Pasha responded by expressing gratitude for Japan's chivalrous act of returning the

---

36    *Nihon jinmei daijiten*, <http://kotobank.jp/hanrei/nihonjinmeijiten/01.html>, accessed
      3 December 2012.

37    No. 49. *Toruko shucchō ni kan shi hōkoku no ken*, Secret No. 1, from Minister Uchida in
      Turkey to Foreign Minister Uchida, Gaimusho hensan, *Nihon gaikōmonjō*, 35–37.

38    Ibid.

survivors from the Ertuğrul disaster. He also noted the difficulties over treaty relations even though the Turkish people sympathized with Japan and that the Turkish government had sincerely desired close friendship and a commercial and navigation treaty. Uchida adopted an apologetic tone, acknowledging that Japan had to make sure it was considered equal to other Western countries on the capitulations question, but emphasizing that Japan was happy to abolish the privileges, provided there was agreement among other countries.

Uchida engaged in more revealing conversations with his counterpart from Ankara. Bekir Sami responded to Uchida's appointment to Istanbul in very favorable terms despite the fact that technically Japan was an "enemy" of Ankara. He told Uchida that the Turkish general public felt extremely strong friendship toward Japan, therefore "you will be considered as the representative of a friendly country not an enemy." Uchida expressed his sympathy for Turkey's plight, as it had lost territory and sovereignty as a result of the war. However, he cautioned that, although military power might restore both for the moment, in the long run diplomacy would provide a more advantageous revision of the treaty. Bekir Sami replied that the Treaty of Sèvres was very harsh and that, if implemented, it would deprive Turkey of its independence, and perhaps even its survival.[39]

Shortly before Uchida arrived in Istanbul on 18 April 1921 to join the Allies officially, the Le Temps paper in Paris published a complimentary article on Uchida's appointment as a favorable event that showed that Japan will "support Turkey's independence." The article also noted that Japan hoped to use the Ottoman capital in order to observe Russia's plans for expansion to the South. This positive view of Uchida was indicative of the swift change of mood that was taking place in France, which became the first Allied country to abandon its claims under the Sèvres Treaty on 9 March 1921 when it signed the Cilicia Peace Treaty. France later withdrew from some occupied territories under the terms of the Franko-Turkish Agreement of 20 October.[40] The Le Temps article was reported on in the Turkish papers in Istanbul, which ensured a positive welcome for Uchida.

He spent the next weeks in an energetic schedule of meetings with the High Commissioners of the European powers; diplomats; religious leaders of the Jewish, Armenian, and Greek communities; and commanders of the French, Italian, and British occupation forces. He also visited the Yildiz

---

39    Ibid.

40    Ibid.; No. 41. *Uchida kōshi Kunfu funin ni kan shi tan shi kōiteki shasetsukei*, 13 April 1921, Telegram No. 553, from Ambassador Ishii in Paris to Uchida, Gaimushō hensan, *Nihon gaikōmonjō*, 32.

Palace to have an audience with Sultan Vahdettin, who praised the Turkish-Japanese friendship. After a brief stay in the famous Pera Palace Hotel, Uchida rented a furnished home on 26 Siraselviler Street as the office of the Japanese High Commissioner. Here, Uchida would receive numerous Turkish visitors, who gave him messages that he relayed to the British side. All in all, Uchida formally took care to act as a member of the victorious Allied countries throughout the talks, but noteworthy was the fact that he had already formed a trusting cordial relationship with Turks from both governments, who appeared to be optimistic that Japan might be able to help them in this quagmire of negotiations.[41]

It is clear from his subsequent telegrams from Istanbul that Uchida frequently played this role of intermediary between the British and the Turkish nationalists. For example, Uchida's 27 October 1921 report to Tokyo recounts his mediation between three key protagonists: Sir Horace Rumbold, the British Ambassador High Commissioner in occupied Istanbul, who was known to have advised Lord Curzon to recognize the Turkish point of view; the representative of the Ankara government and the Vice-President of the Turkish Red Crescent Relief Society, Hamid bey (1870–1943; he adopted the surname Hasancan in the Republic); and the Ottoman government's Foreign Minister Izzet Pasha.[42] Surprisingly, Uchida remained equally friendly with both Turkish governments throughout this episode, and showed that he had become a trusted ear for the nationalists in the informal exchanges between Ankara and London despite the formal position of the Japanese government not to get involved in the conflict among the Allies, Greece, and Turkey in the European theater.

By the early fall of 1921, three factors seem to have pushed the British to moderate their position. First was the quagmire in which the Greek occupation forces found themselves in Anatolia, while second was the swiftness with which the French abandoned both the terms of Sèvres and their occupation of Cilicia. Third, and most interestingly from a global standpoint, was the rise of pan-Islamist movements as embodied in the Khilafat Movement of Indian Muslims. Founded in 1919 to protect the Ottoman Caliphate, the Khilafat formed an alliance with Gandhi's Indian National Congress in 1921 to promote the struggle for Indian independence. When the Indians gave support to fellow Muslims in Turkey, the London authorities felt compelled to adopt

---

41    No. 49. *Toruko shucchō ni kan*, 38.
42    Paul G. Halpern, *The Mediterranean Fleet* (Surrey: Ashgate Publishing, 2011), 328; Mohamed M. El Zeidy, *The Principle of Complementarity in International Criminal Law: Origin, Development, and Practice* (Leiden: Martinus Nijhoff Publishers, 2008), 25–26.

a compromising attitude toward the Turkish nationalists.[43] The first step towards a negotiated settlement was an exchange of 24 British POWs held in Ankara for 51 Turkish prisoners held at Malta, which Rumbold and Hamid arranged through talks in September and October.

During the days leading up to the final Anglo-Turkish prisoner exchange on October 23, Uchida was actively involved in facilitating the prospective peace. In his October 27 telegram, he argued that, in view of the persistence of the Turkish national struggle and the rise of anti-British pan-Islamism, Britain *should change* its policy of suppressing Turkey, otherwise permanent peace in the Near East could not be achieved. He carried these ideas into his meetings with his Turkish and British interlocutors. In one meeting, Uchida asked Huseyin, as an "individual" (not as the official representative of Japan),

> if Turkey insists on the terms of the National Pact and if Britain does really modify the Sèvres Treaty, would Turkey exhort the anti-British movement of Indian Muslims and Muslims in other countries?[44]

Huseyin replied that he would have to ask Ankara. Uchida then met with Izzet Pasha and asked the same question. Interestingly, Izzet Pasha assured him that if Turkey's conditions were accepted it would exhort moderation to the anti-British movement of Muslims in India and other countries. When Huseyin visited Uchida together with Hamid bey on 13 October, Uchida relayed Izzet's response and asked whether they would concur on the question of the Muslim movement. On 14 October, he met this time with Rumbold who, upon Uchida's explanation of his exchanges with the Turks, expressed great interest in knowing Ankara's reply. Rumbold passed on the message that it would be difficult to return Eastern Thrace to Turkey under British and Allied occupation at the moment, but the Greek Army could be pressed to retreat from Asia-Minor and that Smyrna (Izmir) on the Aegean coast could be returned to Turkey. The comment reveals that the British were already ready to abandon the Greek cause in Anatolia.

On 19 October, Hamid came back with Ankara's reply, which suggested that Turkey and Britain should cooperate with respect to restraining the anti-British movement, and proposed that both sides should proceed with peace

---

43    M. Naeem Qureshi, *Pan Islam in British Indian Politics: A Study of the Khilafat Movement, 1918–1924* (Leiden: Brill, 1999), 104.

44    No. 51. *Toruko no kōwa ni kansuru taidō ni tsuki dashin no ken*, Telegram no. 100, from Minister Uchida in Turkey to Foreign Minister Uchida, Gaimushō hensan, *Nihon gaikōmonjō*, 39.

negotiations on the basis of an agreement over conditions. When Uchida passed on this information, Rumbold replied that he did not yet want to start negotiations concerning peace, but asked Uchida to relay his position that the anti-British movement had to be restrained in whatever manner possible. Uchida called on Hamid and passed on Rumbold's comments, upon which Hamid replied that Britain would have to first agree to the demands of the National Pact. However, he added that, although he could not negotiate peace on his own, he personally desired the restitution of friendship between Britain and Turkey. Although these exchanges did not immediately produce formal peace negotiations, they led Uchida to conclude that, if Britain could satisfy Turkey's basic requests, there was hope for friendship between the two countries in the future. He continued to meet with both Hamid bey and Rumbold, and ultimately felt that his mediating had met with some success when he learned that the Minister of Internal Affairs of the Ankara government had banned all anti-British propaganda in Anatolia.[45]

Uchida's exchanges between Ankara and the British continued through the rest of that year. On 29 November 1921, Uchida advised Hamid that the Turkish side should prepare concrete conditions for peace rather than insist on the vague terms of the National Pact. Hamid enthusiastically proposed that Uchida directly inquire as to the opinion of the Allied authorities on the peace conditions that Ankara would relay to him. However, because Uchida believed that Rumbold was unwilling to negotiate through his intercession, he felt at a crossroads and cabled Tokyo for further instructions. Uchida's thinking suggests that he advocated a more active role for Japan in the Near East, which would break from its practice of following the British line in this region. As he explained it, the Japanese imperial government did not consider the Near East as important for its interest as did the Allied countries, but rather preferred to remain an observer of Turkey's peace negotiations. However, Uchida urged that if Japan could play a role by directly receiving Turkey's conditions, and participating in the advancement of Near Eastern peace by mediating with the other parties, it would guarantee itself a secure position in the region in the future.[46]

Uchida continued to be close to the Ankara side, in particular Bekir Sami bey, who had resigned from the post of Foreign Minister but was frequently still sent to Europe for official negotiations with the Allies. On his return from

---

45    Ibid.
46    No. 52. *Toruko zoku no kōwa jōken ni kan shi Toruko yōjin to no kaidan ni tsuki hōkoku oyobi seikun no ken*, Telegram no. 105, from Minister Uchida in Turkey to Foreign Minister Uchida, Gaimushō hensan, *Nihon gaikōmonjō*, 41.

an official trip to France and Italy on 5 December, Bekir Sami dropped by Uchida's office and relayed the carefully prepared explanation of the Turkish position. He explained that Turkey had lost such a large portion of its territory in Mesopotamia, Syria, and Palestine that the Turkish people could not live as an independent nation. He noted that the conditions of the National Pact were the minimum of "our" demands, which meant that there "can be no peace negotiations until the retreat of the Greek Army from Asia Minor and East Thrace." Interestingly, this was a point that Rumbold had previously proposed through Uchida to Ankara.

Bekir Sami also commented on the Muslim protest problem:

> Ankara absolutely does not harbor intentions of intrigue among Muslims or any irredentist designs, but Muslims in foreign countries sympathize with the Turkish national movement, which means, even if one tries to suppress them this will not eliminate their sense of opposition. Britain, which in the past plotted to instigate Greece to invade in order to gain domination, has in turn caused unrest among the Muslims of India and further has invited the animosity of nations in Afghanistan and Persia. If Britain intends to compromise with Turkey, we the Ankara government would be pleased to respond but would want Britain as a victor to extend a hand for a handshake as it would not cause any loss of face to them but as a defeated nation we cannot make the first move.

Two aspects of this meeting were particularly noteworthy. First, noting the sympathetic attitude of France and Italy toward the Turkish nationalist government, Bekir Sami argued that peace in the Near East totally depended on Britain's actions. Second, Bekir Sami referred to Japan as the friend of Islam, an image that circulated globally among Muslims from the days of the 1904–1905 Russo-Japanese War, and insisted that if Japan advanced the peace process, the Turkish people and Muslim peoples of the Far East would be grateful to it.[47]

However, the Japanese government preferred to keep its non-committal position and did not take up the Turkish offer to be the mediator with Greece or the Allies. On 16 December, Foreign Minister Uchida wrote back to Uchida in Istanbul, explaining that there are "delicate matters" between Britain, France, and Italy, which meant that Britain and France would not easily agree

---

47    No. 53. *Toruko no kōwa ni tai suru taido ni tsuki zen gaisō no danwa yōryō hōkoku no ken*, Telegram no. 107, from Minister Uchida in Turkey to Foreign Minister Uchida, Gaimushō hensan, *Nihon gaikōmonjō*, 42.

in the event that the Turkish side announced its conditions for peace. Hence, it was not advisable for Japan to undertake the difficult role of mediation between Turkey and Greece. Even if the Turkish side informally revealed its conditions for peace to Uchida, the Foreign Minister advised him to postpone requesting the conditions of the other sides: in sum, not to mediate between the two.[48]

A second telegram from Foreign Minister Uchida showed that the British authorities were disturbed by Uchida's initiatives in Istanbul. On 28 December, upon receiving instructions from London, the counselor of the British Embassy in Tokyo had visited the Ministry to explain that the British felt troubled by Uchida's close contacts with the Ankara side. Foreign Minister Uchida related that the British counselor read aloud the opinion that,

> the Japanese government should instruct him [Uchida in Istanbul] to pay attention to this matter. I replied that as the Minister I have been informed that your Excellency has had two or three conversations with the unofficial representative of the Ankara government and that it absolutely arose from well-intentioned motives based on the normal judgment of your Excellency. Furthermore I surmised that it was probably nothing other than trying to obtain information about that side. It is because of this situation that you were instructed about a week ago not to go over board too much.

The exchange explicitly showed that the Japanese side carefully heeded the British perspective on the matter, even though the diplomat Uchida's attitude in Istanbul indicated that, like France and Italy, Japan should befriend the Turkish nationalists who had effectively won the military conflict and appeared to be the new political power in the region.[49]

Responding to Minister Uchida's similar query on the matter, Ambassador Ishii in Paris, who had consulted with the French authorities, reiterated the same non-committal policy by advising that Japan should participate in the pending revision of the Sèvres Treaty but must not get involved in the arbitration between Greece and Turkey. Ishii insisted that was a matter that should be

48   No. 56. *Gito kan chōtei mondai ni tai shi fukainyū no taido iji ho kunrei no ken*, Telegram
      No. 37, from Foreign Minister Uchida to Minister Uchida in Turkey, Gaimushō hensan,
      *Nihon gaikōmonjō*, 44.

49   No. 58. *Angora soku to no sesshoku ni tsuki Eikokusoku no ginen wo manekazaru yō rui hō
      shiji no ken*, Telegram No. 39, from Foreign Minister Uchida to Minister Uchida in Turkey,
      Gaimushō hensan, *Nihon gaikōmonjō*, 45.

left to the European Allies. He emphasized that Japan should be an "onlooker" (*bōkan suru*) in this geo-political matter of the Near East and the Balkans, which was the concern of the Europeans.[50]

Although Tokyo urged the maintenance of the status quo in world affairs, Uchida's actions showed that there was an informal undercurrent in Japanese diplomatic activities that acknowledged a new reality. His relations with the Ankara government reflected the fact that the Turkish movement had become the global symbol of national liberation against the established order of European imperialism for many in Asia. Uchida's activities in Istanbul had countered the official stance of the Japanese government to remain quiet so as to be accepted as honorary westerners. Perhaps because his efforts to build ties to the Turkish nationalists had gone against the grain of Japanese policy, Uchida remained in Istanbul during 1922 when the Peace Treaty Council reconvened in Paris.

On 24 July 1923, Ambassador Hayashi Gonsuke in Britain and Ambassador Ochiai Kentarō in Italy represented Japan at the signing of the Lausanne Treaty that annulled the Sèvres Treaty and accepted most of the terms of the Turkish nationalists. The new treaty abolished the capitulations and delineated Turkey's borders mostly as outlined in the National Pact. Under the terms of Lausanne, the Republic of Turkey was proclaimed on 29 October 1923. On 6 August 1924, no longer impeded by the obstacle of the capitulations, Japan officially recognized Turkey. As for Uchida, in recognition of his great efforts in forming good relations with the nationalists, on 31 January 1923, he became the first Japanese Ambassador in Istanbul. On 15 June 1923 he returned to Japan, leaving First Secretary Kasama in charge.[51]

## Conclusion

In 1981 the Turkish diplomat Osman Olcay, who translated the records of the Sèvres preparatory meetings into Turkish, offered a somewhat cynical view of the Japanese Delegation at the Sèvres Preparatory Meetings, arguing that they kept a low profile in order to be accepted as honorary Westerners. However, the informal relations that transpired from 1920 to 1922 suggest that the truth was

50    No. 59. *Gito kan no chōtei mondai ni kan shiteba waga hō wa bōkan shi karu mune hinshin no ken*, Telegram no. 1787, from Ambassador Ishii in France to Foreign Minister Uchida, Gaimushō hensan, *Nihon gaikōmonjō*, 46.

51    Tadahisa Takahashi, "Türk-Japon Münasebetlerine Kisa bir Bakis (1871–1945)," *Türk Dünyasi Araştirmalari* 18 (June 1982): 124–148.

otherwise.[52] The Japanese authorities outwardly maintained the formal posture and publicly declared a non-involvement stance in the post-war reconfiguration of the Near East. But Uchida and his Turkish interlocutors interacted in a form of "twilight diplomacy" following the precedent of Japanese-Turkish relations that had evolved in the late 19th century. The Japanese interest in joining the Straits Commission was in line with the Britain-oriented policy of the Ministry of Foreign Affairs, but the Commission became a venue for forming close contacts with the Turkish nationalists.

Uchida's efforts to form good relations with Ankara and Istanbul displayed a range of Japanese motivations. They showed that the Japanese authorities carefully followed what transpired between the Turkish nationalists and the European powers in order to strengthen Japan's status of equality with the European powers. Moreover, as Bolshevik Russia formed an alliance with Ankara, Japanese leaders sought a stable foothold in the region to keep close watch on Russian activities. The Japanese records also give a clear sense that Japanese like Uchida hoped that Britain would restore order in the region by reaching an accommodation with the new political realities in Turkey. These considerations must have been behind the unassuming but autonomous overtures of Uchida in Istanbul, through which he became a friend of the radicals in Ankara who had defied the Sèvres Treaty as the enemy of Britain.

From the perspective of Japanese history, the above survey shows that the Anglo-Japanese Alliance prevailed through the 1910s and early 1920s as the primary framework of Japanese diplomacy in the Near East. But, developments such as Utsunomiya Tarō's Asianist rhetoric for a Turkish-Islamic line, and Uchida Sadatsuchi's interest in Turkish nationalists, surfaced as the elements of a new Japanese effort to play an independent global role, marking a major shift away from following the nineteenth-century Western imperialist order. The episodes recounted in this essay reinforce Frederick R. Dickinson's assessment in his work on Japan in the Great War, that pan-Asianist views held sway among the power elite in imperial Japan before the outbreak of the China war in 1937 and the establishment of the Great East Asia Co-Prosperity Sphere.[53] In Istanbul, Uchida took an independent path from the British line that no longer appeared convincing in order to answer the reality of the anti-colonial and nationalist movements. His actions, which foreshadowed Japan's new ways of interacting with the West, came out of the global shifts resulting from the war that opened the gate to nationalist movements for independence. Uchida

---

52    Olcay, Foreword, XLIII.
53    Frederick R. Dickinson, *War and National Reinvention: Japan in the Great War, 1914–1919* (Cambridge, MA: Harvard University Asia Center, 1999).

acted as a pragmatic diplomat who remained well within the frame of prudent diplomacy, while he realized the significance of the Ankara radicals as nationalists earlier than his British colleagues did. This realization surely aided the swift finalization of treaty relations between the two countries that ended decades of a lingering diplomatic problem. In a different vein, the new Japanese Asianist language of the post-war era was to privilege the Turkish nationalist struggle in a historical narrative of Asian awakening that would play itself out in future Japanese actions toward the Turkish and Muslim world, as Japan forcefully chiseled out an empire for itself in Asia.

# SECTION 2

## *National and Transnational Networks*

∵

# Women on the Move
## Shifting Patterns in Migration and the Colonization of Taiwan

*Evan Dawley*

### Japanese Women and Imperialism

As women began to constitute a larger percentage of the Japanese settler population in Taiwan, they made distinctive contributions to the colonization of the island. According to an organizational history published in 1941, the founders of the Taiwan Branch of Japan's *Aikoku fujinkai* (Patriotic Ladies' Association; hereafter, AFK) established the group during the early 1900s to achieve the edification of the people of Taiwan, and to support and promote Japanese forces in their campaigns against Taiwan's aborigines.[1] These two goals expressed distillations of the soft and hard sides of Japanese imperialism – cultural transformation and military conquest – that were specific to the context of Taiwan. Moreover, although the goals reflected a Kōminka-era perspective with the prioritization of enlightenment over pacification, they captured the fundamental connection between the Taiwan AFK and the growth of the Japanese Empire. For Taiwan, the decade of the 1910s marked a transitional period for the colony, as social reform and civilian rule gradually replaced military governance and the pacification of aborigine areas. Acting through organizations like the AFK, women settlers exemplified and at times led this shift in Japanese colonial policies, even as they sometimes challenged the restrictions placed upon them by Japan's imperial ideology.

The changes that took place in Taiwan were linked to broader regional and global trends that had their roots in the late 19th century and left an influence on the following decade. Within East Asia, Japan had solidified its position as a

---

\*   I would like to thank Paul Barclay and Ti Ngo for their comments on a previous version of this essay, and the Institute of East Asian Studies at the University of California-Berkeley for giving me the opportunity to present and receive feedback at an early stage of this research. I would also like to thank Eric Luhrs at the East Asia Image Collection at Lafayette College for his assistance in obtaining the images used in this chapter.

1   Kō Ikujo and Ōhashi Suetsaburō, *Aikoku fujinkai Taiwan honbu enkakushi* (Tokyo: Yumani shobō, 2007), vol. 1, 1. This is a reprint of the 1941 original. "Patriotic Women's Association" is also a fair translation, but given the social standing and values of its leaders and members, "ladies" captures the spirit of the word *"fujin"* more accurately.

regional leader through domestic reforms, military victories, and colonial acquisitions. Globally, European dominance, which had seemed unchallengeable in the heyday of imperialism during the 1880s and 1890s, suffered mortal blows from the brutality of the Great War and the anti-imperialist tendencies of both Wilsonianism and Leninism. The globalization of ideas meant that Japan was fully engaged in the modification of colonial discourse that took form in Versailles. Faced with anti-colonial resistance in Korea and anti-Japanese sentiment in China, at the end of the decade the Government-General in Taiwan launched new assimilationist policies. To be sure, the prime mechanisms of control – the military and civilian police forces, and the judicial system – did not disappear, but the colonial project in Taiwan underwent a transformation that reflected both broader trends and local concerns.

The study of Japanese-era Taiwan has seen impressive, but uneven, growth during the past two decades. The range and depth of inquiry have increased thanks in part to the greater availability of a wealth of archival and published sources. The result of this expansion of scholarship has been a much deeper understanding of the workings of the colonial state, the structural foundations of Taiwan's post-1949 economic miracle, and the colonial-era origins of Taiwanese nationalism. However, very little has been written about the lives and experiences of Japanese settlers, or their contributions to the topics that have been receiving greater examination. Several recently published essays do address these subjects through their studies of individual authors, artists, and anthropologists, but these essays have not looked at Japanese women.[2] Perhaps the only major study of Japanese women settlers in Taiwan is a three-volume work by Takenaka Nobuko, one volume for each of the Meiji, Taishō, and Shōwa eras.[3] Takenaka has assembled an impressive body of research that serves primarily as an invaluable resource for other scholars. In short, the subject remains essentially untouched. This essay is a preliminary attempt to fill this gap, and to connect female settlers in Taiwan to the history of Japan's global relations in the 1910s.

---

2  See the contributions by Yen Chuan-ying on Japanese landscape painters, and Faye Yuan Kleeman on the author and ethnologist Nishikawa Mitsuru, in Liao Ping-hui and David Derwei Wang, eds., *Taiwan Under Japanese Colonial Rule, 1895–1945: History, Culture, Memory* (New York: Columbia University Press, 2006). For Japanese anthropologists, see Paul Barclay, "An Historian Among the Anthropologists: The Inō Kanori Revival and the Legacy of Japanese Colonial Ethnography in Taiwan," *Japanese Studies* 21:2 (September 2001): 117–136; and "'Gaining Trust and Friendship' in Aborigine Country: Diplomacy, Drinking, and Debauchery on Japan's Southern Frontier," *Social Science Japan Journal* 6:1 (April 2003): 77–96.
3  Takenaka Nobuko, *Shokuminchi Taiwan no Nihon josei seikatsu shi* (Tokyo: Tabata shoten, 2001).

## Early Colonial Taiwan and Japanese Women Settlers

Japan's rule of Taiwan got off to a rocky start. Although China's Qing Dynasty relinquished control of the island in 1895, a number of the island's residents objected to being transferred from one empire to another. Some officials and literati established a short-lived Republic of Taiwan in an effort to gain international support for their bid to avoid falling under Japanese rule, and a coalition of militia and gentry groups launched an armed resistance that continued sporadically for seven years. Aborigines in Taiwan's mountainous areas remained in conflict with Japanese forces for much longer than that. Japanese soldiers and settlers, particularly during the early years, faced a number of other difficulties, some of them potentially fatal: lack of clean drinking water, a climate to which they were unaccustomed, and a range of diseases including malaria, cholera, and plague. Finally, Japanese administrators needed to figure out how to rule their first colony, incorporate new populations, and make the whole enterprise profitable.

Early colonial officials employed military, administrative, and policing methods to establish and maintain control over the island. Following the successful suppression of the initial island-wide resistance, the military Governors-General launched additional campaigns as necessary, and established permanent garrisons around the island, particularly near areas inhabited predominantly by aborigines.[4] In 1909, colonial authorities embarked on a major aborigine suppression (*seiban tōbatsu*) campaign that targeted tribes in the mountainous regions of northern and eastern Taiwan. After the completion of this effort in 1914, and the suppression of a substantial uprising in 1915,[5] Taiwan saw no significant military engagements until the 1930s. From 1896 onward, under the terms of Law 63, the Taiwan Governors-General had the authority to issue edicts and institute the measures they saw as necessary for pacification and rule. The Government-General set up extensive networks of military and civil police to keep close watch on local society. It also placed some of the responsibility for policing Taiwan onto the indigenous population by effectively adapting an old Chinese security system,

---

4   The Japanese regime restored the Qing Era aborigine boundary line that had demarcated the division between Chinese and mountain aborigine societies. See Lung-chih Chang, "From Island Frontier to Imperial Colony: Qing and Japanese Sovereignty Debates and Territorial Projects in Taiwan, 1874–1906" (Harvard University, 2003).

5   This was the Tapani or Jiaobanian Incident, thoroughly explored by Paul R. Katz, *When Valleys Turned Blood Red: The Ta-pa-ni Incident in Colonial Taiwan* (Honolulu: University of Hawai'i Press, 2005).

the *hokō* (Ch., *baojia*), which put local leaders in charge of securing their communities.[6]

The Government-General also cultivated cooperation from the indigenous residents by protecting some aspects of their culture, promoting some indigenous involvement in Taiwan's economic development, and importing some modern technologies. For the most part the colonial government did not suppress the observance of local religious traditions, at least not until the 1930s, although many Japanese officials and settlers looked down on these things as superstitious and inferior to their own.[7] This forbearance indicated a tendency to move slowly on efforts to assimilate the non-Japanese population; although this tendency derived from Japanese self-interest, it was generally, though not entirely, appreciated by the indigenous residents. On the economic front, while Japanese individuals and businesses, including several of the most powerful *zaibatsu*, derived the largest share of the profits from the colony's main enterprises (agriculture, fishing, and mining), many Taiwanese landowners, businessmen, and traders accumulated significant wealth as the economy expanded.[8] Finally, Governor-General Kodama Gentarō and his Civil Administrator Gotō Shimpei launched significant improvements in public health and medicine, port construction, plumbing and water treatment, intra-island transportation, and public education. For these and other reasons, the vast majority of indigenous residents chose to work within the system rather than overtly oppose it. Thus, during the 1910s, Taiwan was a relatively stable colony, and it produced enough revenue to ensure that it was not a burden on the imperial treasury.

It was also a colony that experienced an overall rise in the settler population, particularly in the numbers of Japanese women from 1905 onward. In 1910, the Japanese population of Taiwan was 98,048, but by 1920 that number had expanded to 166,621, a 70 per cent increase. The increase of female settlers was even more dramatic, rising from 39,468 to 72,819, bringing the ratio of males to females from 1.5:1 down to 1.3:1. Roughly two thirds of this growth occurred during the first half of the decade. One result of this demographic shift was that settler society in Taiwan took on a decidedly more domestic cast. The number of Japanese marriages – those in which the husband was Japanese,

---

6 The effective implementation of the *hokō* system by the Japanese colonial government is explored in Hui-yu Caroline Tsai, *Taiwan in Japan's Empire-Building: An Institutional Approach to Colonial Engineering* (New York: Routledge, 2009).

7 Cai Jintang, *Nihon teikokushugika Taiwan no shūkyō seisaku* (Tokyo: Dōseisha, 1994).

8 Man-houng Lin, "Taiwanese Merchants, Overseas Chinese Merchants, and the Japanese Government in the Economic Relations Between Taiwan and Japan, 1895–1945," *Journal of Asia-Pacific Studies* 4 (2001): 3–20.

the vast majority of which were to women from the home islands – more than doubled from 344 in 1910 to 718 in 1920. More to the point, while roughly a third of Japanese settlers were married in 1905, over 40 per cent were married in 1920; for women, the marriage rate increased from about 30 per cent to almost half.[9] As Hong Yuru suggests, most women came to Taiwan as wives accompanying male officials, businessmen, and other elites.[10] Although a significant number of adult Japanese women settlers had received an education in Japan,[11] only about one quarter of Japanese females between the ages of 16 and 50 worked outside the home during the latter half of the 1910s.[12] The employment opportunities for Japanese women were limited by the absence of the textile industry that absorbed so much female labor in the home islands, and by the presence of a cheap indigenous labor force that took many of the jobs that Japanese women might have performed.[13]

Nevertheless, settler women entered the labor force in increasing numbers during the 1910s. Most Japanese families were well-off enough to afford nannies, usually teenaged Taiwanese girls, to take care of their children, thus freeing up the wives and mothers to work outside of the home. Japanese women found employment in a growing range of jobs including as waitresses, nurses, midwives, flower decoration teachers, tea servers, music teachers, telephone operators, hairdressers, schoolteachers, and office clerks. The medical professions of nursing and midwifery were the most highly paid, and most jobs either required professional training or were in modern workplaces.[14] Even with this broadening range of employment options, most Japanese women in Taiwan remained out of the workplace.

---

9    Taiwan sheng xingzheng changguan gongshu tongji shi, ed., *Taiwan sheng wushiyi nian lai tongji tiyao* (Taipei: Taiwan sheng xingzheng changguan gongshu, 1946), Tables 49 and 65, 77, 155; George W. Barclay, *Colonial Development and Population in Taiwan* (Port Washington, N.Y: Kennikat Press, 1972), Table 61, 213.

10   Hong Yuru, "Riben zhimin tongzhi yu furen tuanti – shilun 1904–1930 nian aiguo furenhui Taiwan zhibu," *Taiwan fengwu* 47:2 (June 1997): 62.

11   By the early 20th century, the compliance rate for primary education among girls in Japan was 97.4 per cent. See Sharon H. Nolte and Sally Hastings, "The Meiji State's Policy Toward Women, 1890–1910," in Gail Lee Bernstein, ed., *Recreating Japanese Women, 1600–1945* (Berkeley: University of California Press, 1991), 157.

12   Taiwan sheng xingzheng changguan, Tables 49, 58, and 59, 77, 127–139.

13   Takenaka Nobuko, *Rizhi Taiwan shenghuo shi: Riben nüren zai Taiwan, Dazheng pian 1912– 1925*, trans. Cai Longbao, *Chuban, lishi yu xianchang* 175 (Taipei: Shibao wenhua, 2007), 117–118. All subsequent citations of Takenaka are from this translation.

14   Ibid., 50–51, 113–117. Takenaka refers to the waitresses as "apron-wearing," a term suggestive of employees in modern restaurants in metropolitan Japan.

When these women settled in Taiwan, they brought with them ideas about their role as colonizers, and about their role as women. As colonizers, Japanese women shared in what Stefan Tanaka describes as a form of Orientalism in defining their relations with other Asian societies. While viewing themselves as backward in comparison to Westerners, Japanese saw Chinese people as even more backward and in need of Japanese leadership if they were to become civilized.[15] On top of this civilizing ideology, the elite women who comprised the majority of Japanese women settlers brought with them the state-sponsored model of modern womanhood: the *ryōsai kenbo* (good wife, wise mother). Although they were not unaware of, nor unaffected by, the contemporary debate swirling in the home islands over the definition of the "new woman," most settler women fit the model of *ryōsai kenbo*, as defined by Sharon Nolte and Sally Hastings: "As Japan passed from the 19th century into the 20th, the ideal woman was one who attended girls' higher school, spent an appropriate amount of time on organized philanthropic and patriotic activities, and used the postal savings system."[16] At times, however, they pushed against the limitations of that ideology.

With these two conceptions of their roles guiding their activities in Taiwan, Japanese women helped to civilize their empire in two main ways. First, they participated directly and indirectly in the control and transformation of the supposedly uncivilized aborigines, and the perhaps more culturally endowed islander elites. The somewhat crude division here between aborigines (*banjin*) and islanders (*hontōjin*) is significant, because it separated the indigenous residents into two main groups. The former was the object of primarily violent suppression during the period under study, while the latter was seen as being in need of civilization, but also as a potential, and even necessary, ally in the colonization of Taiwan. Settler women dealt with these groups in dramatically different ways. Second, as the AFK turned its attention away from suppression and toward transformation, it presaged many of the policies that the civilian-led Government-General would institute during the 1920s. Thus Japanese women played an important role in the shift from military to civil colonization of Taiwan.

### The Taiwan Branch of the AFK and Its Connections to Empire

From its foundation, Japan's AFK had strong connections to the nation's ruling elite and imperial project. The two people most closely associated with its

---

15    Stefan Tanaka, *Japan's Orient: Rendering Pasts into History* (Berkeley: University of California Press, 1993).

16    Nolte and Hastings, 171.

foundation were Okumura Ioko, daughter of an elite family, and Prince Konoe Atsumaro, President of the House of Peers. Okumura conceived of the organization as a group that could boost the morale of Japanese troops while touring China in the wake of the First Sino-Japanese War, and then used her relationship with Konoe and other social, political, and business elites to establish the association in early 1901. The principal officers were noble ladies, including the first chair, Marchioness Iwakura Hisako, and the first president, Princess Kan'in Chieko. In addition, a cohort of prominent men served as advisors and auditors, including Konoe, Hara Kei, Yoshida Shigeru, and Shibusawa Eiichi; in other words, it was a women's association, but men played a key role in facilitating its growth and agenda. In light of such high-profile backing, scholars have often interpreted the association's actions as merely being the implementation of official policies.[17] Although there is evidence for such views, the reality was more complex.

The AFK became one of the largest empire-wide associations of any sort in pre-WWII Japan. It grew rapidly during the first two decades of its existence, drawing hundreds of thousands of members from among middle and upper class women. The expansion to over one million members by 1920 can be attributed to three main factors. First was the aforementioned prestige, which meant that the association received little if any opposition from the state, and second was the manner in which the association spread and expanded. Okumura set up the main office in Tokyo, and branch offices quickly appeared throughout Japan. In each prefecture or municipality, the wife of the governor or mayor served as chair of the local branch, while her husband served as chief advisor. The social stature and political position of local leaders ensured a smooth and rapid growth. Third was the outbreak of the Russo-Japanese War. Okumura's primary initial objective was to support soldiers and aid their families, especially in cases of injury or death. The patriotic furor that accompanied the conflict with Russia gave the group a huge boost in terms of membership and revenues. Funding came in part from dues that, at a base level of one yen per year, limited membership to the middle and upper tiers, at least until those fees were frozen during the 1920s.[18]

In both the home islands and overseas, the AFK was primarily a relief organization. From its founding, its self-appointed task was "to relieve the bereaved of the dead and seriously injured soldiers," and in 1917 the aid

---

17    Keiko Morita, "Activities of the Japanese Patriotic Ladies' Association (*Aikoku Fujinkai*)," in Maja Mikula, ed., *Women, Activism, and Social Change*, Routledge Research in Gender and Society 11 (London: Routledge, 2005), 52; Nolte and Hastings, 160–161.

18    Morita, 53–57.

function expanded to include "other relieving activities depending on local needs."[19] Members met these goals through various specific activities, including holding sending-off and welcome-home ceremonies for soldiers, visiting sick and wounded soldiers in hospitals, consoling bereaved families and providing them with small amounts of money, and sending postcards and care packages (*imonbukuro*) to soldiers at the front. Also, as early as 1906 some local branches began to establish industrial training institutes, in an effort to promote the economic activities of women and direct them toward both supporting military efforts and raising funds that would benefit the families of soldiers. During the 1920s and 1930s, the AFK diversified its activities and became involved in education, medical care for children and pregnant women, and a range of social movement (*shakai undō*) activities associated with government-led programs for rural revitalization and social mobilization.[20] Created initially to aid Japan's soldiers and their families, the association adopted a much broader mandate for social reform that reflected the growth of moral suasion campaigns in interwar Japan.[21]

The history of the AFK in Taiwan highlights the fundamental connections between the association and the creation, expansion, and maintenance of Japan's overseas empire. The war that had provided the troops who had inspired Okumura Ioko to create the AFK also enabled Japan's colonization of Taiwan, thus the association was linked to imperial expansion from its founding. This linkage became manifest when, contemporaneous with the growth of the early 1900s, officials and settlers set up the first outpost of the AFK outside the home islands when they established the Taiwan Branch (*Aikoku fujinkai Taiwan shibu*) in 1905–1906. The Taiwan Branch owed its existence both to the support of Gotō Shimpei, and to the internally-driven spread of the organization.[22] Gotō, who knew about the association through his ties to its President, Iwakura Hisako, encouraged its establishment in Taiwan in two stages. First, he urged the district heads in Taiwan's three most populous regions (Taipei, Taizhong, and Tainan) to set up branches within their jurisdictions, with their wives serving as the district chiefs. Under this guidance, the wife of Taizhong's district head took charge of a local branch in February 1905, and others followed in Taipei and Tainan later that year. He implemented the second stage in

19    Ibid., 57.

20    Ibid., 58–68. See also Nolte and Hastings, 160–161.

21    On moral suasion and women's groups, see Sheldon Garon, *Molding Japanese Minds: The State in Everyday Life* (Princeton, NJ: Princeton University Press, 1997), Chapters 1 and 4.

22    Hong Yuru emphasizes the internal dynamic as the paramount reason for the spread of the AFK to Taiwan; Hong, 56.

July 1906, when he unified these three groups into one island-wide branch under his wife's leadership; Gotō himself became chief advisor.[23]

In order to fund the Taiwan Branch, Gotō and the other founders turned to Taiwan-based sources to provide 70 per cent of the group's budget. Their decision was in keeping with the overall objective of making Taiwan financially self-sufficient, but they also sought to strengthen the ties between the association and both settler and indigenous women. They thought that such bonds were necessary because of the many difficulties faced by women in the colony, both the Japanese settlers who sought to import their way of life, and the islanders who needed to be freed from existing social structures and customs. In fact, the foundational document for the Taiwan AFK emphasized that obtaining most of the funding from within the colony was essential for displaying the "greatness of the motherland" (*bokoku no idai*). The Tokyo office approved the emphasis on local funding in 1907, and in so doing acknowledged that the Taiwan Branch functioned under special circumstances that necessitated this particular financial division. Local sources of funding included money from the overall budget for aborigine suppression, membership fees, donations from Japanese and islanders, and the sale of aborigine handicraft products.[24]

From the beginning, technically all women on the island could join, although as in the home islands, membership fees circumscribed the pool of those able to do so. Those who joined were divided into special, regular, and support members, most of who fell under the last category. The Tainan Branch had roughly 2000 members at its founding, and within about a year it had more than tripled to well over 6000. Women with ancestral roots in China made up the majority, with over 4000, although most of these were in the lowest category of support members. In Taipei and Taizhong, where Japanese settlement was greater than in the south and east, Japanese and islander membership were in greater balance. Japanese women dominated the more prestigious levels, which gave them greater control over the local association, and occupied 23 of 25 leadership positions from the founding of the Taiwan Branch.[25] Throughout the organization's entire existence, only 13 islanders served as officers. Overall membership expanded dramatically during the first decade, from some 10,000 total members at its founding to over 75,000 a decade later. This growth was mostly attributable to a massive influx of islander women, who expanded from about one third to almost 90 per cent of the island-wide membership.[26]

23   Kō and Ōhashi, 6, 19.
24   Hong, 25–26, 59–60.
25   Kō and Ōhashi, 9–18, 23.
26   Hong, 67, 71.

The numerical majority of islander members indicated a mutual sense of benefit, though not a coincidence of interests, that derived from having indigenous elites join the AFK. For islander women, membership helped to advance the social and economic standing of their families. For Japanese settlers, indigenous members provided substantial financial support, greater access to islander society, and an opportunity to spread Japanese customs and traditions (*fūzoku shūkan*) among the indigenous elite.[27] Although islanders comprised the majority of the membership, the Taiwan Branch was by no means a bastion of interethnic equality. Instead, the transformative ethos of the Japanese settlers highlights the way in which Japanese women used the AFK to advance Japan's imperial project.

The Taiwan Branch was not isolated from the larger organization or the empire as a whole, but rather forged tight bonds to both. In spite of the emphasis on local over central funding, articles published in Taiwan consistently reinforced the supremacy of the central branch and the overriding importance of the empire. Both the main island-wide newspaper, the *Taiwan nichinichi shinpō*, and the most important periodical about Taiwan, *Taiwan jihō*, reported on the general meetings of the empire-wide AFK that took place in Tokyo. These reports mentioned the presence of representatives from Taiwan, seemingly to highlight the connections between metropole and colony.[28] Those connections were reinforced when two royal visitors, the Prince and Princess Kan'innomiya, attended the first island-wide general meeting of the Taiwan Branch, in 1916, in their capacities as Directors of the entire association. When she opened the proceedings, Her Imperial Highness exhorted members of the AFK to work as hard as they could to fulfill their national responsibilities and bring benefits to the nation.[29]

At the general meetings in both Taiwan and Tokyo, speakers discussed the most important military undertaking of the Japanese empire at that time: Japan's involvement in World War I. The Taiwan Branch held its initial gathering in conjunction with the local outposts of both the Japan Red Cross and the *Tokushi kango fujinkai* (Women's Charitable Nursing Association; hereafter, TKF), and the 4500 AFK members present listened as His Imperial Highness noted that Taiwan's Red Cross had recently sent aid workers to England, France, and Russia to provide assistance for Allied soldiers.[30] These women acted a bit closer to home by

---

27    Kō and Ōhashi, p. 24.

28    See "Aikoku fujinkai sōkai" and "Aikoku fujinkai sōkai to hontō," *Taiwan nichinichi shinpō*, 30 April 1911, 3, and 23 August 1912, page illegible; and "Zongcai Kan'innomiyahi dianxia lengzhi," *Taiwan jihō*, June 1917, 15–16.

29    "Seki jūjisha oyobi ryō fujinkai," *Taiwan jihō*, May 1916, 90–91.

30    Ibid., 89.

gathering donations of money and supplies to aid the Qingdao Expeditionary Force that seized the German concessions in Shandong Province. As the European conflict spread during the summer of 1914, the chief of the Taiwan Branch responded: "The European War has suddenly spread into East Asia, and moreover, the proclamation of a declaration of war indeed fills us with awe. Everyone hopes that, in view of the present situation, there will be no miscalculation in this association meeting its goals through strenuous and united effort." The members responded with 20,000 yen in donations to support imperial soldiers, especially those who had enlisted from Taiwan.[31] The emphasis on the Taiwan Branch as part of the empire-wide AFK, engaged in activities supporting imperial and Allied troops around the globe, highlighted the contribution made by women settlers in Taiwan to the expansion of Japan's empire.

### The AFK and the Aborigine Suppression Campaigns

The Taiwan Branch devoted itself to providing assistance to the military and police forces responsible for suppressing and controlling Taiwan's aborigines. Okumura Ioko's initial vision for the association was that it would provide aid and comfort for Japan's soldiers and their families during major military campaigns, but the special circumstances of colonizing Taiwan required a slight modification to this goal. According to its foundational document, the Taiwan Branch would give aid not only to the families of those injured or killed in war, but also to those who suffered hardship in the prolonged campaigns to control the mountain aborigines, or while guarding the aborigine frontier line.[32] However, the AFK's relationship to Taiwan's aborigines was not merely one of military conquest; rather, there were layers of complexity that made the Taiwan Branch partially dependent upon the continued survival of those the military campaigns sought to destroy.

In fact, military suppression was not the only policy that the colonial government adopted vis-à-vis aborigines living in both lowland and mountainous areas (the "cooked" and the "raw," according to Chinese and Japanese nomenclature). As Paul Barclay has shown, Japanese authorities quickly adopted the Qing Dynasty technique of promoting intermarriage with aborigine women in the contact zone between settler and aborigine society, as a means of managing relations along the frontier. The Japanese colonial government did the Qing one better by playing the role of marriage broker: "...the government-general embraced interethnic marriage as a solution to the problem of

---

31    Kō and Ōhashi, 92.
32    Ibid., 25.

'Aborigine administration' in Taiwan's rugged mountain interior, where armed resistance to Japanese rule simmered well into the 1910s." Although the female participants in these unions sometimes suffered marginalization and abandonment, and occasionally fatal conflict erupted when Japanese men disavowed their aborigine wives, the practice remained a central part of colonial policy until 1915.[33] From 1909 onward, control through marriage went hand-in-hand with the five-year plan to pacify the aborigine areas through successive military campaigns.

The Taipei-based Taiwan Branch and smaller outposts throughout the island threw themselves into activities in support of the Aborigine Suppression Brigades (*Tōbantai*). Working in conjunction with newspaper companies in Taiwan, the AFK began raising contributions from individuals, organizations, and companies throughout the empire. In fact, the Taiwan Branch took the initiative to publicize the suppression campaign among AFK branches in the home islands, and to solicit donations through those local offices. It also distributed pictures and descriptions of its activities through newspapers in Tokyo, and sought out officials in the Colonial Bureau and Oriental Association (*Tōyō kyōkai*) to garner more support.[34] It used these monies for direct financial aid to wounded soldiers and the families of those who died, and to purchase care packages for distribution to members of the Suppression Brigades. Over the course of the five-year plan, according to its records the AFK disbursed almost 29,000 yen and over 9000 care packages.[35] The AFK's monetary and material assistance to soldiers both strengthened the Taiwan Branch's network throughout the empire, and connected the donors and recipients to each other in a collective sense.

The Taiwan Branch engaged in a range of other activities that further developed its ties to the Suppression Brigades and the empire. Members visited wounded soldiers in hospitals, and as the numbers of injured began to become too large for existing facilities, the AFK joined together with the

---

33    Paul D. Barclay, "Cultural Brokerage and Interethnic Marriage in Colonial Taiwan: Japanese Subalterns and their Aborigine Wives, 1895–1930," *Journal of Asian Studies* 64:2 (May 2005); the quotation comes from p. 325. Barclay points out that the colonial government did not recognize these unions as legal marriages, but in practice there were examples of aborigine women entering Japanese households, and Japanese men entering aborigine homes, which amounted to marriage.

34    "Tōban to aikoku fujinkai," *Taiwan nichinichi*, 10 February 1912, 7.

35    Kō and Ōhashi, 87. Articles on these donations appeared frequently in the *Taiwan nichinichi*, often with remarkably precise details about how much was distributed to each part of the island, and how many people received it. For example, see "Giran fujinkai no katsudō," *Taiwan nichinichi*, 22 October 1910, page illegible.

Government-General and Taipei Hospital to build a new wing, solely for casualties of the suppression campaigns. Not long after the completion of the new wing, it became a formal part of Taipei Hospital, and thus was under the control of the Taiwan Government-General. Perhaps most significantly, beginning in 1908, every year the AFK organized a public observance of the *shōkon* festival at various locations in Taipei, to honor those who had died as part of the Suppression Brigades.[36] This ceremony was inextricably connected to the modern Japanese nation-state, and thus the Japanese Empire, because it had first been observed to honor those who had died in the Bōshin War, during which the forces of the fledgling Meiji state defeated the last of the Tokugawa loyalists.

Although women took part in all of these activities, they were not always in charge of them. Hong Yuru argues that some forms of support, such as working in hospitals and receiving or sending off troops and visiting dignitaries, were controlled by men who worked for the Government-General and served as advisors to the AFK. Moreover, the vast majority of women who participated on a public level were Japanese; islander women rarely got involved, at least prior to 1930.[37] This pattern of male leadership, female action had characterized the association from its founding in 1901, and its replication here suggests that many of the connections between the Taiwan Branch, other branches, and Japanese officials existed between men rather than women.

Nevertheless, the five-year suppression plan coincided with the largest growth of the AFK, among both Japanese settlers and islanders. Two important conclusions emerge from this temporal overlap. One, islander women saw joining the AFK not only as a chance to enhance the status of their families, but also as a means of distancing themselves from Taiwan's aborigines. The fact that the available sources made no mention of the AFK providing aid to soldiers involved in defeating the islander-led Tapani Uprising of 1915 further suggests that islander involvement had much to do with the target of the suppression campaign. Two, Japanese women saw supporting the brigades as the best opportunity they had to contribute to the expansion of Japan's empire, to help it spread into parts of Taiwan that had hitherto remained beyond the reach of the colonial state.

The AFK's relationship with Taiwan's aborigines was, in fact, more complex than simply supporting the goal of military conquest. Although the AFK provided significant aid to those who fought against the mountain aborigines, it also served as a sort of distributor of information about both the lowland and

---

36    Kō and Ōhashi, 59–60, 87–89. Honorees ranged from a low of 43 to a high of 268.
37    Hong, 60–61.

(3 3)    DOMICILES OF SAVAGES OF THE KOBO GROUP IN FORMOSA    家住ノ人蕃社[-ホ-コ]    (製撮許不)

FIGURE 13.1    *Domiciles of savages of the Kobo Group in Formosa.*
SOURCE: FROM THE MICHAEL LEWIS POSTCARD COLLECTION, EAST ASIA IMAGE
COLLECTION, LAFAYETTE COLLEGE, IMAGE LW0352.

upland tribes. The Taiwan Branch took pictures of its various activities and areas of operation, which it then used to publicize itself and to sell for revenue. These pictures included images of aborigines, some of which ended up on postcards like those in Figures 13.1 and 13.2, presumably for Japanese settlers or travelers to send home as evidence of the backwardness of those to whom they were bringing civilization. Also, in its journal, *Taiwan aikokufujin*, the association published an occasional series of pieces about aborigine society. One such story, titled "Aborigine Fairytale: Grandmother's Spoon," contained information about the customs, traditions, and physique of the tribe that produced the tale.[38]

Most significantly, the Taiwan Branch derived a consistent source of income from its sale of aborigine handicrafts and other products. It obtained these goods through barter at designated trading posts along the lowland-highland frontier, where the association exchanged items sought by aborigines. It then took those items and sold them to customers in Taiwan and in the home islands.[39] As a sort of adjunct to the punitive military campaigns, the

---

38    Ying Tangcui, "Seiban otagibanashi: obaasan no saji (Aborigine Fairytale: Grandmother's Spoon)," *Taiwan aikokufujin*, 76 (March 1914), 122–142.

39    Hong, 59–60.

FIGURE 13.2    *Frontier police guards detachment in Mount Bonbon, Formosa.*
SOURCE: FROM THE MICHAEL LEWIS POSTCARD COLLECTION, EAST ASIA IMAGE
COLLECTION, LAFAYETTE COLLEGE, IMAGE LW0354.

Government-General granted the AFK control of these trading posts in order to use economic means to force the tribes into submission. The AFK set rates of exchange that were far above market prices, allowing the organization and the Government-General to turn a considerable profit at the expense of the aborigines. In fact, colonial official Marui Keijirō argued that the exploitative practices instituted by these posts were more likely to cause uprisings than bring the tribes into compliance. On Marui's recommendation, the AFK-run posts were closed in 1914 and replaced by a government-operated monopoly.[40] Nevertheless, the Taiwan Branch continued to derive income from aborigine products for several more years. Although the branch announced at its general meeting in 1916 that it would halt the sale of such items, perhaps because the Government-General sought to curtail its independent activity, it continued to offer aborigine goods at a store in Taipei for at least two more years.[41] It seems

---

40    Paul Barclay, "Profits as Contagion, Production as Progress: Trading Posts, Tribute, and Feasting in the History of Japanese-Formosan Relations, 1895–1917," *International Symposium: Studies on Indigenous Peoples of Taiwan: Retrospect and Prospect in Japan and Taiwan* (Tokyo: Research Institute for Languages and Cultures of Asia and Africa, Tokyo University of Foreign Studies, 2005), L1–L36.

41    Takenaka, 142–143.

that the Taiwan Branch relied on the existence of Taiwan's aborigines for both its financial well-being and a certain amount of its status. That is, because it occupied a position between Taiwan's aborigines and Japanese society, it influenced what Japanese and others knew about these tribes through the trade in aborigine goods and by providing the aborigine artifacts displayed at major expositions in Europe and Japan.[42] This status gave the Japanese women of the Taiwan Branch a certain amount of power and perhaps allowed them to resist the imposition of the state monopoly for as long as they did.

Once the suppression campaign came to an end, and the brigades disbanded, the AFK lost what had been its primary area of operations and a source of some notoriety. Although there were still wounded soldiers to care for and bereaved families to comfort and support, in the absence of a nearby military campaign, the Taiwan Branch reached a sort of identity crisis: what could an association devoted to the military do in a time of relative peace? Having established its position within the web of AFK branches, and its connections throughout the empire, on the basis of its role in the five-year campaign, how would it continue to justify its existence? Fortunately, it had a secondary area of activity to fall back upon, which represented the softer side of Japanese imperialism. Starting in the middle of the 1910s, the AFK turned its attention more and more to the transformation of islander society.

### The AFK, Education and Reform

During the 1910s, members of the Taiwan Branch began to push beyond their military-oriented mandate to engage in social and cultural reform activities. They organized film exhibitions, sponsored and ran performing arts groups, and led postal savings campaigns.[43] They promoted social interaction among Japanese and islander women by sponsoring annual "namecard exchange" events.[44] More importantly, they concentrated on the education of girls living in Taiwan, both islanders and Japanese, promoted vocational training for girls,

---

42    Kō and Ōhashi, 135–136. The expositions included the British-Japanese Expo in London in 1910; an international sanitation exhibition in Dresden in 1911; and three in Tokyo: the Colonial Expo of 1912, the Meiji Memorial Colonial Expo of 1913, and the Taishō Expo of 1914.

43    Takenaka, 142. One cultural activity connected the military and civilian sides of the AFK's activities: a three-day series of dramatic performances, with all proceeds going to the Suppression Brigades. "Fujinkai imon engei," *Taiwan nichinichi*, 21 June 1914, 7.

44    "Fujin meishi kōkankai mōshikomi," *Taiwan nichinichi*, 23 February 1911, 6; and "Yilan furen jiao lihui," ibid., 7 January 1919, 6.

and sought to reform some of the customs and practices of islander women. Through these sorts of activities, Japanese women switched their focus from military suppression to their colonial civilizing mission.

Girls' education became a major focus for the Taiwan Branch during the 1910s. Initially, the AFK established schools and programs designed to train islander girls and women in Japanese language, vocational skills, and household management techniques. As early as 1914, the Taiwan Branch instituted a small program to train islander women in improved sericulture techniques,[45] and the following year it established the first of several Training Centers in a few locations around Taipei. These centers sought to teach Japanese language, tailoring, and handicraft manufacturing to teenage girls who had graduated from public school. The association quickly set up more centers in the rest of the city, and within four years over 300 individuals had graduated from the training courses. Motivated by the slogan, "Japanese begins in the home," AFK members also instituted language-training classes at schools, banks, and other businesses, and ran courses specifically for middle and upper class islander women. As the new colonial schools began to replace older educational institutions, AFK members trained the teachers in Japanese, math, and other subjects, and helped them to find work in the new schools.[46] Although the linguistic instruction did not meet with much success during the 1910s, the Training Centers proved so popular that, in 1920, the AFK merged three existing public schools in Taipei into the Girls' Vocational School, which was open to both islanders and Japanese.[47] Given that education was one of the prime means by which the Government-General sought to transform islanders into loyal Japanese subjects, the AFK's educational efforts linked the Taiwan Branch to a crucial mechanism for colonization.

It was not the only link, for the association also played an important role in cultural transformation outside of the classroom through its involvement in the campaign to eradicate footbinding in Taiwan. The binding of girls' feet in order to keep them small had become widespread in Taiwan during the Qing period, but after the advent of Japanese rule, beginning in the early 1900s, both islanders and Japanese sought to end the practice by convincing women to unbind their feet. The anti-foot-binding campaign was initiated by the Government-General, but islanders became leading participants in the effort. Nevertheless, by the early 1910s, roughly a third of islander women still had bound feet – aborigines never engaged in the practice – and the AFK embarked

---

45    "Aikoku fujinkai to sangyō sōrai," *Taiwan nichinichi*, 21 February 1914, 7.
46    Takenaka, 143–147.
47    Ibid., 144.

on a new campaign to complete the abolition. In 1912, it established programs at public schools in Taipei to convince girls and their parents to unbind their feet. On 24 January 1915, the AFK in Taizhong led a large ceremony in the city park at which women unbound their feet in public.[48] These projects could have put Japanese women settlers at odds with the elite islander women upon which the AFK depended for its growth, since most of them likely had bound feet. However there seems to have been no appreciable objection from islander members, and in fact the membership continued to grow throughout the 1910s.

Although it is difficult to measure the specific influence of these programs on islander society, by concentrating their efforts on reforming local customs, Japanese women settlers placed the Taiwan Branch somewhat ahead of the AFK in the home islands. Keiko Morita suggests that the AFK engaged in social enlightenment activities as early as 1902, when it began publishing its bulletin, *Aikoku fujin* (*Patriotic Ladies*). However, it did so largely for public relations and fundraising, not for social reform.[49] The colonial setting, where Japanese settlers were motivated in part by a desire to change the locals and teach them Japanese ways and customs, gave women there an opportunity to use the AFK in a manner that they had not yet done in the metropole. Even though women settlers joined the work force at a lower rate than women in the home islands, they still moved outside of the home through their involvement with the Taiwan Branch. When they engaged in cultural reform instead of household management, they also went beyond the limits of the *ryōsai kenbo* model of Japanese womanhood. When they continued to sell aborigine products in spite of official injunctions not to, and took advantage of their privileged access to aborigine culture, they carved out prominent space for themselves in Japanese society. Regardless of the results of their reform initiatives, women settlers redirected their main collective organization from support for military campaigns against aborigines to the promotion of social and cultural transformation among islanders – from the hard to the soft side of Japanese imperialism.

## Conclusion

As increasingly numerous representatives of the Japanese empire in Taiwan, women settlers played a similarly larger and more important role in Japan's colonial project during the 1910s. Separated, or perhaps liberated, from the

---

48    Ibid., 108–110. Large events such as this – and there were others – were remarkable for the simple fact that Chinese women had generally hidden their bound feet from public view.

49    Morita, 63.

need to run their households by the availability of cheap domestic labor, they forged public space for themselves through associations such as the Taiwan Branch of the *Aikoku fujinkai*. In the middle of the decade, roughly one in nine Japanese females in the island belonged to the AFK, suggesting that the organization was a key institution in the lives of a large number of women settlers. Through this association, Japanese women contributed to the civilization of empire in two key ways. The first had to do with carrying out the civilizing mission that Japanese took upon themselves in Taiwan, and was seen in the AFK's active support for the aborigine suppression campaigns, its distribution of aborigine products and a limited knowledge of aborigines throughout the empire, and its promotion of educational and cultural reform among islander girls and women. Through these and other ways, Japanese women sought to civilize the newly-colonized subjects of the Japanese emperors. Their second contribution focused more on the character of the Japanese empire itself. Even within the context of aborigine pacification, Japanese women adopted nurturing rather than belligerent roles. Following the supposed completion of the military campaigns around 1915, Japanese women turned more of their attention to social and cultural transformation. As they did so, they adopted the sort of civilizing practices that the Japanese colonial government later instituted under civilian leadership. Thus, they prefigured the burgeoning social programs and social movements that swept Taiwan during the 1920s, a time when the colonial government allowed broader discourse and activism even as it reinforced its programs of assimilation. Women settlers carved out space for themselves in the public arena based upon their privileged position between aborigine and Japanese societies, and between islander women and the Japanese colonial state. In so doing they played roles that were unavailable to women in the home islands, pushed against the limits of state-sanctioned gender roles, and advanced a softer, more civilized form of Japanese imperialism.

Within the global context of Japan's foreign relations of the 1910s, Japanese women settlers highlighted several ways in which that decade was pivotal for Japan's involvement with the world. First and foremost, although in some ways the Russo-Japanese war marked Japan's emergence as a full imperial power capable of holding its own in conflict with a European empire, it took the entire decade of the 1910s for Japan to consolidate its hold over its own colonies. With its colonies seemingly under control, Japan began to play a more confident, collaborative role in international diplomacy, as seen in its participation in the League of Nations and multilateral conferences. Thus the support that the AFK gave to the aborigine suppression campaigns contributed to that confidence. Second, the ascendance of the softer side of Japanese imperialism brought Japan's colonial ideology more in line with the civilizing ethos of the contemporary French empire. This transformative strain had been present in Japanese imperialism from the outset, but it came more to the forefront in the 1920s, and remained in the 1930s when it fused with the militaristic side in the *kōminka* movement and wartime mobilization. Third, the actions of settler women in Taiwan reflected and promoted the global shift in power set in motion by the Great War, after which the European powers began a decades-long process of declining global influence and diminishing control over their colonial possessions. The War did not have a dramatic impact upon women settlers in Taiwan, but rather they helped Japan take advantage of the opportunities that came out of the terrible conflict.

# The Great War and Urban Crisis

*Conceptualizing the Industrial Metropolis in Japan and Britain in the 1910s*

*Susan C. Townsend*

## The Garden City in England and Japan

In Japan and Britain, the 1910s was an important decade during which ideas about urban life, city planning and modernity were recorded, debated, and investigated, culminating in new concepts of national planning in both countries by 1919. Internationally, the origins of contemporary town planning can be traced to the twenty-year period between 1890 and 1910, although it was not firmly established by the time of the outbreak of the First World War. During this period, major industrial cities faced crisis as migrants from the surrounding countryside sought employment opportunities in the growing number of factories and workshops and aspired to the modern lifestyle promised by the city. While each country has its own story to tell, there was an extraordinary diffusion of ideas around the globe in this period.[1] In the case of Japan and Britain ideas travelled not only between the two countries, but beyond their borders and into their empires, whether it be Lutyens' designs in Delhi or Gotō Shimpei's city plan in Taipei, Taiwan. Eventually, with the professionalization of town planning, new conceptions of the industrial metropolis emerged in the 1910s. In particular, this decade saw the dissemination of Ebenezer Howard's Garden City Movement globally, from the first, much studied, example at Letchworth (1903) in England to the "new world" countries of the United States, South America, New Zealand and Australia. In Japan, the businessman and developer Shibusawa Eiichi (1840–1931) in Tokyo, as well as city planners such as Seki Hajime (1873–1935) and garden designers such as Ohya Reijō (1890–1934) in Osaka, were inspired by Ebenezer Howard's concept of the garden city first outlined in *To-morrow: A Peaceful Path to Real Reform* (1898). Howard's utopian vision linking town planning and social reform became an important aspect (both as an ideal and in practice) of the Taishō democracy movement.[2]

---

1  Gordon E. Cherry, "Introduction: Aspects of Twentieth-century Planning," in *Shaping an Urban World*, ed. Gordon E. Cherry, vol. 2 of *Planning and the Environment in the Modern World*, ed. Gordon E. Cherry (London: Mansell, 1980), 1–2.

2  Ken Tadashi Oshima, "Denenchōfu: Building the Garden City in Japan," *Journal of the Society of Architectural Historians* 55:2 (June 1996): 140.

© KONINKLIJKE BRILL NV, LEIDEN, 2014 | DOI 10.1163/9789004274273_016

After the First World War, however, Japanese urban planners increasingly turned away from the Garden City Movement to an idea of the industrial metropolis that embraced urban growth, and suburbanization became the default solution to the urban crisis. The suburb was "discovered" in the late Meiji and early Taishō periods after being prefigured in the literary imagination by writers such as Kunikida Doppo (1872–1908) and Tokutomi Roka (1868–1927). Indeed, the concept of suburb is not natural but "had to be created as a space that addressed the romantic and somewhat greedy urge to escape."[3] British planners, on the other hand, were uncomfortable with the idea of ever-expanding suburbs and continued to promote the garden city idea, especially after Clough Williams-Ellis' *England and the Octopus* (1928) began a plea, backed by architect Patrick Abercrombie (1879–1957), for the "containment" of urban England.

The introduction of the garden city concept (or more specifically its variant form, the garden suburb) to Japan is relatively well known (Sorenson 2001; Hanes 2002; Oshima 1996; Watanabe 1980, 1992).[4] However, the context, development, and criticism of Howard's plans has not been addressed within a comparative framework and little consideration has been given to differences in demographic trends in Japan and Britain which impacted on the reception of the garden city ideal and its implementation in both countries. Moreover, the importation of the garden city idea into Japan was the culmination of a much longer process of thought about the city and urban living dating back to the Tokugawa period. Ideas had emerged which included a Confucian discourse rooted in agrarianism, leading in some cases to a back-to-the-land movement (*dochaku*) led by Kumazawa Banzon (1619–1728) in the 1760s. Partly in response to this Ogyū Sorai (1666–1728) produced one of the first systematic discourses about urban life around 1727. During the early Meiji period, Tokyo emerged as a showcase for modern Western-style experiments in architecture to impress foreigners, which was also one of the primary aims of the Municipal Improvement Act of 1888 that encouraged road widening and paving, better

---

3   Angela Yiu, "'Beautiful Town': The Discovery of the Suburbs and the Vision of the Garden City in Late Meiji and Taisho Literature," *Japan Forum* 18:3 (2006): 316.

4   André Sorenson, "Subcentres and Satellite Cities: Tokyo's 20th Century Experience of Planned Polycentrism," *International Planning Studies* 6:1 (2001): 9–32; Jeffrey E. Hanes, *The City as Subject: Seki Hajime and the Reinvention of Modern Osaka* (Berkeley L.A.: University of California Press, 2002); Oshima, "Denenchōfu"; Shun'ichi Watanabe, "Garden City Japanese Style: The Case of Den-en Toshi Ltd., 1918–1928," in *Shaping an Urban World*, ed. Gordon E. Cherry, (London: Mansell, 1980); and Shun'ichi Watanabe, "The Japanese Garden City," in *The Garden City: Past, present and future*, ed. Stephen V. Ward (London: E & FN Spon, 1992).

water supply, and the dredging of rivers. Inevitably, the Act was based on the idea of Haussmann's Paris (1853–1870), "the leading Western urban model for Tokyo at the time: grand, permanent, and monumental."[5] While not denying the importance of other influences, such as Fritz Schumacher's *Stadtpark* (1914) in Hamburg, "English Town Planning"[6] appealed to Japanese planners in the 1910s because of Britain's long experience of rapid industrial and urban transformation since the Industrial Revolution. Moreover, in both countries the impact of the First World War made the task of finding a solution to the urban problem (*toshi mondai*) even more of a priority. In Britain the challenge was to build homes "fit for heroes" returning from the war, while in Japan, the war accelerated the process of industrialization, pulling people into the towns and cities and exacerbating the problems of overcrowding and attendant social ills. The Rice Riots of 1918 raised the specter of widespread urban discontent as wartime boom turned into post-war inflation and recession.

The aim of this chapter is not to attempt a direct comparison of the responses to urban crisis in Japan and England in the 1910s, but to highlight the growing importance of town planning and the influence of the Garden City Movement in both countries. In this respect, the concept of "travelling theory" is useful for comparative urban studies since it recognises that ideas about space

> get new meanings when they are put in practice in different contexts. Researchers and other people travel and so do theories and concepts. Both are modified by different contexts and experiences. After travelling, the return to the place of origin is never the same.[7]

A prime example of the use of travelling theory is Naho Shiba's comparative study of the early parks movement in Britain and Japan. She shows how British parks were seen as an antidote to the crowded and often insanitary living

---

5   Henry D. Smith, "Tokyo as an Idea: An Exploration of Japanese Urban Thought until 1945," *Journal of Japanese Studies* 4:1 (1978): 54–55.

6   The "English town-planning tradition" refers to city planning exemplified by the Georgian town of Bath in the eighteenth century and the continuity of notions such as the "picturesque" in the planning of industrial or factory villages in the 19th century, such as Titus Salt's Saltaire near Bradford, Lord Lever's Port Sunlight (1888) in Birkenhead and George Cadbury's Bournville (1895) near Birmingham.

7   Peter Clark, and Jussi S Jauhiainen, introduction to *The European City and Green Space: London, Stockholm, Helsinki and St. Petersburg, 1850–2000*, ed. Peter Clark (Aldershot: Ashgate, 2006), 8.

conditions prevailing in Victorian industrial towns, and as a means of improving the health and well-being of industrial workers. Such ideas were first realized in Joseph Paxton's Birkenhead Park on the Wirral Peninsula, England (1847). In Japan, on the other hand, early park building during the Meiji period was intimately connected with the visible signs of the drive towards modernization and Westernization. For example, Honda Seiroku's Hibiya Park (1903) was associated with a desire to demonstrate to the world that Japan was committed to the ideals of *bunmei kaika* (civilization and enlightenment). This contrast is important since it shows that while city planners in both countries considered the provision of green space in the urban environment to be highly desirable, their approaches and the final outcomes were very different.[8]

### Early Planning Concepts

Early Meiji planning ideas were influenced by the findings of the Iwakura Mission between 1871 and 1873. As he travelled across Britain and France, Kume Kunitake, the Embassy's chronicler, noted the massive migration of peasants to industrial cities, causing their populations to swell enormously. In Britain, the Mission visited London before travelling north to Birmingham, Sheffield, Birkenhead, Manchester, Bradford, and Glasgow, which were at the height of their prosperity in the autumn of 1872. While admiring Britain's economic power, Kume came away with the overriding impression of bustling industriousness accompanied by gloom, fog and clouds of black smoke emitted from the forests of domestic chimneys and industrial smoke stacks. As well as environmental degradation he witnessed acute social problems. His frequent visits to courts and prisons gave him the impression that Britain's cities teemed with beggars, prostitutes, child thieves, gangs of ruffians, gamblers, and footpads. Furthermore, "an unending succession of poor men and women throw themselves into London's rivers and canals." It was clear that "the rich get richer day by day, while the poor struggle throughout their lives simply to feed themselves."[9] In contrast he noted the suburbs of Manchester where "the imposing

---

8   Naho Shiba, "A Comparative Study of the Provision of Public Open Space in Industrialising Societies East & West: The Work of Pioneer British and Japanese Park Designers in the Nineteenth and early Twentieth Centuries," (PhD diss., University of Nottingham, 2007), 18.

9   Kunitake Kume, *Britain*, trans. Graham Healey, vol. 2 of Kunitake Kume, *The Iwakura Embassy 1871–73: A True Account of the Ambassador Extraordinary & Plenipotentiary's Journey of Observation Through the United States of America and Europe,* ed. Graham Healey and Chūshichi Tsuzuki (Princeton, N. J.: The Japan Documents, 2002), 26.

residences of the rich stood side by side. Trees, shrubs and flowers grew in pro-
fusion behind their walls, and there were occasional ponds. The effect was one
of refined elegance."[10]

Paris, on the other hand, was the "greatest metropolis of the continent
of Europe, no city in the world with the exception of London can compare
with Paris in size, and in terms of splendour it attains heights unequalled
anywhere else on Earth."[11] Whereas in London "smoke from coal fires pervades the sunlight, and even the rain, too, seemed black," in Paris the air
was fresh since its citizens "all live in the midst of parkland, and wherever
one goes there are celebrated sites for recreation."[12] It is little wonder that
Haussmann's Paris provided a model for early Meiji urban planning when
the emphasis was on national political goals rather than urban practicalities.
However, modernizers such as Fukuzawa Yukichi (1884–1901), Taguchi Ukichi
(1855–1905), and Mori Ōgai (1862–1922) challenged this emphasis, insisting
that the urban challenge be met with modern technology and practical
education.[13]

The practicality of Sir Titus Salt's industrial village of Saltaire, three miles
from Bradford, had impressed Kume. Salt's village, in fact, a small town of
some 5000 souls in 1872, was built on a site that, twenty years earlier, had
been moorland and pasture. While marred by the smoke of the mill built on
the banks of the river Aire, the town provided facilities, including schools,
which benefited the workers as well as Salt's great enterprise. The Mission
observed a similar example, the artisans' quarters around the park of the
Buttes-Chaumont, in the rustic outskirts of Paris where manufacturers and
industrialists had bought cheap land on which to construct dwellings for
their workers. The key to both developments was the availability of cheap land
on the outskirts of cities, which attracted private developers. Roads would
be laid out and rows of houses built after considering the tastes and financial means of the workers whose social standing would also be reflected in
different styles of houses (as at Bournville). In the Paris scheme, workers were
encouraged to save some of their wages in order, eventually, to buy their
houses. Services such as lighting, paving, and water were provided as well as
parks, churches, and schools and so on. Eventually whole communities with
shops, laundries, libraries, and bathhouses would emerge and flourish. Kume

---

10    Ibid., 177.
11    Kunitake Kume, *Continental Europe*, trans. Andrew Cobbing, vol. 3 of *Iwakura Embassy*,
      ed. Healey and Tsuzuki, 33.
12    Ibid., 40.
13    Smith, "Tokyo," 55.

regarded the savings schemes for workers from banks, mutual aid societies, insurance companies and pension funds as particularly "virtuous and laudable" since:

> Without such inducements and support from the upper classes, the workers would squander their money on worthless pursuits, leading a life of debauchery and indolence, eventually falling prey to alcoholism and syphilis until they are no longer able to work, so is it not the case that is all just disposable income anyway?

Indeed, vast profits could be made from the work-force "by setting up labourers' quarters and offering them encouragement and help."[14]

### Taishō Urban Planning and the Garden City Movement

However, such patronizing and moralizing attitudes, together with lauding the profit motives of the capitalist class, sat less easily with the Taishō generation. In the early 19th century, responses to urbanization were varied. They ranged from the deeply personal, for example, the philosopher Miki Kiyoshi's shock and loneliness upon arriving in Tokyo from the countryside in 1917,[15] through university movements such as Mushanokōji Saneatsu's Tolstoy-inspired New Village Movement, to Leftist and Marxist social reform movements influenced by Kawakami Hajime's *Bimbo Monogatari* (Tale of poverty) (1916).[16] Municipal socialists such as Katayama Sen (1859–1933) and Abe Iso (1865–1949) formed a link between the urban modernizers, Taguchi and Mori, of the early Meiji period, and the so-called "bureaucratic reformers" and city planners of the Taishō period.[17] They linked urban planning with social reform; Katayama in *Toshi shakaigaku* (Municipal Socialism) in 1903 and Abe who, in *Toshi dokusen jigyōron* (Municipal Monopoly of Utilities) in 1911, also looked to New Zealand as a model for urban reform.[18]

---

14 Kume, *Continental Europe*, 75–77.
15 *Dokusho henreki* in vol. 1 of *Miki Kiyoshi Zenshū*, ed. Ōuchi Hyōe et. al. (Tokyo: Iwanami shoten, 1966): 381.
16 Susan C. Townsend, *Miki Kiyoshi 1897–1945: Japan's Itinerant Philosopher* (Leiden: Brill, 2009), 55, 98–99.
17 Smith, "Tokyo," 60.
18 Masako Gavin, "Abe Iso and New Zealand as a Model for a 'New' Japan," *Japan Forum* 16, no. 3 (2004): 393–394.

The emergence of modern town planning in Japan and Britain in the 1910s was, in part, a response to rapidly changing demographics. In 1911, the populations of Japan and Britain were roughly similar, as was the rate of increase over the previous four decades. In Britain (including Ireland at this time) the population increased by around 42.8 per cent, from 31.8 million in 1871 to 45.4 million in 1911.[19] In Japan the increase was similar, from 34.8 million in 1872 to 49.9 million in 1911 (see Figure 14.1).[20] While precise estimates are difficult,[21] in 1910 roughly three-quarters of the population of England, the most heavily populated part of the British Isles, lived in areas classified as "urban," in contrast to Japan where even in 1920 only one-third of people lived in settlements over 10,000.[22] Notwithstanding differences in the pace of urbanization in both

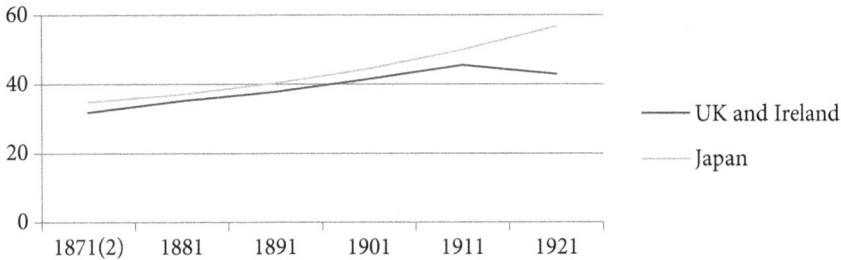

FIGURE 14.1     *Population of UK and Ireland and Japan 1871–1921.*
SOURCES: UK DATA: "CENSUS REPORTS" HTTP://WWW.VISIONOFBRITAIN.ORG.UK/CENSUS/ (ACCESSED 25/01/2012). JAPAN DATA: "POPULATION BY SEX, POPULATION INCREASE AND POPULATION DENSITY (1872–2006)," JAPANESE BUREAU OF STATISTICS, *HISTORICAL STATISTICS OF JAPAN.* HTTP://WWW.STAT.GO.JP/ENGLISH/DATA/CHOUKI/INDEX.HTM (ACCESSED 09/08/2010).

19    1911 Census, <http://www.visionofbritain.org.uk/census/>, accessed 26 February 2012.
20    Statistics for Japan are taken or calculated from Japanese Bureau of Statistics, *Historical Statistics of Japan*, <http://www.stat.go.jp/english/data/chouki/index.htm>, accessed on various dates.
21    Different countries apply varying definitions of "urban" and "rural" areas to their statistical categories. It is generally agreed that "urban" refers to an area of high population density in which residents are primarily engaged in manufacturing and service sectors. Susumu Osada, "The Japanese Urban System 1970–1990," in *Progress in Planning*, 59 (2003): 130–132.
22    André Sorensen, *The Making of Urban Japan: Cities and Planning from Edo to the Twenty-first Century*, (Abingdon, Oxon: Routledge, 2002), 92. Other urban scholars have put the 1920 figure at only 18 per cent living in "urban" districts (Harris 1982; Watanabe, "Planning History in Japan," *Urban History* 7 (1980): 63–75). However, Sorensen's usage of the category "settlements of 10,000 or more" probably gives a more accurate impression of the extent of urbanisation in Japan.

countries, unregulated, unplanned building led to the proliferation of slum conditions.

The most significant differences were in trends relating to population density and distribution. In England and Wales,[23] assuming equal distribution of the population, there were around 251 people per km$^2$ compared to Japan with 131 people per km$^2$ by 1911. However, a 1913 survey revealed already that the "most striking feature of human distribution in Japan appears to be the belt of maximum population that lies along the shores of the Inland Sea and continues, with a little northing, towards Tokyo."[24] By this time high densities of population were situated on the great plains of Kantō, Nobi, and Kansai, in the area now known as the Tokaidō Megalopolis belt. On the Kantō plain Tokyo prefecture had the highest concentration of 1431 people per km$^2$, followed by Osaka prefecture on the Kansai plain with 1210 people per km$^2$. In the rapidly industrializing region around Nagoya on the Nobi plain, however, there were only around 405 people per km$^2$. Continuing changes in population density and increasing land values in areas around these cities had an important impact on the process of suburbanization.

Although England and Wales had, overall, a higher population density than Japan in the 1910s, it was more evenly distributed throughout the country, mostly within 97 "urban" districts. In Japan in 1889 there were 39 areas classified as "cities" or shi, rising to 83 by 1920.[25] In both countries only four cities had populations over half a million: Tokyo, Osaka, Kobe, and Kyoto in Japan, and London, Glasgow, Birmingham, and Liverpool in Britain (see Table 14.1). All Japan's major cities had much higher population densities compared with Britain. Tokyo's population of over 2 million was squeezed into an area of 81.24 km$^2$, giving a population density of 26,307 people per km$^2$, almost twice that of London.

In the 1910s, the population of the merchant capital Osaka suddenly increased as the rapid industrialization prompted by the First World War drew in thousands of laborers from the surrounding countryside. By 1920, 1.25 million people were concentrated into 58.44 km$^2$ (a population density of 21,440 per km$^2$) with many forced to live in slums. It was in Osaka and Tokyo, the most

23   For census purposes England and Wales are often treated separately to Scotland and Northern Island because of major demographic differences.

24   Mark Jefferson, "The Distribution of People in Japan in 1913," Geographical Review 2:6 (November 1916): 368.

25   Japan's municipal designations had imprecise differentiations. Some areas designated as shi had only around 20,000 people while others classified as "towns" or machi had over 50,000 people. The majority of shi (59) had populations between 30,000 and 99,000 while 10 were between 100,000 and 199,000.

TABLE 14.1 *Population trends in the six largest English cities (1891–1911).*

| City | Population increase | | | Percentage increase or decrease in intercensal period | |
|---|---|---|---|---|---|
| | 1891 | 1901 | 1911 | 1891–1901 | 1901–1911 |
| London | 4,277,954 | 4,536,267 | 4,521,685 | 7.3 | -0.3 |
| Liverpool | 644,243 | 704,134 | 746,421 | 9.3 | 6.0 |
| Manchester | 575,741 | 644,878 | 714,333 | 12.0 | 10.8 |
| Birmingham | 478,922 | 523,179 | 525,833 | 9.2 | 0.5 |
| Sheffield | 339,170 | 409,070 | 454,632 | 20.6 | 11.1 |
| Leeds | 367,505 | 428,968 | 445,550 | 16.7 | 3.9 |
| Total 97 urban districts | 13,779,848 | 15,886,874 | 17,251,009 | 15.3 | 8.3 |

Source: 1911 census of England and Wales general report with appendices: Table 9 population 1891, 1901, 1911, in the 97 towns with populations exceeding 50,000 arranged in order of their populations in 1911. http://www.visionofbritain.org.uk/census/table_page.jsp?tab_id =EW1911GEN_M9&show=DB (accessed 30/01/2012).

densely populated cities, that the garden city idea was studied as a solution to overcrowding. This is in contrast to other, smaller cities that dealt with sudden population expansion by expanding their boundaries. For example, Nagoya's population of 157,496 lived in an area of 13.34 km² centered on the old castle town in 1889. By 1921 the city's population had more than doubled and its boundaries had expanded to 149.56 km² through absorbing neighboring towns and villages. While it is often assumed that the First World War stimulated further industrialization and urban growth, Nagoya experienced a mini recession that temporarily halted expansion.[26] However, after 1920, with lower population densities in the surrounding Nobi plain, Nagoya's City Engineer Ishikawa Hideaki (Eiyo) (1893–1955) was able to expand the suburbs more easily than his counterparts in densely-populated Tokyo and Osaka (Table 14.2).[27]

---

26    Nagoya Planning Bureau Foundation, *Nagoya toshi keikaku shi: Taishō 8 - Shōwa 44* (Nagoya: Nagoya Planning Bureau Foundation, 1999) 9, 14–15.

27    In 1920, Ishikawa, was appointed to the Nagoya Regional Commission for Town Planning established under the 1919 planning law. On his tour of Europe in 1923, he met Raymond

TABLE 14.2   *Comparison of population and area of the six largest cities in Japan 1920 and the UK 1921.*

| Japan | | | UK | | |
|---|---|---|---|---|---|
| City | Population | City area (km²) | City | Population | City area (km²) |
| Tokyo | 2,137,201 | 81.24 | London | 4,484,523 | 303.12* |
| Osaka | 1,252,983 | 58.44 | Glasgow | 1,033,526 | 70.58 |
| Kobe | 608,644 | 62.62 | Birmingham | 919,444 | 176.44 |
| Kyoto | 591,323 | 60.43 | Liverpool | 805,066 | 133.54 |
| Nagoya | 429,997 | 37.35 | Manchester | 731,318 | 115.65 |
| Fukuoka | 422,938 | 37.03 | Sheffield | 490,639 | 100.88 |

Sources: Nagoya Planning Bureau Foundation, *Nagoya toshi keikaku shi* (1999), and 1921 UK Census, http://www.visionofbritain.org.uk (accessed 11 November 2011).
* In 1921 statistics for County of London, corresponding to the area now known as Inner London.

While Japanese cities continued to experience rapid population increase throughout the interwar (1905–1931) period, the population of Britain's major cities had already peaked. The 1911 census showed a falling off in the rate of increase, or even diminution of population resident within the boundaries of a number of larger British cities. In England, boundary changes after 1911 incorporated the suburbs – especially in Liverpool, Manchester, and Birmingham – and improved transportation networks enabled the relatively orderly movement of population out to the suburbs and beyond. In addition, some rebuilding of slum areas had already taken place to reduce overcrowding, thus beginning a trend of decentralization in the bigger cities, some two decades or so ahead of Japan.

It was in response to a peak in population densities in English cities in the 1890s, that Howard published *To-Morrow*, and then republished it in 1902 in its more familiar form as *Garden Cities of To-Morrow*. It was subsequently translated into numerous languages. The Garden City and Town Planning

---

Unwin, and discussed a master plan for Nagoya based on the separation of the city's functions. However, it was not until after the Second World War that Nagoya's city engineer, Tabuchi Jūrō, put the plan into full effect. Nori Itō, *Nagoya no Machi: Sensai fukko no kiroko* (Nagoya, 1988), 99.

Association was founded in 1899 to promulgate Howard's ideas.[28] Howard responded to commentaries appearing from 1891 describing the nature of the urban crisis in England. The Dean of Canterbury, Frederick Farrar, lamented the ever expanding cities as the "graves of the physique of our race" with their "houses so foul, so squalid, so ill-drained, so vitiated by neglect and dirt"; while the Fabian and Trade Unionist Tom Mann decried "the congestion of labour in the metropolis...caused mainly by the influx from the country districts who were needed there to cultivate the land."[29] The urban crisis in England was related to the twin evils of overcrowding in the cities and depopulation of the countryside.

Similarly, the consequence of rapid migration of labor into the industrial cities of Japan was nowhere more apparent than in Osaka. Once termed the "Venice of Japan" because of its mercantile heritage and numerous canals and waterways, it was now labeled the "Manchester of the Orient" because of its cotton industry and, increasingly, its slums. The English social reformers Beatrice (1858–1943) and Sidney (1859–1947) Webb visited Osaka in late summer 1911 during a tour of Asia and remarked:

> This flourishing industrial city, with its 5000 factories, its teeming population in crowded, narrow streets, its forest of smoking chimneys, its numerous great stone buildings in 'foreign' style, and, unfortunately, its paupers and its slums, represents the 'new industrialism' of Japan in its most extreme form.[30]

On the one hand they admired Osaka's "progressive" municipal government for constructing an impressive infrastructure (harbor, trams, and ferry boats) and for its sewer and drainage system and daily household refuse collection. One of its main streets (probably Shinsaibashi-suji) struck them as "one of the great streets of the world, a brilliantly lighted narrow thread of busy life through the prevailing gloom of night in a Japanese city."[31] However, since the late 1880s Osaka's slums achieved notoriety after a journalist, Suzuki Umeshirō,

---

28   Patrick Abercrombie, "A Comparative Review of Examples of Modern Town Planning and 'Garden City' Schemes in England," *Town Planning Review* 1:1 (April 1910): 20.

29   Ebenezer Howard, *To-Morrow: A Peaceful Path to Real Reform*, (London: Routledge, 2003), 3–4.

30   Sidney and Beatrice Webb, *The Webbs in Asia: The 1911–12 Travel Diary*, ed. George Feaver, (Basingstoke: Macmillan, 1992), 70. The number of 5000 factories is probably an overestimate since Hanes gives a figure of 3000 factories by 1919. Hanes, *City as Subject*, 195.

31   Webb and Webb, 70.

reported on conditions in the Nagomachi area for the newspaper *Jiji shinpō*. Originally on the agricultural margins, this village had been engulfed as the city spread southwards, and Suzuki highlighted the problems presented by massive immigration of labor from the countryside. However, in the 1880s, as Hanes pointed out, it was a case of "out of sight, out of mind," but later "Osaka graduated from benign neglect to social cynicism" when it demolished slums near the site of the Fifth Industrial Exposition taking place in 1903.[32]

The Webbs were determined to go "slumming," as they put it, and were escorted "in a procession of seven *jinrickshas*" by their English-speaking guide, the Municipal Secretary, a charity official, and two police officers. Proceeding on foot through filthy, dingy and unpaved alleyways they found dwellings as appalling as any in London; "with their dirt and garbage, and foul gutters, evidently full of fleas, dark and destitute of all conveniences." However, they noted that the smell was less offensive than in the London slums, there being "fewer piles of dirty rags, and generally less filthy furniture, as well as cleaner bodies" thanks to public bath-houses. While slum dwellings in Osaka were better ventilated because of the lack of brick walls and glass windows, they were depressingly darker than their London counterparts. Moreover, lack of schooling until the age of six, compounded with exemptions from school attendance due to "poverty" meant that numerous children could be seen in the gutters while many others were sent out to work. Evidence of malnutrition and extreme destitution was rife. Upon further investigation, the Webbs were dismayed to discover that the city authorities were on the point of organizing a system of poor relief not unlike that of the English Poor Law, complete with workhouse-type institutions, which the Webbs had vehemently campaigned against. They determined to send copies of Beatrice's *The Minority Report in Its Relation to Public Health and the Medical Profession*, published in 1910 (part of her protest at the findings of the Poor Law Commission of 1905–1909), and their jointly authored *The Prevention of Destitution* (1911) to the authorities in Osaka. Maintaining that it was the duty of government and local authorities to tackle the causes of poverty and destitution rather than the symptoms, they found "Osaka in this respect, as in its factory conditions, at much the same point as Manchester a hundred years ago." They asked: "Will Japan be able to avoid making all the same mistakes as England made?"[33]

A Japanese Home Ministry official, Ogawa Shigehiro, took the Webbs' advice seriously but failed to draw up a sufficiently detailed plan for an alternative

32    Hanes, *City as Subject*, 183.
33    Sidney and Beatrice Webb, *Travel Diaries*, 72.

welfare system.[34] In the early 1910s Japanese urban planners were confident that they could avoid Britain's mistakes. However, by the late 1910s, many Japanese urban planners "had come to recognize their earlier self-confidence for what it was: hubris. They were shocked out of their smug complacency by one simple fact of Japanese urban life: the looming specter of social problems."[35] In 1913 Ogawa resigned from the Home Office and arrived in Osaka to champion a new system of relief for the city's poor.[36] The following year, Seki Hajime was appointed Deputy Mayor to spearhead major reforms, including expansion of the city limits and a program of modernization and social reform. The economic boom of the First World War years exacerbated the problem: nearly a thousand new factories opened. Floods of immigrant workers or "new arrivals" (*gairaisha*) poured into the heavily polluted slum areas around the factories on city's fringes "where living conditions were so poor that they posed a threat to public morals."[37] The worst areas were those adjacent to factories erected close to the harbor and along the rivers, especially the incorporated districts of Nishinari-gun and Higashinari-gun. Nishinari-gun reported a 47 per cent increase from 170,000 to 250,000 during the First World War and Higashinari-gun a 43 per cent increase from 140,000 to 200,000 turning these areas, according to Hanes, from residential purgatory into something like Hell.[38]

In 1917 another journalist, Murashima Motoyuki, wrote an excoriating exposé of conditions in the slum of Kamagasaki near Imamiya on the southern boundary of Osaka, leading Seki to attack the city's greedy capitalist classes, the very people who put him in power. Seki turned firstly to the British 1909 Housing and Town Planning Act, citing it in its entirety, and consciously invoking the term "town planning" in his proposed reforms.[39] Accordingly, like Katayama and Abe, Seki linked housing, town planning and social reform. The British Act perhaps appealed because, as Cherry pointed out, "it was a comprehensive exercise with integral social objectives."[40] Seki was also familiar with the socialist humanitarianism of the Webbs and the urban idealism of Cadbury

---

34   Kingo Tamai, "Images of the Poor in an Official Survey of Osaka," *Continuity and Change* 15:1 (2000): 100–101.

35   Hanes, *City as Subject*, 217.

36   Tamai, "Images of the Poor," 101.

37   Hanes, *City as Subject*, 195–196.

38   Ibid., 199.

39   Ibid., 197–200.

40   Gordon E. Cherry, *Town Planning in its Social Context* (London: Leonard Hill Books, 1970), 44.

and Howard.[41] Furthermore, the International Garden Cities and Town Planning Association, founded in 1913 and representing eighteen countries, had become a tool for spreading Howard's ideas as well as the English concept of town planning world-wide. In 1914 the Association funded an "Australasian town-planning tour" led by surveyor W.R. Davidge (1879–1961). Whereas Abe believed that Japan should learn from New Zealand, on 1 April 1914, an article in the *Wellington Evening Post* outlined exactly why the "old" countries of the world, particularly Britain, provided a lesson for the "new":

> The effects of overcrowding, slums, poverty, and other social ills are easier to see and understand by reason of their extraordinary intensity. The sharply-drawn lines between pauperism and affluence in the great cities of the world are unmistakable. The tangle of factories, schools, and thousands of homes heaped and huddled together in Greater London, Greater Manchester, and Greater Glasgow are common enough. What strikes home to the colonial imagination is the fact that in all the towns of Great Britain there is the same overpowering disorder, the same chaos of buildings, traffic, docks, railways, factories, houses, and human beings huddled and squeezed together in a congestion both amazing and distressing to the visitor from the Pacific.[42]

For Abe, Britain provided a model for all the wrong reasons and Japanese cities such as Osaka could now be added to the list of "Old World" countries displaying such symptoms. However, that Britain's urban crisis was longer in the making also allowed solutions to emerge and Howard's *To-Morrow* was the product of over a century of urban thought in Britain. Widely regarded as "the most important single work in the history of modern town planning,"[43] it offered a panacea for the evils of overcrowding affecting cities in developing and developed countries the world over. Famously illustrated through his "Three Magnets" diagram, an "extremely compressed and brilliant statement of planning objectives,"[44] Howard's vision is long on architectural detail, but somewhat short on the precise details of social reform. Its most important prescriptions concern acreage, population, and revenue. Garden City would

---

41    Hanes, *City as Subject*, 165.

42    "Better Towns by Sane Planning: A World-wide Movement. New Zealand's Turn," <http://www.makers.org.uk/place/reade>, accessed 25 January 2012.

43    Peter Hall, Dennis Hardy, and Colin Ward, "Commentators' Introduction," in Howard, *To-Morrow*, 1.

44    Peter Hall, "Commentary," in Howard, op. cit., 31.

cover an area of 1000 acres in the middle of a 6000-acre estate, the whole being in a circular form 1240 yards from center to circumference. 30,000 people would dwell within the city with a further 2000 living and working on the agricultural estate supporting it. Housing would be of "varied architecture and design" on "5,500 building lots of an average size of 20 feet by 130 feet." These were in addition to the "ring of very excellently-built houses, each standing in its own ample grounds." Situated on the outer ring of the town are "factories, warehouses, dairies, markets, coal yards, timber yards etc., all fronting on the circle railway which encompasses the whole town." The railway would be no more than 600 yards from any of the city's inhabitants. Most importantly, there would be municipal ownership of land with revenue raised from rents within the city and the surrounding agricultural estate. The retention of revenue from increasing land values would be used for capital projects and the provision of local social welfare administered by the citizens.[45]

However, Howard's vision coincided with a new European conception of the industrial metropolis that bound together socio-cultural change, environment, and town planning in a way that potentially conflicted with the garden city concept. This movement was led by Patrick Geddes, who reported that "the world is now rapidly entering upon a new era of civic development, one in which 'progress' is no longer described as in mere quantity of wealth and increase of population, but is seen to depend upon the quality of these."[46] With the great continental capitals leading the way, Geddes was not promoting a vision of "U-topia," but "Eu-topia." The art was not to imagine an "impossible no-place where all is well," but to make "the most and best of each and every place, and especially of the city in which we live."[47] A few years later, in the very first issue of *Town Planning Review*, its editor S.D. Adshead spoke of a "new era in the history of civic design" which would challenge "middle-class" attempts to turn cities into factories. The well-organized city should take into account the "essentials of existence – 'food,' 'home,' and 'rest'." Zoning into residential districts, business districts, and commercial zones with areas of park and places for pleasure was essential. This concept of town planning had a strong moral undertone and recognized the "essentials of communal existence" upon which depended not only the physical health and prosperity of a city, but also the "intellectual vigour" and "moral force" of the citizen through which law,

45    Howard, *To-Morrow*, 12–13, 14–17.
46    Patrick Geddes, *City Development: A Study of Parks, Gardens, and Culture-Institutes* (Birmingham: The Saint George Press, 1904), 2.
47    Ibid., 3.

order, and custom are brought into play.[48] The International Planning Conference held in Brussels in 1913 confirmed the principle of zoning, which became the basis of both British and Japanese planning laws after the First World War.

However, in the 1910s, the conflict arose because Howard's garden city idea appeared to be diverting the energies of town planning away from ideas about civic development and improving existing towns and cities into creating new garden suburbs and satellites. Supporters of the garden city movement such as Charles Compton Reade (1880–1933) were able to cite evidence from infant mortality rates in England's industrial cities, such as Liverpool with one of the highest infant mortality rates at 125 per 1000, and compare these to Letchworth Garden City with a rate of 50.6 per 1000.[49] George Cadbury, who began constructing his garden village on the green fields of rural Worcestershire in 1879, carried out surveys into the health of Bournville's residents from 1902 comparing data with findings from the poverty-stricken Floodgate Street area of nearby Birmingham. He found that not only were Bournville children two or three inches taller, but they weighed almost 10lbs heavier than the Birmingham children. A survey of death rates for the First World War years 1914–1919 found that the average in Bournville was 7.7 compared to Birmingham, which at 13.7 was slightly better than the average for England and Wales of 14.9, due perhaps to the legacy of Joseph Chamberlain's city improvement scheme in the 1880s. The average infant mortality rate of 51 per thousand births in Bournville was around half that of Birmingham at 101, compared to 97 for England and Wales.[50]

The most vociferous critic of the garden city and its variants was A.T. Edwards, who argued that the whole principal of living in sparsely scattered homes was "profoundly unnatural" leading to the isolation of residents, especially those without their own means of transport for whom "civilisation is their birthright too." Suburbs were "second-rate" and highly regressive, the typical garden suburb was "shoddy and depressing" and their development indicative of a "narrow and pharisaical attitude of mind." Instead industrial towns should be "so beautiful that everybody would wish to stay inside them. If they are unhealthy we must make them healthy. If they are noisy we

48    S.D. Adshead, "An Introduction to Civic Design," *Town Planning Review* 1:1 (April 1910): 10–11.
49    Charles C. Reade, "A Defence of the Garden City Movement," *Town Planning Review* 4:3 (October 1913): 245, 247.
50    Adrian Vaughan and Peter Jordan, *George Cadbury and Bournville*, (Birmingham: Friends of Bournville Carillon, 2004), 13–14.

must take steps to make them less so. If they are too smoky, we must abolish smoke."[51]

Just before it came under attack in Britain, the garden city concept was introduced into Japan in 1907 by a newspaper article "Hanazono Toshi" (Floral garden city) in the *Tokyo Nichi Nichi*. It appealed to Japanese landowners and developers who understood perfectly the potential for accruing profits from appreciating land values and rents that such a scheme offered; not at all what Howard had envisaged. Unfortunately, the term "garden city" was not well understood and later that year the Ministry of Internal Affairs coined the term *den-en toshi* meaning "pastoral city," which fails to capture the nuances of the English concept.[52] Seki was the first Japanese planner to seriously research the English Garden City Movement. In 1913, according to Watanabe, he was the first Japanese planner to make "conceptual distinctions between garden cities, garden suburbs and garden villages."[53] Osaka became an important hub for the diffusion of Howard's garden city ideal. The architect Kataoka Yasushi, for example, visited Letchworth and returned to Japan intent on creating a model of social housing that could be adapted to Japanese conditions.[54] The garden designer and landscape architect Ohya Reijō, a pioneer in integrating town planning and providing green space in the city, became a member of the International Garden Cities and Town Planning Association after meeting Howard and visiting Letchworth in 1920. He incorporated many of Howard's ideas into small-scale housing designs in the 1920s and in his design for Suminoe Park in Osaka in the 1930s.[55] While Howard's *To-Morrow* was the major inspiration, Japanese planners in the 1910s and 1920s also followed Raymond Unwin, the architect of both Letchworth Garden City and Hampstead Garden Suburb, and Thomas Mawson's *Civic Art: A Study in Town Planning, Parks, Boulevards and Open Spaces* (1911) which, although less well known, was in the possession of the Home Office in Japan.[56]

---

51    A.T. Edwards, "A Criticism of the Garden City Movement" *Town Planning Review* 4, no. 2 (July 1913): 153–156.

52    Oshima, "Denenchōfu," 141.

53    Watanabe, "Japanese Garden City," 80.

54    Hanes, *City as Subject*, 219–220.

55    Masayuki Shimizu, "Ohya Reijō: Shodai no midori no toshi keikaku-ka," *Randosukeepu kenkyū*, 60, no. 3 (1997): 205–206; Shiba, "Open Space," 254–256. Namae Takayuki, part-time consultant in the Local Bureau of the Home Ministry, was the first Japanese to stay in Letchworth and to visit Howard in August 1908, and Inouye Tomouchi was the first to translate Howard's concepts and introduce them to Japan in 1906. Watanabe, "Japanese Garden City," 70–71.

56    Shiba, "Open Space," 267.

However, as Watanabe pointed out, "this does not necessarily mean that the English Garden City idea has been correctly understood and sincerely accepted by the planners and people of the world": ideas can be misunderstood or reduced to mere "borrowing of a planning jargon."[57] Indeed, in 1910, Abercrombie pointed out that the many foreigners who flocked to England to see the garden city idea in practice failed to distinguish between Howard's original idea of creating new nuclei in rural areas which had strict limits to growth under full municipal ownership of land, and its variants such as garden suburbs and garden villages.[58] Consequently, no garden cities as such were ever constructed in Japan. The Mino Electric Railway Company sponsored a number of garden suburbs around Osaka in 1911 in the hope of creating a consumer base for itself. However, these were little more than small-scale, conventional suburbs in the guise of *den-en toshi* with nothing resembling Howard's notion of social reform. More suburbs of this type sprang up around Tokyo from 1913 promoted firstly by the Tokyo Trust Co. and then by a company calling itself Den-en Toshi.[59] In 1918, former Finance Minister and entrepreneur Shibusawa Eiichi and publisher Yano Tsuneta (1865–1951) planned the largest such development, Tamagawadai, which is now known as Den-en Chōfu and located about half an hour from Tokyo by express train. Eiichi's son Hideo helped him to realize his dream after visiting Letchworth and St. Francis Wood, San Francisco in 1919.[60] Den-en Chōfu was planned with only white-collar workers in mind as the "average" people who would be able to afford his houses. Eiichi also fully intended to place the enterprise under the control of a non-profit company that he would chair. Considered a risky financial venture at the time, the Den-en Toshi Corporation comprised Shibusawa's personal contacts and acquaintances, who bought up around 390 acres of land along the banks of the Tama River between Tokyo and Yokohama. To offset the financial risks for the project's backers, however, Shibusawa intended to sell the houses and plots to individual owners.[61] In almost every respect there were important differences between the realization of Howard's vision at Letchworth, and Shibusawa's at Den-en Chōfu in terms of the levels of planning, scale, costs, and distribution of benefits between shareholders and residents. According to Watanabe: "In contrast to the British approach, which in effect was mean with the stockholders but generous with the residents, Den-en Toshi was generous with

---

57    Watanabe, "Garden City Japanese Style," 129–130.

58    Abercrombie, "Comparative View," 19.

59    Watanabe, "Japanese Garden City," 75–76.

60    Oshima, "Denenchōfu," 140, 144.

61    Ibid., 143–144.

both." Whereas Den-en Chōfu provided houses with gardens for the wealthy "upper middle class," half the residents in Letchworth could be described as "working class."[62] Shibusawa's model was not the garden city of Letchworth, but the garden suburb of Hampstead. Despite the best efforts of Howard's planning disciples to be true to the idea of creating self-sufficient garden cities that privileged the community over profit, in Japan the resulting towns and suburbs were ultimately shaped by the practicalities of adapting the model to local conditions. Market forces such as escalating land values ultimately compromised the idea. By 1928, Den-en Toshi Corporation had sold all the land parcels and Den-en Chōfu became a victim of its own success and popularity. As land prices rose, Shibusawa's ideals were abandoned and the town became an exclusive, wealthy suburb.

Seki's rising concern that such schemes might be socially divisive by creating wealthy middle-class enclaves was compounded by his firsthand experience of the 1918 Rice Riots, leading him to criticize companies peddling the garden city idea in Japan as being interested only in "promoting suburban, middle-class developments where rising real estate values and well-heeled clients would ensure them huge profits."[63] It is not clear whether this statement included criticism of Shibusawa's plans for Den-en Chōfu, which had been circulating since around 1916. Born 33 years later than Shibusawa, Seki belonged to a generation that had become disenchanted with the uncomfortable mix of philanthropic idealism and pragmatic capitalism displayed by Meiji entrepreneurs such as Shibusawa.[64] Attempts to transfer Howard's utopian ideal into Japan suddenly appeared to Seki to be retrogressive rather than progressive. Since "big cities represented the fulfillment of Japan's promise as a modern industrial nation," why attempt to flee from them? He echoed criticism of the garden city idea in Britain when he claimed that it denied "the necessity of the metropolis." He also claimed that both British and French models of urban planning in general ignored the urban poor living in the spaces between the avenues and grand boulevards. Rather than negating urban growth by building self-contained, self-sufficient garden cities, he formulated a compromise that was, nevertheless, broadly based on Howard's ideal. Characterizing this new approach as "housing-centered pragmatism" he would create satellite towns on the edge of the metropolis that, essentially, would be working-class

---

62    Watanabe, "Japanese Garden City," 78–79.

63    Hanes, *City as Subject*, 225.

64    Indeed, in 1914 when it became known that Seki had been nominated as deputy mayor of Osaka, Shibusawa, who saw in Seki a gifted economist, tried to dissuade him from going into government service, describing it as a thankless task. Hanes, *City as Subject*, 172.

suburbs. Seki's disillusionment with European civilization after the shock of the Great War was one reason for his change of heart and his search for an indigenous solution to the housing problem.[65]

By 1920 Ohya Reijō also realized that Howard's ideals would be very difficult to put into practice in the Japanese context. In keeping with Seki's ideas, his plan was to bring green space into the city together with the provision of high quality housing such as he had seen at Letchworth. He drew up plans for a small group of 13 residences with shops and a common garden for children placed around a square. However, due to restrictions on space these residences were to be built on an area of 750 *tsubo* (0.6 acre) at over twice the density of Unwin's ideal of not more than 12 houses to the acre. The key to Ohya's adaptation was his recognition of the importance of allowing light and air to penetrate both suburban and urban housing developments to create a healthy environment.[66]

The end of the First World War, therefore, provided a stimulus to town planning in both countries, although for slightly different reasons. In Britain, in 1916, the National Housing and Town Planning Council began to consider the problems of post-war reconstruction and, while the slogan "Homes for Heroes" had yet to be invented, housing and post-war reconstruction were intimately linked. The Tudor Walters Report, published in October 1918, called for low-density housing in the suburbs of the type expressed in Unwin's *Cottage Plans and Common Sense* (1902). The need for homes fit for heroes could not be met by private developers and, under the 1919 Housing Acts, most were built by local authorities and public-utility-housing societies.[67] The satellite town at Wythenshawe near Manchester was a prime example of an attempt to create a garden city in the interwar period. Separated from Manchester by a green belt, by the mid-1930s it already had more people than Letchworth and Welwyn Garden City combined, representing "the most striking example of the municipalization of the Garden City."[68]

In Japan, the unedifying spectacle of the Great War broke the illusion of European superiority that had so impressed Meiji urban planners, and a new generation of urban visionaries turned to their own resources in order to find solutions to the problems posed by rapid urbanization. While the war itself had little direct impact on the Japanese City Planning and Urban Building

---

65    Ibid., 224–226, 229.

66    Shiba, "Open Space," 254–256.

67    Mervyn Miller, *Raymond Unwin: Garden Cities and Town Planning* (Leicester: Leicester University Press, 1992), 161–162, 179.

68    Ibid., 184.

Laws proclaimed in 1919, one of the reasons for creating it was the unplanned, sprawling nature of suburban development exacerbated by the economic boom of the war years. In Tokyo the suburban population increased from 420,000 in 1905 to 1,180,000 in 1920.[69] However, much of this growth took place toward the periphery of the 23 wards. What could be termed the outer suburbs (*Santama*) beyond the 23 wards, Saitama, Chiba, and Kanagawa, emerged only in the early 1920s.[70] Plans were largely completed by the summer of 1923 to control suburban development through the use of Land Readjustment (LR).[71] However, not only were these plans destroyed during the Great Kantō Earthquake, but huge numbers of people were relocated to the suburbs ruining any chance for planned suburbanization to take place.[72]

## Conclusion

In the decade of the 1910s, the great industrial cities of England and Japan experienced an urban crisis which caused ideas about the links between town planning, housing and social reform to converge, but only temporarily. Howard's *To-morrow* presented a new way of conceptualizing the industrial metropolis which attempted to balance town and country. After the First World War, however, it became apparent that Howard's ideas would have to be modified to take account of Japan's higher population densities, which were concentrated in the Tokyo and Osaka (Hanshin) areas. In 1919, the novelist Satō Haruo (1892–1964) was inspired by the Garden City Movement to write "Japan's first utopian novel."[73] However, he had his protagonist admit that the "Beautiful Town" of the novel's title "is an impossibility."[74] Ultimately, even the English examples of Letchworth and Welwyn Garden City (1919) diverged considerably from Howard's original concept as the "social reformism of the garden city idea was quickly converted into an environmental reformism."[75] As the concept

---

69    Sorensen, *Urban Japan*, 124.

70    Gary D. Allinson, *Suburban Tokyo: A Comparative Study in Politics and Social Change* (Berkeley: University of California Press, 1979).

71    For a detailed explanation of LR see André Sorensen, "Land Readjustment and Metropolitan Growth: An Examination of Suburban Land Development and Urban Sprawl in the Tokyo Metropolitan Area" *Progress in Planning* 53 (2000), 217–330.

72    Sorensen, *Urban Japan*, 124–125.

73    Elaine Gerbert, introduction to *Beautiful Town*, by Haruo Sato (Honolulu: University of Hawai'i, 1996), 3.

74    Sato, *Beautiful Town*, 55.

75    Stephen V. Ward, "The Garden City Introduced," in *Garden City*, ed. Ward, 24.

"travelled" to Japan it was further modified by local experiences of urbanization, morphing into new varieties of suburbanization.

Perhaps the greatest influence of the Garden City Movement was not on
housing and the ideal of self-supporting satellites that would help to check the
growth of urban sprawl, but on the parks movement in Japan. According to
Shiba, Howard's ideal gave town planners and park designers such as Ohya
new perspectives on the concept of open or green space within the city.[76] As
Tokyo grew exponentially throughout the 20th century, the Kantō Region
Metropolitan Structure Plan of 1940 with its radial structures, greenbelt, garden suburbs, industrial promotion areas, and agricultural areas appeared to be
a curious throwback to Howard's original scheme. Moreover, the first 1958
National Capital Region Development Plan also included a broad greenbelt in
emulation of Abercrombie's desires to contain urban development in his
Greater London Plan.[77]

In the 21st century, however, the garden city ideal is far from forgotten and
has enjoyed a resurgence. In Japan, a new garden city project was instituted in
2001 at a conference held in Kobe to mark the 100th anniversary of the garden
city concept. As a result, the experimental Mitsuike Community Project has
constructed 60 residential lots, a green park and community hall within the
grounds of a municipal golf course in a rural part of Kobe. The project is small
and the language *so* 21st century: "The term healthy urban planning refers to
the idea that a city is more than its buildings, streets and open spaces. Instead
it is a dynamic social entity whose health is closely linked to those who reside
in it."[78] But the vision first expressed by Howard and echoed and adapted by
British and Japanese town planners in the 1910s is still "travelling," perhaps one
day to return to its place of origin in a more contemporary form.

---

76    Shiba, "Open Space," 302
77    Sorenson, "Subcentres," 15–16.
78    World Health Organisation, "Healthy Urban Planning," <http://www.who.int/kobe_centre/
      publications/urban_planning2011.pdf>, accessed December 2, 2012.

# Gender and the Great War

## Tsuda Umeko's Role in Institutionalizing Women's Education in Japan

*Chika Shinohara*

### Introduction

Building a national school system was a centerpiece of Japan's modernization during the *Meiji* period (1868–1912). This attempt to strengthen the
nation by educating its citizens was extended to females when girls' schools
were built throughout the country. By the time of the Great War (1914–
1918), Japanese women's higher education had been developed into a
gendered institution. Existing studies in the early 20th century crystallized
Japan's success in developing gendered education and centralized its
cultural uniqueness. What is missing in this picture is the sociological
institutional perspective that such cultural and structural transformations
of education and gender roles occurred along with Japan's interactions
with the outside world and initial adjoining into world society.[1] In the
imagined community, Japan shaped and institutionalized its national
education, receiving and responding to the emerging global norm.[2]
Moreover, the process did not only foster education for women by training
"good wives, wise mothers" (*ryōsai kenbo*)[3] for the nation *per se*, but also
introduced an emerging global norm of "women's rights" into a modernizing society.

As it began its voyage into the modern world in the mid-19th century,
Japan sent five young women including Tsuda Umeko (1864–1929) – a female
icon of the particular time – to the United States as part of the Iwakura

---

1  John W. Meyer, "Reflection: Institutional Theory and World Society," in *World Society:
The Writings of John W. Meyer*, eds. Georg Krucken and Gili S. Drori (Oxford: Oxford
University Press, 2009), 36–37; Andrew Gordon, *Fabricating Consumers: The Sewing
Machine in Modern Japan* (Berkeley & Los Angeles: University of California Press, 2012),
78, 84.
2  Benedict Anderson, *Imagined Communities* (London: Verso, 1983[2003]), especially 1–8,
83–111.
3  Kimi Hara and Kumiko Fujiwara-Fanselow, "Educational Challenges Past and Present," in
*Transforming Japan: How Feminism and Diversity Are Making a Difference*, ed. Kumiko
Fujiwara-Fanselow (New York: Feminist Press, 2011), 71–76.

© KONINKLIJKE BRILL NV, LEIDEN, 2014 | DOI 10.1163/9789004274273_017

Embassy (1871–1873).[4] This first Japanese women's study abroad added to Japan's education and international networks, and that later affected its developments in the wartime gender ideology and national educational system. The stories of Tsuda and other women educators are important to enhance our understanding of gender and war, and of women's contributions to the early modern history of education. Exploring Japan's interactions with the wider world, this socio-historical analysis of women's education and their roles introduces the preliminary diffusion processes of "women's rights" into Japan and its former colonies. This chapter, hereafter, illustrates the new institutionalization process of women's higher education in Japan and its establishment as a national system toward the Great War period.

## Japanese Education and the Great War

Research on women and education in Japan's modernization history has been predominantly focused on the gendered cultural development – the "good wife and wise mother" ideology. As the nation-state was being established with its growing nationalism,[5] education for good wives and wise mothers restricted women's roles primarily to home and family in order for Imperial Japan to "enrich the country and strengthen the army" (*fukoku kyōhei*).[6] Japan successfully utilized education as a tool to enforce gender specific roles upon women and men, effectively creating clear and rigid gender stratification in its private and public spheres. Such Japanese gendered education has been perceived as producing strategic outcomes, which could be later recognized in militant Japan's victories in wars during the early 1900s. Sociological work on nationalism and gender points at war itself as innovating and progressing gendered Japan as a nation.[7] Similarly, contemporary research on gender and work have also drawn attention to Japan's gendered education and social structures as contributing to its achievement over business war in the postwar

---

4   Andrew Gordon, *A Modern History of Japan: From Tokugawa Times to the Present, Second Edition* (Oxford & New York: Oxford University Press, 2009), 87–89; Kunitake Kume, Tsuzuki Chushichi, and R. Jules Young, *Japan Rising: The Iwakura Embassy to the USA and Europe 1871–1873* (Cambridge: Cambridge University Press, 2009), xi, xvii, 7.

5   Gordon, *A Modern History of Japan*, 134–137.

6   Hara and Fujiwara-Fanselow, "Educational Challenges," 75; Gordon, *A Modern History of Japan*, 70–72.

7   Chizuko Ueno, *Engendering Nationalism* (Tokyo: Seidosha, 1998), 29.

period.[8] While the whole world was moving into the time of war, world movements for women's rights were emerging simultaneously. Since the 19th century, women had started organizing themselves into movements for social reforms and for their own rights in Europe and North America. With such a global women's rights movement occurring all around, the institutionalization of Japanese women's education began as the world moved into the Great War.

Although international movements for women started affecting various aspects of the social, economic, and political lives of peoples in the world at that time, examining Japanese women's education and its relationship with the wider world would provide an intriguing case to study local social transformations of the emerging Far East in history. An observational research, *The Educational Systems of Japan* (1906), published by a British researcher, William Hastings Sharp, reported on Japanese education in the earlier 1900s; women's schooling and social status in Japan had gone through a great progress influenced from the outside.[9] Such a social change in women's education and rights were in part promoted through information sources affected by international movements and, thus, by Japan's connection with the international community. How did such a new normative value come into a local society and then become institutionalized greatly, influencing local Japanese? Answering the question, this work introduces Japan's growing interactions with the world, particularly focusing on women such as Tsuda Umeko, and their roles and development processes of women's schools as a national institution in Japanese society toward and during World War I. In particular, I argue that women's education in Japan not only advanced the gender ideology at that time, but also fostered the emergence and institutionalization of a counter ideology, women's rights and careers, extending and continuing the normative value to contemporary society. This chapter, therefore, traces the new-institutionalization process of women's education in Japan toward and during the Great War.

### First Japanese Women's Study Abroad – Tsuda Umeko's Journey to the United States

The dawn of Japanese women's higher education started with a Japanese Government-funded ten-year project with young women students. They were

8 Mary C. Brinton, *Women and the Economic Miracle* (Berkley, CA: University of California Press, 1993).

9 William Hastings Sharp, *The Educational System of Japan* (Bombay: Central Government Press, 1906), 302–327; William Hastings Sharp, *Aru Eikokujin no mita Meijikōki no Nihon no Kyōiku*, trans. Manabu Ueda (Kyoto: Kohrosha, 1995), 239–248.

sent to the United States with the Iwakura Embassy (1871–1983) in order to experience and study American life, and bring such knowledge and skills back to Japan. The Japanese *Meiji* Government sent a number of students to Europe and North America so that they would be educated and, with the knowledge they gained, construct a new and powerful society, right after the *Meiji* Restoration – opening the country to the world with its political restoration and revolutionary socio-cultural and economic transformation immediately before and after 1868. The Iwakura Embassy, led by the Foreign Minister Prince Iwakura Tomomi (1825–1883), was just such a group of those high-class dele-gates sent first to the United States and then to Europe. Their missions were negotiating and making agreements of treaties, and exploring the "new" world for modernizing Japan's political, economic, and social institutions, including national education.[10]

As the youngest member in the Iwakura Mission, Tsuda Umeko later estab-lished the Women's Institute for English Studies (*Joshi Eigaku Juku*) or forerun-ner of Tsuda College (*Tsuda Juku Daigaku*) in 1900 and dedicated herself to women's career education, and she devoted her life to these endeavors through-out the 1910s.[11] With the knowledge and resources she gained from her study-abroad experiences, she contributed greatly to the formation of Japanese women's higher education. Previously, historians and educational specialists of the *Meiji* (1868–1912) and *Taishō* (1912–1925) periods of Japan studied Tsuda Umeko and often introduced her and her school as the only pioneer in Japanese women's education. They trivialized her as an outlier, challenging to the Japanese nationalistic "good wife, wise mother" ideology. Such centralization of one individual and crystallization of her work under our contemporary val-ues have been critiqued and problematized as blinding an important part of social history of gender and education.[12] Therefore, this study extends its view to stories of other women as well, and introduces institutionalization pro-cesses of Japanese women's education toward the 1910s.

Figures 15.1A/B show Tsuda Umeko when she was eleven years old in Philadelphia and when she started her own school in Tokyo. Born in pre-modern Japan (1864), the Japanese *Meiji* Government's Hokkaido Development

---

10    Kume, Chushichi, and Young, *Japan Rising*, xi, xvii, 7.

11    Takako Yamazaki, *Tsuda Umeko* (Tokyo: Yoshikawa Kobunkan, 1962); Barbara Rose, *Tsuda Umeko and Women's Education in Japan* (New Haven & London: Yale University Press, 1992).

12    Yuko Takahashi, *Tsuda Umeko no Shakaishi* (Tokyo: Tamagawa University Press, 2002), 9–10; Sally Ann Hastings, "Women Educators of the Meiji Era and the Making of Modern Japan," *International Journal of Social Education* 6 (1991): 83–94.

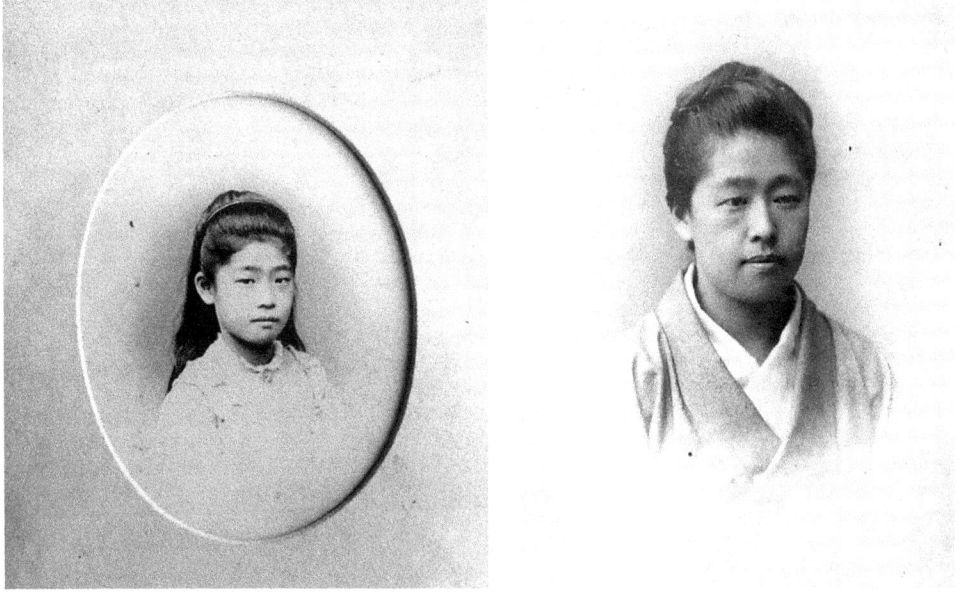

FIGURE 15.1    A. Tsuda Umeko, age 11 in Philadelphia and B. Tsuda Umeko when she started her
               own school in Tokyo (1901) (photos: Tsuda College Archive).

Agency sent Tsuda Umeko (age six) and four other Japanese girls, Yamakawa
Sutematsu (eleven), Nagai Shigeko (eight), Ueda Sadako (fourteen), and
Yoshimasu Ryoko (also fourteen), to the United States as a mission for learning about American women's lifestyles and modern education in 1871.[13]
Figure 15.2 shows the five Japanese girls in Chicago. Tsuda Umeko as a little
girl studied in the United States for over 10 years (1871–1882) staying with an
American family, Charles and Adeline Lanman, in Washington D.C. As a
teenager, she returned to Japan after completing her education at a private
girls' school, the Archer Institute. She did not simply travel for her own education and experiences, but was sent on a national mission for the development of women's education in Japan. A number of internationally connected
women made advancing Japanese women's higher education possible during the Great War period. Tracing Tsuda Umeko's and other key women's
contributions to women's education toward the Great War, the following
shows the social history of female education and its new institutionalization
processes in Japan.

---

13    Yamazaki, *Tsuda Umeko*; Takahashi, *Tsuda Umeko no Shakaishi*, 27.

FIGURE 15.2    *Five Japanese girls in Chicago* (1872): *Nagai Shigeko, Ueda Sadako, Yoshimasu Ryoko, Tsuda Umeko, Yamakawa Sutematsu ( from left to right) (photo: Tsuda College Archive).*

## Prevalence of Girls' Education in Pre-Modern and Modernizing Japan

The historical legacy of pre-modern Japanese teaching culture provides an explanation for the relatively fast institutionalization of girls' education in the early modernization period. European and American visitors to Japan before the Great War recorded that women's status and educational levels at that time were comparatively high. For example, Sharp, one who visited and researched Japan in 1904 states,

> [M]ost foreign residents who are in a position to judge appear to think that Japanese women are fairly well off, often better off than women of the middle class in Europe or America, who are simply household drudges, and that they enjoy a considerable amount of freedom. Whether this is due to foreign influence or not, is disputed; but it seems difficult to believe that foreign example and modern education are not working a silent change in this respect.[14]

Prior to modernization, Japan's literacy rate among the masses was already high, especially in urban areas, such as in *Edo*, which is now known as the capital city of Japan, Tokyo. Since the middle of the *Edo* period (1603–1867) in pre-modern Japan, *terakoya* or small scale tutoring schools had already developed for children's reading, writing, and basic math skills among the ordinary. Such schools spread all over Japan, even in farming and fishing villages, increasing their numbers to somewhere between ten thousand and a hundred thousand by the beginning of the *Meiji* period. In urban Japan – cities such as Tokyo, Kyoto, and Osaka – historians today assume that around 70 to 80 percent of children studied in such tutoring schools for at least a few years. Although gender disparities did exist, statistics show that approximately 88 percent of girls in Tokyo (to 100 percent of boys) learned at *terakoya,* as well as 74 percent of girls in Kyoto and 53 percent of girls in Osaka.[15] In particular, girls in pre-modern Tokyo were known to have often studied for more years at schools than boys did. Both school attendance and literacy rates in Japan were relatively high in the world while the Japanese *Meiji* Government began expanding its modernization and new-institutionalization of education nationwide. Hence, pre-modern Japan already had a good basis for developing more formalized

---

14    Sharp, *The Educational System of Japan*, 309.
15    Masashi Fukaya, *"Terakoya no Joshikyōiku,"* in *Zōho: Ryōsaikemboshugi no Kyōiku* (Tokyo/Nagoya: Reimeishobo, 1981), 34.

women's higher education further, as well as for promoting more widespread social acceptance of women's education in general.

Figure 15.3 visualizes how the school enrollment numbers for girls and boys in Japan grew while the new educational system developed between 1873 and 1920. The compulsory school enrollment rates are estimated by the total number of the pupils' age group, as provided by the Japanese Ministry of Education's historical census data on school enrollments by gender. Toward the late 1910s this data shows the numbers of girls and boys enrolled in elementary schools exceeding four million (solid areas in Figure 15.3). The enrollment rates for both boys and girls (lines in Figure 15.3) show that Japan had already achieved close to perfect elementary school enrollments for girls by the time Japan and the world start moving into the Great War. Free compulsory education since 1900 contributed to the high enrollments afterwards.[16] These statistics tell that by the First World War Japan had minimized the enrollment disparity between girls and boys and thus established a good basis for developing higher

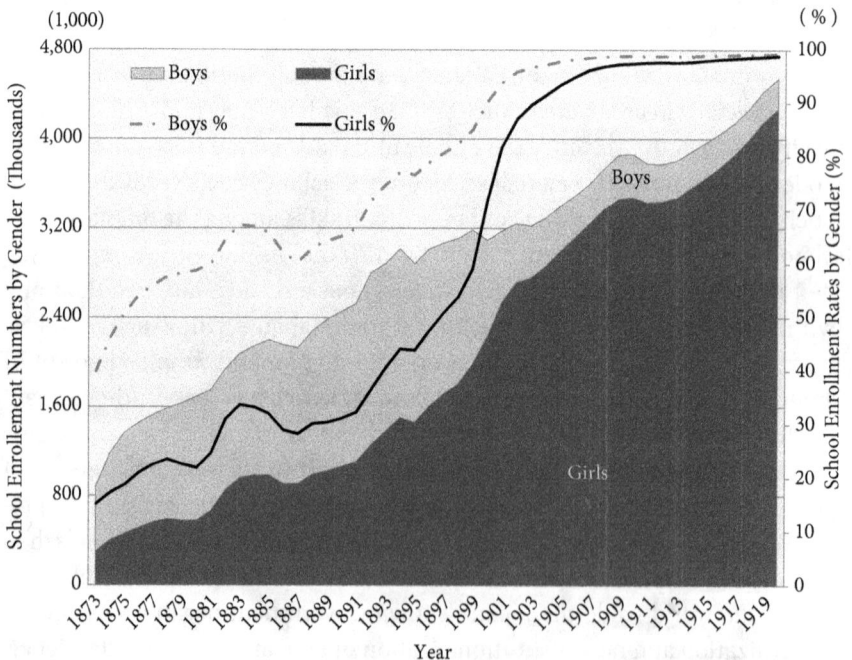

FIGURE 15.3    *Elementary school enrollments for girls and boys in Japan 1873–1920. Data: Ministry of Education, Japan (Ed.). Gakusei Hyakunenshi Shiryōhen. (Tokyo: Teikoku Chihō Gyōsei Gakkai, 1981).*

---

16    For more detailed historical background, see Gordon, *A Modern History of Japan*, 67–68.

education amongst all citizens, regardless of gender. Although elementary education for girls in Japan had already been institutionalized nationwide by the early 1900s, women's secondary and higher education did not enjoy as much substantial development. While some of those earlier educated women abroad coming back to Japan devoted their lives to religious missionary work, several returned with their knowledge acquired abroad and contributed to female education within the country. Therefore, the historical record of urban girls' *terakoya* attendance and the early modernizing girls' school enrollment data suggest the effects of well-formed education for girls from the pre-modern time and the importance of continuity in this respect.[17]

### Japanese Women's Education and Rights Prior to the Great War

The continuity of girls' learning culture from pre-modern Japan resulted in the relatively fast growth of the elementary school enrollment rate for girls in a rapidly modernizing Japanese society before the First World War period. Although Japanese secondary education for girls was not separated from that for boys in its national policy up until 1890, the institutionalization of gendered education for secondary and higher levels took place with other educational reforms during the term of Education Minister Inoue Kowashi (1844–1895). Table 15.1 shows a summary of the institutionalization process of women's education and legal rights in Japan during the life of Tsuda Umeko. Prior to the Great War, women's education in Japan had three distinct phases.[18] In the first of these, Japan showed no clear national policy for women's education, while missionary schools only began to be established in urban Japan and the first Japanese women, including Tsuda Umeko, left with the Iwakura Mission for the United States (see Phase 1 in Table 15.1). The second of these phases, however, would reflect an exciting and momentous period in emerging women's education and rights in Japan.

In 1882, Yamakawa Sutematsu – one of the five young women with the Iwakura Mission – completed her study at Vassar College, thus becoming the first woman from Japan to earn a degree in the United States. Back in Japan, she soon married Oyama Iwao (1842–1916), the Minister of War, and later

17 Martha Tocco, "Made in Japan: Meiji Women's Education," in *Gendering Modern Japanese History*, eds. Barbara Molony and Katheleen Uno (Cambridge and London: Harvard University Press, 2005), 39–60.

18 Kayo Umemura, "*Kōtō Jogakkōrei Seiritsu no Shisōteki Kiban*," in *Nihon Joseishi Ronshū 8: Kyōiku to Shisō*, ed. Sōgō Joseishi Kenkyūkai (Tokyo: Yoshikawabunkan, 1998), 159–194.

TABLE 15.1  *Japanese women's education and rights during Tsuda Umeko's life (1864–1929).*

| Year/period | Women's education and rights in Japan during Tsuda Umeko's life time |
|---|---|

**Phase 1 – no clear national policy (1860s–1870s)**

| | | |
|---|---|---|
| 1864 | Edo | Tsuda Umeko born |
| 1868 | Meiji | |
| 1870 | | · 1st Christian Missionary Schools for Girls & Women |
| 1871 | | · 1st Women's Study Abroad – Tsuda and others, with the Iwakura Embassy |
| | | · 1st National Secondary School for Girls – Tokyo Girls' School |
| 1872 | | · 1st National Secondary School for Girls-Tokyo Girls' School |
| 1875 | | · 1st Women's Teaching School – Tokyo Women's Normal School |

**Phase 2 – emerging period (1879–1894)**

| | |
|---|---|
| 1882 | · 1st Japanese woman earned a college degree in the US – Yamakawa Sutematsu |
| 1885 | · "Expansion of Women's Rights" became a social issue |
| | · 1st Secondary Schools for Girls – Meiji Jogakko, Peeresses' School...etc. |
| |     Tsuda taught at Peeresses' School in Japan |
| 1889 | · No Political Rights for Women (Meiji Constitution of Japan) |
| |     Tsuda studied at Bryn Mawr College (1889–1892) in the US |
| 1893 | · Gender Equality for Education ("About Girls' Education") |
| 1894 | 1st Sino-Japanese War (1894–1895) |

**Phase 3 – establishing period (1895–1909)**

| | |
|---|---|
| 1895 | · Separation of Gender in Education (Regulation for Girls' High School) |
| |     Tsuda wrote "Japanese Women & the War," in the New York Independent |
| 1898 | · Further Restriction of Women's Rights (Meiji Civil Code of Japan) |
| |     Tsuda attended Oxford University and visited the US, London, and Paris |
| | · Gendered Education Policy (Law for Girls' High School) |
| 1900 | · Women Banned from Political Activisms & Organizing (Public Peace Police Law) |
| | Boxer Rebellion (1900–1901) |

| Year/period | Women's education and rights in Japan during Tsuda Umeko's life time |
|---|---|
| 1904 | · *Joshi Eigaku Juku* (forerunner of Tsuda College) established |
|  | Russo-Japanese War (1904–1905) |
| 1905 | · Girls' Elementary School Enrollment reached the vast majority (+90%) |
| Phase 4 – unresting period (1910–1918, 1919- through the end of WWII) | |
| 1911 | · "Blue Stockings (*Seitō*)" Movement (Hiratsuka Raicho and others) began |
| 1912    Taishō | · "Good Wife, Wise Mother" Ideology & Policy |
| 1913 | · 1st Women's Admission Allowed to National University (Tohoku University) |
|  | Tsuda attended Christian Students' Federation Conference in the US |
| 1914 | Great War (1914–1918) |
| 1918 | · Tokyo Women's College established |
| 1919 | · Social Movement and Demand for Women's Higher Education starts |
| 1926    Shōwa | |
| 1929 | Tsuda Umeko passed away |

*Sources:* (1) Ministry of Education, Japan (Ed.). Gakusei Hyakunenshi Shiryōhen. (Tokyo: Teikoku Chihō Gyōsei Gakkai, 1981). (2) Ministry of Education, Japan (Ed.). Gakusei Hyakunenshi. (Tokyo: Teikoku Chihō Gyōsei Gakkai, 1981). (3) Yamazaki, Takako. Tsuda Umeko. Tokyo: Yoshikawa Kobunkan, 1962. (4) Umemura, Kayo. "Kōtō Jogakkōrei Seiritsu no Shisōteki Kiban," In Nihon Joseishi Ronshū 8: Kyōiku to Shisō, ed. Sōgō Joseshi Kenkyuūkai, 159–194. (Tokyo: Yoshikawakobunkan, 1998).

became a trustee of the Peeresses' School and co-founder of the Women's Institute of English (later Tsuda College) with Tsuda Umeko.[19] This Japanese woman's achievement in earning a college degree was a notable historic milestone that marked an emerging period of Japanese gendered education. As the expansion of Japanese women's rights became a social issue in the rising Freedom and People's Rights Movement (*Jiyū Minken Undō*) during the 1880s, private and public women's schools emerged (see Phase 2 in Table 15.1). Until then, there were only a few women's secondary schools in Japan and only one government founded school for girls, Tokyo Girls' School (1872); the only other

---

19    The Sutematsu Yamakawa Oyama Collection in Vassar College Libraries.

options would have been Christian missionary schools and those for daughters of upper-class families, such as the Peeresses' School (*Kazoku Jogakkō*) and a short-lived private school Meiji Girls School (*Meiji Jogakkō*) established in 1885.

In 1893 the Japanese Ministry of Education issued its first legal statement on the matter, entitled "About Girls' Education" (*Joshikyōiku ni Kansuruken*, Ministry of Education's Instruction Number 8, July 22, 1893). It reported that throughout the country "only 25 percent of girls were enrolled in schools when 50 percent of boys were." While addressing gender inequality in this respect and encouraging more girls to be educated in its school system, it simultaneously suggested adding sewing courses to girls' elementary education, as "sewing is the most necessary for women's life." Although it agreed that "education should not have discriminatory practices between boys and girls" – a symbolic legal statement for gender equality in education – the statement "About Girls' Education" separated girls' schools to be independent and different national institutions from boys'. Japan's gender-specific education as a national policy started with this legal statement. Hence, the Japanese government statistics and policy then tell that Japan encouraged female education in general and institutionalized girls' formal schooling with a symbolic legal statement for gender equality. In sum, since the onset of its modernization at the end of the 19th century, Japan had begun institutionalizing a new school system following its Western counterparts and, in particular, the 1880s through the mid-1890s was an emerging period for Japanese women's education (see Phase 2 in Table 15.1).

The emerging period of gendered education in Japan recorded a short time reflecting an open attitude toward women's rights and gender equal education before Japan began devoting itself to a series of war efforts and heading toward the Great War period. To catch up with Europe and the United States, political leaders in Japan explored new women's social roles and effective education in order to produce "wise mothers" who would raise future Japanese children – such children raised by well-educated "wise mothers" would eventually contribute to the creation of a richer nation with its stronger army (*fukoku kyōhei*). Those who studied abroad earlier brought back knowledge about relatively high women's status and education in the West.[20] Developing education for girls and women was regarded as a crucial national strategy, while Japan rushed its social, political, and economic transformations for national development: first replacing the *Tokugawa* Shogunate and abolishing feudalism,

---

20    Gordon, *A Modern History of Japan*, 87–89. Also found in the literature of that time such as Yukichi Fukuzawa, *Onna Daigaku Hyouron* (Tokyo: Jijishimposha, 1899). Reprint in *Onna Daigaku Hyouron: Shin Onna Daigaku* (Tokyo: Kodansha, 2001).

then implementing the parliamentary political system with the emperor as the ruling head, adopting a capitalist economy, and institutionalizing a new education system. Although critics argue that such a positive view toward gender roles in the West was the Japanese elites' blindness about women's status disparities by social class and racial groups, Japanese pioneers at that time appeared eager to grasp and apply what had been observed in the West for Japanese women's education and society.[21] In sum, the first women's liberation movement in Japan continued until after the first Sino-Japanese War (1894–1895).

The subsequent years between 1895 and 1909 marked the establishing period of Japanese gendered education as a national institution (see Phase 3 in Table 15.1). In 1895, the Regulation for Girls' High School (*Kōtō Jogakkō Kitei*, Ministry of Education's Ordinance Number 1, January 29, 1895) legally established separation of gender in Japanese secondary schools. While the promulgation of the civil code (1898) further restricted women's legal rights, education was legally separated by gender, and the "good wife, wise mother" ideology became a dominant value in women's education, evident in the content of women's education curriculums. As the majority of girls started enrolling into primary schools in the 1890s, the Law for Girls' High School (*Kōtō Jogakkō Rei*, Imperial Ordinance Number 31, February 8, 1899) came into effect in 1899. Following these, Japan brought itself into two international conflicts, the Boxer Rebellion (1900–1901) and the Russo-Japanese War (1904–1905). Gender separated education with gendered curriculums and legal restriction of women's rights were established partially as a reaction to the earlier rushed social change for modernization and Westernization. Moreover, the establishment process was formed by the nation's involvements in the two aforementioned conflicts, before Japanese women's education moved into its next period – one of unrest – toward the Great War.

### Tsuda Umeko and Border Crossing of Women's Education into Japan

While the historic transformation of girls' schooling had been occurring prior to the Great War, Tsuda Umeko and a number of women and men – Japanese and non-Japanese – had taken part in the formation of female education in various ways and crossed borders, bringing Western cultural values of education and gender relations into Japanese society. Biographies of Tsuda Umeko

---

21    Takahashi, *Tsuda Umeko no Shakaishi*, 58–59.

and other Japanese women who studied abroad have been published else-where.[22] Thus, here I briefly summarize her life and others where it pertains to Japan's international links which fostered women's education in Japan prior to the war. Tsuda Umeko, born into a pre-modern noble *samurai* war-rior family, was not only fortunate enough to have resourceful international networks, but was also able to create links between the local Japanese and the international community. She lived and studied in the United States for over ten years, since she was six years old. Her father Tsuda Sen (1837–1908) was a progressive thinking *samurai* who studied English and Dutch, and was appointed by the Tokugawa Shogunate as an interpreter in the Foreign Affairs Bureau of the Regime in 1862 along with Fukuzawa Yukichi (1834–1901), one of the most influential writers and educators of *Meiji*-era Japan, and others in 1867.[23] Having such a unique family background at that time, Tsuda Umeko joined four other girls to form the Iwakura Embassy in 1871 for their journey to the United States. Other girls sent with Tsuda Umeko, such as Yamakawa Sutematsu and Nagai Shigeko also came from families with international experiences.[24] One British educator in early 1900s intro-duced the Iwakura Mission and Japanese social attitude towards women's education:

> As early as 1871 the Emperor approved a proposal to send a few girls of good families to America to be educated, on the express ground that the better education of the sex would tend to raise it in public esteem; to which other leaders of Japanese opinion added that a permanent improvement in future generations presupposes an improvement in the parents of both sexes, and that all countries which have attempted to work with the male sex alone have fallen signally behind in the march of progress.[25]

---

22    Yamazaki, *Tsuda Umeko*; Takako Yamazaki, "Tsuda Ume," in *Ten Great Educators of Modern Japan: A Japanese Perspective*, ed. Benjamin C. Duke (Tokyo: University of Tokyo Press, 1989), 125–148; Yoshiko Furuki, *The White Plum: A Biography of Ume Tsuda, Pioneer in the Higher Education of Japanese Women* (New York: Weatherhill, 1991); Rose, *Tsuda Umeko*; Kinuko Kameda, *Tsuda Umeko: Hitori no Meikyōshi no Kiseki* (Tokyo: Soubunsha, 2005); Kinuko Kameda, *Tsuda Umeko to Anna C. Hartshorne: Futakumi no Chihimusume no Monogatari* (Tokyo: Soubunsha, 2005).

23    Yamazaki, "Tsuda Ume," 130.

24    Takahashi, *Tsuda Umeko no Shakaishi*, 27–30. Two other girls left the US soon after their arrival due to health conditions.

25    Sharp, *The Educational System of Japan*, 305.

While Tsuda Umeko was in the United States she took advantage of her unique opportunity, and through her father's social network, she built her own social capital, constructing her own social and professional networks with educators, the wealthy, and elite political figures that would provide her great support and valuable resources for her life-long contributions to Japanese women's education. The closest of those associates were Yamakawa Sutematsu and her host sister, Alice Mabel Bacon (1858–1918),[26] who later went to Japan to support Tsuda Umeko's establishment of her school. Anna C. Hartshorne (1860–1957) was another important supporter for Tsuda Umeko's life in the United States and for the development of Tsuda College.[27] Tsuda Umeko's friends in the United States became important sources for her return to study for a higher degree in later years and to collect donations from American women for Japanese women's education. Itō Hirobumi (1841–1909), the first Prime Minister of Japan, was among Tsuda Umeko's circle of networks from the first visit to the United States with the Iwakura Embassy.[28] He was a "mentor and respectful person," noted in her "Personal Recollections of Prince Itō."[29] Prime Minister Itō provided her a job as an English tutor for the Itō family, and later recommended her to work for a women's school called *Tōyōonnajuku*, and again recommended her to work at the Peeresses' School in 1885. Just as Alice Bacon did, Itō Hirobumi influenced Tsuda Umeko to devote her life to women's education. Through such personal networks, she gained information and resources to help establish the first stage of women's education in Japan. After her teaching experience at the Peeresses' School and others, she started her own school in 1900, the Women's Institute for English Studies.

Christian missionaries were among the first to bring Euro-American gender ideology and education into modernizing Japan (see 1870, Phase 1 in Table 15.1). Their schools include Ferris School for Girls (established in 1870), United School for Girls (1871), Aoyama Institute for Girls (1874), Kobe Institute for Girls and Heian Institute for Girls (both 1875), Tokyo Academy for Girls (1876), Rikkyo Institute for Girls (1877), Doshisha School for Girls (1878), and Kassui School for Girls and Poole School for Girls (both 1879).[30] Missionary schools for

26    Alice Mabel Bacon, *Japanese Girls and Women* (London: Gay and Bird, 1891). Reprint in
      *West Encounter with Japanese Civilization 1800–1940, Volume 10* (Richmond, Surrey: Japan
      Library, Curzon Press, 2000).
27    Kameda, *Tsuda Umeko to Anna C. Hartshorne*, 123–197.
28    Yamazaki, "Tsuda Ume," 106–113.
29    Yamazaki, "Tsuda Ume" (1989), 111; Fumio Nakajima and Tsuda College, eds., *Tsuda Umeko
      Bunsho* (Tokyo: Tsuda College, 1980), 489–498.
30    Yamazaki, "Tsuda Ume."

girls soon became popular among upper class daughters. Daughters and wives of elite political families, such as Iwakura, Itō, Saigō, and Date were among those educated at a Toyo Eiwa School for Girls (*Tōyō Eiwa Jogakkō*).[31] Some of those women educated at such missionary schools later traveled to North America and Europe for higher education. In 1890 Hirata Toshiko and in the following year Watabane Tsuneko received undergraduate degrees from colleges in the United States.[32] The two Christian women were educated at Kobe Institute for Girls (forerunner of Kobe College or *Kobe Jogakuin Daigaku*) and devoted themselves to Christian missionary lives in Japan. To summarize, border crossing of people and flowing Western cultural values of education into Japanese society had surely played an important part in the historic transformation of female education in Japan.

### New-Institutionalization of Education and Diffusion of Women's Rights Norms

The historic transformation and new institutionalization process of women's education in Japan had started receiving Western cultural norms and reshaping Japanese education prior to World War I. Emerging at that time were the development of higher education and social movements for women's rights in Europe and the United States. The global cultural diffusion – either of education or women's rights – in recent world history indicate globalization of cultural and structural features of Western society.[33] New-institutionalists have shown the importance of national society's links with world society in the development of higher education and women's rights in the 20th century.[34] Indeed, Japan around the Great War period expanded its connections to world society developing women's education and enrollments.

---

31   Toshiaki Tachibanaki, *Josei to Kyōiku: Joshi Kōtō Kyōiku no Ayumito Yukue* (Tokyo: Keisōshobō, 2011), 12–13.

32   Chizuko Usui, *"Nichibei Kindai Joshikyōiku no Kankeihikaku,"* in *Joshikyōiku no Kindai to Gendai: Nichibei no Hikakukyōikugakuteki Shiron* (Tokyo: Kindai Bungeisha, 1994), 38–39.

33   George M. Thomas et al., *Institutional Structure: Constituting State, Society, and the Individual* (Newbury Park, CA: SAGE Publications, 1987); John W. Meyer et al., "World Society and the Nation-State," *American Journal of Sociology* 103 (1997): 144–181.

34   Evan Schofer and John W. Meyer, "The Worldwide Expansion of Higher Education in the Twentieth Century," *American Sociological Review* 70 (2005): 898–920; Nitza Berkovitch, *From Motherhood to Citizenship: Women's Rights and International Organizations* (Baltimore: John Hopkins University Press, 1999).

World women's movements and organizing had begun developing since the late 1800s throughout the post-WWI period. The International Council of Women, for instance, was founded in 1888. Focusing its activities exclusively on women's political rights, the first international organization, the International Woman Suffrage Alliance, was established in 1904. The first internationally organized women's movements group had a great effect on women's international activism in general, leading to the subsequent establishment of twenty-two international women's organizations by the time of the First World War.[35] As history tells, soon after the war, women's organizations gained greater power and alliance through the League of Nations (1920–1946) and the International Labour Organization (1919-to date).[36] It was only later that such movements expanded and became more widely recognized through such organizational networks. Hence, women's education in Japan then was not completely independent from such social change. Although the advancement of the "good wife, wise mother" ideology tends to be emphasized in studies of women and education in early 1900s Japan, this study delves into the process of the emerging and institutionalizing Japanese women's education from an alternative angle. A counter ideology and global norms of women's rights had been fostered and simultaneously challenged through education in the same society.

Previously, socio-historical investigations on women's rights growth in Japan have shown how Japan's links with the international society had advanced Japanese women's legal rights and social attention to the particular issue.[37] Additionally, even a symbolic legal statement eventually shaped negative social reactions to women's rights violations, showing stronger resistance among the educated and younger women in globalizing contemporary Japan.[38]

---

35    Berkovitch, *From Motherhood to Citizenship*, 22.

36    Nitza Berkovitch, "The Emergence and Transformation of the International Women's Movement," in *Constructing World Culture: International Nongovernmental Organizations Since 1875*, eds. John Boli and George M. Thomas (Stanford, CA: Stanford University Press, 1999), 100–126.

37    Jennifer Chan-Tiberghien, "Global Norms Concerning Women's, Children's, Minority Rights," in *Gender and Human Rights Politics in Japan: Global Norms and Domestic Networks* (Stanford, CA: Stanford University Press, 2004), 20–38; Chika Shinohara, "Global Pressure, Local Results: the Impact of CEDAW on Working Women in Japan," *Journal of Workplace Rights* 13 (2009): 449–471.

38    Christopher Uggen and Chika Shinohara, "Sexual Harassment Comes of Age: A Comparative Analysis of the United States and Japan," *The Sociological Quarterly* 50, (2009): 201–234; Chika Shinohara, "How Did Sexual Harassment Become a Social Problem in Japan? The Equal Employment Opportunity Law and Globalization," in *Advances in*

Such links and interactions with world society helped develop women's education by disseminating information and resources and, I argue, fostered the
emergence process of global norms such as women's education and rights in
Japan moving toward the Great War.

### Japanese Women Educators – Local-International Linkages

Such international networks are fostered by formal and organizational levels,
and also by personal levels. Upon Japan's emerging period into the world in the
late 1890s to the early 1900s, a few Japanese women had personal networks
with those outside the country. Yet, their links with the outside world played
crucial roles for advancing education for women in Japan. As presented earlier,
secondary and higher education for Japanese women started with missionaries and was pioneered by Christian Japanese educators such as Tsuda Umeko,
Yamakawa Sutematsu, Yasui Tetsu – a founder of Japan Women's University
(introduced later in this chapter), and Hatoyama Haruko (1861–1938).[39]

Tsuda Umeko played an important role as an ambassador representing
Japanese women and networking between Japan and international women's
organizations. She traveled abroad five times not just for her own education
but also for Japan's advancement in women's education. In 1889 after spending
seven years of her life back in Japan, she again left for the United States for college education (Biology, Bryn Mawr College) and raised funds for women's
education. She returned to Japan in 1892. Back to the United States in 1898, her
third visit there was to participate in the International Convention for Women's
Club with Watanabe Fudeko,[40] another pioneer woman of Japanese education
particularly for children with disabilities. Representing Japanese women,
Tsuda Umeko made a speech at the International Convention for Women's
Club in Denver, Colorado.[41] She visited the United Kingdom and Germany

---

*Gender Research, Volume 13: Perceiving Gender Locally, Globally, and Intersectionally*, eds.
Vasilikie Demos and Marcia Texler Segal (Bingley: Emerald Group Publishing Limited,
2009), 267–309.

39    She was a founder of Kyoritsu Women's Occupational Institute (forerunner of Kyoritsu
      Women's University or *Kyōritsu Joshi Daigaku*, 1886); Rie Hatanaka, *Taishōki Joshi
      Kōtōkyōiku no Kenkyū: Keihanshin wo Chūshin nishite* (Tokyo: Kazamashobo, 2004), 247.

40    "*Tsuda Umeko, Watanabe Fudeko ga Tobei: Bankoku Fujin Kyokai Taikai e Shusseki*," *Yomiuri
      Shimbun*, June 3, 1898, Ladies Page, Morning Edition.

41    Umeko Tsuda, "*Denver Kaiginiokeru Supichi* (Convention Speech)," in *Tsuda Umeko
      Bunsho*, eds. Fumio Nakajima and Tsuda College (Tokyo: Tsuda College, 1980), 481–484.

afterwards and studied at a women's school in Oxford until June of the following year. In 1907 she travelled the United States and Europe, and returned to
Japan by way of India, Colombo, Singapore, and Hong Kong. Her final visit to
the United States was in 1913 when she attended an International Christian
Students Convention in New York. During these visits abroad and also at home
in Japan, she introduced Japanese culture and social change to American
newspapers by giving speeches at international conferences and writing works
about Japanese women and education.

One of her works is a piece entitled "Japanese Women and the War (Sino-
Japanese War)." Tsuda Umeko, recommended by Alice Bacon, wrote an essay
in the *New York Independent* in May 1895 introducing Japanese women and
their roles in contributing to the nation and war.[42]

> [...]the women of Japan are making their greatest sacrifice for their
> country – the voluntary offering of what is dearest to them, in the lives of
> their best loved ones. The husbands, brothers and sons who are sent out
> to danger and to death are given most ungrudgingly. No woman dares to
> utter a word of regret. [...] It is marvelous to see the self-control and for-
> titude exercised. [...]
>
> BY TSUDA UMEKO, May 1895 in *The New York Independent*

The newspaper comments on the essay replied:

> ...From reading the article on Japanese women in the war by Miss Umé
> Tsuda, no one would suspect that she was not born to the use of the
> English language. But she is a Japanese who was sent to this country
> twenty years ago to be educated, and has since devoted herself to teach-
> ing as head of the English Department in the Peeresses' School in Tokio
> [Tokyo]. She has lately returned to her position after a visit of three years
> to this country, which was spent in study at Bryn Mawr College. It is thus
> Western culture has entered Japan through its young women as well as its
> young men.
>
> COMMENTARY ON TSUDA UMEKO, May 1895 in *The New York Independent*

This essay and the newspaper commentary provide not only a picture of wom-
en's situation in Japan moving into the time of war, but also information on

---

42    Umeko Tsuda, "Japanese Women and the War," in *Tsuda Umeko Bunsho*, eds. Fumio
      Nakajima and Tsuda College (Tokyo: Tsuda College, 1980), 49–63.

Japan's links and interactions with the United States and the rapidly changing world. Japanese newspapers occasionally reported Tsuda Umeko's whereabouts and opinions on issues such as women's education and voting rights to the public as well. Such local-international networks fostered an awareness of women's important social roles, impacts, and their rights, particularly among highly educated women in Japan. Later educated women started to join women's movements for their rights while the "good wife, wise mother" ideology and policy began to stay and strengthen with growing nationalism in Japan during the Great War.

## International Networks and Women's Education in Japan

The decade of the Great War was the beginning of global travels in the world. A growing number of people in the world started traveling by steamer ship from one continent to another. In 1909, a group of Japanese business leaders and their families dubbed the Shibusawa Business Mission, for instance, traveled to the United States. Among them was one of the first woman Japanese sociologists, Takanashi Taka (Tanaka Takako) (1886–1966). She was a niece of Shibusawa Eiichi (1840–1931) – the greatest contributor to Japan's business education[43] – and she was also known as the wife of liberal philosopher Tanaka Ōdō (1867–1932). In 1918, she wrote *The Status of Women Under Modern Conditions of Japanese Life* and earned a Master's Degree in Sociology at the University of Chicago. Later she became a professor at Japan Women's University (*Nihon Joshi Daigaku*). As the economy recovered and expanded during the Great War and toward the end of the war, growing numbers of Japanese made trips to the American and European continents. Some studied while abroad; others simply enjoyed visiting new worlds; and some others migrated for new business and work opportunities as well.

Yasui Tetsu (1870–1945) was another internationally networked female educator who dedicated her life to Japanese and Thai women's education during this time. In Japan today, she is best known as a president of Tokyo Women's Christian University (*Tokyo Joshi Daigaku* 1918-to present). She first studied and later taught at the first Japanese government-established women's school, Tokyo Women's Normal School (forerunner of Ochanomizu University). Later she learned English from Tsuda Umeko, left for Britain for her study in education and psychology at Cambridge Training College and Oxford in the 1890s,

---

43    Hatanaka, *Taishōki Joshi Kōtōkyōiku*, 250.

and upon returning from Britain she taught at Tsuda Umeko's school.[44] For three years from 1904, she contributed to the formation of female education in Thailand as the first principal of Rajini School. Yasui Tetsu later again studied back in the United Kingdom before herself serving for the establishment of the first Christian women's university in Japan during the 1910s.

Increasing numbers of Japanese studied abroad toward the Great War era. Figure 15.4 shows changes in numbers of Japanese students who studied abroad (bars in Figure 15.4), and European and American instructors who taught in Japan (line with squares in Figure 15.4) between the 1900s and 1920s. These increasing numbers represent students and instructors funded by the Japanese Ministry of Education. In the coming war period, as the national economy emerged and benefited from the Great War, both the Japanese students sent abroad and instructors invited from Europe and the United States began growing in numbers, as Figure 15.4 shows. The number of women students funded by the Japanese Ministry of Education stayed extremely small (numbers marked on the top of bars in Figure 15.4), however. In 1912, for

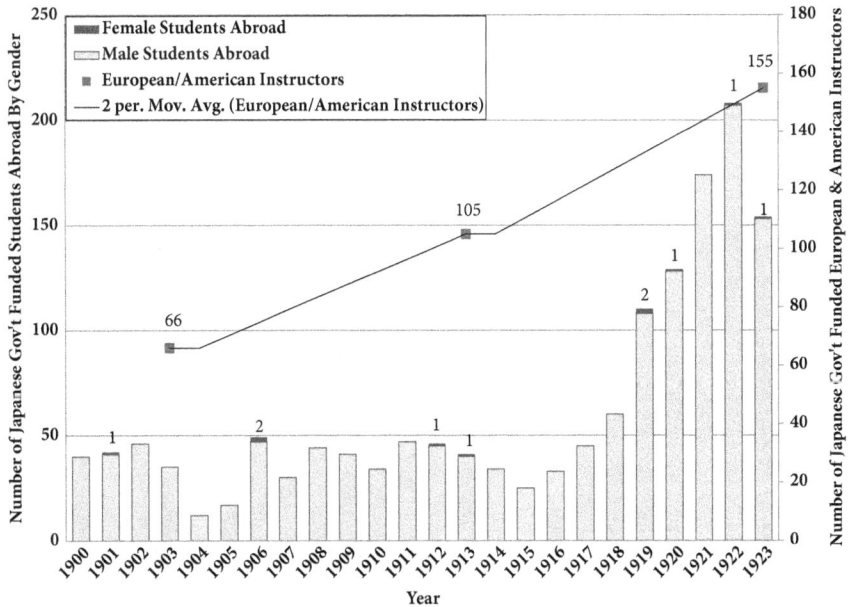

FIGURE 15.4    *The Japanese government funded European/American instructors and Japanese students abroad 1900–1923. Data: Ministry of Education, Japan (Ed.). Gakusei Hyakunenshi Shiryōhen. (Tokyo: Teikoku Chihō Gyōsei Gakkai, 1981).*

---

44    Yamazaki, *Tsuda Umeko*, 239–244, 300–303.

instance, a Japanese female student in the East Coast of the United States reported that she knew the total of fourteen to fifteen Japanese women students at women's colleges like Vassar, Cornell, Wellesley, and Smith, and many of them were receiving scholarships and other funding from their colleges.[45] The majority of Japanese women students who studied abroad were funded privately and/or supported by their colleges.

### Great War Shaping Women's Education: Socially Expected Women's Roles in the 1910s

Figure 15.5 shows growing numbers of Girls High Schools and female high school students in Japan between 1870s and 1920s. The constant increase of schools and students can be seen until the early 1910s, despite the economic downturn of that time. Following the war, it shows a sharp growth of the schools and students towards the Great War and thereafter. One major reason

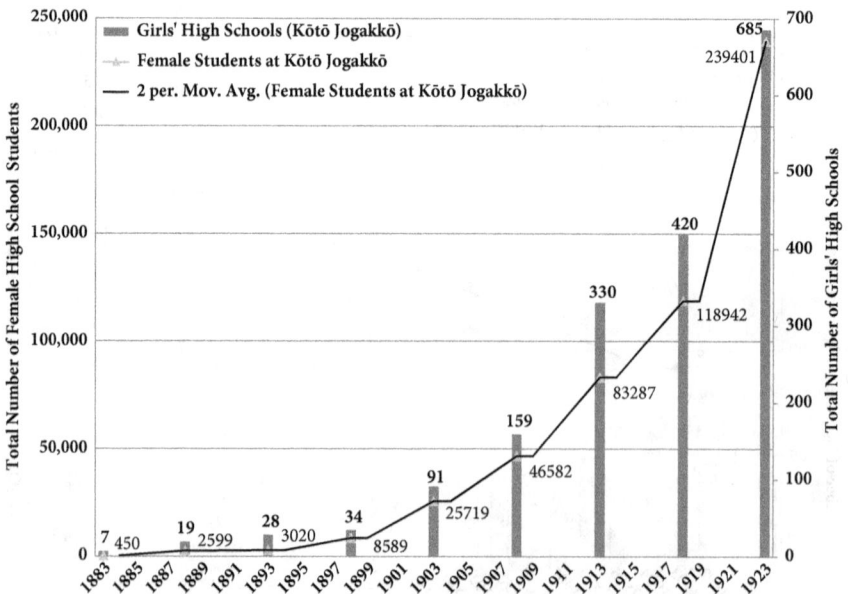

FIGURE 15.5    *Public & private girls' secondary schools (Kōtō Jogakkō) and students in Japan. Data: Ministry of Education, Japan (Ed.). Gakusei Hyakunenshi Shiryōhen. (Tokyo: Teikoku Chihō Gyōsei Gakkai, 1981).*

45    *"Fujin no Ryūgakusei Seikatsu," Yomiuri Shimbun*, September 12, 1912, Ladies Page, Morning Edition.

for the sky rocketing increase of girls' education after the Great War was that Japan's economic growth benefited not only upper class girls with family education and wealth, but other girls with less advantageous backgrounds as well. Growing urban middle class girls gradually became able to proceed to secondary education. Yet, it was less than five percent of girls who proceeded to secondary education (*kōtō jogakkō*) in 1905. It was only after 1920 that ten percent of girls in Japan began receiving secondary education, which means a small number of upper class girls continued their education after the first few years of elementary school during the Geat War.

Yamakawa Kikue, a student of Tsuda Umeko during the early 1910s who later became a women's movement activist, recalls:

> While Tsuda Umeko was teaching at Peeresses' School, as the old American teaching, she actually had a cane. Although she would never use it, she was literally "teaching with a cane." And then, girls from noble class families were her students and they never show dedication for studying at all. [...eventually] she ended up quitting the job.[46]

By 1910, "women students (*jogakusei*)" experienced social popularity (*jogakusei boom*). The Japanese media – newspapers and magazines – reported intensively about women students and their particular fashion styles. More women proceeded to secondary education and the institution of education in Japan started developing into a gendered institution, as the national policy clearly separated women's schools and education from those of men's under the law and as the Japanese society moved into the time of war. Female students during the 1910s had already experienced the nation at war since their childhood: the First Sino-Japanese War (1894–1895), Boxer Rebellion (1900–1901, Hokushin Incident or Yihetuan Movement), Russo-Japanese War (1904–1905), and the Great War (1914–1918).

Many of the highly educated women in Japan then perhaps gave little consideration to the "flip-side" of women, education, and war. Their background, experience, and social position might have provided little conflicting feeling about women's rights and nationalism. Tsuda Umeko's writings show how she intended to harmonize quality education for women students, women's rights and leadership, and locality for the nation, rather than simply challenging competitive claims between women's rights and their loyal citizenship dedicating life for war. There appears little contradiction between the two. It is

---

46    Hisako Kuroiwa, *Meiji no Ojōsama* (Tokyo: Kadokawa Sensho, 2008), 23.

perhaps because she was an elite class woman raised and educated to devote her life for the Japanese nation-state. As part of the status group, elite women working for the establishment of women's higher education had little sense that the nation states they belonged to were also imperial oppressors of other women in the imperial world and historical time. Other female educators of that time like Miwata Masako and Yamawaki Fusako, who had distance from American education and Western feminist values did not voice against the Japanese state; yet they appeared to stay independent and dedicated themselves as educators when they worked close to the national authority.[47] It is important to reconsider today how Imperial Japan and war shaped and oppressed the lives and education of underclass women in Japan and women in its colonies.[48] In sum, war surely shaped women's education and gender ideology or socially expected gender roles in the 1910s.

## Education in Japan's Colonies – A Case of Korea

When school enrollment rates for boys and girls in Japan reached the vast majority, children in Japan's colonies – Korea and Taiwan – at that time still experienced hardship for basic education. National newspapers began reporting the numbers of schools established and enrollment conditions in the 1910s Korea and Taiwan.[49] Japan's *de facto* colonization of the Korean Peninsula began from the early 1900s, though officially Japan colonized Korea from 1910 and for 36 years until the end of WWII.[50] Japan designed separate national educational policies for Japanese children and children in the colonies. For instance, in Korea children were required to start schooling at the age of eight, instead of six, and the content of education was mainly the Japanese language and farming. Starting in 1919, the policy turned to be more assimilation-oriented. As expected, the school enrollment rates of Korean children during the 1910s were quite low. As Table 15.2 shows, only five percent of boys and one percent of girls in the Peninsula received formal education during the 1910s; while the rates increased in the 1920s, still 25 percent of boys and five percent

---

47   Hastings, "Women Educators," 83–94.
48   Takahashi, *Tsuda Umeko no Shakaishi*, 151–152.
49   "Chōsenjin Gakkō Seitosū," *Yomiuri Shimbun*, February 9, 1914, Education Page, Morning Edition; "Taiwan Kyōiku Zento," *Yomiuri Shimbun*, February 21, 1916, Political Administration Page, Morning Edition.
50   For historical details and processes of Japan's foreign relations and policies, see Michael A. Barnhart, *Japan and the World Since 1868* (London: Edward Arnold, 1995), 21–46.

TABLE 15.2   *Elementary school enrollments in Japan and colonized Korea during the 1910s.*

|        | Korea (1912–1919) | Japan (1910–1919) |
|--------|-------------------|-------------------|
| Girls  | 0.56%             | 97.95%            |
| Boys   | 4.78%             | 98.92%            |

Data: Ministry of Education, Japan (Ed.). Gakusei Hyakunenshi Shiryōhen. (Tokyo: Teikoku Chihō Gyōsei Gakkai, 1981). Table 4 on Page 172 in Kim, Puja. Shokuminchiki Chōusen no Kyōiku to Jendā: Shūgaku Fushūgaku wo meguru Kenryokukankei. (Kanagawa: Seori Shobō, 2005).

of girls studied at school.[51] Even toward the Second World War, less than half of Korean children received formal basic education.

The huge gender gap was a concern; yet, education and schooling had very different meanings in Korea. Schooling meant forced education in Japanese, the language of the colonizers. Particularly for Korean girls, poverty and Korean gender expectation (girls' education as unnecessary) shaped extremely low rates of female school enrollments. Emerging Japanese nationalism, policy enforcement, and growing Korean ethnic identities, later in the 1920s, consequently and slowly increased school enrollment rates of Korean students. One example is Oh Ki-Moon born in 1911.[52] In her personal history interview, she revealed the following: she had learned Korean Hangul character writing from her grandmother and then wanted to go and study at school to learn the Japanese language in order to contribute to the resistance movement against Japan, after the emergence of March 1 Resistance Movement (*Samil Undong* or *Sanichi Dokuritsu Undō*) in 1919. Yet, in the end, her father did not allow her to be educated any further. Even though the complex cultural, historical and gender power relations affected the actual schooling situations of girls in colonies at first, this example tells us that women's education and their rights were perceived as a possibility for younger generations in particular. Thus, later the school enrollment rates and number of schools gradually increased even in a historically disadvantaged area like Korea, as new institutionalists of education would expect. Yet, the large gender disparity for school enrollment stayed even after the Great War.

---

51   Puja Kim, *Shokuminchiki Chōusen no Kyōiku to Jendā: Shūgaku Fushūgaku wo meguru Kenryokukankei* (Kanagawa: Seori Shobō, 2005), 73.

52   Kim, *Shokuminchiki Chōusen*, 97.

## Conclusion

Toward the Great War era, as Japan connected with the outside world, it rapidly institutionalized its female schooling receiving and responding to the global norms of women's education and rights. The social acceptance of women's formal education originated from pre-modern urban Japan's social environment and girls' learning culture. Japan also learned from other countries' failures of not educating females well enough and began preparing itself for female schooling quite early. The first Japanese women's study abroad took place in 1871 as part of the Iwakura Mission, sending five young female students to the United States on a ten-year project. In the late 1800s, only a quarter of girls received formal school education nationwide; by the beginning of 1900s, however, the enrollment rate reached the vast majority. In the emerging period of education in Japan, Christian missionary schools and Christian educators provided young women with higher education. Although the advancement of the "good wife, wise mother" ideology tended to be emphasized in studies of gendered education in the particular period, this study delved into the process of the institutionalizing of women's education from an alternative angle in Japan. The global norm of women's rights, a counter ideology, had been fostered and challenged through education in the same society. This socio-historical investigation illustrated such cultural and structural transformations of education and gender roles along with Japan's interactions with, and initial involvement into, world society.

As Japan moved into the time of international conflicts and the Great War, its educational policy and legal codes began clearly separating female education from that of males'. Yet, it is important to note that the very first national legal statement on female education in 1893 clearly included a symbolic statement supporting gender equality and female formal schooling. Exploring Japan's interactions with the wider world toward and throughout the Great War, this chapter introduced sociological institutional analyses of women's education, and examined the outset of diffusion processes of female schooling and rights into modernizing Japanese society. The gendered aspect of education in Japan has received much scholarly attention; nevertheless, "rights" consciousness has also been internalized, particularly among younger women in Japan during the time of the Great War. Furthermore, those seeds of women's education and rights planted in the *Meiji* and *Taishō* periods have grown to be the strong roots of gender equality demanded in Japanese society today.

# The Science Room as an Archive

*Taisho Japan and WWI*

*Hiromi Mizuno*

In 1918, the Ministry of Education ordered, for the first time, all junior high schools in Japan to incorporate students' experiments into teaching and to secure a designated science room in a school building. This was part of the "science boom" in Japan brought about by WWI. With this and other guidelines, the Japanese government launched the first major science education reform since the Civilization and Enlightenment years of the Meiji period.

Historians have documented the ways in which the Great War fundamentally shaped modern science in Japan.[1] Scholars have also examined the science education reform during the Great War years, mainly at the elementary school level through textbooks and supplemental guidebooks.[2] This chapter examines one radical curriculum change during the Great War years that has received little attention from scholars: the introduction of students' experiments to the classroom at the middle school level.[3]

Kishiwada Junior High was one of the schools that immediately responded to the urging of the Ministry of Education by building new science classrooms in 1918. Located in the city of Kishiwada in Osaka's Senshū region, home of the booming textile industry, Kishiwada Junior High (thereafter Kishikō, as locals call it) provided post-compulsory education to boys in the southern half of the prefecture as well as the northern part of the neighboring Wakayama prefecture. While belonging to the oldest and more prestigious group of junior high schools, the so-called "number schools" in the prefecture, Kishikō was neither the wealthiest nor the most elite among them. Nonetheless, as a result of the science education reform, Kishikō acquired multiple rooms for various science subjects.

---

1  For example, see James Bartholomew, *Formation of Japanese Science* (New Haven: Yale University Press, 1993).

2  For example, see Hori Shichizō, *Nihon no rika kyōiku shi* (Tokyo: Fukumura shoten, 1961), and Itakura Kiyonobu, *Nihon rika kyōiku shi* (Tokyo: Daiichi hōki, 1963).

3  Middle schools [中等学校] in prewar Japan consisted of junior high schools, normal schools, girls' higher schools, and various kinds of practical schools; among them, junior high schools and normal schools were the target of the curricular change I discuss. In this chapter, I focus on junior high schools, where boys who graduated from the compulsory elementary schools went. Most junior high schools became high schools 高等学校 after WWII.

© KONINKLIJKE BRILL NV, LEIDEN, 2014 | DOI 10.1163/9789004274273_018

This chapter uses Kishikō's science rooms as an archive for Taisho Japan's relation to the Great War and the world. The approach is unique in the history of science education in Japan, in which the textbook-focused approach has been the norm. Also, while scholarship has conventionally examined either university-level research activities or the elementary school curriculum, this chapter focuses on the middle schools, as their dramatic expansion in the 1910s and 1920s was indeed a significant indicator of economic changes, the formation of the new middle class, and industrial growth during Taisho Japan.

Kishikō offers rare access to the science education reform of the WWI years because the school has kept the records of purchasing experiment tools, specimen collections, and room furniture since Meiji years. It has also preserved more than 100 experiment tools and specimen collections from the Meiji, Taisho, and Showa periods. This is a uniquely rich treasure box for historians. Some elite former high schools, namely the Third High (present Kyoto University) and the Fourth High (Kanazawa University), maintain excellent collections of this sort, but former junior high schools rarely kept any such physical trace of science curriculum of the past. Kishikō's collection is most likely one of the largest – and quite possibly one of the few existing – collections from former junior high schools in Japan.[4]

The experiment room and materials at Kishikō attest to the moment in Japanese history when hands-on experiments by students – now a standard feature of the science curriculum – became the focus of pedagogy for the first time. In this regard, Kishikō's science rooms tell a story of the New Education movement, an international movement in the late-19th and early-20th century by such educators and intellectuals as John Dewey, Maria Montessori, Francis Parker, inspired by Johann Heinrich Pestalozzi, Johann Friedrich Herbart and others, who wanted to develop a child-centered pedagogy based on children's desire to learn and their participation through practical work.[5] In Japan, the

4  I thank Mrs. Oguchi Etsuko, a former Kishikō teacher and independent scholar, and Mrs. Kakimoto and Mr. Karatsu, physics teachers at Kishikō, for sharing various materials and time. The original objects of the photos as well as school records used in this chapter are all stored at Kishikō's archival room. The cataloguing of preserved instruments was done and published in 2002 by Mr. Yasufumi Nakaoka, a former physics teacher at Kishikō. The Third High collection is particularly well known and well catalogued. See Yukiko Nagahira, *Kindai nihon to butsuri jikken kiki: Kyoto daigaku shozō Meiji Taishoki butsuri jikken kiki* (Kyoto: Kyoto daigaku shuppankai, 2001).

5  The "new education" movement was also called the "new school" movement in England, and the "progressive education" movement in the US. For the New Education movement in Japan, see Sekai kyōikushi kenkyūkai, *Nihon kyōiku shi*, vols. I and II (Toyo: Kōdansha, 1975); Nagao Tomiji, ed., *Shin kyōiku undō no riron* (Tokyo: Meiji tosho, 1988); Kiuchi Yōichi,

New Education Movement developed into the Taisho Liberal Education movement [*Taishō jiyū kyōiku undō*] of the 1920s, culminating in the establishment
of such alternative schools as Seijō Elementary School and Jiyū Gakuen and
new media for children such as Suzuki Miekichi's magazine *Akai tori*. "New
Science," *shin rika*, was a part of this international movement. While the New
Science Education Movement in Japan has rarely received attention from
scholars, it provides an interesting case in which liberal ideals of New Science
were materialized by the government that deemed science education also
important but for more practical purposes. The honeymoon between the state
and the liberal science educators was short-lived, and its results were disap-
pointing to most advocates of New Science.

Yet, the school science room, the physical trace of this honeymoon, tells
more about Japan in the 1910s. I locate the Kishikō's science classrooms at the
intersection of the Great War and the international education movement, as
well as that of Japan's industrial growth and colonial expansion. My goal is to
connect the school science room to WWI through a set of networks that become
visible by examining various factors behind the new science room. They are
the networks of educators, of commercialized educational materials, of the
empire, and of what I call pedagogical seeing.

## The Room: State Policy and the New Science Education Movement

In 1918, Kishikō was very proud to have completed its new science rooms:

> Our school wanted to use this opportunity to improve teaching environ-
> ment for biology, not just physics and chemistry, within the budget allo-
> cated for the latter subjects. We built a new biology room, remodeled the
> old biology room into a chemistry room for both lecture and experiment;
> we remodeled the physics storage room into a physics experiment room;
> the physics room with stair seating now became an exclusively physics
> lecture room. We furnished shelves in each room to store tools. This way,
> without any problem, we were able to upgrade all rooms for biology,
> physics, and chemistry. ...As a result, our school came to possess science
> rooms that were worthy of pride for a junior high school.[6]

"Nihon ni okeru herubaruto-ha kyōikugaku no juyō to tenkai," in *Kindai kyōiku shisō no
tenkai*, eds. Hayashu Tadayuki and Morikawa Naoshi (Tokyo: Fukumura shuppan, 2000).

6  Kōshi hensan iinkai, *Kishidawa kōtōgakkō no daiisseiki* (Kishiwada, Osaka: Osaka furitsu
   kishiwada kōtō gakkō, 1997), 183.

One room for biology, one room for chemistry, and two rooms for physics – four rooms assigned specifically for the science curriculum in a local junior high school: sounds extravagant indeed (Figure 16.1).

Science rooms, together with those ubiquitous drawings of room layout, are the quintessential visual embodiment and footprints of the New Science Education Movement in Taisho Japan. This is clear from pages of *Rika Kyōiku* [Science Education], a journal that began in 1918. Dedicated to the New Science Education ideals, this was the first journal in Japan that specialized in science pedagogy. Drawings of the science room layouts frequently appeared as part of the reports that various schools throughout the nation sent to the editors; they proudly demonstrated, through such submissions, their commitment to the new education.

New Science Education ideals had been introduced to Japan by the turn of the century, but the explicit promotion of student experiments began to be published in the early 1910s. Tanahashi Gentarō's 1913 publication, *Science Education Pedagogy* [Shin rika kyōjuhō], is considered the pivotal text in this movement. A great advocate of Henry Armstrong's "heuristic method" (translated to "discovery method" in Japanese), Tanahashi emphasized the importance of giving an opportunity for children to "discover" on their own through direct observation and experimentation. This book was written after his time

FIGURE 16.1    *Kishiko at the time.*

spent studying abroad in Germany and the US, and he tirelessly advocated the necessity of experiment rooms that "in the West, even elementary schools, let alone junior high schools, have."[7] Throughout the 1910s and early 1920s, New Science promoters in Japan devoured pedagogical theories by Johann Heinrich Pestalozzi, Johann Friedrich Herbart, Henry Armstrong, Liberty Hyde Bailey and John Dewey, and discussed new developments such as New Schools, Nature Studies, and general science education in the US and Europe. Those who studied abroad passionately reported back the latest trends they observed at schools and science museums in major cities such as Chicago, New York, Berlin, and Paris, as well as smaller cities like Gary, Indiana, that were receiving international attention. The New Education was a buzzword both in the West and in Japan.

To many advocates, students' direct experience with natural phenomena, rather than memorization of the textbook or passive observation of the teacher's demonstration, was the key to a truly scientific education. For them, this was not about an efficient accumulation of scientific facts in the student's brain. It was meant to be a more holistic, fundamental education to create a thinking person with the independent, scientific, and civic mind. Students' hands-on experimentation and the well-equipped science room that enabled it were deemed essential to this ideal.[8]

In Japan, for many advocates, the ultimate objective of the New Science Education Movement was to nurture the scientific spirit among the Japanese people, as a critical challenge to the Meiji curricula by the authoritarian, bureaucratic state and its militarism. For example, Sano Riki, professor of architecture at Tokyo Imperial University, advocated science as "the only thing that would secure the future of the nation" against "empty

---

7  Tanahashi Gentarō, *Shin rika kyōjuhō* (1913), quoted in *Nippon kagaku gijutsushi taikei*, v. 9, ed. Nihon kagakushi gakkai (Tokyo: Daiichi hōki shuppan, 1965), 380. Tanahashi carried on the New Science Education Movement in his own way even after he became the director of the Tokyo Museum (predecessor of the National Science Museum). For Tanahashi, see Miyazaki Jun, *Tanahashi Gentarō: Hakubutsugaku ni kaketa shōgai* (Seki, Gifu Prefecture: Gifuken hakubutsukan tomo no kai, 1992).

8  Sally G. Kholstedt, *Teaching Children Science: Hands-On Nature Study in North America, 1890–1930* (Chicago: University of Chicago Press, 2010). It is interesting to note that, unlike the important contribution that women educators made to the American Nature Studies movement, the Japanese counterpart lacked a significant woman figure. See also John L. Rudolph, "Turning Science to Account: Chicago and the General Science Movement in Secondary Education, 1905–1920." *Isis*, v. 96, n. 3 (September 2005): 353–389. It is also interesting that WWI does not play any significant role in these American movements in the accounts by Kohlstead and Rudolph.

patriotism...constructed through the education that renders dying in the war into the sole ethics." Likewise, Sawayanagi Seitarō founded Seijō Gakuen in 1917, a famed alternative school of the Taisho Liberal Education Movement with a very progressive curriculum, to challenge the authoritarian and bureaucratic politics. Wada Yaezō, who was in charge of the science curriculum at Seijō Gakuen, was trained at a liberal arts college in the US, not at a Japanese normal school. Wada argued that the purpose of science education should be "to develop and nurture the scientific intelligence to secure and improve the life of the people [kokumin] for the next generation."[9]

While the New Science Education promoters assumed that the revision of science education would take a long time in Japan, the onset of WWI betrayed this pessimism. As the war continued in Europe, Japan was no longer able to import crucial industrial and pharmaceutical materials from Europe. This posed a serious challenge to a Japanese economy that had relied so heavily on Western products and resources. The Japanese government immediately issued special directives and established various ad hoc commissions for the purpose of promoting domestic research and development (R&D), leading to the opening of numerous research centers, an increase in university chairs in the fields of science and engineering, the establishment of private research funding, and so forth. "Domestic production" became a key phrase for solving the immediate problems as well as for determining the future direction of Japan.[10]

The government and industry considered science education crucial for this new direction. Expecting the practical result along the lines of the Meiji slogan "Wealthy Nation, Strong Military," the Taisho government expanded the science curriculum. At the elementary school, science now began at the 4th grade rather than the 5th grade. At the middle school, hours for science increased from four hours a week in the fourth and fifth years to additional two hours a week in the third year as well.

The Diet also approved the special budget of 205,220 yen in 1917 to finance new science room constructions at the nation's junior high schools and normal schools. The following year, the Ministry of Education issued "the Guideline for Student Experiment in Physics and Chemistry at Middle Schools," requiring all the junior high schools and normal schools to incorporate student experiments into the classroom. The 1918 Guideline stipulated in detail which lessons in physics and chemistry textbooks needed to be accompanied by what kind of

9      *Nippon kagaku gijutsu taikei*, v. 9, 383.
10     See Bartholomew, *Formation of Japanese Science*, for details.

practical work.[11] Renowned biologist Oka Asajirō described this sudden promotion of science as follows:

In the past, shortsighted politicians and businessmen treated science as
if it were a hobby of dilettantes, paying no attention to its benefit. Now,
facing the great problem [caused by the war in Europe], people suddenly
started talking about science, just like a herd of birds flying up at once,
and loudly demanding the promotion of scientific research.[12]

New Science Education promoters welcomed this state initiative. Tanahashi
Gentarō responded by writing in his *Revised New Science Pedagogy* in 1918 that
"I assumed that it would take a decade or some decades for Japan to accept
student experiments in the classroom, but due to the European War, it was all
of sudden put into practice, only several years after [the initial publication of
this book]. I am deeply satisfied."[13] In the words of one junior high teacher in
Hiroshima, "for us the science teachers, this is the most rewarding time in our
profession."[14]

Local governments were even more enthusiastic about the promotion of
science education than the central government in Tokyo. When the central government requested supplemental budgets from each prefectural government,
prefectural governments responded immediately and enthusiastically, though
the amount of funding they came up with varied greatly. For example, Ishikawa
Prefecture set aside 29,000 yen within its 1918 budget, but Iwate Prefecture only
set aside 13,000 yen.[15] Nationally, the total of 1,689,569 yen was contributed
from prefectural governments. The total of 377 schools in the nation – 232

11    Monbushō, "Chūgakko butsuri oyobi kagaku seito jikken yōmoku" in *Nihon kagaku gijut-
      sushi taikei*, Vol. 9: 388–389. Nagata Eiji, *Shin rika kyōiku nyūmon* (Tokyo: Hoshinowa kai,
      2003): 34–37. The 1917 supplemental budget did not cover any Girls Higher Schools.
      However, most Girls Higher School did incorporate student experiment into curriculum
      as much as they could. About 20% of Girls Higher Schools were furnished with the experi-
      ment room separate from the instruction room. Matusno Sachiko and Isozaki Tetsuo,
      "Rika kyōikushi ni okeru jendaa no mondai, zenpen," *Rika kyōikugaku kenkyū*, v. 44, n. 2
      (2004): 40–41.
12    Oka Aasajirō, "Rika kyōiku no tettei," *Tōa no hikari* (September 1918), quoted in *Rika
      kyōikushi shiryō* (Toko: Tokyo Hōrei shuppan, 1986–1987), vol. 1: 221–222.
13    *Nippon kagaku gijutsushi taikei*, v. 9, 381.
14    Ooshima Chinji, "Chūgakko ni okeru rikagakuka setsubi mondai," *Gakkō kyōiku*, vol. 5,
      no. 5 (March 1918): 2.
15    Kataoka Shūji & Isozaki Tetsuō, "Taishō-ki no chūgakkō kagaku seitojikken ni kansuru
      chiiki jittaishi kenkyū," *Nihon kyōka kyōiku gakkaishi*, vol. 26, no.3 (Dec 2003): 12.

public junior high schools, 53 private junior high schools, and 12 normal schools – applied for the special funding. One school received anywhere between 420 yen and 8917 yen. The average amount per school was 2600 yen, of which only 550 yen came from the central government's budget.[16] This reflected the expectation these local governments held that the science education should contribute to local industry and economy.

Building new science experiment rooms was costly because the rooms required water, gas, and electricity, in addition to various equipment, storage space, specialized benches, and ideally a dark room. One of the most extravagant cases was Hiroshima Higher Normal School's Junior High, which spent as much as 19,115 yen to construct chemistry and physics experiment rooms from scratch.[17] Yet, this figure was not completely outrageous. In Ōita Prefecture, 14% of the schools spent more than 10,000 yen on room construction.[18] When funding from the governments failed to cover all the costs, some prefectures raised tuition.[19]

As a result of this new policy, most junior high schools in the nation obtained a science room. According to a survey conducted in 1921, only 13% of junior highs lacked a room specifically designated for science experiments. As there were 385 junior high schools in Japan at the time, a simple calculation reveals that only about 50 schools in the entire nation had no separate science room. The majority of the junior high schools were equipped with one or two science rooms, multi-tasking them for physics, chemistry, and biology. On the other end of the spectrum were about 15% of the schools that had the luxury of having three or four separate rooms to be used for each subject of science, as was the case of Kishikō.[20]

Kishikō teachers must have been very pleased with the expansion of the science rooms, as the New Education movement was popular there too. According to the school chronicle,

> The new trend of the New Education influenced Kishiwada as well. Workshops and study groups were frequently held at each school, across

16    These figures are based on "Rika jikken hojokin no wariate," *Gakkō kyōiku*, v. 55 (May 1918), 82, and "Rika jikkenhi hojo," *Tokyo Asahi shimbun*, Janary, 17, 1918. Also see Kataoka and Isozaki. Initially there was a debate as to how much private schools should benefit from this distribution of funding. "Rikagaku shisetsu hi," *Tokyo Asahi shimbun*, January 14, 1918: 4.

17    Kataoka & Isozaki, 14.

18    Kataoka & Isozaki, 12.

19    Kataoka & Isozaki, 14; Sakai Yūsuke and Isozaki Tetsuo, "Rikagaku seito jikken ni kannsuru rekishiteki kenkyū: Shizuoka ken no chūgakko oyobi shihan gakkō no jittaishi o chūshin toshite," *Rika kyōikugaku kenkyū*, vol. 46, no. 1 (2005): 45.

20    Kataoka & Isozaki, 15.

the city, and across the prefecture, to exchange ideas about theoretical and practical aspects of the New Education.... When a national conference or workshop took place, teachers went whether it was in [nearby cities like] Nara and Akashi or remote cities such as Hiroshima, Tokyo, and Nagano, using their own pocket money.[21]

Records show that Kishikō teachers also went to lecture at workshops for elementary school teachers.[22] Kishikō's rich collection of science materials was in part a result of these teachers who used their own pocket money to learn and teach the latest educational trend and pedagogical techniques. Although we do not have a record of how much Kishikō received for the new science rooms, the scale of the construction indicates a large amount. This was no doubt assisted by the fact that the Senshū region was economically supported by the booming textile industry.[23]

In other words, those newly constructed science rooms at Kishikō embodied the educators' desire to introduce the student-centered *learning* environment, the government's demand for an effective *teaching* environment for an internationally competitive Japan, and the local government's expectation for more vigorous economy.

Student experiment required more than the physical space of the room. Experiment instruments were also a necessary part of the science room. The next section will place the science room at the intersection of the growing domestic industry of scientific instruments, and the formation of a new middle class that composed the student body at junior high schools in Taisho Japan.

### The Physics Experiment Room : Capitalism and the Rise of the New Middle Class.

Kishikō purchased a variety of experiment materials for the physics and chemistry curricula in 1918 and 1919. The surviving school ledger gives us an excellent look at what tools and materials educators purchased. In 1918, Kishikō spent

21    *Kishidawa kōtōgakkō no daiisseiki*, 174.

22    *Kaihō*, vol. 21 (November 1919): 1. *Kaihō* was the monthly school journal of Kishiwada Junior High.

23    Its largest spinning factory, Kishiwada Bōseki, is remembered for the 1930 strike by Korean and Japanese factory girls. Kim Ch'an-jŏng, *Chōsenjin jokō no uta* (Tokyo: Iwanami shinsho, 1982). Prefectures and areas that had budgetary problems could not allocate much funding for the student experiment requirement, as was the case with Shizuoka Prefecture. See Sakai & Isozaki.

335 yen on physics; it made no purchase specifically for chemistry. In 1919, the expense for physics was 444 yen 40 sen, while chemistry was 103 yen 22 sen. The most expensive purchases included a generator (dynamo) for 290 yen, a voltage converter for 280 yen, and an electric bulb for 140 yen, all for physics experiments. Since the previous years' expenses had been much smaller, we can assume that these 1918 and 1919 purchases were made with help of the government special funding (Figure 16.2). Some items were clearly for student experiments, such as an order of fifty-five burette tables in 1918.

Yet, if we also examine Meiji entries on the ledger, it becomes immediately clear that this was not the only time that Kishikō purchased expensive materials for the science curriculum. In fact, Kishikō purchased experiment tools most actively in the 1900s, well before the government initiative; especially during the years following the opening of the school in 1897, Kishikō spent even more than during the Taisho period (Figure 16.3). The late Meiji purchases included very expensive items, such as a projector (magic lantern) in 1901 for 300 yen (including sets of educational slides), and a Crookes tube for 380 yen for a teacher to demonstrate an experiment of electrostatic discharge. This indicates that Kishikō was probably able to use most of the supplemental funding during WWI for the room construction and remodeling, as the school had already accumulated decent sets of materials over the last two decades. Subsequently, it is possible to speculate that the 1918 ordinance by the Ministry of Education mattered most crucially to those junior high schools that were newly established and needed to furnish science rooms from scratch.

And there were many such schools, as middle school education expanded dramatically in Taisho Japan. From 1917 to 1926, the number of junior high schools jumped about by 1.6, from 329 to 518. The number of students increased at an even higher pace, as the 1917 revision of the Junior High School Edict increased the enrollment cap per school from 600 to 800. In 1895, only 5% of boys in Japan went on to the middle school level. By the end of the Taisho period, the figure reached almost 20%. In actual numbers, students who attended junior high schools more than doubled from 147,467 in 1917 to 316,759 in 1926. This was the case for girls too. In 1895, only 1.3% girls went to a middle school (girls' higher school, girls' normal school, or equivalent practical schools); in 1925, the figure was 14.1%. The middle-school student enrollment, for both boys and girls, continued to increase through prewar years. As the income level of the Japanese increased, more Japanese went beyond the compulsory elementary school.[24]

---

24    See Monkashō, Chapter three "Chūgakko Kōtō jogakkō no hatten," in *Gakusei hya-kunenshi* <http://www.mext.go.jp/b_menu/hakusho/html/others/detail/1317552.htm>,

FIGURE 16.2 *Rotating mirror purchased by Kishiko in 1918 [photo taken by the author].*

Thus, the Ministry of Education's ordinance to promote student experiment at the junior high level should not be understood as targeting only the small

accessed Oct 3, 2011); and Kikuchi Shōji, "Darega chūtō gakkō ni shingaku shitaka: Kindai nihon ni okeru chūtō kyōiku kikai saikō," *Osaka daigaku kyōikugaku nenpō*, vol. 2 (1997).

FIGURE 16.3    *Vacuum pump purchased by Kishiko in late Meiji.*

number of the nation's elite. Middle schools, especially junior highs, were increasingly becoming part of ordinary middle-class life in Taisho Japan. It makes sense that New Science Education promoters tended to speak as if junior high education were part of the fundamental, civic education. As I quoted earlier, advocates such as Wada considered it to be part of the "people's life" of the next generation, not as the specialized, privileged preparation for high school entrance examination for the tiny elite.

Consequently, the function of junior high school was greatly debated during WWI years and in the 1920s. As more and more young Japanese went on to attend junior high schools, its significance as the place for the higher civic education gained more attention. Since only a small percentage of junior high graduates went on further to high schools (prep schools for college), more educators and policy makers began to think that the role of junior high schools should be the producer of the solid middle strata of the Japanese population and labor force, rather than that of the elite leaders of the nation. At the same time, however, since the competition to enter high schools became fiercer (a larger number of junior high students competing over the limited spots in high schools), preparation for the entrance exams became a more urgent agenda for junior high schools.[25] These two goals were not compatible, with a competing priority over the efficient memorization of information necessary for entrance examinations vs. the fundamental understanding of the natural laws that called for time-consuming student experiment.[26] The junior high science room, therefore, was not only the embodiment of the promotion of science education but also contained competing visions for the role of the middle school education that directly reflected the formation of a new middle class in Taisho Japan.

Another important dimension of the physical space of the school science room is experiment tools. The dominant supplier of experiment tools at Kishikō was a company named Shimadzu Corporation [Shimadzu Seisakusho]. This was the case with most schools of all levels, including elementary schools as well as prestigious high schools such as the Third High and the Fourth High, especially in the Kansai region where the company headquarters were located. The government could not even have conceived of mandating all junior high schools to utilize student experiments, had there not been the availability of reasonably-priced domestic supplies of experiment materials and the maturity of that industry. This material factor behind the government policy should not be taken lightly. Shimadzu Corporation's growth as the pioneer in this area was a pre-requisite for the science education reform during WWI in Japan.

Shimadzu Corporation was established in 1875 by Shimadzu Genzō in Kyoto.[27] Son of a craftsman of Buddhist alters, Genzō transformed his craft knowledge of metal and wood works into a new business in scientific instruments, with an amazing entrepreneur vision and training received from Gottfried Wagener, a government-hired chemical engineer from Germany whose office, Seimikyoku (an industrial chemistry laboratory later to be

---

25    One new public junior high school in Tokyo attempted to resolve this tension by "training the person with characters [*jinkakusha*] by prioritizing scientific observation skills as the foundation of daily life...when science education these days regrettably inclined to become too practical..." This Sixth Junior High in Tokyo proposed to incorporate a more holistic "nature studies" approach rather than relying on the existing division of the school subjects, to use the reader materials to acquire scientific knowledge, and to visit the newly built Riken [National Physics and Chemistry Research Institute] across the street as part of field trips. "Rikagaku to shutosuru shinsetsu no furitsu gochū," *Tokyo Asahi shimbun*, December 17, 1918: 5.

26    Kinoshita Michiko, "Kindai nihon no chūtō kyōiku: *Kyōiku jiron* ni miru daiichiji sekaitaihen kaishi zengo no kyōikukan," *Shikan*, 144 (March 2001), 119–121.

27    This is the same Shimadzu Corporation where Tanaka Kōichi, Nobel Prize laureate in chemistry in 2002, is employed.

incorporated into the Third High School), was located across the street from Genzō's store. By the early 1880s, Genzō began manufacturing a wide range of scientific and medical instruments, won prizes at various industrial fairs in Japan, and established his name in the industry of scientific and educational instruments.

Under his son, Shimadzu Genzō Jr., who succeeded him in the business, the company developed into the first-rate corporation in Japan. Born gifted in mechanical and physical engineering, Genzō Jr. grew up in his father's store and Wagener's lab. At the age of fifteen, Genzō succeeded in manufacturing the electric generator in 1885 by modeling after the Wimshurst influence machine, which had been perfected by James Wimshurst only a few years earlier. Genzō Jr.'s machine immediately became available to schools in Japan as the "Shimadzu electricity" and was used widely for decades. At the age of nineteen, Genzō Jr. began teaching at the Kyoto Normal School. Meanwhile, Shimadzu expanded its business by building new branch stores in Osaka, Okayama, and Kanazawa and by adding more space to its factories and main store front in Kyoto, with the entire second floor dedicated to displaying instruments and demonstrating experiments.[28]

The 1890s and 1900s, the decades of Shimadzu's rapid growth, coincided with the establishment of higher education in Japan, especially in the Kansai region. Newly opened schools included the Third High in 1894, Osaka Industrial College [Osaka kyōgyō daigaku] in 1896, Kyoto Imperial University and especially its College of Science and Engineering in 1897, and Nara Women's Normal School in 1908. The earliest junior high schools in Kansai opened their doors during those decades, including Kishikō in 1897. Shimadzu grew as the higher education system in Japan did. By 1906, its catalogue listed more than 3000 instruments in a wide range of areas including mechanics, electromagnetics, thermology, acoustics, optics, radium, and chemistry.[29]

Until the mid-Meiji period, most scientific instruments in Japan were imported from Europe and the US. They were expensive. British products were in general the most expensive, followed by German products. Starting in the mid 1880s, however, domestic products began to enter the market. According to records of Third High School, among its experiment and research instruments acquired between 1898 and 1924, fifty recorded items were domestic products, with 36 of them by Shimadzu.[30] By the 1900s, when Kishikō made

---

28   Shimadzu seisakusho, *Shimadzu seisakusho shi* (Kyoto: Shimadzu seisakusho, 1967), 9–10, 13.

29   *Shimadzu seisakusho shi*, 20–21.

30   *Kindai nihon to butsuri jikken kiki*, 75.

numerous purchases, the school was able to procure a wide range of materials from Shimadzu (specimen, physics lab tools, so forth) for a more affordable price. Approximately half of all Kishokō's materials were made by or purchased via Shimadzu.

The ascendance of Shimadzu did not happen automatically. Since the mid Meiji period, Shimadzu marketed its products aggressively, by holding experiment demonstrations throughout the nation at various meetings and conferences related to education. Once the state announced the new guideline for student experiments, Shimadzu added a new line of experiment tools accordingly, such as measuring scales and experiment benches. That is, things that had been imported so far, Shimadzu took an aggressive initiative to mass-produce, anticipating the needs created by the curriculum change. Shimadzu also successfully marketed its storage batteries useful for newly constructed school experiment rooms. Scholarship on science education rarely pays attention to companies such as Shimadzu, but it is worth considering the role that these companies and their marketing strategies might have played in the promotion of students' experiments in Japan.

Shimadzu greatly profited from the state promotion of science in Japan during the Great War. It met the urgent needs created by the blockage of European imports as well as the drastic expansion of research centers, higher educational institutions in science and engineering, the mandate for student experiments at junior high and normal schools, and the "experiment boom" among elementary and girls' schools. In the absence of German products, for example, Shimadzu's GS Storage Battery, developed in the 1900s, came to receive orders from the Navy and the Ministry of Transportation, as well as from research centers and schools. To solve "the national crisis," Shimadzu made its battery section into a new buttery company, with a financial help of Mitsubishi. Shimadzu itself became a corporation in 1917, with the backing of powerful finance houses in Kansai, as its market expanded to include the colonies. At the end of the war, Shimadzu Corporation was one successful business that supplied scientific instruments to the empire.

### The Specimen Collection: The Empire and Pedagogical Seeing

Biology was not a subject included in the government science education reform, but it was an important subject for the New Science Education movement. In the final Section I invite the reader to Kishikō's biology room, where WWI enriched its specimen collection as well.

Kishikō's biology room boasted a rich specimen collection of insects, animals, plants, and minerals. The school record shows that it had already accumulated a good collection by the mid 1910s. This may have something to do with one teacher who taught biology in 1899–1901 at Kishikō, Kuriyama Shōhei. Kuriyama was a skilled collector-researcher of plants and sea creatures and a friend of Minakata Kumagusu, one of the most internationally renowned Japanese naturalists at the time. Kuriyama remained an active collector-researcher during his Kishikō years; we know this because his specimen of a *myra cleris galil* (tenaga kobushi gani) submitted in 1899 from Kishiwada is still preserved in the Tokyo Imperial University Natural History Museum. Kishikō's numerous tools for dissection as well as various specimens of plants, animal body parts, and stuffed animals were probably ordered by him during his three-year tenure. His personal role, however, should not be over-emphasized, as many materials, including nice Leica microscopes, were also purchased after he had transferred to another school.

Kishikō's collection in fact testifies to the wide distribution of specimen boxes and jarred animals in formalin at the junior high level by the 1910s. As explained earlier, New Science advocates considered direct observation of natural objects as an important pedagogical process. Shimadzu's role here, just like its role in physics and chemistry experiment instruments, was immense. Shimadzu established a new Specimen Production section in 1891, steadily expanded it over the years, and dominated the market well before the science education promotion during WWI. Kishikō was one of many schools in the nation that contributed to Shimadzu's sales by continuing to order new sets of specimen collections as the company expanded its repertoires.

An immense impact on Kishikō's biology room by WWI is apparent. For example, as we have seen, the school managed to use the government supplement funding for physics and chemistry to build a new biology room as well. Kishikō also purchased a particularly large number of mineral, botanical, and animal specimens in 1917, 1918, and 1919, along with physics and chemistry experiment equipment.

New purchases for the biology class included more than 50 specimens that the school principal, Miura Kikutarō, collected during his trip in 1918 to Nan'yo, the South Pacific region that Japan occupied due to German retreat. It is worth noting that a local junior high principal was touring Nan'yo already, before the official conclusion of the war. Most likely, Miura joined an "observation trip" orchestrated by the local government or the military for educators, as this was a common way for schoolteachers to visit the Empire. We know, for example, that Miura's successor, Principal Ochiai, went to Manchuria three times as part of his official duty.[31]

Principal Miura, upon returning from his 10-day trip to Nan'yo on September 4, gave a lecture titled "About Newly Occupied Nan'yo" in front of the entire school. In detail, he explained Nan'yo's geography, peoples, customs, natural resources and their significance for the Japanese Empire. His lecture was full of numbers (as to specific locations of islands, population of the native peoples, etc) and detailed names. "There are those who speak of birth control these days," Principal Miura spoke: "But I disagree. Our population should be larger, and we should send our energetic youth abroad to the south and the north." He ended his talk with a message: Japanese capitalists seem to exploit native laborers, but such phenomena darkens the future of Japan and should be amended. Together with this story, Principal Miura brought back specimens of a hawks bill turtle, a long-tail tropicbird, a sea shell of *Cassis cornutus* – all stuffed and preserved – as well as a boxed collection of tropical plants native in Nan'yo and many more: the total of more than fifty sets of specimen. They were displayed at school first and then used for class.[32]

The natural history materials in the classroom, therefore, were not simply a collection of dead animals and stones simply stuffed in wooden boxes. These specimens came with narratives and meanings attached, of the Nan'yo as an exotic place with tropical plants, rare creatures, important natural resources, unfamiliar peoples, and most importantly of the triumphant Japanese Empire that now occupied such a far-away territory. They transformed Kishiko students into the scientific Japanese who could categorize those fauna, flora, and native peoples into the systematic knowledge with academic names. They bridged the periphery of the empire and a not-so-urban region of the metropole, erasing the physical as well as psychological distance that might have hindered those boys from becoming adventurers and honorable capitalists.

---

31    Ochiai's third trip was to participate in the All Junior High School Principals Conference of Greater Japan, held in Shinkyo in 1934. *Kishiwada kōtō gakkō no daiisseiki*, 181. Records show that as early as 1906, three teachers and six students from Kishiko visited Manchuria and Korea. For school trips at other schools, see Song An'nei, "Hyōgoken kyōikukai ni yoru kyōin no 'shina mansen shisatsu ryokō,'" *Shakai shisutemu kenkyū*, v. 21: 115–142. See also Ueda Takuji, "Meijiki o shutoshita 'kaigai kankō ryokō' nit suite," *Nagoya gaikokugo daigaku gendai kokusai gakubu kiyō*, vol. 6 (March 2010).

32    His talk was later published in *Kaihō*, vol. 21 (November 1918), "Supplement": 1–15. Quote on page 14.

We may say that the newly acquired specimen collections from Nan'yo provided a "pedagogical seeing" of the empire. The prevalence of pedagogical seeing in Taisho Japan is well documented by scholars who have studied fairs and exhibitions.[33] During the decade and half of Taisho, there held at least 116 major exhibitions and fairs.[34] It is, perhaps, possible to say that commercialized imperial spectacle and pedagogical seeing defined Taisho culture. Iwan Rhys Morus argues that seeing – and its power to convince the viewer – was a central aspect of science as the process of knowledge-making and knowledge-legitimizing in the 19th century Europe.[35] This was true even after science became a firmly established field of knowledge. In Taisho Japan, too, seeing was considered crucial for the scientific education of the masses, as Tanahashi Gentarō and New Science promoters argued.

The Japanese indeed saw a great deal of "science" in numerous fairs and exhibitions. Take, for example, the most popular fair in Taisho Japan, the Tokyo Taisho Exhibition of 1914 that attracted 6,470,000 visitors during the four months of its opening. As the mission of this fair was to showcase the progress Japan made since the Meiji Restoration, science and technology was a major display factor. Visitors saw the first domestically produced Japanese car, DAT, the predecessor of Datsun; the cable car that went over Shinobazu-no-ike; the first escalator in Japan; and various agricultural and industrial technologies in pavilions such as the Coal Mine Pavilion (the first pavilion devoted to the industry). Even an entertainment pavilion, the Island of Beauties, was advertised as the "application of science," as the clever use of light and mirrors magically illuminated beautiful women like magic lanterns.[36] The fantastic technological and scientific advancement was displayed side by side with the pavilions from the Japanese empire such as the Taiwan Pavilion and the Korea Pavilion.

The symbiosis of science and the empire on the fairground was seen at many other popular exhibitions. The Peace Exhibition of 1922, held at Ueno Park to commemorate the end of WWI, featured the "water airplane," the modified glider that roamed around on the water of Shinobazu-no-ike with the Asahi beer advertisement; and a real airplane produced by Japanese at the Airplane Pavilion. Also occupying this exhibition space, along with other

---

33    For example, see Yoshimi Shun'ya, *Hakurankai no seijigaku: manazashi no kindai* (Tokyo: Chūō kōronsha, 1992).

34    Yasuda Masahiko and Yasuda Toshiyuki, "Ehagaki ni miru taishō jidai no hakurankai," *Tezukayama gakuin daigaku kenkyū ronshū*, no. 42 (2007): 34–35.

35    Iwan Rhys Morus, "Seeing and Believing Science," *Isis*, v. 97 n. 1 (March 2006): 101–110.

36    Yamada and Yasuda, 40.

industrial and technological pavilions, were colonial pavilions such as the Nan'yo Pavilion, the Korea Pavilion, and the Manchu-Mongolian Pavilion.[37]

Kishikō's science classroom belonged to this Taisho Japan. Students did not have to travel to a far-away exhibition to see the flora and fauna of Nan'yo; the empire came to them in boxes of specimen, together with the principal's story of the place and its significance to the empire. It is possible to assume that many other schools' science rooms were connected to the empire through this pedagogical seeing, as Kishikō was one of numerous schools whose principals and teachers were invited to join the tour of Nan'yo and other parts of the empire.

### Beyond the Science Room

Despite initial enthusiasm, New Education Science movement promoters were disappointed by the lack of any immediate effect of student experiments on children's learning. One most frequently mentioned reason was the lack of teachers capable of effectively guiding student experiments. For example, Kanbe Isaburō, in his 1922 book, *Learning-Centered New Pedagogy of Science*, lamented that many teachers simply transferred the burden of doing the experiments to the student. He also criticized that teachers often cared more about strictly following the guideline instruction than using experiments as an opportunity to induce their curiosity and questions.[38]

Disappointment like Kanbe's was shared by elementary school teachers who quickly dominated the New Science Education movement. It was probably and ironically because of the lack of special government funding that elementary school educators actively discussed and exchanged ideas about how to make simple experimental tools by themselves and how to guide students within the confines of limited resources. In the words of Ujiie Yuuki, the author of *Detailed Instruction of Science Experiments in Elementary School*, "it was a big mistake to think that students' scientific mind would be nurtured if they conducted experiments by themselves."[39] The frustration turned to despair when in the 1930s the reactionary emphasis on ultra-nationalist spiritualism in education dumped the New Science Education movement and the succeeding Liberal Education movement.

---

37    Yamada and Yasuda, 49–51.

38    Kanbe Isaburō, *Rika no shin shidōhō* (1922), in *Nippon kagaku gijutsushi* vol. 9, 395.

39    Nagata, *Shin rika kyōiku nyūmon*, 36.

As Ujiie's words reveal, however, the sense of disappointment came from their assumption that doing experiments would automatically lead students to the "scientific mind," a kind of independent, critical mind they envisioned. While it is understandable that child-centered learning and self-discovery were meant to challenge the more authoritarian style of textbook memorization, conducting experiments as told by teachers does not inherently entail an exercise of a critical mind or democratic politics.

Mark Lincicome in his study of the "international education movement" in Japan between 1905 and 1931 argues that scholarship has painted too dominating a picture of the powerful school system disseminating emperor-centered nationalism. As a result, he maintains, it "tends to overlook, downplay, or dismiss evidence of challenges to the status quo that was allegedly established by the early 1890s. To appreciate the dynamic, even contentious history of educational development in Japan *after* 1890, and its convoluted role in the dissemination of nationalism and the formation of Japan's imagined community before World War II, requires that those challenges be examined more closely."[40] I agree with Lincicome, but the New Science Education movement examined in this chapter complicates this picture. The New Science Education movement shared the same pedagogical ideals with the other new education movements but was supported and materialized as part of the state promotion of science. It embodied both challenges to and support of the state's agenda, thereby refusing to be located in the binary of the emperor-centered nationalism and internationalism that Lincicome sets up.

This rejection of the binary illuminates the ambiguous place of science in wartime Japan (both World Wars) and in Taisho liberalism. Science experiments continued to be utilized at a higher rate in the curriculum. According to one survey, in 1921, after most junior high schools built science rooms, only 11 percent of the junior high schools fully incorporated student experiments into the third year curriculum as stipulated, 24% for the fourth year, and 32% for the fifth year. By 1928, however, the figure increased to 83% of all junior high schools.[41] This indicates that, while the immediate impact of the 1918 curriculum change was disappointingly limited to contemporary observers, its long-term effect – the normalization of student experiments – was far-reaching. At the same time, the high percentage of student experiments in the late 1920s did not convince the successors of New Education teachers, Taisho Liberal

---

40      Mark E. Lincicome, "Nationalism, Imperialism, and the International Education Movement in Early Twentieth-Century Japan," *Journal of Asian Studies*, v. 58, No. 2 (May 1999): 338–360 (the quote on 339).

41      Katagiri & Isozaki, 16.

Education reformers, that science education in Japan had improved. Their continuing frustration with the science curriculum, in fact, would later lead them to celebrate the next major science education reform in 1941, as the wartime government mobilized effective science pedagogy for total war. The tension between the wartime state ideology – emperor-centered ultra-nationalism – and liberal ideals of individuality and creative thinking was noticeable but ignored. Historians generally portray this as a hard-won triumph of liberal educators whose Taisho Movement failed but nonetheless persisted beyond the dark period of the 1930s. However, as I have argued elsewhere, science education could easily be mobilized for the production of the scientifically capable imperial subject obedient to the state and imperial duties. The vision of a scientific Japan, including the concept of the scientific mind, was something that could easily be co-opted into the state's goal of a militarily and economically competitive empire.[42] The case of the New Science Education movement in Taisho Japan demonstrates that the cooperation between the liberal education movement and the wartime government was already set in the years of WWI.

If we step outside of the science rooms, Kishikō's history does reveal something of which New Education advocates might have approved. Kishiko held theme-based educational fairs annually during the Taisho period. As seen in the list below, most of the themes were related to science and technology (in parenthesis are teachers who supervised the production):

> 1915 Measurement Fair (math and science teachers)
> 1916 Transportation Fair (geography teachers)
> 1917 Time Fair (math and science teachers)
> 1918 Letters Fair (reader and English teachers)
> 1919 Earth Fair (math, science, natural sciences, geography teachers)
> 1920 Energy Fair (math and science teachers)
> 1921 Measurement Fair (math and science teachers)[43]

For these fairs, students conducted their own research, consulted with experts at universities and research institutions, organized information, and presented it with visual display. In other words, here we actually see students actively involved in knowledge making for the public. Nearby elementary schools made a field trip to Kishikō fairs, Kyoto University professors were invited to give

42    Hiromi Mizuno, *Science for the Empire: Scientific Nationalism in Twentieth-century Japan* (Stanford: Stanford University Press, 2009).

43    *Kishiwada kōtō gakkō no daiisseiki*, 186–188. The pamphlet is mentioned on 188.

FIGURE 16.4    *Cover of a Kishiko student fair book, Records of the Earth Fair, 1918 (photo taken by the author).*

public lectures, and other schools borrowed materials and information from Kishikō in order to hold fairs on similar themes. Some fairs even resulted in publications such as a little booklet, "Report from the Earth Fair," that came out of the 1919 Earth Fair (Figure 16.4).[44]

It is impossible to read adequate and accurate meanings out of these school events here, as we have such scant records of science fairs at junior high schools in Taisho Japan. There is no indication that these events were promoted by the government, but there is also no information about how much students' initiative took place or what these fairs meant to the students. The science fairs at Kishikō were discontinued after 1921. Yet, these extra-curricular student activities strongly suggest that historians need to look not just at textbook and policy changes, but also at various events and activities that took place in and beyond the science classroom in order to better understand the New Science Education movement and the wartime state promotion of science.

In addition, rather than seeing the student experiment from the perspective of a success or failure of the liberal education, we want to pay attention to the colonial, commercial, and industrial networks that constituted the new space of the science rooms in Taisho Japan. This space was materialized not only due to the international education movement and the state wartime promotion of science, but also due to the availability of inexpensive experiment instruments that were domestically produced and vigorously marketed by Shimadzu. The space tells a story of a Japanese company taking advantage of WWI, transforming Japan reliant on European imports to a nation of competitive domestic supplies, and growing to be the dominant corporation for the empire. The space was also composed of specimen collections brought back from Nan'yo, the newly acquired territory of the Japanese empire, and an increasing number of students whose family background was becoming more middle-class than elite. Direct observation of the nature through these specimens provided a pedagogical seeing of the empire to students. The science room in Taisho Japan was a dynamic space. For a historian, it is a place composed of physical, intellectual, and political traces of various networks and stories of Taisho Japan, an archive of a sort.

44    *Kishiwada kōtō gakkō no daiisseiki*, 188.

# Of World History and Great Men
## A Japanese Village and Its Worlds

*Martin Dusinberre*

## The Demands of the Times

In March 1910, the public library of Murotsu village in Yamaguchi prefecture, western Japan, received three significant donations: 40 new books on "great men" (*ijin*), 30 books for the library's household section, and 400 books for the children's section, including a series on world history.[1] The latter were a gift from Yoshizaki Eisuke (1878–1952), scion of one of the oldest and most important households in Murotsu. In the 18th and 19th centuries, the Yoshizakis had made their fortunes as sake-brewers and merchants, and successive household heads served intermittently as "port elders" during the period when Murotsu, located in the southeast of what was then the Chōshū domain, became a key Inland Sea port in the "Western Circuit" trade route (established in the 1670s). As merchants, administrators, landowners, moneylenders, political leaders, local mediators and much more besides, Yoshizaki Eisuke's ancestors were typical of the *gōnō* ("rich farmer") class whose members did so much to stimulate Japan's protoindustrial and later regional industrial development in the 19th and early 20th centuries.[2] From both a local and a national perspective, therefore, Yoshizaki's 1910 gift to his village library, worth 50 yen, was nothing unusual. Indeed, along with fellow villager Yoshida Shūzō (1854–1939), who was also descended from an elite merchant household and who in 1910 was the Murotsu village postmaster, Yoshizaki would give generously to a variety of village causes until at least the mid-1930s. Both men were quick to respond to Home Ministry exhortations in the early 1900s that local elites contribute more to local infrastructure investments, including new administrative buildings and educational facilities.[3]

---

1　*Kifu-bo Murotsu-son yakuba*, Section 11. This is an uncatalogued document, incorrectly recorded as number 30, from the Murotsu Yakuba Monjo archive (hereafter MYM), currently held in the Kaminoseki Town Municipal Board of Education. All translations of the Murotsu archives are my own.

2　Edward E. Pratt, *Japan's Protoindustrial Elite: The Economic Foundations of the Gōnō* (Cambridge, MA: Harvard University Asia Center, 1999); see also Naofumi Nakamura, *Chihō kara no Sangyō Kakumei: Nihon ni okeru Kigyō Bokkō no Gendōryoku* (Nagoya: Nagoya daigaku shuppankai, 2010), chapter 5.

3　Carol Gluck, *Japan's Modern Myths: Ideology in the Late Meiji Period* (Princeton: Princeton University Press, 1985), 166.

© KONINKLIJKE BRILL NV, LEIDEN, 2014 | DOI 10.1163/9789004274273_019

But in the same month that Yoshizaki Eisuke gave a series of books on world history to his local library, there was a novel development in the village – one that highlighted Murotsu's own place in the world. On 28 March, the village council, which included both Yoshizaki and Yoshida among its elected representatives, passed a resolution to build a new assembly hall for the Murotsu municipal elementary school. In a subsequent "Statement of Aims" (April 1910), local bureaucrats explained both their rationale for this major project and also their plans for how to finance it. The "Statement" is a remarkable insight into the hopes and expectations of one group of village administrators at the beginning of the 1910s, and I quote it in full:

> At present, the speedy development of the nation and the dynamic progress of the times know no rest. It is to be expected that in national education, which is the basis of such progress, each locality compete in striving for the betterment of facilities and in planning for the vitality of humanity, such that local municipalities may achieve smooth development and there may be no delay in the progress of the state. Yet in a village such as our own Murotsu, these dynamics, alongside the extension of compulsory education, have together caused an increase in the number of children now entering school, suddenly revealing the paucity of our school facilities. In this financial year, as the accompanying council resolution states and as a matter of utmost urgency, we shall first construct general school buildings, of which the most necessary is the construction of an assembly hall appropriate both to house the Imperial Portrait and to be a venue for ceremonies. Moreover, within a few years we must construct additional buildings – and also a [new] village library, which will directly impact on school education.
>
>   Certainly, we cannot avoid the demands of the times. Nevertheless, in considering the financial strength of our village, it goes without saying that we cannot possibly deal with the burden of spending well over 10,000 yen for such education infrastructure at a time when we must also budget for future expenditures – such as the establishment of water mains, the dredging of the port, the construction of seawalls, and the repair of roads. As a result, we appeal for the assistance of all volunteers who harbor a deep sense of hometown love. We shall rely upon the cooperation of Murotsu villagers resident in Korea and Manchuria for the most sacrosanct and important building among those to be constructed, namely the assembly hall. That the assembly hall may be completed in this way – that by its construction we may mark the development of village education and not lag behind the progress of the times – is the

unceasing and passionately felt hope of the entire village population here in Murotsu.

Now more than ever, village conditions are steadily improving and we are attempting to chart the course of our livelihoods in new directions. At this time, if we are fortunate enough to obtain assistance and cooperation in our plan for education infrastructure, which is the basis of village affairs, it will greatly add to the fundamental spirit of the village population and stimulate yet more activities in all the village facilities – both from inside and outside the village. It will count as a marvelous municipal accomplishment, and it will be a permanent way of acknowledging His Imperial Majesty's munificent favor. Ah! The beautiful mountains and rivers, with the towering Mt. Ōza and the swirling waters of Yanagiura bay: truly, our beloved hometown is always in the hearts of Murotsu villagers living overseas. We fervently pray that through the understanding and intervention of every passionate, hometown-loving volunteer, we may be able to perfect the superior nature of our village and the educational aesthetic of our people.[4]

The "Statement" marked a shift in village affairs: for construction projects as big and as expensive as a new assembly hall, the rich farmer elites could not bear the burden of fundraising alone. In the absence of central government support for such projects and with top-down pressures on local governments to prioritize infrastructure investments of the sort listed in the "Statement" (water mains, roads, port improvements), local bureaucrats needed new streams of revenue; they needed, in short, a "new generation" of hometown patriots.[5]

On a first reading, it is easy to overlook the global scope of the "Statement" by focusing instead on its domestic implications. For example, it would be possible to read it through the lens of rural distress in the second decade of the 20th century. In 1910, Nagatsuka Takashi published *The Soil*, a novel set in Ibaraki prefecture, in which he offered a searing account of rural poverty and tenant impotence, both factors that led to increased tenant union militancy in

---

4  MYM 772. Unless otherwise stated, all other references to the Korean Hall project come from MYM 772.

5  James C. Baxter, *The Meiji Unification through the Lens of Ishikawa Prefecture* (Cambridge, MA: Council on East Asian Studies, Harvard University, 1994), 188, 193; Kenneth B. Pyle, *The New Generation in Meiji Japan: Power and Purpose in a New Era* (Stanford: Stanford University Press, 1987).

the 1920s.[6] From this perspective, the hope that Murotsu "not lag behind the progress of the times" may conversely be read as an expression of anxiety, in which attempts to "chart the course of our livelihoods in new directions" were unlikely to succeed – farming, port commerce and fishing would remain the village's principal forms of occupation throughout the 1910s[7] – and thus the gap between rural localities such as Murotsu and expanding cities such as Osaka and Tokyo would continue to widen. Rather than passively accepting the impersonal forces of "development," however, village officials were now attempting to control and direct the "demands of the times" (*jisei no yōkyū*).[8]

A second interpretation might focus on how the "Statement" speaks to the wider history of compulsory education in the Meiji era (1868–1912) – a period whose first two decades were characterized, as Brian Platt demonstrates, by local authorities often acting in defiance of central government directives. Indeed, the physical site of the school in Japanese villages – especially consolidated elementary schools that served a number of distinct hamlets, each with their own identities – often provoked intense local passions.[9] These tensions notwithstanding, the "Statement" makes clear that the basic Meiji aim of educating all Japanese children for six years (up from four in 1907) was succeeding by 1910, as demonstrated by the greater pressures on school facilities and the consequent realization of their "paucity." Indeed, graduation rates for boys in Murotsu village increased from 75 per cent in 1894 to 84 per cent in 1910, and from 45 per cent to 90 per cent for girls in the same period (nationally, the school attendance rate was 85 per cent in 1910).[10]

This focus on schoolboys and schoolgirls suggests a third possible interpretation of the "Statement," as framed by Julia Adeney Thomas. Early in her chapter, "Naturalizing Nationhood," Thomas imagines a schoolboy sitting "disconsolately on the stump of a venerable old tree that used to shade his village's

---

6    Takashi Nagatsuka, *The Soil: A Portrait of Rural Life in Meiji Japan*, trans. Ann Waswo (Berkeley: University of California Press, 1989 [1910]).

7    MYM 496.

8    For discourses of *jisei* in this period, see Kenneth B. Pyle, "The Technology of Japanese Nationalism: The Local Improvement Movement, 1900–1918," *The Journal of Asian Studies*, 33:1, (1973), 53–54.

9    Brian Platt, *Burning and Building: Schooling and State Formation in Japan, 1750–1890* (Cambridge, MA: Council on East Asian Studies, Harvard University, 2004), 206–213, 255–259.

10   MYM 496. For national rates, see Ann Waswo, "The Transformation of Rural Society, 1900–1950," in *The Cambridge History of Modern Japan*, vol. 6, ed. Peter Duus (Cambridge: Cambridge University Press, 1988), 560.

shrine." The tree has been felled under the central government's "one shrine per village" policy, but the boy is more worried by "the tediousness of his ethics textbook proclaiming him and his school fellows to be children of the paternal emperor. ...The boy, fidgeting on his tree stump, is subject to the new national articulation of nature that places him in a landscape centered on Tokyo and in a genealogical relationship to that new imperial center through his multiple fathers."[11] The Murotsu "Statement" appealed to local sensibilities of nature through its reverence of Mt. Ōza, the "Emperor's Seat" that towers 527 meters above the village, whence the child Antoku (reigned 1180–1185) apparently kept watch for the pursuing fleet of the enemy Genji clan. But as in Thomas's formulation of nature and nation, this evocation of the home village was framed by reference to "His Imperial Majesty's munificent favor," and indeed the central motivation for constructing an assembly hall in the village school was to house the Imperial Portrait, which would gaze down at the increasing number of children entering school.[12]

In all three interpretations – rural distress, education policy, and visions of nature and emperor – the central tension is between the local and the national. But what makes the "Statement" particularly striking is its explicit appeal to "Murotsu villagers resident in Korea and Manchuria"; that is, an additional dynamic exists between the local and the *inter*national, in which the "center" in the 1910s was simultaneously the imperial state and Murotsu village. In what follows, I examine this local-international interplay by focusing on the transnational relationship between the local community and the Japanese diaspora, thus going beyond the historiography of the countryside and the city in early 20th-century Japan. In the case of Murotsu village, that diaspora numbered more than 500 by the 1910s, out of a total population of 2700.[13] Although these numbers did not make Murotsu unusual (western Japan was notable for its high levels of overseas emigration from at least the 1880s onward),[14]

---

11    Julia Adeney Thomas, "Naturalizing Nationhood: Ideology and Practice in Early Twentieth-Century Japan," in *Japan's Competing Modernities: Issues in Culture and Democracy, 1900–1930*, ed. Sharon A. Minichiello (Honolulu: University of Hawai'i Press, 1998), 115–116.

12    For the "imperial gaze," see Takashi Fujitani, *Splendid Monarchy: Power and Pageantry in Modern Japan* (Berkeley: University of California Press, 1996), *passim*.

13    For the total village population, see Kaminoseki Chōshi Hensan Iinkai, *Kaminoseki chōshi* (Kaminoseki: Kaminoseki-chō yakuba, 1988), 404. Hereafter abbreviated as *KC*.

14    See, for example, Kimura Kenji, *Zaichō Nihonjin no shakaishi* (Tokyo: Miraisha, 1989); Alan Takeo Moriyama, *Imingaisha: Japanese Emigration Companies and Hawaii, 1894–1908* (Honolulu: University of Hawai'i Press, 1985).

what *is* remarkable about Murotsu is the survival of a rich collection of village documents from the 1870s to the 1930s. These documents enable us first to delve behind the numbers and to trace, through the assembly hall appeal, the networks of communication between the hometown and its diaspora communities in the 1910s. By then reconstructing the life stories of two major overseas donors to the Murotsu village elementary school – one from Korea and one from Hawai'i – I hope to show something of the motivations of "hometown-loving volunteers" from beyond the borders of the Japanese nation. Such men may indeed have been inspired to philanthropy by a desire to acknowledge the Emperor's munificence, but I argue that there was also a more straightforward ambition, namely the desire to be seen by fellow villagers as a "great man" oneself.

This chapter therefore offers a social history perspective of the 1910s by focusing on "ordinary people" in what might at first sight appear to be a peripheral backwater of rural Japan. Such a perspective highlights the ways in which the ties between the periphery and the center in 1910s Japan were deepened by the transnational connections of the local community to the outside world, such that the "international" became a key element in the figurative and physical construction of the nation at a local level. That is, world history in the 1910s belonged not just in books in the village library; as any Murotsu schoolchild could have told you, it was all around, in transformed school facilities and in daily classroom life.

### Banking on the Diaspora Network

While Europe descended into war in 1914, a native of Nagano prefecture, Takano Tatsuyuki, saw his new song published by the Ministry of Education in that year's *Common Elementary School Songbook* (*Sixth Grade*). Takano's lyrics beautifully captured the zeitgeist of the early 20th century, as thousands of Japanese migrated each year from the countryside to the cities and then nostalgically recalled their eponymous "Furusato" (hometown):

> That hill where I chased rabbits,
> That river where I fished for carp,
> Even now they appear like a dream:
> The *furusato* I can't forget.

For their part, Murotsu bureaucrats engaged in some analogous tugging of nostalgic heartstrings with their repeated appeal, in the 1910 "Statement of Aims," to "volunteers who harbor a deep sense of hometown love" (*aikyō*).[15] Through their evocation of beautiful mountains and rivers, they invited Murotsu villagers resident in Korea to embark on what Jun Uchida, in a different colonial context, has termed "a sentimental journey" back to the hometown.[16]

But the Murotsu Assembly Hall appeal was based on more than just sentiment and poetic imagery. An additional, eight-point document, "Guidelines Concerning the Solicitation of Donations for the Assembly Hall Construction," issued in the same month that Japan annexed Korea, reveals some of the organizational principles of a campaign that aimed to raise the vast sum of 2540 yen (equivalent to just under half of the village's annual expenditure in 1909).[17] The "Guidelines" open by noting that the new building will be called "The Korean Hall" so as to commemorate the philanthropy of Murotsu villagers residing on the Korean peninsula. Donations will be solicited and collected by 31 December 1910, for construction to begin in financial year 1911, and donors' names and contributions will be recorded somewhere appropriate "for eternity." Recent photographs of each donor will be kept in an album in the assembly hall and when construction is completed, a large ceremony will be held so that all villagers may express their gratitude. An official report will also be sent to all donors at the end of the project.

All these points presumed the existence of a large and prosperous emigrant community in Korea, and the ability of Murotsu village bureaucrats to communicate efficiently with those emigrants. A handful of extant letters from the peninsula enables us to trace the contours of such an emerging diaspora network. The letters suggest that sometime in April or May 1910, Murotsu mayor Sakō Gisaku first wrote to a select group of 30 settlers who had apparently been prevailed upon to form a fundraising committee.[18] These committee members were based in Pusan, Mokp'o, Kunsan, Inch'ŏn, Seoul, P'yŏngyang, Chinnamp'o, Wŏnsan, and Ch'ŏngjin – a geographical spread that illustrates the extent of

15   For discussion of "Furusato" and other hometown-nostalgia songs from the early 20th century, see Narita Ryūichi, *"Kokyō" to iu monogatari* (Tokyo: Yoshikawakō bunkan, 1998), 2–17. The alternative transliteration of *furusato* is *kokyō*, which shares its second character with *aikyō*, or "hometown love."

16   Jun Uchida, "A Sentimental Journey: Mapping the Interior Frontier of Japanese Settlers in Colonial Korea," *The Journal of Asian Studies*, 70:3 (August 2011): 706–729.

17   MYM 496.

18   The 30 committee members are listed in MYM 298; the letters are separate from but folded into the pages of MYM 772. I am very grateful to Takashima Chiyo (Kwansei Gakuin University) and Ishiyama Hideo (formerly of the Edo-Tokyo Hakubutsukan) for deciphering these letters.

rural Japanese emigration to the Korean peninsula even before the annexation. With his letter, Mayor Sakō enclosed the "Statement of Aims," which usually provoked comments of thanks and admiration. In a joint letter dated 11 June 1910, for example, Asami Suketarō and Yamazaki Shikazō (based in Seoul) wrote, "We are both deeply grateful for the great efforts of every volunteer, starting with the Mayor, on behalf of Murotsu village."[19] Perhaps more importantly, Mayor Sakō also enclosed some kind of register and requested that committee members return it once they had filled in the names of other Murotsu residents that they knew to be living in their area. From the eastern port city of Ch'ŏngjin, for example, Inoue Takesaburō wrote back to the mayor on 7 July 1910, apologizing for not having replied sooner. He was, he explained, "extremely busy with administrative preparations for starting the telephone network." (By way of comparison, Murotsu's own telephone network would not be established until the late 1920s, thanks to a major donation from postmaster Yoshida Shūzō: Inoue's work on the Ch'ŏngjin network was thus an example of colonial infrastructure projects considerably outpacing those in the metropole.) In his reply, Inoue enclosed a list of all Murotsu villagers living in the city (the list does not survive), and he furthermore promised personally to pass on the mayor's letter to a fellow villager by the name of Kunishige Kōsuke.

Although Kunishige did not ultimately make a donation to the assembly hall appeal, his knowledge of the project, through the mediation of Inoue, was one example of the network of contacts between Murotsu and Korea that was established during the second half of 1910. Indeed, by the end of the year, village officials had contacted 184 Murotsu villagers resident in Korea, including 60 women (a third of whom were married to non-Murotsu Japanese).[20] I have calculated elsewhere that this number was equivalent to just under a third of Murotsu's total households having a household member resident on the Korean peninsula. In addition, a quarter of village households contained a member previously or currently resident in Hawai'i. Thus, more than half of Murotsu's households boasted some kind of emigrant connection to the outside world in the early 1910s, a fact that underlines the highly transnational character of the wider Murotsu community.[21] Equally, the volume of paperwork preserved in the Murotsu archives attests to the extent that village bureaucracy itself also became a transnational enterprise in the years after

19    Asami Suketarō and Yamazaki Shikazō to Mayor Sakō, 11 June 1910.

20    MYM 298.

21    Martin Dusinberre, "Unread Relics of a Transnational 'hometown' in Rural Western Japan," *Japan Forum*, 20:3 (2008): 313.

1910, as administrators sent fundraising letters, logged replies, checked the actual payment of donations, and so on – all activities that traversed the borders between Japan and the wider world. On occasion, the logistical challenges of keeping track of villagers resident not only in Korea but also in Hawai'i, North America, China, and Brazil seemed to get the better of apparently overworked bureaucrats, even after they moved into the spacious new village office in 1914 (built with a major donation from postmaster Yoshida Shūzō). Thus, one set of statistics for overseas villagers in the 1910s omits Korean emigrants, while another list includes Korea and Hawai'i but not China, and moreover has a number of errors, meaning that the total number of 534 overseas villagers in the one year that the two lists coincide – 1917 – is almost certainly an underestimate.[22]

Mayor Sakō and the members of the village council clearly banked on the expectation that members of the expatriate community in Korea would have deep pockets to fund the assembly hall appeal. They were not to be disappointed in the long run, but in the short run there were frustrating cases of vagueness and delay. One committee member wrote, "Regarding my donation, I will make it very soon, but in the meantime I am sending...the name list to you."[23] This was on 2 August 1910, but his eventual donation – of five yen – was not received in Murotsu until five months later. Still, at least he met the nominal deadline of 31 December. Other correspondents were less punctilious: Asami Suketarō and Yamazaki Shikazō (Seoul) did not make their respective payments of five yen and 120 yen until February 1911; Inoue Takesaburō (Ch'ŏngjin) contributed five yen in September 1911; Asami Shintarō (P'yŏngyang) transferred 80 yen only in July 1913. Indeed, more than three-quarters of the 94 eventual donors made their payments to the village only after the end of the 1910 financial year.[24]

These delays throw light on one surviving letter from Yamamoto Atsuzō, a sake merchant in Mokp'o. Writing in May 1913 to the new Murotsu mayor, Yoshizaki Eisuke (who donated the world history books), Yamamoto acknowledges an apparent follow-up to Mayor Sakō's original appeal. "Concerning the Elementary School Assembly Hall, I too planned to make a small donation, but I was dissatisfied with the amount," he writes. Now, in response to Yoshizaki's request for more money to complete the formal entrance to the Assembly Hall, he explains:

---

22    MYM 496, MYM 1127.
23    Ueshige Kaneroku to Mayor Sakō, 2 August 1910.
24    MYM 298, MYM 772. In total, 3203 yen was raised.

> [I]t has only been a short time since I came to Korea, and I have not yet achieved my goals. For that reason, with great embarrassment I am sending a postal order for 10 yen, which I hope you will accept.
>
> This is truly a very small amount of money, so I absolutely do not need to receive a letter of thanks from the [Yamaguchi] governor. Please do not make my donation public: I have no objection to your using my money under some other name.[25]

Dissatisfaction, embarrassment, unfulfilled goals, and requests for anonymity in the homeland: despite the fact that 10 yen was actually the median donation for Murotsu villagers, Yamamoto was not the only Japanese emigrant to Korea to discover a gap between his expectations and the reality on the ground – a gap that was brought into unsettling focus by his hometown's assembly hall appeal.[26]

On the other hand, the Murotsu appeal could serve as a marker of how far some emigrants had come since arriving on the peninsula. One correspondent, Suzuki Taneichi, wrote to Mayor Sakō in June 1910 to congratulate him on his work "for the nation" and to pledge his support for the school campaign. Suzuki and Sakō (both born in 1874) had a history of working together. In October 1894, along with two other Murotsu merchants, they had composed an impassioned petition to the then mayor of the village, in which they lamented the decline of the Murotsu port from the heady days of the "Western Circuit" years:

> The fact is, despite us being called the most prosperous port in the Chūgoku region, world conditions have been transformed: the domains have been replaced by the prefectural system, the coming and going of official ships has stopped, most shipping has become steam-powered, goods are transported directly to meet demand, and both commercial shipping and merchants are no longer coming.[27]

By 1910, these problems had become Sakō's responsibility as mayor of the village. But Suzuki, too, was in a new position: from complaining passively about "world conditions" in the 1890s, at the beginning of the 1910s he was himself

---

25   Yamamoto Atsuzō to Mayor Yoshizaki, 16 May 1913. There is some confusion over Yamamoto's given name, which appears as Atsutarō in MYM 298.

26   On this gap, see Helen J.S. Lee, "Writing Colonial Relations of Everyday Life in Senryu," *positions* 16:3 (Winter 2008): 605–608.

27   MYM 112; *KC*, 450.

out in the world, demonstrating the transformation of his own fortunes through his benefaction of 150 yen to the assembly hall appeal.

### A Korean "Success" Story

One hundred and fifty yen was a lot of money in February 1912, when Suzuki Taneichi finally made his postal transfer. It was, to be precise, equivalent to more than four months' salary for the then principal of Murotsu elementary school.[28] Other than amorphous feelings of "hometown love" and a sense of loyalty to his contemporary Sakō Gisaku, what might have impelled Suzuki to make such a large donation? One hint may be found in the aforementioned "Guidelines Concerning the Solicitation of Donations": the names of benefactors will be recorded "for eternity," their photographs will be kept in an album in the assembly hall and they will be feted in a large ceremony upon completion of the project. In other words, a generous donation would elevate the profile of the donor and give him/her a photographic presence in the same "sacrosanct" space as that of the Emperor himself.

Without knowing more of Suzuki's personal history, it is difficult to tell why a higher profile might have been particularly appealing to him, other than serving to tickle his ego. We do, however, know a lot more about his distant relative, Kōno Takenosuke, who owned the sundries store in Chinnamp'o that Suzuki managed at the time of the appeal. Kōno was born in Murotsu in March 1867, the third son of Kōno Naozō. In keeping with other Murotsu elites from the Edo period, Naozō was a wholesale agent and merchant in the port area of the village – his spacious main house neighbored that of later postmaster Yoshida Shūzō, but was only half as big – and he also served on the first village assembly from 1878 onward. After Naozō's death in 1884, his first son, Mangorō, continued the family business. But in 1886, the "wind of death" once again blew over the household, taking with it not only Mangorō but also the family's second son. Thus, at the tender age of nineteen, Takenosuke was left as head of the household and of the family business.

Kōno's starting position was strong. In addition to the main house, he owned at least eight other properties throughout the village. In 1887, he paid the top rate of village business tax – even the Yoshida household was only in the second band for business tax, suggesting that merchant profits were even greater

---

28   MYM *Sonritsu shōgakkō kyōin meibo* (uncatalogued document). The principal's monthly salary in academic year April 1911–March 1912 was 35 yen.

for Kōno than for his neighbor – and in the following year, the Kōno household was ranked joint-sixth out of 581 households on which the local household tax was levied.[29] According to Takenosuke's hagiographic entry in the 1917 *Yamaguchi Dictionary of Biography*, however, "Due to his youth and lack of experience, he made repeated mistakes, and saw that business would become impossibly difficult in his hometown [...]"[30] There is no elaboration of these "mistakes" (*shippai*) in the text, which focuses instead on his "hopes for great success in the future" when he left Murotsu and initially crossed to Pusan in March 1895; and surviving tax records only hint at his troubles in 1893, when the Kōno household had dropped to band fifteen of household tax (from band five in 1888) – a rate that still left it in the top 13 per cent of Murotsu taxpayers.[31] It is possible that the dictionary of biography exaggerated Kōno's troubles in Japan so as to underline the opportunities for "great success" in the imperial colonies – a message that complemented central government aims to increase the number of settlers to Korea in the 1910s.[32] But if it really is true that business had become "impossibly difficult" by the end of 1894 – and Suzuki and Sakō penned their lament on the port economy in October of that year – then the Kōno household's fall from grace was both spectacular and swift.

In Korea, by contrast, Kōno quickly established new business networks, taking advantage of the opportunities created by both the Sino-Japanese (1894–1895) and Russo-Japanese (1904–1905) wars.[33] By 1910, according to a different dictionary entry, there was "no one who did not know Kōno within the world of Inch'ŏn trade and commerce."[34] Despite the misfortune of not one but two fires burning down his Inch'ŏn main store in 1907, he quickly restored his assets to their former level, and his businesses included branch stores in P'yŏngyang and Chinnamp'o (under the management of Suzuki Taneichi). Moreover, he helped establish the Inch'ŏn Yamaguchi Association in 1905 with a grant of 150 yen, and by 1910 he was serving as its honorary vice-chair, a position that he held until 1915.

---

29  MYM 93.

30  Izeki Kurō, *Gendai Bōchō jinbutsu-shi* (*ji*) (Tokyo: Hattensha, 1917), 48.

31  MYM 112.

32  Such rags-to-riches stories were also a theme of settlers' autobiographies: Jun Uchida, *Brokers of Empire: Japanese Settler Colonialism in Korea, 1876–1945* (Cambridge, MA: Harvard University Asia Center, 2011), 93–94.

33  For more on Kōno in Korea, see Martin Dusinberre, *Hard Times in the Hometown: A History of Community Survival in Modern Japan* (Honolulu: University of Hawai'i Press, 2012), 93–95. On p. 95, I have mistakenly cited the merchants' petition as having been written in July 1894, not October.

34  Munei Shinsei, *Bōchō no jinbutsu* (*jō*) (Kudamatsu: Bōchō jitsugyōsha, 1910), 249.

All these activities may well have made Kōno's name widely recognized as a "success" story within the 11,000-strong Japanese community in Inch'ŏn, but back in the motherland, Murotsu villagers more likely remembered his "mistakes" and the precipitous decline of a once influential household. Therefore, with his enormous donation of 300 yen and his work as a member of the assembly hall fundraising committee in 1910–1911, Kōno may have hoped to restore the once-good name of his household within his hometown community. Such philanthropy also triggered a virtuous cycle of good will and prosperity between the metropole and the colony. Murotsu elementary school, most obviously, got a "superior" new assembly hall. For his part, Kōno received a certificate of merit and the gift of some wooden sake cups from the Governor of Yamaguchi prefecture as a token of thanks for his donation. This official recognition likely improved his ability to build new, international business networks, such as his establishment of the Inch'ŏn office of the New Zealand Fire Insurance Company in September 1913. In turn, his work for major corporations, including Standard Oil and numerous up-and-coming Japanese companies, and his track-record of post-1910 benefactions both to Murotsu and to the Inch'ŏn community, further raised his social standing at home and abroad.[35] It was this standing that was reflected in Kōno's eight-page entry in the *Yamaguchi Dictionary of Biography*, a book on "great men" to be found on public library bookshelves even a century later.

### Bluster and Bucks in Hawai'i

Kōno Takenosuke's biographical entry makes brief mention of the long-anticipated ceremony held to celebrate the completion of the Korean Hall project in 1913. At that time, the whole school population – exactly 400 pupils and their seven teachers – would have crammed into the new building, which measured 63.5 *tsubo* (210 square meters), admiring its cornice ceiling, its pine-laid flooring, its 1.3 meter-long sash windows, and of course the Imperial Portrait – now of the Taishō Emperor – on a raised dais at the front.[36]

---

35  In Inch'ŏn, Kōno financed the development of a city park in 1914; in Murotsu, he made donations towards road repairs (1917), rice relief (1918) and the village police service (1920).

36  MYM 772. The student Figures I cite are from academic year 1913–1914; there were 414 students in year 1912–1913 (MYM 496). The exact date of the celebration ceremony is unclear: contracts in MYM 772 indicate that construction of the hall was due to be completed in February 1912, but the fundraising effort continued until July 1913.

But eleven pupils who were due to graduate from the elementary school in academic year 1913–1914 were absent from the ceremony. These eleven, including Suzuki Taneichi's son, had all been withdrawn from school to join their parents in Korea. In Suzuki's case, his son left for Chinnamp'o after only a year of education in Japan; as Table 17.1 reveals, nearly fifty other pupils curtailed their Murotsu schooling to join their parents in Korea by the middle of the decade. By the end of the 1910s, children who should have been educated in Murotsu but who in fact resided overseas numbered between 15 and 20 every academic year. When we add to these figures returnees from overseas, we see that across the decade, almost a fifth of nominal Murotsu students (19 per cent) had some kind of personal experience of the world outside Japan.

One such "international" child, a young girl who may have attended the Korean Hall ceremony and who certainly enjoyed the new school facilities from April 1913 onward, was Fuyuki Mitsuyo (born 1906).[37] Her father, Fuyuki Sakazō, was born in Murotsu in c.1869. Two decades later, in September 1889, he was one of 997 Japanese nationals to board the *Yamashiro-maru* from Yokohama and cross the Pacific on the ninth government-sponsored crossing of Japanese emigrants to the Kingdom of Hawai'i. Fuyuki thus joined 29,000 other Japanese who went to Hawai'i on the program between 1885 and 1894, including over two hundred emigrants from Murotsu village itself. As emigrant number 8051, he worked on the Hana sugar plantation in Mau'i island for several years before returning home to Murotsu in 1897 and marrying his first cousin Sumi (born 1881). By 1903, the couple was back in Hawai'i, this time on Kaua'i island. At the time of the US Federal Census in 1910, the family was living in Eleele, on the southern coast of the island, where Sakazō worked as a "salesman" at the McBryde Sugar Company plantation store.

The next part of the story appears simple on paper but is rather more complex in terms of interpretation. Not long after the birth of their sixth child in June 1912, Sakazō and Sumi sailed back to Murotsu leaving only their eldest son, Shin'ichi (born 1901), in Hawai'i. Fuyuki Mitsuyo and her older sister Fusayo (born 1904) entered school in April 1913. Between May and August 1913, Sakazō purchased three houses in Seto, a narrow district hemmed in between the Inland Sea straits and the small hill on which stood the elementary school itself. On 12 March 1914, Sakazō was the first donor in a new campaign to raise money for the construction of new facilities at Murotsu elementary school. With his pledge of 400 yen, he was also, by some distance, the principal donor to the campaign. In May 1914, he returned to Kaua'i and to his son, and over the

---

37   Fuyuki is a pseudonym.

TABLE 17.1   *Total number of students due to complete schooling. Data from MYM 917–922, 932, 933.*

| | 1910 | 1911 | 1912 | 1913 | 1914 | 1915 | 1916 | 1917 | 1918 | 1919 | 1920 | 1921 | Total |
|---|---|---|---|---|---|---|---|---|---|---|---|---|---|
| *Total number of students due to complete schooling (A)* | 88 | 71 | 97 | 56 | 57 | 89 | 95 | 106 | 93 | 88 | 88 | 108 | 1036 |
| School attendees in Hawai'i/USA | 0 | 0 | 0 | 0 | 1 | 3 | 6 | 1 | 4 | 7 | 7 | 11 | 40 |
| School attendees in Korea | 0 | 0 | 0 | 0 | 0 | 1 | 7 | 2 | 10 | 12 | 10 | 14 | 56 |
| School attendees in Taiwan/China | 0 | 0 | 0 | 0 | 0 | 0 | 1 | 2 | 1 | 1 | 1 | 2 | 8 |
| Students who left for Hawai'i/USA before completion | 1 | 0 | 0 | 0 | 0 | 0 | 0 | 0 | 1 | 0 | 0 | 1 | 3 |
| Students who left for Korea before completion | 3 | 8 | 15 | 11 | 3 | 7 | 5 | 7 | 4 | 2 | 4 | 4 | 73 |
| Students who left for Taiwan/China before completion | 0 | 0 | 2 | 0 | 3 | 0 | 0 | 0 | 1 | 0 | 0 | 0 | 6 |
| Number of returnees from Hawai'i/Japanese Empire | 0 | 2 | 2 | 0 | 0 | 0 | 0 | 1 | 1 | 1 | 1 | 3 | 11 |
| *Total number of students with overseas connection (B)* | 4 | 10 | 19 | 11 | 7 | 11 | 19 | 13 | 22 | 23 | 23 | 35 | 197 |
| *Percentage of students with overseas connection (B÷A)* | 4.5 | 14.1 | 19.6 | 19.6 | 12.3 | 12.4 | 20.0 | 12.3 | 23.7 | 26.1 | 26.1 | 32.4 | 19.0 |

next nine months, more than thirty Murotsu villagers residing in Hawai'i and the mainland USA pledged money to the elementary school appeal. Construction on what became known as the "America-Hawai'i Hall," which may in fact have been a classroom building rather than an assembly hall, began in July 1915 and was completed in January 1916. A month later, Sakazō donated 13.7 yen to his home village to mark the accession of the Taishō Emperor, and in August 1918 he donated 10 yen towards Murotsu's rice relief fund. By this time, Sakazō had become "Clerk" at the general store of the McBryde Sugar Company in Eleele, a position that he held until August 1921, when he returned to Murotsu for a brief, nine-month visit.[38]

This story is intriguing for several reasons. First, when Murotsu bureaucrats wrote in their 1910 "Statement of Aims" that local development and the progress of the state came from "each locality compet[ing] in striving for the betterment of facilities," it is unlikely that they had in mind competition between the "local" diaspora communities in Korea and North America. Yet reading between the lines of Fuyuki's career in the 1910s, I suspect this is exactly what happened. During his period back in Murotsu between 1912 and 1914, Fuyuki would have seen the splendid new Korean Hall on the hill just behind his new houses; he would also have seen the ways in which the Murotsu expatriates in Korea were feted by local bureaucrats for their contributions to the welfare of the village, and the esteem with which villagers now presumably spoke of men such as Kōno Takenosuke and Suzuki Taneichi. As a man with cash to burn – not everyone could afford to buy three new houses within a three-month period, nor indeed to ferry their families across the Pacific – he may have been looking for opportunities to invest in his hometown community. That his name was always the first to appear on the repeated lists of donors drawn up by village bureaucrats makes me think that he played an important role in organizing donations from his compatriots in Hawai'i and further afield – and that he may even have suggested the idea of a new fundraising campaign to village leaders in the first

---

38    For Fuyuki's early life in Hawai'i, see the Diplomatic Record Office archives of the Japanese Ministry of Foreign Affairs: 3-8-2-5/14; and *Hawai imin*, vol. 3. For the school records of his children, see MYM 919 and MYM 920. For his land purchases, see the *Tochi daichō* of the Yanai branch of the Ministry of Justice Legal Affairs Bureau. Records concerning the America-Hawai'i Hall are in MYM 773. For details of his life in Kaua'i, I have referred to the US Federal Censuses of both 1910 and 1920, and to the Honolulu Passenger and Crew Lists (1900–1959), all accessed through <http://www.ancestry.com>. I am particularly grateful to Marylou Bradley of the Kaua'i Historical Society for her generous assistance concerning Fuyuki's life in Eleele, and to Murakami Tomoko, daughter of Fuyuki Mitsuyo and granddaughter of Fuyuki Sakazō, for her help with family genealogy.

place. In any case, through the construction of a 116 *tsubo* (380 square meter) America-Hawai'i Hall to rival the smaller Korean Hall, Murotsu elementary school became a site of competition in the mid-1910s between different constituencies of the village diaspora located in different parts of the Pacific world.

What is more, Fuyuki's pledge of 400 yen in March 1914 was quite a statement of intent from someone who, unlike Kōno Takenosuke, could never claim to have come from an elite background. So far as I can tell, it was the single largest promise of philanthropy by any villager in Murotsu in the 1910s, larger even than any single benefaction made by Yoshizaki Eisuke or Yoshida Shūzō in that period. To a certain extent, then, Fuyuki was demonstrating how much he had come up in the world by being out in the world. To put this in context, we can compare him to his namesake in Kaminoseki village, just across the straits from Murotsu. Fuyuki Shukutarō, who was born in 1870 and was thus almost a contemporary of Sakazō (the two were not related), was the most senior paid bureaucrat in the Kaminoseki village office at the beginning of the 1910s, earning 17 yen a month by the time that he stepped down for ill health in April 1911.[39] Had Fuyuki Sakazō not gone to Hawai'i in 1889 and instead worked his way up the village bureaucracy, a senior position by his early forties would have been considered a successful career. Yet here he was, in 1914, pledging an amount equivalent to two years' worth of his namesake's salary.

There is something odd, however, about a store salesman from Hawai'i being in a position to pledge even more money to his hometown than a fabulously wealthy businessman in Korea. By the standards of the time, especially by the Murotsu standards of the time, Fuyuki Sakazō was clearly well-off. When he returned to Honolulu in May 1914, for example, he was in possession of more than $50 in cash – a sum that Murotsu bureaucrats calculated, during the America-Hawai'i Hall fundraising campaign, to be equivalent to 100 yen.[40] Even so, after the major strike of 1909, Japanese plantation workers in Hawai'i were only paid a basic wage of $20 a month.[41] As a store worker, and especially later as a clerk, Fuyuki would have been paid considerably more than this basic rate, and he may also have worked on commission. But it is still difficult to see how he could have acquired the capital to pledge at least six to eight months' salary to the Murotsu elementary school construction project, especially as he had a seventh child to support by the time that he returned to Hawai'i in 1914.

---

39   Kaminoseki yakuba monjo 66 (stored in the Kaminoseki Town Municipal Board of Education). Some senior bureaucrats worked gratis in this period.

40   MYM 1127, MYM 773.

41   Yukiko Kimura, *Issei: Japanese Immigrants in Hawaii* (Honolulu: University of Hawai'i Press, 1988), 91–92.

Most intriguing of all, there is no evidence in the surviving Murotsu archives that Fuyuki ever actually paid the sum that he had pledged in March 1914. He *did* pay 10 yen to the Murotsu rice relief fund in August 1918, but that was a much more modest amount – one dwarfed by the 200 yen donated to the same fund by Kōno Takenosuke. We are left, therefore, with the possibility that Fuyuki was all bluster and no buck: a man who served as cheerleader for the America-Hawai'i Hall without contributing to it himself.

Ultimately, however, perhaps that did not matter. Fuyuki's pledge was a public statement (indeed, village officials mistakenly recorded it as 500 yen in a circular they published in August 1914). On the one hand, it undoubtedly served to galvanize other prosperous Murotsu expatriates in Hawai'i, the USA, and even Canada to make more modest contributions to the appeal, contributions that reached almost 2000 yen by the end of the campaign, and that indeed led to the marked "betterment of [school] facilities" by January 1916. On the other hand, in a period of retrenchment and "local improvement" in rural Japan, when the 1908 Boshin Rescript had urged Japanese to be "frugal in the management of their households...to abide by simplicity and avoid ostentation, and to inure themselves to arduous toil without yielding to any degree of indulgence,"[42] a public pledge of several hundred yen enabled men such as Fuyuki and Kōno to be ostentatious while avoiding ostentation, and to enjoy the simple indulgence of having helped out their beloved hometown community.


### Conclusion

Historians, in their wilder moments (if that is not an oxymoron), like to imagine the subjects of their enquiries freed from the constraints of documents and historical veracity. So in a spirit of indulgence, let us imagine a scene from early 1920, when young Fuyuki Mitsuyo takes a quick stroll from her home in Seto to the Murotsu village post office. There, postmaster Yoshida Shūzō will give her the latest remittance to arrive from her father Sakazō, in Hawai'i. As she dawdles back home along the narrow main street that skirts the historical port, perhaps she hums to herself the tune of "Furusato," which she has recently learned in sixth-grade classes at school.[43]

---

42 Quoted in Sheldon Garon, *Molding Japanese Minds: The State in Everyday Life* (Princeton: Princeton University Press, 1997), 9.

43 Fuyuki Mitsuyo did in fact regularly go to the Murotsu post office to pick up remittances from her father; personal correspondence with Murakami Tomoko, May 2011.

Yoshida Shūzō's presence as village postmaster in 1920, the election of
Yoshizaki Eisuke as village mayor in 1913 (a post he would hold until 1925), and
the philanthropy of both men throughout the 1920s and 1930s, remind us that
Edo period elites continued to play an influential role in Japanese rural life well
into the 20th century.[44] Nevertheless, the histories presented in this chapter
suggest that hometown life was also changing by the 1910s as a new generation
of villagers forced their way into the local public consciousness. They did so by
pledging considerable amounts of money to improve the educational welfare
of the village and thus to prevent Murotsu from lagging behind "the progress of
the times" (*jisei no shinpo*). Most importantly, they were in a position to make
such contributions because of their transnational careers in Korea, Hawai'i,
North America, and beyond. Thus, one conclusion about Japan and the wider
world in the 1910s is that the successes of the Japanese overseas diaspora facilitated increased social mobility within the hometown as world conditions were
embraced, household fortunes were restored, and plantation laborers became
property owners. To a greater extent than in the hometown community, work
in the outside world offered opportunities for Suzuki Taneichi, Kōno
Takenosuke and Fuyuki Sakazō to become "self-made men" by the end of the
Meiji period. Thanks to international labor networks, the appearance of parve-
nus and the nouveaux riches (*narikin*) in the 1910s was therefore a phenomenon that occurred in the countryside as well as in the cities.[45] Conversely, the
embarrassment expressed by Yamamoto Atsuzō in his letter of 1913 was partly
due to the realization that unlike many of his fellow villagers in Korea and
beyond, he had not (yet) achieved this desirable new socioeconomic status.

A second conclusion is that although the history of large-scale Japanese
emigration to Asia and the Americas dated back to the 1880s, and although the
benefits of overseas wage remittances were felt by individual households in
the homeland almost immediately,[46] the accumulation of overseas wealth to
the extent that emigrants could become philanthropists took much longer.
Thus, the true impact of this diaspora in *institutional* terms only began to be
felt in the homeland from the 1910s onward. The Korean Assembly Hall appeal
led to the first major group donation to Murotsu from the overseas village community in the years 1910–1913, and it was quickly followed by the America-
Hawai'i Hall appeal of 1914–1915. Several members of the Asia-Pacific diaspora

---

44   See also Simon Partner, *The Mayor of Aihara: A Japanese Villager and His Community,*
     *1865–1925* (Berkeley: University of California Press, 2009).

45   Earl Kinmonth, *The Self-Made Man in Meiji Thought: From Samurai to Salary Man*
     (Berkeley: University of California Press, 1981); Uchida, *Brokers of Empire*, 2.

46   Moriyama, *Imingaisha*, 25.

similarly contributed to Murotsu's rice relief fund in 1918, while in neighboring
Kaminoseki village, overseas group donations led to a new school radio in 1926,
a new elementary school assembly hall in 1929, and an entirely new school for
Iwaishima district in 1934. Indeed, group donations to Murotsu from the
Hawaiian diaspora would continue until the mid-1950s, when mainly second-
generation Japanese-Americans (including Fuyuki Sakazō's first son, Shin'ichi)
raised funds to build a new junior high school in the village.[47] As the 1910
"Statement of Aims" made clear, "*national* education" (*kokumin kyōiku*) was the
basis of "*national* development" (*koku'un no hatten*, emphasis added). But from
the philanthropic era of the 1910s onward, the material culture of Murotsu and
Kaminoseki villages' elementary schools would be truly *trans*national in character. So, too, would the experiences of a significant minority of the children
attending school. What, one wonders, did "Furusato" mean to Hawaiian
returnee Fuyuki Mitsuyo? Was her "home" Mt. Ōza and the swirling waters of
Yanagiura bay, or the sugarcane fields of Eleele, with the deep gulch of the
Hanapepe river rising toward the central Kaua'i mountains? These questions
highlight the overlapping dynamics of local, national and transnational history
as we try to reconstruct a Japanese village and its worlds in the 1910s.

William Blake once wrote of seeing "a world in a grain of sand." The micro-
historical approach of this chapter has similarly attempted to reveal a world in
the sandy grounds of Murotsu village elementary school. My aim has not been
to suggest that Murotsu was "typical" of every Japanese village in the 1910s, any
more than Fuyuki Mitsuyo was typical of every Japanese schoolgirl. Rather, the
extraordinary details of transnational village life as revealed by the surviving
Murotsu archives enable us to pose wider historical and historiographical
questions about our study of early 20th century Japan than might at first sight
be supposed by a study of "local" history. My first question, therefore, para-
phrasing David Igler in his work on the eastern Pacific world in the first half of
the 19th century, is to ask whether Murotsu and other parts of rural Japan were
in fact "international before [they] became national."[48] Take, for example, the
"Song of Celebration" composed for the opening of the America-Hawai'i Hall
in February 1916 – a song that Fuyuki Mitsuyo must also have sung:

In the middle of the playground,
Looking up from beside the willow tree,

---

47  *Murotsu chūgakkō dai ni-ki kōji kifu meibo* (1955), not catalogued in MYM.
48  David Igler, "Diseased Goods: Global Exchanges in the Eastern Pacific Basin, 1770–1850,"
    *The American Historical Review*, 109:3 (2004), 696. Igler takes this idea, in turn, from Karen
    Ordahl Kupperman.

Our eyes are astonished by the America-Hawai'i Hall.
This beautiful structure was built
with the pure fortunes
of people living in America and Hawai'i –
"May our *furusato*
become yet better," they nostalgically hoped.
So every day, in this building
where we learn of people's toils,
Let us single-mindedly
work, apply ourselves, and unfailingly become
good Japanese
As a token of our gratitude.[49]

Iambic pentameter it is not – not in Japanese and certainly not in translation – but the song does suggest that the desire to become "good Japanese" at home was stimulated in significant ways by the actions of villagers living overseas; or, to rephrase using Igler's terminology, the "international" aspect of daily village life by the 1910s was in some ways a precondition for Japan's "national" development. This is important because for many years our analysis of rural life in the early 20th century has been framed by Kenneth Pyle's observations concerning the role that the "Local Improvement Movement" (1906–1918) played in stimulating national loyalties at a local level.[50] But where did transnational households such as the Fuyuki family fit into this model of emerging Japanese state nationalism? Perhaps we need to see the 1910s not just as a period of local and regional identities coalescing into a national culture, but also of Japan's transnational communities helping fund the material culture of the nation-state.

The second question is to consider how the momentous world events of the 1910s described elsewhere in this volume were actually perceived in a tiny village such as Murotsu. A traditional, "great men" view of history would suggest that the key event in 1910 concerning Japan's relationship with the outside world was the annexation of Korea. Yet the evidence of this chapter suggests that the plan to construct a new assembly hall, and to target villagers living on the peninsula as potential donors, constituted a much more concrete imagination of Korea in the local bureaucratic consciousness than abstract questions of annexation and sovereignty. Similarly, although Europe stumbled into a

---

49    MYM 773. The word "toil" (*tsutome*) is written in phonetic hiragana; its homonym may also
       be translated as "duty."

50    Pyle, "The Technology of Japanese Nationalism."

world war in 1914, the "wider world" for many Murotsu villagers in that year would have been symbolized more by plans to build an America-Hawai'i Hall in the elementary school grounds than by photographs of an assassination in Sarajevo. To make these points is not to belittle the significance of the Korean annexation or of the Great War in our study of Japan in the 1910s; rather, it is to suggest that a social history of international affairs must acknowledge lesser known events – and lesser known "great men" (and women) – in the world perspectives of "ordinary people."

# Buddhism and the Twenty-One Demands

*The Politics behind the International Movement of Japanese Buddhists*

Yoshiko Okamoto

## Introduction

The modern age for Japanese Buddhists began with the so-called *haibutsu kishaku* movement that sought to expel Buddhism from the center of religious authority in Japan. In the years immediately following the Meiji Restoration of 1868, the new government turned against Buddhism, resulting in a nation-wide campaign to destroy Buddhist temples, images, and texts. In place of Buddhism, Shinto was declared to be Japan's national religion.[1] Prior to this, Buddhists had argued against the spread of Christianity, seeing it as politically and morally dangerous. Religious reform was undertaken in an attempt to demonstrate that Buddhism was crucial to the defense and integrity of the new nation state. Overseas missionary work to propagate Japanese Buddhism was one of these new initiatives. This chapter deals with attempts in the early 20th century to spread Buddhism abroad, an endeavor in which Buddhist leaders and government officials were sometimes in agreement, but sometimes found themselves at odds in advancing Japan's international reputation as a modern state. It focuses on two Buddhist movements connected with diplomatic relations between Japan, China and the United States in 1915 when the Japanese government presented the Twenty-One Demands to China. On the one hand, in 1915, Japanese Buddhist missionaries hosted an international conference in San Francisco to cope with the anti-Japanese sentiments in the West Coast and to make an appeal for world peace. On the other hand, in Japan, Buddhists lobbied to acquire the legal right to propagate Buddhism in China.

## 1 The 1915 San Francisco World Buddhist Conference

### 1.1 *Buddhism and Japanese Immigrants in California*

One of the new purposes of modern Buddhism was to establish its identity as a global religion. Japanese Buddhist leaders undertook their first steps on the

---

1  James Edward Ketelaar, *Of Heretics and Martyrs in Meiji Japan: Buddhism and its Persecution* (Princeton: Princeton University Press, 1990).

world stage at the Parliament of the World's Religions at the Columbian Exposition in Chicago in 1893. This parliament began with the self-evident assumption of Christian superiority over other of the worlds' religions; in fact, the meeting allowed leaders of non-Christian religions to show off their teachings and values, giving birth to a sustained interest in Eastern spiritualism among peoples in the United States and Europe. To Japanese Buddhist leaders, the parliament was important as an opportunity to present their Buddhism as "Japanese Buddhism," derived from but distinct to doctrines imported from India via China and Korea in ancient times.[2]

In 1915, twenty-two years after the parliament, some Japanese Buddhists succeeded in hosting a World Buddhist Conference in San Francisco, inviting distinguished monks and scholars from Japan, India, Ceylon, Burma, Hawai'i and the mainland of the United States. The conference, held between 2 August and 7 August 1915 on the occasion of the Pan-Pacific International Exposition to celebrate the completion of the Panama Canal, attracted the participation of Japanese residents as well as many curious ordinary Americans. The host was the Buddhist Mission to North America (BMNA) headed by Uchida Kōyū (1876–1960), the chief Nishi Hongan-ji missionary of the Buddhist Church of San Francisco.

In 1899, as the number of Japanese immigrants settling in the West Coast of the United States grew, the first Nishi Hongan-ji[3] missionaries arrived in San Francisco and opened a branch of Kyoto Nishi Hongan-ji, making it the first Buddhist temple in mainland United States. This was later renamed the Buddhist Church of San Francisco and became the staging ground for Japanese Buddhist missionary work. Other branches of the Buddhist Church were established in towns and cities up and down the West Coast. Buddhist missionaries worked largely for Japanese immigrants preaching sermons and conducting funeral services. For the missionaries, who provided spiritual support to the Japanese community, to host a multi-cultural event such as the World Buddhist Conference was a major achievement.

The highlight of the conference was the adoption, on 6 August, of a resolution that consisted of five points. The first three points urged that (1) Buddhists make efforts to introduce the essence of Eastern civilization to the world for

---

2  Judith Snodgrass, *Presenting Japanese Buddhism to the West: Orientalism, Occidentalism, and the Columbian Exposition* (Chapel Hill: University of North Carolina Press, 2003).

3  In 1881, Nishi Hongan-ji declared "Shinshū Hongan-ji-ha" to be their official name. Higashi Hongan-ji chose "Shinshū Ōtani-ha" that same year. In this chapter, however, I use "Nishi Hongan-ji" and "Higashi Hongan-ji" to avoid confusion since I am dealing with their activities before and after 1881.

the purpose of fusion of East and West and the rapprochement of humankind; (2) Buddhists in and out of the United States cooperate with each other to propagate Buddhism to the American people for the purpose of Japan-US friendship; and (3) Buddhists must strive to correct the misunderstanding that Buddhist missionary work contributes to anti-Japanese feelings in the United States.[4] These points demonstrate that the purpose of the conference was to open up the Japanese community and make the teaching of Buddhism known to white American society, thereby hoping to deal constructively with a growing anti-Japanese movement in the West Coast.

In fact, when Uchida assumed his appointment in 1905, the Japanese community in the West Coast was confronted by the harsh realities of racial prejudice. After the Russo-Japanese War, Japan did not conform to the American "open door" policy in Asia. Its refusal to allow "equal opportunity" in Manchuria resulted in repeated attempts to exclude Japanese immigrants from entry into the United States. On 18 April 1906, a major earthquake struck San Francisco, resulting in one of the worst natural disasters to hit the United States. The Buddhist Church of San Francisco devoted itself to the relief of Japanese immigrants. Soon after this emergency, in October, the San Francisco City Board of Education adopted a resolution to refuse admission of Japanese pupils to public schools. The California Alien Land Law, which was rejected in 1909 and in 1911, but adopted in 1913, accelerated the movement against Japanese immigrants.[5] The plan to hold the World Buddhist Conference began in early July 1914.[6] In holding the conference, Uchida stove to improve this situation and make peace with the white Christian society.

Furthermore, it is equally important to examine the fourth point that requested President Woodrow Wilson to make efforts for an early end to the ongoing war in Europe:

---

4  Sōkō Bukkyō-kai Bunsho-bu ed., *Sōkō Bukkyō-kai kaikyō sanjūnen kinen-shi*, 1930, reprinted edition in *Bukkyō kaigai kaikyō shiryō shūsei Hokubei hen*, vol. 1 (Tokyo: Fuji Shuppan, 2008), 95–96.

5  Roger Daniels, *The Politics of Prejudice: The Anti-Japanese Movement in California and the Struggle for Japanese Exclusion* (Gloucester, Mass.: Peter Smith, 1966). Minohara Toshihiro, *Kariforunia-shū no hainichi undō to Nichibei kankei* (Tokyo: Yūhikaku, 2006).

6  A meeting of the missionaries from the Buddhist churches in the West Coast and representatives of believers was held from 8 July to 10 July 1914. A plan to hold the World Buddhist Conference as well as to establish BMNA as the headquarters of missionary work in North America was placed on the agenda. "Kaikyō honbu enkaku" (1898–1935), Terakawa Hōkō ed., *Hokubei kaikyō enkaku-shi*, Hongan-ji Hokubei Kaikyō Honbu, 1936, reprinted edition in *Bukkyō kaigai kaikyō shiryō shūsei Hokubei hen*, vol. 2 (Tokyo: Fuji Shuppan, 2008), 14.

The ongoing European war is an unprecedented incident in human history. As the extension of this war will result in unlimited enlargement of the situation with the dreadful and cruel tragedy, we the gathering of Buddhists from around the world, as believers of the gospel of peace and philanthropy, unceasingly pray for the immediate end to this cruel war and for the recovery of world peace. Therefore, in the name of the World Buddhist Conference held in San Francisco, representing Buddhists from throughout the world, on the occasion of the Pan-Pacific International Exposition, we express the ardent wish that his excellency the President of the United States of America Woodrow Wilson do his best from his prominent position, based on his lofty spirit in the cause of humanity, to guide the mind of peoples at war to peace.[7]

The fifth point of the resolution, which was also adopted, requested that Uchida and two Sōtō Zen sect monks who were invited from Japan, Hioki Mokusen (1847–1920) and Yamagami Sōgen (1878–1957), should visit the White House in order to deliver the fourth resolution directly to the President. They left for Washington D.C. soon after the conference and met with President Wilson on 23 August to carry out this mission. America had not yet entered the war (it would not do so until 17 April 1917) and President Wilson was known for his attempts at mediation. At the World Buddhist Conference, Japanese Buddhists in the West Coast took action not only to redress the American exclusion of Japanese immigrants, but also to make a direct appeal to President Wilson concerning the war that was engulfing the entire world. Since the Buddhist missionaries began to make plans for the conference (July 1914) right after the Sarajevo Incident on 28 June, it can be assumed that the idea for a peace appeal must have evolved simultaneously with the progress of the war.

Before Hioki departed for the United States, he expressed his desire that the conference discuss possibilities of a peaceful solution to the world at war and report these results to President Wilson.[8] Embracing this sense of mission, Hioki also met with Prime Minister Ōkuma Shigenobu (1838–1922) and Foreign Minister Katō Takaaki (1860–1926) before leaving for the United States. They agreed with Hioki's idea based on Buddhist ideals and requested him to give the President their regards.[9] This indicates that the plan to meet with President

---

7   *Sōkō Bukkyō-kai kaikyō sanjūnen kinen-shi*, 96. My translation.
8   "Bukkyō-kai meika no tobei," *Chūgai Nippō*, 14 July 1915.
9   Takashina Ryūsen ed., *Hioki Mokusen zenshi den* (Tokyo: Daihōrinkaku, 1962), 273, 287–290.

Wilson had been formulated before Hioki's departure and that the idea of making a peace proposal may have originated at this time, although details regarding the addition of this appeal to the resolutions are unknown.

### 1.2    The Twenty-One Demands and Japanese-American Diplomacy in 1915

What did the conference and the resolutions of the Japanese Buddhists mean in the context of international politics and Japanese-American diplomacy in 1915?

Japan entered the war on the side of the Allies on 23 August 1914. In October, Japanese naval forces seized German possessions in the South Seas, including the Mariana, Caroline, and Marshall islands. Qingdao and Jiaozhou Bay in Shandong Province, German leased territories of the Republic, fell to Japanese forces in November. On 18 January 1915, the Ōkuma Cabinet presented the Twenty-One Demands to the government of Republic of China under President Yuan Shikai.

The demands of the Japanese government on China consisted of fourteen articles in Groups One through Four, including the confirmation of Japan's new acquisitions in Shandong Province, the extension of the Lushunkou lease-hold and Japan's interests in South Manchurian Railway zone, the expansion of Japan's interests in southern Manchuria and eastern Inner Mongolia, the joint management by Japan and China of Hanyeping Company, China's major iron-manufacturing company. Moreover, there were seven rather sensitive articles in Group Five that seriously intruded into questions of Chinese sovereignty. After the difficult negotiations with the Chinese government, in which some of these demands were eliminated or revised, the Ōkuma Cabinet presented an ultimatum to China on 7 May 1915. The day that the Yuan regime accepted Japan's ultimatum, 9 May, is now remembered in China as a national day of humiliation.

The demands in Group Five, some of which infringed upon areas of Chinese sovereignty (for example, Japanese military, political, and financial advisors were to be appointed to central government positions), and some of which conflicted with the interests of the United States and Britain (for example, Japan was to be consulted first whenever foreign capital was needed for the construction of railways, mines and harbor works in Fujian Province, and given the rights to construct railways in South China), were initially concealed from the Western powers when the original Twenty-One Demands were presented to China on 18 January, 1915. The Chinese government immediately sought to reject the Group Five demands, stalling for time and leaking the contents of Group Five to the Western powers. In turn, Japan's attempt to conceal the last group of demands was the cause of diplomatic friction with Britain and the United States, and threatened to tarnish Japan's image in international opinion.[10]

Diplomatic officials in the United States were confused when they learned of the secret provisions and contents of the Group Five demands. In February, President Wilson, William J. Bryan, the Secretary of State and other leading persons in charge of diplomacy attempted to understand Japan's intentions. Bryan did not protest when Chinda Sutemi, the Japanese ambassador, explained that the articles in Group Five were not really "demands" but merely "requests." On the other hand, Paul S. Reinsch, the American Minister to China, sent reports, sometimes exaggerated, of Japan's intention to make excessive demands, based on information which he received from Chinese diplomats and Western journalists in Beijing. Although President Wilson was cautious about the accuracy of information received from Reinsch, he remained suspicious about the Group Five demands. Nonetheless, the first Bryan Note delivered to the Japanese diplomatic mission on 13 March did not express major opposition to the provisions.[11]

Soon afterwards, new information arrived that changed matters. Japan dispatched additional troops to Shandong during the middle of March to pressure the Chinese government to accept the Group Two demands concerning south Manchuria and east Inner Mongolia. The White House, however, mistook this as a measure to force China into accepting the Group Five demands. Moreover, a twenty-one page telegram arrived on 8 April signed by leading American missionaries and teachers in Beijing condemning Japan's demands and petitioning the president for American assistance to China in order to resist the Japanese demands. These events increased President Wilson's suspicion of Japanese motives. After the Chinese government accepted the ultimatum on 9 May, President Wilson made it clear that the government of the United States would not recognize any treaty that infringed upon American vested rights and the principles of the "open door," "equal opportunity" and "territorial integration" in Manchuria as detailed in the second Bryan Note of 11 May.[12]

By August 1915, when the World Buddhist Conference was held in San Francisco and the three Buddhist priests met with President Wilson in

---

10 Shimada Yōichi, "Taika nijūikkajō yōkyū: Katō Takaaki no gaikō shidō II," *Seijikeizai shigaku*, no. 260 (December 1987): 23–36.

11 Takahara Shūsuke, *Wiruson gaikō to Nihon: Risō to genjitsu no aida, 1913–1921* (Tokyo: Sōbunsha, 2006), 31–48.

12 Kitaoka Shin'ichi, "Nijūikkajō saikō: Nichibei gaikō no sōgo sayō," *Nenpō kindai Nihon kenkyū*, no. 7 (1985): 127–147.

Washington, American views of Japan were highly negative. An aggressive image of Japan, forcing excessive demands on China in the absence of the European powers during the war, had been growing in the American mind via journalism, and it is no wonder that appeals for "world peace" by Japanese Buddhists might be the object of suspicion and disbelief.

Nonetheless, in the midst of this cold season of Japanese-American relations, Uchida Kōyū may well have been sincere in his wish to improve relations between white American and the Japanese community in the West Coast of the United States. Hioki, on the other hand, visited Qingdao after the bloody campaign of October 1914 in order to console the souls of the war victims. His visit to Washington was less driven by politics; as a man of religion, he simply wished to see an end to war.

In the spring of 1915, while the BMNA was busy preparing for the conference in San Francisco, Buddhists in Tokyo were intimately concerned about the course of negotiations between Japan and China. Much hinged on the fate of the twenty-first demand, Article Seven of the infamous Group Five, asking the Chinese government to "recognise the right of preaching by Japanese in China." A group of Buddhists had made strenuous efforts hoping to acquire the formal right to propagate Japanese Buddhism in China. It is ironic that while Japanese Buddhists in the United States held an international conference aiming at peace and reconciliation, some Buddhists in Japan were engaged in promoting demands to China that served to worsen Japanese-American relations.

## 2      Diplomacy and Early Japanese Buddhist Missionary Work in Late Qing China

### 2.1      *The Beginnings of Missionary Work by Higashi Hongan-ji in China*

Before dealing with Buddhist activities in 1915 regarding the right to propagate religions in China, this section examines how Japanese Buddhists began missionary work in late Qing China and the sorts of diplomatic problems that ensued.

Among the various sects of Japanese Buddhism, Nishi and Higashi Hongan-ji were the most enthusiastic in pursuing missionary work abroad. Higashi Hongan-ji was the first to embark on the propagation of Buddhism in China and Korea.

Ogurusu Kōchō (1831–1905), a Higashi Hongan-ji monk, went to Beijing via Shanghai in July 1873 to investigate the state of contemporary Chinese Buddhism. He had read literature on the doctrine of Christianity and warned that its spread in East Asia would bring social disorder and decline in Buddhism.

This was a major motive behind his trip to China as well as a common concern of Japanese Buddhist thinkers. Since the late Edo period, Higashi and Nishi Hongan-ji had collected information on Christian missionary work in China. In 1868, the year of the Meiji Restoration, Hongan-ji representatives recommended that the government continue to prohibit the propagation of Christianity and championed the role of Buddhism in protecting the Japanese nation state.[13]

In Beijing, Ogurusu learned Chinese, associated with Chinese Buddhists and exchanged views. Ogurusu had a grand design of a Buddhist league that would consist of Japan, China and India with the goal to resist the threat of Christianity that accompanied Western imperialism across Asia. He was disappointed when Chinese Buddhists failed to take up his call for united action. In the end, Ogurusu concluded that the "degenerate" state of Chinese Buddhism was responsible for this lethargic response, and felt it necessary to "save" China by spreading Japanese Shinshū Buddhist doctrine.[14]

Ogurusu returned to Japan because of illness in August 1874. In May 1876, the headquarters of Higashi Hongan-ji requested Ogurusu to meet with Foreign Minister Terashima Munenori in order to obtain government understanding and support for Higashi Hongan-ji's missionary work in China. Terashima consented to this request and encouraged Ogurusu.[15] However, since the Sino-Japanese Treaty of Amity concluded in 1871 did not include provisions concerning the Japanese right to propagate religions in China, it may be that Terashima did not have a full grasp of the legal problems that needed to be overcome before Buddhists could engage in missionary work in China.

In July 1876, Higashi Hongan-ji dispatched six missionaries including Ogurusu to Shanghai. With the support of the Japanese consulate, the missionaries leased a house in the British concession and established the Higashi Hongan-ji Branch Temple in Shanghai. In this temple, they also opened a school for young monks from Japan to learn Chinese. They gave daily sermons at the temple and managed to attract the interest of local Chinese people. However, limited financial and personnel resources prevented them from accomplishing remarkable results among the Chinese people. Their main work was in meeting the demands of Japanese residents such as funeral services and

---

13  Kojima Masaru and Kiba Akeshi eds., *Ajia no kaikyō to kyōiku* (Kyoto: Hōzōkan, 1992), 24–27; Dake Mitsuya, "Senzen no Higashi, Nishi Hongan-ji no Ajia kaikyō," *Kokusai shakai bunka kenkyūjo kiyō*, no. 8 (May 2006): 295–296 and n. 3.

14  Chen Jidong, "Kindai bukkyō no yoake: Shinmatsu, Meiji bukkyōkai no kōryū," *Shisō*, no. 943 (November 2002): 92–97.

15  Satō Saburō, *Kindai Nicchū kōshō-shi no kenkyū* (Tokyo: Yoshikawa Kōbunkan, 1984), 223.

management of cemeteries, schools and hospitals. Because of an internal dispute within Higashi Hongan-ji in Japan, the early missionaries to China had to withdraw in December 1883. In 1885 they resumed work in Shanghai although their activities again centered on services for Japanese residents.

After the Sino-Japanese War of 1894–95, as the number of Japanese residents involved in military service and their families increased in China, other sects dispatched missionaries. Japanese residential areas, often connected with the military, formed the initial bases for the activities of Japanese Buddhist missionaries. A major enlargement of missionary work began in South China. Nishi Hongan-ji sent military missionaries to Taiwan during the Sino-Japanese War and afterwards began to propagate Buddhism not only among Japanese residents but also among the Taiwanese people. Nishi Hongan-ji increased its base there after the annexation of Taiwan in 1895. And after the Russo-Japanese War of 1904–05, it launched missionary bases in Shanghai, Hankou, Chengdu, and Beijing.[16] Higashi Hongan-ji extended its activities to Quanzhou in Fujian Province and then established branches in Zhejiang, Jiangsu and Guangdong. The activities in those areas showed that they had not abandoned propagation among the Chinese people. The Nichiren sect, after sending its first missionary to Shanghai in 1890, was forced to withdraw due to poor results, but resumed activities in 1899 establishing a branch in Shanghai. The Shingon sect started its work by dispatching a missionary to Dalian in 1908 and gradually expanded its activities. However, the expansion of Japanese Buddhist activities in China during a period of nationalistic movements such as Boxer Rebellion naturally invited conflict between the Japanese Buddhists and Chinese people and political authorities.

### 2.2    Troubles Caused by Japanese Buddhist Missionaries and the Ambiguous Convention on the Right to Preach

After the defeat in the Arrow War in the late 1850s, the Qing government concluded the Treaty of Tianjin (1858) with Russia, the United States, Britain and France. Britain already had the right to propagate Christianity in the interior of China and had demanded the protection of missionaries by local authorities according to the most-favored-nation provision added to the 1843 Treaty of Nanjing. Russia, the United States and France obtained the same right with the Treaty of Tianjin. On the one hand, the ignorance and prejudice of Christian missionaries with regard to native religion and customs and rumors associated with the strange behavior of missionaries were the cause of much trouble and

---

16    Nose Eisui, "Kindai Shinshū Hongan-ji-ha no Chūgoku ni okeru katsudō," *Indogaku bukkyōgaku kenkyū*, vol. 56, no. 2 (March 2008): 22–23.

sometimes intense anti-Christian activity. On the other hand, the extraterritorial rights enjoyed by Christian churches not only applied to missionaries but also to Chinese followers so that sometimes lawbreakers were part the mix of church membership. Central and local governments constantly agonized over how to deal with these frequent troubles that threatened the destruction of social and political order.

In the early period of Japanese missionary work in China, Japanese ministers and consuls in China and government officials in Japan operated on the basis of an ambiguous recognition of the right to propagate religions. Government officials, as in the case of Foreign Minister Terashima, did not place importance on any formal stipulation of rights, perhaps because of the long history of shared Buddhist exchange that had existed between China and Japan.[17] As for the Qing government, although it did not admit the formal propagation of Japanese Buddhism, Japanese missionary work was implicitly condoned. Local authorities similarly dealt with each matter without a consistent policy.

Kikuchi Shūgon (1855–1944), a missionary from Higashi Hongan-ji in Zhili, questioned the ambiguous attitudes of both governments and made a formal appeal that the right to preach be clarified when he returned to Japan in June 1881. Rejected at first, Kikuchi persisted and ultimately gained an interview with Iwakura Tomomi, the Minister of the Right. Kikuchi's proposal convinced Higashi Hongan-ji headquarters of the importance of this matter. Although Iwakura ordered the head of Higashi Hongan-ji to let Kikuchi consult with Foreign Minister Inoue Kaoru, a satisfactory outcome was not reached.[18]

Negotiations for the revision of the Sino-Japanese Treaty of Amity, which was to expire in April 1883, finally began in 1886. At that point, the Japanese government did not seek to clarify rights regarding the propagation of religions in China. For the Japanese government, the revision of the treaties with Western powers was more important. Negotiations between the two governments remained inconclusive until Japan was able to conclude, after the Sino-Japanese War, the Sino-Japanese Treaty of Commerce and Navigation in 1896. With its enhanced status gained by victory in war, Japan was able to include the most-favored-nation provision that had up to then been the privilege of the Western powers.

Japanese Buddhist missionary activity in China increased rapidly in the early years of the 20th century, but so did incidents of anti-Japanese behavior.

---

17    Satō, *Kindai Nicchū kōshō-shi no kenkyū*, 230.

18    Ibid., 231–233.

In South China, particularly in Fujian and Zhejiang Province, a number of anti-Japanese Buddhist movements took place, sometimes connected with financial corruption and claims of moral depravity; like the Christian missionaries, Japanese Buddhists and their converts were slandered because of protection and privileges afforded them by their foreign nationality.[19]

On 24 August 1900, an incident happened which was unusual but crucial in strengthening suspicions about Japanese Buddhist activities among Chinese central and local governments. During the Boxer Rebellion, Ueno Sen'ichi, the consul in Amoy, requested the Japanese navy in Taiwan to dispatch warships for the protection of Japanese residents when a Higashi Hongan-ji temple in Amoy was burned down. The Japanese navy sent the warships and attempted to land at Amoy but failed. It turned out later that the fire was set by a Higashi Hongan-ji monk connected with the Governor-General of Taiwan.

After this incident, the fact that Buddhist missionaries were operating without the formal right to propagate religions became a major bone of contention between the Qing and Japanese governments. The gap in interpretation of treaty provisions between the two governments was exposed, causing diplomatic dispute whenever trouble with Japanese missionaries occurred. The Japanese Ministry of Foreign Affairs insisted that Japanese missionaries had equal rights with other treaty powers who had the right to propagate religions in China under the most-favored-nation provision in the Sino-Japanese Treaty of Commerce and Navigation. Rejecting this interpretation, the Qing government asserted that there was no article in the treaty to stipulate that Japan had the right and that the religion Western powers were allowed to propagate was Christianity, thereby disqualifying Buddhism.[20]

Japanese ministers and consuls in China were not only troubled by negotiations with the Qing government, but sometimes equally troubled with their own dealings with the "wicked" Japanese missionaries. While Christian missionaries overseas generally had the financial and moral support of missionary headquarters in their respective countries, Japanese Buddhist missionaries were not similarly privileged. A lack of funds led some missionaries to collect money illicitly from their Chinese followers. Furthermore, there was a conspicuous case that made headline news both in China and Japan in 1906. As many

---

19   As for the various problems and details of the negotiations between the Japanese consulate and Chinese central and local governments, see ibid., and Iriye Akira, "Chūgoku ni okeru Nihon bukkyō fukyō mondai: Shinmatsu Nicchū kankei no ichi-danmen," *Kokusai seiji*, vol. 64, no. 2 (April 1965).

20   Ibid., 89–96.

as thirty-five Chinese temples in Zhejiang Province suddenly decided to belong to Higashi Hongan-ji in order to escape from *Miaochanxingxue*, an education policy in late Qing to utilize temple properties for establishing schools. This case provoked the antipathy of the Qing government. The consulate in Hangzhou ordered the deportation of the Higashi Hongan-ji monk who took the lead in this case. The Ministry of Foreign Affairs in Japan sent notification to the headquarters of each sect requesting the improvement of personnel for missionaries overseas. These provisions, however, did not result in any remarkable change for the better.[21]

For China, in addition to problems caused by Christian missionary work under the provisions of the unequal treaty system, the activities of Japanese Buddhist missionaries only made a bad situation worse. It was impossible for China, even after the 1911 Revolution that ended the Qing dynasty, to admit the right to propagate Japanese Buddhism. And for the Japanese Ministry of Foreign Affairs, troubles over Buddhist missionaries in China and disputes with the Chinese government accompanying those troubles were annoying diplomatic obstacles.

## 3      Postponement of Issues Relating to Religion in the Twenty-One Demands

When the Japanese government presented the Twenty-One Demands to China, Japanese Buddhists were seemingly given a chance to acquire propagation rights. The nature of treaty negotiations between Japan and China had drastically changed from the time when Kikuchi Shūgon first pointed out the ambiguity of Japanese right to preach in China at the government in 1881. Negotiations on this matter were carried out as part of the new series of demands on China, backed up by Japan's participation in the Great War on the side of the Allies.

The seven "demands" in Group Five were a grab bag of miscellaneous items, derived from a variety of groups interested in China including the army, political parties and voluntary organizations. According to the initial formulation of Group Five, as detailed in a document entitled "Propositions Relating to the Solution of Pending Questions and Others," the articles relating to Buddhism included: "2. The Chinese Government to recognise the right of land ownership for the purpose of building Japanese hospitals, temples, and schools

---

21      Satō, *Kindai Nicchū kōshō-shi no kenkyū*, 254–269.

thereon in the interior China"; and "7. The Chinese Government to recognise the right of preaching by Japanese in China."[22]

Among the various proposals for the demands, the one written by *Tōa Dōshikai* [Association of Comradeship for East Asia] in Kumamoto,[23] and the one by Kanda Masao (1879–1961), the correspondent to the *Ōsaka Asahi Shinbun* in Beijing,[24] included an article to give the Japanese the right to propagate religions in China. Kanda, who had experience as an educator in Sichuan and who was well-connected with both Japanese and Chinese government leaders, was knowledgeable in Chinese affairs.

There is no accurate record detailing how the right to propagate religions in China was eventually included in the initial Group Five. Its placement as the very last demand may indicate that the matter was considered less important compared with other demands. But without a doubt the matter was regarded as a longstanding diplomatic issue requiring some sort of solution.

How, then, were negotiations for the articles relating to religion conducted? On 16 February, 12 and 22 April 1915, Katō Takaaki dispatched telegrams to Hioki Eki (1861–1926), the Minister to China in Beijing, regarding compromises made with regard to Group Five. The 16 February telegram notes that "as for Article Two on the right of land ownership for the purpose of building Japanese hospitals, temples, and schools, and Article Seven on the right of preaching by Japanese, you should exact a promise that the Chinese government must give favorable consideration at some other day."[25] Thus Katō ordered Hioki to extract a future concession for these articles from the Chinese government.

Afterwards, these articles were brought into negotiation between Hioki and the foreign officers of the Chinese government at their sixteenth meeting on 30 March. As Hioki reported, they discussed Articles Two and Seven together and arguments regarding the right to propagate religions went on more than two hours. And as Hioki concluded, "after all, the Chinese government was far from giving the Japanese the right to propagate religions so that it seems to be quite difficult to get their agreement on this matter."[26] Following these words, Hioki entered into a long description of the reasons why the Chinese government was unwilling to compromise on this matter as conveyed by Lu Zhengxiang, the Minister of Foreign Affairs.

---

22　"Gaimushō Happyō" on 7 May 1915, *Nihon gaikō monjo* [*Henceforth cited as NGM*], Taishō 4 [1915]. vol. 3-1, 400.

23　Dated 1 September 1914, *NGM*, T3 [1914], vol. 2, 909–914.

24　Dated 10 October 1914, *NGM*, T3 [1914], vol. 2, 929–935.

25　From Katō to Hioki on 16 February 1915, *NGM*, T4 [1915], vol. 3-1, 166. My translation.

26　From Hioki to Katō on 30 March 1915, *NGM*, T4 [1915], vol. 3-1, 272. My translation.

According to Lu, the Chinese government wished to prevent problems similar to those caused by Christian missionaries because they might be the cause of future diplomatic discord between China and Japan. Moreover, it was unnecessary for China to import Buddhism from Japan since it already existed in China. Lu feared that doctrinal disputes between Chinese and Japanese Buddhists might cause conflict and social unrest. Finally, just as Christian missionaries interfered in legal and administrative incidents by protecting their Chinese followers, Japanese Buddhists might come to China with political ambitions and conspire with Chinese monks, drawing them into illegal and potentially dangerous activities. Therefore, Lu concluded that the Chinese government must request the Japanese government not to persist in this matter. Hioki attempted to refute Lu's claims. He explained that so long as the Chinese government admitted Christians to preach in China, it was the Japanese government's duty to give the Japanese people the same right as enjoyed by the Western powers. Moreover, Hioki stated that extending Japanese Buddhists the right to preach in China would instead advance the cause of friendship between Japan and China, precisely because they shared the same religion. The possibility of troubles arising should not be an excuse to refuse the right to propagate Buddhism since there would necessarily be appropriate means to ameliorate these troubles. In the end, no agreement was reached, but Hioki vowed that the Japanese government would not abandon the matter.[27]

During talks after the meeting, as Hioki reported, Cao Rulin, the Vice Foreign Minister suggested his personal view that granting rights of land ownership for hospitals and schools might be possible.[28] But even this suggestion excluded "temples" from Article Two.

Due to the firm rejection of the right to propagate religions at the sixteenth meeting and Cao's suggestion to consider Article Two, the seventeenth meeting on 1 April dealt with Article Two without "temples."[29] At this point, the right to propagate religions was in effect shelved.

On 12 April Katō directed Hioki to record the statement in the minutes that the Japanese government would restart negotiations for the right to propagate religions another day.[30] Katō's 22 April telegram on the "final revisions" reminded Hioki that the issue of religious propagation was not dead.[31]

---

27    Ibid., 272–273.
28    Ibid., 273.
29    From Hioki to Katō on 2 April 1915, *NGM*, T4 [1915], vol. 3-1, 280.
30    From Katō to Hioki on 12 April 1915, *NGM*, T4 [1915], vol. 3-1, 315.
31    From Katō to Hioki on 22 April 1915, *NGM*, T4 [1915], vol. 3-1, 339.

Among the articles of Group Five, Article Six regarding the capitals in Fujian Province was revised and an arrangement reached. But others provoked the ire of the Chinese government and made negotiations rough going, so that it drove the Japanese government to issue an ultimatum in May. Owing to a hint from Britain that it was considering the abrogation of the Anglo-Japanese Alliance and instructions from elder statesmen such as Yamagata Aritomo, Katō withdrew or postponed the unsettled articles of Group Five.[32] When Katō wrote the proposal for the ultimatum on 4 May to be submitted to the council of the elder statesmen (*Genrō kaigi*), he stated clearly that "the right of land ownership for temples is to be withdrawn."[33] And the ultimatum included the following statement: "the question of the freedom of preaching by Japanese missionaries, will be left for future discussion."[34]

### 4       The Activities of Buddhists for the Right to Propagate Religions in China

#### 4.1     *The Appeal of the Bukkyōto Yūshi Taikai*
As described above, at the seventeenth meeting in Beijing on 1 April, the negotiations over the right to propagate religions was in effect shelved. Almost a month later, in Japan, some pro-Buddhist activists established the Bukkyōto Yūshi Taikai, an association for lobbying and protesting the importance of acquiring the right to propagate Buddhism in China.

This association, with headquarters in Asakusa, consisted of monks, lay Buddhists, journalists, politicians and pan-Asianist activists. On 30 April, they held a gathering and presented a resolution to be printed in the newspapers. It declared that "the only way" to "maintain eternal peace in East Asia and activate humanity and benevolence" is to "fuse the thoughts of Japanese and Chinese peoples and thereby advance friendship." Moreover, "the Buddhism shared in Japan and China in common invites spiritual exchange; it deems that they [the Chinese people] should rely upon us [Japanese] under a relationship as close and cooperative as that of lips and teeth; we must ensure that they listen to us under our guidance in the right direction. Only in this way can we achieve true and righteous results." The document proceeded to relate that it

---

32    Shimada Yōichi, "Taika nijūikkajō yōkyū," Inoue Mitsusada et al. eds., *Nihon rekishi taikei 5 Kindai II* (Tokyo: Yamakawa Shuppansha, 1989), 63 and n. 6.

33    From Katō to Hioki on 6 May 1915 (Appendix 2, Proposal written on 4 May), *NGM*, T4 [1915], vol. 3-1, 385. My translation.

34    "Gaimushō Happyō" on 7 May 1915, ibid., 405.

would be a "national dishonor" if Japan does not share equally with the Western powers the right to propagate religions.[35]

At this gathering, fifteen persons were selected as members of the executive committee. Five of them asked for interviews with Ōkuma, Katō and Ichiki Kitokurō, the Minister of Education on 1 May. At the Ministry of Foreign Affairs, the five representatives lodged a petition with Matsui Keishirō, the Vice Foreign Minister who met with them instead of Katō. Four other representatives visited the branches of major Buddhist sects in Tokyo to explain their purpose and gain their cooperation.[36]

When they were informed that the right to propagate religions would be postponed in the final plan for the treaty, the executive committee held a meeting on 11 May. They determined to send their resolution to members of the Diet for the purpose of making inquiries regarding the support of individual Diet members, to make a proposition in the Diet, to give public speeches, to cooperate with other Buddhist associations or voluntary groups throughout Japan, and to organize a center of operations in Japan for missionary activities in China so as to connect the activities of all Buddhist sects. Additionally, it was decided that Mizuno Baigyō, a monk who was familiar with Chinese affairs, would immediately write a book to publicize the importance of the matter.[37]

The core members of this association were Andō Masazumi (editor-in-chief of *Tōkyō Asahi Shinbun*, 1876–1955), Tamura Hōryō (monk, Nichiren sect), Shibata Ichinō (monk, Nichiren sect, 1873–1951), Tomita Kōjun (monk, Buzan school of Shingon sect, 1875–1955), Mizuno Baigyō (monk, Nishi Hongan-ji, 1878–1949), Ōmori Zenkai (monk, Sōtō sect, 1871–1947), Tanaka Zenryū (monk, Higashi Hongan-ji, 1874–1955), Shimaji Daitō (monk, Nishi Hongan-ji, 1875–1927), Watanabe Kaigyoku (monk, Jōdo sect, 1872–1933), Takashima Beihō (lay Buddhist, 1875–1949), Tanaka Shashin (lay Buddhist, 1863–1934), Wada Yūgen (lay Buddhist, journalist, 1882–1942), Tatsuguchi Ryōshin (lay Buddhist, member of the House of Representatives, 1867–1943), Sasaki Yasugorō (member of the House of Representatives, 1872–1934), Itō Tomoya (Kokuryū-kai, member of the House of Representatives, 1873–1921) and Ogawa Heikichi (member of the House of Representatives, 1870–1942). It is curious that most of them were born around 1870 except for Tanaka Shashin and Wada Yūgen.

---

35    "Bukkyōto funki," *Tōkyō Asahi Shinbun*, 1 May 1915. My translation.
36    "Bukkyōto no kakushō hōmon," *Chūgai Nippō*, 5 May 1915.
37    "Taishi fukyōken mondai no zengo undō," *Chūgai Nippō*, 15 May, 1915. Mizuno in effect published a book in July entitled *Shina ni okeru Ōbei no dendō seisaku* (Tokyo: Bukkyōto Yūshi Taikai, 1915).

Andō Masazumi was born into a Higashi Hongan-ji temple and became a longstanding leading activist for strengthening the ties between Buddhists and the nation state. Lay Buddhist journalists such as Andō and Wada, who worked for *Chūgai Nippō*, a newspaper of religious matters, made use of space in the papers for making their activities known.

The monks among the members were not only from Higashi and Nishi Hongan-ji but also from other sects that had begun missionary work later than both Hongan-ji sects. The group also included activists such as Mizuno Baigyō and Itō Tomoya who were engaged in various activities concerning Japan-China relations and associated with the leaders of the 1911 Xinhai Revolution. Itō belonged to Kokuryū-kai, the pan-Asian nationalist group.

One important point is that some leading figures of this movement were Diet members and activists who advocated a strong foreign policy. They belonged to Kokumin Gaikō Dōmeikai [National Alliance for Diplomacy], a voluntary group that was formed right after Japan's takeover of Qingdao in November 1914 and often brought pressure on the government's foreign policy. Andō, Tanaka Shashin, Tanaka Zenryū, Itō, Sasaki and Ogawa were the members. Ogawa in particular, the central figure of Kokumin Gaikō Dōmeikai, was famous for his condemnation of the government's foreign policy in speeches on the Diet floor. He spoke on behalf of the Bukkyōto Yūshi Taikai when the government decided to postpone a decision on preaching rights in China.[38]

The movement to support Buddhist activities in China joined forces with advocates of a strong foreign policy in an attempt to influence Japan's demands on China. The members of the Bukkyōto Yūshi Taikai severely criticized the Chinese government for its refusal to permit Japanese Buddhists to preach in China. At the same time, it found the Japanese government at fault for its weak-kneed approach; and the Japanese populace was similarly reproached for its low level of interest in the future of Buddhism in China. Finally, they complained that even some Buddhist sects were lukewarm when asked for support.

### 4.2    *Defending Japanese Buddhist Activities in China*
The logic of the Bukkyōto Yūshi Taikai on behalf of the propagation of Japanese Buddhism in China reflected the imperialistic nature of their demand. It had the following four points.

---

38    After the Chinese government accepted the ultimatum, Ogawa insisted that the postponement of solving the matter of the right to propagate religions in China was a "big failure" (*Chūgai Nippō*, 16 May 1915).

First of all, Bukkyōto Yūshi Taikai members justified the right to propagate Buddhism in China by referring to connections between Christian missionary activity and the encroachment of Western imperialism in East Asia. For example, they were astonished at the fact that Germany was able to dispatch troops and occupy Jiaozhou Bay in 1897, citing the murder of two German missionaries as an excuse. Initially, Japanese Buddhists sought to undertake missionary activity in China as a way of dealing with the crisis brought on by this combination of Christianity and Western imperialism. Later, however, Japan itself adopted an expansionist agenda in competition with the West. On the one hand, members of the Bukkyōto Yūshi Taikai were both afraid of, but also interested in, the way that Western powers sought to advance their interests by means of the right to propagate Christianity. According to Watanabe: "Look, Western nations realize that in China it is necessary to win the minds of the people. Therefore they place importance on the right to propagate Christianity and have done everything possible to protect their missionaries."[39] The group criticized the Japanese government's ignorance of the importance of this matter. On the other hand, they concealed Japan's own imperialist agenda and emphasized the importance of being a "good neighbor" to China and showing "proper guidance" through the spread of Buddhism.[40]

The Bukkyōto Yūshi Taikai was also wary of the political engagement of Christian missionaries in China. For example, as noted above, American missionaries in China sent a long telegram to President Wilson seeking to convey their opposition to Japan's demands.[41] Such activities were the subject of critical press reports in Japan.[42]

Second, Bukkyōto Yūshi Taikai members mobilized the concept of "freedom of religion" as a "universal principle of modern civilization" (bunmei no tsūgi) in demanding equal standing with other treaty powers in China. As Andō declared: "freedom of religion is not only obtained but fully realized when one

---

39  Bukkyōto Yūshi Taikai, "Shina naichi fukyōken mondai sengen-sho" written by Watanabe Kaigyoku, Shin bukkyō, vol. 16, no. 6 (June 1915): 548. My translation.

40  Ibid., 547–551.

41  The copies of the dispatch from American missionaries and teachers in Beijing to the president were distributed to the foreign correspondents, including members of the Japanese press (Lo Hui-Min ed., The Correspondence of G.E. Morrison 2, 1912–1920 (Cambridge: Cambridge University Press, 1978), 442–443). Japanese correspondents including Kanda Masao may have received a copy and dispatched it to Japanese news agencies.

42  For example, "Shina bukkyō dendō ni tsuite, waga kirisutokyōto no kyōryoku wo nozomu," Ōsaka Shinpō, 26 April 1915.

can propagate religion to the people of a treaty country."[43] The Bukkyōto Yūshi Taikai insisted that it was proper that rights given to the Japanese people should be guaranteed when they were in China.

Third, they emphasized Japan's special historical, cultural and geographic relationship with China. Together, Japanese people could advance "peace in the East" in a way that the Christian nations could not. Mizuno expressed his belief by saying that Japan and China shared "the same region, same script, same race, same creed," and that "a shared Buddhism will lead us to mutual reliance and solidarity in dealing with spiritual matters as the essence of humanity."[44] Andō asserted, "Japanese Buddhism has its root in China so that the sources of our doctrine and faith would never change despite changes in international relations due to temporal measures. ...This is something very different from Christianity in China in which differences in principle leads to conflict with Chinese thought and social uprisings."[45]

As seen above, the Bukkyōto Yūshi Taikai took advantage of seemingly contradictory approaches. At once they identified with Christian nations in protesting their freedom to preach alongside other treaty powers. But at the same time, they stressed Japan's long history of cultural exchange in East Asia that distinguished them from the Christian missionaries. Thus they based their claim both on their identification with the modern nations of the West and on their differences as an Eastern country with a long and unique tradition of Asian cultural exchange.

Fourth, Bukkyōto Yūshi Taikai members regarded Chinese Buddhism as "degenerate" and expressed a sense of mission to "revive" it. As Shimaji put it, "present-day Chinese Buddhism is disordered and corrupt. It is the mission of Japanese Buddhists to radically put it in order and purify it."[46] This view was common in justifying Japanese Buddhist missionary work in China. This mission was called "requital of gratitude" (hōon), as Takashima reasoned that "Japan had received much spiritual and material benefits from China in the past. Thus, it is Japan's turn to repay China for the benefits in the future. ... Metaphorically speaking, Buddhism was a bride from China so that present-day Japanese Buddhism is a child of the Chinese bride and her Japanese

43 Andō Tecchō (Masazumi), "Fukyōken mondai 1," *Tōkyō Asahi Shinbun*, 15 May 1915. My translation.
44 Mizuno, *Shina ni okeru Ōbei no dendō seisaku*, 106. My translation.
45 Andō, "Fukyōken mondai 7," *Tōkyō Asahi Shinbun*, 21 May 1915. My translation.
46 Shimaji Daitō, "Naze Shina e bukkyō no gyakuyunyū wo yōsuruka," *Chūgai Nippō*, 8 May 1915. My translation.

bridegroom."[47] These two statements seem to be saying different things, but in fact display a similar sense of cultural superiority over the Chinese. Despite disguising Japanese Buddhism as a "child" and heaping expressions of gratitude for blessings received from China, the attitude is clearly one of self-righteous paternalism toward Chinese Buddhism.

### Conclusion

Japanese attempts to propagate Buddhism in China were justified by an imperialist logic that increasingly dominated the relationship between the two countries in the early 20th century. In August 1915, when the World Buddhist Conference was held in San Francisco, the activities of the Bukkyōto Yūshi Taikai were in full swing. While Japanese Buddhists in California were confronted by racial prejudice and anti-Japanese behavior, Buddhists in Japan enthusiastically sought to impose demands on China, focusing on the right to propagate Buddhism, that not only worsened relations with China, but with the United States as well. The Twenty-One Demands was a crucial turn for Buddhists to pour their sense of mission into thus imperialistic mold.

On 23 October 1915, a memorial service for Ogurusu Kōchō, who had died in 1905, was held at the branch temple of Higashi Hongan-ji in Tokyo. At this occasion, a report was given on the activities of the Bukkyōto Yūshi Taikai. Hioki Mokusen, who had just returned from the United States was invited to the ceremony but was unable to attend due to a busy schedule. Instead, the manuscript of his speech was read out. Admiring Ogurusu, the pioneer of propagation of Japanese Buddhism in China, members of the Bukkyōto Yūshi Taikai delivered fervent speeches to urge more strenuous efforts to secure the right to preach in China.[48]

In fact, even if Japanese Buddhists were able to obtain legal rights in China, the quality of missionary work may not have improved substantially. Moreover, despite the slogan of "peace in East Asia" and "friendship between Japan and China," Japanese Buddhism did not have the capability to exert influence in China where anti-Japanese nationalism was on the rise. Even Andō could not help but worry whether Japanese monks had "the strength in reserve" to assume the heavy responsibility for "spiritual matters" in Japanese-Chinese

---

47    Takashima Beihō, "Shina naichi fukyōken no kakutoku," *Shin bukkyō*, vol. 16, no. 5 (May 1915): 523–524. My translation.

48    "Taishi kyōken[sic] mondai no kogō," *Chūgai Nippō*, 27 October 1915.

diplomatic relations.[49] Limitations of financial and personnel resources did not allow Japanese Buddhists to compete with their Christian counterparts.

The activities of the Bukkyōto Yūshi Taikai did not produce appreciable results. Eventually, on the occasion of the Washington Naval Conference on 4 February 1922, when the Japanese government reluctantly agreed to the return of former German leased-territories in Shandong Province and to the abandonment of priority for Japanese investments in Manchuria and Mongolia, the postponed items from Group Five, including the right to propagate religions, were withdrawn. Nonetheless, Japanese Buddhists continued their activities in China despite the absence of legal arrangements.

Although the activities of the Bukkyōto Yūshi Taikai did not have a strong influence on the realities of ever-changing diplomatic priorities, their discourse displayed a modern Buddhist nationalism that corresponded positively with imperialistic attitudes toward China. As Japanese military operations expanded in China in the 1930s, Buddhism was closely linked to organized national policy for pacification work among the Chinese people and for the moral edification for Japanese residents. Since the establishment of Manchukuo in 1932, Nishi Hongan-ji rapidly increased its presence in Manchuria and North China. Higashi Hongan-ji, too, developed branches in North China after the Lugouqiao (Marco Polo Bridge) Incident of 7 July 1937. Buddhist activities followed pace with the course of Japanese military invasion. Under the Asian Development Board (*Kōa-in*), an organization established directly under the Cabinet in 1938, Buddhists and Christians alike were mobilized in an attempt to win over the hearts and minds of the Chinese people.[50] The legal arrangements for the propagation of religions in China were long left undone as Japanese Buddhists cooperated wholeheartedly in the military's attempt to bring about a new order in Asia.

---

49    Andō, "Fukyōken mondai 7."
50    Kiba Akeshi, "Kindai ni okeru Nihon bukkyō no Ajia dendō," Nihon Bukkyō Kenkyū-kai
       ed., *Nihon no bukkyō vol. 2, Ajia no naka no Nihon bukkyō* (Kyoto: Hōzōkan, 1995), 227–230.

# Railroad Workers and World War I
## Labor Hygiene and the Policies of Japanese National Railways

*Chaisung Lim*

### Introduction

After successfully operating the first train line between Yokohama and Shinbash of Tokyo in 1873, the Japanese government built a national railroad network by working with the privately owned railroad businesses. When the Japanese National Railroad (JNR) was founded in 1907 after taking over 17 private railroad companies, an integration of railroad facilities and operation systems became a pressing issue. As a result, the number of railroad employees reached approximately 90,000, up from 30,000. And the President, Koto Shinpei, strongly advocated "JNR Familism" for all employees coming from different backgrounds. However, it could not have been possible to properly operate the nationwide railroad network if the familism – the close relationship between the railroad company and its employees – had not covered any substantive issues on a personal basis. In other words, as the day and night running of trains resulted in more complex tasks for workers, it became necessary to keep all field workers healthy and robust so that those workers could fully display their capabilities.

As railways spread disease from one region to another, the JNR was required to keep railroad cars and stations clean all the time and provide health and hygiene services to all field workers, including medical checkups, nutrition care, disaster prevention, occupational disease treatment, and social insurance. But these health and hygiene policies were not perfect from the start, and specific measures were not offered until concerns were voiced about the deterioration in health among employees. Meanwhile, the JNR was capable of building an excellent labor hygiene system, which came to be referred to as an "advanced system" by other sectors. The labor hygiene system was not limited to Japan. With the expansion of Japan's railroad network to its colonies, the labor hygiene system was also introduced to other parts of the Japanese empire.

The purpose of this article is to elucidate the process of building a labor hygiene system by reviewing the changes in the hygienic conditions of the employees of the prewar JNR, and the subsequent actions taken by the JNR authorities. Although there have been studies of the labor hygiene systems in the spinning and mining industries before the war, little attention has been

© KONINKLIJKE BRILL NV, LEIDEN, 2014 | DOI 10.1163/9789004274273_021

paid to the labor hygiene of the railway industry.[1] To the best of my knowledge, the 1992 article by Hazime Matsufuzi is the sole academic paper about the JNR.[2] However, since his study was intended only as an academic analysis on "Railway Labor Hygiology" rather than as a review of the history of "Railway Labor Hygiene," it focuses primarily on the research conducted by hygiene research institutes before and after the war. In addition, Sōsuke Fujiwara's 1960 article analyzed the mutual aid association and concluded that the association, as a comprehensive protection measure for labor living, laid the foundation for the development of "JNR Familism."[3] Although Fujiwara's analysis is insightful, he does not examine the question of labor hygiene from the perspective of labor force preservation. Elsewhere, I argue that the modern labor hygiene system was based on the colonial employment structure and it was established in a manner so as to give priority to Japanese employees.[4]

This chapter is divided into three parts. The first section reviews how the hygiene system was first developed in the JNR after the nationalization of railroads. Then, the next section examines the impact of the First World War on railroad workers. In the third section, I discuss the measures taken by the JNR authorities to improve the health of the workers.

### Nationalization of Railways and Establishment of its Labor Hygiene System

During the Russo-Japanese War, the main-line railway network in Japan was operated by a dozen or more railway companies and as a result, the operation of railroad cars, communication with crew members, fare calculation and other things became extremely complicated. Accordingly, there was an urgent need for operating a state-run main-line network. For this reason, the Japanese government decided to purchase 17 private railroad companies and in March 1907, the JNR was founded. With the birth of the national railroad organization, the number of employees quadrupled from 28,878 in March 1906 to 90,491 in

---

1   See, for example, Osamu Isihara, "Female Factory Workers and Tuberculosis," *Gazette of National Medical Association*, No. 322 (1913), 1–118.

2   Hazime Matufuzi, "History of Labor Hygiene in Japanese Railway," *Science for Labor*, 68, 3 (1992), 102–114.

3   Sōsuke Fujiwara, *The Change of Labor Policy by Prewar JNR* (Tokyo: Investigation and Research Study Division, Japanese Association of Labor, 1960), 1–52.

4   Chaisung Lim, "The Development of Labor Hygiene in Colonial Korea, 1910–1945: The Health Conditions of Korean National Railways (KNR) Employees," *Seoul Journal of Korean Studies*, 24(1) (2001): 51–86.

November 1908. Then, as the number of employees surpassed 100,000, there was a growing need for an efficient labor management.[5]

In particular, the authority officials thought that the employees from the privately-owned railroad companies experienced dramatic changes in their wages due to the shift of their status, and thus would be likely to feel insecure.[6] Additionally, in each railroad company, the continuation of employment was not guaranteed for the executives and high-grade employees and as a result, there existed a high level of dissatisfaction among many high-level employees. In the past, given that the locomotive engineers of JNR on the Tohoku Line had held a walkout, the sense of uneasiness was high.

As a response, some measures were taken that included "inspiring the cooperative spirit, promoting proper communication between the upper and lower sides and then sweeping away anxiety over status" and "building appropriate welfare facilities, promoting a relief system and thereby eliminating any future concerns."[7] These measures were later described as the JNR Familism, that is, the railroad company should help its employees in the spirit of one big family. For the leaders of the JNR, familism meant that the "family members" should follow the orders of the leaders and not be overcome by individual interests. During the prewar period, the JNR Familism played an important role in the labor-management relations, and in the process of implementing the familism, the German labor insurance system was studied. But, when the Ministry of Finance and the Bureau of Legislation were seeking a compromise in legislation, it was pointed out that it would be premature to initiate the compulsory insurance system and therefore it would be unfair if the system was applied only to the JNR workers. Consequently, the insurance act was abandoned in February 1907.[8] As an alternative, the relief association system – a first step toward social insurance – was implemented, along with the establishment of Imperial Government Railways.

According to the plan, the JNR relief association (known as mutual aid association in 1918) paid relief funds to the families of those who had died, or to those who had sustained disabilities while on duty. To be certain of having a sufficient fund, the workers paid 3% of their wages to the JNR relief association and the government paid 2% worth of the workers' salary. There was a plan for

---

5  Department of Health, Secretariat, Minister of Railways, *The 50-Year History of National Railways Mutual Aid Association* (Tokyo: Ministry of Railways, 1938), 8.

6  See Isaburo Yamakata, "Nationalization of Railways at A High Speed" [18 July 1906], in *The 50-Year History of National Railways Mutual Aid Association*, 8–13.

7  Ibid., 8–13.

8  Ibid., 44–45; see also *The 50-Year History of National Railways Mutual Aid Association*, 32.

insuring for the injuries, death, and senility but then, the absence of financial resources and the data on disease relief activities caused a delay in implementing the insurance project. Mitsuyoshi Sato, the president of the Japanese Association of Railway Medicine stated that the mutual aid association was only a starting point in railway hygiene.[9] As seen in Figure 19.1, there were three types of association members. The A-type members included all field workers under the age of 50 who paid the association dues until the age of 55. The B-type members included employees, except all field workers, who joined the association and were not eligible for the government subsidy. The C-type included employees under age 15 or over age 50 and employees who had worked for the company for six months or less. The C-type members were exempted from paying the dues. As for the A and C types, full membership was required and the criteria for type A was broad enough to include more employees in the JNR relief association.

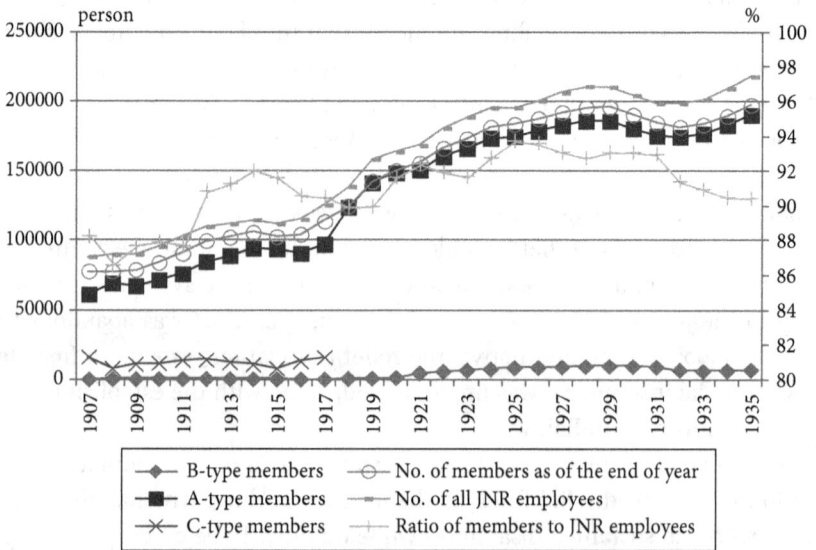

FIGURE 19.1     *Trend in the number of association members per type (Unit: person, %).*
SOURCE: NATIONAL RAILWAYS MUTUAL AID ASSOCIATION, *THE 50-YEAR HISTORY OF NATIONAL RAILWAYS MUTUAL AID ASSOCIATION* (TOKYO: NATIONAL RAILWAYS MUTUAL AID ASSOCIATION, 1958), 108–109 (NOTE: ONLY RATIO OF MEMBERS IS EXPRESSED WITH %).

9  Japanese Association of Railway Medicine, "Article about the 1st General Meeting of Japanese Association of Railway Medicine," *Gazette of Japanese Association of Railway Medicine*, 1, 3 (1915): 85.

What was the health condition of the railroad workers? According to the available data, the mortality rate was 7–9‰ and the injury-causing mortality rate 2‰ (Figure 19.5).[10] The operation accidents accounted for a majority of the diseases and injuries sustained while on duty. Of course, as illustrated in Figure 19.2, the numbers of accidents and casualties per one million train-km decreased in the long term but the numbers of annual accidents and casualties reached over 3000 and over 2000 respectively. Furthermore, a lot of accidents, which resulted in diseases and injuries while on duty, occurred in railway workshops and were not related to the operation of trains. The data shows that the frequency of accidents in the railway workshops was higher than that in other workplaces (Figure 19.3). With regards to the trend in disease and injuries while on duty, the mortality rate caused by disease amounted to 4–5‰. In short, two-thirds of death was caused by disease.

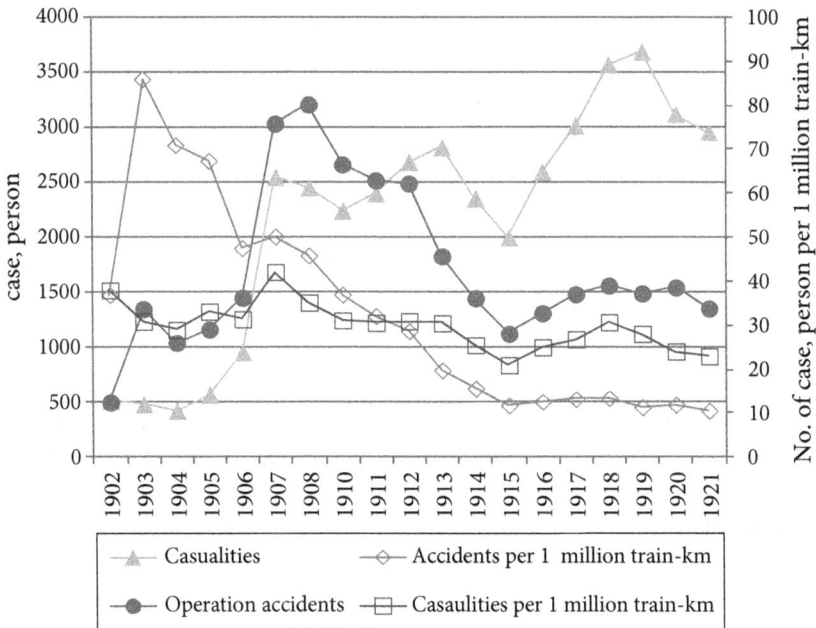

FIGURE 19.2    *The number of cases of operation accidents and toll of casualties in the JNR (Unit: case, person).*
SOURCE: JAPANESE GOVERNMENT RAILWAYS, *JAPANESE GOVERNMENT RAILWAYS YEARBOOK* (TOKYO: JAPANESE GOVERNMENT RAILWAYS, ANNUAL EDITION); MINISTRY OF RAILWAYS, *RAILWAY STATISTICS* (TOKYO: MINISTRY OF RAILWAYS, ANNUAL EDITION). NOTE: DATA OF 1909 IS MISSING.

10    A per mil (‰) is a tenth of a percent (%) or one part per thousand.

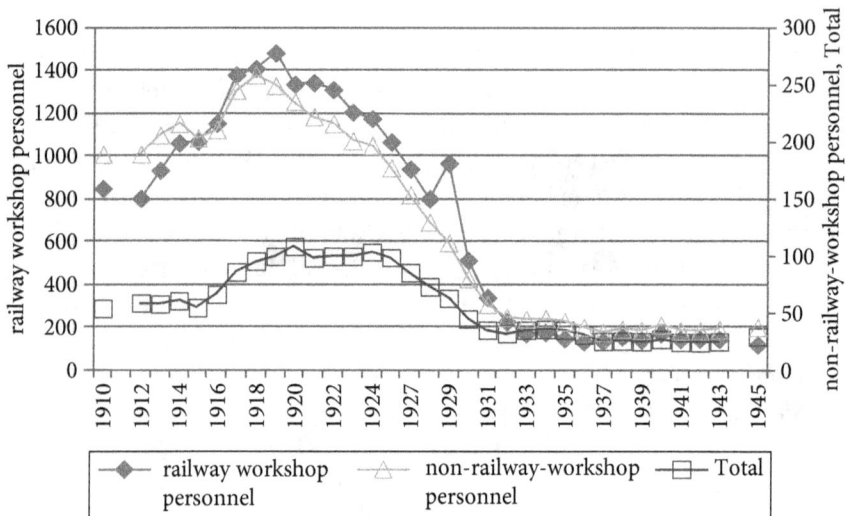

FIGURE 19.3    *Rate of Injury on duty per 1000 employees (Unit: ‰ [per mil]).*
SOURCE: JAPANESE GOVERNMENT RAILWAYS, *JAPANESE GOVERNMENT RAILWAYS YEARBOOK*
(TOKYO: MINISTRY OF RAILWAYS; DEPARTMENT OF HEALTH, SECRETARIAT, MINISTER OF
RAILWAYS, ANNUAL EDITION); *THE 30-YEAR HISTORY OF NATIONAL RAILWAYS MUTUAL AID
ASSOCIATION* (TOKYO: MINISTRY OF RAILWAYS, 1938), 665–666; JAPANESE ASSOCIATION OF
RAILWAY MEDICINE, "GENERAL AFFAIRS OF THE DEPARTMENT OF HEALTHCARE AND
GENERAL AFFAIRS," *GAZETTE OF JAPANESE ASSOCIATION OF RAILWAY MEDICINE*, 3,
10 (1917), 20.

Regarding the cause of death, in 1910 respiratory disorders were the major
cause (2.3‰), followed by digestive disorders (1.0‰), neurological disorders
(0.8‰), circulatory disorders (0.4‰), acute infectious diseases (0.3‰), and
urogenital disorders (0.3‰).[11] When the mortality rate was examined in detail
per individual diseases, the rate was the highest in pulmonary tuberculosis
(1.5‰), followed by beriberi (0.4‰), pneumonia (0.4‰), meningitis (0.2‰),
peritonitis (0.2‰), typhoid (0.2‰), and cerebral hemorrhage (0.2‰), excluding the rate of 1.7‰ in injury after being pinned by a vehicle. Given that tuberculosis included other diseases, in addition to pulmonary tuberculosis, such as
tuberculous meningitis, when all these tuberculous diseases were combined
together, tuberculosis amounted to 20.1% of all causes of death.

The information about the mortality rate per work system is not available
for the initial period but the rate in 1913 is available. The overall mortality rate
was 7.05‰ (2.48‰ for diseases and injuries sustained while on duty, 4.49‰
for diseases and injuries sustained while off duty). In the case of the railway

---

11    *Japanese Government Railways*, annual edition, 1910.

workshop personnel who accounted for 7.41‰ in the workforce (0.85‰ for
diseases and injuries sustained while on duty, 6.26‰ for diseases and injuries
sustained while off duty), the rate of disease and injuries sustained while on
duty was high but the rate of mortality caused by diseases and injuries was not
that high.[12] On the other hand, with regards to the death caused by diseases
and injuries while off duty, the railway workshop personnel showed a remarkably higher rate compared to those in other workplaces. As a result, measures
were taken early on to improve the hygienic conditions in railway workshops.
After the success in 1907 of founding an emergency treatment clinic at Ōmiya
Railway Workshop, clinics (16 centers in 1914) were quickly established and in
May 1911 Jōban Hospital was opened.[13] These medical institutions were managed by the relief association.

In addition, the Department of Health of the Secretariat was set up in the
headquarters of the national railways in 1908 with the goal of supervising matters related to the recuperation of employees, the mutual aid association, the
recreation facilities for employees, medical checkups, railways hygiene, railway hospitals, sanatoria, clinics, and part-time physicians. Furthermore, in July
1913, in each regional bureau of railways, part-time hygiene employees were
added to the general affairs department (Section of Healthcare), directly
responsible for general affairs related to health and hygiene at a director's command.[14] Under the leadership of the Department of Health of the headquarters and the Section of Health of Bureau of Railways, the Council for General
Insurance Affairs, the Consultation Meeting for Part-Time Hygiene Employees
and the Consultation Meeting on Medicine Preparation were held annually to
discuss medical examinations, enforcement of the Factory Act, the prevention
of infectious diseases, and the responses to diseases and injuries incurred
while on duty.

Meanwhile, the number of patients increased annually. For instance, the
number of patients with diseases and injuries while on duty increased from
3976 in 1907 to 13,475 in 1913. In hospitals, the number of inpatients and relevant

---

12    *Japanese Government Railways Yearbook* (Tokyo: Japanese Government Railways, 1913).
13    The name of Jōban Hospital was originated from using an overhead line in Jōban Bridge.
      Japanese Association of Railway Medicine, "General Affairs of the Department of Healthcare
      and General Affairs," *Gazette of Japanese Association of Railway Medicine*, 3,10 (1917): 20;
      National Railways Mutual Aid Association, *The 50-Year History of National Railways Mutual
      Aid Association* (Tokyo: National Railways Mutual Aid Association, 1958), 474.
14    August 1916, Directive No. 79, Regulation on Department of Bureau of Railways. See also
      Japanese Association of Railway Medicine, "Article about the 1st General Meeting of
      Japanese Association of Railway Medicine," *Gazette of Japanese Association of Railway
      Medicine*, 1, 3, Tokyo (1915): 86.

man-days were 498 and 14,273 respectively in 1911, 426 and 16,853 in 1913.[15] The
number of outpatients and relevant man-days were 5279 and 36,727 respectively
in 1911. And the figures increased to 6204 and 55,883 in 1912 and 7538 and 60,381
in 1913. The surgery department had the biggest number of inpatients, followed
by the ENT department. On the other hand, the internal medicine department
had the most number of outpatients, followed by the ENT department or surgery department. Meanwhile, the types of outpatients were not identified but
when it comes to the number of inpatients, the majority of inpatients came
from the Type-1 employees who suffered from diseases and injuries while on
duty (236 persons in 1912) and from the Type-3 employees who suffered from
diseases and injuries while off duty (164 persons). The Type-2 passengers who
had the diseases and injuries while on duty or while traveling were few in number (5 persons). And the numbers of Type-3 patients (147 persons), who were
family members of the employees, were fewer than those of the employee
patients. In the case of the Types-1 and 2, the medical costs were paid for by the
JNR but for the other cases, the patients had to pay their medical expenses.

Although the number of patients increased, the medical institutions and
the relief association in charge of handling the patients suffered from unstable
management. As the number of employee patients rapidly increased, the hospitals continuously operated at a loss. Consequently, the relief association
recorded the deficits of 8000 yen in 1908 and 10,000 yen in 1909 and after that,
the association recorded the surplus of 4000 yen in 1911, 38,000 yen in 1912, and
154,000 yen in 1913. However, the surplus could not fully cover the costs of running the hospitals.[16] To generate more revenue, "the Edict on the Recuperation
of Employees (No. 105)" was announced in June 1914 and accordingly, the existing Jōban Hospital and 15 workshop clinics were separated from the relief association and then changed into the Tokyo Railway Hospital. After that, the
governmental workshop clinics were directly managed by the JNR.[17] In the end,
the JNR was able to provide more stable medical services.

Additionally, "Regulations on Physical Checkup and Health examination"
(30 November 1914, President's Directive, No. 1079) was prepared. Based on the
Standards for Physical Checkup, patients were divided into the four types of A,
B, C, and D and those belonging to A, B, and C were accepted while those

---

15   The man-days of patients are calculated by multiplying the number of patients with the
     days of medical treatment.
16   The profit and loss surplus rate against asset was –8.95% in 1908, –0.81% in 1909, 0.25% in
     1910, 1.84% in 1911, and 5.97% in 1912. See *The 50-Year History of National Railways Mutual
     Aid Association*, 44, 457–458.
17   Ibid, 47.

belonging to D were not accepted. New employees belonging to A were assigned to special duties such as being station masters, operation clerks, and train dispatchers. After employment, the medical examination became annual and was based on the examination result, and it was decided whether employees could perform their assigned duties.[18]

## Outbreak of World War I and Deterioration in Health of Employees

Before analyzing the impact of World War I on the health services to the JNR workers, it is necessary to review the workload of JNR employees. As is well known, the industrialization of the heavy chemical sector and the economic growth after the outbreak of the First World War led to a dramatic increase in the national railroad transportation. The volume of railroad traffic increased from 166.09 million passengers and 35.84 million tons of freight in 1914 to 245.23 million passengers and 49.53 million tons of freight in 1917, and to 405.82 million passengers and 57.53 million tons of freight in 1920. Consequently, a lot of labor force was required.[19] However, during WWI, the slow rise in the wages of the national railroad workers resulted in a decrease in the real wage (30.9 yen in 1914, 33.7 yen in 1915, 31.2 yen in 1916, 27.6 yen in 1917, 22.9 yen in 1918, and 20.0 yen in 1919). As a result, the JNR faced a very flexible labor force.[20] In other words, the turnover rate of employees had gone up from 18.6% in 1914 to 27.2% in 1918 and the employment rate exceeded the turnover rate, increasing from 22.5% to 37.9% over the same period. This situation inevitably resulted in an increase in operation accidents. As shown in Figure 19.3, the highest rate of injuries on duty was found in the year of 1918. As the age of employees got lower and the length of service of employees got shorter, the skill level of employees went down, which led to an increase in the number of accidents.

Data is available about the number of patients in Kobe Railway Hospital. When it comes to the age-specific composition (Figure 19.4a), the occurrence

---

18    Japanese Association of Railway Medicine, "General Affairs of the Department of Healthcare and General Affairs," *Gazette of Japanese Association of Railway Medicine*, 3, 10 (1917): 20.

19    Ministry of Railways, *Railway Statistics* (Tokyo: Ministry of Railways, 1920).

20    For the real wage, the wage per employee is measured by the consumer price index (CPI) (1934–36 = 100). For the employment rate, it is calculated by dividing the number of incoming members by the number of current members of mutual aid association in the previous year. For the turnover rate, it is calculated by dividing the number of the total outgoing members except voluntary outgoing numbers and transferred non-field workers by the number of the current members of mutual aid association in the previous year.

of diseases and injuries while on duty was high for employees in their 20s. When examining the term of service until the injuries (Figure 19.4b), it is clear that the group of employees who worked for one year or less amounted to 51.2%, indicating that the cause of injuries was the lack of skill. According to Tadao Harada, surgeon at Kobe Railway Hospital, "in many cases, even apprentices were involved in the most dangerous work of train coupling. This is shown in tragic accidents where a high number of patients who lost their legs and arms in operation room were apprentices. The injuries were caused by being pinned under train vehicles or their abdomens were caught in vehicles."[21] In the case of transportation and operation personnel, it is reported that "despite the fixed break time, the workers often kept on working due to work culture and consequently they are likely to have accidents."[22] To cut working hours, starting from 1919, more workers were added and the "three eight-hour shift system" was introduced.[23]

In particular, the injury rate in the railway workshops surpassed 1000‰ (Figure 19.3) which was 20 times higher than that of all national railroad employees (100‰). The rate of diseases and injuries while on duty at the railway workshops was higher among young workers than older workers. When the rate was investigated per occupation, steam boiler manufacture, lathes, and assembly were found to have higher numbers, followed by smithing and casting. And lower numbers were found in seamsters and painters.[24] In short, the numbers of injured workers show a clear difference in age and occupation. In addition, the results varied greatly depending on whether clinics existed or not. If there was a clinic, workers who were slightly wounded would receive treatment more quickly. In addition, a high rate of injury was found between 10:00 AM and 03:00 PM when workers received less attention. The increase in demand in the efficiency of vehicle repair during World War I resulted in a great number of accidents incurred on duty.

The rate of injury peaked around 1918, but it was not the only cause that brought about the increase in the death of employees. According to Figure 19.5,

21    Tadao Harada, "Statistical Observation on 1,000 Trauma Patients," *Gazette of Japanese Association of Railway Medicine*, 5, 3 (1919): 2.
22    Japanese Association of Railway Medicine, "Relaxed Working Hours for Transportation Employees at Japanese Government Railways," *Gazette of Japanese Association of Railway Medicine*, 5, 7 (1919): 33.
23    Ibid, 33.
24    Taijō Takamatsu, "A Numerical Observation of Railway Workshop Workers' Injuries in Each Railway Workshop by Japanese Government Railways," *Gazette of Japanese Association of Railway Medicine*, 4, 8 (1918): 1–5.

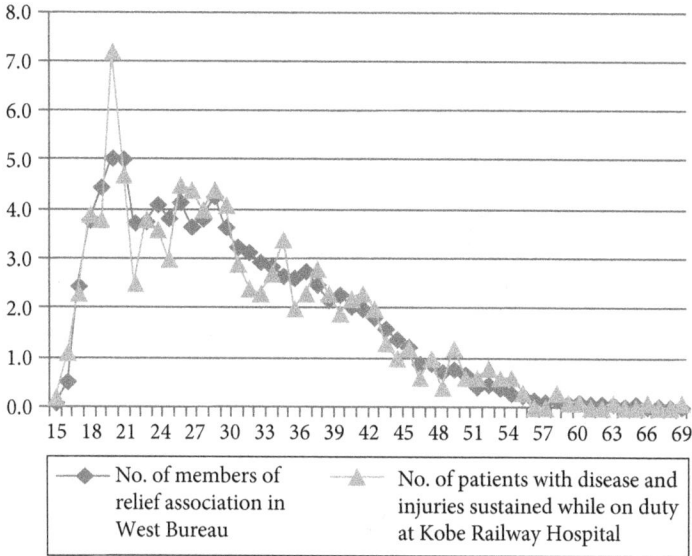

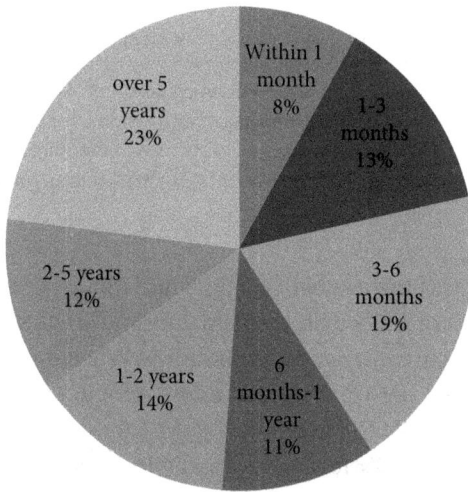

FIGURE 19.4    *The age-specific composition of patients with disease and injuries sustained while on duty in Kobe Railway Hospital and the term of service by the patients until having injuries (1915–18). A. Age-specific composition (unit: %). B. Term of service till injury (unit: %).*

SOURCE: JAPANESE GOVERNMENT RAILWAYS, *JAPANESE GOVERNMENT RAILWAYS YEARBOOK* (TOKYO: JAPANESE GOVERNMENT RAILWAYS, ANNUAL EDITION); TADAO HARADA, "STATISTICAL OBSERVATION ON 1000 TRAUMA PATIENTS," *GAZETTE OF JAPANESE ASSOCIATION OF RAILWAY MEDICINE*, 5. 3 (1919), 1–12.

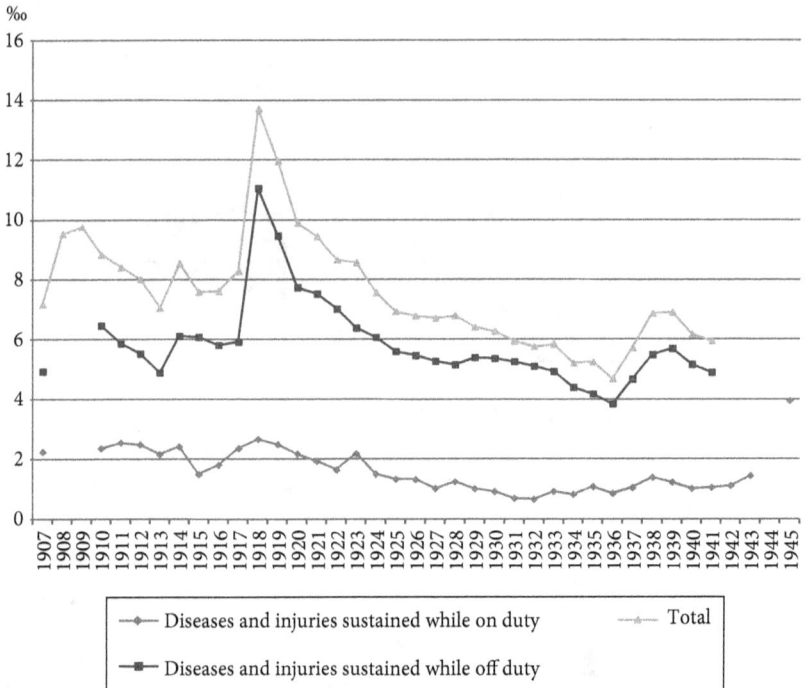

FIGURE 19.5   *The mortality rate of mutual aid association (unit: ‰).*
SOURCE: JAPANESE GOVERNMENT RAILWAYS, *JAPANESE GOVERNMENT RAILWAYS YEARBOOK*
(TOKYO: JAPANESE GOVERNMENT RAILWAYS, ANNUAL EDITION); MINISTRY OF RAILWAYS,
*RAILWAY STATISTICS* (TOKYO: MINISTRY OF RAILWAYS, ANNUAL EDITION).

the mortality rate was highest between 1918 and 1919. When the causes of the high mortality rate are divided between on duty and off duty, it is clear that the off duty mortality figures increased dramatically. When the numbers of deaths in 1918 were recorded per work system, a total of 1716 employees were found dead, with 717 employees from stations (3.99‰ for diseases and injuries sustained while on duty, 10.11‰ for diseases and injuries sustained while off duty), 382 employees from the locomotive section (2.14‰, 11.49‰), 239 employees from the railway maintenance section (3.17‰, 10.61‰), 225 employees from workshops (0.58‰, 13.64‰), 8 employees from ships (0‰, 8.36‰), and 145 employees from others (0.57‰, 11.72‰).[25] In all work systems, the number of deaths among station employees was higher while off duty. Furthermore, in terms of deaths caused by official duties, the number for station employees

25   Japanese Government Railways, *Japanese Government Railways Yearbook* (Tokyo: Japanese Government Railways, annual edition).

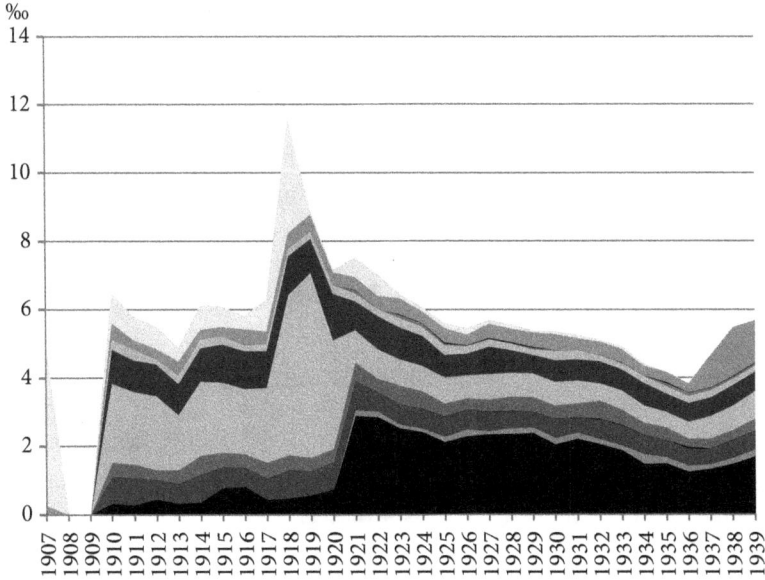

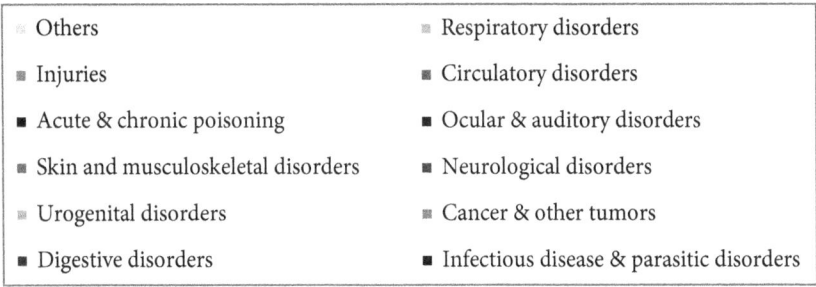

FIGURE 19.6     *The mortality rate per cause of diseases and injuries sustained while off duty
(unit: ‰).*[26]

SOURCE: JAPANESE GOVERNMENT RAILWAYS, *JAPANESE GOVERNMENT RAILWAYS YEARBOOK*
(TOKYO: JAPANESE GOVERNMENT RAILWAYS, ANNUAL EDITION); MINISTRY OF RAILWAYS,
*RAILWAY STATISTICS* (TOKYO: MINISTRY OF RAILWAYS, ANNUAL EDITION).

was higher. One of the explanations for the high number is that the station
employees originally outnumbered the others and also because many train
couplers who were responsible for connecting vehicles lost their lives at

---

26      A variety of infectious diseases (in addition to officially designated infectious diseases) belonging to respiratory disorders, including tuberculosis have been classified into infectious diseases
since 1921. Circulatory disorders include blood dyscrasia and blood-forming organ-related diseases. Skin and musculoskeletal disorders include rheumatic disease and nutrition disorder.
Suicide till the year of 1916 was classified into injury based on the later classification.

work. In 1925 when the automatic couplers were installed, the number of employees killed or hurt was cut in half to 109. In terms of the mortality rate, the workshops with poor working conditions showed a higher rate compared to other systems.

With regard to the causes of the rise in the mortality rate, the higher numbers were found for respiratory disorders, followed by digestive disorders, neurological disorders, acute infectious diseases, circulatory disorders, and urogenital disorders. A similar result to the overall trend is shown in the causes of death while off duty. It is also worth noting that the respiratory disorders were related to the global pandemic of Spanish Influenza. According to Akira Hayami, the flu pandemic that happened twice in Japan had killed more than 450,000 people.[27] The reason was that the Department of Heath of the JNR failed to respond to the flu in its initial stage, causing unnecessary casualties. According to the numbers collected between January and February 1920 when the outbreak of second pandemic occurred, the number of patients suffering from the flu reached 14,445 and 256 of them died due to the flu. Also shown in the statistics is that the mortality rate of patients affected by the pandemic was 17.7‰. The number of absentees affected by the pandemic stood at 2551 in the mid-January 1920, which was equivalent to 1.81% of total employees.[28]

According to Akira Hayami, the number of additional deaths was estimated at 1087.[29] Of course, the death toll of all employees was likely to increase slightly because the estimation was based on the mutual aid association members accounting for over 90% of all employees. Considering that those who were killed in 1917 already amounted to 943, it was inevitable that the added demand for medical services during the Spanish Influenza dealt a blow to the labor hygiene system of the JNR.[30] After the outbreak of Spanish Influenza, the

27    Akira Hayami, *Japan Hit by the Spanish Influenza Pandemic: Mankind and the First World War of the Virus* (Tokyo: Hujiwara Shoten, 2006), 239–240.

28    Department of Health, Secretariat, Minister of Railways, "Overview of Influenza Prevention Facility," *Gazette of Japanese Association of Railway Medicine*, 8, 12 (1922): 2.

29    The basis of Akira Hayami's argument is that the number of Spanish Influenza death toll is equal to (A) minus (B). (A) is the three-year respiratory disorders and other death tolls between 1918 and 1920. (B) is the three-year respiratory disorders and other death tolls between 1915 and 1917. But he didn't take into account the increase of population. It is important to note that the 30.2% rate of increase in the numbers of aid association for estimating the exact death toll. The number of Spanish Influenza death toll should be calculated by ((A) minus (B)) × (1 minus 0.302).

30    Due to this, starting from 1921, influenza and tuberculosis (one of chronic infectious diseases) were counted as infectious diseases, in addition to acute infectious diseases.

Department of Heath of the JNR implemented preventive measures on 28 October 1918. In December 1919 when there were signs of the reoccurrence of the pandemic, the Department distributed 150,000 handouts to call general employees' attention to the pandemic and proposed measures, such as brushing teeth, wearing a mask, washing hands, disinfecting the residential space of patients, classifying culinary utensils, and disinfecting bedding and clothes, to prevent the spread of diseases.[31] In January 1920, the JNR decided to distribute water to employees for teeth brushing. The company also gave employees masks and vaccinations.[32] In May 1921, Masao Fukuda, head of the Health Department, called all field workers' attention to improving hygiene. He said that "everyone should start and end a day with cleanliness, not allowing germs to affect our health."[33]

As stated above, after the foundation of the JNR, under the leadership of the Department of Health of the headquarters, the labor hygiene was controlled through the two systems of railway hospital and relief association in the spirit of the JNR Familism. But the health system was critically challenged during WWI. JNR Familism, although efficient in the past, could not deal with the high volumes of death and injuries during the WWI period. It was because the JNR Familism was designed to deal with internal instability which had arisen from the nationalization of private railways, and was for attaining the organizational integration of a national rail system. However, it could no longer function efficiently when the number of employees increased rapidly and when the employees' morbidity and mortality rates climbed swiftly during the war. In other words, it was because the health demands of WWI were so great that the old concept of the JNR Familism was rendered obsolete.

### Expansion of the Labor Hygiene System and Health of Employees

Immediately following WWI, the JNR undertook a number of measures to improve on its health prevention program. In addition to the Tokyo Railway

---

The dramatic fluctuation among respiratory disorders and infectious diseases seen in Figure 19.6 is resulted from the change in a way of counting.

31   Department of Health, Secretariat, Minister of Railways, "Overview of Influenza Prevention Facility," *Gazette of Japanese Association of Railway Medicine*, 8, 11 (1922): 7–8.
32   It was not possible to expect vaccination would be able to stop the influenza because scientists had not found Pfeiffer's bacillus as a pathogen.
33   Masao Fukuda, "Improvement of Railway Employees' Awareness toward Hygiene and 'Cleanliness First'," *Gazette of Japanese Association of Railway Medicine*, 7, 6 (1921): 1–5.

Hospital were added Kobe Railway Hospital (March 1915), Sapporo Railway Hospital (October 1915), Moji Railway Hospital (April 1917), Sendai Railway Hospital (February 1921), Nagoya Railway Hospital (May 1923), Kobe Railway Hospital, and Osaka Branch Hospital (October 1923). Furthermore, thanks to adding more scientists and doctors, the medical team was expanded to include a total of 252 members with 150 railway physicians and 102 pharmacists in April 1925.[34] Despite being affected by the Great Kanto Earthquake, Tokyo Railway Hospital secured a medical team composed of physicians, pharmacists, and nurses, and the hospital steadily expanded its facilities. At Tokyo Railway Hospital, almost all the medical costs were paid for by the railway authorities and the patients were only charged with a small percentage of the entire medical cost, including medicines, operation and meals.

From Figures 19.7 and 19.8, it is clear that the medical services were rapidly expanded after WWI. However, from the employees' perspective, the number of Type-1 patients hardly increased in 1920s and as a result, even when the Type-3 patients were included from the second half of 1920s, there were few changes. In short, the rise in the number of patients from the second half of the 1920s was linked to the rise in the number of Type-3 employees' family patients in terms of both inpatients and outpatients. This expansion means, in essence, a full implementation of "JNR Familism." In terms of the number of inpatients, an overwhelming majority of inpatients were held by the surgery department in the early days but as the rate of accidents decreased, the number of inpatients decreased relatively. At the same time, the internal medicine department witnessed a rise in the number of inpatients. This is related to an increase in the number of employee patients and the family members of employees. Meanwhile, in the case of the number of outpatients per department, the internal medicine and ophthalmology departments had a higher number of outpatients while the patients treated by various departments were kept at a certain level.

This trend was particularly clear in the railway clinics at railway workshops and large workplaces. Managers, physicians, assistants and nurses were assigned to clinics. Consequently, the number of clinics, even those not equipped with branch organizations and facilities for hospitalization, increased from 16 in 1914, to 65 in 1924, to 106 in 1934 and the number of patients also increased from 196,693 in 1914 to 1.5 million in 1924, to 3.3 million in 1934. In addition, sanatoria were installed in four hot springs including Arima, Betbu, Iizuka, and

---

34    Japanese Association of Railway Medicine, "Article about the 1st General Meeting of Japanese Association of Railway Medicine," *Gazette of Japanese Association of Railway Medicine*, 1, 3 (1915): 21.

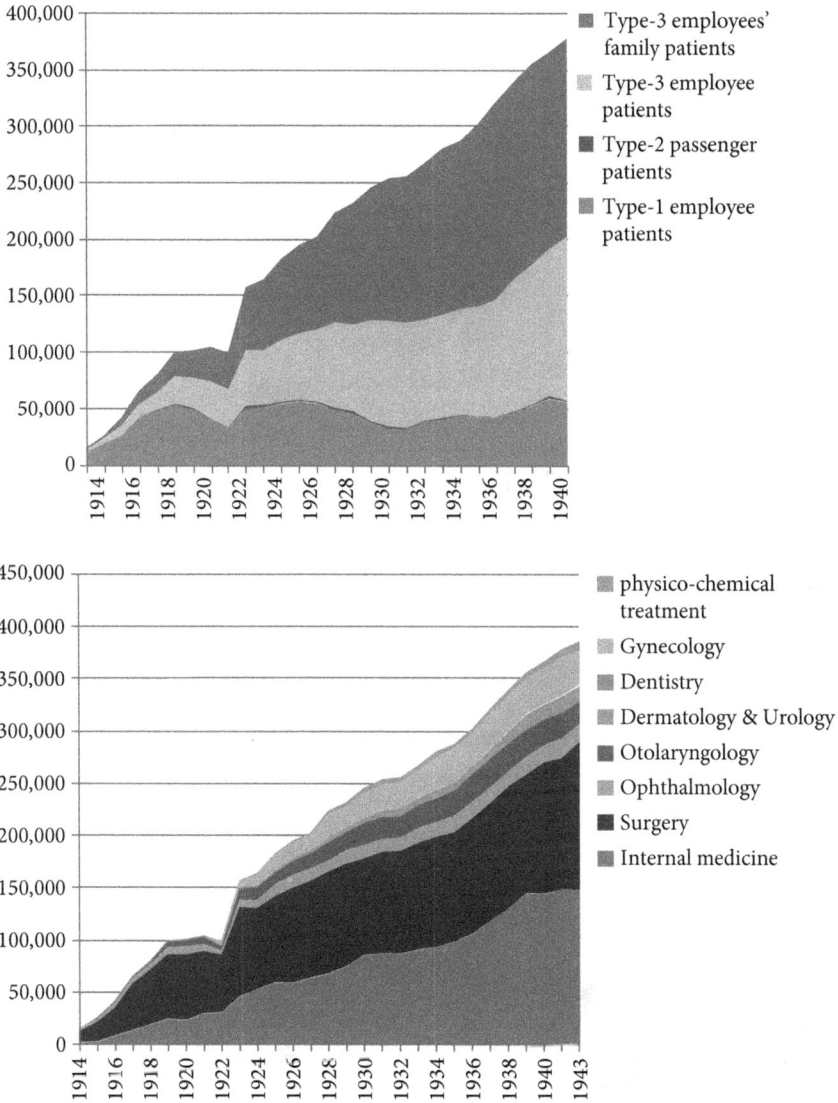

FIGURE 19.7    *The number of inpatients at railway hospitals (unit: man-days) A. Per type. B. Per department.*

SOURCE: JAPANESE GOVERNMENT RAILWAYS, *JAPANESE GOVERNMENT RAILWAYS YEARBOOK* (TOKYO: JAPANESE GOVERNMENT RAILWAYS, ANNUAL EDITION); MINISTRY OF RAILWAYS, *RAILWAY STATISTICS* (TOKYO: MINISTRY OF RAILWAYS, ANNUAL EDITION).

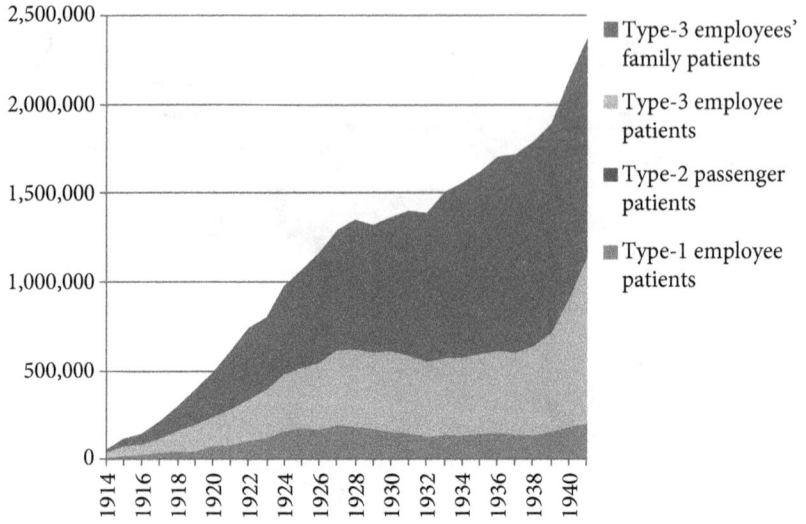

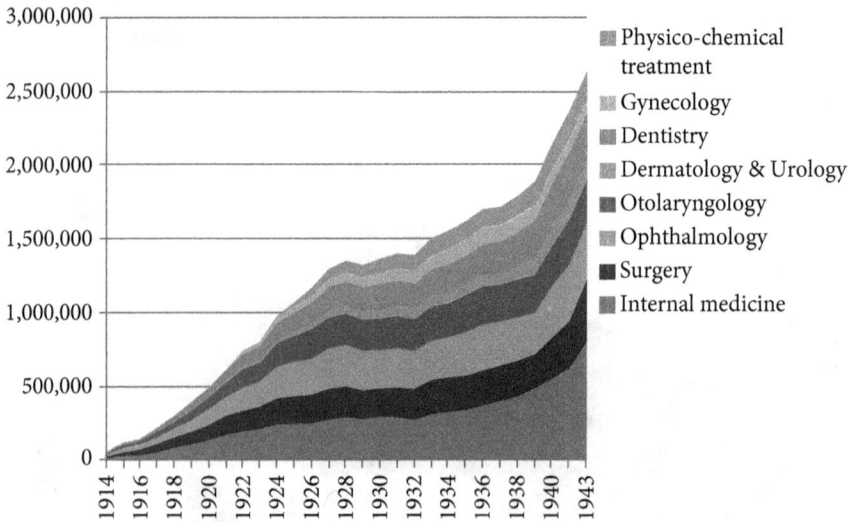

FIGURE 19.8    *The number of outpatients at railway hospitals (unit: man-days). A. Per type.*
*B. Per department.*

SOURCE: JAPANESE GOVERNMENT RAILWAYS, *JAPANESE GOVERNMENT RAILWAYS YEARBOOK*
(TOKYO: JAPANESE GOVERNMENT RAILWAYS, ANNUAL EDITION); MINISTRY OF RAILWAYS,
*RAILWAY STATISTICS* (TOKYO: MINISTRY OF RAILWAYS, ANNUAL EDITION).

Noboribetsu, providing hot-spring therapy and physio-chemical treatment.[35] Part-time physicians were assigned to places where it was difficult to build railway hospitals and clinics.[36] To further improve the health services, a hygienic laboratory was built to undergo physico-chemical and medical studies and experiments related to railway hygiene. As a part of the measures to prevent fatigue among railroad crew, communal lounges and baths were installed at 2141 and 2540 places respectively in 1927, thereby making a significant contribution to reducing the number of accidents among employees.[37]

In addition, the railway authorities made several attempts to increase wages. The national railways increased the basic salary between 1917 and 1919 and at the same time, provided extra allowances, special bonuses, and additional salaries for long service (for employees who had worked for the company for over five years). As a result, the real wage increased from 20 yen in 1919 to 36.3 yen in 1920 and afterwards continued to rise, amid deflation at the beginning of 1930s. Additionally, when the relief association accumulated a surplus of almost 1 million yen in 1916, JNR authorities used a portion of the surplus to establish the medical relief system to take care of workers who suffered from diseases and injuries while off duty. The new relief system was considered at the time to be "a visionary trail of health insurance system." To that end, the employee relief association's medical regulation, which stipulated the provision of medical costs, was prepared in 1916.[38] Considering that the conventional relief put more emphasis on the life insurance aspect, such as relief for those disabled, invalid, dead and infirm, the name of the association was changed from the relief association to the mutual aid association in 1918 and the membership system was changed from the A, B, and C types previously into A and B types, with the A type for compulsory membership and B type for

---

35  Kiyotake Kagechika, "Medical Work and Hygiene Facilities in 1923," *Gazette of Japanese Association of Railway Medicine*, 10, 9 (1924): 3.

36  In June 1919, some of the railway physicians working for the JNR's directly managed medical institutions received a salary equivalent to that of high-grade officials (51) and others received the salary of clerical officials (57). See Japanese Association of Railway Medicine, "Limited in Number of Railway Physicians," *Gazette of Japanese Association of Railway Medicine*, 5, 6 (1919): 24.

37  Yukisuke Shibama, Yukisuke, "Reduced Causality Accident of and Rehabilitation Facility for JNR Employees," *Field-Work Research Data*, 3, 5 (1929): 1–13.

38  With half amount of medical costs as standard, ① For those who receive treatment while working, five sen per day (sen = 1/100 yen), ② For those who receive treatment during cessation from work, 10 sen (daily-paid job) and 5 sen (monthly-paid job), ③ For those who are hospitalized, 40 sen per day (daily-paid job), 20 sen per day (monthly-paid job). But, the medical costs were subsidized only within 60 days per year.

voluntary membership.[39] In the case of the relief fund for workers who suffered from diseases and injuries while on duty, benefits for seriously injured patients were increased. Concerning the second-grade patients who suffered from diseases and injuries while on duty, a pension system was set up. For employees with diseases and injuries while off duty, disease relief funds were raised and disease allowance and aid for specific conditions (e.g., the retirement from JNR due to pulmonary tuberculosis) were introduced to give the system more flexibility. In the same year, a purchasing division was created in the mutual aid association, providing daily necessities and food. As a result, many workers were able to receive extensive medical treatment and were supported economically by the mutual aid association at the end of World War I.

It was in 1920 that the pension system was introduced to all members of the association. The expanded pension system not only provided a retirement pension (whole life annuity of over 20-year-long membership holder) and a terminal retirement pension (15–20 year long membership holder, maximum period of 15 years), it also provided a pension for those who had disabilities and permanent invalidity owing to diseases and injuries sustained while off duty.[40] In addition, the system provided the pension to those who suffered from diseases and injuries while on duty as well as to the bereaved family. More importantly, the disease benefits were expanded.[41] Eventually, coverage was extended to those workers who suffered from diseases and injuries while off duty. Meanwhile, membership dues (3/100 for Type-A, 5/100for Type-B) and government subsidies (3/100) were increased to give the JNR more financial resources. With additional financial resources, the railway authorities were able to provide more services. As a result, the existing five types of relief funds, including relief funds for diseases and injuries sustained while on duty, disease relief funds, death relief funds, retirement relief funds, and old-aged relief funds, were expanded into six types, including the benefits for diseases and injuries sustained while on duty, invalidity benefits, disease benefits, retirement benefits, bereaved family's benefits, and calamity benefits. After that, the

39    Department of Health, *The 50-Year History of National Railways Mutual Aid Association* (Tokyo: Ministry of Railways, 1938), 169–177.
40    A majority of Invalid pension holders died within 1~2 years after being entitled to the pension. Kazue Mawatari, "On the Relocation and Return of Invalid Pension Recipient," *Gazette of Japanese Association of Railway Medicine*, 22, 1 (1936), 4–5.
41    National Railways Mutual Aid Association, *The 50-Year History of National Railways Mutual Aid Association* (Tokyo: National Railways Mutual Aid Association, 1958): 21–22.

pension for retirees aged over 40 increased to one-third of the annual wage amount.[42]

A result of revamping the system was that the range of recipients and the amount of benefits were increased dramatically (Figures 19.9 and 19.10). In terms of the number of recipients, before 1919 the medical care funds and the disease relief funds gave out the highest numbers of supports, followed by the retirement relief funds. After 1920, the disease benefits and the health benefits ranked top, followed by the retirement funds or benefits. In terms of the amount of funds, before 1919 the largest amounts were given out through the relief funds for diseases and injuries sustained while on duty and the death relief funds. After 1920, the largest amounts were dispensed from the retirement pension. In 1926, this trend was accelerated due to the increase in the pension amount.

Consequently, both the rate of injury incurred while on duty and the mortality rate went down from 1920s to the first half of 1930s (Figures 19.3 and 19.5). With the decrease in turnover rate of employees during the economic recession, the number of long-term employed persons went up. Furthermore, various measures including shorter working hours, the addition of fatigue recovery facilities (such as lounges, communal baths), the supply of protective equipment (masks, gloves, safety goggles), nationwide installation of automatic couplers, and safety campaigns led by the accident prevention society, the injury and accident prevention committee, the safety committee, and the disaster prevention association, led to better health conditions among employees.[43] Following the rise in real wage, the standard of living of the national railroad workers was significantly improved.

### Conclusion

The above analysis shows that as the national railways company expanded in managing the economy and ruling a country, it was expected to provide health care to all field workers. However, due to the difficulties in securing medical

---

42   The Field Workers Committee (established in May 1920) representing the position of workers strongly insisted the increase in pension and as a result, an annual wage amount increased from one-fourth to one-third in compliance with New Pension Act (1923). See Department of Health, Secretariat, Minister of Railways, *The 50-Year History of National Railways Mutual Aid Association* (Tokyo: Ministry of Railways, 1938), 4–5.

43   Yukisuke Shibama, "Reduced Causality Accident of and Rehabilitation Facility for JNR Employees," *Field-Work Research Data*, 3, 5 (1929): 1–13.

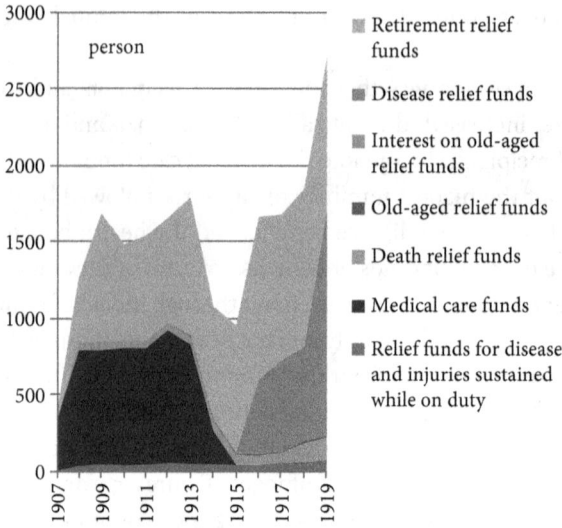

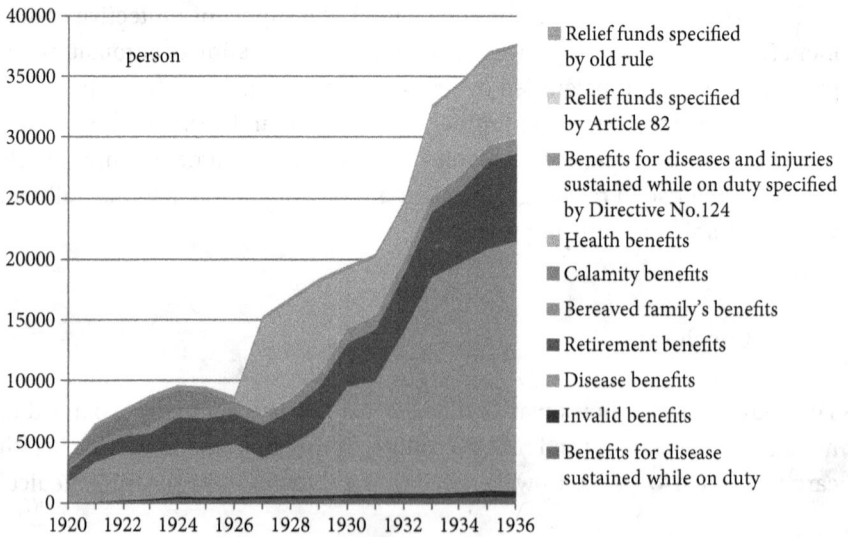

FIGURE 19.9 *The number of recipients of each relief fund and benefit of mutual aid association (unit: person).*

SOURCE: DEPARTMENT OF HEALTH, THE 30-YEAR HISTORY OF NATIONAL RAILWAYS MUTUAL AID ASSOCIATION (TOKYO: MINISTRY OF RAILWAYS, 1938), 422–423.

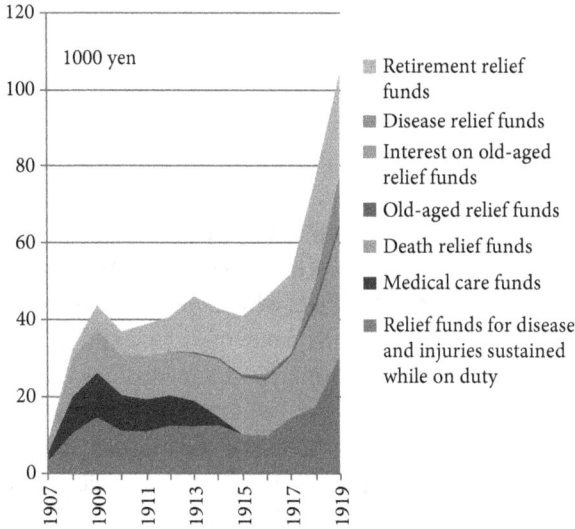

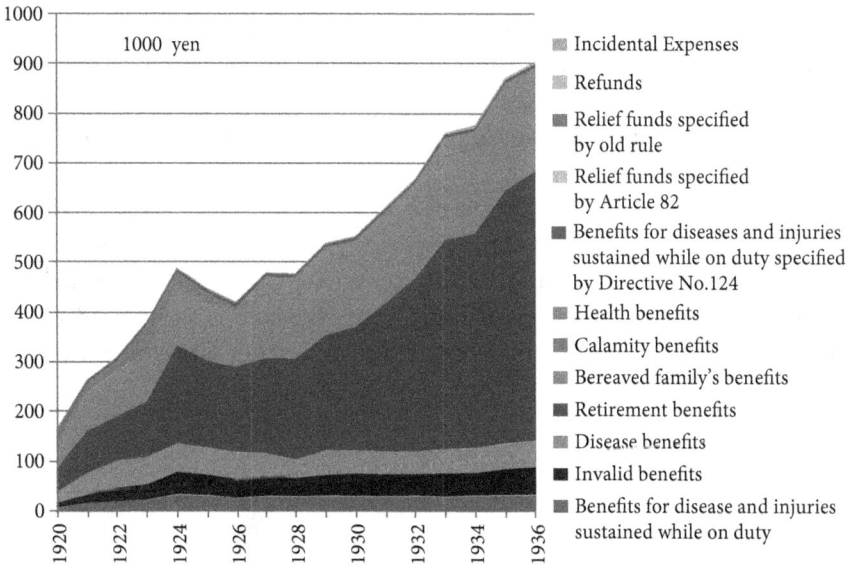

FIGURE 19.10 *Trend of each relief fund and benefit of mutual aid association (unit: 1000 yen).*
SOURCE: DEPARTMENT OF HEALTH, THE 30-YEAR HISTORY OF NATIONAL RAILWAYS MUTUAL
AID ASSOCIATION (TOKYO: MINISTRY OF RAILWAYS, 1938), 422–423.

services outside the organization, it needed to establish a comprehensible hygiene control system including the relief association and the railway hospitals. The relief association system, which was known as "JNR Familism," lay the foundation for creating a more comprehensive healthcare system later. The relief association system not only provided fringe benefits but also contributed to stabilizing the labor-management relation.

Spurred by WWI, efficient railroad management was pursued to cope with the increase in transportation demand. However, because of high turnover, the age and the term of service of employees declined, which inevitably led to the deterioration in the quality of labor. As a result, the rate of disease and injuries went up. In addition, Spanish Influenza was running rampant, dealing another blow to the health-care system. In response, the JNR expanded the medical system, pension, and medical insurance and established the mutual aid association system. Throughout WWI, many employees were able to participate in benefitting the internal medical system supported economically by the JNR authorities.

Under the new system, more people were able to have access to medical services. And at first, benefits were provided only to the employees who suffered from diseases and injuries while on duty. Later, they were expanded to include first the employee patients who had diseases and injuries while off duty, and then later, employees' family members. Accordingly, "JNR Familism" seems to be fully implemented.

Because of these results, from the perspective of JNR, the physical condition of railroad workers did not simply mean a disease-free condition. Rather, healthy workers were valued when they recovered from illness with the help of appropriate medical treatment. In other words, the railway authorities' ability to provide health services underwent a sea change before and after WWI.

# Sovereignty and Imperial Hygiene
## Japan and the 1919 Cholera Epidemic in East Asia

*Yuehtsen Juliette Chung*

Cholera is notoriously a water-borne epidemic. Whether it has been an indigenous and endemic disease in East Asia for millennia is a subject of dispute.[1] In Japan, cholera is written *ko-re-ra* in Japanese katakana コレラ (虎列刺), which displays a conspicuous marker of its foreign origin. Such usage first appeared around 1789–1801 when Udakawa Genshin (1769–1834) translated a Dutch medical text and called it *Seisetsu Naika senyō* (the outline of western internal medicine). Chinese medical texts had classified symptoms of repeated vomiting and purging, shivering with cold extremities, suffering from great thirst, severe cramps and abdominal pain, and recorded this perennial summer disease as *huoluan* (霍亂). The description of symptoms as such certainly fits into our current understanding of cholera. In the literature of the disease's origin, "cholera" was first mentioned in Sanskrit texts around 400 BC. However, given our knowledge of the evolution of species, it is inconceivable that the *vibrio cholerae* bacterium discovered by Robert Koch in 1882 would have retained an identical genetic structure for millennia. The most reliable account of "cholera" closest to the modern understanding of this disease was the record of an 1817 occurrence that arose in the Ganges delta in Bengal and swept over all of India. In the 1820s, it spread out across China, Japan, Asiatic Russia and America.[2]

The outbreak of the cholera epidemic in 1919 swept over China, Japan, Thailand, India, Afghanistan, Russia and Sweden. In East Asia, it was first introduced from the Philippines to the Chinese ports Swatow and Foochow, and rampaged through Japan, Taiwan, Korea, Shanghai, Hong Kong and Manchuria. Below is a list of the approximate dates when the first cholera cases appeared in each city:[3]

---

1  Kerrie L. MacPherson, "Cholera in China (1820–1930): The Aspect of International Epidemics" collected in the edited volume of Chinese environmental history entitled *Jijian suozhi: Zhuoguo huanjingshi lunwenji* (Institute of Economics, Academia Sinica, 1995), 747–795. The issues MacPherson was interested in are the evolutionary process and mapping routes of such disease. However, the most problematic obstacle for this pursuit is the difficulty in the disease identification for such a vast terrain and long span of time.

2  Mark Harrison, *Disease and the Modern World: 1500 to the Present Day* (Cambridge: Polity Press, 2004), 100–101.

3  Wu Liande, "1919 Cholera Epidemic in China" in *Manchurian Plague Prevention Service, Memorial Volume 1912–1932* (Shanghai: National Quarantine Service, 1934), 251–265.

| Fuzhou | July 7 |
|---|---|
| Shanghai | July 15 |
| Yingkou (Newchwang) | July 22 |
| Shenyang | July 24 |
| Dalian | August 3 |
| Harbin | August 5 |
| Changchun | August 15 |
| Jilin | August 16 |
| Langfang | August 15 |
| Fengtai | August 15 |
| Tianjin | August 20 |
| Beijing | August 20 |
| Sansing | August 22 |
| Tokyo, Osaka, Moji | August 28 |
| Seoul (Korea) | August 29 |

The Manchurian port of Yingkou recorded its first case on July 22, and Harbin on August 5. Within six weeks, 13,000 cases had been reported in Harbin alone, with 4500 deaths.[4] A Chinese newspaper, *Chenbao* (Morning Post), reported over twenty thousand deaths in Fuzhou city during the same season.[5] It was a synchronic phenomenon in terms of the timing of the outbreak in each area.

According to Iijima Wataru's study, the statistics of cholera patients and death tolls in 1919 are shown in the table below:

| 1919 Cholera | Patients/deaths | Patients/deaths |
|---|---|---|
| Japan | 407/356 | Yokohama 5/2 |
| Taiwan | Taiwanese 3586/2533 | Japanese 181/118 |
| Korea | Japanese 272/179 | Korean 16,617/11,339 |
| Shanghai International Settlement | Chinese deaths 648 | Foreign deaths 32 |
| Hong Kong | Chinese deaths 41 | Foreign deaths 5 |

Source: Iijima Wataru, *Pesuto to kindai chugoku: eisei no "seidōka" to shakai henyō* (Tokyo: kenbunshupan, 2000), 238–239.

---

4  Wu Liande, *Cholera: A Manual For the Medical Profession in China* (Shanghai: National Quarantine Service, 1934), 27.

5  Deng Tietao, *Zhongguo fangyi shi* 中國防疫史 (History of Chinese Epidemic Prevention) (Nanning: Kuangxi kexu jishu chubanshe, 2006), 424. The *Morning Post* reported the occurrence of cholera cases on June 23, 1920.

Japan obviously did not suffer as much as other parts of the East Asian region in 1919. Such success derived from the wartime experience of comprehensive quarantine and segregation of water and food sources between the Japanese and the local population when Japan was occupying Qingdao. In comparison, the Chinese were unable to ward off the dissemination of cholera since the Chinese quarantine regulations only targeted commercial ships and did not apply to the junk trade, which unintentionally turned junks into free carriers of infectious pathogen among Chinese coastal cities and between North China and Korea. However, only three years earlier, in 1916 cholera ravaged Japan, with reports of 10,371 cases with 7482 deaths, including 110 cases and 78 deaths in Yokohama. At that time, Taiwan only had 34 cases and 16 deaths; Korea 2066 cases and 1254 deaths; Shanghai 100 deaths; and Hong Kong 10 deaths. As the statistics further show, Japan did not reproduce its success of 1919, because it reported 4969 patients and 3417 deaths in 1920.[6]

The above table shows not only the inadequacies of the mechanism of disease control but also the limits of the public hygienic regulations in the region. Most importantly, it shows a nonsynchronic development of hygienic modernity in relation to the synchronic phenomenon of epidemic cholera in the East Asia region. This chapter argues that the history of Japan's colonial expansion was a two-way course and that in terms of hygienic modernity, its experience in the colonies came back to shape the metropolitan administration. During the "long 1910s," a regional network of disease prevention regimes was integrated and driven by the common and synchronic battle against cholera, rather than by the influence of the Great War. Hence, the following sections explore different types of preventive measures employed in the region. They also examine the coalition and the competition between the Japanese quarantine regime and Chinese regional quarantine services, all of which were shaped by the development of cholera epidemic. Such coalition and competition indicate the ascendance of the Japanese over the British as dominant in the region.

### Cholera and Japan's Quarantine Regime

Public health as a signifier of modern civilization and as a foundation for political legitimacy has been a dominant aspect of governance that involves the state in penetrating and intervening in all aspects of the lives of its national subjects. It is not far-fetched to imagine modern epidemics as a driving force

---

6   Iijima Wataru, *Pesuto to kindai chugoku: eisei no "seidōka" to shakai henyō* (Tokyo: kenbunshu-pan, 2000), 238–239.

leading the state to mobilize its resources, to restructure social organizations and social space, and to devise new technologies in order to overcome the disintegrated parts and transform the nation into a holistic body. In Japan, to achieve the prevailing standards of public health in modern civilization, public hygiene (*eisei* 衛生) emerged as a new form of knowledge distinct from traditional teachings of nourishing the individual's life and health (*yōjō* 養生). Among other epidemics, cholera has been described as "the mother giving birth to modern hygiene."[7] In 1822, cholera first visited Japan from India, but Japan did not suffer much since only a few ports with limited foreign trade were exposed to such disease. The 1858 visit of cholera, after Japan opened five ports to the US and the western powers, devastated Japan's coastal areas and caused over 800 deaths in Nagasaki, roughly 10,000 deaths in Osaka, and 30,000 deaths in Tokyo.[8] The third attack in 1876–1879 ravaged extensively and claimed 105,786 victims. Such tremendous casualties proved the failure of the traditional medical system of individual self-care and the inadequate preventive measures in existing personal hygiene.

Since 1858, the Bureau of Hygiene actively introduced and disseminated information drawn from foreign literature on hygiene, especially regarding the British implementation of public hygiene, which Japanese hygienists considered the most appropriate model for emulation, since the British road to the system of public hygiene and the Public Health Act of 1848 were also driven by the ravages of cholera.[9] Japan lacked the fundamental infrastructure of water works, sewage systems, environmental hygiene, and sanitary industry that existed in Britain, and Nagayo Sensai 長与専齋 (1838–1902, the first director of the Hygiene Bureau and well-known as the pioneer of Japanese public hygiene) reckoned that Japan was unable to allocate a huge fund in a short period to implement maritime quarantine and port sanitation. However, in 1873, under the threat of cholera outbreak in Thailand and Singapore, the Home Ministry coordinated with the Ministries of Finance, Education, and Foreign Affairs, and gained the support from various foreign embassies to adopt 14 regulations of port quarantine. These regulations included establishing quarantine

---

7  Abe Yasunari, "'Eisei' toiu chitsujo 衛生という秩序" in *Shippei, kaihatsu, teikoku iryō: Ajia ni okeru byōki to iryō no rekishigaku* (Tokyo: Tokyo daigaku shuppankai, 2001), ed. by Masatoshi Miichi et al., 107–130.

8  Yamamoto Shūnichi, *Nihon korerashi* (Tokyo: Tokyo daigaku shuppankai, 1982), chap. II, 14–26.

9  Kanbayashi Shigenobu, "公衆衛生の確立における日本と英国: 長与専斎とE チャドウィックの果たした役割 (Establishment of Public Health in Japan and Britain: The Roles Played by Sensai Nagayo and Edwin Chadwick)" in *Ninhon Ishigaku zasshi* (Journal of Japanese History of Medicine), 47 (2001, Dec) issue 4: 665–696.

hospitals to treat patients from foreign ships entering Japanese ports; building temporary shelters for infected residents in the overpopulated cities; and authorizing physicians, hygiene staff, and police officers to identify infected individuals and households and subsequently apply sanitation and quarantine to the infected ones. The regulations also imposed fines and penalties in the cases of violation such as relocating the patients, littering infected materials, and disposing of infected corpses without official permission.[10]

As soon as Japan received the report of a cholera outbreak in Xiamen in July, 1877, the Bureau of Hygiene in the Home Ministry incorporated these 14 regulations and propagated the *Guide for the Prevention of Cholera* written by Nagayo to local government offices. Admonishing his fellow countrymen with the traditional rhetoric of individual self-care, Nagayo added an epidemic report system networked by the police forces and local governments. He followed the national borderlines externally, and the county and prefecture borderlines domestically, to map out a monitoring system for epidemic control. Nagayo reckoned that, because the Japanese archipelago was surrounded by sea, it would be possible to prevent the spread of imported epidemics by imposing strict port quarantine measures. Moreover, the unequal treaties with Western powers reinforced Nagayo's plans because they bound Japan to impose port quarantine.[11]

In 1878 the Bureau prepared Provisional Rules for the Prevention of Cholera (*Korera yobō no yukai*), which granted the quarantine officers more authority and imposed fines and prison terms upon physicians in cases of not revealing infected patients. In 1879 the Bureau officially promulgated the Rules for the Prevention of Cholera at the Ports, which included 22 regulations with detailed instructions to fight against cholera and five other infectious diseases (dysentery, intestinal typhus, diphtheria, typhoid and smallpox). The draft of the Rules was circulated among foreign councils with whom Japan had signed various unequal treaties to solicit their support. The United States accepted the Rules, while Britain vetoed, and Germany and France proposed revision. The British diplomat Sir Harry Smith Parkes (1828–1885) complained to the Japanese government that the Rules did not clearly specify their applicability to ships of foreign origin, and that the regulations were too obscure and insufficient for foreigners to follow. For instance, the Rules stated that all ships, crews and passengers from any ports of epidemic outbreak would be indiscriminately quarantined for seven days when arriving in Japan. In this time,

---

10    Kanbayashi, "公衆衛生の確立における日本と英国" and Kōseishō ed. *Ken'eki seido hyakunenshi* (Tokyo: Kōseishō Kōshū eiseikyoku, 1980), Chap. I.

11    Abe Yasunari, "'Eisei' toiu chitsujo."

the crews, passengers and cargos would be allowed to disembark without any disinfection if they received a clean bill of health. Parkes insisted that Japan revise and establish a separate category of Rules specifically applicable to British carriers, while the Japanese protested that the request was an intervention into Japanese administrative authority. Parkes counter-argued that the British legation could not violate the Quarantine Act proclaimed by the British court and hence was bound to follow the British regulations. What Britain demanded at the time was the right to uphold a higher yardstick for quarantine measures. The subsequent development of Japanese quarantine regulations to some extent yielded to international conditions and consents. In terms of technology, infrastructure, and the legal system of maritime quarantine, Britain obviously took the lead in these developments, and Japan was unable to compete on a par in its formative period.[12] The most notable regulations that Japan borrowed from Britain were that infected bodies should be cremated immediately; fees levied for cargo and carrier disinfection and fumigation; infected objects and personal belongings should be demolished; and warships would stand by each port. Although the quarantine regulations at this formative stage were nominal instead of realistic, they nonetheless set an imperious tone for the regime of disease control in decades to come.

In 1880, the Bureau displayed the extension of its responsibility from medicine to nation-wide sanitation and published an explanation of the Rules for the Prevention of Cholera. Facing the fact that villagers would not reveal the cases of patients and deaths, for fear of antiseptic sanitation and fumigation and being put away in the quarantine hospitals, the Rules exhorted that the epidemic of cholera would not only threaten the loss of one's life but also the death of hundreds of thousand residents in entire villages and cities. Using the conventional moral code of self-care, the Bureau tried to raise public awareness of community hygiene as every citizen's duty. Each individual was locked in concentric circles of the social body while the nation-state presided at the center to administer the preventive measures along the domestic and external borderlines. While each citizen safeguarded his own health, everyone altogether safeguarded the nation's health and hence the nation's wealth.[13]

*Eisei*, later interpreted as "hygiene" by Nagayo's successor Gotō Shimpei (1857–1929) in his work "Principles of National Hygiene" ("Kokka eisei genri" 國家衛生原理) in 1889, became the *eisei* of the nation-state (*kokka*) and saw the nation-state as a sublimated form, analogous to the human body. Upon such a

---

12   *Ken'eki seido hyakunenshi*, 28–29. One case in point, Yokohama was the only port in Japan carrying steam boilers for sanitation purpose during this period.

13   Abe Yasunari, "'Eisei' toiu chitsujo."

form the evolutionary force could manifest itself in the change from ignorance to enlightenment, from shamanistic superstition to sanitation, from treatment to prevention, from prolonging life to enriching life, and from savage to civilized. In order to function and achieve perfect physiological harmony, the nation-state as an organism would coordinate various organs in times of peace, and in times of turmoil would defend its life (the majority's *eisei*) and sacrifice the survival of individuals.[14] It was this very principle of totality, which required forsaking the individual's life and subsuming it into a meaningful whole, that brought forth the historical synthesis of individual body and social body to form the national body, a body acted upon by public hygiene. Such a principle espoused the reshuffling of Japanese hygiene personnel and the police system in 1886 in the name of effective management. With the hygiene personnel's supervision, the police took over the executive force to administer affairs of quarantine and epidemic prevention, such as tracking down the epicenter of disease outbreak, sanitizing infected households, and dispatching infected patients to quarantine hospitals or shelters.[15] Japanese officials carried this managerial approach over to their Japanese colonies after Japan defeated Qing China in 1894 and acquired the colonies of Taiwan in 1895 and Korea in 1910.

Japanese rule in colonial Taiwan was largely envisioned by Gotō Shimpei, who became the first administrator of the colonial government in Taiwan and the preeminent architect of the Japanese empire. Facing pressing problems in Taiwan – among them "bandits," "savages," epidemics, language barriers, and a lack of harbors and transportation – Gotō formulated his vision of empire through the "biology politics" doctrine.[16] He perceived the foundation of biology and scientific progress – as embodied in trade, industry, sanitation, policing, communication, and education – to be the essence of colonial management. On the basis of this doctrine, he believed that Japan would become the "fittest" in the international struggle by devising appropriate schemes for improving the quality of life so as to achieve glory in the management of Taiwan.

The initial implementation of hygienic facilities began in 1896 when the sanitary engineer William K. Burton (1856–1899) arrived in Taiwan to build sewage and clean water systems for the Japanese residential areas first, and

---

14   Gotō Shimpei, "Kokka eisei genri" in *Kagaku no shisō*, II (Tokyo: Chimaku shobō, 1964), 289–303.

15   *Ken'eki seido hyakunenshi*, 35–36.

16   Bo Liang, *Jishu yu diguo yiyanjiu: Riben zai Zhongguo de zhimin keyan jigou* (Researches on technology and imperialism: Japanese colonial scientific research institutes in China) (Jinan: Shandong jiaoyu chuban she, 2006), 234.

later extended them to major cities in the island.[17] The colonial government extended the Japanese quarantine regulations to Taiwan in 1896 and in 1897 it instituted pestilence-prevention measures for eight major acute epidemic diseases.[18] In addition, the colonial police system incorporated the household registration system and took exclusive control over quarantine and epidemic prevention measures.[19] The local prefecture governments financed such prevention measures by collecting public sanitation fees from taxes on the use of markets.[20] Compared to the dual systems of sanitary/police personnel management in Japan's homeland, the police in Taiwan upheld an often tougher centralizing (often militarizing) control over hygiene administration.[21] Before the issuance and enforcement of quarantine regulations, the colonial government often called for corvee and donations from the gentry elites and local village heads for public works such as sewers, street sanitation, and local clinics. Subsequently, local elites criticized police coercion as a ruthless form of colonial tyranny. After 1896, there were often complaints of police brutality, and incidents in which local villagers concealed and disguised the corpses of diseased patients as suicide victims, or buried the corpses without official reports. There were also horrendous rumors that the quarantine hospitals were death camps, which impelled local residents to flee elsewhere.[22]

In Korea, under the influence of the Japanese advisors, the Joseon Dynasty created a sanitary police system in 1894 as part of its Gabo modernization project. This incorporation of the police force into epidemic control might have

---

17 Lu Zheqi, "A Research on the Modernity Influence by Sanitation Engineer William Kinninmond Burton in Taiwan Cities during the Japanese Governance of Taiwan" (Masters Thesis in Chinese, Chung Yuan Christian University, 1999).

18 Zhang Xiurong ed., *Rizhi Taiwan yiliao gongwei wushi nian* (Five Decades of Public Hygiene and Medicine in Colonial Taiwan) (Taipei: National Taiwan University Press, 2012), 308.

19 Fan Yanqiu, "Riju qianqi Taiwan gonggong weisheng zhi xingcheng, 1895–1920: yizhong zhidumian de guancha (Public hygiene in Colonial Taiwan, 1895–1920: a case study of epidemic prevention)" (M.A. Thesis, National Normal University, 1994).

20 Hui-yu Caroline Ts'ai, *Taiwan in Japan's Empire Building: An Institutional Approach to Colonial Engineering* (New York: Routledge, 2009), 110–113.

21 Fan Yanqiu, "Riju qianqi Taiwan zhi gonggong weisheng: yi fangyi wei zhongxin zhi yanjiu 1895–1920."

22 Ibid., 80–83. A recent memoir of Monk Jingxin documented the brutality of Japanese police hunting down the diseased patients with cholera, smallpox, dysentery and typhoid fever and employing euthanasia during his childhood. See Monk Jingxin's lecture collection in *Jingxin zhanglao yanjiang xuanji* (Kaohsiung: Chin Jei Buddhist Association, 1996), 13.

been out of necessity or a historical coincidence. In times of epidemic outbreak, police had more authority in limiting the flow of vehicles and people,
especially since the sanitary sector was often understaffed. Public hygiene and
epidemic control were practices rooted in the West and few Koreans were
trained professionally in Western medicine. The Gabo modernist reformers
perceived hygiene in a way similar to Gotō Shimpei's vision of a civilizing mission of progress in which an individual's privileges were forsaken for the public
good. The police were the most appropriate tool to implement such a vision.[23]
The dual system of administrative supervision and police execution in Korean
epidemic control encountered a setback during the political feud between the
Gabo reformers and the royalists in 1896 and resumed again in 1902 when cholera ravaged Korea. In 1906, the role of police in sanitation was reinforced when
the Department of Sanitation was transferred to the National Police Agency
and in 1910 the gendarme police were assigned a specified function of sanitation to be responsible for epidemic prevention, food inspection and public
health. The hygienic officers' duties included port quarantine, inoculation,
food hygiene, swimming pool water inspection, medicine, and cemetery, cre-
mation, sewage and slaughterhouse patrol.[24]

Later that year, the Department of Sanitation was abolished when Japan
formally annexed Korea, and in 1919, the colonial government changed the
administrative chief of epidemic prevention ordinance from the Provincial
Police Director to Provincial Governor in the name of the new "Cultural Policy"
with which Japan would help Korea to achieve "independence" in a distant
future. However, such a nominal shift did not affect the *de facto* structure in
which the administrative officials played a supplementary role to the police in
undertaking epidemic control activities in colonial Korea.[25] In 1916, the police
legislated the regulation of household investigation compounded by hygiene
inspection. Such legislation elicited complaints from the local populace, who
objected to police interference in raising domestic farm animals when they

---

23    Park Yunjae, "Anti-Cholera Measures and the Development of Sanitary Police System in
       Korea, 1890s–1920s" in 近現代アジアにおける健康の社会経済史–疾病,開発,医療.
       公眾衛生, 153–162.

24    Keun-Sik Jung, "Chaoxian zhimindi weisheng jingcha xingcheng yu yanbian ji yichan:
       cong zhimindi tongzhi jiaodu guancha"(The formation and transformation of Korean
       hygienic police and its legacy: an observation from colonial governmentality), collected
       in Fan Yanqiu ed. *Duoyuan xiangqian yu chuangzao zhuanhua: Taiwan gonggong weish-
       eng bainian shi* (A Centennial history of Taiwan's public health)(Taipei: Yuanliu publish-
       ing, 2011), 35–77.

25    Park Yunjae, "Anti-Cholera Measures and the Development of Sanitary Police System in
       Korea, 1890s–1920s."

investigated the village privies. The colonial government commented in the 1920 annual report on cholera that the joint forces of the police and quarantine doctors patrolled each household daily to locate cholera victims quickly during the 1919–1920 outbreak, and highlighted that such success was only achieved in Korea.[26] The sentiment against Japanese rule and its epidemic control mechanism sparked a movement to establish a private isolation hospital in Korea in the early 1920s in order to promote traditional Korean medicine and to relieve local Koreans' anxiety of infection and fear of the quarantine wards.[27]

## Chinese Maritime Customs and Quarantine Service

The dominance of the police force in the sanitation and epidemic control systems in Japan and colonial Taiwan and Korea was contingent upon the circumstance of an integrated national-state. Owing to its perennial struggles against foreign encroachments and internal rebellions and civil wars, both state-building and hygienic practices in Qing and Republican China staggered along a path to modernity.

The Chinese Maritime Customs Service was founded in 1854 when British, French, and American diplomats decided to assist the Qing court in collecting international trade duties in Shanghai, which was one of five treaty ports opened to the West by the Sino-British Treaty of Nanjing of 1842. In 1853, in the midst of the Taiping Rebellion (1850–1864), a group of rebels attacked the city of Shanghai, destroyed the customs house and forced the official in charge of customs (*daotai*) to flee. Although the customs house ceased to function, the treaties with Britain, America and France remained in force and so foreign merchants had to pay duties to the Chinese government. The British and American consuls required their nationals to declare exports and imports at the consulates and to make a commitment to the eventual payment of the required duties. This expedient measure generated complaints among the British and American merchants, since the merchants of other nationalities

---

26    Keun-Sik Jung, "Chaoxian zhimindi weisheng jingcha xingcheng yu yanbian ji yichan: cong zhimindi tongzhi jiaodu guancha."

27    Park Yunjae and Shin Dong-hwan, "A Study on the Movement for Establishing a Private Isolation Hospital under the Rule of Japanese Imperialism," in *Korean Journal of Medical History* (1998)7: 37–45. This movement only succeeded partially in that a ward of contagion study was established. The partial failure was due to the causes of insufficient fundraising among the pro-Japanese upper class and opposition hold by local community.

were free from such legal obligation. After the British regained control of Shanghai, the British, American and French consuls swayed the *daotai* to return and reopen the customs house. In addition, the consuls proposed to help re-establish the customs service with foreign recruits and the *daotai* accepted their proposal on June 29, 1854.

The arrangement was that Westerners, predominantly British in its initial phase, would staff an Inspectorate, which would be an organ of the Qing bureaucracy and which assessed the duties payable on all imports. One reason why the British, the American, and the French set up the system was to prevent preferential treatment of merchants from nations without treaties with China, or with better connections than themselves. Following the Second Opium War of 1858–60, between the Qing and Britain and France, new treaties put the Customs Service on a new legal basis to extend its operations to additional ports such as Nanjing, Yingkou, Yantai, Tianjin, Hankou, Zhenjiang, Danshui, Taizhong, Jiujiang and Shantou. Under the stewardship of Sir Robert Hart (1835–1911, an Irish-born British diplomat and the Inspector General of Customs from 1863 to 1908), the Maritime Customs Service grew into one of the largest bureaucracies of the Qing Dynasty and its Republican successors. By the last decade of the 19th century, the Service supervised around fifty Customs Houses and many more substations across China. Customs revenue amounted to one third of all central revenue from then to the outbreak of the Second Sino-Japanese War in 1937. Its staff ultimately reached more than 10,000 members, with Europeans, Americans, and also Japanese after the First Sino-Japanese War, dominating its higher ranks until 1929, when a policy of signification was introduced that halted the hiring of foreign staff the next year.

Quarantine as an imaginary vision of the geo-body of a nation is a perfect situation of nationalist expression bound for territorial marking and citizenship making.[28] Quarantine service is essential to the security of trade, and had inaugurated the public hygiene campaigns in modern China. According to the report of Sir Frederick Maze, Commissioner and later Inspector General of China's Maritime Customs, quarantine as a special function of the Chinese Maritime Service began from 1873 in Xiamen and Shanghai, where ships and Chinese migrant workers went back and forth to Southeast Asia, where cholera rampaged in Thailand and Malaysia. Quarantine was under Customs supervision and the foreign consuls, rather than the Chinese territorial authorities, had magisterial jurisdiction over the vessels of their corresponding nationalities. The local *daotai* appointed the Customs Medical Officer to serve as Port

---

28    The term "geobody" was coined by Thongchai Winichakul in his *Siam Mapped: A History of the Geo-Body of a Nation* (Honolulu: University of Hawai'i Press, 1994).

Health Officer, but he would have to inform the Harbor Master, who would in turn inform his superior officer and obtain the approval of the consul in question. When the 1873 outbreak occurred, the Customs Medical Officers in Xiamen were Dr. Patrick Manson and his brother David, who reported the cholera rampage:

> In consequence of the cholera prevailing in India and the Straits Settlements, a quarantine was established for some time for vessels coming from infected ports. The crews were inspected before entering the inner harbour, but unfortunately in no instance did anything like a history of cholera present itself so as to make isolation necessary.[29]

In 1874, the commissioner of the Xiamen Customs, George Hughes, witnessed the turmoil and deliberated over the need for epidemic prevention. He then drafted the quarantine regulations in three languages (Chinese, English and French) and, with the agreement of the local consuls, put them into practice. According to these regulations, the determination of an infected port rested with the Superintendent of Customs and the foreign consuls. Declaration of Infection was shown by the hoisting of a yellow flag in the foremast of the vessel, which would then proceed up the river to Shanghai. More specifically, the rules provided that:

1.  All vessels from Singapore, Bangkok and other cholera-infected places had to anchor at a specified point and to remain there until inspected by the Customs Medical Officers.
2.  Such vessels were forbidden to shift their berths, land passengers, baggage or any article whatsoever until a Customs permit to do so had been issued.
3.  Punishment for any infraction of these regulations was to be "as the law directs by the Consular officer concerned."[30]

At the turn of the nineteenth century, Shanghai was made up of three distinct and independent administrative units: the International Settlement, the French Settlement, and the Chinese City. Each of these units played an equally significant part as far as the health of the port is concerned. The International Settlement had an efficient Public Health Department conducted along the

---

29  Wu Lien-teh, *Plague Fighter: The Autobiography of a Modern Chinese Physician* (Cambridge: W. Heffer & Sons Ltd., 1959), 404.

30  Wu Lien-teh, *Plague Fighter: The Autobiography of a Modern Chinese Physician*, 404–405.

best British lines with a laboratory staff of well-trained men. The French Settlement had a Sanitary Service run in accordance with French practices, but the Chinese City had hardly any organized attempt at health administration. Authority for health in the port was vested in the Commissioner of Customs, who was assisted by a Port Health Officer stationed at Wusong. The latter was entirely dependent upon the health organizations of the city for his information as to the prevalence of infectious diseases.[31]

Customs stations in other cities subsequently and respectively established their own quarantine services without one unified regime to administer the entire system of imperial hygiene. Ningbo in 1894 declared against Hong Kong and Canton regarding the presence of plague; Shantou issued its first sanitary laws in 1883; Yingkou established a sanitary service in 1899; Tianjin obtained the Viceroy's approval for opening a quarantine station at Dagu at the same time; and Hankou promulgated sanitary regulations in 1902–04. When the Manchurian Plague Prevention Service was established in 1912, it assumed all responsibility for the control of epidemic diseases (particularly plague and cholera) in that region. In addition to the establishment of regional quarantine services, the administrative organs experienced gradual centralization, seen in the 1917 establishment of the Central Office of Epidemic Prevention within the Health Division, and its subsequent promotion and incorporation into the Ministry of Internal Affairs in 1919. The renowned anti-plague hero, Dr. Wu Lien-teh, held the directorship of the National Quarantine Service from 1919 onward. That same year, the Maritime Customs appropriated $60,000 for the construction of a quarantine hospital at Yingkou and $24,000 for annual operating expenses. In 1923, the port of Andong received $45,000 for constructing a modern quarantine station at Shantou-Longkou, together with an annual allowance of $20,000 for upkeep. Both stations were then under the aegis of the Manchurian Plague Prevention Service, which also controlled quarantine work.[32] During this period, these port authorities felt themselves constrained to impose quarantine on vessels from particular places even against the wishes of the consul, leaving to the latter the responsibility of refusing to assist in enforcing the regulations against vessels of his nationality.

The on-site practice of sanitation and quarantine enforcement was subject to the source of funding, and administrative coordination between the customs stations and local governments. The Commissioner of the Shanghai Customs station, L. Rocher, once complained about the quarantine service:

---

31    See Circular 245 for the establishment of quarantine service.

32    Wu Lieh-teh, *Plague Fighter*, 406.

The whole system is most unsatisfactory. It is obviously asking the impossible when we expect one Health Officer to attend to the whole needs of the port; but we are certainly in no position to ask those concerned to authorize the engagement of an assistant...As far as I can see the only satisfactory solution would be to put the Sanitary Service here on the same footing as the Manchurian Plague Prevention Service. The latter gets a fixed annual grant from revenue, is administered by a group of Doctors under Dr. Wu Lien Te[teh], and the Commissioner guards the funds.[33]

The disintegration of the quarantine service in China explained why Shanghai and Harbin had sufficiently reliable statistics during the 1919 cholera outbreak, while other ports' statistics are unavailable. The director of the National Quarantine Service, Dr. Wu Lien-teh, had consistently called for assistance from the police force for the epidemic control activities based on his administrative experience in the Manchurian Plague Prevention Service and the successful anti-plague campaigns of 1911 and 1921. However, his objectives did not materialize until the Customs' quarantine service become a uniform administration after the Nationalist Government established itself in Nanjing in 1928 and created the Ministry of Health. Subsequently, it established the Central Cholera Bureau in 1935.

Nevertheless, local populations often viewed the prevailing quarantine regime in negative terms. They felt constrained in their mobility within and without national borders, compelled by the daily routine of bodily hygiene inside and beyond their households, and slighted in their Sino-Western encounters, especially in the foreign concessions. The gentry elites showed their ambivalence: on the one hand, they embraced the civility of modern hygiene, but on the other hand, they felt disgraced by the cultural inferiority of their compatriots and their filthy living environments under the threat of imperialist encroachment. Chu Renxun (1874–1928), a resident of Tianjin, lamented the national disgrace when he reported his observation of twenty people, including a scholar and a merchant, being forced into street cleaning during the international occupation of Tianjin in 1900.[34] Hence hygiene was in this context a marker symbolizing the violation of national sovereignty and personal dignity. In the area of the Japanese concession in Tianjin, the Japanese bacteriologist Tsuzuki Jinnouke observed the 1902 cholera epidemic and

---

33    Despatch No. 22,659 to Inspector General, Shanghai, May 23rd, 1929.
34    Ruth Rogaski, *Hygienic Modernity: Meanings of Health and Disease in Treaty-Port China* (Berkeley: University Of California Press, 2004), 175.

attributed the cause to the flies transporting human excreta in areas where the Japanese concession was heavily populated by Chinese residents and surrounded by Chinese markets. Like most Westerners' earlier admonition for ethnic segregation, Tsuzuki warned against Sino-Japanese contact.[35] However, there was an important tension. On the one hand, foreigners lodged official complaints that Chinese people relieved themselves openly in the streets, while, on the other hand, Chinese complained of police oppression and concealed cholera deaths and disposed of bodies in secret, or dumped the bodies in rivers, to avoid such harassment.[36]

In Shanghai, Chinese residents cohabitated with foreigners, which produced confrontations when their priorities diverged. Property disputes over a Chinese cemetery in the French Concession arose in 1874 and 1898 when the French authorities decided to construct new streets across the cemetery. Disputes also arose when foreigners feared that Chinese coffins temporarily deposited on the ground in the Ningbo Pagoda district were the source of various epidemics.[37] In 1910, the Municipal Council enforced household investigation and street sanitation to prevent the spread of Manchurian plague. However, the Municipal hygienic inspecting team was confronted by thousands of local residents. The police arrested twelve perpetrators and stipulated new quarantine regulations to fine family members who refused relocation when the patients of an epidemic disease were confirmed. Given the overcrowded housing condition in Shanghai, such stipulations further instigated Chinese residents' discontent and resistance.[38] In the eyes of foreign observers, the Chinese people were physically and culturally obscene. In 1912, when Nakajima Tan published *China's Destiny of Partition*, he observed the Chinese in Shanghai and commented that the Chinese across the entire country would remain hopelessly filthy for centuries to come.[39]

Due to domestic turmoil and foreign encroachments in China, the period between the two World Wars marked a high tide of Chinese emigration,

---

35    Ibid., 181–182.

36    Ibid., 179–180.

37    Zhen Zeqing, "Zuotian de kangzheng: Jindai Shanghai fangyi lueying (Yesterday's social protest: A brief review of epidemic prevention in modern Shanghai)," in *Shanghai Archive* (2003): no. 4, 51–53.

38    Ibid. The Shanghai Municipal Council used both sticks and carrots to enforce the quarantine regulations. For instance, the Council awarded a tael of silver when a case of cholera was reported to the police.

39    Hu Cheng, "The Image of the 'Unsanitary Chinese': Different Narratives of Foreigners and Chinese – Observations Based on Hygiene in Shanghai, 1860–1911," *Bulletin of the Institute of Modern History Academia Sinica*, no. 56 (2007): 1–43.

especially to southeast Asia. The number of emigrants setting out from Shantou and Hong Kong alone was 3,800,000 from 1918–31.[40] When travelling within and without the national borders, Chinese emigrants encountered ruthless quarantine treatments before embarkation and disembarkation. Under the effect of unequal treaties signed with various imperial powers, China's Maritime Customs could not single-handedly enforce the quarantine measures without the consensus and approvals of foreign consuls. The inspection of Chinese travelers was not only subject to the quarantine requirements of emigration but also to the regulations of immigration authorized by the foreign ports. For instance, in 1904, Chinese emigrants and travelers, men or women, were required by the Singaporean authorities to submit to full-body inspection by removing all clothes. The Chinese consul Sun Shiding had negotiated with the British Consul in Beijing for better treatment in 1906.[41] In 1911, Chinese crew members and emigrants to the Philippines were required to be power-washed and to have their luggage fumigated under the supervision of American medical officers before embarkation at the Chinese ports. Before disembarkation in the Philippines, Chinese travelers were inspected and stool-sampled. Should they fail the inspection, they would be grounded in the temporary shelters for months, awaiting deportation back to China. In 1915, the British colonial authority in Singapore required Chinese immigrants to be vaccinated, physically examined, and certified with a clean bill of health before embarkation.[42] According to the report of National Quarantine Service at Xiamen in the 1930s, the quarantined diseases for emigration were not limited to the epidemic diseases such as cholera, bubonic plague, typhoid, smallpox and yellow-fever. The restrictions also extended to ordinary illness such as trachoma, eczema, scabies and other dermatological problems.[43] Obviously, the quarantine regimes, both the domestic and the international, not only monitored the flows of diseases but also screened and controlled the movement of human migration. As the Great War was the driving force for massive human migration and an even more boisterous flows of pathogens, the 1910s marked a turning point for integrating regional health regimes and networks

40    Zhu Guohong, "A Historical Demography of Chinese Migration," in *The Chinese Overseas* (London and New York: Routledge, 2006), volume One, 139–167.

41    Iijima Wataru, *Pesuto to kindai chugoku*, 266. Cai Peirong, *Qingji zhu Xinjiapo lingshi zhi tantao, 1877–1911* (Singapore: Bafang wenhua qiye, 2002), 150–151.

42    Lian Xinhao, "Jindai haigang jianyi yu dongnanya huaqiao yimin (Modern port quarantine regimes and Chinese emigration to Southeast Asia)" in *Huaqiao Huaren lishi yanjiu*, S1(1997): 43–52.

43    Ibid.

of control to battle the vicious cholera epidemic, as well as other communicable diseases, despite the fact that the affected nations were fighting against one another.

## International Organization and Coalitions in Epidemic Control

The scientific and technological advances before the Great War ultimately frustrated people's desire to create a disease-free world, as individual nations manipulated these developments for more formidable international competition. Contrasting with this centrifugal force of science and technology, the centripetal power of medicine draws nations into international coalitions because microbes do not recognize the boundaries of nations and races, but rather create losses of human life and trade throughout the world system of capitalism. The key centripetal instrument has been the World Health Organization (WHO). Although the WHO was not established until 1948, it was the culmination of international health cooperation since the opening of the first International Sanitary Convention 1851. Cholera has been the driving force for international health organizations and was, in fact, the sole subject of discussion during the 19th century.[44] The specific goals at that time were to protect the colonial powers from the possible importation of epidemic diseases from their endemic regions, and to protect shipping and trade from the irrational and unjustified restrictions of various sanitary-quarantine measures.[45]

The twelfth International Sanitary Convention was held in 1911–12 in Paris, with participation by 41 countries, including China, Siam, Japan and various Euro-American countries. The significance of this Convention was to obligate all contracting countries "not to exceed the measures specified under the convention against the importation of cholera, plague and yellow fever, while at the same time they should observe the rules of notification of other states about epidemics and take measures against the dissemination of the diseases."[46] However, the Convention was only ratified by 15 governments by the disruption of the Great War. Thereafter, the postwar urge for a new world order rendered the quarantine concept of erecting barriers against contagion invalid and gave rise to a new vision of public health that all efforts should be towards

44    N. Howard-Jones, "The Scientific Background of the International Sanitary Conference, 1851–1938," in *WHO Chronicle*, 28(1974), no. 4: 159–171.

45    Oleg P. Schepin and Waldemar V. Yermakov, *International Quarantine* (Madison: International Universities Press, 1991), 179.

46    Ibid., 192.

eliminating the foci of infection at their points of origin. This objective could
be accomplished only by well-organized health services in all countries.[47] The
creation of the League of Nations in 1921 allowed the establishment of the
Epidemic Commission and the Health Section in the League, and steered their
task forces towards this new vision. The embodiment of this new view of international health was the League's support for China to plan a national health
program, beginning in 1926.[48]

In East Asia, the consensus of notifying other nations with accurate epidemiological information, reached during the twelfth International Sanitary
Convention, encountered a central difficulty: there was no single centralized
system monitoring the information and promoting mutual understanding
between states. In Japan, the East Asian regional network of epidemic prevention heavily relied upon two main institutions. These were the colonial government in Taiwan and its team of tropical medicine experts, which administered
medical philanthropic work across the region, and the South Manchuria
Railway Company survey team.[49]

One other network of disease reporting was framed by the Japanese consular branch offices. Upon the outbreak of diseases subject to quarantine, the
overseas offices reported back to the Ministry of Foreign Affairs and the MFA
would provide the Hygiene Bureau of the Home Ministry with monthly and
weekly reports, which were subsequently circulated to other offices concerned
with the interests of commerce.[50] Japan's trade had been increasing since its
seizure of Taiwan in 1895. In order to segregate Taiwan's trade with mainland
China, and to secure its integration into the Japanese economy, the colonial
government constructed regular shipping routes between Taiwan's coast and
Japan, and between Japan and China, respectively. The routes were managed
by two entities, the Japan Mail and the Osaka shōsen kaisha.[51] These two shipping companies were merged with two other companies into the Nisshin kisen
kaisha in 1907 and were invested with Japanese state capital. Including the
Yangzi River area, its vessels carried the second greatest tonnage in 1911, after
the British. During the period of the Great War, Nisshin kisen replaced the
British and German liners and subsequently ranked as the major shipping

47    N. Howard-Jones, "The Scientific Background of the International Sanitary Conference,
      1851–1938," in *WHO Chronicle*, 28(1974), no. 11: 495–508.
48    Ka-che Yip, *Health and National Reconstruction in Nationalist China: the Development of
      Modern Health Services, 1928–1937* (Ann Arbor: Association for Asian Studies, 1995), 53–56.
49    Iijima Wataru, *Pesuto to kindai chugoku*, 268–269.
50    Ibid., 275–276.
51    Dai Baocun, *Jindai Taiwan haiyun fazhan shi* (Taibei: Yushan publishing, 2000), 130–132.

company dominating maritime transportation in East Asia.[52] Hence, Japan was keen to access reports on disease promptly and regularly, and to find solutions that reconciled trade profits with quarantine security.

Compounding the growing diplomatic hostility between China and Japan, China did not have a unified government to administer the comprehensive quarantine service and public health system during the 1910s and early 1920s.[53] These tensions had been sparked by the Twenty-One Demands of 1915, the occupation of Shandong Peninsula during the Great War, and the verdict of the Versailles Peace Conference. The philanthropic activities in China performed by the American Rockefeller Foundation filled in this medical vacuum and helped set up medical colleges, hospitals and fellowships for students and visiting scholars to study abroad. Most importantly, the Foundation generously donated $50,000 to set up the Eastern Epidemiological Intelligence Bureau, stationed in Singapore, in 1925. It provided an additional $125,000 to sponsor the Bureau's subsequent five years of health surveys and monthly health reports, which circulated in the region.[54] The Rockefeller Foundation's interest in the development of China's resources coincided with expanding American economic-political involvement in China, anxiety over the disappearing American frontier, religious zeal centered on Christianity's perceived responsibility to the "heathen" world, and an optimistic vision of changing the world through American progressive ideology.[55]

In spite of the international animosity that prevailed after the War, humanity was exalted in a very difficult time of epidemics. An outbreak of cholera in Harbin in 1919 caused 60 Japanese deaths, 705 Russian, and 3738 Chinese. Dr. Wu Lien-teh later recalled that, during the struggle to combat the disease in Harbin, the Japanese did not have their own hospital, so their Consul-General

---

52    Zhu Yingui, "1895 nianhou riben lunyun shili zai changjiang liuyu de kuozhang" in *Zhongguo jindai lunchuan hangyunye yanjiu* (Beijing: Zhongguo shehui kexue chubanshe, 2008), 91–119. Nissin Kisen increased its shipping income 6.9 times since 1907, and its area of transportation expanded not only to North China, but also Central and South China.

53    During the era of warlord politics, the Beijing government did establish a central division of epidemic prevention in 1919. However, its administration was only limited to the region controlled by the northern clique of warlords.

54    Iijima Wataru, *Pesuto to kindai chugoku*, 275.

55    Qiusha Ma, *The Rockefeller Foundation and Modern Medical Education in China, 1915–1951* (Ph.D. Dissertation, Case Western Reserve University, 1995), chapter III: "China: A New Frontier for the Rockefeller Philanthropy." For the RF's funds to other developing countries, see Shirish N. Kavadi, *The Rockefeller Foundation and Public Health in Colonial India, 1916–1945: a Narrative History* (Bombay: Foundation for Research in Community Health, 1999).

had asked for permission to send his sick nationals to Wu's hospital. Wu placed one entire block of wards at their disposal and under the hospital's care. The American Red Cross contributed $1000 to the hospital while the Japanese supplied 225 pounds of carbolic acid for disinfection.[56]

The frequent occurrence of epidemic outbreaks in the endemic parts of Asia posed a severe threat of their possible exportation to other regions and hindered international trade and ship transportation among countries in southeast Asia. In August 1922, the Japanese delegates to the League of Nations' Health Section proposed to organize a special commission to survey the region by collecting data on the morbidity of plague, cholera, and smallpox. They also sought to track shipping routes for their spread of infection, and to render quarantine measures uniform in the major ports. Subsequently, the call for a more effective system to monitor the region's epidemiological information was pressed by the countries that had previously applied quarantine measures to ships (implying possible hindrance of trade interest).[57] In June 1924, the League of Nations officially endorsed the establishment of a Sanitary Bureau in Singapore and in February 1925, twelve representatives from different countries and territories convened to examine the working plan and budgets. The Bureau officially opened in March 1925. The number of ports sharing the information of epidemic diseases increased from 35 to 183, including ports in Africa, Australia, Oceania and America.[58]

### Concluding Remarks

Michel Foucault argued in *Discipline and Punish* that the social condition of epidemics produced some of the earliest examples of disciplinary government, rendering subjects normalized through mechanisms of bodily training and self-surveillance.[59] The practice of quarantine was embedded in the interest of rendering populations governable through public health projects in the modern world, as commerce extended worldwide. Such practices were also bound up with the development of administrative governments that captured the imagination of a national "geo-body" as they outwardly classified, communicated, and enforced artificial territorial boundaries, and inwardly projected a

---

56    Wu Lien-teh, *Plague Fighter: The Autobiography of a Modern Chinese Physician* (Cambridge: W. Heffer & Sons, 1959), 432–435.

57    Schepin and Yermakov, *International Quarantine*, 221–224.

58    Ibid., 225–226.

59    Michel Foucault, *Discipline and Punish* (Penguin, 1991), 198.

series of expectations for modern citizenship of healthy individuals on their populations. These territorial and human boundaries only came to be meaningful in the arenas of commercial regulation and customs control, and as sites of medico-legal border control and quarantine.[60]

Both Japan and China, though late comers in their pursuit of modernity, became integrated into the modern world through a full consciousness of the nation-state, characterized in part by statistics and population management, to define themselves and their power. The developmental process of this full consciousness sets the stage for what Foucault called a biopolitics, "that gave rise to comprehensive measures, statistical assessments, and interventions aimed at the entire social body or at groups as a whole" to achieve the goals of health, longevity, reproductivity, economy and security. These teleological objectives in turn justify the executive agency to decide, select and control the grouping of governable/ungovernable, fit/unfit, desirable/undesirable. However, such exercise of biopolitics in Japan came to police the lines of global racial distribution and differentiation, while in China it did not.[61]

The above sections suggest several conclusions. First, the quarantine services and the mechanisms of public hygiene that developed in East Asia were driven initially by the quest for national survival and popular sentiments for "Strengthening and enriching the Nation" (*Fuguo Qiangbing/Fukoku gyōhei*). Second, quarantine services and public health institutions are ways in which the national goals of epidemic-disease prevention and health can be approached as the symbols of modernity and as self-identification as one nation among others. Third, quarantine services along national borders impose exclusion and penalty in order to keep the undesired peoples and communicable microbes out of national terrains, and juxtapose an inward parallel of selecting desirable social elements and disciplining national citizens. The comprehensive set of these approaches can be understood as the biotechnology of modern governance. Fourth, the political effect of quarantine enforcement in the colonies was achieved by the combination of police forces and hygienic administration. Such a model was advocated for emulation by the hygienists in both China and the Japanese metropole. Fifth, from the view

---

60    Alison Bashford, *Imperial Hygiene: A Critical History of Colonialism, Nationalism and Public Health* (New York: Palgrave MacMillian, 2004), 115.

61    See the excellent example in Bashford's *Imperial Hygiene*. Bashford's book not only explores the colonial practice of racial divide and the technology of securing the boundaries, enclosure and segregations of hygienic, eugenic, imperialist/nationalist imagination; she also probes into the practice of interior frontiers in the zone of tropics in Australian context.

of international politics, the competition and coalition among the regional quarantine regimes indicated the ascendance of the Japanese over the British in the region during the 1910s. We also learn that international coalitions are the best medicine for humanity, just as Gabriel Garcia Marquez's novel, *Love in the Time of Cholera*, suggested. From a broad perspective of medicine and public hygiene in East Asia, the "long 1910s" marks a turning point for an integration of regional health development and network of control despite the Great War.

# Fighting on Two Fronts
*Japan's Involvement in the Siberian Intervention and the Spanish Influenza Pandemic of 1918*

*Sumiko Otsubo*

## Introduction

In the spring of 1918 when the Great War was about to come to a close, the Spanish Influenza broke out in the US. The first wave was relatively benign, but in August a second highly lethal strain quickly swept through many parts of the world. By spring 1920, the pandemic had killed as many as 100,000,000 people, ten times as many as the war had claimed in soldiers.[1] It is estimated that as many as 450,000 individuals fell victim to the disease in Japan.[2] It was also in August 1918 that Japan began sending over 70,000 troops to Siberia, from Japan proper, and also from its base in Manchuria, as part of the Allied effort to support White Russians against the Bolshevik revolution.[3] Although the fatal fall wave of the Spanish Influenza coincided with this mass mobilization, little is known about the Japanese Imperial Army's role in the spread of the flu pandemic in eastern Eurasia.

The paucity of information regarding Spanish influenza in Siberia can be attributed to traditional national approaches to studies of the pandemic. To overcome these limitations, the present study will examine casualty and health records compiled by the Imperial Japanese Army (IJA), the largest

---

1   John M. Barry, *The Great Influenza: The Story of the Deadliest Pandemic in History* (New York: Penguin Books, 2004), 4; Hew Strachan, *The First World War* (New York: Penguin Books, 2003), 337.

2   Hayami Akira, *Nihon o osotta Supein infuruenza: Jinrui to uirusu no dai-ichiji sekai sensō* (Tokyo: Fujiwara Shoten, 2006), 13. The third wave, which is not dealt with in this essay, was in full swing between the end of 1919 and spring 1920. My classifications of the first, second, and third waves generally correspond with Hayami's with different names. Hayami calls the first the forewarning (*sakibure*), the second the earlier outbreak (*zen ryūkō*), and the third the later outbreak (*kō ryūkō*).

3   Existing scholarship in Japanese and western languages are well reviewed in recent studies on the Siberian Intervention. See Izao Tomio, *Shoki Shiberia shuppei no kenkyū: "Atarashiki kyūseigun" kōsō no tōjō to tenkai* (Fukuoka: Kyushu Daigaku Shuppankai, 2003), 3–13; and Paul E. Dunscomb, *Japan's Siberian Intervention, 1918–1922* (Lanham, MD: Lexington Books, 2011), 1–30.

© KONINKLIJKE BRILL NV, LEIDEN, 2014 | DOI 10.1163/9789004274273_022

constituent of the multinational Siberian Intervention. There are two objectives for this study. First, it will identify how and when the fall wave ravaged northeastern Asia. This chapter will aim at situating the region on the global map of the pandemic diffusion pattern. Focusing on greater eastern Siberia, including parts of Russia, China, and Korea, to which the IJA sent and moved troops for the intervention in the fall of 1918, we will document that the deadly autumn wave of Spanish Influenza first appeared inland near the border of Siberia and Manchuria in early September 1918 and traveled along the Trans-Siberian Railroad system to the Asian east coast rather than breaking out first at Vladivostok, the disembarkation port of multi-national forces. Second, by investigating the IJA's efforts to fight on two fronts, military and epidemiological, this essay will argue that despite a political vacuum and desolate tundra, Siberia connected Japan to the wider world virally, through the modern technologies of trains and steamships. In this context, we will explore the question of what these viral links mean in evaluating the decade of the 1910s and history.

### About the *Shiberia Shuppei Eiseishi*

The IJA left detailed medical records of the killed, wounded, and diseased for later generations to study.[4] Controlling infectious diseases was a crucial military consideration, since poor hygienic conditions in battlefronts and the ensuing deaths by illness was usually much greater than that of the numbers killed in action.[5] The eleven-volume *Shiberia shuppei eiseishi* [History of Hygiene in the Siberian Expedition, hereafter referred to as the *Eiseishi*] published between 1923 and 1924 contains remarkably detailed flu-related information and statistical data of people, mostly men, on the move around Japan,

4   For example, Rikugun-shō, ed. *Meiji sanjūshichihachi-nen sen'eki rikugun eiseishi* (Tokyo: Rikugun-shō, 1924) deals with the Russo-Japanese War (1894–5) and Rikugun-shō, ed. *Taishō san-nen sen'eki eiseishi* (Tokyo: Rikugun-shō, 1917) deals with the Battle of Qingdao (1914) against Germany. Alfred W. Crosby notes, "in all previous wars more American soldiers had died of disease than in combat...." See Crosby, *America's Forgotten Pandemic: The Influenza of 1918*, 2nd ed. (New York: Cambridge University Press, 2003), 3.

5   Except for the Twelfth Division, which lost 350 soldiers in the Yufta campaign, all the Japanese army divisions sent to the Siberian Intervention suffered more deaths by illness than deaths in combats between August 1918 and October 1920. See the chart "Shidanbetsu shibō joeki," in *Shiberia shuppei eiseishi*, vol. 2, *Kanja tōkei* (Tokyo: 1924), n.p. and Yamazaki Chiyogorō's self-published memoir, *Shiberia shussei Yufuta jissenki: Chizome no yuki*, new ed. (1927; Tokyo: Yamazaki Chiyogorō, 1934).

Siberia, Manchuria and Korea. The *Eiseishi*, a geographically transnational document, is especially suited to an analysis of pandemic transmission in northeastern Asia where national boundaries were unstable and systematic national and local statistics and records were scarcely kept.[6] There is another quality which makes this document superior. In Japan, influenza was not a reportable infectious disease and was sometimes diagnosed as other respiratory diseases, but in Siberia it was designated as a wartime infectious disease that allowed the families of victims to qualify for a military pension. Therefore, careful diagnosis and counting were a priority for the IJA from the onset of the intervention.[7] According to the *Eiseishi*, between 3 August 1918 and 31 October 1920, 102,329 patients – 84,653 outpatients (82.73 per cent) and 17,676 inpatients (17.27 per cent) – received medical care. Reflecting progress in medicine, sanitation, and prevention, the numbers of contagious disease patients in wars had been steadily declining since the Sino-Japanese War (1894–95). The exception to this rule was influenza (*ryūkōsei kanbō*) during the Siberian Intervention. Among 102,329 patients in greater eastern Siberia, 12,331 (or 12.05 per cent) saw doctors because of flu. Influenza was the major killer, claiming the lives of 330 out of 956 deaths by illness (34.52 per cent).[8] The *Eiseishi*, in spite of its greater geographical coverage and promising statistical quality and quantity, has not been utilized to assess the transmission of the 1918 pandemic.[9]

---

6   Hayami Akira notes that there was no separate set of statistical data for Kantō-shū (Guandong leasehold in Manchuria), which was not an official Japanese territory. See Hayami, *Nihon o osotta Supein infuruenza*, 377–423; and see also Naimushō Eiseikyoku, ed. *Ryūkōsei kanbō* (Tokyo: Naimushō Eiseikyoku, 1922), reprinted as Naimushō Eiseikyoku, ed. *Ryūkōsei kanbō: "Supein kaze" dai ryūkō no kiroku*, Tōyō Bunko 778 (Tokyo: Heibonsha, 2008), 116–130. Crosby notes that "[t]here is no record of how many died [of Spanish Influenza] in the whole of Russia...." See his *America's Forgotten Pandemic*, 149.

7   Hayami, *Nihon o osotta Supein infuruenza*, 76–77, 103–104, 234–239. On 20 August 1918, shortly after Japan began sending troops to Siberia and a few weeks before the second wave of the pandemic arrived, the Japanese Imperial Army made an announcement listing influenza as one of the sixteen infectious diseases that would make families eligible for a military pension. The following day, they issued more detailed instructions, including a special note directing military physicians to provide a death certificate using the military pension form for influenza instead of using a regular death certificate as a substitute. In early December, after confronting the severe October outbreak, the authorities further instructed medical personnel to diagnose croupous pneumonia as influenza since it was a common complication of influenza. See *Shiberia shuppei eiseishi*, vol. 1, *Eisei kinmu*, vol. Ge (Tokyo: 1924), 393–394.

8   *Shiberia shuppei eiseishi*, vol. 5, *Senbyō* (Tokyo: 1924), 1–5.

9   A recent preliminary study of Izao Tomio, focusing on Yamaguchi Prefecture and exploring the connection between the pandemic and domestic politics, uses the *Eiseishi*. See his

## Modern Transportation: Steamship and Railroad

The Spanish Influenza outbreak was a markedly modern phenomenon. One of the main reasons it reached such pandemic proportions was the increasingly widespread use of modern transportation technologies and the movement of troops and supplies for the war. It also revealed the limited knowledge of modern medicine in the early 20th century. Medical experts, following the late 19th-century development of germ theory, worked hard to identify a bacterium causing the pandemic. It was not until 1933 that scientists discovered that influenza was caused by a virus, not a bacterium. Historian Alfred Crosby describes their inability to contain the 1918 influenza as "the greatest failure of medical science in the 20th century or, if absolute numbers of dead are the measure, of all time."[10] In the decade of the Great War, the flu virus traveled from person to person through coughs, as overcrowded railroad and steamships transported soldiers across continents and oceans. Referring to the relationship between maritime transportation and the second wave of influenza, historian Geoffrey W. Rice notes, "[h]ealth inspectors went to some lengths in Japan to establish how the influenza had arrived, and the culprit they finally identified was the Hozan-maru from Siberia, which had docked at Urashio [Vladivostok]."[11] Home Ministry official, Mr. Taniguchi, maintained that "the epidemic of Fukui started on October 9 at Tsuruga, and came into the port of Urashio on a ship, the Hozan-maru, from Siberia."[12]

The Spanish Influenza peaked in November 1918 worldwide, and it is important to investigate how the Siberian Intervention served to transport the virus around greater eastern Siberia and into Japan proper. After reviewing the Home Ministry's 1922 report on the pandemic, virologist Nishimura Hidekazu attributed the lack of information concerning flu outbreaks during the Siberian

---

     "Shiberia Shuppei ni okeru Supein Infuruenza no mondai," *Yamaguchi Kenritsu Daigaku Gakujutsu Jōhō* 17.4 (March 2011): 1–12.

10    Crosby, *America's Forgotten Pandemic*, 10.

11    Geoffrey W. Rice, "Japan and New Zealand in the 1918 Influenza Pandemic: Comparative Perspectives on Official Responses and Crisis Management," in *The Spanish Influenza Pandemic of 1918–19: New Perspectives*, eds. Howard Phillips and David Killingray (London: Routledge, 2003), 73–85, esp. 74.

12    Geoffrey W. Rice and Edwina Palmer, "Pandemic Influenza in Japan, 1918–19: Mortality Patterns and Official Responses," *Journal of Japanese Studies* 19, no. 2 (Summer 1993): 389–420, esp. 401. The description is based on "Kanbō no sanjō o shisatsu seru bōekikan no hōkoku," *Tokyo Asahi*, November 2, 1918. The inspection tours by Home Ministry officials are also covered in "Ryūkō kakuchi ni mukatte bōekikan o haken," *Tokyo Asahi*, October 25, 1918.

Intervention to military censorship.[13] In his 2006 monograph on Spanish
Influenza in Japan, demographic historian Hayami Akira devotes a ten-page
section to exploring the relationship between the Siberian Intervention and
the pandemic.[14] Analyzing flu casualty data in various newspaper articles,
including the news concerning recently discovered Siberian field hospital
medical records, Hayami suspects that available statistical figures grossly
underreported actual numbers.[15] American historian Alfred Crosby has found
it odd that influenza is not mentioned in the pages of *The Medical Department
of the United States Army in the World War* which deals with the American
forces in Siberia, since "there can be no doubt that influenza did ravage Siberia
and the Pacific provinces of Russia."[16]

While these scholars have recognized the importance of the Siberian
Intervention and Siberia in the diffusion of influenza and lamented inadequate
information, others have not. Editors of the groundbreaking collected volume,
*The Spanish Influenza Pandemic of 1918–19*, Howard Phillips and David Killingray
write: "Russia's vast Euro-Asian land mass was not immune from the virus,
although civil war and revolution, and raging typhus, meant that little attention

---

13    Nishimura Hidekazau, "Kaisetsu," in *Ryūkōsei kanbō: "Supein kaze" dai ryūkō no kiroku*, ed.
Naimushō Eiseikyoku, Tōyō Bunko 778 (1922; Tokyo: Heibonsha, 2008), 444–454, esp. 451.
Crosby theorizes that the name "Spanish Influenza" resulted from the absence of wartime
censorship in nonbelligerent Spain. See Crosby, *America's Forgotten Pandemic*, 26.

14    See "Shiberia shuppei to infuruenza," in Hayami, *Nihon o osotta Supein infuruenza*, 284–293.

15    See Hayami, *Nihon o osotta Supein infuruenza*, 285. In 2005, epidemiologist Kawana
Akihiko of International Medical Center of Japan (IMCJ) discovered nearly 700 medical
records on the Spanish pandemic flu together with other things stored in a few carton
boxes at the medical history depository of the IMCJ hospital. They were medical records
and hospitalization registries of the Tokyo First Army Hospital (a predecessor of the IMCJ
Hospital) and the Fifth Japanese Garrison Hospital, Krasnoyarsk, Russia. See "Kyū Nihon-
gun de mōi Supein kaze," *Yomiuri*, May 17, 2005; quoted in Hayami, *Nihon o osotta Supein
Infuruenza*, 285 and Note 20 on p. 324; Nishimura, "Kaisetsu," 452; Kondō Tatsuya, "Karute
no hozon," *Nihon byōinkai zasshi* 52, no. 8 (August 2005), 79; and Akihiko Kawana, Go
Naka, Yuji Fujikura, Yasutaka Mizuno, Tatsuya Kondo, and Koichiro Kudo, "Spanish
Influenza in Japanese Armed Forces, 1918–1920," *Emerging Infectious Diseases* 13, no. 4
(April 2007): 590–593, esp. 590. Though both Kawana and Kondō do not explain why
these medical flu records were stored at the IMCJ much, I suspect that they were originally
gathered in order to compile *Shiberia Shuppei eiseishi* in the 1920s as the Tokyo First Army
Hospital (*Tokyo Dai-ichi Eiju Byōin*) housed its editorial office after November 1922 when
the original editorial space at the Army Medical School (*Rikugun Gun'i Gakkō*) had
become too small. See *Shiberia Shuppei eiseishi*, Vol. 1, *Eisei kinmu*, Zoku-hen, (Tokyo:
1924?), Attachment 1, 3.

16    Crosby, *America's Forgotten Pandemic*, 150.

was given to influenza. The movement of refugees undoubtedly helped to exacerbate the transmission of influenza and total deaths there may have reached 450,000."[17] They referred to refugees but not to soldiers. Furthermore, in the same volume, Wataru Iijima concluded that "between 1918 and 1920, the Spanish flu did hit China's eastern ports and cities, some quite severely," but "it did not explode from there into the interior, as elsewhere in Asia, largely because of limited population mobility."[18] Likewise, Robert Perrins, in his study examining the development of the Japanese colonial port city of Dalian in the Japanese leasehold of Guandong in southern Manchuria, describes the fall wave of influenza among "the military personnel" stationed at "the naval base in Ryojun (Port Arthur)," also in Guandong, in mid-October 1918. Together with the third wave in spring 1919, "one-third of the local population had been infected, and of these, 3354 had died as a direct result of the influenza virus."[19] Iijima's view, though tentative, disregarded the large-scale wartime traffic between northern Manchuria, part of China, and the Transbaikal region of Siberia involving the mobilization of Japanese troops stationed in Port Arthur along the South Manchurian Railway, connecting Dalian and the Chinese Eastern Railway at Harbin.

In order to grasp the traffic situation across the long Russo-Chinese border, it is important to understand the railway system there. (See Figure 21.1). The Chinese Eastern Railway (completed in 1903), a part of the Trans-Siberian Railway system, was a direct short-cut to Russia's Pacific port city Vladivostok. Until the 1916 completion of the Amur line, an alternative northern detour going through exclusively Russian provinces, the Chinese Eastern had been the only link between Chita, a city in the Transbaikal region in Siberia, and Vladivostok.[20] At Harbin in Manchuria, the Chinese Eastern was connected to the South Manchurian Railroad. A branch line of the South Manchurian between Mukden and the Sino-Korean border city of Andong (now Dandong)

17    Howard Phillips and David Killingray, "Introduction," in *The Spanish Influenza Pandemic of 1918–19: New Perspectives*, eds. Phillips and Killingray (London: Routledge, 2003), 1–25, esp. 7.
18    Wataru Iijima, "Spanish Influenza in China, 1918–20: A Preliminary Probe," in *The Spanish Influenza Pandemic of 1918–19: New Perspectives*, eds. Howard Phillips and David Killingray (London: Routledge, 2003), 101–109, esp., 109.
19    Robert J. Perrins, "Doctors, Disease, and Development: Engineering Colonial Public Health in Southern Manchuria, 1905–1926," in *Building a Modern Japan: Science, Technology, and Medicine in the Meiji Era and Beyond*, ed. Morris Low (New York: Palgrave Macmillan, 2005), 103–132, esp. 116.
20    The portion of the northern route of the railway linking Vladivostok and Khabarovsk was called the Ussuri line. Details about the railroad system in greater Siberia can be found in Hara Teruyuki, *Shiberia Shuppei: Kakumei to Kanshō, 1917–1922* (Tokyo: Chikuma Shobō, 1989), 30–58.

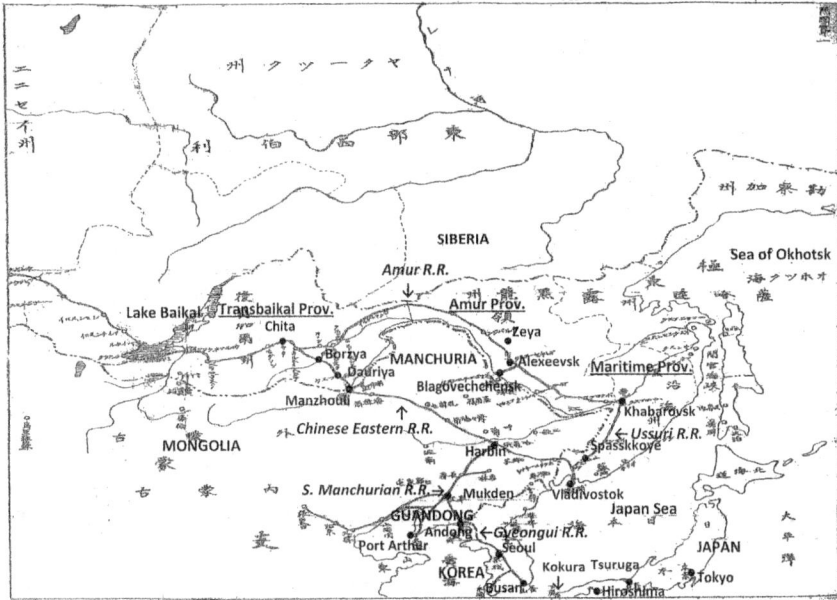

FIGURE 21.1    *Map of Northeast Asia.*
SOURCE: KENPEI SHIREIBU, *HI SHIBERIA SHUPPEI KENPEISHI FUROKU,*
TOKYO: KENPEI SHIREIBU, 1928), APPENDIX MAP 1. COURTESY OF WASEDA
UNIVERSITY LIBRARY.

was connected to the peninsula's Gyeongui Line, linking Seoul to Europe
through Manchuria and Siberia. Thus, the Chinese Eastern was a transnational
railroad going in and out of Russia's Siberia and China's Manchuria. Because of
Japan's colonization of Korea and leasehold in Guandong, together with control over the South Manchurian Railway, obtained as a result of the Russo-
Japanese War (1904–05), the Japanese empire had access to Siberia and the
Trans-Siberian Railway.

Today historians such as Iijima and to some degree Perrins suggest the introduction of influenza to China by sea. However, at the time of the pandemic,
western anatomists working in Seoul, in Japan's colonial Korea, observed that
the vicious influenza came to the peninsula "from Europe, via Siberia," in
late September, 1918.[21] "[T]he absence of studies of major regions of the

---

21    Frank W. Schofield and H.C. Cynn, "Pandemic Influenza in Korea with Special Reference
      to its Etiology," *Journal of the American Medical Association* 72, no. 14 (April 5, 1919): 981–
      983, esp. 981. Influenza outbreaks in Chin'nanpo (today's Nam'po, Pyongyang's seaport),
      Busan, and Seoul in September 1918 were recorded without details in Naimushō
      Eiseikyoku, ed. *Ryūkōsei kanbō: "Supein kaze" dai ryūkō no kiroku,* Tōyō Bunko 778 (1922;

globe" including Russia and inland China[22] made the border area of these two countries one of the darkest corners of the history of the 1918–19 flu pandemic.


### The Siberian Intervention

Even before the Russian Revolution and the Siberian Intervention, the geopolitics of northeast Asia were already fluid with Japan's imperial ambitions and China's political change in the 1910s. Japan annexed Korea in 1910. When the Great War broke out in the summer of 1914, Japan promptly joined the British side against the Central Powers led by Germany. Japan then moved to take over Qingdao, a German leased territory in northeast China. In 1915, Japan submitted the Twenty-One Demands to the fragile new Chinese republic which emerged after the fall of the Qing dynasty (1644–1911). New China also faced an internal challenge of fragmentation.

In the history of World War I, the year 1917 was pivotal for two reasons. First, Russia effectively dropped out of the Great War because of the Revolution; second, the US entered the war. By signing the Treaty of Brest-Litovsk with Germany in March 1918, Bolshevik leaders formally pulled Russia out of World War I. This let Czech Legions, formerly fighting for Czarist Russia against Germany and Austria in an attempt to establish their own nation independent from the Austro-Hungarian Empire, seek to join the French on the Western Front. They had to avoid trespassing on German-controlled areas lying between Russia and France. The shortage of ships in Europe forced them to travel eastward, taking control of towns along the Trans-Siberian Railroad.[23] They planned to return to Europe from Vladivostok via North America; they were going to transit North America by train and then take ships back over to Europe.[24] German and Austrian prisoners of war, released by the Bolsheviks, were returning to Europe westward and had skirmishes with the Czechs. In the name of rescuing the Czechs, Britain and France, hoping to recreate a new Eastern Front, requested the US and Japan to intervene, and in July each agreed

---

Tokyo: Heibonsha, 2008), 57. The Gyeongbu Line had connected Seoul and Busan since 1905.

22  Phillips and Killingray, "Introduction," 24.

23  Sugawara Sagae, *Shiberia shuppeishi yō* (Tokyo: Kaikōsha, 1925), 16–18.

24  Major General William S. Graves led the American Expeditionary Forces in the Siberian Intervention. See his memoir, *America's Siberian Adventure 1918–1920* (New York: Peter Smith, 1941), 37.

to send a small force of about 7000 to Siberia.[25] For Japan, this was the beginning of a costly war which accomplished little.[26] The stated goal for this intervention was quickly lost.[27] The Czechs reached Vladivostok as early as 28 June but there were no arrangements made for ships to take them from Vladivostok.[28] In May, two months before Tokyo's decision to participate in the intervention, Japan had secured a military agreement with China allowing Japan to move its army divisions stationed in China to Siberia.[29] The IJA hoped to establish a non-communist government as a buffer zone between Japan and Red Russia in eastern Siberia.

The IJA first dispatched 9000 troops from the Twelfth Division from Kokura, Kyushu, to Vladivostok in early August 1918. They were deployed in the Maritime and Amur provinces in eastern Siberia. According to this "official" storyline, the IJA soon sent an additional 10,000 troops to Vladivostok so as not to be overwhelmed by 15,000 enemy forces in the Maritime province. Beginning on August 23, 7000 Japanese troops, together with 3000 British, French, Czech, and White Russians led by an Ussuri Cossac named Ivan Kalmikoff launched an Allied attack against the Bolsheviks at Kraevski. Red Russian forces retreated north to Khabarovsk and then westward to the Amur region via rail and steamboat. After the Ussuri campaign, while Americans, Chinese, and Japanese troops chased revolutionary Russians to Khabarovsk, and then to the Amur cities of Alexeevsk and Blagoveschchensk.[30] As we will see, one of the fall outbreaks of influenza developed during this chase.

In mid-August, Japan also began mobilizing the Guandong Garrison (the Seventh Division originally from Hokkaidō) from northern Manchuria to the Transbaikal province of Siberia, where another Cossack leader, Grigory Semyonov, backed by the Czechs and Japanese, was trying to establish an anti-revolutionary provisional government. When the Third Division from Nagoya came to the region by the end of September, part of the Guangdong troops moved to the western Transbaikal region. It was the stronghold of the red forces, estimated to be about 30,000, including 1800 German and Austrian

25 Sugawara, 14–21. For political and diplomatic details, see Hosoya Chihiro, *Shiberia shuppei no shiteki kenkyū* (1955; Tokyo: Iwanami Shoten, 2005), 200.

26 Hara, *Shiberia Shuppei*, i, and ii.

27 Ibid., 277–297.

28 Graves, *America's Siberian Adventure*, 44, 61, Sugawara, *Shiberia shuppeishi yō*, 64, and Hara, *Shiberia Shuppei*, 343–349.

29 *Shiberia shuppei eiseishi*, vol. 1, *Eisei kinmu*, vol. Jō (Tokyo: 1924), 2–3, Sugawara, *Shiberia shuppeishi yō*, 13.

30 Sugawara, *Shiberia shuppeishi yō*, 1–67.

soldiers and 1000 Bolsheviks near Chita, 8500 Germans and Austrians near Verkhneudinsk (today's Ulan-Ude) and 8000 Bolsheviks near Daurya.[31] Semyonov's troops, the Czechs and the Japanese met near the border of Siberia, Manchuria, and Mongolia, and advanced to the Transbaikal city of Chita in early September. Thus, by the end of September, Japan had established control over both the Chinese Eastern and Amur lines, though skirmishes with partisans continued.[32]

Altogether, at the beginning of November, there were 72,400 Japanese troops in greater eastern Siberia. In addition, an infantry battalion from the Nineteenth Division, an IJA's garrison force in northern Korea, was sent to southern Ussuri. The three Siberian provinces were put under Japanese (and Allied) control, and few anticipated major offences during the severe winter there. The IJA determined that transport, mountain and field artillery units in Siberia were unnecessary, and ordered 13,800 men to return home in November, when the influenza pandemic was at its worst.[33]

Until the spring 1920 Allied withdrawal, Siberia saw a total of 350,000 Allied troops come and go. (Japan did not withdraw then.) In addition to White Russian forces, Americans, and the Japanese troops, there were over 60,000 Czecho-Slovaks, 1000 British, 4000 Canadians (who arrived in January 1919), 5000 Chinese, 1850 French, and 2000 Italians, among others.[34] In addition, the British dispatched troops from their colonies in Asia, the Hindus, as the French did with their Vietnamese. Many foreign troops landed in Vladivostok in the summer of 1918.[35] Thus, Vladivostok could have been the place where the second, more deadly wave of flu virus arrived.

## The 1918 Spring and Fall Wave of the Spanish Influenza

Let us briefly review how Spanish Influenza spread around the world. Although the true geographical origin of Spanish influenza is unclear,[36] the "epidemic of

31    Hosoya, *Shiberia shuppei no shiteki kenkyū*, 205; and Sugawara, *Shiberia shuppeishi yō*, 35–36.

32    Sugawara, *Shiberia shuppeishi yō*, 57–59.

33    Hosoya, *Shiberia shuppei no shiteki kenkyū*, Note 26, 305.

34    Takahashi Osamu, "'Shiberia shussei nikki' kaisetsu," in Matsuo Katsuzō, *Shiberia shussei nikki* (Nagoya: Fūbaisha, 1978), 13–34, esp. 33–34; and Benjamin Isitt, "Mutiny from Victoria to Vladivostok, December 1918," *Canadian Historical Review* 87, no.2 (2006): 223–264, esp. 237 and 262.

35    Takahashi Osamu, *Hahei*, vol. 2 (Tokyo: Asahi Shinbun, 1973), 12.

36    Naimushō Eiseikyoku, *Ryūkōsei kanbō*, 41. The *Eiseishi* lists Madrid, the western front in Europe, or Russia as a possible place from which the 1918 influenza pandemic

grippe" in the United States in the spring of 1918, is well recorded.[37] By late July, the mild spring flu virus had disappeared both in the United States and in Japan.[38]

The second wave in the fall was more serious and "gave rise to a high mortality, not only in Europe, but also in America and other parts of the world."[39] Crosby asserts that "[i]n the latter part of August 1918, the Spanish Influenza virus mutated, and epidemics of unprecedented virulence exploded in the same week in three port cities thousands of miles apart: Freetown, Sierra Leone; Brest, France; and Boston, Massachusetts." Freetown, the capital of the British colony and protectorate of Sierra Leone, served as a West African coaling station for ships traveling between Europe, South Africa, and the Far East. Starting around 24 August, "an estimated two-thirds of the native population contracted the disease," and "1,072 died of influenza and complications" in and around Freetown. Beginning about 24 August, Brest, a major disembarkation port for American soldiers, experienced an outbreak of the second wave of influenza. Spanish influenza came back to the eastern American coast city of Boston on 27 August.[40] In the very same month of August 1918, when the supposedly mutated and more deadly virus began to ravage the world, the Allied Intervention into Siberia officially began.

### The Japanese Imperial Army and Spanish Influenza in Northeast Asia

Soon after the first wave of the virus had lost its momentum in late July, the first group of Japanese soldiers left Kokura and arrived in Vladivostok on 12 August after a two-day voyage. The first group of Americans got there a week

---

originated. See *Shiberia shuppei eiseishi*, vol. 5, *Senbyō*, 126. Citing a medical textbook, Christopher Langford refers to a theory tracing the pandemic's origin to Russia. See his "Did the 1918–19 Influenza Pandemic Originate in China?" *Population and Development Review* 31, no. 3 (2005): 473–505, esp. 475. See also his reference, Karl G. Nicholson, Robert G. Webster and Alan J. Hay, eds. *Textbook of Influenza* (Oxford: Blackwell Science, 1998), 7.

37   Crosby, *America's Forgotten Pandemic*, 18.

38   *Shiberia shuppei eiseishi*, vol. 5, *Senbyō*, 28–32, Hayami, *Nihon o osotta Supein infuruenza*, 48.

39   Bruce Low, "Incidence of Epidemic Influenza during 1918–1919 in Europe and the Western Hemisphere," in Ministry of Health, *Reports on Public Health and Medical Subjects*, No. 4, *Report on the Pandemic of Influenza* (London: His Majesty's Stationary Office, 1920), 202–348, esp. 202.

40   Crosby, *America's Forgotten Pandemic*, 37–40.

later.[41] Their arrival did not prompt any immediate influenza outbreak on the east coast of Siberia. Instead, the Japanese Army recorded its first encounter with the Spanish Influenza inland near the border of Siberia and Manchuria in early September. A Seventh Division medical officer Takahashi Kichiji reported that the local Russian population (*Rokoku jūmin*) in Konduy and Borzya began suffering from influenza, which sometimes developed into pulmonary pneumonia resulting in death. This was about two weeks after the second wave of influenza was reported in Brest, France and at least a month before the fall wave began spreading in the home islands of Japan.[42] It was also about a week before Japanese troops from Vladivostok advanced to meet their counterparts from Manchuria.[43] Borzya was on the Chinese Eastern Railroad southeast of Chita. Nearby Konduy was located northwest of Manzhouli. The Seventh Division from Guandong was setting up there in response to enemy concentration in the area.[44]

The first flu patients among the Japanese appeared among soldiers who belonged to the 25th Infantry Regiment stationing in Borzya, nearby Byrka, and Olovyannaya in mid-September. Olovyannaya was another town along the Chinese Eastern line, close to Chita. Then the epidemic broke out among cavalrymen, artillerymen, engineers, and flying corps men stationed in Dauriya, Byrka, Olovyannaya in Siberia, and Monzhouli and Harbin in Manchuria. By early November there were a total of 1255 patients.[45]

---

41  About the voyage of Twelfth Division soldiers, see Matsuo Katsuzō, *Shiberia shussei nikki* (Nagoya: Fūbaisha, 1978), 36.

42  *Shiberia shuppei eiseishi*, vol. 5, *Senbyō*, 127. A summary of influenza epidemic during the Siberian Intervention can be found in Sanbō Honbu, *Hi Taishō 7-nen naishi 11-nen Shiberia shuppeishi (Fukkoku)*, vol. Chu (vols. 3–4 in original) (1941; reprint Tokyo: Shinjidaisha, 1972), 1083–1084. Hayami Akira suspects that the mutated influenza (the second wave influenza virus) first arrived in Japan in late September or early October. The 26 September issue of a local newspaper, *Shin Aichi*, reported that about four hundred soldiers of the Ninth Infantry Regiment in Ōtsu, Shiga, came down with influenza on that day. (The Ninth Infantry Regiment belonged to the Sixteenth Division based on Kyoto.) On 9 October, the *Osaka Mainichi*, reported that exercises were cancelled due to a pestilent flu which struck more than half of those who were in the Second Infantry Regiment in Mito. (The regiment belonged to the Fourteenth Division.) Hayami finds that many flu cases started being reported all around Japan starting in mid-October. See Hayami, *Nihon o osotta Supein Infuruenza*, 99–102.

43  American troops led by William Graves generally stayed in the Maritime and Amur regions. Sugawara, *Shiberia shuppeishi yō*, 66.

44  See the significance of and the level of population concentration in this area prior to and during the intervention in Hara, *Shiberia Shuppei*, 238–240, 311–312.

45  *Shiberia shuppei eiseishi*, vol. 5, *Senbyō*, 127–129.

The Third Division, which had just arrived in the eastern Transbaikal province of Russia, also reported that the flu first appeared among locals living near railroad cities of Borzya and Olovyannaya. From there the virus jumped to Japanese soldiers who were stationed nearby and traveled mainly southeastward along the Chinese Eastern Railway line all the way to Harbin, which was a junction city of the South Manchurian Railroad.[46] A medical officer saw influenza patients virtually at every logistics station starting in mid-October, and the situation was especially bad among travelling soldiers. Both Japanese soldiers and the local Chinese population were severely affected by the flu. For a while there were twenty to thirty deaths every day among the Chinese at Harbin. Many died by coughing up blood, and it was medically confirmed that they died of influenza-turned-into-pneumonia.[47]

In late September, a number of soldiers in the Third Field Artillery Regiment of the Third Division, which was being transported west of the Manchurian city of Qiqihar, caught influenza, which spread to other units. The flu struck soldiers in the unit transporting food in early October after they left Kuancheng (Kanjōshi or Chōshun in Japanese) for the north. Also in early October, men in the Fifty-first Infantry Regiment were brought down by the flu while traveling westward by rail from Mukden (Hōten in Japanese and Shenyang in Chinese) to Peschanka via Chōshun. In October, the flu rapidly spread among infantrymen and artillerymen stationed in Siberian cities such as Mogocha and Berezovka.[48] According to Japanese army observations, the flu first moved from the southern Transbaikal region to the north and then into southern Manchuria. A Chinese source indicates that the second wave of influenza was widespread enough to delay Mukden farmers from harvesting.[49]

As noted, observers in Seoul stated that the influenza pandemic had come to the peninsula "from Europe, via Siberia," traveling along the South Manchurian Railway, in late September 1918.[50] The timing seems somewhat early.[51] In any case, Seoul was connected to Mukden, a South Manchuria Railway station, through the Gyeongui Line, so influenza originating in Borzya and Konduy could have been carried to Korea along rail lines. Hayami Akira

46 Ibid.
47 *Shiberia shuppei eiseishi*, vol. 1, *Eisei kinmu*, vol. Ge, 62–63.
48 *Shiberia shuppei eiseishi*, vol. 5, *Senbyō*, 127–129.
49 Langford, "Did the 1918–19 Influenza Pandemic Originate in China?," 480, 496.
50 Schofield and Cynn, "Pandemic Influenza in Korea," 981.
51 The Home Ministry identifies the beginning of the second wave flu outbreak in Korea as "early fall." See Naimushō Eiseikyoku, *Ryūkōsei kanbō*, 116. According to Hayami, one of the earliest Korean reports on flu in Seoul was published on October 17. Hayami, *Nihon o osotta Supein Infuruenza*, 389–391.

also notes the flu outbreaks in Mukden and Port Arthur starting around 10 October.[52] Robert Perrins has discussed the second wave of Spanish Influenza among the military personnel in Port Arthur, the southernmost station of the South Manchurian Railway in mid-October.[53] It was likely that influenza moved into the leasehold by rail, even though its arrival by sea remains a possibility.

Influenza also moved back beyond the originating points of Borzya and Olovyannaya in southern Transbaikalia to the north, near Chita, and then westward to the Krasnoyarsk region, located more than 1200 miles (or 2000 km) west of Chita along the mainline of the Trans-Siberian Railroad. It also traveled eastward along the Amur line to Mogocha, an eastern Transbaikal city. Generally speaking, the disease moved along rail lines along with Japanese troops.

Later in September, the flu epidemic was again found among local residents in the Maritime province city of Spasskoye, south of Kraevski and northeast of Vladivostok along the Ussuri line. The Twelfth Division of the Imperial Japanese Army occupied this Russian coastal region. In late September, soldiers stationed in Spasskoye who worked on the trains began to be infected by influenza, which quickly attacked other units. A physician first suspected that soldiers might be developing influenza on October 8 and took the precaution of preventing soldiers who displayed symptoms from transporting food between Tygda and Zeya, both located in the western Amur province. But healthy soldiers working on the transport soon began coming down with flu-like symptoms during their train ride. Medical Officer Matsubara Tamotsu promptly separated the sick from the healthy by designating a quarantine train. Despite all these measures, however, the disease broke out among the soldiers in charge of military horses while traveling by rail. With an unexpected cold wave in mid-October, the number of flu patients increased and influenza spread southward to other units along the Amur-Ussuri lines toward Vladivostok. By late October, virtually all the units in the Twelfth Division were affected by the epidemic.[54]

Some patients were lucky to have a mild flu and recovered after a few days. Others were not so fortunate. In October, there were many cases in which influenza developed into pneumonia resulting in death.[55] Some Spasskoye-based soldiers lasted less than 48 hours from the time of their admission to the

52    Hayami, *Nihon o osotta Supein Infuruenza*, 405–407.
53    Perrins, "Doctors, Disease, and Development," 116.
54    *Shiberia shuppei eiseishi*, vol. 5, *Senbyō*, 127–129.
55    Ibid., 127–129, 132–133.

Fourth Field Hospital. The hospital admitted 318 patients between 30 September 1918 and 6 March 1919. Among them, 35 died and 45 were sent back to Japan. Although the reasons why they died or were sent back home are not explained, the dates when the inpatients were sent home are available and indicate that 26 of 45 patients left Siberia between 6 October and 1 November 1918. This means that approximately 58 per cent of patients were shipped home during the month of October.[56] In the middle of the virulent influenza outbreak, gravely sick and wounded soldiers in eastern Siberia were sent back to Japan as early as 6 October. Until 10 November, almost all official military ships from Vladivostok, Dalian and Busan (Korea) went to two ports, Moji near Kokura and Ujina near Hiroshima. The Hiroshima Army Hospital (*Hiroshima Eiju Byōin*) reported that they treated eight returnees on 15 September, but by early October the number of inpatients had increased to 240. By 1 November, the number of inpatients exceeded 1000, well beyond the hospital's capacity of 300. Although the hospital originally separated returnees from soldiers at home, the influenza outbreak and the increase of returnees quickly caused this distinction to collapse.[57] *Ōsaka Mainichi* reported that a transport ship arrived at Moji on 4 November from Vladivostok carrying the bodies of eleven men, all of whom had developed pneumonia within two days of catching flu. Two Buddhist monks, accompanying these bodies from Siberia, commented on the deadly nature of the influenza outbreak on the continent, "On the 26th of last month, as many as 27 died of flu. We had been busy with funerals every day."[58] The quarantine station at Ninoshima Island off Hiroshima began its operation on 10 November.[59] After that, virtually all military ships had to go there first.

For civilians, the flu found a different route between Vladivostok and Japan. As previously noted, the influenza epidemic of Tsuruga, Fukui started on 9 October after the arrival of the Hozan-maru from Vladivostok. The Hozan-maru connected Tsuruga, a small port facing the Japan Sea, and Vladivostok through its regular weekly service. In fact, a new group of Japanese Red Cross nurses had left Tsuruga on the Hozan-maru on 28 September and arrived at

56　See an attached map with charts, "Enkaishū Kokuryūshū hōmen kanja shūyō kōsō hyō," in *Shiberia shuppei eiseishi*, vol. 1, *Eisei kinmu*, vol. Ge, n.p.

57　Ibid., 327, 343–344.

58　"Shiberia shuppei no heishi mo gisei," *Osaka Mainichi* 4 November, 1918, in *Taishō nyūsu jiten*, vol. 3 *Taishō 6-nen-Taishō 7-nen*, ed. Taishō nyūsu jiten henshū iinkai (Tokyo: Mainichi Komyunikēshonzu, 1987), 355.

59　*Shiberia shuppei eiseishi*, vol. 1, *Eisei kinmu*, vol. Ge, 226–227. Later in April 1919, another quarantine station began operating in Hakodate. See the same volume, 300.

Vladivostok two days later.[60] It seems likely that the steamship picked up the
influenza virus already prevalent in the Siberian coast in early October and
brought it to Japan on its next round trip if not earlier.[61] By mid-October, influenza outbreaks began being reported in many places in Japan.[62] Steamships
from Vladivostok to Tsuruga, Moji, and Ujina are some of many possible
sources bringing in the virus to Japan.[63] Though the worst effects of the epidemic on the war fronts was experienced between mid- to late-October,[64] the
IJA, getting ready for winter, began withdrawing nearly 14,000 soldiers from
Siberia in November before the outbreaks there were completely over. The
Influenza virus of continental origin must have traveled to Japan easily along
with the returning soldiers.

An issue requiring further investigation is the relationship between human
and horse flu. In his journal, Matsuo Katsuzō, a Twelfth Division soldier from
Kokura, wrote that on 26 October when he arrived in Arkhara, he met a transport soldier heading for Spasskoye from Blagovechchensk. He told Matsuo that
further inland the daily temperature dropped to lower than –30°C (–22°F) and
more than ten transport soldiers had died of influenza. These human deaths
occurred simultaneously with fifteen or sixteen horse deaths.[65] A newspaper

60    "Daiichi kangofu soshiki kyūgohan zōha," *Hakuai* 378 (October 10, 1918), 4–5. Regarding
      Hozan-maru's schedule, see Kenpei Shireibu, *Shiberia Kenpeishi Furoku* (Tokyo: Kenpei
      Shireibu, 1928); 85. Business owner Horie Naozō in Vladivostok frequently noted the arriv-
      als and departures of the Hozan-maru in his diary. His diary from 1918 can be found in
      Horie Machi, *Haruka naru Urajiosutokku: Meiji-Taishō jidai no Nihonjin kyoryūmin no
      sokuseki o otte* (Osaka: Shinpū Shobō, 2002), 151–191.

61    The Home Ministry's report refers to an allegation that a ship from North America arriv-
      ing at Yokohama on 2 September might have brought the flu virus to Japan. Considering
      that the first American cases of the second wave influenza were found in Boston, on the
      Atlantic coast of the United States, on 27 August, and the flu outbreak in Japan did not
      start until late September at the earliest, this theory seems difficult to support. See
      Naimushō Eiseikyoku, *Ryūkōsei kanbō*, 103.

62    Hayami, *Nihon o osotta Supein Infuruenza*, 101.

63    Geographer Sugiura Yoshio analyzes spatial diffusion of the Spanish Influenza in Japan.
      He found that many southwestern prefectures, including those with the ports used for the
      Siberian Intervention, experienced the peak influenza outbreak in November and that
      the peak was moving eastward and northward. See his "Waga kuni ni okeru 'Supein kaze'
      no kūkanteki kakusan ni kansuru ichi kōsatsu," *Chirigaku hyōron* 50, no. 4 (1977): 201–215,
      esp. 203.

64    *Shiberia shuppei eiseishi*, vol. 5, *Senbyō*, 127–129, 132–133.

65    Matsuo, *Shiberia shussei nikki*, 128. Soldiers and military horses could have been packed in
      a limited number of roofed and heated Trans-Siberian Railroad trains in wartime settings.
      At least that was the case during the Russo-Japanese War. See Hara, *Shiberia Shuppei*, 46.

article dated 15 November reported that a Twelfth Division transport battalion chief who had returned home commented on the flu deaths of twenty-six soldiers and one hundred or so horses, clearly linking horse deaths to influenza.[66] The official history of the intervention also noted that an unusually large number of horses, 989, belonging to the Twelfth Division, died of illness in October 1918 when temperatures dropped so suddenly. Curiously, 430 horses got sick while they were engaged in the transportation project between Zeya and Tygda, not too far away from Blagovechchensk. From these 430, 98 were diagnosed to have nasal catarrh, which could be related to influenza. 140 of the 430 died, and it was likely that these 140 included the dead horses mentioned by Matsuo and the transport battalion chief. By November, the number of horse deaths seemed substantially reduced compared with September and October, because, according to the army, horses "became acclimated."[67]

Equine influenza during the Spanish influenza pandemic was also reported elsewhere, including France and the United States.[68] At a health conference of the Allies (*Rengōkoku Eisei Kaigi*) in Paris in late March 1919, experts pointed out that different animal species, including monkeys, cats, dogs, and horses, were infected with influenza.[69] It is important to analyze the relationships between the 1918 influenza's species-crossings in war settings.

### Conclusion

By closely examining medical records of the Imperial Japanese Army during the Siberian Intervention, this essay has traced the diffusion patterns of the

---

66   "Kōhō kinmu no nankō: Sentō butai ni otorazu konku," *Fukuoka Nichinichi Shinbun*, November 15, 1918, quoted in Hayami, *Nihon o osotta Supein Infuruenza*, 288–289.

67   Sanbō Honbu, *Hi Taishō 7-nen naishi 11-nen Shiberia shuppeishi (Fukkoku)*, vol. Chu, 1089.

68   Crosby, *America's Forgotten Pandemic*, 296. Viral links between equine and human influenza-like disease were historically prevalent between 1648 and 1916. See David M. Morens and Jeffery K. Taubenberger, "Historical Thoughts on Influenza Ecosystems, or Behold a Pale Horse, Dead Dogs, Failing Fowl, and Sick Swine," *Influenza and Other Respiratory Viruses* 4 (2010): 327–337.

69   Noted in Naimushō Eiseikyoku, *Ryūkōsei kanbō*, 47. Pigs are known as the mixers of various A-type virus common to certain species. In the 1990s, Jeffrey K. Taubenberger identified that the 1918 Spanish Influenza was a strain of influenza A type; more specifically, it was a subtype H1N1, endemic among pigs. Taubenberger writes about "simultaneous outbreaks of influenza in humans and pigs," "around the world during the second wave" and "the avian association with the 1918 flu." See his "Genetic Characterisation of the 1918 'Spanish' Influenza Virus" in *The Spanish Influenza Pandemic of 1918–19: New Perspectives*,

deadly second wave in greater eastern Siberia and Japan and placed them in a global context. Over 70,000 Japanese troops arrived at their battlefronts after travelling through Vladivostok and Guandong starting 12 August 1918, about two weeks before the first cases of the fall outbreak was reported in war-torn France at the other end of the Eurasian continent. The *Eiseishi* identified the earliest flu outbreak among Russians around Konduy and Borzya near the border of Siberia and Manchuria in early September. Japanese soldiers along with revolutionary Russians, Germans, and Austrians were concentrated in the area. Soon Japanese soldiers became new hosts for the treacherous flu virus. The virus seemed to travel eastward along the Chinese Eastern and southward along the South Manchurian Railway and its branch lines, possibly to the Guandong cities of Dalian and Port Arthur, and Korean cities, claiming the lives of Chinese and Korean people. On the east coast, the first flu outbreak was recorded in Spasskoye, north of Vladiostok in late September. The flu found its way down to Vladivostok, not the other way around. The major disembarkation port of multi-national forces, Vladivostok, was not the place where the fall wave of the 1918 influenza began to move westward to inland Siberia. Vladivostok, however, seemed to be one of the major sources of the flu virus arriving to Japan. In November, at the peak of the Spanish Influenza's virulence, the IJA winterized its operations and sent back about 14,000 soldiers from greater Siberia to Japan. A large number of men traveled with silent nano-companions across the eastern Asian continent and the Japan Sea.

Generally, the second wave of influenza in northeast Asia moved from west to east along the Trans-Siberian Railroad. Steamships also helped the virus continue its eastward journey from Vladivostok to Japan. In his classic study of cholera epidemics in 19th century America, noted medical historian Charles Rosenberg observed that cholera, originally endemic to India, could not have traveled extensively had it not been "an unprecedented development of trade and transportation."[70] While European Russia and Vladivostok had already been connected by rail, the 1910s saw wartime turmoil rather than peacetime trade. The Great War and the Russian Revolution, followed by the Civil War and the Allied Intervention, encouraged increased trans-continental traffic there. Japan's large scale wartime mobilization allowed the virus to travel much

---

eds. Howard Phillips and David Killingray (London: Routledge, 2003), 39–46, esp. 29. Among the total of 1965 hospitalized Japanese flu patients in greater Siberia before October 1920, 388 were transport soldiers and 64 were cavalrymen working closely with horses. *Shiberia shuppei eiseishi*, vol. 5, *Senbyō*, 126.

70    Charles E. Rosenberg, *The Cholera Years: The United States in 1832, 1849, and 1866 with A New Afterword* (1962; Chicago: University of Chicago, 1987), 2 and 241.

more quickly by putting soldiers in contact with local peoples, foreign forces, and animals.

Despite the political vacuum and desolate tundra, despite preventive efforts to contain the disease, and despite the debatable political significance of the Siberian Intervention, it is clear that the Siberian Intervention served as a microbiological link between Japan and the wider world because of the trans-continental railroad system and steamship, the crown jewels of modernity. The railroad, steamship and the desire to defend and expand capitalism and impe-rialism militarily are defining characteristics of the early days of the modern era. Ironically, this study also sheds light on the deficiencies of modern (pre-viral) knowledge and (pre-tank) technology in the 1910s. It suggests the unsuc-cessful search for the cause and cure as well as the possibility of horses as a facilitator of influenza's spread in the era before the age of the mass use of tanks and other mechanized vehicles in warfare.

The examination of Japan's military and epidemiological struggles during the Siberian Intervention has made the presence of a biological zonal space in greater Siberia visible. A great number of outsiders of different ethnic, racial, cultural, linguistic, and ideological origins came to Siberia to share this space with the existing inhabitants of the region because of the Great War, the Russian Revolution, and the Siberian Intervention. The mobilization of war horses, together with humans, must have put stress on the ecosystem there.[71] The zone was geographically transnational and existed only temporarily out-side the framework of sovereign states. The history of this space, which is potentially rich and worthy of historical inquiries, had been virtually lost between the cracks of teleological national histories, including those of Russia, China, Korea, and Japan.[72]

This study also illuminates the uniqueness of viral links. Although young men, forced to breathe air infused with the influenza virus in crowded trains, ships, and barracks because of war, were the prime targets, the 1918 virus did not discriminate against ideologies, races, ethnicities, classes, or sexes, and quickly travelled worldwide disregarding man-made national boundaries. Spanish Influenza defied human control efforts and extended its reach assisted

---

71  See, for example, Mark Fiege, "Gettysburg and the Organic Nature of the American Civil War," in *Natural Enemy, Natural Ally*, eds. Richard P. Tucker and Edmund Russell (Corvallis, OR: Oregon State University Press, 2004), 93–109.

72  Though generally they are not focused on biological elements or the decade of the 1910s, exciting new studies exploring trans-border connections of this region began being pub-lished. See, for instance, Sakon Yukimura, ed., *Kindai Tōhoku Ajia no tanjō: Kokyō-shi e no kokoromi* (Sapporo: Hokkaidō Daigaku Shuppankai, 2008).

by animal hosts. The global diffusion of the killer influenza was an "unintended" consequence of such human activities as war, civil war, nation-building, (political or economic) empire-building, and improved transportation technologies. It is important to look at the viral links supported by the non-sovereign state space in Siberia from a "supraterritorial" and "less anthropocentric" perspective in order to understand the patterns of infectious disease mutations and diffusions as well as their environmental implications.[73]

### Acknowledgements

I would like to thank the editors of this volume, Tosh Minohara, Tze-ki Hon, and Evan Dawley, for giving me the opportunity to explore this subject. I am also grateful for helpful comments on the earlier drafts of this chapter from James Bartholomew, Kevin Doak, Joseph Wicentowski, and the audience of the January 2011 American Historical Association meeting, March 2011 Association for Asian Studies meeting, and February 2012 Midwest Japan Seminar.

---

73    The concept of the "supraterritorial" nature of "transborder" interactions is discussed in Lance Saker, Kelley Lee, Barbara Cannito, Anna Gilmore, and Diarmid Campbell-Lendrum, *Globalization and Infectious Diseases: A Review of the Linkages*, TDR/STR/SEB/ST/04.2 Special Topics No.3 (Geneva, Switzerland: World Health Organization on behalf of the Special Programme for Research and Training in Tropical Diseases, 2004), 5.

# Changing Mutual Perceptions of China-Japan Relations in the 1910s in Chinese and Japanese Textbooks

*Caroline Rose*

## The Significance of the 1910s for Sino-Japanese Relations

The 1910s witnessed changes in the national consciousness in both China and Japan as a result not only of the events taking place on the international stage, but also of shifts in their bilateral relationship. The decade of the 1910s represented one of the most tumultuous periods in Sino-Japanese relations before the 1937–1945 conflict. After a flowering of relations between China and Japan in the early 1900s when the Chinese government sent students to Japan in an attempt to emulate Japan's successful modernization program, the relationship became increasingly strained by Japan's imperialist ambitions. In particular, Japan's issuing of the Twenty-One Demands in 1915 and the ensuing anti-Japanese boycotts and demonstrations in China were followed a few years later by the outcome of the Paris Peace Conference in 1919, at which the Western powers judged in favor of Japan's retention of the rights it had seized from Germany in Shandong in 1914, and which in turn led to the May Fourth Movement in China.

The significance of this period in Sino-Japanese relations has perhaps been overshadowed by the subsequent descent to war and the atrocities inflicted by the Japanese Imperial Army on the Chinese people. However, the 1910s, specifically the Twenty-One Demands, Japan's occupation of Shandong during World War One, and the ongoing "Shandong Question" at the Paris Peace Conference, are important because they marked a change in Japan's posture towards China. Japan's harder position in turn provoked popular anti-Japanese protests in China and produced a more cohesive national consciousness, giving "Chinese nationalism a strong anti-Japanese tinge."[1] Hattori Ryūji argues that, whereas Japan had previously "considered its

---

1  Kawashima Shin, "A Prototype of Close Relations and Antagonism: From the First Sino-Japanese War to the Twenty-One Demands," in *Toward a History Beyond Borders: Contentious Issues in Sino-Japanese Relations*, ed. Yang Daqing et al. (Cambridge, Massachusetts and London: Harvard University Press, 2012), 76.

relations with the other powers before planning a response," such as during the Boxer Rebellion or the Xinhai Revolution, the Twenty-One Demands saw Japan positioning itself "in direct opposition to China alone."[2] The result was to make "Chinese nationalism focus on the 'sole enemy' of Japan.[3] Similarly, Callahan argues that for the Republic of China, still in its infancy when faced with the Twenty-One Demands, the "Japanese empire presented a credible threat to territorial integrity and civilizational security."[4] The increasing tension between China and Japan from the late 19th century to the early 20th century and the "strongly antagonistic relationship" that developed, has, as Kawashima Shin points out, "continued to exert influence into the twenty-first century."[5] Indeed, China's anti-Japan protests and widespread calls for boycotts of Japanese goods in 2012 have strong echoes of the demonstrations held across China in 1915 and 1919, and the re-emergence of "national humiliation" as a central theme in Chinese textbooks in the 1990s harks back to the sentiments expressed in textbooks produced in the wake of the Twenty-One Demands.

Given the importance of the 1910s in China-Japan relations, this chapter explores how the events have been integrated into Chinese and Japanese "national stories" since 1945, using textbooks as the medium through which to understand the part that the 1910s have played in official narratives. Textbook content provides a record of the ways in which governments wish to impart the nation's official history to the younger generation and induct them into a pre-formulated national identity. Robert Culp's reference to textbooks of China's Republican period is equally applicable to Japanese textbooks of the same era, and indeed contemporary textbooks in both countries, in that they "are valuable artifacts for understanding historical, and consequently, national consciousness."[6]

The chapter begins by first reviewing the content of Chinese and Japanese textbooks produced in the 1910s, and highlights the diametrically-opposed narratives that emerged in each country. On the one hand, Chinese textbooks came to identify the Japanese aggressor as one threat, if not the main threat to

---

2 Hattori Ryūji, "Japan's Continental Expansion Policy and the Chinese National Revolution Movement," *Japan – China Joint History Research Report* (provisional translation), 2011: 66.

3 Kawashima, "A Prototype of Close Relations," 77.

4 William A. Callahan, "National Insecurities, Humiliation, Salvation, and Chinese Nationalism," *Alternatives* 29 (2004): 211.

5 Kawashima, "A Prototype of Close Relations," 78.

6 Robert Culp, "'China – The Land and its People': Fashioning Identity in Secondary School History Textbooks, 1911–37," *Twentieth Century China*, 26:2 (2001): 17.

Chinese sovereignty in the 1910s, bound up in a discourse focusing on the need for the Chinese people to resist Japan and stem the national humiliation brought upon China by its inept, self-interested government. On the other hand, in Japan, textbooks considered China weak, guileful, and therefore a threat to Japanese, and by extension, Asian stability that Japan had a responsibility to protect. Thus, the portrayal of China and Japan as the increasingly negative "other" in each other's textbooks in the 1910s reflected the developing national consciousness in both countries, highlighting, on the one hand, China's discourse of national humiliation, and, on the other, Japan's narrative of national hubris.

The chapter then considers the ways in which the events of the 1910s have been represented in post-World War Two (WWII) Chinese and Japanese textbooks, in order to identify how the period has been situated in the dominant historical narratives. As tumultuous as the events were at the time, the decade of the 1910s has largely been eclipsed by the atrocious events of the 1930s and 1940s. Nevertheless, the 1910s have remained part of the textbook narratives of Sino-Japanese relations. Not surprisingly, however, the decade has been viewed very differently in China and Japan, and has also been subject to changing historiographical trends in each country. In Chinese historiography, Japan's actions in China in the 1910s have become part of a bigger, linear picture. The Twenty-One Demands, and what they represented, are often described as one in a series of Japanese assaults on China that started in 1894 (or according to some accounts, in 1874 with the Taiwan Expedition), "inevitably" culminating in the 1937–1945 war. In Japanese historiography, by contrast, the events form part of an often unconnected set of developments in Japan's history of modernization and in China-Japan relations. These different positions, what Kawashima terms a "results-oriented" view (Chinese) versus a "process-oriented" view (Japanese), point to a continued dissonance in narratives, and explain some of the difficulties experienced by both sides in attempting to reconcile history.

The "meta-trends" in Chinese and Japanese historiography have also influenced textbook content, though this is much more apparent in the Chinese case than the Japanese case. Broadly speaking, in post-WWII Japanese textbooks, the story of Japan in China in the 1910s has become embedded in a larger story of national movements in East Asia and elsewhere. Japan's direct role in sparking popular protests in China, as well as a longer-term view of Japanese actions in China, tend to be sidestepped. In Chinese textbooks, while the Twenty-One Demands became a symbol of China's national humiliation and were quickly integrated into the official narrative through history education and textbooks in the 1910s, the national humiliation narrative waxed and waned as new historical realities emerged.[7] Thus, as Republican China gave way to Communist China, and as a new, Marxist, historiography came to dominate after WWII, the decade of the 1910s lost its narrative of victimization. However, the powerful symbolism of "one hundred years of humiliation" was pressed into service in Chinese history and popular education in the 1980s, with a renewed emphasis on the role of imperialist Japan in 1910s China. By the 2010s, however, the humiliation narrative appears once again to have waned, at least in terms of the prescribed curriculum, and reference to the Twenty-One Demands in some Chinese history textbooks has become limited to explanatory footnotes.

### The Clash of National Narratives in the 1910s: Humiliation Versus Hubris

In the late 19th/early 20th centuries, both China and Japan embarked on significant reforms of their respective education systems, and started to introduce guidance for, and controls over, school textbooks, the content of which would soon come to reflect the emerging national narratives of each country. For China, in the late Qing and early Republican periods this was readily seen in its evolving story of national humiliation and a call to arms for patriotism amongst schoolchildren and loyalty to the newly-formed state. For Japan, the narrative developed into one of national hubris, particularly after its victories in the Sino-Japanese and Russo-Japanese wars produced an emerging sense of superiority and an embrace of the civilizing mission in East Asia, and also emphasized the need for a patriotic and loyal citizenry.

### China's "Anti-Japanese Textbooks" and the First Textbook Issue

One of the most important reforms enacted by the late Qing was the abolition of the examination system and the establishment of a new school system. As a result, textbook production in China boomed in the early 1900s, with a proliferation of textbook publishers emerging to satisfy the market for new school subjects. Despite the variety of textbooks that became available, Peter Zarrow nonetheless notes the "general similarities [in textbook content] that reflected

---

7   See Paul A. Cohen, *China Unbound: Evolving Perspectives on the Chinese Past* (London and New York: RoutledgeCurzon, 2003) and Callahan, "National Insecurities," 199–218, for excellent accounts of the malleability and political utility of the national humiliation narrative.

both official regulations and elite consensus."[8] Late Qing history textbooks "conveyed a sense of national identity deeply rooted in the past," emphasized political unity, and promoted patriotism.[9] For the first time, history was being "designed systematically for the inculcation of children."[10] They followed a "rise and fall" narrative that reflected the dynastic cycle but was imbued more with a sense of nation within an "evolutionary framework,"[11] within which the "unity of empire" and the "protection of borders, or resistance to barbarian pressure" became dominant themes.[12]

The portrayal of Japan held a central position within this emerging narrative. Late Qing/early Republican textbooks reflected the developing contradictions between Japan being perceived as a model, and Japan as a threat. Descriptions of Japan appeared not just in Chinese history textbooks, but also, as with the textbooks published by Wenming Shuju, across the curriculum in subjects such as world history, geography, language, and even math.[13]

Over time descriptions of Japan as a model of military and political reform were overshadowed by the notion that Japan represented a persistent and present threat to China. Kō Toran argues that the content of Chinese geography textbooks are particularly useful in identifying the changes in contemporary perceptions of Japan from the late Qing to the early Republican period, since they contained a wide range of information, not just about Japan's natural environment, but also about politics, economics, how people lived, and national characteristics. Late Qing "Chinese Geography" (*Benguo dili*) textbooks recounted the "pain" inflicted in China by Japan through the unequal treaty but Japan was otherwise treated in much the same way as the European powers. In the "Foreign/Overseas Geography" (*Waiguo dili*) Japan received the most coverage of all Asian countries because it was the "strongest country in the East."[14] The period of Meiji growth, the characteristics of the Japanese, and even Japan's rule in Taiwan received positive evaluations in this textbook.

---

8   Peter Zarrow, "The New Schools and National Identity: Chinese History Textbooks in Late Qing," in *The Politics of Historical Production in Late Qing and Republican China*, eds. Tze-ki Hon and Robert J. Culp (Leiden, Boston: Brill, 2007), 22.

9   Ibid., 23.

10  Ibid., 25.

11  Ibid., 35.

12  Ibid., 27.

13  Xu Bing, "Seimatsu no Chūgoku kyōkasho ni miru Nihonjin zō," *Chūgoku 21*, 22 (2005): 111–112.

14  Kō Toran, "Seimatsu Minkokuki chiri kyōkasho no Nihonzō," in *Modern China: Textbooks and Japan*, eds. Namiki Yorihisa et al. (Tokyo: Kenbun shuppan, 2010), 269–270.

However, this characterization changed with the publication of new textbooks in the early Republican period. For example, Commercial Press's six-volume "New Geography" (*Gongheguo jiaokeshu xindili*) published in 1912, notes Japan's increasing proximity to Chinese borders with its annexation of Korea in 1910, an increasingly tense political and industrial situation, and the loss of China's "stronghold" on the Liaodong peninsula.[15] Although the new textbook gave reduced coverage to Japan, it especially emphasized Japan's military preparations underway since the Meiji period. In other textbooks, such as Zhonghua Shuju's "New China Geography Textbook" (*Xinzhi Zhonghua dili jiaokeshu*), Japan is described as having the same ambitions in China as the other great powers, and appears as the "invader," stealing bits of territory one by one.[16] In the aftermath of the Twenty-One Demands, Commercial Press's "Practical Geography Textbook" (*Shiyong dili jiaokeshu*) states: "Unfortunately there is some territory that has been leased and ceded to foreign countries. This humiliation must not be forgotten."[17]

The apparent "anti-Japanese" tone of Chinese textbooks became the subject of a diplomatic dispute between China and Japan in September 1914, at about the same time as Japan dispatched Japanese troops to capture Germany's possessions in Shandong. On 26 September, the Japanese ambassador in China issued a complaint, on the basis of critical editorials in the Tokyo *Nichi Nichi Shimbun* and the Osaka *Mainichi Shimbun*, about the anti-Japanese tone of a primary school textbook in use in China.[18] The Japanese ambassador commented on the regrettable nature of the textbook and suggested that it harmed the close relationship between the two countries. In response, the Chinese Education Minister explained the textbook authorization process in China and argued that the "textbook" in question was in fact not a textbook since it had not been through the authorization process, and was therefore not allowed to be used in schools. The minister stressed the friendly nature of China-Japan relations since the beginning of the Republican period, and assured his counterpart that the problematic book was not indicative of the general mood. In this spirit of friendship (*qinren shanlin*), the Chinese government agreed to carry out a survey and make immediate revisions, issuing a directive to the education board later that month.[19] This mandate temporarily resolved the

---

15    Ibid., 271.

16    Ibid., 275.

17    Ibid., 275.

18    Sunayama Yukio, "'Shina haiNichi kyōkasho' hihan no," in *Modern China*, eds. Namiki Yorihisa et al., 333.

19    Xu Bing, "Minguo shiqi ZhongRi jiaokeshu jiufen kaolüe," *Riben xuekan* 2 (2001): 131.

issue, although Tokyo subsequently tasked Japanese diplomatic staff in China with surveying Chinese teaching materials.[20]

Japanese complaints about the content of Chinese textbooks re-emerged after the Twenty-One Demands of 1915, which quickly became textbook fodder and came to play a central role in the production of a new "national humiliation" discourse. Luo Zhitian notes, in particular, the impact of the Twenty-One Demands on educational content:

> The Twenty-one Demands was not the first "national humiliation" in modern Chinese history. Nor was it the first time the Chinese stressed commemoration of the humiliation. But, it was the first time to have a National Humiliation Day; it was *the first time to include national humiliation into school texts; and it was the first time to stress the importance of education, both "spiritual education" in school and popular education, as a vehicle to arouse people's patriotism to such an extent* (author's italics).[21]

Thus, after the Twenty-One Demands, the curriculum emphasized the need to resist Japan's invasion, inculcate an awareness of China's humiliation, develop esteem for the military arts, and revere the truth.[22] New textbooks introduced from 1916 expressed these concepts, in particular the "New-style Textbooks" (*Xinshi jiaokeshu*) produced by Zhonghua Shuju, some of which dealt specifically with Japan's seizure of German leased territory in Shandong, the Twenty-One Demands, and Japan's plans for China. In late 1916, the Japanese government once again protested about the anti-Japanese tone and requested that the problematic textbooks be banned.[23] In response, the Chinese Education Ministry, at the behest of the Foreign Ministry, asked the publisher to revise the text. Though reluctant to do so, the company ultimately made some concessions to the Japanese.[24]

It should be noted that while the Twenty-One Demands became incorporated into some history textbooks in the late 1910s, the ways in which they were recorded, and remained in the public consciousness, fluctuated over time. As Cohen describes, the Twenty-One Demands were remembered and forgotten a number of times early in the 20th century, as the political situation and

---

20    Sunayama, "Shina haiNichi kyōkasho," 337.
21    Luo Zhitian, "National Humiliation and National Assertion: The Chinese Response to the Twenty-One Demands," *Modern Asian Studies* 27:2 (1993): 312.
22    Sunayama, "Shina haiNichi kyōkasho," 338.
23    Ibid., 332.
24    Ibid. 339.

accompanying "master narratives" themselves changed.[25] As we will later see in the discussion of post-WWII textbook content, the revival of the national humiliation discourse in the 1990s, followed by a revision to the history curriculum in 2001, produced another phase of remembering, and forgetting, the Twenty-One Demands.

### Views of China in Japan's Textbooks in the 1910s

Had the Chinese government scrutinized the content of Japanese textbooks in the 1910s, it would have found much to complain about. Harry Wray's studies of the content of Japanese history and geography textbooks published from 1903 to 1941 provide the most comprehensive surveys and analysis of Japanese textbook depictions of China as Japan evolved to its modernized and militarized form. As in China, Japan's education system and textbook content also underwent centralization and reform in the early part of the twentieth century, as government officials and textbook compilers grappled with the problem of the lackluster nature of Japanese patriotism, and the "lack of ideals among the youth."[26] As a result, new textbooks were produced that aimed to inculcate a greater sense of loyalty to the state and emperor. The new narrative emphasized native values, traditions and ideologies, stressed the importance of territoriality and the need to be kept safe from external threats.

The elementary-level textbooks compiled by the Japanese Ministry of Education for use from 1903 contained relatively little treatment of China, perhaps as a means of de-emphasizing Japan's association with Asia as whole. However, what descriptions there were of China revealed an attitude that was "explicitly and implicitly the least favorable, hopeful, or balanced of any subsequent textbook edition" and served to juxtapose images of modern Japan with those of a backward China.[27] China's outdated political institutions, military weakness, and "Middle Kingdom" consciousness were key themes.

The textbooks produced in 1910 showed a renewed interest in, and greater coverage of, East Asia as a whole, reflecting contemporary ideas about Japan's

---

25 Cohen, *China Unbound*, 144–184.

26 Harold J. Wray, "Changes and Continuity in Japanese images of the *kokutai* and attitudes and role towards the outside world, a content analysis of Japanese textbooks, 1903–1945" (PhD diss., University of Hawai'i, 1971), 171.

27 Harry Wray, "China in Japanese Textbooks" in *China and Japan: Search for Balance since World War I*, eds. Alvin D. Coox and Hilary Conroy (Santa Barbara, California: ABC-Clio Press, 1978), 116.

self-perceived civilizing mission in East Asia, and the importance of China to peace in East Asia. The lure of the China market is noted within the context of the opportunities it brought to the potential development of the national economy, but the textbooks continued to adopt a negative and condescending attitude to China which was not seen to be making sufficient progress in its own reform efforts.[28] They characterized China as smug, insincere and guileful in diplomacy, and framed China's weakness and guile as an increasing threat to stability in the region.[29] The textbook content reflected the dominant narrative of the time whereby Japan had turned China into a "negative object for comparison," thereby affirming Japan's own civilized, advanced self.[30]

In the 1918–23 version of Japanese textbooks, internal tensions within Japan played out on the pages of the history and morals textbooks on the one hand (which emphasized loyalty to the *kokutai*) and geography and language textbooks on the other (which emphasized internationalism and international cooperation). Wray outlines the main ways in which these textbooks differed from their predecessors, for example, in attempting to synthesize the open nationalism of the 1903 editions with the family-nation concept of the 1910 texts; with a de-emphasis on the military; with an attempt to meld internationalism with "more material on the nation and nationalism"; and with an emphasis on Japan's "national destiny" to "develop and preserve East Asia."[31] Of particular interest here is the omission of specific details of the developments of the 1910s in Japan, which saw the emergence of a much more pluralist, fractious society. The image created in textbooks, however, is Japan as a traditional, harmonious, predominantly rural and peaceful society. The textbooks contain no information on what might otherwise be viewed as humiliations inflicted on Japan by the West, such as the pressure on Japan to drop the fifth group of Twenty-One Demands, to pull out of Siberia, and to return its gains in Shandong to China after the Washington Conference. Instead the textbook "authors studiously avoided mentioning insults to Japanese honor with the exception of the treatment of the unequal treaties."[32] Here the contrast with the Chinese adoption of a national humiliation narrative is marked.

Wray notes the emergence of a patriotic education movement after 1916 that called for greater emphasis on national history and moral education. In 1919, the number of hours allocated to history classes was increased, and the

---

28 Wray, "China in Japanese Textbooks," 118.
29 Wray, "Changes and Continuity," 161–174.
30 Kawashima, "A Prototype of Close Relations," 55.
31 Wray, "Changes and Continuity," 180.
32 Ibid., 183.

history textbook after 1922 was expanded and contained more references to the virtues of loyalty, filial piety, and heroism etc.[33] At the same time, Wray points out that this was not a chauvinistic or isolationist nationalism and that the textbooks recognized the "limitations of Japanese personality, culture and history," while also acknowledging achievements made by other societies and "Japan's indebtedness to China, Korea, and India in earlier times."[34] Reflecting the internationalism of the post-WWI period, the textbooks emphasized the need for cooperation and the expansion of trade as a benefit to the Japanese economy. In this regard, the texts emphasized Japan's greater ties in Manchuria for its expanding role in East Asia, as well as the importance of cooperative relations with China to keep the West out with mutual benefit. The depiction of a weak and defenseless China, however, remained firmly in place, with the responsibility for the peace and security of East Asia ultimately falling to Japan, thus rationalizing Japan's reasons for entry into the war against Germany.[35]

Simply put, Chinese and Japanese textbook content of the 1910s reflected dominant views of each other as shaped by specific events, and the imperatives of government leaders to construct images of the other as a means of creating a strong national identity and patriotic citizens. In the case of China this emerged in the form of the national humiliation narrative, and in Japan in the form of a narrative emphasizing Japan's role as a modernized force for good in the region struggling against the dangers of a backward China. As the next section will show, some of these themes have reappeared in textbook content in the post-WWII period.

## One Century On: Changing Depictions of the 1910s in Contemporary Chinese and Japanese Textbooks

Although China's History Teaching Outlines (*jiaoxue dagang*; later to be renamed Curriculum Standards, *kecheng biaozhun*) have undergone several revisions since the 1950s, three broad historiographical phases can be discerned which have influenced textbook accounts of China's interaction with Japan in the 1910s.[36] During the Mao period, Marxist historiography dominated, with an

---

33    Ibid., 189–191.

34    Ibid., 211.

35    Ibid., 237–240.

36    The complete set of Chinese Teaching Outlines and Curriculum Standards, up to 2000, can be found in Renmin jiaoyu chubanshe kecheng jiaocai yanjiusuo, *Ershi shiji Zhongguo zhongxiaoxue kecheng biaozhun, jiaoxue dagang huibian: Lishi juan* (Beijing: Renmin jiaoyu chubanshe, 2001).

emphasis on class struggles, internal enemies, imperialist and capitalist invasions, and the role of the Communist Party of China (CPC). In the Deng Xiaoping/Zhao Ziyang era, from the early 1980s through to the late 1990s, the socialist spiritual civilization movement stressed the need to develop citizens who would be loyal to the Party and the nation. History textbook content, as a result, placed less emphasis on internal divisions in China, and greater emphasis on external aggressors. This period saw a return of the national humiliation discourse. From the late 1990s, a more tempered program of patriotic education was implemented, characterized more by a focus on China's reforms and modernization, its ascending global role and the need to develop internationally-minded citizens.

While the changes in Chinese official historiography since the 1950s map more or less directly on to changes in textbook content, as described below, the same is not true of the relationship between Japanese historiography and textbook content. Julian Dierkes argues that history textbooks, under the strict control of bureaucrats in the Ministry of Education through the textbook authorization system adopted an empiricist historiographical approach, characterized by a fact-based neutrality often at odds with the academic and popular debates over war responsibility and Japan's path to modernization. Similarly, Duus notes the lack of a "strong overarching narrative giving students interpretive guidance" in addition to a "muted, neutral, and almost bland" tone of textbook content when compared to American or Chinese equivalents.[37] While the coverage of the 1910s in Japanese textbooks is by no means extensive, such developments as Japan's entry into WWI, its actions in China, and the impact of the Paris Peace Conference have nonetheless consistently appeared in most middle school history textbooks since the 1950s. While changes have been incremental over time, it is possible to discern variations in nuance, detail and the use of language both in line with the particular stance of the textbook authors, and the changes made to the national curriculum, or Course of Study (COS).

### The 1910s and Japan in Modern Chinese History Textbooks

In Chinese history textbooks in use from the late 1950s to the early 1980s, the history syllabus as a whole conformed to the standard narrative, which included an emphasis on historical materialism, the weakness of the Qing and

---

37    Peter Duus, "War Stories" in *History Textbooks and the Wars in Asia: Divided Memories*, eds. Gi-Wook Shin and Daniel C. Sneider (London and New York: Routledge 2011), 110–112.

the Nationalist governments, the Maoist victory, and the CPC rule.[38] The narrative relating specifically to the 1910s was one of Japan attempting to monopolize China, using the excuse of the declaration of war against Germany to dispatch troops to Shandong, and take the Jiaoji railway and Qingdao by force. However, the texts gave more negative attention to domestic figures, such as Yuan Shikai and warlord Duan Qirui, than they did to Japan.[39] The textbooks depicted Yuan Shikai as a self-seeking individual who, wishing to become monarch, sought Japanese support and put up no resistance to the Japanese invasion.[40] They provided the details of the Twenty-One Demands, including those in group five, and cited Yuan's personal ambitions as the reason he accepted "nearly all" of the Demands. The Demands were described as aiming "to bring about the extinction of China," and both Japan's imperialist invasion and Yuan's actions in selling out China were presented as responsible for arousing the Chinese people's indignation both at home and overseas. The texts described the boycott of Japanese goods and the "high level of patriotic fervor" amongst the proletariat.[41]

The narrative further described how Japan's aggressive actions continued after Yuan's death, through its financial support for warlord Duan Qirui, seen "as a means of gaining control over the Chinese military, political system, economy, and diplomacy" by getting Duan to declare war on Germany.[42] Duan strengthened his links to Japan by handing over various railway and mining rights in the Northeast of China and Inner Mongolia, and acknowledging Japan's claims to Germany's former possessions in Shandong – in sum "selling out" to Japan as Yuan had previously done.[43] The extent of Japan's economic invasion of China received considerable coverage in Mao period textbooks, with details of the geographic breadth of Japan's investments, and the extent to which Japan controlled Chinese companies. The reader was told that, after WWI, the expansion of Japanese and US economic interests outstripped that of other nations, leaving them, along with the UK, as the "three main aggressors in China."[44] Thus the main characters of the 1910s in Mao era textbooks were: Japan as one of a number of external aggressors; a power-hungry president and

---

38    Alisa Jones, "Changing the Past to Build the Future: History Education in Post-Mao China" (Ph.D. diss., University of Leeds, 2007), 132.

39    Renmin jiaoyu chubanshe (People's Education Press, hereafter PEP), *Zhongguo lishi* (*Di san ce*) (Beijing: Renmin jiaoyu chubanshe, 1957), 111–113.

40    PEP, *Zhongguo lishi* (*Di san ce*) (Beijing: Renmin jiaoyu chubanshe, 1979), 87–88.

41    Ibid., 88–89.

42    Ibid., 91–92.

43    Ibid.

44    Ibid., 95–96.

warlord governments as the "internal others" – traitors who brought crisis upon the people; the people themselves, who engaged in struggles against external and internal oppressors; and, finally, the intellectuals who played leading roles in the May Fourth Movement and the emergence of the Communist Party. While the characters have remained the same in subsequent narratives, the weight and responsibility attributed to each has altered in accordance with the revised Teaching Outlines/Curriculum Standards.

From the mid-1980s, Zhao Ziyang's program of socialist spiritual civilization placed greater emphasis on history and geography education in the curriculum to help students understand China's "national condition" (*guoqing*). After 1986, when relations between the PRC and Taiwan began to improve, the depiction of the Nationalists became more positive, and the 1911–1949 period underwent substantial revision in textbooks. Of particular note, the 1988 Outline re-positioned the end date of "Modern History" to 1949, as opposed to 1919. Alisa Jones suggests that this new periodization adhered to "the emphasis on the rise-and-fall narrative in which the CPC is depicted, if not exactly as a new dynasty, as representative of a new social order and a fresh start for a beleaguered nation."[45] It also converged with the "national humiliation" boom, and neatly encapsulated China's humiliations within the one hundred year period from the 1840s. The 1988 Outline also placed greater emphasis on cultural history and the "great men" of history, thereby promoting "patriotism and national self-confidence through nurturing pride in China's past glories."[46] Yet what was particularly noteworthy about the 1988, and indeed all subsequent Outlines and Curriculum Standards, was the lack of specific reference to the events of the 1910s, with the exception of the May Fourth Movement. The guidelines removed the section on the "Anti-Yuan Shikai Struggle," made no specific reference to the Twenty-One Demands, and the "May Fourth Patriotic Movement" reverted to the "May Fourth Movement." Thus, the 1988 Outline appeared to be moving towards a softening of the anti-Yuan/Duan line in addition to adopting a different approach to the Twenty-One Demands.

Despite this apparent softening, the People's Education Press textbooks of the 1990s displayed a negative shift in tone regarding the nature of the Japanese invasion, and the response of the Chinese leadership. In the description of the events of 1915, for example, the emphasis of the narrative shifted away from Yuan Shikai's weakness and ambition, and more towards the scheming of the Japanese. Yuan was presented in a more sympathetic light, since he "could not dare to oppose" the Japanese who were playing on his aspirations to become

---

45    Jones, "Changing the Past," 201.
46    Ibid., 145.

emperor. Similarly, while the new description of Duan Qirui referred to his own attempts to utilize Japanese loans to build up the power base of his Anhui clique, it was the Japanese who tried in vain (*wangtu*) to strengthen their control over China. This narrative shift fits with the contemporaneous revival of the national humiliation theme, and portrayed Yuan and Duan as being victims of Japanese manipulation. It also correlated with Cohen's analysis of the humiliation discourse of the 1990s, where the emphasis was "much less on the defects of the Chinese body politic that facilitated imperialist incursion and much more on the Chinese people's defiant struggle against it."[47] Indeed, the teachers' guide accompanying the PEP textbook explained that China's modern history signified a century of imperialist invasion and humiliating semi-colonialism marked by unequal treaties through which the great powers seized Chinese territory, controlled China's economic lifeline, and suppressed the Chinese revolutionary struggle. In addition, the guide explains, this is also a period signifying the Chinese people's ceaseless resistance of foreign invasion.[48]

The next major set of revisions to Chinese textbooks were implemented on the basis of the 2001 provisional Curriculum Standard that allowed for much greater textbook pluralism and enabled Beijing Normal University (BNU), rather than the PEP, to design the national curriculum. The new guidelines deal very briefly with the 1910s within the description of the May Fourth Movement, which is itself subsumed in the unit on the rise of the New Culture Movement. The brief instructions provided in the "guidance on content" state that students should have an "outline of the basic facts of May Fourth, and understand the spirit of May Fourth," followed by an understanding of the significance of the establishment of the CPC, the Northern Expedition, and the Nanjing government. Thus there is no specific unit that deals with World War I, Japan's actions in Shandong, the Twenty-One Demands, or the anti-Yuan and anti-Duan struggles, as had previously been the case, and the humiliation narrative is toned down.

Textbook publishers have interpreted the 2001 Curriculum Standard in different ways, suggesting that the liberalization of the textbook market has provided scope for some variation of the national story, albeit still within the parameters set down by the Ministry of Education. Chapter Two of PEP's 2006 *Zhonguo lishi* (authorized in 2001) traces China's modernization, from the Self-strengthening Movement through to the New Culture Movement.

---

47    Cohen, *China Unbound*, 167.

48    Renmin jiaoyu chuban lishishi, *Zhongguo lishi jiaoxue zhidao yu cankao (di er ce)* (Beijing: Renmin jiaoyu chubanshe, 1993), 10.

The description of the May Fourth Movement starts with China's participation in the Paris "Peace Conference" (quotes in original) which was "in fact a conference aimed once again at carving up colonial territory" by the victorious powers of the UK, US, France, Japan and others. China's "just demands" to have all its rights returned, and the Twenty-One Demands repealed, were refused through the manipulation of the UK, France and the US.[49] Furthermore, Germany's former rights were handed to the Japanese. Once the news reached home, "fury erupted in the hearts of the Chinese people like a volcano." There follows a detailed description of the protests themselves as they spread across the country that presents them as the beginning of China's new democracy revolution. However, the content of the Twenty-One Demands themselves, and details about their origins, receive no explanation in this unit, or indeed anywhere else in this volume. The Huadong Shifan Daxue textbook follows a similar outline to the PEP textbook, with no description of WWI, its impact on China, or China's involvement, and the wording of the section on the Paris Peace Conference is strikingly similar to that of the PEP text.[50]

In contrast, the 2007 BNU textbook refers to the refusal of Chinese proposals at the Paris Peace Conference to have all foreign rights in China revoked, and to have the Twenty-One Demands repealed. The Demands are then explained, *in a footnote,* as "unequal treaties forced upon the Yuan Shikai government in an attempt by Japan in 1915 to take sole control over China."[51] This textbook also provides background information to explain when and why Germany took the Shandong possessions initially, and why Japan invaded Shandong in WWI. The discussion of the Shandong question at the Paris Peace Conference is also described, with Japan's threat to walk out of the talks described as a means of getting the other countries to acknowledge its rights in Shandong. Thus, "even though China was participating as a victor, it was treated as a defeated nation!"[52]

The 2007 Sichuan Chubanshe textbook describes the "Patriotic struggle of Beijing students" as being sparked by the "diplomatic failure of the Chinese at the Paris Peace Conference,"[53] and as with the PEP text, the UK, France and the

49  PEP, *Zhongguo lishi* (Beijing: Renmin jiaoyu chubanshe, 2006), 46.

50  Huadong shifan daxue chubanshe, *Zhongguo lishi (Chuzhong ernianji)* (Shanghai: Huadong shifan daxue chubanshe, 2007), 49–50.

51  Beijing Normal University (BNU) *Lishi (Banianji shang)* (Beijing: Beijing shifan daxue chuban, 2007), 63.

52  Ibid.

53  Sichuan jiaoyu chubanshe, *Zhongguo lishi (Banianji shangce)* (Chengdu: Sichuan chubanshe, 2007), 49.

US are seen to have manipulated the conference and "unreasonably rejected China's requests," instead transferring the rights to Japan. In common with the BNU textbook, though, the Twenty-One Demands are explained in a footnote: "[I]n 1915, using the ploy of supporting Yuan Shikai's bid to become emperor, the Japanese issued the Twenty-One Demands aimed at destroying China. Yuan Shikai accepted nearly all of them." One of the aims of the May Fourth Movement, according to this textbook was to demand that revenge be taken on the "pro-Japanese" negotiators at the Paris Peace Conference who "sold the country out."[54]

Thus, in Chinese textbooks authorized after 2001, specific details of Japan's role in China in the 1910s and the nature and impact of the Twenty-One Demands are largely absent. The event that first generated the national humiliation campaign in 1915 and made its first entry into textbooks as an important reminder to the country's youth of the shame brought on the country by Yuan Shikai's capitulation to the Japanese has now been excised from the narrative in some cases, or else has become, quite literally in others, a mere footnote in history.

### The 1910s and China in Japanese History Textbooks

As a number of studies of Japanese post-war textbooks have highlighted, with the exception of the early post-Occupation period (before the Ministry of Education (MOE) regained control over textbook content and authorization), there have been no radical changes to the content of Japanese history textbooks. Christopher Barnard's description of high school history textbook content as the product of a "naturalized ideology" which grew out of lengthy and complex negotiations between the textbook author and the MOE holds equally true for middle school history textbooks considered in this section.[55] Similarly, Dierkes argues that there is an accepted narrative that has changed very little since the late 1950s, producing stability in history textbook content in spite of changes in global trends in history education. Thus, in his study of portrayals of the nation (ranging from the origins of human life in Japan to post-war reconstruction), "no entirely new areas for discussion were introduced nor were any eliminated, and the episodes included appeared very much in the

54  The reference is to Cao Rulin, Lu Zongyu, and Zhang Zongxiang. Sichuan chubanshe (2007), *Zhongguo lishi*, 50.
55  Christopher Barnard, *Language, Ideology, and Japanese History Textbooks* (London and New York: RoutledgeCurzon, 2003), 61.

same light throughout the post-war era."[56] In analyzing Japanese textbook content, then, one is often looking for subtle shifts in nuance, the addition or omission of a word or phrase, or even a change of grammatical structure, as the following snapshot of textbooks authorized in the 1950s, 1980s and 2000s demonstrates.

Until the early 1970s, the two world wars were dealt with in one or two discrete chapters. The first post-Occupation COS (1955) required fairly broad but also detailed coverage of WWI, its background, and effects, stating that students should understand the changes in Japan's international status through a study of *fukoku kyōhei* (rich country, strong army) ideology, the Sino-Japanese War, the Russo-Japanese War, treaty revision, and the world before and after WWI. This last category included the Chinese 1911 Revolution, the Russian Revolution, the League of Nations and efforts for peace, and other key developments. The revised COS of 1958 provided more explanation on how to deal with "Japan's rising status in international affairs" in the early 1900s, part of which was to touch upon the colonization of Africa and Asia, and "Japan's relations with China before and after the establishment of the Republic." In dealing with WWI, authors were to cover Japan's situation after the Versailles Treaty, and the failings of the Versailles system that led to new conflicts. In the 1968 COS, this had been altered to include Japan's entry into WWI, the establishment of the League of Nations, the naval/arms reduction conferences and the post-WWI international efforts for peace.[57]

The textbooks in use in the mid-1950s offered largely similar accounts, though with some variations or additional details on the causes and effects of Japan's actions in China. In Osaka shoseki's (1956 authorized) textbook, Japan:

> taking advantage of the fact that the Powers had no time to think about Asia, attempted to make major advances onto the mainland. In an attempt to expand their rights in Shandong, then Manchuria and Inner Mongolia, Japan issued the Twenty-One Demands. A weak Chinese government had no choice but to accept them, but the Chinese people showed their dissatisfaction through an anti-Japanese movement (*haiNichi, kōNichi undō*).[58]

---

56    Julian Dierkes, *Postwar History Education in Japan and the Germanys: Guilty Lessons* (London and New York: Routledge, 2009), 154.

57    The entire set of Japan's Courses of Study are available online at <http://www.nier.go.jp/guideline/>.

58    Osaka shoseki, *Chūgaku shakai: Kako to genzai (shita)* (Osaka: Osaka shoseki, 1956), 85–86.

Similarly Gakkō Toshō's 1952 authorized text, co-authored by Ienaga Saburō, stated that an anti-Japanese movement erupted in China after Japan made the Twenty-One Demands.[59] Kyōiku Shuppan's 1954 text provided a separate section on the Twenty-One Demands and, in contrast to other texts, explained that Japan took advantage of warlord rule and lack of unity in China to present the Demands, the aim of which was to gain sole occupation of Manchuria, Inner Mongolia and Shandong, and to gain authority over military and commercial interests. While the Chinese government initially refused, the textbook explains, it:

> had no choice but to capitulate when the Japanese threatened the use of force. As a result, Japan strengthened its powers in China but the anti-Japanese movement thereafter gained strength. In addition, the Western powers, fearing that Japan was going to use this [anti-Japanese movement] to invade Asia, monitored the situation, thereby gradually deepening the conflict between Japan and powers.[60]

Tokyo shoseki's 1954 textbook described the worsening of Chinese people's sentiment towards Japan on the basis of the Twenty-One Demands, leading to an anti-Japanese movement and calls for the boycott of Japanese goods, which in turn "dealt a large blow to Japanese capitalism."[61] Nihon shoseki's textbook, also authorized in 1954, similarly described Japan's attempt to take advantage of European pre-occupation with war "to advance in to China," presenting Yuan Shikai with the Twenty-One Demands "which he was forced to accept. In response, the Chinese people, resentful of the weak attitude of their government, launched a strong anti-Japanese movement."[62]

Thus, on the whole the narratives agree on the nature of Japan's "advance" into China and all indicate Yuan Shikai's lack of choice in having to accept the Twenty-One Demands, which in turn sparked anti-Japanese protests in China. They also reflect the fairly liberal environment of early post-Occupation Japan, before the 1955 textbook campaign ushered in a tightening up of the authorization process by the Ministry of Education.

The 1977 cos moved away from a strict chronological approach, and also introduced a new section on the rise of national movements, for example,

---

59   Gakkō toshō, *Chūgaku Nihonshi* (Tokyo: Gakkō toshō kabushiki kaisha, 1952), 139.

60   Kyōiku shuppan, *Rekishi no nagare* (Tokyo: Kyōiku shuppan, 1954), 80–81. This textbook erroneously cited the Japan-US alliance as the reason for Japan's entry to wwi.

61   Tokyo shoseki, *Atarashii shakai: Nihon no shakai no hatten* (Tokyo: Tokyo shoseki, 1954), 159.

62   Nihon shoseki, *Jidai to seikatsu (shita)* (Tokyo: Nihon shoseki kabushiki kaisha, 1954), 202.

in China and Korea. In the textbooks based on this curriculum, the events of the 1910s tended to be subsumed under the heading of the newly labeled "Taishō 'Democracy'" which "did not discuss the First World War as being relevant to a definition of this period, given Japan's very limited and opportunistic involvement in that conflict."[63] Furthermore, the tendency of textbook authors to treat the Taishō years "as a chronology of political events that seemed to come about in temporal succession, but with no causal connection"[64] resonates with Kawashima's description of the process-oriented approach to Japanese historiography. The wording relating to the 1910s in the 1977 COS was retained more or less *verbatim* in the next three Courses of Study (1989, 1998 and 2008), with some additions to make the curriculum more student-friendly.

In Tokyo shoseki's textbook authorized in 1980, the basic narrative remained largely intact: Japan, seeing that the Western countries were not able to focus their attention on Asia, presented the Twenty-One Demands to China in an attempt to expand Japan's rights in Manchuria and Mongolia, and take over Germany's rights in Shandong. In addition, the textbook explained that "Japan increased its naval strength and took a tough position, such that China had no choice but to accept most of the demands. The Chinese people's animosity towards such actions increased and a movement calling for people not to buy Japanese goods spread everywhere."[65] A change in language is of note here. For example there was no use of the causative in the 1980 edition: China, and not Yuan Shikai, accepted, rather than China was made to accept; and the phrase "anti-Japanese movement (*haiNichi undō*)" is omitted. The new section on Asian national movements included a description of the May Fourth Movement that stemmed from the decision taken at the "Paris Peace Conference to transfer German rights in China to Japan, which caused student protests in Beijing. This movement, supported by the masses, developed into a people's movement against imperialism."[66] However, the text did not mention anti-Japanese protests specifically in this context. It further explained that British and US fears of a Japanese advance into China produced an agreement at the Washington Conference to respect China's independence and territory, and allow all countries "equal access to economic activities." The explanation noted that this was of "particular benefit to the US and UK as large economic powers"

---

63    Julian Dierkes, "Teaching Portrayals of the Nation: Postwar History Education in Japan and the Germanys" (PhD diss, University of Princeton, 2003), 401.

64    Dierkes, *Postwar History*, 147.

65    Tokyo shoseki, *Atarashii shakai* (*rekishi*) (Tokyo: Tokyo shoseki kabushiki kaisha, 1984), 255.

66    Ibid., 260.

and, furthermore, "it was also decided" that Japan's rights in China should be returned.[67] Unlike the textbooks of the 1910s in which, as Wray noted, there was a studious avoidance of "insults to Japanese honour," the 1980 text hinted at Japan's rather disadvantageous and unequal position vis-à-vis the great powers. The nuance was also different to Tokyo shoseki's 1954 textbook, which described Japan's status as having increased because of WWI, and depicted the various agreements reached at Washington and London as mutual agreements concluded in a positive environment in favor of arms reduction.[68]

The 2005-authorized Tokyo shoseki textbook, based on the 1998 COS, and the most recent version authorized in 2011, based on the 2008 COS, for use from April 2012, are almost identical. These textbooks are of note because the narrative appears to reinstate some detail about the immediate causes and effects of Japan's actions in China in the 1910s. While the description of the Versailles Treaty, in the section on WWI in Europe, merely states that "Japan maintained the rights in Shandong previously owned by Germany,"[69] the later section dealing with Asian national movements provides more detail about how Japan gained such rights, with the additional explanation that forcing the Twenty-One Demands on China (the use of causative is restored in these versions) "was a violation of Chinese sovereignty."[70] An explanatory panel summarizes some of the Twenty-One Demands relating to Germany's former interests in Shandong, the extension of Japan's leases in Lüshun, Dalian and the South Manchurian Railway (SMR), and the granting of mining rights in South Manchuria and Inner Mongolia. Significantly, however, there is no reference to group five of the Demands. The developments at the Paris Peace Conference and the response in China are more clearly stated in the description of the May Fourth Movement, and longer-term political developments in China, such as the formation of the Nationalist party under Sun Yat-sen and its cooperation with the Communist Party, are also included, indicating a shift back towards a slightly longer-term perspective of the impact of the events of the 1910s.

Yang Biao's comprehensive study of all the Japanese middle school history textbooks published in the 2000s discusses the different treatment of the Twenty-One Demands. While, in his view, the textbooks achieve some objectivity overall, he is critical of the fact that the textbooks do not contain descriptions of the final set of demands since these were "central to the contradictions

---

67    Ibid.
68    Tokyo shoseki (1954), *Atarashii shakai*, 161.
69    Tokyo shoseki (2006), *Atarashii shakai*, 188.
70    Ibid., 190.

between China and Japan."[71] The tendency for Japanese textbook descriptions of the Taishō period to omit the "causal connections" (noted by Dierkes) is also of concern to Yang, who suggests that emphasizing the rise of anti-Japanese sentiment in China, without specifying the cause, will have an effect on how Chinese students think about Japan, and Sino-Japanese relations.[72] In addition, Yang takes some of the textbooks to task for their choice of "soft" language. For example Tokyo shoseki uses such terms as "transfer" or "retain" in reference to the rights in Shandong, which plays down Japan's aim to monopolize China and, he suggests, gives students the mistaken impression that Japan had merely inherited Germany's rights, thereby overlooking the aggressive nature of Japan's actions in Shandong.[73]

### Conclusion

This chapter has described the changing portrayals of the events of the 1910s in China-Japan relations in Chinese and Japanese textbooks over time. The perceived importance of the actual events of the decade, as imparted through the medium of textbooks, and in terms of Chinese and Japanese historical, political, social and economic development, has varied over the last hundred years in accordance with the dominant themes in the national stories of each country. The humiliation discourse, which found its way into Chinese textbook content in the 1910s, re-emerged eighty years later as a powerful and symbolic tool for the CPC to signal a new way of thinking about China's present, through the lens of the past. Textbooks, accordingly, moved away from Mao-period historiography by downplaying China's internal divisions, and emphasizing instead the duplicity of the Japanese imperialists.

Post-WWII democratic Japan, on the other hand, has not revived its pre-war dominant narrative (though some would argue otherwise). Indeed, some of Japan's post-Occupation textbooks were able to be fairly expansive in their descriptions of the 1910s and there was perhaps greater variety of expression across the different textbook publishers. However, the "naturalization" that took place through the authorization process, along with the various changes in the Courses of Study, produced an accepted narrative, as far as MOE textbook examiners are concerned, which has undergone relatively little change since

71   Yang Biao "Riben zhongxue lishi jiaokeshuzhong youguan Zhongguo neirong yanjiu" (unpublished report, 2007), 41.
72   Ibid., 42.
73   Ibid.

the late 1950s. The dominance of empiricist, fact-oriented historiography noted in Dierkes' study applies to a certain extent to the findings here, where the focus on dates and events tends to provide little or no *long-term* "analysis of the causes or teleology of historical developments."[74]

The most recent round of curriculum reforms in both China and Japan has produced more changes in Chinese textbooks than Japanese. In China, since 2001, the swing of the humiliation pendulum appears to be moving in the other direction as far as textbook content is concerned, and textbook pluralization has meant that authors have interpreted the curriculum in different ways – some laying (slightly) more emphasis than others on the events of 1915 and their relationship to the May Fourth Movement. On the whole though, Japan has been absented from current Chinese middle school textbooks in their descriptions of the 1910s, either as an invading force intent on the complete subjugation of China, or through its capitalist advance or "economic invasion" of China. In contrast to Kawashima's observations of the dominant view held by Chinese historians involved in the Joint History Project that Japan's continental expansion tends to be seen as a sequence of related events and incidents, the narrative in some of the current textbooks, while positioning the two wars of invasion as book ends, nonetheless fails to trace the intermediate steps that led from 1894 to 1937.

The disappearance of the Twenty-One Demands and a less critical assessment of Japanese behavior in China in the 1910s in current Chinese textbooks perhaps support Luo's argument about the "true" impact of the Demands themselves on China's self-perception and evolution, in that they "probably contributed more to China's domestic development than to the rise of nationalism against foreigners in China. The narrative of the anti-Japanese movement reveals Chinese societal change, concerns of improvement of domestic politics, and anxiety of intellectual development, as much as the rise of nationalism."[75] It is these societal changes and political and intellectual developments, rather than the humiliating actions of an imperialist aggressor, which form the core of China's current narrative of the 1910s in the middle school history curriculum. There is an irony in the fact that current Japanese textbooks have more to say about the Twenty-One Demands than do some Chinese textbooks, and that they have retained a position in the Japanese narrative despite the otherwise peripheral role of WWI in the coverage of the Taishō democracy.

The reduced emphasis on national humiliation in current Chinese textbooks may point towards an official discouragement of an active remembering

---

74    Dierkes, *Postwar History Education,* 5.
75    Luo, "National Humiliation," 315.

of Japan's role in this period of Chinese history. However, events of the 2010s in China-Japan relations such as the anti-Japanese demonstrations over the disputed Diaoyu/Senkaku islands, and the negative Chinese reaction to the return to power of Abe Shinzō as prime minister of Japan, suggest that popular sentiment in China, seen, for example, in the form of banners calling for citizens to 'Love China, Boycott Japanese Goods' or remember 'National Humiliation Day', show that the leitmotifs of the past remain very firmly in the present.

# Global Competition for Power and Wealth
## The Chinese Views of the World before and after the Great War

*Tze-ki Hon*

### Chinese World Views of the 1910s

In his seminal work, *China and the Great War*, Xu Guoqui argues that Chinese intellectuals before WWI suffered from "diplomatic romanticism" because they considered the global system of nation-states as "an arena of justice in which every country would be welcome and entitled to equal treatment."[1] Xu points out that Chinese intellectuals failed to take note of cut-throat competitions among European powers in their pursuit of power and wealth. He further suggests that this "idealization" of the nation-state system came to an end when the Chinese government was forced to accept unfavorable treaty terms in the Versailles Settlement of 1919.[2] This "awakening" occurred after the Chinese realized that the global system of nation-states was based on territorial boundaries and capital accumulation, rather than social evolution and progress in civilization.

In this chapter, I will expand on Xu's argument by comparing Chinese geographical writings in the early 20th century. As with many places outside of Europe, the Chinese developed a keen interest in world geography during the 19th and 20th centuries when their country was incorporated into the global system of nation-states.[3] This Chinese interest in world geography coincided with their struggle in defining their country's position in a world dominated by Western powers. To demonstrate the relationship between spatial knowledge and the global system of nation-states, I will examine writings which appeared in the *Journal of Geographical Studies* (Dixue zazhi, 1910–37), the

---

1   Xu Guoqi, *China and the Great War: China's Pursuit of a New National Identity and Internationalization* (Cambridge, UK: Cambridge University Press, 2005), 74–77.

2   Ibid., 273–281.

3   Michael Guyer and Charles Bright date the dominance of the global system of nation-states from 1850 to 1991, a period which they call "the long 20th century." Before 1850, they argue, the globe was divided into "a series of overlapping, interacting, but basically autonomous regions." In contrast, from 1850 to 1991, the globe was intricately integrated giving rise to "a new ordering of relations of domination and subordination among all regions of the world." See Michael Guyer and Charles Bright, "World History in a Global Age," *American Historical Review*, vol. 100 no. 4 (October 1995), 1034–1060, especially 1045–1052.

© KONINKLIJKE BRILL NV, LEIDEN, 2014 | DOI 10.1163/9789004274273_025

flagship publication by the first professional association for geographers, Chinese Geographical Society (Zhongguo dixue hui).

The *Journal of Geographical Studies* is chosen because it offers firsthand materials that cover the first three decades of the 20th century – a pivotal period when the Chinese significantly changed their view of the world. When the journal was first launched in 1910, China was in the process of adopting what Martin W. Lewis and Kären E. Wigen called "the myth of the nation-state."[4] Following the European arguments for social evolution, many Chinese concluded that forming a nation-state was the only way to join the "civilized" world by participating in fair and open competitions.[5] After WWI, however, this belief in joining the civilized community was greatly challenged. Disillusioned by China's unfair treatment in the Versailles Settlement, the Chinese discovered that the nation-state system was controlled by Western powers eager to protect their own interests at all costs. From the mid 1920s to mid 1930s, the journal continuously published articles that argued that adopting Western domestic political practices would not win recognition for China in international affairs. Instead, the Chinese should focus on recovering sovereignty through diplomatic negotiations, treaty revisions, and if all else failed, armed resistance.[6] As Prasenjit Duara points out, this shift from joining global evolution to protecting China's geo-body fueled an "anti-imperialist nationalism" in China.[7]

As we shall see, the writings in the *Journal of Geographical Studies* both affirm and modify Xu Guoqi's argument. They affirm Xu's findings that there was indeed a fundamental shift in the Chinese view of the world before and after WWI. But the writings in the *Journal of Geographical Studies* also complicate Xu's argument by demonstrating that rather than one being "idealistic" and the other "awakened," the two Chinese views were equally valid descriptions of the nation-state system. When the Chinese understood the nation-state system as *a hierarchy in time* for human evolution, they believed

---

4   Martin W. Lewis and Kären E. Wigen, *The Myth of Continents: A Critique of Metageography* (Berkeley: University of California Press, 1997), 8.

5   For a discussion of how the standard of civilization shaped the international relations during the 19th and early 20th centuries, see Gerrit W. Gong, *The Standard of 'Civilization' in International Society* (Oxford: Clarendon Press, 1984).

6   William C. Kirby, "The Internationalization of China: Foreign Relations at Home and Abroad in the Republican Era," *China Quarterly* 150.2 (1997): 439–441.

7   Prasenjit Duara, "Transnationalism and the Predicament of Sovereignty: China, 1900–1945," *American Historical Review* 102.4 (October 1997): 1030–1051; Duara, *Sovereignty and Authenticity: Manchukuo and the East Asian Modern* (Lanham, MD: Rowman & Littlefield, 2003), 1–40.

that China should join the global network of exchange and competition that moved humankind forward to a higher stage of civilization. In this understanding, land was continuous and ambiguous.[8] It was a broad category that included minerals and raw materials that human beings shared to better their lives, individually and collectively. When the Chinese understood the nation-state system as *a hierarchy in space* in competing for power and wealth, they believed that territorial boundaries must be clearly marked to protect national sovereignty.[9] In this understanding, land was specific and concrete. It constituted a territory to denote a nation's sovereign rights, and legitimized a regime of power for control and coercion within set borders.

Certainly these two views of land (*tudi*) are not mutually exclusive, and in many instances they overlap and coexist. They refer to two different aspects of the nation-state system: a collective enterprise for human evolution and a series of competitions to sort out winners and losers. At a given moment, however, the relationship between the two views varied due to domestic concerns and international relations. Sometimes, one view was dominant over the other; at other times, the two views appeared to be in conflict. Yet, despite the different combinations, the changes in the Chinese view of the world demonstrate that the nation-state system is full of tension and contradictions. As a complex structure for power and wealth, the nation-state system is fair and open in some respects, and monopolistic and bellicose in others.

### The Global Network

Similar to many journals and newspapers of early 20th-century China, the publication of the *Journal of Geographical Studies* reflected the drastic changes in the Chinese conceptions of time and space. When the first issue of the *Journal of Geographical Studies* appeared in 1910 in the Beijing-Tianjin area,

---

8  My discussion of the different Chinese understanding of land is inspired by Henri Lefebvre's *The Production of Space*, translated by Donald Nicholson-Smith (Oxford: Blackwell, 1991). I am particularly intrigued by Lefebvre's three meanings of space: spatial practice, representation of space, and the space of representation (see *Production of Space*, 26–46). For a discussion of Lefebvre's concept of space, see David Harvey, *Cosmopolitanism and the Geographies of Freedom* (New York: Columbia University Press, 2009), 133–165.

9  Elsewhere I have discussed the characteristics of a hierarchy in time and a hierarchy in space. See "From a Hierarchy in Time to a Hierarchy in Space: The Meanings of Sino-Babylonianism in Early Twentieth Century China," *Modern China* 36.2 (March 2009), 139–169.

seventy years had passed after China opened its ports and cities to Westerners. Now ocean-going ships traveled directly from London to Shanghai, ending the centuries-long separation of three discrete zones – the Atlantic Ocean, the Indian Ocean, and the South China Sea. Within China, steam ships had replaced sailing junks to carry passengers and goods along the Yangtze River, greatly reducing the travel time from weeks to days, and from days to hours.[10] Although China was still behind other countries in building railroads, thousands of miles of rail tracks had been laid by the end of the 19th century, crisscrossing north, central, and south China.[11] The combined speed of land, river, and sea transportation gave rise to what David Harvey calls the "time-space compression" in which distance was shortened when travelers and goods could reach their destinations faster.[12]

At the turn of the 20th century, the veteran columnist and political reformer Liang Qichao (1873–1929) described the impact of this "time-space compression" in his usual crisp and vivid language. "In present days," he wrote, "we have nations coexisting like next-door neighbors and continents linked together like friends in the same room."[13] In the early 1900s, in addition to Liang's striking metaphors of "next-door neighbors" (*bilin*) and "sharing the same room" (*tongshi*), the sense of proximity to lands and peoples far away was also conveyed in a variety of ways such as "the ten thousand countries of the globe" (*diqiu wanguo*), "the world" (*shijie*), and "the stage of the five continents" (*wuzhou zhi wutai*). The metaphor of a "stage" (*wutai*) was particularly poignant in highlighting the proximity of far-flung lands when they were connected through intricate networks of roads, railway, canals, waterways, and shipping lines. It evoked an image of people from different places sharing the same spot and the same time – being on stage together.[14]

---

10   For the changes in China's domestic and international shipping industries after 1842, see Chen Zhengshu, "Yanjiang chengshi jiaotong jiegou jindaihua," in Zhang Zhongli, Xiong Yuezhi, and Shen Zuwei, eds., *Changjiang yuanjiang chengshi yu Zhongguo jindaihua* (Shanghai: Shanghai renmin chubanshe, 2002), 272–304.

11   For railroad construction in north, central, and south China, see ibid, 304–315.

12   For the concept of "space-time compression" (or 'spacetime'), see David Harvey, *Cosmopolitanism and Geographies of Freedom* (New York: Columbia University Press, 2009), 133–165.

13   Liang Qichao, "Lun baoguan youyi yu guoshi" (1989). In *Yinbinshi quanji, wenji* 1 (Beijing: Zhonghua shuju, 1989 reprint), 100.

14   For the implications of stage in China at the turn of the 20th century, see Rebecca Karl, *Staging the World: Chinese Nationalism at the Turn of the Twentieth Century* (Durham: Duke University Press 2002), 1–52.

In early 20th-century China, this sense of proximity and simultaneity was greatly enhanced by mechanized print technology that allowed the presses to produce large numbers of leaflets, pamphlets, books, newspapers, and magazines in a short time. The Chinese "print capitalism," as Christopher Reed has suggested, triggered a rapid expansion of the print market that combined the traditional print culture with the efficiency of modern machines.[15] With the convenience of modern transportation, many of these printed products were distributed rapidly from the coast (where most of the presses were located) to various parts of the country. For the majority of Chinese who could not afford to travel, their sense of proximity and simultaneity was developed mainly from reading journals and newspapers. Through journals and newspapers, events that happened hundreds of miles away were rendered as though they happened locally. More important, in reading the same stories, readers in different parts of China could participate in what Benedict Anderson calls the "homogeneous empty time."[16] Liang Qichao once described the "homogeneous empty time" as "connectivity" (*tong*). Drawing on Chinese traditional medicine, he compared the "homogeneous empty time" to the invisible nervous system in a human body that connects and energizes limbs, organs, and the brain. When "connected" by newspapers, Liang told us, one could stay home and reach the world.[17]

When the term "geography" (*dixue* or *dili*) first appeared in China in the late 19th century, it referred to this vibrant connectivity facilitated by the global system of nation-states. Originally an ancient Chinese term but acquiring a modern meaning via Meiji Japan, geography delineated the boundary and sovereignty of a nation-state on the one hand and depicted the world as an integrated entity on the other.[18] Thus, from the beginning, geography was closely related to state-making and nation-building, fostering an imagination of the globe as a unity divided in separate spatial entities. In one of the early textbooks, *Textbook for Chinese Geography* (Zhongguo dili jiaokeshu, 1905), the author Liu Shipei (1884–1919) described the location of China:

15   Christopher Reed, *Gutenberg in Shanghai: Chinese Print Capitalism, 1876–1937* (Honolulu: University of Hawai'i Press 2004), 1–9.

16   For the concept of "homogeneous empty time," see Benedict Anderson, *Imagined Communities: Reflections on the Origin and Spread of Nationalism,* revised edition (London: Verso, 1991), 22–36.

17   Liang Qichao, "Lun baoguan youyi yu guoshi" in *Yinbinshi quanji, wenji* 1, 101.

18   Hou Yongjian, *Lishi dili xue tansuo* (Beijing: Zhongguo shehui kexue chubanshe, 2004), 145–178.

China is located in the southeast of Asia. In the south it begins at latitude 18° 13' N, and in the north at latitude 53° 50' N. In the east it starts at chang 18° 15' E measured from the east of Beijing, and in the west longitude 42° 11' E. From north to south, its length is more than 7100 *li*. From east to west, its length is more than 8800 *li*. Its total size is 3,262,882 square *li*. It is indeed the biggest country in Asia.[19]

Although ending with a self-congratulatory note about China being the "biggest country in Asia," Liu's discussion of China's location was a sharp break from the traditional view of the tributary system. Rather than presenting China as the center of a multileveled tributary order and the protector of its dependent states,[20] Liu employed standard geographic coordinates to locate his country, implying that China's location was relative to that of others. As a nation, Liu implied, China was not superior to any country.

To further clarify his point, Liu Shipei continued with a detailed description of China's boundaries and its neighbors:

In the east, China is surrounded by Bo Hai, the Yellow Sea and the Eastern Sea, facing Korea, Japan, and Taiwan. In the southeast, China is surrounded by the Southern Sea. In the south, it is connected with Annam, Laos, and Burma. In the southwest, it is linked to India...In the west, it is joined with the Himalayas and Russian Central Asia. In the north, it is linked to the Russian Siberia. In the northeast, it is connected with the Russian Eastern Sea region and Korea.[21]

Using deserts, mountains, and oceans as natural markers, Liu located China's boundaries in all directions. But unlike the previous paragraph, the purpose of this mapping of boundary was not to show the huge size of China, but to describe the location of sovereign countries surrounding the Chinese borders. On the list of sovereign countries, Liu included former Chinese territory

19   Liu Shipei, "Zhongguo dili jiaokeshu," *Liu Shensu yishu* (Hangzhou: Jiangsu guji chuban-she, 1936; repr., 1997), 2276.
20   For a discussion of the Chinese tributary system as a multilayered and multifaceted structure of diplomatic and trade relations, see Takeshi Hamashita, "The Tribute Trade System and Modern Asia," in *Japanese Industrialization and the Asian Economy*, ed. A.J.H. Latham and Heita Kawakatsu (London: Routledge, 1994), 91–107; Takeshi Hamashita, "Tribute and Treaties: Maritime Asia and Treaty Port Network in the Era of Negotiations, 1800–1900," in *The Resurgence of East Asia: 500, 150, 50 Years Perspective*, ed. Giovanni Arrighi, Takeshi Hamashita, and Mark Selden (London: Routledge, 2003), 17–50.
21   Liu Shipei, "Zhongguo dili jiaokeshu," *Liu Shensu yishu*, 2276.

(e.g., Taiwan) and erstwhile tributary states (e.g., Korea and Annam). Although not explicitly stated, Liu accepted the Westphalian sovereign-state system wherein boundary and sovereignty are based on mutual recognition and legal agreements among states.[22]

### The Age of Imperialism and Colonialism

Five years later, in 1910, it was the Westphalian sovereign-state system that was the main focus of the *Journal of Geographical Studies*. Published by the Chinese Geographical Society in Beijing, the goal of the journal was to define China's role in the nation-state system. In their pronouncement on publishing the journal, the editors explained their view of the nation-state system:

> Human beings have to work the land to obtain food, and to form groups to survive. Nevertheless, owing to fierce competition in natural selection, human beings must go outside of their territories to invade others. As a result, the size of a group's territory is relative to the rise and fall of the group's power. It is up to the people of each group to decide whether they want to expand their territory by a hundred *li* per day, or to lose a hundred *li* per day. As for the cause [for the rise and fall of power], it is due to the level of geographical knowledge of each group. Thus, the level of geographical knowledge has a direct impact upon a country, and it can cause havoc to a race. It is indeed [a manifestation of] the natural law of selection based on competition.[23]

Judging by the history of China since 1840, it is surprising to see the editors of *Journal of Geographical Studies* condone seizure of lands through imperialist domination. More perplexing still is their aloofness to the loss of territory of a weak nation such as China. Seemingly unconcerned with the safety of their own country, they discussed the "natural law of selection" (*gongli*) that

---

22    In the study of international relations, the Peace of Westphalia of 1648 is considered the beginning of the sovereign-state system in which states guarantee one another their exclusive authority within their own geographic boundaries. For a summary and a critical analysis of the Westphalia sovereign-state system, see Stephen D. Krasner, "Rethinking the Sovereign State Model," in *Empires, Systems and States: Great Transformations in International Politics*, ed. Michael Cox, Tim Dunne, and Ken Booth (Cambridge, UK: Cambridge University Press, 2001), 17–42.

23    "Zhongguo dixue hui qi," *Journal of Geographical Studies* 1910, no. 1:1.

rewarded strong nations and punished weak nations. They seemed to suggest that China, being a weak nation, had to accept loss of its land for its backwardness and tardiness in global competition.

To a 1910 reader, however, the fluctuation in the size of a nation might not have been as ominous as it appears to us today. It was true that for more than half a century since the Opium War, late Qing China had been repeatedly defeated by foreign powers and had subsequently lost land. On the other hand, since the natural law of selection should always be fair and just, China might lose land now because she was weak, but would gain back land when she become strong and powerful. China's loss of land was not understood to be permanent. What was considered permanent was the "natural law of selection" that rewards winners and punishes losers.

In 1910s China, another way to describe the "natural law of selection" was to "catch up with the world in social evolution." Known to the Chinese through Yan Fu's (1853–1921) translation of Edward Jenks' *A History of Politics*, the scientific law of social evolution states that in terms of political institutions, all human communities develop from tribal alliances through feudal empires to nation-states; in terms of economic structure, all human communities develop from hunting and gathering through agriculture to industrial production; in terms of social system, all human communities develop from tribes through patrilineal families to professional classes.[24] As Yan Fu pointed out in 1904, Europeans might have been slow in the earlier stages of social evolution, but they subsequently became more advanced than other peoples because they mastered the skills of building a nation-state, an industrial economy, and an equal and mobile society. As a result, Europeans were destined to be leaders in modern times because they possessed advanced science and technology.[25] In comparison, China had clearly been "fast [in social evolution] in the beginning but slow at the end" (*shizhou er zhongchi*).[26] China entered the age of feudalism quite early on by practicing large-scale farming and adopting the patrilineal family structure. Yet, it had been stuck in the "Dark Ages" from the Qin (221–204 BCE) to the Qing (1644–1911). As a result, by the 1910s, China was considered to be at least five hundred years behind Europe in social evolution.

Viewing imperialism and colonialism from the perspective of social evolution, the editors of the *Journal of Geographical Studies* tried to explain the source of China's problems since the Opium War.

---

24    Yan Fu, *Shehui tongquan* (Beijing: Shangwu yinshuguan, 1981 [1904]), x.
25    Ibid.
26    Ibid.

In recent decades, imperialist powers crossed the oceans to acquire new territories and to expand their races. Despite China's huge size and its rich natural resources, we have suffered setbacks in diplomacy in facing the strong enemies and have had numerous problems on the border. At this time, even if we decide to clearly mark our boundaries and vigorously defend them, we will not be able to do so. Alas, when a lazy farmer does not work on his lands, his neighbors will come to use them; when an old fisherman falls asleep after a drink, other fishermen will come to steal his nets. In our time, all of us are in a sinking ship and gathered under a fallen roof. Without choice, we must take action to respond to our times.[27]

Instead of condemning the Western imperialist powers for aggression and expansion, the leaders of the Chinese Geographical Society put the blame on the Chinese. They criticized them for not knowing the fierce competition that characterized the modern age. Likening the Chinese to a lazy farmer and a drunken fisherman, they admonished them for failing to compete with Western powers. Living in an age of imperialism and colonialism, they asserted, the Chinese had no other alternative but to join the global competition for lands and resources by modernizing their political and social systems (Figure 23.1).

### The Versailles Settlement

This idealistic picture of imperialism and colonialism was predicated on an assumption that the nation-state system was always open and fair. As a "measurement of civilization" in *a hierarchy in time*, nation-states represented human progress from imperial autocracy to political liberty, from agricultural production to industrial production, and from disorganized society to a bounded community. Thus, as a system promoting progress in civilization, the international community invited everyone – Africans, Asians, Europeans, Muslims – to join the global march for "liberty, equality and fraternity."

What was missing in this rosy picture of nation-states was the vested interest of the Western states to protect their territories and markets. As Giovanni Arrighi points out, because of the twin logics of territorialism and capitalism, nation-states have to compete with one another to acquire land and wealth.[28]

---

27    "Zhongguo dixue hui qi," 1.
28    Giovanni Arrighi, *The Long Twentieth Century: Money, Power, and the Origins of Our Times* (London: Verso, 1994), 33–43.

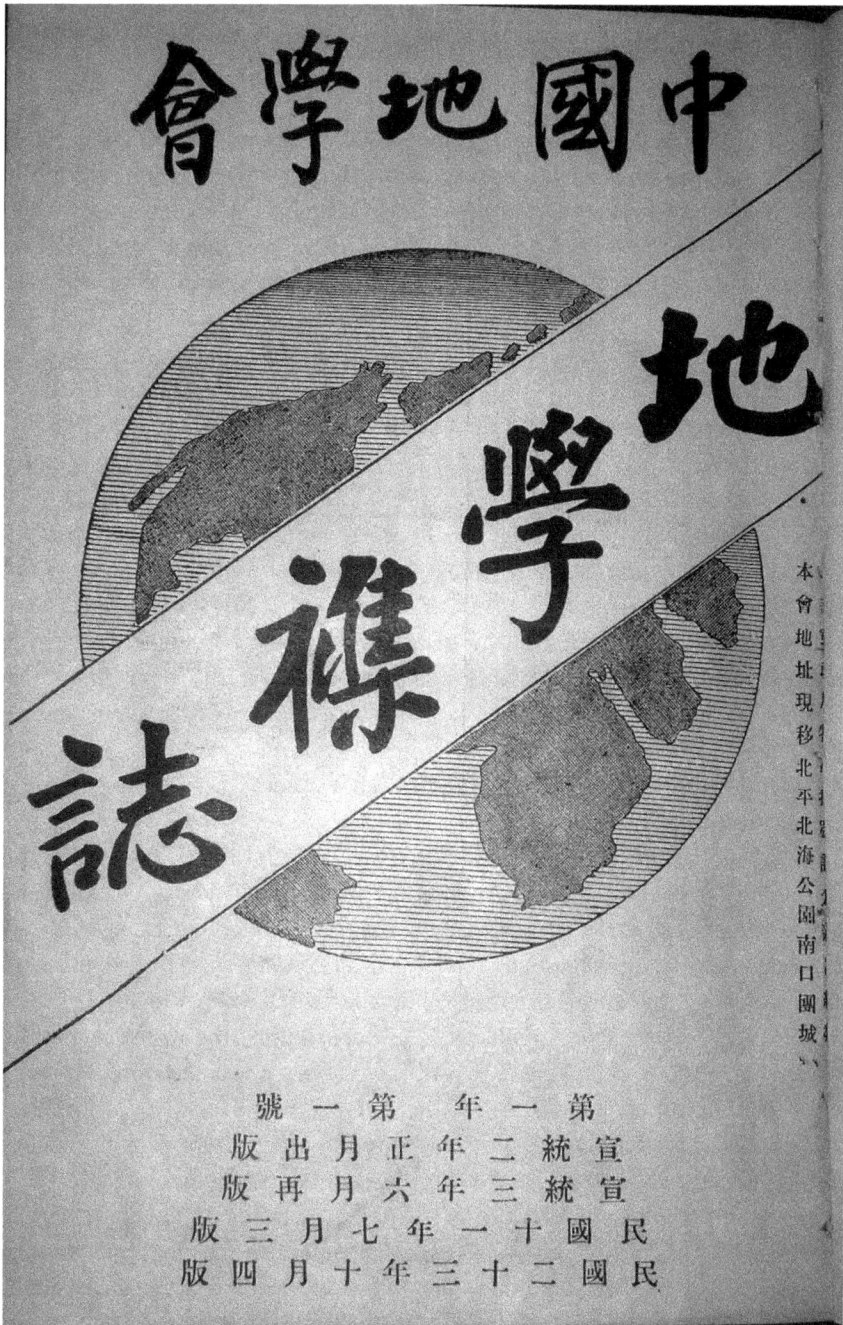

FIGURE 23.1 *The cover of January 1923 issue of Journal of Geographical Studies where the world is presented as a globe.*

Rather than "a measurement of civilization," Arrighi points out, the nation-state is a "container of power."

> Territorialist rulers identify power with the extent and populousness of their domains, and conceive of wealth/capital as a means or a by-product of the pursuit of territorial expansion. Capitalist rulers, in contrast, identify power with the extent of their command over scarce resources and consider territorial acquisitions as a means and a by-product of the accumulation of capital...Territorialist rulers tend to increase their power by expanding the size of their container. Capitalist rulers, in contrast, tend to increase their power by piling up wealth within a small container and increase the size of the container only if it is justified by the requirements of the accumulation of capital.[29]

What is significant about the twin logics of territorialism and capitalism is that they are mutually reinforcing and intricately interdependent. When a nation pursues land, it is also looking for ways to accumulate capital. Conversely, when a nation is intent upon accumulating capital, acquiring land is an effective way to amass a large amount of wealth swiftly. In Charles Tilly's terms, these dialectics of territorialism and capitalism give rise to the "logics of coercion and capital" whereby a nation-state has to be both a political structure of war-making and an economic structure of capital concentration.[30]

In China, the twin logics of territorialism and capitalism became clear to the Chinese after the Versailles Settlement. Disillusioned by the decision of the Allied powers to transfer the German colonies in Shandong to Japan, they saw the Versatile Settlement as an attempt by Britain, France, and Italy to preserve their power in the world system. Despite the promise of national liberation and national sovereignty in Wilson's Fourteen Points, the Chinese saw the redrawing of the world map as a ploy of the Western powers to stop non-Western countries from gaining their national independence.

To draw readers' attention to the unfair treatment of China in the Versailles Settlement, the editors of the *Journal of Geographical Studies* changed their view on imperialism and colonialism. From 1919 to 1923, they continuously published articles to urge the Chinese government to reclaim Qingdao (the major seaside city in Shandong) and prevent the expansion of Japanese

---

29    Ibid., 33.
30    Similar argument is found in Charles Tilly, *Coercion, Capital, and European States, AD 990–1990* (Cambridge, UK: Basil Blackwell, 1990), 1–37.

influence in Shandong Province.[31] To push the issue, they also called attention to the return of Lüshun (Port Arthur) and Dalian from Russia to China in 1923. Deeply troubled by the Japanese attempt to delay the return of the two port cities when the Russian lease expired, the editors published "An Emergency Announcement from the Chinese Geographical Society" in the combined third and fourth issue of 1923. In the "emergency announcement," the editors of the *Journal of Geographical Studies* called on readers to follow the event closely, making sure that the Chinese government would take necessary measures to reclaim the two strategically located harbors. To highlight the urgency of the matter, the editors broke the rules of the journal by printing a full-page "Editors' Advertisement" in the same issue. In the advertisement, the editors told readers "not to forget March 26 1923, the day when the Russian lease expired and we should claim back Lüshun and Dalian."[32] In the following issue, the combined fifth and sixth issue of 1923, the editors continued to mobilize public opinion by publishing excerpts of news reports and announcements around the country that demanded the return of the two ports[33] (Figure 23.2).

### Protectors of the Land

Of the writers for *Journal of Geographical Studies*, Bai Meichu (also known as Bai Yueheng, 1876–1940) was most aggressive in presenting the image of "the protectors of the land." Serialized from 1928 to 1930, he published a long essay entitled "A Study of Pian Ma" (*Pian Ma kao*) chronicling the British attempts to occupy an unmarked patch of land between Burma and Yunan. What provoked Bai to write the article was the British decision in 1922 to officially claim Pian Ma as part of the British-controlled Burma. To mark their sovereignty over Pian Ma, the British set up a military outpost on Mount Savages (*Yeren shan*). Although few Chinese had heard of Pian Ma or Mount Savages, Bai regarded the British move as an overt action of aggression, violating the territorial sovereignty of the young Chinese Republic. For this reason, Bai wrote the long article urging his readers to put pressure on their government to claim back Pian

---

31  "Qingdao zuijin guancha (Recent Observations of Qingdao," *Journal of Geographical Studies* 1919, no. 9–10: 9a-10b; Tong Yi, "Shandong zhi houhuan," *Journal of Geographical Studies*, 1920, no. 7: 12–18; "Riben jingying Shandong neidi zhi diaocha," *Journal of Geographical Studies*, 1921, nos. 6–7: 67–89; "Zuijin Qingdao Riren zhuang lüe," *Journal of Geographical Studies*, 1921, nos. 6–7: 89–91.

32  *Journal of Geographical Studies*, 1923, no. 3–4.

33  *Journal of Geographical Studies*, "Lüda shouhui sheng zhong zhi dianwen zhailu," 1923, nos. 5–6.

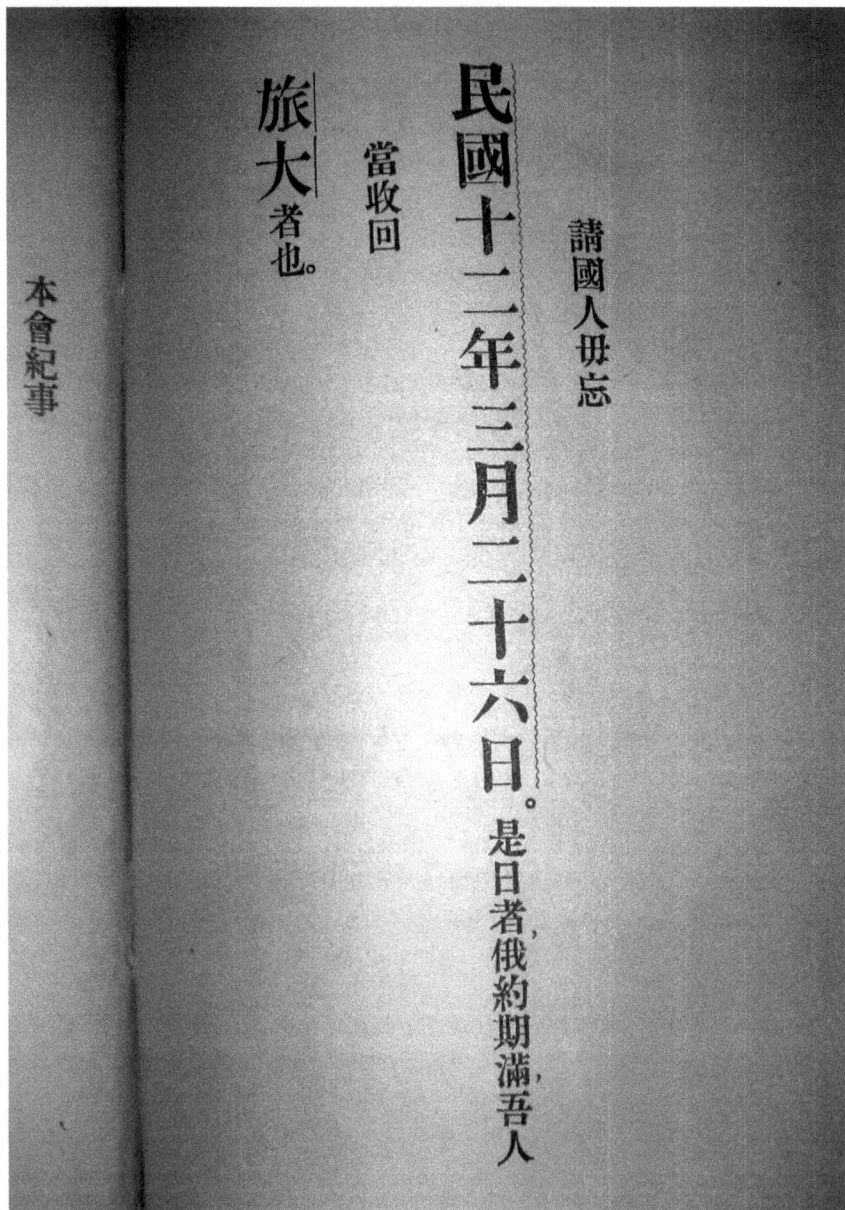

FIGURE 23.2    *The full-page "Editors Advertisment" on the return of Lüshun and Dalian. Note that the editors of* Journal of Geographical Studies *started the advertisement with a plea urging "our countrymen not to forget [Lüshun and Dalian]."*

Ma so that "the weaknesses of our citizens will not be exposed in front of the world."[34]

What is most striking is Bai's suggestion for resolving the Pian Ma controversy. First, Bai did not see the British action as an expression of the "natural law of selection" in social evolution. Second, he did not find the lackadaisical response from the Chinese government as being appropriate, even though the British Empire was clearly more powerful than the nascent Chinese Republic. Knowing fully China's long odds in standing up against the mighty British Empire, Bai recommended the use of force to drive the British out of Pian Ma. He wrote:

> In negotiating with a tiger for its skin, the tiger will bite us if we take a peaceful measure. It is better to ask hunters to use arrows and spikes to catch the tiger. In asking a thief to return the stolen goods, we will be killed if we pursue peaceful negotiation. It is better to ask soldiers to take up guns to catch the thief. So, we must wage a war to take back our Mount Savages in Pian Ma.[35]

What is revealing about Bai's belligerence is that he took his position for granted. He did not hesitate to urge his government to pursue military action against the British. The two metaphors he used – negotiating with a tiger for its skin, and asking a thief to return the stolen goods – were intentionally simplistic to make the point that it was useless to talk with aggressors. Aggressors, as the two metaphors imply, only know aggression and their goal is to get what they want at all costs. The only way to save one's life and one's property is to use violence to stop violence.

Underlying Bai's belligerence was a different view of the global system of nation-states. For him, the global system of nation-states was no longer fair and open. Instead, the global system was monopolized by a small group of ruthless aggressors who employed different measures – secret alliances, closed-door negotiations, legal tricks, and the show of force – to keep their power and to prevent others from competing with them. In this monopolistic system, the late-starters, such as China, would always be the targets of the predators, unless they overturned the rules of the game by challenging the established powers.[36]

---

34      Bai Meichu "Pian Ma kao," *Journal of Geographical Studies*, 1929 no. 2: 153.

35      Ibid., 167–168.

36      Xu Guoqi traces the change of Chinese views of international relations during the Versailles Settlement, and describes the shift as the end of "an age of innocence." See *China and the Great War*, 1–18, 273–281.

In 1920s China, there were a number of factors that contributed to this somber view of a sinister world. First, the introduction of Communism into China in the late 1910s and early 1920s – particularly Lenin's argument for imperialism being the highest stage of capitalism – provided a theoretical explanation for monopolistic state-capitalism.[37] Second, the brutal British suppression of labor protests in Shanghai in 1925 offered a fresh reminder of the hypocrisy of "civilizing missions" in foreign settlements and colonies. Third, the continuing attempts by the Japanese to expand their spheres of influence in Manchuria and the North China Plain suggested to the Chinese that their country had become a site of the global inter-state competition for land and wealth. Above all, by the mid 1920s the Chinese scientists had learned a great deal about mineral and other natural resources that could be extracted from Chinese land. Thus, land that was formerly considered to be uninhabitable, remote, unproductive, and unusable became a valuable asset when new technologies were developed in excavation, communication, and transportation. Suddenly the vast Chinese territory, previously regarded as a liability in terms of national defense and racial harmony, was treated like a precious commodity that would fuel the rise of China.[38]

While we do not know which factor or factors actually contributed to Bai Meichu's belligerence, it is clear that in "A Study of Pian Ma" he based his argument squarely on a new understanding of land. In recommending the Chinese to take up arms against the British, Bai deliberately reminded his readers of China's vast territory and its large population.

---

37   For a theoretical discussion of the differences between laissez-faire capitalism and state capitalism, see Frederick Pollock, "State Capitalism: Its Possibilities and Limitations," in *Critical Theory and Society*, edited by Stephen Eric Bronner and Douglas Mackay Kellner (New York: Routledge, 1989), 95–118. For a historical account of the transition from laissez-faire capitalism to state capitalism, see Jerry A. Frieden, *Global Capitalism: Its Fall and Rise in the Twentieth Century* (New York: W.W. Norton, 2006), 127–172; Ronald Findley and Kevin H. O'Rourke, *Power and Plenty: Trade, War, and the World Economy in the Second Millennium* (Princeton: Princeton University Press, 2007), 365–428. For a discussion of how the emergence of the monopolistic state capitalism led to a change in non-Westerners' view of the world order, see Cemil Aydin, *The Politics of Anti-Westernization in Asia: Visions of World Order in Pan-Islamic and Pan-Asian Thought* (New York: Columbia University Press, 2007), 71–92.

38   "Qiongya zhi kuangchan," *Journal of Geographical Studies,* 1921, no. 8: 45–53; Yao Cunwu, "He wei dili huanjing? Dili huanjing yu renlei shenghuo you ruohe zhi guanxi," *Journal of Geographical Studies,* 1922, no. 3: 1–17; "Ouzhou guojie bianqian ji yu kuangwu zhi yingxiang," *Journal of Geographical Studies,* 1923, nos. 3–4: 1–6.

China has one tenth of the world's land and one fourth of its population. The Chinese are clever, prudent, and hard working...Thus, readers should not be afraid of the current powerful countries such as Britain, the United States, France, Germany, Italy, and Japan. Considering the recent rapid expansion [in our country's industry and infrastructure], it is hard to predict what our country will look like in hundreds of years. We should not underestimate our country's potential by saying that we will not be the rulers of the world.[39]

Certainly, Bai knew that in the late 1920s, China could not match Britain in economic and military power. He also knew that the Guomindang leaders in Nanjing would not wage a war against Britain for a small patch of land in the far corner of the country's southwest borders. However, he saw the Pian Ma controversy as another example of imperialistic aggressions against China. For him, Pian Ma might not be worth defending due to its remote location, yet a line had to be drawn in stopping foreign aggressions. Given so much potential and real value in their land, Bai suggested that the Chinese must take action to protect their territory as soon as possible, and they should start that process with Pian Ma.

### Conclusion

The story of the rise of Chinese nationalism is familiar to us. In the past two decades, we have seen many insightful studies showing how the Chinese turned from being cosmopolitan to being fervently nationalistic and racially prejudicial.[40] The rise of Chinese nationalism is vividly summarized by John Fitzgerald as a process of narrowing the horizon, of reducing "one China" to "one state," and equating "one state" to "one party."[41] A result of this narrowing of the horizon is the creation of a nationalist historiography that does not give a full account of the diversity, complexity, and multiplicity of the Chinese people. As Peter Perdue points out, the blindness of Chinese nationalist historiography is that it stresses China's differences from the rest of the world only

---

39    Bai Meichu, "A study of Pian Ma," *Journal of Geographical Studies*. 1929, no. 2: 167–168.

40    See Dikötter, *Discourse of Race in Modern China*; Dikötter, *Construction of Racial Identities in China and Japan*; Prasenjit Duara, *Rescuing History from the Nation: Questioning Narratives of Modern China* (Chicago: University of Chicago Press, 1995).

41    John Fitzgerald, *Awakening China: Politics, Culture, and Class in the Nationalist Revolution* (Stanford: Stanford University Press, 1996), 1–22.

by discussing "its vast size and population, and its long continuous recorded history, epitomized in the Chinese phrase *dida, renduo,* and *lishichang* (large country, many people, long history)."[42] Furthermore, to explain away Chinese problems in the 20th century, Chinese historians focus on China being a victim – the victim of feudalism, of Confucian orthodoxy, and, above all, of Western colonialism.[43] In many respects, the development of geographical studies appears to reflect the same narrowing of horizon and the adoption of a self-inflicted victim mentality in Chinese nationalist historiography. When it was first introduced into China in the 1900s, geography was deemed a new discipline that helped China to join the global process of social evolution. By the 1920s, it was turned into a study of territorial sovereignty and national defense.

However, as recent studies have shown, the trajectory of Chinese nationalism has to be understood in the broader context of the transformation of the global system of nation-states.[44] What this study shows is that for many Chinese of the early 20th century, the nation-state system was full of contradictions and incongruities. On the one hand, it presented itself as a "measurement of civilization" in *a hierarchy in time* denoting human progress from barbarism to civilization. As a measurement of civilization, it invites everyone – Africans, Asians, Europeans, Muslims – to join the global march for liberty, fraternity, and equality. On the other hand, after WWI, the nation-state system promoted *a hierarchy in space* in which strong nations were allowed to acquire lands and resources without regard for the territorial sovereignty of weak nations.

As shown in this chapter, it was this tension between *a hierarchy in time* and *a hierarchy in space* of the nation-state system that caused tension and confusion in the Chinese perception of the world. When the Chinese understood the nation-state system as *a hierarchy in time* for human evolution, they willingly joined the global network of commerce and communication in the hope of catching up with the West politically, socially, and culturally. When the Chinese understood the nation-state system as *a hierarchy in space* for acquiring wealth and land, they were keen to protect China's territorial sovereignty and natural resources. With this understanding, we must look at Chinese nationalism more carefully. Before we blame the Chinese for narrowing their horizon and adopting a victim mentality, we should first examine the nation-state system that is fair and open in some respects, and monopolistic and bellicose in others.

---

42   Peter C. Perdue, "A Frontier View of Chineseness," in Arrighi, Hamashita, and Selden, eds., *Resurgence of East Asia,* 52.

43   Ibid., 52.

44   Arif Dirlik, *Global Modernity: Modernity in the Age of Global Capitalism* (Boulder, CO: Paradigm, 2007); Rebecca Karl, *Staging the World*; Ban Wang, *Illuminations from the Past: Trauma, Memory, and History in Modern China* (Stanford: Stanford University Press, 2004).

# Compiled Bibliography

Akashi, Motojirō. *Rakka ryūsui: Colonel Akashi's Report on His Secret Cooperation with the Russian Revolutionary Parties during the Russo-Japanese War.* Selected chapters translated by Inaba Chiharu, ed. Olavi K. Fält and Antti Kujala. Helsinki: Finnish Historical Society, 1988.

Aksakal, Mustafa. *The Ottoman Road to War in 1914: The Ottoman Empire and the First World War.* Cambridge: Cambridge University Press, 2008.

Albertini, Luigi. *The Origins of the War of 1914,* translated by Isabella M. Massey, 3 vols. London: Oxford University Press, 1957.

Allinson, Gary D. *Suburban Tokyo: A Comparative Study in Politics and Social Change.* Berkeley: University of California Press, 1979.

Archiwum Akt Nowych (The Central Archives of Modern Records), Warsaw.

Arrighi, Giovanni. *The Long Twentieth Century: Money, Power, and the Origins of Our Times.* London: Verso, 1994.

Arrighi, Giovanni, Takeshi Hamashita, and Mark Selden, eds. *The Resurgence of East Asia: 500, 150, 50 Years Perspective.* London: Routledge, 2003.

Asada, Sadao. "Between the Old Diplomacy and the New, 1918–1922: The Washington System and the Origins of Japanese-American Rapprochement," *Diplomatic History,* 30(2), April 2006: 211–230.

Åselius, Gunnar. *The "Russian Menace" to Sweden: The Belief System of a Small Power Security Élite in the Age of Imperialism.* Stockholm: Almqvist & Wiksell International, 1994.

Bacon, Alice Mabel. *Japanese Girls and Women.* London: Gay and Bird, 1891. Reprint in *West Encounter with Japanese Civilization 1800–1940,* Volume 10. Richmond, Surrey: Japan Library (Curzon Press), 2000.

Bailey, Thomas. "California, Japan, and the Alien Land Legislation of 1913," *Pacific Historical Review,* 1, 1932: 36–59.

Barclay, Paul D. "Cultural Brokerage and Interethnic Marriage in Colonial Taiwan: Japanese Subalterns and Their Aborigine Wives, 1895–1930," *Journal of Asian Studies,* 64(2), May 2005: 323–360.

Barnhart, Michael A. *Japan and the World Since 1868.* London: Edward Arnold, 1995.

Barrett, John, *Panama Canal, What it is, What it means (1913).* Washington, DC: PanAmerican Union, 1914.

Bartholomew, James. *Formation of Japanese Science.* Yale University Press, 1993.

Baryshev, Eduard. *The Epoch of Russo-Japanese Alliance, 1914 to 1917: The Truth about an "Exceptional Friendship."* Fukuoka: Hana Shoin, 2007.

Bashford, Alison. *Imperial Hygiene: A Critical History of Colonialism, Nationalism and Public Health.* New York: Palgrave MacMillian, 2004.

Berkovitch, Nitza. "The Emergence and Transformation of the International Women's Movement." In *Constructing World Culture: International Nongovernmental Organizations Since 1875*, edited by John Boli and George M. Thomas, 100–126. Stanford, CA: Stanford University Press, 1999.

Best, Anthony. "The 'Ghost' of the Anglo-Japanese Alliance: An Examination into Historical Myth-Making," *The Historical Journal*, 49(3), Sept. 2006: 811–831.

Birdsall, Paul. *Versailles Twenty Years After*. Hamden, CT: Archon Books, 1962.

Bjørn, Claus and Carsten Due-Nielsen. *Dansk udenrigspolitiks historie 3: Fra helstat till nationalstat, 1814–1914*. København: Gyldendal Leksikon Danmarks nationalleksikon, 2003.

Braisted, William Reynolds. *The United States Navy in the Pacific, 1909–1922*. Austin: University of Texas Press, 1971.

Burkman, Thomas W. *Japan and the League of Nations: Empire and World Order, 1914–1938*. Honolulu: University of Hawai'i Press, 2008.

Callahan, William A. "National Insecurities, Humiliation, Salvation, and Chinese Nationalism," *Alternatives*, 29, 2004: 199–218.

Challinger, Michael. *Anzacs in Arkhangel: The Untold Story of Australia and the Invasion of Russia, 1918–19*. Melbourne and London: Hardie Grant Books, 2010.

Chan, Lau Kit-Ching. *Anglo-Chinese Diplomacy in the Careers of Sir John Jordan and Yuan Shih-k'ai 1906–1920*. Hong Kong: Hong Kong University Press, 1978.

Chiba, Isao. *The Formation of Old Diplomacy: Japanese Diplomacy 1900–1919*. Tokyo: Keisō Shobō, 2008.

———, ed. *Selected Papers of Katsura Tarō*. Tokyo: University of Tokyo Press, 2010.

———, ed. *The Letters of Katsura Tarō*. Tokyo: University of Tokyo Press, 2011.

Chuman, Frank F. *The Bamboo People: The Law and Japanese-Americans*. Del Mar: Publisher's Inc., 1976.

Clyde, Paul H. *Japan's Pacific Mandate*. New York: Macmillan, 1935.

Cohen, Paul A. *China Unbound: Evolving Perspectives on the Chinese Past*. London and New York: RoutledgeCurzon, 2003.

Coletta, Paolo E. "'The Most Thankless Task': Bryan and the California Alien Land Law Legislation," *Pacific Historical Review*, 36, 1967: 163–187.

Cooper, Frederick and Ann Laura Stoler, eds. *Tensions of Empire: Colonial Cultures in a Bourgeois World*. Berkeley: University of California Press, 1997.

Cooper, John Milton, ed. *Reconsidering Woodrow Wilson: Progressivism, Internationalism, War, and Peace*. Washington: Woodrow Wilson Center Press; Baltimore: Johns Hopkins University Press, 2008.

Craft, Stephen G. *V.K. Wellington Koo and the Emergence of Modern China*. Lexington, KY: The University Press of Kentucky, 2004.

Cronon, E. David, ed. *The Cabinet Diary of Josephus Daniels, 1913–1921*. Lincoln: University of Nebraska Press, 1963.

Crosby, Alfred W. *America's Forgotten Pandemic: The Influenza of 1918.* 2nd ed. New York: Cambridge University Press, 2003.

Culp, Robert. "'China-The Land and its People': Fashioning Identity in Secondary School History Textbooks, 1911–37," *Twentieth Century China*, 26(2), 2001: 17–62.

Curry, Roy Waston. *Woodrow Wilson and Far East Policy.* New York: Octagon Books, 1948.

Daniels, Roger. *Politics of Prejudice: The Anti-Japanese Movement in California and the Struggle for Japanese Exclusion.* Berkeley and Los Angeles: University of California Press, 1962.

Department of Health, Secretariat, Minister of Railways. *The 30-Year History of National Railways Mutual Aid Association.* Tokyo: Ministry of Railways, 1938.

——. *Statistics on Employees' Diseases.* Tokyo: Ministry of Railways, Annual edition.

Dickinson, Frederick. *War and National Reinvention: Japan in the Great War, 1914–1914.* Cambridge, MA: Harvard UP, 1999.

Dierkes, Julian. *Postwar History Education in Japan and the Germanys: Guilty Lessons.* London and New York: Routledge, 2009.

Dirlik, Arif. *Global Modernity: Modernity in the Age of Global Capitalism.* Boulder, CO: Paradigm, 2007.

Donaghy, Greg and Patricia Roy, eds. *Contradictory Impulses: Canada and Japan in the Twentieth Century.* Vancouver: University of British Columbia Press, 2008.

Duara, Prasenjit. "Transnationalism and the Predicament of Sovereignty: China, 1900–1945," *American Historical Review*, 102(4), October 1997: 1030–1051.

Dunscomb, Paul E. *Japan's Siberian Intervention, 1918–1922.* Lanham, MD: Lexington Books, 2011.

Duus Peter. *The Abacus and the Sword: The Japanese Penetration of Korea, 1895–1910.* Berkeley: University of California Press, 1995.

Edström, Bert. "Storsvensken i Yttersta Östern: G. O. Wallenberg som svenskt sändebud i Japan, 1906–1918." University of Stockholm, Center for Pacific Asia Studies, *Working Paper* 52 (August 1999).

Elleman, Bruce A. *Wilson and China: A Revised History of the Shandong Question.* Armonk, NY; London, England: M. E. Sharpe, 2002.

Esenbel, Selçuk. *Japan, Turkey, and the World of Islam: The Writings of Selçuk Esenbel.* Folkestone: Brill Global Oriental, 2011.

Fifield, Russell. "Disposal of the Carolines, Marshalls, and Marianas at the Paris Peace Conference," *American Historical Review*, 51, 1946: 472–479.

Fifield, Russel H. *Woodrow Wilson and the Far East: The Diplomacy of the Shantung Question.* Hamden, CT: Archon Books, 1965.

Gaimushō, ed., *Nihon gaikō bunsho*, Volume 3, *Taishō sannen* [1914]. Tokyo: Gaimushō, 1966.

Gavin, Masako. "Abe Iso and New Zealand as a Model for A 'New' Japan," *Japan Forum*, 16(3), 2004, 385–400.

Gelfand, Lawrence E. *Inquiry: American Preparation for Peace*. New Haven: Yale University Press, 1976.

Gluck, Carol. *Japan's Modern Myths: Ideology in the Late Meiji Period*. Princeton: Princeton University Press, 1985.

Gong, Gerrit W. *The Standard of 'Civilization' in International Society*. Oxford: Clarendon Press, 1984.

Gooch, G.P. and Harold Temperley, eds., *British Documents on the Origins of the War, 1898–1914*, 11 vols. London: His Majesty's Stationery Office, 1926.

Gordon, Andrew. *Fabricating Consumers: The Sewing Machine in Modern Japan*. Berkeley & Los Angeles: University of California Press, 2012.

Guyer, Micheal and Charles Bright. "World History in a Global Age," *American Historical Review*, 100(4), October 1995: 1034–1060.

Hall, Catherine, ed. *Cultures of Empire: Colonizers in Britain and the Empire in the 19th and 20th Centuries: A Reader*. New York: Routledge, 2000.

Hanes, Jeffrey E. *The City as Subject: Seki Hajime and the Reinvention of Modern Osaka*. Berkeley L.A.: University of California Press, 2002.

Hara, Teruyuki. *Siberian Intervention: Revolution and Interference, 1917–1922*. Tokyo: Chikumashobō, 1989.

Harris, C.D. "The Urban and Industrial Transformation of Japan," *Geographical Review*, 72(1), 1982: 50–89.

Harvey, David. *Cosmopolitanism and Geographies of Freedom*. New York: Columbia University Press, 2009.

Hattori, Ryūji. *Higashi Ajia kokusai kankyō no hendō to Nihon gaikō, 1918–1931*. Tokyo: Yūhikaku, 2001.

Hayami, Akira. *Nihon o osotta Supein infuruenza: Jinrui to uirusu no dai-ichiji sekai sensō*. Tokyo: Fujiwara Shoten, 2006.

Hellner, Johannes. *Minnen och dagböcker: Joh. Hellner med inledning och kommentar*, ed. Wilhelm Odelberg. Stockholm: P. A. Norstedt & Söners förlag, 1960.

Hirama, Yoichi, *Dai ichiji sekai taisen to Nihon*. Tokyo: Keio gijuku daigaku shuppankai, 1998.

Hon, Tze-ki and Robert J. Culp. *The Politics of Historical Production in Late Qing and Republican China*. Leiden, Boston: Brill, 2007.

Hong, Yuru. "Riben zhimin tongzhi yu furen tuanti - shilun 1904–1930 nian aiguo furen-hui Taiwan zhibu," *Taiwan fengwu*, 47(2), June 1997: 53–72.

Hori, Shichizo. *Nihon no rika kyôiku shi*. Tokyo: Fukumura shoten, 1961.

Hosoya, Chihiro. *Historic Study on Siberian Intervention*. Tokyo: Iwanami Shoten, 2005.

Hujiwara, Sōsuke. *The Change of Labor Policy by Prewar JNR*. Tokyo: Investigation and Research Study Division, Japanese Association of Labor, 1960.

Iijima, Wataru. "Spanish Influenza in China, 1918–20: A Preliminary Probe." In *The Spanish Influenza Pandemic of 1918–19: New Perspectives*, edited by Howard Phillips and David Killingray, 101–109. London: Routledge, 2003.

——. *Pesuto to kindai Chugoku: eisei no "seidōka" to shakai henyō*. Tokyo: kenbunshu-pan, 2000.

Ikei, Masaru and Sakamoto Tsutomu, *Kindai Nihon to Toruko sekai*. Tokyo: Keisōshobō, 1999.

Iriye, Akira. *After Imperialism: The Search for a New Order in the Far East, 1921–1931*. Cambridge, MA: Harvard UP, 1965.

Isihara, Osamu. "Female Factory Workers and Tuberculosis," *Gazette of National Medical Association*, 322, 1913: 1–118.

Isitt, Benjamin. *From Victoria to Vladivostok: Canada's Siberian Expedition, 1917–19*. Vancouver: University of British Columbia Press, 2010.

Itō, Masanori, ed., *Katō Takaaki den*, 2 vols. Tokyo: Katō haku denki hensan iinkai, 1929.

Izao, Tomio. *Study on Primary Siberian Intervention: Appearance and Development of New Salvation Army*. Fukuoka: Kyūshū University Press, 2003.

Jansen, Marius B., ed. *The Cambridge History of Japan Volume 5: The Nineteenth Century*. Cambridge: Cambridge University Press, 1989, online 2008.

Japanese National Railways. *A History of One Hundred Years of Japanese National Railways*, Vol. 5. Tokyo: Japanese National Railways, 1972.

Japanese Government Railways. *Japanese Government Railways Yearbook*. Tokyo: Japanese Government Railways, Annual edition.

Kachi, Teruko O. *The Treaty of 1911 and the Immigration and Alien Land Law Issue between the United States and Japan, 1911–1913*. New York: Arno Press, 1978.

Kaigunshō, Kaigun daijin kanbō, eds., *Kaigun gunbi enkaku*.Tokyo: Gannadō shoten, 1970.

Karl, Rebecca. *Staging the World: Chinese Nationalism at the Turn of the Twentieth Century*. Durham: Duke University Press 2002.

Kataoka, Shuji and Isozaki Tetsuo. "Taisho-ki no chugakkô kagaku seitojikken ni kans-uru chiiki jittaishi kenkyû," *Nihon kyôka kyôiku gakkaishi*, 26(3), Dec 2003: 11–22.

*Katō Gensui denki hensan iinkai*, eds., *Gensui Katō Tomosaburō den*. Tokyo: Miyata Mitsuo, 1928.

Kawamura, Noriko. *Turbulence in the Pacific: Japanese-US Relations during World War I*. Westport, CT: Praeger Publishers, 2000.

Kawashima, Shin. "A Prototype of Close Relations and Antagonism: From the First Sino-Japanese War to the Twenty-One Demands." In *Toward a History beyond Borders: Contentious Issues in Sino-Japanese Relations*, edited by Yang Daqing, Liu Jie, Mitani Hiroshi, and Andrew Gordon, 53–80. Cambridge, Massachusetts and London: Harvard University Press, 2012.

Kawashima, Shin. "Nitchū rekishi kyōdō kenkyū no mittsu no isō: nandai wa doko ni atta ka." In *Nitchū Rekishi Ninshiki*, ed. *Kasahara Tokushi*, 73–92, Tokyo: Bensei shup-pan, 2010.

Ketelaar, James Edward. *Of Heretics and Martyrs in Meiji Japan: Buddhism and Its Persecution*. Princeton: Princeton University Press, 1990.

Kimura, Kenji. *Zaichō Nihonjin no shakaishi*. Tokyo: Miraisha, 1989.

Kimura, Masato. *Zaikai Network and Japan-United States Diplomatic History*. Tokyo: Yamakawa Shuppansha, 1997.

Kirby, William C.K. "The Internationalization of China: Foreign Relations at Home and Abroad in the Republican Era," *China Quarterly*, 150(2), 1997: 439–441.

Kitaoka, Shinichi. "Gotō Shinpei as a Diplomacy Leader." In Modern Japan Research Society ed. *Annual Report Study on Modern Japan 2: Modern Japan and East Asia*. Tokyo: Yamakawa Shuppansha Ltd., 1980.

———. *Gotō Shinpei: Diplomacy and Vision*. Tokyo: Chuokoron-sha, 1988.

Kiyonobu, Itakura. *Nihon rika kyôiku shi*. Tokyo: Daiichi hôki, 1963.

Kjellén, Rudolf. *Stormakterna*, vol. 2. Stockholm: Hugo Gebers förlag.

———. *Den stora Orienten: Resestudier i Österväg*. Göteborg: Åhlén & Åkerlunds förlag, 1911.

Kō,Ikujo and Ōhashi Suetsaburō. *Aikoku fujinkai Taiwan honbu enkakushi*, 2 vols. Tokyo: Yumani shobō, 2007.

Kojima, Masaru and Kiba Akeshi eds., *Ajia no kaiky to kyiku*, Kyoto: Hzkan, 1992.

Kôshi hensan iinkai. *Kishidawa kôtôgakkô no daiisseiki*. Kishiwada. Osaka: Osaka furitsu kishiwada kôtô gakkô, 1997.

Kurobane, Shigeru. *Nichirō sensō to Akashi kōsaku*. Tokyo: Nansōsha, 1976 [1983].

Lafeber, Walter. *The Panama Canal, the Crisis in Historical Perspective*. New York: Oxford University Press, 1978.

Liao, Ping-hui and David Der-wei Wang, eds. *Taiwan under Japanese Colonial Rule, 1895–1945: History, Culture, Memory*. New York: Columbia University Press, 2006.

Lim, Chaisung. "The Development of Labor Hygiene in Colonial Korea, 1910–1945: The Health Conditions of Korean National Railways (KNR) Employees," *Seoul Journal of Korean Studies*, 24(1), 2011: 51–86.

Link, Arthur S. *Wilson: The Struggle for Neutrality, 1914–1915*. Princeton: Princeton University Press, 1960.

———, ed. *The Papers of Woodrow Wilson, 1913*, vol. 27. Princeton: Princeton University Press, 1978.

Louis, William Roger, *Great Britain and Germany's Lost Colonies, 1914–1919*. Oxford: Clarendon Press, 1967.

Lowe, Peter. *Great Britain and Japan, 1911–15: A Study of British Far Eastern Policy*. London: Macmillan & Co., 1969.

Luo, Zhitian "National Humiliation and National Assertion: The Chinese Response to the Twenty-One Demands," *Modern Asian Studies*, 27(2), 1993: 297–319.

Magee, Gary B. and Thompson Andrew S. *Empire and Globalization: Networks of People, Goods and Capital in the British World, c. 1850–1914*. Cambridge: Cambridge University Press, 2010.

Mageli, Eldrid Ingebjørg. *Towards Friendship: The Relationship between Norway and Japan, 1905–2005*. Oslo: Oslo Academic Press, 2006.

Mahan, Alfred. The Panama Canal and Sea Power in the Pacific, *Century Magazine*, June 1911.

Matsuhuzi, Hazime. "History of Labor Hygiene in Japanese Railway," *Science for Labor*, 68(3), 1992: 102–114.

Matsumoto Teruo, "Pōrando no Siberia kojitachi" (Polish Orphans from Siberia), *Polonica*, 5, 1994: 62–81.

Matsuo, Katsuzō. *Shiberia shussei nikki*. Nagoya: Fūbaisha, 1978.

Matsusaka, Yoshihisa Tak. *The Making of Japanese Manchuria, 1904–1932*. Cambridge, MA and London: Harvard University Asia Center, 2001.

Maxwell, Lloyd W., *Discriminating Duties and the American Merchant Marine*. New York: Wilson, 1926.

McClain, Charles, ed. *Japanese Immigrants and American Law: The Alien Land Law and Other Issues*. New York: Garland Publishing, 1994.

Meehan, John D. *The Dominion and the Rising Sun: Canada Encounters Japan, 1929–1941*. Vancouver: University of British Columbia Press, 2004.

——. *Nikka kankei shi, 1929–1941: Sensou ni mukau Nihon Kanada no shiza kara*, trans. Kenki Adachi, Kunihiro Haraguchi and Toshihiro Tanaka. Tokyo: Sairyusha Press, 2006.

Minichiello, Sharon A., ed. *Japan's Competing Modernities: Issues in Culture and Democracy, 1900–1930*. Honolulu: University of Hawai'i Press, 1998.

Ministry of Foreign Affairs (Gaimushō). *Gaikōmonjō*, 1921 Volume III Part I Section 2. "Dōmei oyobi rengōkoku to To-koku to no Se-buru jōyaku gunjiyō jōkō nado jisshi narabi Gi-To ryōkokukan suru ken."

——. *Toruko jijō* (Conditions in Turkey). Tokyo: Gaimushō seimukyoku dainika, 1911.

Ministry of Railways. *Railway Statistics*. Tokyo: Ministry of Railways, Annual edition.

Minohara, Toshihiro. *Kariforuniashu no hainichiundou to nichibeikankei: Iminmodai wo meguru nichibeimasatsu, 1906–1921*. Tokyo: Yuhikaku, 2006.

Mizuno, Baigy. *Shinu ni okeru bei no dend seisaku*. Tokyo: Bukky to y shi taikai, 1915.

Mizuno, Hiromi. *Science for the Empire: Scientific Nationalism in Twentieth-century Japan*. Stanford: Stanford University Press, 2009.

Molodyakov, Vasily. *Gotō Shinpei and History of Russo-Japanese Relations: New Opinion Based on New Russian Documents*. Tokyo: Fujiwara-Shoten, 2009.

Morita, Keiko. "Activities of the Japanese Patriotic Ladies' Association (*Aikoku Fujinkai*)." In Maja Mikula, ed., *Women, Activism, and Social Change*, 49–70. London: Routledge, 2005.

Nagahira, Yukio. *Kindai nihon to butsuri jikken kiki: Kyoto daigaku shozô Meiji Taishoki butsuri jikken kiki*. Kyoto: Kyoto daigaku shuppankai, 2001.

Nagoya Planning Bureau Foundation. *Nagoya toshi keikaku shi: Taishō 8 – Shōwa 44.* Nagoya: Nagoya City, 1999.

Naimushō, Eiseikyoku, ed. *Ryūkōsei kanbō.* Tokyo: Naimushō Eiseikyoku, 1922. Reprinted as Naimushō Eiseikyoku, ed. *Ryūkōsei kanbō: "Supein kaze" dai ryūkō no kiroku.* Tōyō Bunko 778. Tokyo: Heibonsha, 2008.

Nakamura, Naofumi, *Chihō kara no Sangyō Kakumei: Nihon ni okeru Kigyō Bokkō no Gendōryoku.* Nagoya: Nagoya daigaku shuppankai, 2010.

Namiki, Yorihisa, Osato Hiroaki, and Sunayama Yukio, *Kindai Chūgoku, kyōkasho to Nihon.* Tokyo: Kenbun shuppan, 2010.

Naraoka, Sochi. *Kato Takaaki to Seito Seiji: Nidai Seitosei eno Michi.* Tokyo: Yamakawa shuppansha, 2006.

National Railways Mutual Aid Association. *The 50-Year History of National Railways Mutual Aid Association.* Tokyo: National Railways Mutual Aid Association, 1958.

*Nihon gaikō bunsho*, 1918/vol. 3. Tokyo: Nihon kokusai rengō kyōkai, 1969.

Nish, Ian. *The Anglo-Japanese Alliance: The Diplomacy of Two Island Empires, 1894–1907.* London: Athlone Press, 1968.

——. *Alliance in Decline: A Study in Anglo-Japanese Relations, 1908–23.* London: Athlone Press, 1972.

——. *Japanese Foreign Policy, 1869–1942: Kasumigaseki to Miyakezaka.* London and Boston: Routledge and Kegan Paul, 1977 [reprint 2002].

Nolte, Sharon H. and Sally Hastings. "The Meiji State's Policy Toward Women, 1890–1910." In Gail Lee Bernstein, ed. *Recreating Japanese Women, 1600–1941,* 151–174. Berkeley: University of California Press, 1991.

O'Brien, Philips Payson, ed., *The Anglo-Japanese Alliance, 1902–22.* London: RoutledgeCurzon, 2004.

Olin, Spencer C. "European Immigrant and Oriental Alien: Acceptance and Rejection by the California Legislature of 1913," *Pacific Historical Review,* 35, 1966: 303–315.

Osada, Susumu. "The Japanese Urban System 1970–1990," *Progress in Planning,* 59, 2003: 125–231.

Oshima, Ken Tadashi. "Denenchōfu: Building the Garden City in Japan," *Journal of the Society of Architectural Historians,* 55(2), 1996: 140–151.

Pałasz-Rutkowska Ewa, Romer Andrzej, T. *Nihon Pōrando kankeishi.* transl. Shiba Riko. Tokyo: Sairyūsha, 2009.

Park, Yunjae and Shin, Dong-hwan. "A Study on the Movement for Establishing a Private Isolation Hospital under the Rule of Japanese Imperialism," *Korean Journal of Medical History,* 7, 1998: 37–45.

Partner, Simon. *The Mayor of Aihara: A Japanese Villager and His Community, 1865–1925.* Berkeley: University of California Press, 2009.

Paul, Rodman W. *The Abrogation of the Gentlemen's Agreement.* Cambridge: The Society [Harvard University], 1936.

Perry, John C. *Facing West: Americans and the Opening of the Pacific.* Westport: Praeger, 1994.

*Prawo międzynarodowe i historia dyplomatyczna. Wybór dokumentów.* comp. L. Gelberg, vol. 2. Warsaw: PWN, 1958.

Pringsheim, Klaus H. *Neighbours across the Pacific: Canadian-Japanese Relations, 1870-1982.* Oakville, ON: Mosaic Press, 1983.

Pugach, Noel H., Paul S. Reinsh. *Open Door Diplomat in Action.* New York: KTO Press, 1979.

Pyle, Kenneth B. "The Technology of Japanese Nationalism: The Local Improvement Movement, 1900–1918," *The Journal of Asian Studies*, 33(1), 1973: 51–65.

Reed, James. *The Missionary Mind and American East Asia Policy 1911–1915.* Cambridge, Mass.: The Council on East Asian Studies at Harvard University, 1983.

Rice, Geoffrey W. "Japan and New Zealand in the 1918 Influenza Pandemic: Comparative Perspectives on Official Responses and Crisis Management." In *The Spanish Influenza Pandemic of 1918–19: New Perspectives*, edited by Howard Phillips and David Killingray, 73–85. London: Routledge, 2003.

Rice, Geoffrey W. and Edwina Palmer. "Pandemic Influenza in Japan, 1918–19: Mortality Patterns and Official Responses," *Journal of Japanese Studies*, 19(2), Summer 1993: 389–420.

*Rika kyôiku (1918–1932). Rika kyôikushi shiryô.* Toko: Tokyo hôrei shuppan, 1986–1987.

Rogaski, Ruth. *Hygienic Modernity: Meanings of Health and Disease in Treaty-Port China.* Berkeley: University of California Press, 2004.

*Rok 1920. Wojna polsko-radziecka we wspomnieniach i innych dokumentach.* Warsaw: PIW, 1990.

Rose, Barbara. *Tsuda Umeko and Women's Education in Japan.* New Haven & London: Yale University Press, 1989.

Roy, Patricia E. *The Oriental Question: Consolidating a White Man's Province, 1914–41.* Vancouver: University of British Columbia Press, 2003.

Samizade, Süreyya (Erdogan), *Day Nippon Büyük Japonya.* Istanbul: Matbaa-I Osmaniye, 1917.

Sato, Haruo. *Beautiful Town* (F. B. Tenny, Trans.) Honolulu: University of Hawai'i Press, 1996.

Sat, Sabur, *Kindai Nicch ksh-shi no kenky.* Tokyo: Yoshikawa kbunkan, 1984.

Schencking, J. Charles. *Making Waves: Politics, Propaganda, and the Emergence of the Imperial Japanese Navy, 1868–1922.* Stanford: Stanford University Press, 2005.

Schepin, Oleg P. and Waldemar V. Yermakov. *International Quarantine.* Madison: International Universities Press, 1991.

Schofer, Evan and John W. Meyer. "The Worldwide Expansion of Higher Education in the Twentieth Century," *American Sociological Review*, 70(6), 2005: 898–920.

Sharp, William Hastings. *The Educational System of Japan.* Bombay: Central Government Press, 1906.

Shiba, Naho. "A Comparative Study of the Provision of Public Open Space in Industrialising Societies East & West: The Work of Pioneer British and Japanese Park Designers in the Nineteenth and early Twentieth Centuries" (PhD Thesis, University of Nottingham, 2007).

*Shiberia shuppei eiseishi*. 11 vols. n.p. [Tokyo?]: 1923–24.

Shimadzu seisakusho, *Shimadzu seisakusho shi*. Kyoto: Shimadzu seisakusho, 1967.

Shimazu, Naoko. *Japan, Race and Equality: The Racial Equality Proposal of 1919*. New York: Routledge, 1998.

Shimizu, Masayuki. "Ohya Reijō: Shodai no midori no toshi keikaku-ka," *Randosukeepu kenkyū*, 60(3), 1997: 203–206.

Shinohara, Chika. "Global Pressure, Local Results: the Impact of CEDAW on Working Women in Japan," *Journal of Workplace Rights*, 13(4), 2009: 449–471.

Snodgrass, Judith, *Presenting Japanese Buddhism to the West: Orientalism, Occidentalism, and the Columbian Exposition*. Chapel Hill: University of North Carolina Press, 2003.

Sk Bukky-kai Bunsho-bu, ed., *Sk Bukky-kai kaiky sanjnen kinen-shi*, 1930. Reprinted edition in *Bukky kaigai kaiky shiry shsei Hokubei hen*, vol. 1. Tokyo: Fuji shuppan, 2008.

Sorensen, André. *The Making of Urban Japan: Cities and planning from Edo to the Twenty-first century*. Abingdon, Oxon: Routledge, 2002.

Sugawara, Sagae. *Shiberia shuppeishi yō*. Tokyo: Kaikōsha, 1925.

Sugiura, Yoshio. "Waga kuni ni okeru 'Supein kaze' no kūkanteki kakusan ni kansuru ichi Kōsatsu," *Chirigaku hyōron*, 50(4), 1977: 201–215.

Takahara, Shusuke. *Wiruson gaikō to Nihon: risō to genjitsu no aida, 1913–1921*. Tokyo: Sōbunsha, 2006.

Takashina, Rysen, ed., *Hioki Mokusen zenshi den*. Tokyo: Daihrinkaku, 1962.

Takenaka, Nobuko. *Rizhi Taiwan shenghuo shi: Riben nüren zai Taiwan, Dazheng pian 1912–1925*. Trans. Cai Longbao. *Chuban, lishi yu xianchang* 175. Taipei: Shibao wenhua, 2007.

Targowski, Józef. *Pamiętniki 1883–1921*.

Tillman, Seth B. *Anglo-American Relations at the Paris Conference*. Princeton: Princeton University Press, 1961.

Ts'ai, Hui-yu Caroline. *Taiwan in Japan's Empire Building: An Institutional Approach to Colonial Engineering*. New York: Routledge, 2009.

Tsuda, Umeko. *Tsuda Umeko Bunsho*, edited by Fumio Nakajima and Tsuda College. Tokyo: Tsuda College, 1980.

Tsurumi, Yūsuke. *Authentic Biography: Gotō Shinpei*, 8vols. Tokyo: Fujiwara-shoten, 2004–06.

Uchida, Jun. *Brokers of Empire: Japanese Settler Colonialism in Korea, 1876–1945*. Cambridge, MA: Harvard University Asia Center, 2011.

Uchida Yasuya Denki Hensan Iinkai, ed. *Uchida Yasuya*. Tokyo: Kajima kenkyūjo shuppandai, 1968.

Utsunomiya, Tarō. *Nihon rikugun to Ajia seisaku rikugun taishō: Utsunomiya Tarō nikki*, 3 vols. Tokyo: Iwanami shoten, 2007.

Walker, Samuel H. *The Panama Canal and Restoration of American Merchant Marine.* Washington: 1912.

Waswo, Ann. "The Transformation of Rural Society, 1900–1950." In *The Cambridge History of Modern Japan*, vol. 6, edited by Peter Duus. Cambridge: Cambridge University Press, 1988.

Watanabe, Shun'ichi. "The Japanese Garden City." In *The Garden City: Past, Present and Future*, edited by S.V. Ward, 69–87. London: E & FN Spon, 1992.

Woodhouse, Eiko. *The Chinese Hsinhai Revolution: G.E.Morrison and Anglo-Japanese Relations, 1897–1920.* London: RoutledgeCurzon, 2004.

Wray, Harry, "China in Japanese Textbooks." In *China and Japan: Search for Balance Since World War I*, edited by Alvin D.Coox and Hilary Conroy, 113–132. Santa Barbara, California: ABC-Clio Press, 1978.

Wu, Lien-teh. "1919 Cholera Epidemic in China." In *Manchurian Plague Prevention Service, Memorial*, Volume 1912–1932, 251–265. Shanghai: National Quarantine Service, 1934.

——. *Cholera: A Manual for the Medical Profession in China.* Shanghai: National Quarantine Service, 1934.

——. *Plague Fighter: The Autobiography of a Modern Chinese Physician.* Cambridge: W. Heffer & Sons, 1959.

Xu, Bing. "Minguo shiqi ZhongRi jiaokeshu jiufen kaolue," *Riben xuekan*, 2, 2001: 125–138.

Yamazaki, Takako. *Tsuda Umeko.* Tokyo: Yoshikawa kobunkan, 1962.

Yip, Ka-che. *Health and National Reconstruction in Nationalist China: The Development of Modern Health Services, 1928–1937.* Ann Arbor: Association for Asian Studies, 1995.

Yiu, Angela. "'Beautiful Town': The Discovery of the Suburbs and the Vision of the Garden City in Late Meiji and Taisho literature," *Japan Forum*, 18(3), 2006: 315–338.

Yoshimura, Michio. *Japan and Russia.* Tokyo: Hara Shōbō, 1968.

Young, Louise. *Beyond the Metropolis: Second Cities and Modern Life in Interwar Japan.* Berkeley: University of California Press, 2013.

Żółtowska, Janina, *Inne czasy, inni ludzie.* n.p.: n.d.

Zōsen kyōkai, *Nihon kinsei zōsen shi.* Tokyo: Hara shobō, 1973.

# Index

www.ingramcontent.com/pod-product-compliance
Lightning Source LLC
Chambersburg PA
CBHW070620270326
41926CB00011B/1760